Fodor's

OREGON

WELCOME TO OREGON

Rugged beauty, locavore cuisine, and indie spirit are just some of Oregon's charms. The Pacific Northwest darling is home to hip Portland, whose happening foodie and arts scenes are anchored by an eco-friendly lifestyle. Smaller cities draw you in, too: you can sample microbrews in Bend, see top-notch theater in Ashland, and explore maritime history in Astoria. Miles of bike paths, hikes up Mt. Hood, and rafting in the Columbia River Gorge thrill outdoor enthusiasts. For pure relaxation, taste award-winning Willamette Valley wines and walk windswept Pacific beaches.

TOP REASONS TO GO

★ **Portland:** Terrific food, eclectic music, boutique hotels, and culture galore.

★ **Seafood:** Fresh crab, sea scallops, razor clams, oysters, and salmon.

★ **Wine:** Perfect Pinot Noir, Pinot Gris, and more in the Willamette Valley and beyond.

★ **The Coast:** Scenic strands, tidal pools, whale sightings, headland walks.

★ **Mountains:** From majestic Mt. Hood to the mighty cliffs surrounding Crater Lake.

★ **Scenic Drives:** In the Cascade Range, along the Pacific, through evergreen forests.

Fodor's OREGON

Design: Tina Malaney, *Associate Art Director*; Erica Cuoco, *Production Designer*

Photography: Jennifer Arnow, *Senior Photo Editor*

Maps: Rebecca Baer, *Senior Map Editor*; Mark Stroud (Moon Street Cartography), David Lindroth, *Cartographers*

Production: Angela L. McLean, *Senior Production Manager*; Jennifer DePrima, *Editorial Production Manager*

Sales: Jacqueline Lebow, *Sales Director*

Business & Operations: Chuck Hoover, *Chief Marketing Officer*; Joy Lai, *Vice President and General Manager*; Stephen Horowitz, *Head of Business Development and Partnerships*

Writers: Margot Bigg, Andrew Collins, Jon Shadel

Editor: Salwa Jabado

Production Editor: Jennifer DePrima

7th Edition

ISBN 978-0-14754-678-4

ISSN 1523–8776

All details in this book are based on information supplied to us at press time. Always confirm information when it matters, especially if you're making a detour to visit a specific place. Fodor's expressly disclaims any liability, loss, or risk, personal or otherwise, that is incurred as a consequence of the use of any of the contents of this book.

SPECIAL SALES

This book is available at special discounts for bulk purchases for sales promotions or premiums. For more information, e-mail specialmarkets@penguinrandomhouse.com.

PRINTED IN THE UNITED STATES OF AMERICA

10 9 8 7 6 5 4 3 2 1

CONTENTS

Fodor's Features

CONTENTS

MAPS

ABOUT THIS GUIDE

Fodor's Recommendations

Everything in this guide is worth doing—we don't cover what isn't—but exceptional sights, hotels, and restaurants are recognized with additional accolades; Fodor's Choice★ indicates our top recommendations. Care to nominate a new place? Visit Fodors.com/contact-us.

Trip Costs

We list prices wherever possible to help you budget well. Hotel and restaurant price categories from $ to $$$$ are noted alongside each recommendation. For hotels, we include the lowest cost of a standard double room in high season. For restaurants, we cite the average price of a main course at dinner or, if dinner isn't served, at lunch. For attractions, we always list adult admission fees; discounts are usually available for children, students, and senior citizens.

Hotels

Our local writers vet every hotel to recommend the best overnights in each price category, from budget to expensive. Unless otherwise specified, you can expect private bath, phone, and TV in your room. For expanded hotel reviews, facilities, and deals, visit Fodors.com.

Top Picks		Hotels & Restaurants	
★	Fodor's Choice	🏨	Hotel
Listings		⤴	Number of rooms
⊠	Address	¶⊙¶	Meal plans
⊠	Branch address	W	Restaurant
☎	Telephone	⚓	Reservations
🖶	Fax	👔	Dress code
⊕	Website	▭	No credit cards
✆	E-mail	$	Price
🎫	Admission fee		
☉	Open/closed times	**Other**	
Ⓜ	Subway	⇨	See also
⊹	Directions or Map coordinates	☞	Take note
		⛳	Golf facilities

Restaurants

Unless we state otherwise, restaurants are open for lunch and dinner daily. We mention dress code only when there's a specific requirement and reservations only when they're essential or not accepted.

Credit Cards

The hotels and restaurants in this guide typically accept credit cards. If not, we'll say so.

EUGENE FODOR

Hungarian-born Eugene Fodor (1905–91) began his travel career as an interpreter on a French cruise ship. The experience inspired him to write *On the Continent* (1936), the first guidebook to receive annual updates and discuss a country's way of life as well as its sights. Fodor later joined the U.S. Army and worked for the OSS in World War II. After the war, he kept up his intelligence work while expanding his guidebook series. During the Cold War, many guides were written by fellow agents who understood the value of insider information. Today's guides continue Fodor's legacy by providing travelers with timely coverage, insider tips, and cultural context.

EXPERIENCE
OREGON

WHAT'S WHERE

Numbers refer to chapters.

2 Portland. With its pedestrian-friendly Downtown and great public transit, Portland is easy to explore. The city has become a magnet for fans of artisanal food, beer, wine, and spirits, and its leafy parks and miles of bike lanes make it a prime spot for outdoors enthusiasts.

3 The Oregon Coast. Oregon's roughly 300 miles of rugged shoreline are every bit as scenic as the more crowded and famous California coast. Oregon Dunes National Recreation Area, the Oregon Coast Aquarium, Cannon Beach, and the Columbia River Maritime Museum are key highlights.

4 The Willamette Valley and Wine Country. Just beyond Portland city limits and extending south for 120 miles to Eugene, the Willamette Valley is synonymous with exceptional wine-making.

5 The Columbia River Gorge and Mt. Hood. Less than an hour east of Portland, the Columbia Gorge extends for about 160 miles along the Oregon-Washington border. Sailboarding, kitesurfing, hiking, and white-water rafting abound. Just 35 miles south of Hood River, iconic Mt. Hood is renowned for hiking and skiing.

6 Central Oregon. The swath of Oregon east of the Cascade Range takes in a varied landscape, with the outdoorsy city of Bend as the regional hub. Make time for the quirky mountain town of Sisters and world-famous rock climbing and hiking in Smith Rock State Park.

7 Crater Lake National Park. The 21-square-mile sapphire-blue expanse is the nation's deepest lake and a scenic wonder. You can drive the loop road around the lake, hike, or take a guided boat tour.

8 Southern Oregon. Artsy Ashland and Old West–looking Jacksonville have sophisticated restaurants, shops, and wineries. Nearby, Oregon Caves National Monument is a fascinating natural attraction, while Klamath Falls has some of the best birding and wildlife-viewing in the state.

9 Eastern Oregon. The vast and sparsely populated eastern reaches of the state promise plenty of memorable sights and recreational opportunities for those who make the effort. The Wild West town of Pendleton (famed for its annual rodeo), the picturesque mountain town of Joseph, and historic Baker City are among the top destinations here.

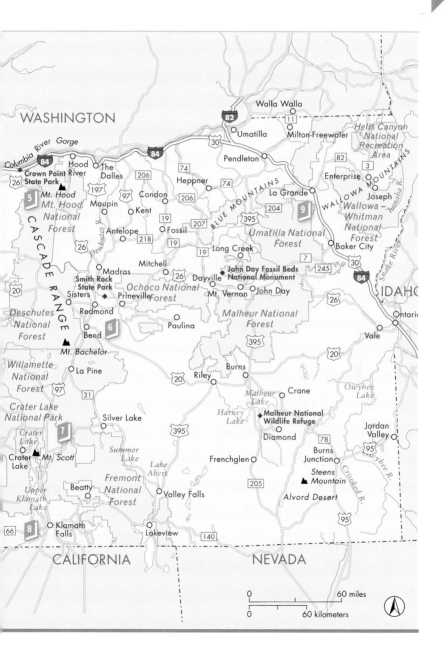

OREGON PLANNER

Fast Facts

Packing It's all about the layers here, as the weather can morph from cold and overcast to warm and sunny and back again in the course of a few hours, especially in spring and fall.

Safety The most dangerous element of Oregon is the great outdoors. Don't hike alone, and make sure you bring enough water plus basic first-aid items. If you're not an experienced hiker, stick to tourist-friendly spots like the more accessible parts of the designated parks. When driving, take care to use only designated and maintained roads and check road conditions ahead of time when planning to pass through mountainous terrain from fall through spring—many roads over the Coast and Cascades ranges are closed in winter.

Taxes Oregon has no sales tax—even in restaurants—making it a popular destination for shoppers, although many cities and counties levy a tax on lodging and services. Room taxes vary from about 6% to 11%.

Getting Here and Around

Most visitors arriving by plane fly into Portland, home of the state's largest airport. There are smaller regional airports in Bend, Coos Bay, Eugene, Medford, and Pendleton. A smaller number of visitors arrive by Amtrak, which has major service connecting Portland, Salem, Eugene, and Klamath Falls with San Francisco, Seattle, and Spokane.

Major interstate highways connect Oregon with neighboring Washington, Idaho, and Northern California, making it easy to include the state as part of a regional Pacific Northwest road trip to Seattle, Vancouver, and environs. Interstate 5 is Oregon's major north–south freeway, and Interstate 84 cuts east–west across the northern part of the state from Portland through the Columbia Gorge and then southeast toward Boise, Idaho. Other major roads through the state, all of them offering plenty of beautiful scenery, include U.S. 101 up and down the coast, U.S. 97 north–south along the eastern edge of the Cascade Range, and U.S. 20 and U.S. 26, both of which run east–west from the coast through the Willamette Valley, over the Cascades, and across the state's vast eastern interior.

The only destination within Oregon that's genuinely easy to visit without a car is Portland, which is served by a superb public transportation system that includes buses, streetcars, and light rail.

Top Festivals

Portland is the state's festivals hub, with many events taking place Downtown on the city's scenic Willamette riverfront, but you'll find plenty of engaging festivals elsewhere. Also keep in mind that Oregon is wild about farmers' markets—most towns in the state have one from spring through fall, and Portland has dozens. There's often live entertainment, arts and crafts, and prepared food at these bustling outdoor markets.

Spring. Portland's **Cinco de Mayo** festival celebrates its sister-city relationship with Guadalajara, Mexico, and runs a full weekend in early May. Arguably the most famous event in the state, the **Portland Rose Festival** consists of numerous events and parties throughout late May and early June, culminating in a huge parade.

Summer. Among the many big gatherings in Portland each summer, many taking place along the riverfront, check out **Portland Gay Pride** in mid-June, the wildly colorful **World Naked Bike Ride** in late June, the **Waterfront Blues Festival** over July 4 weekend, the **Oregon Brewers Festival** in late July, and the **Bite of Oregon** food festival in early August.

Summer kicks off on the coast with the **Astoria Music Festival,** held over two weeks beginning in late June. Jazz fans head to central Oregon in early July for the lively **Bend Summer Festival,** and wine lovers flock to McMinnville, in the Willamette Valley, to sample fine regional vintages in late July during the **International Pinot Noir Celebration.** Autumn is just around the corner with the arrival of the **Oregon Wine Experience** in Jacksonville in late August and the **Oregon State Fair** in Salem in late August and early September.

Fall. Portland's **Feast** has rapidly become one of the most talked-about international culinary festivals in the country, with events and meals prepared by both local and national star chefs. The **Pendleton Round-Up** is one of the most prestigious and downright fun rodeos in the country, drawing upwards of 60,000 participants and spectators in September. In coastal Bandon each September, the **Cranberry Festival** comprises a fair and parade. The **Sisters Folk Festival** brings top-name artists to this scenic mountain town near Bend, which hosts its bustling **Bend Fall Festival** in late September–early October.

Winter. In late January, foodies partake of numerous delicious events throughout the Willamette Valley during the **Oregon Truffle Festival.** Although it sounds like a short-term seasonal event, Ashland's famed **Oregon Shakespeare Festival** actually runs from late February through early November. In mid-February, **Oregon WinterFest** in Bend celebrates the region's winter sports with a mix of outdoors activities and indoor concerts. Late February's **Newport Seafood and Wine Festival** is a tasty time to visit the coast. Film lovers will enjoy the **Portland International Film Festival,** featuring works from throughout the world each February, which coincides with the acclaimed **Portland Jazz Festival.**

When to Go

There's no more scenic and enjoyable time to visit just about any part of Oregon than summer, which promises the driest, sunniest weather and mild temperatures, as well as lush, verdant terrain and the majority of the state's key festivals and gatherings—it's also the only time the road encircling Crater Lake is open. You should plan for occasionally intense (but dry) heat waves in the valleys, from Ashland clear north to Portland as well as east through the Columbia Gorge. Even in summer, fog and rain can sometimes overpower the coast for a few days at a time.

Spring and fall, however, can be just as beautiful, with blooming flowers and fall foliage, and with fewer crowds in popular spots at the coast, Columbia Gorge, and Willamette Wine Country.

During the winter months, from the coast to the Cascades (including Portland and the Willamette Valley), rain and gray skies are the norm and quite common in spring and fall. Winter is also the best time for whale- and storm-watching along the coast and bird-watching in southeastern Oregon.

OREGON TODAY

Politics

After years as one of the country's "battleground" states, Oregon has steadily become more Democrat: nearly all of the state's major officeholders are Dems, and Portland and Eugene are considered two of the most progressive cities in America. In 2014, the state legalized same-sex marriage and passed a ballot initiative making Oregon the third state in the country to legalize marijuana for personal consumption (as opposed to medical use). However, in rural areas, especially the eastern two-thirds of Oregon and southern sections of the coast, you will encounter decidedly more conservative attitudes, with a mix of socially right and libertarian types. A fair share of self-described Oregon conservatives favor same-sex marriage and marijuana legalization, but retain a strong distrust of what they perceive as big-government regulation—this is especially true among Oregon farmers and ranchers. On the other hand, the Republican Party seldom fields candidates for mayoral and city council elections in the state's largest city, which has half-jokingly been dubbed the "People's Republic of Portland" for its decidedly left-of-center vibe.

Eating

It's hard to think of another part of the country with a culinary scene that's both incredibly inventive and sustainable while still eschewing high prices and formality. Oregon chefs have been at the forefront of the locally sourced and seasonal dining movement, especially those in Portland, Eugene, Ashland, and stretches of the northern coast and Columbia Gorge. Farmers' markets thrive all over the state, and restaurants flock to them for local produce such as hazelnuts, marionberries, pears, and chanterelle mushrooms as well as for artisan products ranging from aged goat cheese to spicy kimchi. Even in small towns like Joseph, Grants Pass, and Depoe Bay, you'll find stellar eateries with oft-changing menus featuring sophisticated Northwestern fare. But the best part is that most of the hottest chef-driven spots around the state offer meals that cost a fraction of what you'd pay for comparable cuisine in San Francisco or even Seattle.

Drinking

Oregon is beyond merely beer-obsessed, although craft ales are clearly at the forefront of the state's assiduous attention to beverages. Portland is well regarded for longtime breweries like Bridgeport and Widmer, but you're more likely to find serious fans hanging out at newer, smaller spots like Commons Brewery and Ecliptic Brewing. Many of the most acclaimed beer makers are outside the Portland area—consider Rogue in Newport, Pfriem in Hood River, Deschutes in Bend, Yachats Brewing in Yachats, Ninkasi in Eugene, and Terminal Gravity in Enterprise. Beyond beer, the state ranks third in the nation in wine production, and plenty of *vino* aficionados consider Oregon Pinot Noirs among the world's best, with Pinot Gris and Chardonnay also earning a great deal of praise. The Willamette Valley, just south of Portland, has been producing top wines for a few decades now; new wineries are also popping up increasingly in the Columbia Gorge and southern Oregon's Rogue Valley. You'll also find coffeehouses sourcing and house-roasting high-caliber, single-origin beans in virtually every neighborhood in Portland, in every good-size town elsewhere in the state, and even in a few small villages (like Sleepy Monk in Cannon Beach and Red Horse in Joseph). Finally, there's Oregon's fast-growing bounty of microdistilleries, with Portland once again at the forefront but with towns as varied as outdoorsy Bend and remote Brookings also joining the action.

Environmentalism

Oregon's embrace of eco-friendly practices permeates just about every aspect of the state. Sustainable design plays an increasing role in real-estate projects—according to the U.S. Green Building Council, the state ranks sixth in the country for LEED-certified "green" construction. Oregon's most populous city, Portland, has become a prime example in promoting high-density development and reining in suburban sprawl; the city maintains a strict urban growth boundary, which was instituted in the early 1970s as part of a then-novel statewide policy. The state is home to thousands of square miles of undeveloped wilderness—Oregon ranks behind only Alaska, Nevada, Utah, and Idaho in its percentage (60.4%) of public lands. As you travel around, it's easy to encounter examples of this eco-conscious ethic, especially in terms of the fast-growing number of hotels, farms, restaurants, coffee roasters, breweries, and wineries that adhere strictly to environmentally friendly practices.

The Outdoors

Oregon offers plenty of activities for outdoor enthusiasts. Just 60 miles east of Portland, Mt. Hood (the state's highest mountain) is the only place in the Lower 48 where you can ski year-round (although trails are limited in summer). There are three different facilities on this mammoth, snowcapped mountain. Timberline Lodge Ski Area is the one that remains open year-round, and its runs pass beside the venerable 1930s Timberline Lodge.

Nearby Mt. Hood Skibowl has less interesting terrain but the most night-skiing acreage in the country. Around the north side of the mountain, you'll find the most challenging, extensive, and interesting terrain at Mt. Hood Meadows Ski Resort, which offers some 2,150 acres of winter snowboarding and ski fun. Of the many excellent places for white-water rafting in Oregon, the Rogue River offers some of the most thrilling rides. Several outfitters offer trips along this frothy, 215-mile river in the southwestern part of the state, from half-day adventures well suited to beginners to multiday trips that include camping or overnights in local lodges. The lush Silver Falls State Park, about 25 miles east of Salem, is so impressive that serious campaigns to admit it to the national park system have taken place recently. In the meantime, it's something of a secret treasure. The 8,700-acre swath of skyscraping old-growth Douglas firs climbs into the foothills of the Cascade Range, where rain and melting snow supply the torrent that roars through 14 different waterfalls, several of them more than 100 feet tall.

OREGON
TOP ATTRACTIONS

Cannon Beach
(A)The nearest town on the dramatically rocky, windswept Oregon Coast from Portland also happens to be one of the most idyllic communities in the coastal Northwest. This town, anchored by 235-foot-tall Haystack Rock, is rife with beachside hiking trails, fine-art galleries, and cafés specializing in organic coffee, Oregon wines, and fresh-caught seafood. Nearby Oswald West and Ecola State Parks have some of the most stunning beaches and hiking trails in the state.

Columbia River Gorge
(B)The 110-mile section of the breathtaking Columbia River provides some of the Pacific Northwest's most spectacular vistas. Towering cliffs on both the Washington and Oregon sides of the river form a dramatic backdrop, and meandering highways line both banks. Water and wind sports abound, and a growing wine-making, craft-brewing, and culinary scene has flourished in recent years.

Columbia River Maritime Museum, Astoria
(C)At this dazzling, contemporary facility in the steadily gentrifying town of Astoria, where the northern Oregon Coast meets the Columbia River, you can tour a fully operational U.S. Coast Guard lightship, and check out engaging exhibits on local shipwrecks, marine life, and how the mighty Columbia has driven the economic and cultural development of the Pacific Northwest.

Crater Lake National Park
(D)The deepest lake in the United States is also the clearest, a fact readily grasped as soon as you behold this searing-blue body of water. It's closed much of the year due to snow, but in summer this 21-square-mile lake is southern Oregon's foremost attraction—the nearly century-old Crater Lake Lodge, perched on the southern shore, makes a memorable overnight and dinner venue.

High Desert Museum, Bend

(E) Evocative and intricate walk-through dioramas and an indoor-outdoor zoo with creatures great and tiny convey the high desert's past and present in a delightfully airy and family-friendly space just south of Bend.

Mt. Hood

(F) Just 60 miles east of Portland, the state's highest mountain is the only place in the Lower 48 where you can ski year-round. There are five different facilities, Timberline Lodge Ski Area being the most scenic.

Oregon Sand Dunes

(G) The 41 miles of rolling bluffs that make up Oregon Dunes National Recreation Area bring out the kid in visitors of all ages. You can hike, ride horseback, and race on a dune buggy on these massive mountains of sand, some of them climbing nearly 500 feet higher than the surf. There's great boating and fishing (plus several excellent seafood restaurants) in the nearby town of Florence.

Powell's Bookstore, Portland

(H) The Downtown Portland legend is the world's largest bookstore carrying both new and used titles, and with its coffeehouse, late hours, and endless aisles of reading, it's also a prime spot for literary-minded people-watching.

Willamette Valley Wine Country

(I) Within easy day-tripping of Portland, this swath of fertile, hilly countryside is home to more than 500 wineries and has earned a reputation as one of the finest producers of Pinot Noir in the world—some say the best outside Burgundy. Winemakers in these parts also produce first-rate Pinot Gris and Chardonnay.

IF YOU LIKE

Hidden Food and Wine Finds

As the state—and especially greater Portland—continues to develop cachet for its superb restaurants, farmers' markets, wineries, and microbreweries, it's worth making the effort to venture a bit off the beaten path to find some genuine only-in-Oregon culinary treats.

Clear Creek Distillery, Portland. Clear Creek paved the distillery way with its unique spirits—the pear brandy or cherry Kirschwasser make a perfect nightcap, and a sip of Douglas fir *eau de vie* will deliver you right to the heart of an Oregon forest.

Josephson's Smokehouse, Astoria. Once the heart of Oregon's salmon-canning industry, the endearingly raffish town of Astoria is still a prime destination for seafood lovers. Drop by Josephson's for hot- and cold-smoked salmon, prawns, halibut, and albacore.

Pfriem Family Brewers, Hood River. This up-and-coming craft brewery offers a Belgian-inspired take on Oregon's hoppy brewing style by creating some of the most distinctive and well-respected beers in the state. The modern tasting room on the Columbia River also serves tasty contemporary pub fare.

Rogue Creamery, Central Point. This small but nationally renowned dairy in an otherwise nondescript town near Medford produces phenomenal blue cheeses in several varieties (from Smokey Blue to Oregonzola) plus a delectable lavender-infused cheddar; a small kitchen also serves gourmet grilled-cheese sandwiches.

Sleepy Monk, Cannon Beach. Portland's Stumptown Coffee is Oregon's most famous coffee roaster, but true aficionados rave about this tiny, organic coffeehouse in Cannon Beach—the dark, bold Bogsman Brew blend is heaven in a cup.

Offbeat Museums

Although you'll discover a plethora of art and history museums, Oregon fascinates visitors with its diverse selection of lesser-known, quirky museums.

Columbia River Maritime Museum, Astoria. The observation tower of a World War II submarine and the personal belongings of the passengers of area shipwrecks are among the exhibits inside, while outdoors on the riverside dock you can tour the lightship *Columbia,* which formerly plied the region's waters as a floating lighthouse.

Evergreen Aviation & Space Museum, McMinnville. Engrossing facts about aviation complement an awesome assortment of flying machines at this expansive repository best known as the home of Howard Hughes's "flying boat," the *Spruce Goose,* which has a wingspan longer than a football field and its end zones.

High Desert Museum, Bend. Evocative and intricate walk-through dioramas and an indoor–outdoor zoo with creatures great and tiny convey the high desert's past and present in a delightfully airy and family-friendly space.

National Historic Oregon Trail Interpretive Center, Baker City. With a simulated span of the legendary Oregon Trail, this well-designed museum offers a thorough and vivid look at life for the some 300,000 pioneers who entered Oregon from the Midwest during the 19th century.

Western Antique Aeroplane & Automobile Museum, Hood River. Two massive hangars make up this museum filled with beautifully restored and still working vintage planes and cars dating back as far as the 1910s.

Distinctive Lodging

In Oregon you can stay in hip, urban neighborhoods, along the beach, in the woods, or atop snow-covered mountains. Accommodations include elegant, full-service boutique hotels, luxury alpine retreats, historic bed-and-breakfasts, cozy ski chalets, rustic national park cabins, and funky local motels.

The Allison Inn & Spa, Newberg. Elegant yet refreshingly contemporary, this 80-room boutique resort and spa has finally given Oregon's scenic Willamette Valley accommodations worthy of the region's ethereal Pinot Noirs.

Caravan—The Tiny House Hotel, Portland. A complex of about a half dozen ingeniously designed and truly minuscule (80 to 160 square feet) houses, Caravan is situated along hip and artsy Northeast Alberta Street. Each of these bungalows-on-wheels has a kitchenette.

Heceta Head Lighthouse, Florence. Occupying the same dramatic promontory as a working lighthouse, this Queen Anne–style bed-and-breakfast has views of the Pacific that inspire many a marriage proposal.

McMenamins Kennedy School, Portland. The quirky McMenimans company has adapted dozens of buildings around Oregon as pubs, restaurants, and hotels—from a former asylum to this 1915 elementary school in a funky northeast Portland neighborhood.

Timberline Lodge, Mt. Hood. This iconic 60-room lodge on the upper slopes of Oregon's highest peak is buried beneath many feet of snow for much of the year. Admire the 96-foot stone chimney in the lobby.

Majestic Mountaintops

Oregon is studded with conical mountain peaks, which are strung along its Cascade Range from the Columbia River down to the California border. The summits, most of them topped with snow all year-round, make for memorable photography subjects. Those who venture closer, however, will discover some of the state's best opportunities for recreation.

Mt. Ashland. The first soaring peak you encounter upon crossing into southern Oregon on Interstate 5, this 7,533-foot peak has great skiing much of the year, and also rewards visitors with fantastic views of the Rogue Valley.

Mt. Bachelor. This 9,065-foot peak offers some of the best downhill skiing and snowboarding in the West—consider the impressive 3,265-foot vertical drop. In summer, you can ride a chairlift to the Pine Marten Lodge for panoramic vistas across the shimmering Cascade Lakes.

Mt. Hood. One of Oregon's most recognizable land features, the snowy, conical Mt. Hood rises to some 11,245 feet (the tallest in the state) and is visible from Downtown Portland, more than 50 miles away.

Neahkahnie Mountain. Although it tops out at just 1,680 feet, this craggy peak is one of the most dramatic along the state's coastline. Trails leading to the top draw hikers from nearby Manzanita and Cannon Beach, and the views up and down the coast are mesmerizing.

Steens Mountain. A striking sight in eastern Oregon's otherwise rather level high desert, this 9,700-foot peak was created from a massive block of fractured lava and is largely devoid of vegetation. Hikers here have been known to spot golden eagles and bighorn sheep.

FLAVORS OF OREGON

Short of tropical fruit, there aren't too many types of food that don't grow somewhere in Oregon. Myriad fish and shellfish species dwell off the coast, while tree fruits line the windswept Columbia Gorge, and berries grow wild and on farms in the fertile Willamette Valley. A host of other fruits, vegetables, greens, and produce thrive in the temperate climate. Ranch lands, dairy farms, and acres of wheat and other crops round out an abundance that changes with the seasons.

Natural Bounty

Few states can match Oregon's agricultural diversity, which is good news for both chefs and food-crazy locals.

Nuts: There's a reason why hazelnuts—also known as filberts—are the official state nut. Oregon produces 99% of the country's hazelnuts, which add a toasty-sweet flavor to meat, salads, desserts, coffee drinks, and more.

Berries: Blueberries, blackberries, and strawberries thrive in the lush Willamette Valley. But the state is home to lesser-known berries highlighted in local preserves, baked goods, and sweet sauces. Subtly tart loganberries are a cross between blackberries and red raspberries. Marionberries have a slightly earthy flavor, and are sometimes dubbed "the Cabernet of blackberries."

Produce: Farmers' markets and restaurant menus are filled with locally grown staples like chanterelle mushrooms, rhubarb, kale, spinach, onions, lemon cucumbers, green beans, potatoes, peaches, cherries, apples, and pears.

Cheese: Open an Oregonian's refrigerator and you're likely to find a fat yellow brick (or a diminutive "baby loaf") of Tillamook cheddar from the century-old collective of coastal creameries. The state's broad swaths of grazing lands generate milk that fuels dozens of artisanal cheese producers. Some of the country's best blue cheese comes from the Rogue Creamery in southern Oregon.

Seafood

With 362 miles of coastline, bays, tide flats, and estuaries, Oregon has a stunning variety of fish and shellfish off its shores. Restaurants and locals are attuned to the seasons, from the start of Dungeness season to the best months for oysters.

Salmon: Oregonians know king salmon as chinook salmon, but make no mistake—the largest Pacific salmon reigns as the prize catch of the state's native cuisine. Silvery coho salmon also swim in the state's coastal rivers. Oregon salmon is phenomenal simply grilled or roasted. Perhaps the most indigenous way to cook salmon is to smoke it, a practice that dates back to Native American dwellers.

Crab: Dungeness crab may be named for a town in Washington, but Oregon harvests more of these prized crustaceans than any other state. They are a delicacy simply boiled and served whole, but picked meat often appears in crab cakes or as a focal point in modern regional dishes.

Shellfish: Low tide on Oregon's beaches can yield thin razor clams or a variety of bay clams. Mussels also grow in clusters along rocky coastal stretches while oysters are harvested in several spots. Mussels and clams are delicious steamed (perhaps in an Oregon wine or beer) or in a creamy chowder. Oysters are enjoyed raw on the half shell or lightly battered and fried.

Ocean fish: Pacific halibut, sole, rockfish, hake, lingcod, and the prized albacore tuna are all fished off the Oregon Coast. The Columbia River also offers up freshwater favorites like steelhead trout and Columbia River sturgeon.

Pacific Northwest Restaurants

Chefs across the country are in the throes of the farm-to-table movement, but in Oregon the close connection between chef and producer has long bypassed trend status. It's simply how things are done. Restaurants like **Clyde Common, Higgins,** and **Paley's Place** have been producing organic, locally sourced dishes since well before these approaches became national ideals.

Cuisine here tends to be modern and unfussy—a simple, slightly edgy celebration of what grows nearby. Dishes can have Asian, French, or other global influences, but the ingredients ground them solidly in the Northwest. But there is perhaps no more authentically Oregon preparation of meat or fish than cooking it with a crust of hazelnuts.

Portland is assuredly the epicenter of the state's restaurant scene, but wine-country tourism has helped spread noteworthy cuisine to the Willamette Valley, Hood River and the Columbia Gorge, Bend, the Rogue Valley, and the coastal wine region.

Since it was first inhabited, Oregon has looked to the ocean to feed its population. Nevertheless, eastern Oregon cattle ranches provide a ready supply of sustainably raised beef that chefs love to showcase. The recent nose-to-tail dining trend has generated interest in other meats, including rabbit, pork, goat, and lamb, sourced from Oregon farms.

Wine

Pinot Noir grapes have been the central force of Oregon wine-making since the industry took root in the 1960s. Frustrated by Pinot's poor performance in California, a few intrepid winemakers headed north to test out Oregon's cooler climate. The Willamette Valley's climate is similar to that of France's Burgundy region, where Pinot Noir grapes have reigned for centuries. The rich farmland on the valley floor isn't optimal for grape growing; most vineyards spread across the hillsides that ring the valley, taking advantage of higher elevation, thinner soil, and cool ocean breezes.

Oregon played a central role in America's rediscovery of this famously finicky grape. Today the state is the country's top producer of Pinot Noir. Oregon has 16 official wine-growing regions, though the vast majority of wineries are clustered in the Willamette Valley. Grapes also flourish in parts of southern Oregon and the Columbia Valley along the Washington border.

After Pinot Noir, **Pinot Gris** is the second most prevalent wine varietal in the state. The delicate and dry yet fruity white wine is somewhat of an unsung hero, since its darker Pinot cousin earns so much acclaim. Chardonnay, Merlot, and Riesling round out the state's top wines. Oregon wines are generally highly affordable, and deliver a great value for the money, although top Pinot Noirs can cost a pretty penny.

Unencumbered by the wine-making traditions of France, or even California, Oregon vintners have taken the lead in growing organic grapes and producing wines using sustainable methods.

PORTLAND WITH KIDS

Many of Oregon's best kids-oriented attractions and activities are in greater Portland. Just getting around the Rose City—via streetcars and light-rail trains on city streets and kayaks, excursion cruises, and jet boats on the Willamette River—is fun. For listings of family-oriented concerts, performances by the Oregon Children's Theatre, and the like, check the free *Willamette Weekly* newspaper.

Museums and Attractions

On the east bank of the Willamette River, the **Oregon Museum of Science and Industry** (OMSI) is a leading interactive museum, with touch-friendly exhibits, an Omnimax theater, the state's biggest planetarium, and a 240-foot submarine moored just outside in the river. Along Portland's leafy Park Blocks, both the **Oregon History Museum** and the **Portland Art Museum** have exhibits and programming geared toward kids.

In Old Town, kids enjoy walking amid the ornate pagodas and dramatic foliage of the **Lan Su Chinese Garden**. This is a good spot for a weekend morning, followed by a visit to the **Portland Saturday Market**, where food stalls and musicians keep younger kids entertained, and the cool jewelry, toys, and gifts handcrafted by local artisans appeal to teens. Steps from the market is the **Oregon Maritime Museum**, set within a vintage stern-wheeler docked on the river. And just up Burnside Street from the market, **Powell's City of Books** contains enormous sections of kids' and young adults' literature.

Parks

Portland is dotted with densely wooded parks—many of the larger ones have ball fields, playgrounds, and picnic areas. The most famous urban oasis in the city, **Forest Park** (along with adjoining **Washington Park**) offers a wealth of engaging activities. You can ride the MAX light rail right to the park's main hub of culture, a complex comprising the **Oregon Zoo, Portland Children's Museum,** and **World Forestry Discovery Center Museum.** Ride the narrow-gauge railroad from the zoo for 2 miles to reach the **International Rose Test Garden** and **Japanese Garden.** From here it's an easy downhill stroll to **Northwest 23rd and 21st Avenues'** pizza parlors, ice-cream shops, and bakeries.

Outdoor Adventures

Tour boats ply the **Willamette River,** and a couple of marinas near OMSI rent **kayaks** and conduct **drag-boat races** out on the water. There are also several shops in town that rent **bikes** for use on the city's many miles of dedicated bike lanes and trails. There's outstanding **white-water rafting** just southeast of Portland, along the Clackamas River. On your way toward the Clackamas, check out **North Clackamas Aquatic Park** and **Oaks Amusement Park,** which have rides and wave pools galore.

Nearby **Mt. Hood** has camping, hiking, and biking all summer, and three of the most family-friendly ski resorts in the Northwest—**Timberline** is especially popular for younger and less experienced boarders and skiers. From summer through fall, the pick-your-own berry farms and pumpkin patches on **Sauvie Island** make for an engaging afternoon getaway—for an all-day outing, continue up U.S. 30 all the way to **Astoria,** at the mouth of the Columbia River, to visit the **Columbia River Maritime Museum** and **Fort Stevens State Park,** where kids love to scamper about the remains of an early-20th-century shipwreck.

ECOTOURISM IN OREGON

The word *ecotourism* is believed to have been coined by Mexican environmentalist Héctor Ceballos-Lascuráin in 1983. According to Ceballos-Lascuráin, ecotourism "involves traveling to relatively undisturbed natural areas with the specific object of studying, admiring, and enjoying the scenery and its wild plants and animals." His original definition seemed a bit too general, so in 1993 he amended it with a line that stressed that "ecotourism is environmentally responsible travel."

Natural beauty abounds in Oregon, which has been a pioneer in sustainability and conservation. Famously "green" Portland is a model of eco-friendly urban planning, with its superb public transit, network of urban-growth boundaries, multitude of bike lanes, and abundance of LEED-certified buildings. Outside the city, six of the state's ski areas (Mt. Ashland, Mt. Bachelor, Mt. Hood Meadows, Timberline, and Anthony Lakes) are members of the **Bonneville Environmental Foundation's Ski Green Program.**

Travel-related businesses that embrace the principles of environmental sustainability are common throughout Oregon. The state's tremendous stock of forests, parks, and preserves is a big reason there's been such a push here to balance growth with preservation.

Travel Portland is one of the few tourism organizations in the country with its own public relations manager dedicated solely to promoting environmentally responsible travel.

Accommodations

Oregon has dozens of accommodations committed to sustainable design and operating practices. Many smaller properties are members of **OBBG Green** (⊕ *www.obbg.org/oregon-green-travel.php*), which is made up of about 15 bed-and-breakfasts that qualify as eco-friendly.

Food and Beverages

Oregon has been a leader in the movement toward producing food, beer, and wine using sustainable practices and emphasizing local and organic ingredients. One excellent resource for learning about organic and sustainable pick-your-own farms and farmers' markets around the state is **Oregon Tilth** (⊕ *tilth.org*).

Two statewide organizations dedicated to sustainability in wine-making are **Low Input Viticulture & Enology** (⊕ *www.liveinc.org*) and **Oregon Certified Sustainable Wine** (⊕ *www.ocsw.org*). Dozens of wineries around the state have been recognized for their environmentally friendly practices. Additionally, local breweries with eco-friendly reputations include **Deschutes, Hopworks, Ninkasi, Pfriem,** and **Full Sail.**

Tours

EcoShuttle (⊕ *www.ecoshuttle.net*) is an environmentally oriented charter tour company that arranges winery, brewery, and ecotours. The popular Willamette River boat-tour company **Portland Spirit River Cruises** (⊕ *www.portlandspirit.com*) is a recognized member of Travel Portland's green resources program, as is **Portland Walking Tours** (⊕ *www.portland-walkingtours.com*). To gain a better sense of the progress Oregon's logging industry has made toward sustainable practices, be sure to visit the **World Forestry Center Discovery Museum** in Portland's Washington Park.

GREAT ITINERARIES

BEST OF OREGON TOUR

With 10 days, you can get a taste of Oregon's largest city, eco-conscious Portland, while also getting a nice sense of the state's geographical diversity—the mountainous and sweeping coast, gorgeous Crater Lake, the rugged Cascade Mountains, and the eastern high-desert regions.

Days 1 and 2: Portland

Start by spending a couple of days in Portland, where you can tour the museums and attractions that make up **Washington Park**, as well as the **Lan Su Chinese Garden** in Old Town, and the excellent museums and cultural institutions along Downtown's leafy **Park Blocks**. This city of vibrant, distinctive neighborhoods offers plenty of great urban exploring, with Nob Hill, Hawthorne, and the Mississippi Avenue Arts District among the best areas for shopping, café-hopping, and people-watching. If you have a little extra time, consider spending a couple of hours just south of the city in the **Willamette Valley Wine Country**—it's an easy jaunt from Portland.

Days 3 and 4: Oregon Coast

(1½ hours by car from Portland to Cannon Beach)

Leave Portland early on Day 3 for the drive west about 100 miles on U.S. 30 to the small city of **Astoria**, which has several excellent spots for lunch and the **Columbia River Maritime Museum**. Pick the main scenic highway down the Oregon Coast, U.S. 101, and continue south, stopping at **Fort Stevens State Park** and the **Fort Clatsop National Memorial**. End the day in charming **Cannon Beach** (26 miles south of Astoria), which has a wealth of oceanfront hotels and inns, many with views of one of the region's seminal features,

235-foot-tall **Haystack Rock**. Be sure to check out the stunning beach scenery at nearby **Ecola State Park** and **Oswald West State Park**.

The following morning, continue south down U.S. 101. In **Tillamook** (famous for its cheese), take a detour onto the **Three Capes Loop**, a stunning 35-mile byway. Stop in small and scenic **Pacific City** (at the south end of the loop) for lunch. Once you're back on U.S. 101, continue south to **Newport**, spending some time at the excellent **Oregon Coast Aquarium** as well as Oregon State University's fascinating **Hatfield Marine Science Center**. Your final stop is the charming village of **Florence**, 160 miles (four to six hours) from Cannon Beach.

Day 5: Eugene

(2½ hours by car from Florence to Eugene with detour at Oregon Dunes)

Spend the morning driving 20 miles south of Florence along U.S. 101 to scamper about the sandy bluffs at **Oregon Dunes National Recreation Area** near Reedsport. Then backtrack to Florence for lunch in Old Town before taking Highway 126 east for 60 miles to the attractive college city of **Eugene**, staying at one of the charming inns or bed-and-breakfasts near the leafy campus of the University of Oregon. Take a walk to the summit of **Skinner Butte**, which affords fine views of the city, and plan to have dinner at one of the top-notch restaurants at the **5th Street Public Market**. Budget some additional time in Eugene the following morning to visit two excellent University of Oregon museums, the **Jordan Schnitzer Museum of Art** and the **Oregon Museum of Natural History**.

Days 6 and 7: Crater Lake and Ashland

(3 hours by car from Eugene to Crater Lake National Park or Prospect)

From Eugene, take Interstate 5 south for 75 miles to Roseburg, and then head east along Highway 138 (the Umpqua River Scenic Byway), which twists and turns over the Cascade Range for 85 miles to the northern entrance of **Crater Lake National Park**. Once inside the park, you can continue along Rim Drive for another half hour for excellent views of the lake. Overnight in the park or in nearby **Prospect**.

The following morning, take the lake boat tour to **Wizard Island** and hike through the surrounding forest. In the afternoon, head southwest on Highway 62 to Interstate 5, and then on to **Ashland**, 95 miles (about two hours) from Crater Lake. Plan to stay the night in one of Ashland's many superb bed-and-breakfasts. Have dinner and attend one of the **Oregon Shakespeare Festival** productions (mid-February through early November).

Days 8 and 9: Bend

(3½ hours by car from Ashland)

Get an early start out of Ashland, driving east along scenic Highway 140, which skirts picturesque **Upper Klamath Lake,** and then north on U.S. 97, stopping if you have time at **Collier Memorial State Park,** to reach the outdoorsy resort town of **Bend**. Here you can spend two nights checking out the parks, mountain hikes, microbreweries, and restaurants of the state's largest city east of the Cascades. Be sure to visit the outstanding **High Desert Museum**, the **Old Mill District**, and **Mt. Bachelor Ski Area.**

Day 10: Hood River

(3 hours by car from Bend)

From Bend, continue north up U.S. 97, and then northwest up U.S. 26 to **Mt. Hood,** 105 miles total. Have lunch at the historic **Timberline Lodge,** admiring the stunning views south down the Cascade Range. Pick up Highway 35 and drive around the east side of Mt. Hood and then north 40 miles up to the dapper town of **Hood River,** in the heart of the picturesque Columbia Gorge. Spend the night at one of the attractive inns, and try one of this town's stellar restaurants for dinner. From here it's just a 60-mile drive west along a scenic stretch of Interstate 84 to reach Portland.

FIVE SCENIC OREGON DRIVES

Cascades Lakes Scenic Byway

2 to 4 Hours This mountainous 66-mile tour, which is closed in winter due to snow, passes shimmering mountain lakes and prime geological examples of how glaciers and volcanoes have contributed to Oregon's rugged landscape. The route begins just west of **Bend** on Forest Road 46, which climbs up into the Cascades and through the towering evergreens of **Deschutes National Forest** before turning south by **Devil's Lake.** The road ends at Highway 58, about 80 miles southeast of **Eugene.**

The High Desert: Bend to Baker City

5 to 8 Hours Bend, across the state's consistently sunny high desert, is popular year-round for its stunning big-sky panoramas. Follow U.S. 97 north to **Redmond** (from which you could easily detour to **Cline Falls State Park** for a picnic, or up to the rugged hiking of **Smith Rock State Park).** Next turn east on U.S. 26 and follow the road through verdant ranch lands around **Prineville** and into the pine-forested ridges of **Ochoco National Forest.** Continue into eastern Oregon through the **Painted Hills** unit of **John Day Fossil Beds National Monument,** with its fascinating geological formations, and on through such historic gold-mining centers as **John Day,** and—via scenic U.S. 26 and Highway 7—**Baker City.**

Historic Columbia River Highway

1 to 3 Hours Historic Columbia River Highway (U.S. 30) opened in 1922 and is considered a masterful feat of highway engineering, as it climbs over verdant riverside bluffs and passes beside several massive waterfalls. The longest continuous stretch of road extends from **Troutdale,** just east of Portland, and climbs and dips for 22 miles parallel to the Columbia River, ending just west of **Bonneville Dam.** Be sure to stop by **Vista House at Crown Point,** with its 30-mile views up and down the Gorge.

The Southern Coast: U.S. 101 from Brookings to Florence

4 to 6 Hours You'll spy some of the most majestic maritime scenery in the West on the stretch of U.S. 101 that extends north from the Oregon/California border for 160 miles to Florence. You'll first arrive in the pretty fishing village of **Brookings,** through panoramic views from **Samuel H. Boardman State Park,** quaint **Port Orford,** and **Oregon Dunes National Recreation Area** in **Reedsport.** Finish just north in picturesque Florence, which lies on the Siuslaw River and has a charming Old Town with several fine restaurants.

Washington County's Vineyard and Valley Scenic Tour

3 to 6 Hours This meandering series of country roads passes through the heart of Washington County, the nearest patch of the Willamette Wine Country to Portland, which makes it perfect for an afternoon drive—interspersed with some first-rate wine tasting. The 50-mile route begins just off U.S. 26, Exit 61, in Swiss-settled **Helvetia,** turns south through **Forest Grove's** pastoral wine country, and then finishes with a turn through the fertile **Tualatin Valley,** passing by vintage general stores and historic taverns.

WHALE-WATCHING
IN THE PACIFIC NORTHWEST

The thrill of seeing whales in the wild is, for many, one of the most enduring memories of a trip to the Pacific Northwest. In this part of the world, you'll generally spot two species—gray whales and killer "orca" whales.

About 20,000 grays migrate up the West Coast in spring and back down again in early winter (a smaller group of gray whales live off the Oregon coast all summer). From late spring through early autumn about 80 orcas inhabit Washington's Puget Sound and BC's Georgia Strait. Although far fewer in number, the orcas live in pods and travel in predictable patterns; therefore chances are high that you will see a pod on any given trip. Some operators claim sighting rates of 90 percent; others offer guaranteed sightings, meaning that you can repeat the tour free of charge until you spot a whale.

COMMON PACIFIC NORTHWEST SPECIES

0   20   40   60   80   100 (ft)

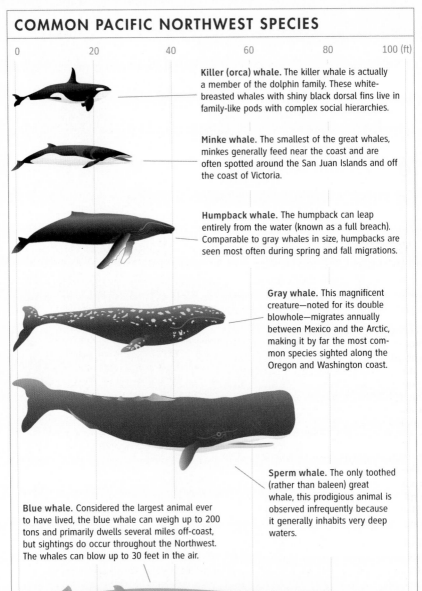

Killer (orca) whale. The killer whale is actually a member of the dolphin family. These white-breasted whales with shiny black dorsal fins live in family-like pods with complex social hierarchies.

Minke whale. The smallest of the great whales, minkes generally feed near the coast and are often spotted around the San Juan Islands and off the coast of Victoria.

Humpback whale. The humpback can leap entirely from the water (known as a full breach). Comparable to gray whales in size, humpbacks are seen most often during spring and fall migrations.

Gray whale. This magnificent creature—noted for its double blowhole—migrates annually between Mexico and the Arctic, making it by far the most common species sighted along the Oregon and Washington coast.

Sperm whale. The only toothed (rather than baleen) great whale, this prodigious animal is observed infrequently because it generally inhabits very deep waters.

Blue whale. Considered the largest animal ever to have lived, the blue whale can weigh up to 200 tons and primarily dwells several miles off-coast, but sightings do occur throughout the Northwest. The whales can blow up to 30 feet in the air.

TAKING A TOUR

Spotting an orca in the Haro Strait between British Columbia and Washington

CHOOSING YOUR BOAT

The type of boat you choose does not affect how close you can get to the whales. For the safety of whales and humans, government regulations require boats to stay at least 100 meters (328 feet) from the pods, though closer encounters are possible if whales approach a boat when its engine is off.

Motor Launches. These cruisers carry from 30 to more than 80 passengers. They are comfortable, with washrooms, protection from the elements, and even snack-and-drink concessions. They can be either glass-enclosed or open-air.

Zodiacs. Open inflatable boats, Zodiacs carry about 12 passengers. They are smaller and more agile than cruisers and offer both an exciting ride bouncing over the waves and an eye-level view of the whales. Passengers are supplied with warm, waterproof survival suits. Note: Zodiac tours are not recommended for people with back or neck problems, pregnant women, or small children.

Most companies have naturalists on board as guides, as well as hydrophones that, if you get close enough, allow you to listen to the whales singing and vocalizing. Although the focus is on whales, you also have a good chance of spotting marine birds, Dall's porpoises, dolphins, seals, and sea lions, as well as other marine life. And, naturally, there's the scenery of forested islands, distant mountains, and craggy coastline.

MOTION SICKNESS

Seasickness isn't usually a problem in the sheltered waters of Puget Sound and the Georgia Strait, but seas can get choppy off the Washington and Oregon coasts. If you're not a good sailor, it's wise to wear a seasickness band or take anti-nausea medication. Ginger candy often works, too.

THE OREGON AND WASHINGTON COAST

A full breach in open waters is a thrilling sight

WHEN TO GO

Mid-December through mid-January is the best time for viewing the southbound migration, with April through mid-June the peak period for the northbound return (when whales swim closer to shore). Throughout summer, several hundred gray whales remain in Oregon waters, often feeding within close view of land. Mornings are often the best time for viewing, as it's more commonly overcast at this time, which means less glare and calmer seas. Try to watch for vapor or water expelled from whales' spouts on the horizon.

WHAT IT COSTS

Trips are generally 2 hours and prices for adults range from about $25 to $40.

RECOMMENDED OUTFITTERS

Depoe Bay, with its sheltered, deepwater harbor, is Oregon's whale-watching capital, and here you'll find several outfitters.

Dockside Charters (☎ 800/733–8915 ⊕ www.docksidedepoebay.com) and **Tradewind Charters** (☎ 800/445–8730 ⊕ www.tradewindscharters.com) have excellent reputations. Green-oriented **Eco Tours of Oregon** (☎ 888/868–7733, ⊕ www.ecotours-of-oregon.com) offers full day tours that depart from Portland hotels and include a stop along the coast at Siletz Bay, a 75-minute charter boat tour, lunch, and stops at state parks near Newport and Lincoln City.

Along the Washington coast, several of the fishing-charter companies in Westport offer seasonal whale-watching cruises, including **Deep Sea Charters** (☎ 800/562–0151 ⊕ www.deepseacharters.net) and **Ocean Sportfishing Charters** (☎ 800/562–0105, ⊕ www.oceansportfishing.com).

BEST VIEWING FROM SHORE

Washington: On Long Beach Peninsula, the North Head Lighthouse at the mouth of the Columbia River, makes an excellent perch for whale sightings. Westport, farther up the coast at the mouth of Grays Harbor, is another great spot.

Oregon Coast: You can spot gray whales all summer long and especially during the spring migration—excellent locales include Neahkanie Mountain Overlook near Manzanita, Cape Lookout State Park, the Whale Watching Center in Depoe Bay, Cape Perpetua Interpretive Center in Yachats, and Cape Blanco Lighthouse near Port Orford.

PORTLAND

WELCOME TO PORTLAND

TOP REASONS TO GO

★ **Play in the parks:** Head to Washington Park's Japanese Garden and International Rose Test Garden; stroll along the Willamette in Tom McCall Riverfront Park, or ramble amid the evergreens atop Mt. Tabor.

★ **View works of art:** Take part in either the First Thursday Pearl District and Last Thursday Alberta Street art walks if you can. Galleries stay open late, often with receptions and openings.

★ **Float on:** Gaze at Portland's gorgeous skyline in the afternoon light, while gently gliding down the Willamette River aboard the *Portland Spirit*.

★ **Sample the liquid assets:** Visit a few of the dozens of superb local producers of craft spirits and beer, artisanal coffee and tea, and fine wine.

★ **Eat locally:** Plenty of visitors to Portland build their entire daily itineraries around eating; food trucks, cafés, and restaurants showcase the city's farm-to-table, locavore ethic.

1 Downtown. At the center of it all, Portland's Downtown boasts the Portland Art Museum, Pioneer Courthouse Square, and the Portland Farmers' Market along with notable restaurants.

2 Old Town/Chinatown. This is the area for Asian-inspired public art and the Lan Su Chinese Garden. It's also home to the Portland Saturday Market, North America's largest open-air handicraft market.

3 Pearl District. Bordering Old Town to the northwest is Portland's trendy and posh neighborhood teaming with upscale restaurants, bars,

2

5 Forest Park. Forest Park is the largest forested area within city limits in the nation. Trailheads are easily accessible from Nob Hill.

6 West Hills and South-west. This neighborhood is home to Washington Park, which contains many must-sees, including the Hoyt Arboretum, International Rose Test Garden, Japanese Garden, and Portland Children's Museum.

7 North. The "fifth quadrant," North Portland sits on the peninsula formed by the joining of the Willamette River and the Columbia River. Part working-class, part trendy, North Mississippi Avenue and North Williams Street are hip dining and drinking destinations.

8 Northeast. Containing the Rose Garden basketball arena, the Lloyd Center Mall, the Alberta Arts District, and some of the city's least and most affluent neighborhoods, Portland's Northeast quadrant is quite diverse.

9 Southeast. The vibrant pockets of foodie-approved restaurants make the South-east a Portland cultural must-see. This neighborhood is also kid-friendly with the OMSI science museum and Mount Tabor Park.

GETTING ORIENTED

Geographically speaking, Portland is relatively easy to navigate. The city's 200-foot-long blocks are highly walk-able, and mapped out into quadrants. The Willamette River divides east and west and Burnside Street separates north from south. "Northwest" refers to the area north of Burnside and west of the river; "Southwest" refers to the area south of Burnside and west of the river; "Northeast" refers to the area north of Burnside and east of the river; "Southeast" refers to the area south of Burnside and east of the river. As you travel around the Portland metro-politan area, keep in mind that named east and west streets intersect numbered avenues, run north to south, and begin at each side of the river. For instance, S.W. 12th Avenue is 12 blocks west of the Willamette. Most of Downtown's streets are one-way.

and shopping, along with pricey condos and artists' lofts. Don't leave Portland without visiting Powell's City of Books here.

4 Nob Hill. From offbeat to upscale, this neighbor-hood's shopping, restau-rants, and bars draw a sophisticated crowd.

Updated by Andrew Collins

What distinguishes Portland, Oregon, from the rest of America's cityscapes? Or from the rest of the world's urban destinations for that matter? In a Northwest nutshell: everything. For some, it's the wealth of cultural offerings and never-ending culinary choices; for others, it's Portland's proximity to the ocean and mountains, or simply the beauty of having all these attributes in one place.

Strolling through Downtown or within one of Portland's numerous neighborhoods, there's an unmistakable vibrancy to this city—one that is encouraged by clean air, infinite trees, and a blend of historic and modern architecture. Portland's various nicknames—Rose City, Bridgetown, Beervana, Brewtopia—tell its story.

Rich cultural offerings, prime historic and modern architecture, endless recreational activities, and a friendly feel make Portland alluring for just about everyone. But it seems that Portland's food scene is one of its biggest attractions these days. It's true that Portland's filled with amazing restaurants—though it's not necessarily the recipes that are causing all the commotion. Rather, it's the locavore movement—using ingredients that are raised, grown, or foraged within a reasonable distance—that's got diners and chefs excited. Often, diners experience savory fish, fowl, or pasta dishes made with seasonal fruit and vegetable accompaniments that have just been plucked from the vine or ground.

PORTLAND PLANNER

WHEN TO GO

Portland's mild climate is best from June through September. Hotels are often filled in July and August, so it's important to book reservations in advance. Spring and fall are also excellent times to visit. The weather usually remains quite good, and the prices for accommodations, transportation, and tours can be lower (and the crowds much smaller) in the most popular destinations. In winter, snow is uncommon in the city but abundant in the nearby mountains, making the region a skier's dream.

Average daytime summer highs are in the 70s; winter temperatures are generally in the 40s. Rainfall varies greatly from one locale to another. In the coastal mountains, for example, 160 inches of rain fall annually, creating temperate rain forests. Portland has an average of only 36 inches of rainfall a year—less than New York, Chicago, or Miami. In winter, however, the rainy days may never seem to end. More than 75% of Portland's annual precipitation occurs from October through March.

GETTING HERE AND AROUND

AIR TRAVEL

It takes about 5 hours to fly nonstop to Portland from New York, 4 hours from Chicago and Atlanta, and 2½ hours from Los Angeles. Flying to Seattle takes just under an hour, and flying to Vancouver takes just over an hour.

Portland International Airport (PDX) is an efficient, modern airport with service to most major national and a handful of international destinations. It's a relatively uncrowded facility, and both check-in and security lines tend to proceed quickly. It's also easily accessible from Downtown Portland, both by car and public transit.

Portland International Airport *(PDX)*. This is the city's—and the region's— major airport. You'll find a pretty good selection of local restaurants and shops inside the terminal. ⊠ *7000 N.E. Airport Way, Portland* ☎ *877/739–4636* ⊕ *www.pdx.com.*

GROUND TRANSPORTATION

Taking the MAX, Portland's light rail train, to and from Portland International Airport is straightforward. The Red Line MAX stops right at the terminal, and the approximately 35- to 45-minute ride to Downtown costs $2.50. Trains run daily from early morning until around midnight—MAX won't be available to some very late-arriving passengers, but it generally runs early enough to catch even the first flights of the day out of Portland, which typically depart around 6 am. You purchase your ticket before boarding at one of the vending machines in the terminal and at every MAX stop; tickets are also good on TriMet buses and the Portland Streetcar, and transfers within 2½ hours of the time of purchase are free.

Contacts TriMet/MAX. ☎ *503/238–7433* ⊕ *www.trimet.org.*

CAR TRAVEL

Portland is a fairly easy city to navigate by car, and if you're planning to explore neighboring regions—such as the coast, Willamette Wine Country, and Columbia Gorge—it's best to do so by car, as public transportation options to these areas, especially the coast, is limited. That said, parking Downtown can get expensive and a car isn't necessary for getting around the city itself. One practical strategy is going without a car during the days you plan to spend in the city center, and then renting a car just for those days when you're venturing outside of the city or exploring some of the East Side neighborhoods, which have ample free parking. Most major rental agencies have Downtown offices, and renting Downtown can save you plenty of money, as you avoid paying the hefty taxes and surcharges that airport agencies charge.

Portland is easily reached via the West Coast's major interstate highway, Interstate 5, which connects Portland to Seattle (which is a three-hour drive north) and Eugene (a little over a two-hour drive south). Interstate 84 begins in Downtown Portland and runs east into the Columbia Gorge and eventually to Idaho. U.S. 26 is the main route to the Oregon Coast west from Downtown, and to Mt. Hood going east. Bypass freeways are Interstate 205, which links Interstate 5 and Interstate 84 before crossing the Columbia River north into Washington, and Interstate 405, which arcs around western Downtown. Most city-center streets are one-way, and some Downtown streets—including 5th and 6th avenues—are limited primarily to bus and MAX traffic (with just one lane for cars, and limited turns).

PARKING   Compared with other major U.S. cities, Portland has ample parking, even Downtown, both metered and in garages. The most affordable and accessible option is to park in one of several city-owned "Smart Park" lots. Rates start at $1.60 per hour (short-term parking, two hours or less) to $5 per hour (long-term parking, weekdays 5 am–6 pm), with a $15 daily maximum; weekends and evenings have lower rates. The best part about Smart Park is that hundreds of participating merchants validate tickets, covering the first two hours of parking when you spend at least $25 in their establishments.

There are numerous privately owned lots around the city as well; fees for these vary and can be quite pricey, and Downtown hotels also charge significantly (as much as $30 to $40 nightly).

Downtown street parking is metered only, and enforcement is vigilant. You can use cash or a credit card to pay ($1.60 per hour) at machines located on each block; display your receipt on the inside of your curbside window. Metered spaces are mostly available for one to three hours, with a few longer-term spaces available on certain streets.

Outside of the Downtown core, you'll find plenty of free street parking, although time limits (usually an hour to three hours) are enforced in some busier, commercial parts of town, including the Pearl District and most of Nob Hill. On the east side of the river, unmetered parking is the norm.

TAXI TRAVEL

Taxi fare is $2.50 at flag drop plus $2.90 per mile; each additional passenger is charged $1. Car-share services like Uber and Lyft cost significantly less than cabs, which sometimes cruise Downtown streets, but it's far more reliable to phone for one or book Uber or Lyft on your smart phone. The major companies are Broadway Cab, New Rose City Cab, Portland Taxi Company, and Radio Cab. The trip between Downtown Portland and the airport takes about 30 minutes by taxi, and the fare averages $35–$43, versus $20–$28 using Uber or Lyft.

Taxi Contacts Broadway Cab. ☎ 503/333-3333 ⊕ www.broadwaycab. com. **New Rose City Cab.** ☎ 503/282-7707 ⊕ www.newrosecitycabco.com. **Portland Taxi Company.** ☎ 503/256-5400 ⊕ www.portlandtaxi.net. **Radio Cab.** ☎ 503/227-1212 ⊕ www.radiocab.net.

TRIMET/MAX TRAVEL

TriMet operates an extensive system of buses, streetcars, and light-rail trains. The North–South streetcar line runs from Nob Hill through the Pearl District, Downtown, and Portland State University campus to South Waterfront. The A and B Loop streetcar lines cross the Willamette River to the East Side via Steel Bridge and the new Tilikum Crossing Bridge.

Metropolitan Area Express, which everybody simply calls MAX, links the eastern and western Portland suburbs with Downtown, Washington Park and the Oregon Zoo, the Lloyd Center district, the Convention Center, and the Rose Quarter. When the Tilikum Crossing Bridge opened in fall 2015, an extension of Downtown's MAX Green line was extended to S.E. Division Street, Sellwood, and the suburbs south of the city. From Downtown, trains operate daily from about 5 am–1 am, with a fare of $2.50 for up to 2½ hours of travel (transfers to other MAX trains, buses, and streetcars are free within this time period), and $5 for an unlimited all-day ticket, which is also good system-wide. A 7-day visitor pass is also available for $26, and a 30-day pass costs $100. The ticket for riding without a fare is stiff.

Upon boarding TriMet buses, the driver will hand you a transfer ticket that's good for up to 2½ hours, on all buses, MAX trains, and streetcars. Be sure to hold onto it whether you're transferring or not; it also serves as proof that you have paid your fare. If you're in town for a while, consider downloading the TriMet app, which allows you to buy tickets on your smart phone. The most central bus routes operate every 10 to 15 minutes throughout the day. Bikes are allowed in designated areas of MAX trains, and there are bike racks on the front of all buses that everyone is free to use.

Contacts TriMet/MAX. ⊠ *Ticket Office at Pioneer Courthouse Sq., 701 S.W. 6th Ave., Downtown* ☎ *503/238–7433* ⊕ *www.trimet.org.*

TOURS
BIKE TOURS

Portland is famously bike-friendly, with miles of dedicated bike lanes and numerous rental shops. There are also a couple of great companies that offer guided rides around the city, covering everything from eating and brewpub-hopping to checking out local parks and historic neighborhoods.

Cycle Portland Bike Tours and Rentals. Trust your guide at Cycle Portland to know Portland's popular and lesser-known spots. Tour themes include Essential Portland, Foodie Field Trip, Brews Cruise, and several others. A well-stocked bike shop is on-site and serves beer on tap. Bike and helmet are included with tours. ⊠ *117 N.W. 2nd Ave., Old Town* ☎ *503/902–5035, 844/739–2453* ⊕ *www.portlandbicycletours.com* 🖃 *From $40.*

FAMILY **Pedal Bike Tours.** This reliable company takes riders into the heart of the city and out to the beauty that surrounds it, from the Columbia Gorge to the Willamette Wine Country. If one of the many tours offered here doesn't meet your criteria, custom tours are available, too. Bikes and helmets are included with each tour. ⊠ *133 S.W. 2nd Ave., Downtown* ☎ *503/243–2453* ⊕ *www.pedalbiketours.com* 🖃 *From $59.*

BOAT TOURS

Portland Spirit River Cruises. Two major rivers lined with pleasant scenery make Portland Spirit River Cruises an engaging tour option. There are brunch, lunch, and dinner cruises, as well as those centered on themes like holidays, tea parties, or live music. Some cruises have a sightseeing option that doesn't include the meal and are less expensive. The company also offers high-speed Explorer Cruises from June through September, which take in about 120 miles of sights along both the Willamette and Columbia rivers; these depart and return to Downtown Portland. Additionally, departing from the town of Cascade Locks (a one-hour drive east of Portland), the stern-wheeler *Columbia Gorge* cruises the Columbia Gorge. ⊠ *Foot of S.W. Salmon St., at Tom McCall Waterfront Park, Downtown* ☎ *503/224–3900, 800/224–3901* ⊕ *www. portlandspirit.com* 🖃 *From $28.*

WALKING TOURS

Walk the Portland beat with guides who share their personal Portland knowledge, including history, food, brews, arts, and sights.

Food Carts Portland. Get to know the city's famed food-cart scene by tagging along with Brett Burmeister, a true expert on the subject. This 90-minute tour is not just a great way to sample bites from some favorite carts, but also an opportunity to learn more about the culture behind the carts. The tour starts at a predetermined Downtown food cart. ⊕ *www.foodcartsportland.com/tours* 🖃 *From $50.*

Portland Walking Tours. A slew of tours are offered by this well-established company, but it's the Beyond Bizarre tour that generates the most buzz. Ghost-hunter wannabes and paranormal junkies make this a popular tour that often sells out during the peak season. If it's unavailable, there's also the Underground Portland tour, which highlights the sinister history of Portland, along with a few other options, including tours that focus on the local food scene. Departure points vary depending on the tour. ☎ *503/774–4522* ⊕ *www.portlandwalkingtours.com* 🖃 *From $23.*

VISITOR INFORMATION

Travel Portland Information Center. ⊠ *Pioneer Courthouse Sq., 701 S.W. 6th Ave., Downtown* ☎ *503/275–8355, 877/678–5263* ⊕ *www.travelportland.com.*

EXPLORING

One of the greatest things about Portland is that there's so much to explore. This city rightfully boasts that there's something for everyone. What makes discovering Portland's treasures even more enticing is that its attractions, transportation options, and events are all relatively accessible and affordable.

DOWNTOWN

Portland has one of the most attractive, inviting Downtown centers in the United States. It's clean, compact, and filled with parks, plazas, and fountains. Architecture fans find plenty to admire in its mix of old and new. Whereas many urban U.S. business districts clear out at night and on weekends, Portland's Downtown is decidedly mixed-use, with plenty of residential and commercial buildings, and an appealing mix of hotels, shops, museums, restaurants, and bars. You can easily walk from one end of Downtown to the other, and the city's superb public transportation system—which includes MAX light rail, buses, and the streetcar—makes it easy to get here from other parts of the city. A day pass is recommended.

TOP ATTRACTIONS

FAMILY

Fodor's Choice

★

Governor Tom McCall Waterfront Park. Named for a former governor revered for his statewide land-use planning initiatives, this park stretches north along the Willamette River for about a mile from near the historic Hawthorne Bridge to Steel Bridge. Broad and grassy, Waterfront Park affords a fine ground-level view of Downtown Portland's bridges and skyline. Once an expressway, it's now the site for many annual celebrations, among them the Rose Festival, classical and blues concerts, Gay Pride, Cinco de Mayo, and the Oregon Brewers Festival. The arching jets of water at the **Salmon Street Fountain** change configuration every few hours, and are a favorite cooling-off spot during the dog days of summer. ■TIP→ Both the Hawthorne Bridge and Steel Bridge offer dedicated pedestrian lanes, allowing joggers, cyclists, and strollers to make a full loop along both banks of the river, via Vera Katz Eastside Esplanade. ✉ *S.W. Naito Pkwy. (Front Ave.), from Steel Bridge to south of Hawthorne Bridge, Downtown* ⊕ *www.portlandoregon.gov/parks.*

Oregon Historical Society Museum. Impressive eight-story-high trompe l'oeil murals of Lewis and Clark and the Oregon Trail invite history lovers into this Downtown museum that relates the state's story from prehistoric times to the present. A pair of 9,000-year-old sagebrush sandals, a covered wagon, and an early chainsaw are displayed in "Oregon My Oregon," a permanent exhibit that provides a comprehensive overview of the state's past. Other spaces host large traveling exhibits and changing regional shows. The center's research library is open to the public Tuesday through Saturday; its bookstore is a good source for maps and publications on Pacific Northwest history. ✉ *1200 S.W. Park Ave., Downtown* ☎ *503/222–1741* ⊕ *www.ohs.org* ◻ *$11.*

Pioneer Courthouse Square. Often billed as the living room, public heart, and commercial soul of Downtown, Pioneer Square is not entirely square, but rather an amphitheater-like brick piazza. Special seasonal, charitable, and festival-oriented events often take place in this premier people-watching venue, although over the years, as other parts of Downtown (the Park Blocks, the Pearl District) have become more trendy, the square has lost a bit of its prominence. Directly across the street is one of Downtown Portland's most familiar landmarks, the classically sedate **Pioneer Courthouse**; built in 1869, it's the oldest public building in the Pacific Northwest. A couple of blocks east of the square,

Downtown

← TO PROVIDENCE PARK

S.W. Pine St.
S.W. Oak St.
S.W. Stark St.
S.W. Washington St.
S.W. Alder St.
MAX LIGHT RAIL
S.W. Morrison St.
S.W. Yamhill St.
S.W. Taylor St.
S.W. Salmon St.
S.W. Main St.
S.W. Madison St.
S.W. Jefferson St.
S.W. Columbia St.
S.W. Clay St.
S.W. Market St.
S.W. Mill St.
Harrison St.

S.W. 12th Ave.
S.W. 11th Ave.
S.W. 10th Ave.
S.W. 9th Ave.
S.W. Park Ave.
S.W. Park Ave.
6th Ave.
Transit Mall
5th Ave.
Transit Mall
S.W. 4th Ave.
S.W. 3rd Ave.
S.W. 2nd Ave.
S.W. 1st Ave.
S.W. Naito Pkwy. (Front Ave.)
MAX LIGHT RAIL

CENTRAL CITY STREETCAR

First Congregationalist Church ◆

South Park Blocks

S.W. Broadway
26
26
S.W. 6th Ave.
S.W. 5th Ave.
S.W. 4th Ave.
S.W. 3rd Ave.

BUS

Salmon Street Fountain ◆

Hawthorne Bridge

Willamette River

KEY
—○— Max Light Rail
- ← - Streetcar
.... Bus
🚲 Bike only

0   1/4 mile
0   1/4 kilometer

Pioneer Square and Pioneer Courthouse

you'll find **Pioneer Place Mall,** an upscale retail center that spans four city blocks. ⊠ *701 S.W. 6th Ave., Downtown* ⊕ *www.thesquarepdx.org.*

Portland/Oregon Information Center. You can pick up maps and literature about the city and the state here at the Portland/Oregon Information Center. Easy to miss, the center is located between the water features, through the glass doors, at Pioneer Courthouse Square. TriMet (⊕ *www.trimet.org*) also operates a desk inside the information center, selling passes and tickets for buses, light rail, and the streetcar. ⊠ *701 S.W. 6th Ave., Downtown* ☎ *503/275–8355, 877/678–5263* ⊕ *www. travelportland.com* ☾ *Closed Sun. Nov.–Apr.*

Fodor's Choice **Portland Art Museum.** The treasures at the Pacific Northwest's oldest arts
★ facility span 35 centuries of Asian, European, and American art—it's an impressive collection for a midsize city. A high point is the Center for Native American Art, with regional and contemporary art from more than 200 indigenous groups. The **Jubitz Center for Modern and Contemporary Art** contains six floors devoted entirely to modern art, including a small but superb photography gallery, with the changing selection chosen from more than 5,000 pieces in the museum's permanent collection. The film center presents the annual Portland International Film Festival in February and the Northwest Filmmakers' Festival in early November. Also, take a moment to linger in the peaceful outdoor sculpture garden. Kids under 17 are admitted free. ⊠ *1219 S.W. Park Ave., Downtown* ☎ *503/226–2811, 503/221–1156 film schedule* ⊕ *www. portlandartmuseum.org* ⊟ *$19.99* ☾ *Closed Mon.*

Portland Farmers' Market. On Saturday year-round, local farmers, bakers, chefs, and entertainers converge at the South Park Blocks near the PSU campus for Oregon's largest open-air farmers' market—it's one of the most impressive in the country. It's a great place to sample the regional bounty and to witness the local-food obsession that's revolutionized Portland's culinary scene. There's plenty of food you can eat on the spot, plus nonperishable local items (wine, hazelnuts, chocolates, vinegars) you can take home with you. There's a smaller Wednesday market, May through November, on a different section of the Park Blocks (between S.W. Salmon and S.W. Main). On Mondays, June through September, the market is held at Pioneer Courthouse Square, and at other times the Portland Farmers' Market is held in different locations around town, including Nob Hill/Northwest, Kenton/North Portland, King/Alberta, and Lents/Southeast, and some 40 other farmers' markets take place throughout metro Portland—see the website for a list. ⊠ *South Park Blocks at S.W. Park Ave. and Montgomery St., Downtown* ☏ *503/241–0032* ⊕ *www.portlandfarmersmarket.org* ☉ *Closed Sun.–Fri.*

West End. A formerly rough-around-the-edges section of Downtown, sandwiched between the Pioneer Square area and the swanky Pearl District, this triangular patch of vintage buildings—interspersed with a handful of contemporary ones—has evolved since the early 2000s into one of the city's most vibrant and eclectic hubs of retail, nightlife, and dining. Hip boutique hotels like the Ace, McMenamins Crystal, and Sentinel rank among the city's trendiest addresses. Along Stark Street, formerly the heart of Portland's LGBT scene, there's still a popular gay bar, but now you'll also find noteworthy restaurants and lounges like Clyde Common, Bamboo Sushi, Multnomah Whiskey Library, and Super Bite and connecting bar, Kask. Among the indie-spirited shops, check out Cacao chocolate shop, Frances May clothier, and Union Way—an enclosed pedestrian mall with a handful of upscale boutiques. ⊠ *S.W. 13th to S.W. 9th Aves., between W. Burnside St. and S.W. Alder St., Downtown* ⊕ *www.wepdx.com.*

WORTH NOTING

Portland State University. The only public university in the city takes advantage of Downtown's South Park Blocks to provide trees and greenery for its 28,000 students. The attractive, compact, but steadily growing campus, between Market Street and Interstate 405, spreads west from the Park Blocks to 12th Avenue and east to 5th Avenue. Seven schools offer undergraduate, masters, and doctoral degrees. Close to the Portland Art Museum and Oregon Historical Society Museum, PSU doesn't have any major attractions of its own, but the campus blends almost imperceptibly with a pretty part of Downtown, and it's the site—along the leafy South Park Blocks—of the city's largest farmers' market on Saturday mornings. ⊠ *Park Ave. and Market St., Downtown* ☏ *503/725–3000* ⊕ *www.pdx.edu.*

OLD TOWN/CHINATOWN

The Skidmore Old Town National Historic District, commonly called Old Town/Chinatown, is where Portland was born. The 20-square-block section, bounded by Oak Street to the south and Hoyt Street to the north, includes buildings of varying ages and architectural designs. Before it was renovated, this was skid row. Vestiges of it remain in parts of Chinatown; older buildings are gradually being remodeled, and lately the immediate area has experienced a small surge in development. Portland doesn't have a gay district per se—the scene permeates just about every neighborhood of this extremely LGBT-welcoming city. But you'll find the highest concentration of Portland's gay nightspots in Old Town (and a few others close by in Downtown). MAX serves the area with a stop at the Old Town/Chinatown station.

Fodor's Choice **Lan Su Chinese Garden.** In a twist on the Joni Mitchell song, the city of
★ Portland and private donors took down a parking lot and unpaved paradise when they created this wonderland near the Pearl District and Old Town/Chinatown. It's the largest Suzhou-style garden outside China, with a large lake, bridged and covered walkways, koi- and water lily–filled ponds, rocks, bamboo, statues, waterfalls, and courtyards. A team of 60 artisans and designers from China literally left no stone unturned—500 tons of stone were brought here from Suzhou—in their

Lan Su Chinese Garden, Old Town/Chinatown

efforts to give the windows, roof tiles, gateways, including a "moon-gate," and other architectural aspects of the garden some specific meaning or purpose. Also on the premises are a gift shop and an enchanting two-story teahouse, operated by local Tao of Tea company, overlooking the lake and garden. ⊠ *239 N.W. Everett St., Old Town* ☎ *503/228–8131* ⊕ *www.lansugarden.org* ⊠ *$9.50.*

FAMILY **Oregon Maritime Museum.** Local model makers created most of this museum's models of ships that once plied the Columbia River. Contained within the stern-wheeler steamship *Portland*, this small museum provides an excellent overview of Oregon's maritime history with artifacts and memorabilia. The Children's Corner has nautical items that can be touched and operated. The *Portland* was the last steam-powered stern-wheel tugboat operating in the United States, and volunteer-guided tours include the pilot house and engine room. ⊠ *Portland steamship, Foot of S.W. Pine St., in Waterfront Park, Old Town* ☎ *503/224–7724* ⊕ *www.oregonmaritimemuseum.org* ⊠ *$7* ⊘ *Closed Sun.–Tues.*

Fodor's Choice **Pine Street Market.** In a city where restaurants rank among the top sight-
★ seeing attractions, the 2016 opening of this bustling food hall in a handsome late-Victorian Old Town building was met with shouts of glee. In one massive room, nine small restaurants with counter service offer visitors the chance to sample the creations of some of Portland's most celebrated chefs. Highlights include one of the first U.S. branches of Tokyo's famed **Marukin Ramen, OP Wurst** gourmet hot dog stand (from Olympia Provisions), Israeli street snacks at **Shalom Y'all** (from John Gorham of Tasty n Sons fame), and a soft-serve ice cream stand called **Wiz Bang Bar** operated by Salt & Straw. Bring your appetite,

and brace yourself for long lines on weekends. ⊠ *126 S.W. 2nd Ave., Old Town* ⊕ *www.pinestreetpdx.com.*

FAMILY

Fodor's Choice

★

Portland Saturday Market. On weekends from March to Christmas Eve, the west side of the Burnside Bridge and the Skidmore Fountain area hosts North America's largest ongoing open-air handicraft market. If you're looking for jewelry, yard art, housewares, and decorative goods made from every material under the sun, check out the amazing collection of works by talented artisans on display here. The market also opens for holiday shopping during the three days preceding Christmas Day, a period known as the Festival of the Last Minute. Entertainers and food booths add to the festive feel (although be careful not to mistake this market for the food-centric PSU Portland Farmers' Market, which also takes place on Saturday, on the other side of Downtown). If taking the MAX train to the market, get off at the Skidmore Fountain stop. ⊠ *2 S.W. Naito Pkwy. at foot of S.W. Ankeny, in Waterfront Park, Old Town* ☎ *503/222–6072* ⊕ *www.portlandsaturdaymarket. com* ⊘ *Closed Jan., Feb., and weekdays.*

PEARL DISTRICT

Bordering Old Town to the west and Downtown and the West End to the north, the trendy Pearl District comprises a formerly rough-and-tumble warren of warehouses and railroad yards. Much of the Pearl is new construction, but dozens of the district's historic industrial buildings have been converted into handsome, loft-style housing and commercial concerns, too. You'll find some of the city's most buzzed-about restaurants, galleries, and shops in this neighborhood—the monthly First Thursday evening art walk is an especially fun time to visit. The Portland Streetcar line passes through here, with stops at ecologically themed Jamison Square and Tanner Springs parks.

FAMILY

Jamison Square Park. This gently terraced park surrounded by tony Pearl District lofts contains a soothing fountain that mimics nature. Rising water gushes over a stack of basalt blocks, gradually fills the open plaza, and then subsides. Colorful 30-foot tiki totems by pop artist Kenny Scharf stand along the park's west edge. There are tables and chairs in the park and wading in the fountain is encouraged. The streetcar stops right at the park. ⊠ *N.W. 10th Ave. and Lovejoy St., Pearl District* ⊕ *www.portlandoregon.gov/parks.*

NEED A
BREAK

✕ **Nuvrei.** You'll find some of the tastiest sweets in town at this cozy patisserie and café a few blocks south of Jamison Square. Try the bacon-cheddar biscuit topped with smoked bacon, fried egg, and raspberry jam, and don't miss the little macaron bar downstairs. ⊠ *404 N.W. 10th Ave., Pearl District* ☎ *503/972–1700* ⊕ *www.nuvrei.com.*

NOB HILL

Fashionable since the 1880s and still filled with Victorian houses, Nob Hill is a mixed-use cornucopia of old Portland charm and new Portland retail and dining. With its cafés, restaurants, galleries, and boutiques,

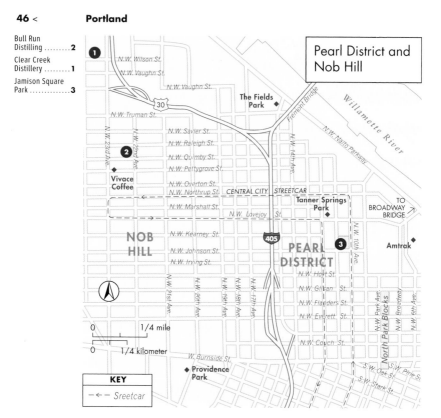

Pearl District and
Nob Hill

it's a great place to stroll, shop, and people-watch. A quite trendy neighborhood in the 1980s and '90s, Nob Hill feels more established but no less inviting today. At the southern end of 23rd, on the blocks nearest Burnside, you'll mostly encounter upscale chain shops, whereas more independent and generally less pricey retail proliferates farther north. More restaurants and nightspots, along with a handful of shops, line N.W. 21st Avenue, two blocks east of 23rd, and more recently, the formerly industrial area known as Slabtown and located in and around the intersection of N.W. 21st and N.W. Raleigh has morphed into a warren of shiny new condos and sceney bars and restaurants. The Portland Streetcar runs from Legacy Good Samaritan Hospital on 23rd, connecting with the Pearl District and Downtown.

Bull Run Distilling. This exceptional small-batch spirits producer joins the more established Clear Creek as yet another highly quaffable reason to explore Nob Hill. In Bull Run's cozy tasting room, sample such acclaimed spirits as Medoyeff Vodka, Temperance Straight Bourbon Whiskey, and Aquavit. ⊠ *2259 N.W. Quimby St., Nob Hill* ☎ *503/224–3483* ⊕ *www.bullrundistillery.com* ⊘ *Closed Mon. and Tues.*

Fodor's Choice   **Clear Creek Distillery.** A pioneer in what has become an internationally
★   acclaimed local distillery scene, this producer of high-quality spirits is tucked down a quiet street in an industrial area just north of Nob Hill.

Just ring the bell and someone will unlock the wrought-iron gate and let you into a cozy tasting room where you can sample Clear Creek's world-famous Oregon apple and pear brandies, distinctive Douglas Fir Brandy, and other liqueurs and grappas. ■ TIP→ **If the peaty, highly prized McCarthy's Oregon Single Malt Whiskey is available, grab a bottle—they sell out fast.** ✉ *2389 N.W. Wilson St., Nob Hill* ☎ *503/248–9470* ⊕ *www.clearcreekdistillery.com.*

FOREST PARK

One of the largest city parks in the country, Forest Park stretches 8 miles along the hills overlooking the Willamette River west of Downtown. More than 80 miles of trails through forests of Douglas fir, hemlock, and cedar (including a few patches of old growth) offer numerous options for those looking to log some miles or spend some time outside.

Fodor's Choice
★

Forest Park. One of the nation's largest urban wildernesses (5,157 acres), this city-owned, car-free park has more than 50 species of birds and mammals and more than 80 miles of trails through forests of Douglas fir, hemlock, and cedar. Running the length of the park is the 30-mile Wildwood Trail, which extends into adjoining Washington Park (and is a handy point for accessing Forest Park), starting at the Vietnam Veteran's Memorial in Hoyt Arboretum. You can access a number of spur trails from the Wildwood Trail, including the 11-mile Leif Erikson Drive, which picks up from the end of N.W. Thurman Street and is a popular route for jogging and mountain biking. ■ TIP→ **You can find information and maps at the Forest Park Conservancy office, at 210 N.W. 17th Avenue, and website.** ✉ *Leif Erikson Dr. entrance, End of N.W. Thurman St., Nob Hill* ☎ *503/223–5449* ⊕ *www.forestparkconservancy.org.*

Portland Audubon Society. The 150-acre sanctuary has a few miles of trails, including one known for ample woodpecker sightings, as well as access to the miles of trails in the adjoining Forest Park. There's also a hospital for injured and orphaned birds here, as well as a gift shop stocked with books and feeders. The society supplies free maps and sponsors a flock of bird-related activities, including guided bird-watching events. ✉ *5151 N.W. Cornell Rd., Forest Park, Northwest* ☎ *503/292–6855* ⊕ *www.audubonportland.org.*

WEST HILLS AND SOUTHWEST

Forming a natural western border of Downtown and Nob Hill, the West Hills extend as a high (up to around 1,000 feet in elevation) ridgeline from Southwest to Northwest Portland. Part of this lofty neighborhood is residential, containing some of the largest and finest homes in the city, many of them with knockout views of the Downtown skyline and Mt. St. Helens and Mt. Hood in the distance. Technically, Downtown Portland is in the city's Southwest quadrant, as are most of the attractions included in the West Hills section of town. But when locals mention Southwest, they're generally referring to the area south and southwest of Downtown, a mostly middle- to upper-middle-class

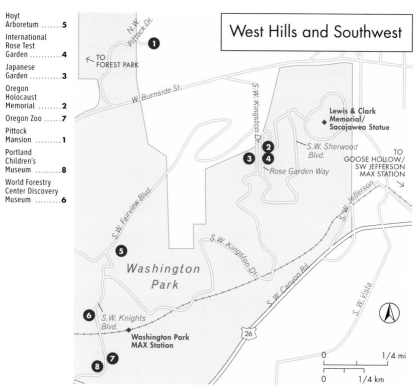

residential district with a few commercial pockets. One notable section is RiverPlace and, a bit farther south, South Waterfront, which both hug the Willamette River. A formerly industrial tract, this area has been rapidly developed since the early 2000s into a contemporary mixed-use neighborhood of both mid- and high-rise glass-and-steel condos, office buildings, a huge expansion of prestigious Oregon Health and Science University, the new Tilikum Crossing Bridge, and a growing but still limited number of restaurants, hotels, and shops. RiverPlace begins just south of Hawthorne Bridge and is easily accessed from Tom McCall Waterfront Park—there's a pretty pedestrian promenade along the river, with a handful of sidewalk cafés and boutiques.

TOP ATTRACTIONS

Hoyt Arboretum. Some 12 miles of trails, which connect with others in Washington Park and Forest Park, wind through the 189-acre arboretum, which was established in 1928 and contains more than 2,000 species of plants and one of the nation's largest collections of coniferous trees; pick up trail maps at the visitor center. Guided 90-minute tours ($3 suggested donation) are offered most Saturdays at noon from April through October. Also here are the Winter Garden and a memorial to veterans of the Vietnam War. The visitor center is a half mile from the Washington Park MAX station. ⊠ *4000 S.W. Fairview Blvd., Arlington Heights, West Hills* ☎ *503/865–8733* ⊕ *www.hoytarboretum.org* ⌕ *Free.*

FAMILY **International Rose Test Garden.** This glorious park within Washington Park
Fodor's Choice comprises three terraced gardens, set on 4½ acres, where more than
★ 10,000 bushes and some 550 varieties of roses grow. The flowers, many
of them new varieties, are at their peak in June, July, September, and
October. From the gardens you can take in highly photogenic views of
the Downtown skyline and, on fine days, the Fuji-shaped slopes of Mt.
Hood, 50 miles to the east. Summer concerts take place in the garden's
amphitheater. It's a pretty but hilly 30- to 40-minute walk from Downtown, or you can get here via MAX light rail (either to Washington Park
or Kings Hill/S.W. Salmon Street stations); then transfer to Bus No. 63
or Washington Park shuttle (May–October only). ⊠ *400 S.W. Kingston
Ave., West Hills* ☎ *503/227–7033* ⊕ *www.rosegardenstore.org.*

Fodor's Choice **Japanese Garden.** One of the most authentic Japanese gardens outside
★ Japan, this serene landscape unfolds over 12½ acres of Washington
Park, just a short stroll up the hill from the International Rose Test
Garden. Designed by a Japanese landscape master, there are five sepa-
rate garden styles: Strolling Pond Garden, Tea Garden, Natural Garden,
Sand and Stone Garden, and Flat Garden. The Tea House was built in
Japan and reconstructed here. An ambitious expansion designed by
renowned Japanese architect Kengo Kuma added a tea garden café,
library, art gallery, and a new gift shop in 2017. The east side of the
Pavilion has a majestic view of Portland and Mt. Hood. Take MAX
light rail to Washington Park station, and transfer to Bus No. 63 or the
Washington Park Shuttle (May–October only). ■ TIP→ The noon public
tours, given daily March–October and weekends November–February,
are given by knowledgeable volunteers. ⊠ *611 S.W. Kingston Ave.,
West Hills* ☎ *503/223–1321* ⊕ *www.japanesegarden.com* 🎟 *$9.50.*

FAMILY **Oregon Zoo.** This beautiful animal park in the West Hills, famous for
its Asian elephants, is undergoing a two-decade-long series of major
improvements and expansions to make the zoo more sustainable and
provide more stimulating spaces, education and conservation opportunities, as well as improved guest amenities and event spaces. New in
recent years are the Condors of the Columbia habitat, which includes a
deep pool for condor bathing, a 30-foot aviary, and an elevated viewing
area to see the condors in flight; and the Elephant Lands area, which
features feeding stations, mud wallows, varied terrain, and deep pools
to keep the elephants active, as well as one of the world's largest indoor
elephant facilities. A state-of-the-art Zoo Education Center opened in
2017, and polar bear, primate, and rhino habitats are planned by 2020.
Other major draws include an Africa Savanna with rhinos, hippos,
zebras, and giraffes. Steller Cove, a state-of-the-art aquatic exhibit, has
Steller sea lions and a family of sea otters. Also popular are the chim-
panzees, a penguinarium, and habitats for beavers, otters, waterfowl,
and reptiles native to the west side of the Cascade Range. In summer a
narrow-gauge train operates from the zoo's new train station, chugging
along a track past several animal exhibits and through the woods to a
station near the International Rose Test Garden and the Japanese Garden. Roughly 15 summer concerts, often featuring nationally known
pop stars, take place at the zoo from mid-June through August. Take the
MAX light rail to the Washington Park station. ⊠ *4001 S.W. Canyon*

Rd., West Hills ☎ *503/226–1561* ⊕ *www.oregonzoo.org* ✉ *Mar.–Sept., $14.95; Oct.–Feb. $9.95.*

Pittock Mansion. Henry Pittock, the founder and publisher of the *Oregonian* newspaper, built this 22-room, castlelike mansion, which combines French Renaissance and Victorian styles. The opulent manor, built in 1914, is filled with art and antiques. The 46-acre grounds, northwest of Washington Park and 1,000 feet above the city, offer superb views of the skyline, rivers, and the Cascade Range, including Mt. Hood and Mt. St. Helens. The mansion is a half-mile uphill trek from the nearest bus stop. The mansion is also a highly popular destination among hikers using Forest Park's and Washington Park's well-utilized Wildwood Trail. ✉ *3229 N.W. Pittock Dr., West Hills* ☎ *503/823–3623* ⊕ *www. pittockmansion.com* ✉ *$10.*

WORTH NOTING

Oregon Holocaust Memorial. This memorial to those who perished during the Holocaust bears the names of surviving families who live in Oregon and southwest Washington. A bronzed baby shoe, a doll, broken spectacles, and other strewn possessions await notice on the cobbled courtyard. Soil and ash from six Nazi concentration camps is interred beneath the black granite wall. The memorial is operated by the Oregon Jewish Museum and Center for Holocaust Education, which is currently closed but will be moving into a new permanent home in Old Town at 724 N.W. Davis Street in summer 2017, hosts rotating history and art exhibits, films, concerts, and lectures. ✉ *S.W. Washington Way and S.W. Wright Ave., West Hills* ☎ *503/226–3600* ⊕ *www.ojmche.org.*

FAMILY **Portland Children's Museum.** Colorful sights and sounds offer a feast of sensations for kids of all ages where hands-on play is the order of the day. Visit nationally touring exhibits; catch a story time, a sing-along, or a puppet show in the Play It Again theater; create sculptures in the clay studio; splash hands in the waterworks display; or make a creation from junk in the Garage. The museum shares the same parking lot as the zoo and can also be reached via the MAX light rail Washington Park stop. ✉ *4015 S.W. Canyon Rd., West Hills* ☎ *503/223–6500* ⊕ *www. portlandcm.org* ✉ *$10.75.*

FAMILY **World Forestry Center Discovery Museum.** This handsomely designed, contemporary museum across from the zoo contains interactive and multimedia exhibits about forest sustainability. A white-water raft ride, smoke-jumper training simulator, and Timberjack tree harvester all provide different perspectives on Pacific Northwest forests. On the second floor the forests of the world are explored in various travel settings. A canopy lift ride hoists visitors to the 50-foot ceiling to look at a Douglas fir. ✉ *4033 S.W. Canyon Rd., West Hills* ☎ *503/228–1367* ⊕ *www. worldforestry.org* ✉ *$7* ☽ *Closed Tues. and Wed. in early Sept.–late May.*

NORTH

Somewhat dismissed historically as the city's "fifth quadrant," North Portland has come into its own in recent years, as the comparatively low cost of real estate has made it popular with young entrepreneurs, students, and other urban pioneers. Marked by a 31-foot-tall roadside statue of the strapping lumberman Paul Bunyan (on the National Register of Historic Places), the neighborhood occupies the peninsula formed by the confluence of the Willamette River (to the west) and the Columbia River (to the north). In the working-class, port-side neighborhood of St. Johns (where you can view one of the city's most beautiful river crossings, the St. John Bridge), old-school barbershops and hardware stores sit alongside a steadily growing mix of hipster-favored shops, restaurants, and cafés. Farther south (and closer to Downtown), North Mississippi and North Williams avenues, which are about 10 short blocks apart, have become home to some of the hottest food, drink, and music venues in the city.

Fodor's Choice
★

North Mississippi Avenue. One of North Portland's strips of indie retailers, the liveliest section of North Mississippi Avenue stretches for several blocks and includes a mix of old storefronts and sleek new buildings that house cafés, brewpubs, collectives, shops, music venues, and an excellent food-cart pod, Mississippi Marketplace. Bioswale planter boxes, found-object fences, and café tables built from old doors are some of the innovations you'll see along this eclectic thoroughfare. At the southern end of the strip, stop by the ReBuilding Center, an outlet for recycled building supplies that has cob (clay-and-straw) trees and benches built into the facade. About a 10-minute walk east and running parallel to North Mississippi, the bike-friendly North Williams corridor is an even newer thoroughfare of almost entirely new, eco-friendly buildings and condos rife with trendy restaurants, nightspots, and boutiques. Highlights here include Tasty n Sons, Lark Press letterpress printing studio and shop, the People's Pig barbecue, and Hopworks BikeBar and eco brewpub. You could easily spend a few hours taking in both neighborhoods—both have outstanding food scenes, while North Mississippi is stronger on retail. To get here on MAX light rail, get off at the Albina/Mississippi station. ⊠ *N. Mississippi Ave. between N. Fremont and N. Skidmore Sts., North.*

NORTHEAST

Still the epicenter of the city's relatively small—compared with other U.S. cities the size of Portland—African American community, the inner parts of Northeast have slowly gentrified over the last half century. In the Irvington, Laurelhurst, and Alameda neighborhoods, you'll find some of the largest, most historic homes in town.

Lined with many excellent—and generally quite affordable—restaurants, bars, galleries, and boutiques, Alberta Street has become one of the city's trendiest neighborhoods. It also hosts a bustling street art fair the last Thursday of every month during summer (primarily between 12th and 31st avenues). Nearer to Downtown, the Lloyd Center—both the name of a rather dull shopping mall and the surrounding

North, Northeast and Southeast

N. E. Killingsworth St.
N. E. Alberta St. **2**
N. E. Prescott St.
N. E. Fremont St.
N. E. Knott St.
N. E. Russell St.

N. North Mississippi Ave.
Martin Luther King Jr. Blvd.
N. E. 33rd Ave.
N. E. 42nd Ave.
N. E. Cully Blvd.
N. E. 57th Ave.
N. E. Sandy Blvd.

5

1

TO AIRPORT →
3

99E

HOLLYWOOD
TO I-205 →

Memorial Coliseum
N. W. Naito Pkwy. (Front Ave.)
N. E. Broadway
Weidler St.
♦ Lloyd Center
Halsey St.

Moda Center
Oregon Convention Center

N.E. Glisan St.
E. Burnside St. **5**
4
S. E. Stark St.
S. E. Belmont St.
S. E. Yamill St.

6
7

S. E. 20th Ave.
S. E. 28th Ave.
S. E. 39th Ave.
S. E. 60th Ave.
S. E. 50th Ave.

M. L. King Jr. Blvd.
S. E. Grand Ave.

S. E. Madison St.
S. E. Hawthorne Blvd.

13

Mt. Tabor Park

8

10

9
S. E. Division St.
12
11

S. E. Powell Blvd.

405
S. W. Naito Pkwy. (Front Ave.)

26

0   1 miles
0   1 kilometers

99E

26

S. E. Holgate Blvd.

Lents Park

43

Ross Island

Eastmoreland General Hospital

Reed ♦ College
S. E. Woodstock Blvd.

205

Oaks Bottom Wildlife Refuge

Willamette River

S. W. Macadam Ave.

S. E. 13th Ave.

S. E. Milwaukee Ave.

S. E. Mcloughlin Blvd.

S. E. 52nd Ave.

S. E. 72nd Ave.

S. E. 82nd Ave.

5

— S. E. Bybee Blvd.

EASTMORELAND

S. E. Tacoma St.

2

neighborhood (containing the Oregon Convention Center and Rose Garden) is an unfortunately drab example of late-20th-century urban renewal. The area serves a purpose, as it's home to the bulk of the East Side's hotels, but it lacks the historic charm and indie spirit of other neighborhoods on this side of the river.

East Burnside and 28th Avenue. A roughly T-shaped dining and retail district that's less defined but no less popular and impressive than some of the East Side's other culinary and shopping hot spots (like N.E. Alberta and Division Street), this diverse neighborhood comprises a slew of mostly food-related ventures along East Burnside Street from about 22nd to 28th avenues. Then, where Burnside meets 28th Avenue, you'll find several blocks of first-rate eateries as well as a handful of boutiques in either direction, heading north up to about Glisan Street and south down to about Stark Street. The historic Laurelhurst Theater anchors the intersection of 28th and Burnside, and top foodie haunts in these parts include Heart Coffee Roasters, Davenport, Screen Door, Tusk, Navarre, Alma Chocolate, PaaDee, Laurelhurst Market, Crema Coffee & Bakery (and the small but excellent food-cart pod containing Wolf and Bear's for Middle Eastern food and Le Pantry for French bistro fare), Vino wineshop, Ken's Artisan Pizza, Bamboo Sushi, and Canteen vegan restaurant and juice bar. The neighborhood isn't close to any light-rail stops, but you can get here easily from Downtown via Bus 20, and street parking is free and abundant. ⊠ *E. Burnside St. from 22nd to 28th Aves., and 28th Ave. from N.E. Glisan to S.E. Stark Sts., Kerns, Northeast.*

The Grotto. Owned by the Catholic Church, the National Sanctuary of Our Sorrowful Mother, as it's officially known, displays more than 100 statues and shrines in 62 acres of woods. The grotto was carved into the base of a 110-foot cliff, and has a replica of Michelangelo's *Pietà*. The real treat is found after ascending the cliff face via elevator, as you enter a wonderland of gardens, sculptures, and shrines, and a glass-walled cathedral with an awe-inspiring view of the Columbia River and the Cascades. There's a dazzling Festival of Lights at Christmastime (late November and December), with 500,000 lights and more than 150 holiday concerts in the 600-seat chapel. Daily masses are held here, too. ■ TIP➔ **Hours can vary seasonally so call ahead if visiting late in the day.** ⊠ *8840 N.E. Skidmore St., Northeast ✛ Main entrance: N.E. Sandy Blvd. at N.E. 85th Ave.* ☎ *503/254–7371* ⊕ *www.thegrotto.org* ▱ *Plaza level free; upper level $6.*

NEED A BREAK

✕ **Pix Patisserie.** In a handsome café and bar with a small patio along East Burnside Street, Pix is famous for its sweet treats, including passion-fruit macarons and dark-chocolate truffles. The adjoining Bar Vivant serves authentic Spanish tapas and has one of the most impressive selections of champagne in the country. **Known for:** huge champagne list; late-night desserts. ⊠ *2225 E. Burnside St., Northeast* ☎ *971/271–7166* ⊕ *www. pixpatisserie.com.*

FAMILY **Northeast Alberta Street.** Few of Portland's several hipster-favored East
Fodor's Choice Side neighborhoods have developed as quickly and as interestingly as
★ N.E. Alberta Street, aka N.E. Alberta, aka the Alberta Arts District,
which has morphed from a downcast area into a funky strip of hippie-
driven counterculture into a considerably more eclectic stretch of both
indie arts spaces and downright sophisticated bistros and galleries.
Favorite stops include Pine State Biscuits, Salt & Straw ice cream, the
Bye and Bye bar, Tin Shed Garden Cafe, Barista coffee, Aviary restaurant, Bollywood Theater restaurant, Ampersand art gallery and books,
the Collective Art Gallery, pedX shoes, and Screaming Sky toys and
housewares. Extending a little more than a mile, Northeast Alberta
offers plenty of one-of-a-kind dining and shopping; you'll find virtually
no national chains along here. The area is also home to some of the best
people-watching in Portland, especially during the Last Thursday (of the
month) art walks, held May–September from 6 pm until 9:30 pm. The
Alberta Street Fair in August showcases the neighborhood's offerings
with arts-and-crafts displays and street performances. ■TIP→ Northeast Alberta is about a mile from the smaller but similarly intriguing
North Mississippi and North Williams corridors; fans of indie dining and
shopping could easily spend a full day strolling or biking among both
areas. ⊠ *N.E. Alberta St. between N.E. Martin Luther King Jr. Blvd.
and N.E. 30th Ave., Northeast* ⊕ *www.albertamainst.org.*

SOUTHEAST

Bounded on the west by the Willamette River and on the north by
Burnside Avenue, the city's Southeast quadrant comprises several of
Portland's hottest and hippest neighborhoods. Abundant with shade
trees, Craftsman-style houses, and backyard chicken coops, this neighborhood is industrial close in (the river to 7th Avenue)—an increasingly
trendy food and retail district known as the Central Eastside, which
has also lately blossomed with top-quality artisanal distilleries and
urban wineries—and middle- to upper-middle-class residential farther
out (8th to 82nd). You'll encounter vibrant pockets of foodie-driven
restaurants—as well as bars, coffeehouses, markets, food-cart pods, and
boutiques—along east–west running Division, Hawthorne, Belmont,
Stark, and Burnside streets, making Southeast a Portland cultural must-
see. Other Southeast highlights include the Eastbank Esplanade on the
Willamette River (which connects with Downtown via several historic
bridges), the kid-focused science museum Oregon Museum of Science
and Industry (OMSI), the sleek Tilikum Crossing Bridge, and the beautiful park at Mt. Tabor, an inactive volcanic cinder cone.

TOP ATTRACTIONS

Fodor's Choice **Division Street.** Back in the early 1970s, Division Street (or "Southeast
★ Division," as many locals call it) was earmarked for condemnation as
part of a proposed—and thankfully never built—freeway that would
have connected Downtown to Mt. Hood. For many years, this street sat
forlornly, just a long stretch of modest buildings and empty lots. These
days, Southeast Division—no longer threatened with condemnation—is
one of the hottest restaurant rows in the city, perhaps even the Western

United States, and sleek three- and four-story contemporary condos and apartments are popping up like dandelions. If culinary tourism is your thing, head to the 10 blocks of Southeast Division from about 30th to 39th avenues, where you'll find such darlings of the culinary scene as Pok Pok, Ava Gene's, American Local, an outpost of Salt & Straw ice cream, Little T bakery, Lauretta Jean's, and several others. The main draw here is mostly food-and-drink related; there are several great bars, and the excellent SE Wine Collective urban winery. You'll also find a smattering of other noteworthy restaurants and bars extending all the way to 12th Avenue to the west, and 50th Avenue to the east. As well as "Division" and "Southeast Division," you may hear some locals refer to the neighborhood as "Clinton/Division," referring to Clinton Street, a block south of Division, where you will find lovely early- to mid-20th-century bungalows and houses and a few noteworthy eateries (Broder, La Moule). Clinton Street was once the destination here, but over the past decade, the allure has grown to encompass the entire Southeast Division area. Bus 4 runs crosses the Hawthorne Bridge from Downtown and continues along Division Street; there's also plenty of free street parking in the neighborhood. ⊠ *S.E. Division St. from 30th to 39th Aves., Southeast.*

Fodor's Choice ★ **Hawthorne District.** Stretching from the foot of Mt. Tabor to S.E. 12th Avenue (where you'll find a stellar food-cart pod), with some blocks far livelier than others, this eclectic commercial thoroughfare was at the forefront of Portland's hippie and LGBT scenes in the '60s and '70s. As the rest of Portland's East Side has become more urbane and popular among hipsters, young families, students, and the so-called creative class over the years, Hawthorne has retained an arty, homegrown flavor. An influx of trendy eateries and shops opening alongside the still-colorful and decidedly low-frills thrift shops and old-school taverns and cafés make for a hodgepodge of styles and personalities—you could easily spend an afternoon popping in and out of boutiques, and then stay for happy hour at a local nightspot or even later for dinner. Highlights include a small (but still impressive) branch of Powell's Books, Bagdad Theater & Pub, Rachel's Ginger Beer, Blue Star Donuts, Gold Dust Meridian bar, Apizza Scholls for stellar thin-crust pizzas, and the Sapphire Hotel for late-night dining, but you'll find every kind of business in Hawthorne, from the airy and contemporary Dosha Aveda day spa to the massive and campy House of Vintage retro fashion and furnishings emporium. ■TIP➔ **Bus 14 runs from Downtown along the length of Hawthorne, and there's plenty of free street parking, too.** ⊠ *S.E. Hawthorne Blvd., between S.E. 12th and S.E. 50th Aves., Buckman, Southeast* ⊕ *www.thinkhawthorne.com.*

Fodor's Choice ★ **House Spirits Distillery.** One of the stalwarts of Distillery Row—a group of eight craft spirits producers mostly clustered together in the Central Eastside—this highly respected outfit opened in 2004, moved into a spacious 14,000-square-foot facility in fall 2014, and has earned international acclaim for its Aviation American Gin and Krogstad Festlig Aquavit. Other favorites include Westward Oregon Straight Malt Whiskey made with locally sourced barley, and—apt in java-loving Portland—coffee liqueur produced using pot-distilled rum and the city's fine Stumptown Coffee beans. In the cozy tasting room, you can also browse a fine selection of barware, books, and other booze-related gifts. Tours are offered daily at 3 pm (and additionally at 1 on Saturday). ■TIP→ **Check out the Distillery Row website (www.distilleryrowpdx. com), where you can view a map of other nearby distilleries and order a Distillery Row Passport, which costs $30 but includes a $5 gift card, complimentary tastings and tours at 11 distilleries (Clear Creek, Bull Run, and Aria in Northwest are included), and discounts at a number of restaurants, hotels, and shops around the city.** ⊠ *65 S.E. Washington St., Southeast* ☎ *503/235–3174* ⊕ *www.housespirits.com.*

FAMILY
Fodor's Choice
★

Mt. Tabor Park. A playground on top of a volcano cinder cone? Yup, that's here. The cinders, or glassy rock fragments, unearthed in the park's construction, were used to surface the respite's roads; the ones leading to the top are closed to cars, but popular with cyclists. They're also popular with cruisers—each August there's an old-fashioned soap-box derby. Picnic tables and tennis, basketball, and volleyball courts make Mt. Tabor Park a popular spot for outdoor recreation, but plenty of quiet, shaded trails and wide-open grassy lawns with panoramic views of the Downtown skyline appeal to sunbathers, hikers, and nature lovers. The whole park is closed to cars on Wednesday. ■TIP→ **Just down the hill on the west side of Mt. Tabor, you'll find the lively cafés and restaurants of the hip Hawthorne District.** ⊠ *S.E. 60th Ave. and S.E. Salmon St., Southeast* ⊕ *www.portlandoregon.gov/parks.*

FAMILY
Fodor's Choice
★

Oregon Museum of Science and Industry (*OMSI*). Hundreds of engaging exhibits draw families to this outstanding interactive science museum, which also has an Omnimax theater and the Northwest's largest planetarium. The many permanent and touring exhibits are loaded with enough hands-on play for kids to fill a whole day exploring robotics, ecology, rockets, animation, and outer space. Moored in the Willamette River as part of the museum is a 240-foot submarine, the USS *Blueback*, which can be toured for an extra charge. OMSI also offers some very cool event programming for adults, including the hugely popular monthly OMSI After Dark nights, where "science nerds" can enjoy food, drink, and science fun, and the twice-monthly OMSI Science Pub nights, where local and national experts lecture on a wide range of topics at theater-pubs in Portland. ■TIP→ **OMSI's excellent restaurant, Theory, open for lunch, offers great views of the Willamette River and Downtown skyline.** ⊠ *1945 S.E. Water Ave., Southeast* ☎ *503/797–4000, 800/955–6674* ⊕ *www.omsi.edu* 🎟 *Museum $14, planetarium $7.50, Omnimax $8.50, submarine $6.75, parking $5* ☉ *Closed Mon. early Sept.–mid-June.*

Fodor's Choice
★

SE Wine Collective. Set along Division Street's white-hot restaurant row, this growing collective houses 11 small wineries and has quickly become the city's leading incubator for vino entrepreneurs. The spacious facility includes a large, light-filled tasting bar with glass roll-up doors (offering a peek at the vinification process) and a main wall and bench seating made from old wine barrels. The tasting bar is also a wine bar, so you can sample the artisanal wines produced on-site, or order a flight, glass, or bottle (to go or to enjoy on-site) as well as tasty small plates from an extensive menu. Although Oregon is chiefly known for Pinot Noir,

Pinot Gris, and Chardonnay, the wineries at the collective produce a richly varied assortment of varietals, including a racy Sauvignon Blanc from Pampleau, a supple Gamay Noir from Division Wine Making, and a peppery Cabernet Franc from Willful Wines. ☒ *2425 S.E. 35th Pl., Southeast* ☎ *503/208–2061* ⊕ *www.sewinecollective.com* ☉ *Closed Tues.*

WORTH NOTING

Fodor's Choice
★

Central Eastside. This expansive 681-acre tract of mostly industrial and commercial buildings was largely ignored by all but local workers until shops, galleries, and restaurants began opening in some of the neighborhood's handsome, high-ceilinged buildings beginning in the '90s. These days, it's a legitimately hot neighborhood for shopping and coffeehouse-hopping by day, and dining and clubbing at night, and a slew of high-end apartment buildings have added a residential component to the Central Eastside. The neighborhood lies just across the Willamette River from Downtown—it extends along the riverfront from the Burnside Bridge to south to the Oregon Museum of Science and Industry (OMSI) and Division Street, extending east about a dozen blocks to S.E. 12th Avenue. Businesses of particularly note in these parts include urban-chic coffeehouses (Water Avenue, Coava), breweries (Base Camp Brewing, Cascade Brewing Barrel House, Commons Brewery), shops and galleries, and restaurants (Kachka, Le Pigeon, Revelry, Taylor Railworks, Trifecta Tavern). In the past few years, a number of acclaimed craft distilleries and urban wineries have joined the mix, including House Spirits and New Deal Distillery among the former, and Clay Pigeon and Coopers Hall among the latter. This is a large neighborhood, and some streets are a bit desolate (though still quite safe), but you can reach it via the East Side Streetcar, and walking from Downtown across the Hawthorne or Burnside bridges. If you're coming by car, street parking is becoming tougher with all the new development but still possible to find, especially on quieter side streets. ☒ *Willamette River to S.E. 12th Ave. from Burnside to Division Sts., Southeast* ⊕ *www.ceic.cc.*

FAMILY **Laurelhurst Park.** Completed in 1914 by Emanuel Mische, who trained with the iconic Olmsted Brothers landscaping design firm, resplendent Laurelhurst Park's hundred-year-old trees and winding, elegant paths are evocative of another time, and may trigger an urge to don a parasol. Listed on the National Register of Historic Places, Laurelhurst offers plentiful trails, playgrounds, tennis courts, soccer fields, horseshoe pits, an off-leash area for dogs, a serene pond with ducks, and many sunny and shady picnic areas. Take a stroll around the large spring-fed pond and keep an eye out for blue heron, the city's official bird. On the south side of this 31-acre park is one of the busiest basketball courts in town. Though the park is always beautiful, it is especially so in fall. The trendy dining and café culture of East Burnside and 28th and Belmont Street are within walking distance. ☒ *S.E. 39th Ave. and S.E. Stark St., Southeast* ⊕ *www.portlandoregon.gov/parks.*

Tilikum Crossing Bridge. Downtown Portland's collection of striking bridges gained a new member in 2015 with the opening of this sleek, cable-stayed bridge a few steps from Oregon Museum of Science and Industry (OMSI). Nicknamed "the Bridge of the People" and unusual in

Tilikum Crossing Bridge

that it's open only to public transit (MAX trains, buses, and streetcars), bikes, and pedestrians, the 1,720-foot-long bridge connects Southeast Portland with the South Waterfront district and rewards those who stroll or cycle across it with impressive skyline views. ⊠ *Tilikum Crossing, Southeast ⚓ Eastbank Esplanade just south of OMSI on the East Side, and S.W. Moody Ave. in South Waterfront.*

WHERE TO EAT

These days, rising-star chefs and the foodies who adore them are flocking to Portland. In this playground of sustainability and creativity, many of the city's hottest restaurants change menus weekly—sometimes even daily—depending upon the ingredients they have delivered to their door that morning from local farms. The combination of fertile soils, temperate weather, and nearby waters contributes to a year-round bountiful harvest (be it lettuces or hazelnuts, mushrooms or salmon) that is within any chef's reach.

And these chefs are not shy about putting new twists on old favorites. Restaurants like Le Pigeon, Beast, Ox, Ned Ludd, Tasty n Sons, and Aviary have all taken culinary risks by presenting imaginatively executed, often globally inspired fare while utilizing sustainable ingredients. There's a strong willingness in and around Portland for chefs to explore their creative boundaries.

Menus frequently extend across nations and continents. First-time visitors to Portland always seem to be impressed by the culinary scene's international diversity, especially when it comes to Asian and

Mediterranean fare, but you'll also find outstanding examples of Peruvian, Russian, regional Mexican, and dozens of other ethnic restaurants. Of course, seafood is prevalent, with chefs regularly taking advantage of the availability of fresh salmon, albacore, halibut, crab, oysters, and mussels from the rivers and the Pacific Ocean.

Most of the city's longtime favorites are concentrated in Nob Hill, the Pearl District, and Downtown. But many of the city's most exciting food scenes are on the East Side, along Alberta Street, Mississippi Avenue, Williams Avenue, Fremont Street, Martin Luther King Jr. Boulevard, Burnside Street, 28th Avenue, Belmont Street, Hawthorne Boulevard, and Division Street, and tucked away in many neighborhoods in between. Serious food enthusiasts will definitely want to make some trips to some of these vibrant, if out-of-the-way neighborhoods.

HOURS, PRICES, AND DRESS

Compared to many other major cities, Portland restaurants aren't open quite as late, and it's unusual to see many diners after 11 pm even on weekends, though there are a handful of restaurants and popular bars that do serve late, albeit often with limited bar menus.

One aspect to Portland's dining scene that many locals and out-of-towners find appealing is how reasonably priced top-notch restaurants are. Particularly welcome in Portland is happy hour, when both inventive cocktails as well as small plates of food can be a good value; you can easily put together a fine early—or in some cases late-night—dinner by grazing from the happy-hour menu at a restaurant that also has a bar scene.

In Portland, many diners dress casually for even higher-end establishments—a proclivity that's refreshing to some and annoying to others. In any case, jeans are acceptable almost everywhere.

Reviews have been shortened; for full information visit Fodors.com. Use the coordinate (✛ B2) at the end of each listing to locate a site on the corresponding map.

WHAT IT COSTS IN U.S. DOLLARS			
$	$$	$$$	$$$$
At Dinner	under $16	$16–$22	$23–$30	over $30

Restaurant prices are the average cost of a main course at dinner, or if dinner is not served, at lunch.

DOWNTOWN

$ ✕ **Blue Star Donuts.** The lines outside much-hyped competitor Voodoo

BAKERY Doughnut are longer, but that doesn't mean you should bypass a chance

FAMILY to sample the creative confections at this handsome, light-filled dough-

Fodor's Choice nut shop on the street level of a glassy condo tower in the West End.

★ Part of Micah Camden's nouvelle–fast-food empire (that includes Little Big Burger and Boxer Ramen), Blue Star opens at 7 or 8 each morning

Portland's Food Carts

Throughout Portland at any given mealtime, around 850 food carts are dishing up steaming plates of everything from Korean tacos to shawarma to artisanal cupcakes. While food carts have seen a rise in popularity throughout the country, the culture is especially strong in Portland.

Brightly colored and mostly stationary, the carts tend to cluster in former parking lots in pods ranging from 3 to nearly 60 establishments, oftentimes ringing a cluster of picnic tables or a covered awning. A recent construction boom has led to the closure of some key cart pods, but other pods have opened, often farther from the city center, where land costs less.

With plate prices averaging $6 to $10, cart fare provides a quick, inexpensive, and delicious alternative to traditional sit-down restaurants if you don't mind sitting outside. Cart dining is also an easy way to sample Portland's extensive ethnic food offerings.

For up-to-date information on hours and locations, and the latest on openings, moves, and closures, check out the extensive local blog **Food Carts Portland** (⊕ *www. foodcartsportland.com*), the corresponding FoodCartsPDX iPhone and Droid apps FoodCartsPDX, and the Twitter thread @pdxfoodcarts.com.

TOP PODS

Downtown, S.W. 9th (and 10th) and Alder: Covering more than an entire city block, this Downtown pod, home to nearly 60 carts, is the largest in the city. The spot is lively during the workweek but slower on the weekends. We recommend the signature Thai chicken dish at **Nong's Khao Man Gai**; battered fish-and-chips at **The Frying Scotsman**; the Cheesus double cheeseburger with bacon at **Grilled Cheese Grill**; kielbasa and other Polish classics at **EuroDish**; the seductively delicious Chinese-style breakfast crepes at **Bing Mi!**; and kalua pig at the Hawaiian cart **808 Grinds**.

Southeast, Portland Mercado (S.E. 73rd Avenue and Foster Road): A convivial collection of some 40 businesses, including food carts and crafts and gift vendors, the Mercado is devoted to Latin culture and heritage. Feast on *ropa vieja* and other Cuban delicacies at **Que Bola**; shredded-pork and red-mole tamales at **Mixteca**; and cinnamon-dusted churros at **Don Churro**.

Southeast, Tidbit Food Farm and Garden (S.E. Division and 28th): This beautifully designed cart colony has a large central dining area and a fire pit. Try the Heartbreak Hotel hot dog topped with bacon, cheddar, ketchup, and a fried egg at the **DogHouse PDX**; the blistered-crust wood-fired pizzas (the one with fennel salami is killer) at **Paper Bag Pizza**; and the peanut butter, bacon, banana, and honey Dutch-style waffle at **Smaaken**. You can also grab a pint of local IPA or saison to accompany your meal at **Scout Beer Garden**.

Portland's famous food carts

and remains open until that day's fresh-baked stock of delicious dough-nuts is sold out. **Known for:** wildly inventive doughnut flavors; serving Stumptown Coffee. $ *Average main: $4* ✉ *1237 S.W. Washington St., West End* ☎ *503/265–8410* ⊕ *www.bluestardonuts.com* ✣ *1:B4.*

$$ CAFÉ

✕ **Chizu.** Legendary Portland cheesemonger Steve Jones, who also oper-ates Cheese Bar near Mt. Tabor and the Cheese Annex inside Southeast's Commons Brewery, runs this clever dairy-driven play on a traditional sushi bar. In this Japanese-inspired space, you can create your own plat-ter of some of the world's most special cheeses, or go the "omakase" route: just name your price point, and the knowledgeable staff will create the ultimate cheese feast. **Known for:** hard-to-find local and inter-national cheeses; sushi bar decor. $ *Average main: $19* ✉ *1126 S.W. Alder St., West End* ☎ *503/719–6889* ⊕ *www.chizubar.com* ☾ *Closed Mon. and Tues.* ✣ *1:B4.*

$$$ PACIFIC NORTHWEST Fodor's Choice ★

✕ **Clyde Common.** Gourmands from all walks of life—politicians, rock stars, socialites, and hipsters—eat and drink at this bustling bistro and bar in the Ace Hotel. Long, communal tables dominate the space, which means you never know who you'll end up sitting next to. **Known for:** barrel-aged cocktails; seasonal farm-to-table menu; outstanding week-end brunch. $ *Average main: $25* ✉ *Ace Hotel, 1014 S.W. Stark St., West End* ☎ *503/228–3333* ⊕ *www.clydecommon.com* ✣ *1:B4.*

$$$ ASIAN FUSION Fodor's Choice ★

✕ **Departure Restaurant + Lounge.** This swanky rooftop restaurant and lounge on the top floor of The Nines hotel looks fresh out of L.A.—a look and feel that is, indeed, a departure from Portland's usual no-fuss vibe. The retro-chic interior has an extravagant, space-age, airport-lounge feel, and the outdoor patio—furnished with low, white couches and bright-orange tables and chairs—offers panoramic views of the

Downtown skyline. **Known for:** big-eye tuna poke; fantastic skyline views. [$] *Average main: $24* ✉ *Nines Hotel, 525 S.W. Morrison St., Downtown* ☎ *503/802–5370* 🌐 *www.departureportland.com* ⏲ *No lunch* ✣ *1:C5.*

$$$ PACIFIC NORTHWEST Fodor's Choice ★

🍴 **Higgins.** One of Portland's original farm-to-table restaurants, this classic eatery, opened in 1994 by renowned namesake chef Greg Higgins, has built its menu—and its reputation—on its dedication to local, seasonal, organic ingredients. Higgins' dishes display the diverse bounty of the Pacific Northwest, incorporating ingredients like heirloom tomatoes, forest mushrooms, mountain huckleberries, Pacific oysters, Oregon Dungeness crab, and locally raised pork. **Known for:** house-made charcuterie plate; casual bistro menu in adjacent bar. [$] *Average main: $30* ✉ *1239 S.W. Broadway, Downtown* ☎ *503/222–9070* 🌐 *www.higginsportland.com* ⏲ *No lunch weekends* ✣ *1:B6.*

$$$ PACIFIC NORTHWEST Fodor's Choice ★

🍴 **Imperial.** Tall concrete pillars, exposed brick and ductwork, soft overhead lighting, and rustic wood tables and floors create an industrial-chic vibe at acclaimed this buzzy restaurant inside the hip Hotel Lucia. Open for breakfast, lunch, and dinner, and serving up exemplary contemporary Pacific Northwest fare, menu highlights include Dungeness crab omelet, duck meatballs, grilled king salmon with corn puree and chanterelles, and meaty fare from the wood-fired rotisserie grill. **Known for:** excellent happy hour; creative cocktails; wood-fired rotisserie-grill fare. [$] *Average main: $25* ✉ *Hotel Lucia, 410 S.W. Broadway, Downtown* ☎ *503/228–7222* 🌐 *www.imperialpdx.com* ✣ *1:C4.*

$ DELI FAMILY

🍴 **Kenny & Zuke's Delicatessen.** The reputation of this Jewish deli beside the hip Ace Hotel is based largely on its much-revered pastrami. Cured for seven days, then smoked for 10 hours and steamed for 3, the rich and flavorful meat is best tasted on a rye bread sandwich or, if your appetite is heartier, the warm, sauerkraut-packed Reuben. **Known for:** best Reuben in town; house-made bagels; breakfast all day. [$] *Average main: $14* ✉ *1038 S.W. Stark St., West End* ☎ *503/222–3354* 🌐 *www.kennyandzukes.com* ✣ *1:B4.*

$$$ BISTRO

🍴 **Little Bird Bistro.** Celeb-chef Gabriel Rucker of Le Pigeon fame operates this lively Downtown sister restaurant that's gained a following for its deliciously curated charcuterie board and tender seared duck breast. Other notable dishes include a fried-chicken version of coq au vin and classic steak au poivre with frites, and a decadent Brie burger with spiced ketchup. **Known for:** foie gras available a couple of ways; business lunches; late-night menu. [$] *Average main: $26* ✉ *219 S.W. 6th Ave., Downtown* ☎ *503/688–5952* 🌐 *www.littlebirdbistro.com* ⏲ *No lunch weekends* ✣ *1:D4.*

$$ AMERICAN FAMILY

🍴 **Mother's Bistro & Bar.** Chef and cookbook author Lisa Schroeder dedicates her home-style, made-with-love approach to food to the comforting foods prepared by mothers everywhere. Clearly, the theme resonates, as evidenced by the long waits on weekends, and even some weekday mornings for breakfast, which is arguably the best time of the day to sample Schroeder's hearty cooking; try the wild salmon hash with leeks or the French toast with a crunchy cornflake crust. **Known for:** down-home American comfort fare; fantastic breakfasts; drinks in the swanky Velvet Lounge bar. [$] *Average main: $17* ✉ *212 S.W. Stark*

St., *Downtown* ☎ *503/464–1122* ⊕ *www.mothersbistro.com* ✆ *Closed Mon. No dinner Sun.* ✛ *1:D4.*

$$$

ITALIAN

Fodor'sChoice

★

✕ **Pazzo Ristorante.** The aromas of roasted garlic and wood smoke greet patrons of the bustling, street-level dining room of the Hotel Vintage. The unprepossessing decor of dark-wood and terra-cotta and the menu of deceptively simple contemporary Italian cuisine belie the fact that Pazzo serves some of the most beautifully prepared, flavorful food Downtown: consider the grilled wild prawns with Jerusalem artichokes, fennel-lemon salad, and garlic-mint emulsion, and gnocchi with black truffles, roasted beets, and Gorgonzola. **Known for:** house-made pasta; fresh baked goods at breakfast; steak, venison, and other hearty grills. Ⓢ *Average main: $27* ⊠ *Hotel Vintage, 627 S.W. Washington St., Downtown* ☎ *503/228–1515* ⊕ *www.pazzo.com* ✛ *1:C4.*

$$$$

MODERN
AMERICAN

✕ **Super Bite.** The acclaimed chef duo behind Ox, Greg Denton and Gabi Quiñónez Denton, present an artfully plated selection of globally inspired treats in this refined yet unpretentious West End space. The menu of is divided into smaller bites, shareable plates, and just three quite substantial family-style platters (such as whole fried trout with ginger–black bean sauce, or pork shoulder confit with hazelnut chimichurri). **Known for:** unusual food combinations (beef tongue "spam" musubi, for instance); extensive list of Spanish sherries; plenty of veggie options. Ⓢ *Average main: $35* ⊠ *527 S.W. 12th Ave., West End* ☎ *503/222–0979* ⊕ *www.superbitepdx.com* ✆ *Closed Mon. No lunch* ✛ *1:B4.*

$$$

ECLECTIC

✕ **Tasty n Alder.** The first Downtown venture of celebrated Portland chef John Gorham, this all-day brunch and evening dinner spot serves some of the most interesting food in the city. Designed for sharing, the tapas-style menu draws on global influences and delivers bold, delicious flavors. **Known for:** "grown-up" milk shakes (with alcohol); deftly prepared cocktails; brunch every day. Ⓢ *Average main: $24* ⊠ *580 S.W. 12th Ave., West End* ☎ *503/621–9251* ⊕ *www.tastynalder.com* ✛ *1:B4.*

OLD TOWN/CHINATOWN

$

MEXICAN

✕ **Mi Mero Mole.** Graffiti and murals decorate one concrete wall of this colorful Old Town–Chinatown eatery dedicated to Mexico City–style street food, proof that superb ethnic food still exists in the Chinatown neighborhood (even if none of it, at the moment, is Chinese). This is some of the most flavorful, authentic Mexican food in town. **Known for:** great afternoon (2–6 pm) happy hour; handcrafted margaritas; lots of veggie options. Ⓢ *Average main: $10* ⊠ *32 N.W. 5th Ave., Old Town* ☎ *971/266–8575* ⊕ *www.mmmtacospdx.com* ✆ *Closed Sun.* ✛ *1:D3.*

$

BAKERY

✕ **Voodoo Doughnut.** The long lines outside this Old Town 24/7 doughnut shop, marked by its distinctive pink-neon sign, attest to the fact that this irreverent bakery is almost as famous a Portland landmark as Powell's Books. The aforementioned sign depicts one of the shop's biggest sellers, a raspberry-jelly-topped chocolate voodoo-doll doughnut, but all of the creations here, some of them witty, some ribald, bring smiles to the faces of customers—even those who have waited 30 minutes in the rain. **Known for:** offbeat doughnut flavors; the bacon maple bar

Map 1: Where to Eat and Stay in Central Portland

A B C D

N.W. Northrup St.

Residence Inn—
Pearl District

N.W. Marshall St.

Broadway Bridge

1

N.W. Lovejoy St.

N.W. 18th Ave.
N.W. 17th Ave.
N.W. 16th Ave.
N.W. 15th Ave.

N.W. Kearney St.

N.W. 12th Ave.

Northwest Naito Parkway

N.W. Johnson St.

Jamison
Square

OLD
TOWN

405

N.W. Irving St.

Irving Street
Kitchen

N.W. 11th Ave.

N.W. 10th Ave.

N.W. 9th Ave.

N.W. Hoyt St.

2

0   300 M
0   1,000 ft

N.W. 13th Ave.

Oba!

N.W. Glisan St.

Andina

N.W. Flanders St.

N.W. 14th Ave.

Mediterranean
Exploration Company

N.W. Everett St.

N.W. Broadway

N.W. 6th Ave.

N.W. 4th Ave.

N.W. 3rd Ave.

Society
Hotel

North
Park
Blocks

N.W. Davis St.

PEARL
DISTRICT

Pearl Bakery

N.W. Couch St.

Mi Mero Mole

3

McMenamins
Crystal Hotel

Kenny & Zuke's
Delicatessen

W. Burnside St.

W. Burnside St.

Mark Spencer Hotel

Maurice

Little Bird
Bistro

Voodoo Doughnu

Blue Star Donuts

Clyde Common
Ace Hotel

S.W. Oak St.

Embassy Suites
Portland-Downtown

Benson Hotel

Hotel deLuxe

Super Bite

Tasty n Alder

S.W. Washington St.

S.W. 9th Ave.

S.W. Stark St.

Hotel Lucia

Imperial

Courtyard by Marriott
Portland City Center

4

Chizu

Sentinel Hotel

Pazzo Ristorante
Hotel Vintage

S.W. 16th Ave.
S.W. 15th Ave.
S.W. 14th Ave.

S.W. Alder St.

Hotel Monaco

Mother's
Bistro & Bar

The Westin Portland

S.W. Morrison St.

The Nines

Departure Restaurant + Lounge

S.W. Yamhill St.

Hotel Rose

The Paramount
Hotel

5

405

Heathman
Hotel

S.W. Taylor St.

S.W. 13th Ave.
S.W. 12th Ave.
S.W. 11th Ave.
S.W. 10th Ave.

S.W. Salmon St.

South
Park
Blocks

S.W. Park Ave.
S.W. Park Ave.

S.W. Broadway

S.W. 6th Ave.
S.W. 5th Ave.
S.W. 4th Ave.
S.W. 3rd Ave.

Lowsdale
Sq

S.W. Main St.

S.W. 2nd Ave.

S.W. 1st Ave.

Chapman
Sq

Madison St.

Southwest Naito Park

Higgins

DOWNTOWN

S.W. Jefferson St.

Terry
Schrunk
Sq

6

Map 1: Where to
Eat and Stay
in Central Portland

S.W. Columbia St.

S.W. Clay St.

Hotel Modera

RiverPlace Hotel

A B C D

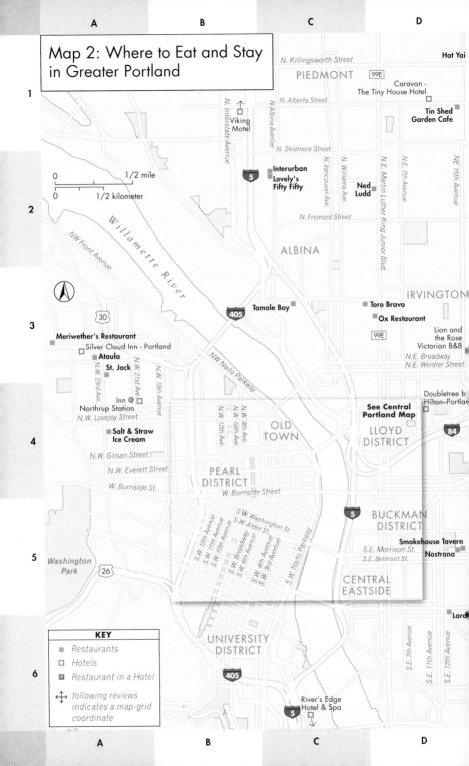

Map 2: Where to Eat and Stay in Greater Portland

KEY

- ■ *Restaurants*
- □ *Hotels*
- ■ *Restaurant in a Hotel*
- ↔ *following reviews indicates a map-grid coordinate*

Hat Yai

Caravan - The Tiny House Hotel

Tin Shed Garden Cafe

Viking Motel

Interurban
Lovely's Fifty Fifty

Ned Ludd

ALBINA

PIEDMONT

IRVINGTON

Tamale Boy

Toro Bravo

Ox Restaurant

Lion and the Rose Victorian B&B

Meriwether's Restaurant

Silver Cloud Inn - Portland

Ataula

St. Jack

Inn @ Northrup Station

Salt & Straw Ice Cream

Doubletree by Hilton-Portland

See Central Portland Map

OLD TOWN

LLOYD DISTRICT

PEARL DISTRICT

BUCKMAN DISTRICT

Smokehouse Tavern

Nostrana

CENTRAL EASTSIDE

Washington Park

UNIVERSITY DISTRICT

Lard

River's Edge Hotel & Spa

N. Killingsworth Street
N. Alberta Street
N. Skidmore Street
N. Fremont Street
N.E. Broadway
N.E. Weidler Street
N.E. Morrison St.
N.E. Belmont St.

N. Interstate Avenue
N. Albina Avenue
N. Vancouver Ave.
N. Williams Ave.
N.E. Martin Luther King Junior Blvd.
N.E. 7th Avenue
NE 15th Avenue

NW Front Avenue
Willamette River
NW Naito Parkway
N.W. 23rd Avenue
N.W. 21st Avenue
N.W. 19th Avenue
N.W. Lovejoy Street
N.W. 12th Ave.
N.W. 10th Ave.
N.W. 9th Ave.
N.W. Glisan Street
N.W. Everett Street
W. Burnside St.
W. Burnside Street

S.W. 12th Avenue
S.W. 11th Avenue
S.W. 10th Avenue
S.W. Broadway
S.W. 6th Avenue
S.W. 4th Avenue
S.W. 3rd Avenue
S.W. Naito Parkway
S.W. Washington St.
S.W. Alder St.

S.E. 7th Avenue
S.E. 11th Avenue
S.E. 12th Avenue

0   1/2 mile
0   1/2 kilometer

doughnut; long lines. $ *Average main: $4* ✉ *22 S.W. 3rd Ave., Old Town* ☎ *503/241–4704* ⊕ *www.voodoodoughnut.com* ✛ *1:D3.*

PEARL DISTRICT

$$$
PERUVIAN
Fodor'sChoice
★

✕ **Andina.** This popular upscale Pearl District restaurant offers an inventive menu—a combination of traditional Peruvian and contemporary "Novoandina" cuisines—served in a large but nook-filled space. The extensive seafood offerings include four kinds of ceviche, grilled octopus, and pan-seared scallops with white and black quinoa. **Known for:** Peruvian-style pisco sours; stylish yet casual lounge; great late-night menu. $ *Average main: $27* ✉ *1314 N.W. Glisan St., Pearl District* ☎ *503/228–9535* ⊕ *www.andinarestaurant.com* ✛ *1:B2.*

$$$
MODERN
AMERICAN
Fodor'sChoice
★

✕ **Irving Street Kitchen.** You might come to this hip Pearl District restaurant set inside a gorgeously transformed warehouse building just because you heard about the rich butterscotch pudding with roasted-banana caramel and peanut butter bonbons (it's available to go, sold in its own adorable canning jar); but chances are, once you see the exposed-brick-and-wood-beam walls, Edison bulb chandeliers, inviting central bar, and patio seats on a converted loading dock, you'll want to stay. And you'll be glad you did. **Known for:** wine by glass dispensed from state-of-the-art taps; terrific weekend brunch; decadent desserts. $ *Average main: $27* ✉ *701 N.W. 13th Ave., Pearl District* ☎ *503/343–9440* ⊕ *www.irvingstreetkitchen.com* ✛ *1:B2.*

$$
MEDITERRANEAN
Fodor'sChoice
★

✕ **Mediterranean Exploration Company.** Developed by cookbook author and celeb-chef John Gorham, this tribute to Mediterranean cuisine occupies a handsome former warehouse on historic 13th Avenue in the Pearl. MEC (for short) is an energy-filled, open space with a mix of communal and individual tables—it's surprisingly affordable considering the quality and portions, particularly if you opt for the $40 tasting menu. **Known for:** reasonably priced tasting menu; Middle East–inspired cocktails; extensive vegetarian options. $ *Average main: $22* ✉ *333 N.W. 13th Ave., Pearl District* ☎ *503/222–0906* ⊕ *www.mediterraneanexplorationcompany.com* ⊘ *No lunch* ✛ *1:B3.*

$$$
LATIN AMERICAN

✕ **Oba!** Many come to Oba! for the upscale bar scene, but this Pearl District salsa hangout with large windows and ample sidewalk seating also serves excellent Latin American cuisine, including coconut prawns, butternut squash enchiladas, achiote braised pork arepas, and filet mignon served with a yuca, gnocchi, and apple cider–molasses reduction. The bar is open late Friday and Saturday. **Known for:** table-side guacamole; flavorful real-fruit margaritas; late-night bar scene on weekends. $ *Average main: $27* ✉ *555 N.W. 12th Ave., Pearl District* ☎ *503/228–6161* ⊕ *www.obarestaurant.com* ⊘ *No lunch* ✛ *1:B2.*

$
BAKERY

✕ **Pearl Bakery.** Known for its excellent pastries and fresh baked breads (which are served at many top restaurants around town), this superb café was the first of the city's true artisan bakeries. It offers light breakfasts and delicious sandwiches (the tomato-basil-mozzarella on a puffy pistolet roll is particularly good) for lunch. **Known for:** flaky, buttery croissants; hearty sandwiches. $ *Average main: $7* ✉ *102 N.W. 9th Ave., Pearl District* ☎ *503/827–0910* ⊕ *www.pearlbakery.com* ⊘ *No dinner* ✛ *1:C3.*

NOB HILL

$$$ ✕ **Ataula.** The son of a chef from Spain's Aragon region, renowned
TAPAS chef-owner Jose Chesa brings his knowledge of and passion for Spanish
cuisine to this small, modern, always-bustling restaurant on a side street
just off Nob Hill's N.W. 23rd Avenue. The food is served tapas-style,
with everything meant to be shared, including the heaping paella plat-
ters, which include a delicious seafood version with prawns, cuttlefish,
mussels, calamari, and more. **Known for:** picturesque sidewalk seat-
ing; the dessert of toasted bread with olive oil, chocolate, and salt;
outstanding wine list. Ⓢ *Average main: $29* ✉ *1818 N.W. 23rd Pl.,
Nob Hill* ☎ *503/894–8904* ⊕ *www.ataulapdx.com* ⊗ *Closed Mon. No
lunch* ✛ *2:A3.*

$$$ ✕ **Meriwether's Restaurant.** The 5-acre Skyline Farm just 12 miles away
PACIFIC grows all the produce for this high-end, yet quaint and unpretentious
NORTHWEST restaurant on the edge of the north end of the N.W. 23rd shopping
district. The farm-to-table offerings include the Skyline Farm beet salad
with spiced coconut, feta, and almonds and lamb chops with couscous,
tomato-carrot stew, yogurt, apricots, and smoked almonds. **Known for:**
Benedicts and other brunch fare made with farm eggs; seasonal desserts
like pumpkin pot de crème; gorgeous heated patio with lush greenery
and birdhouse. Ⓢ *Average main: $28* ✉ *2601 N.W. Vaughn St., Nob
Hill* ☎ *503/228–1250* ⊕ *www.meriwethersnw.com* ✛ *2:A3.*

$ ✕ **Salt & Straw Ice Cream.** In 2011, cousins Kim and Tyler Malek started
CAFÉ a business with a small pushcart and a humble idea—to create unique
FAMILY ice-cream flavors with quality, local ingredients. Today, Salt & Straw Ice
Fodor's Choice Cream has grown into three brick-and-mortar ice-cream parlors around
★ town (and several more in Los Angeles), and it is recognized as one of
the best ice-cream makers in the nation; seasonal, local ingredients drive
the flavors here, and constant experimentation keeps ice-cream lovers
coming back. **Known for:** quick service despite the long lines; local
artisan toppings, such as Woodblock chocolate bars; unusual monthly
specialty flavors. Ⓢ *Average main: $5* ✉ *838 N.W. 23rd Ave., Nob Hill*
☎ *971/271–8168* ⊕ *www.saltandstraw.com* ✛ *2:A4.*

$$$ ✕ **St. Jack.** Serving hearty portions of rich and hearty food, the chic yet
FRENCH cozy Nob Hill restaurant takes its inspiration from the *bouchons*, or
rustic cafés, of Lyon, the culinary capital of France. The pan-seared
scallops, drenched in a cognac, leek, and Gruyère sauce, with a bread-
crumb crunch, make a delicious precursor to the main course, as does
the roasted bone marrow. **Known for:** superbly crafted cocktails; mus-
sels (served with crusty baguettes). Ⓢ *Average main: $28* ✉ *1610 N.W.
23rd Ave., Nob Hill* ⊕ *www.stjackpdx.com* ⊗ *No lunch* ✛ *2:A3.*

NORTH

$ ✕ **Interurban.** A laid-back North Mississippi gastropub with an L-shaped
MODERN indoor bar and a bi-level back patio with lush landscaping and a shaded
AMERICAN pergola, Interurban is both a convivial drinkery and a fine spot for
Fodor's Choice affordable, well-crafted American fare served from mid-afternoon
★ until 2 am (hours start earlier on weekends, with brunch kicking off
at 10 am). The kitchen creates consistently good and creative food,

with starters like venison tartare with house-made potato chips and whiskey-infused chicken-liver mousse with bacon and foie gras. **Known for:** terrific afternoon and late-night happy hour menu; impressive microbrew and cocktail menu; pretty back patio. $ *Average main: $13* ✉ *4057 N. Mississippi Ave., North* ☎ *503/284–6669* ⊕ *www.interurbanpdx.com* ☾ *No lunch weekdays* ✛ *2:C2.*

$ × **Lovely's Fifty-Fifty.** This unpretentious and airy neighborhood spot with
PIZZA   wooden booths and whimsical fire-engine-red chairs is really two deli-
Fodor'sChoice   cious dining options in one: the dining room serves inventively topped,
★   crisp, wood-fired pizzas, and a small takeout counter dispenses home-
made hard and soft-serve organic ice cream. Among the pizzas, you can't go wrong with the pie layered in shaved-and-roasted potatoes, melted leeks, fresh fenugreek, and pancetta, and topped with an egg. **Known for:** innovative flavors of house-made ice cream; perfectly crispy wood-fired pizzas. $ *Average main: $15* ✉ *4039 N. Mississippi Ave., Mississippi, North* ☎ *503/281–4060* ⊕ *www.lovelysfiftyfifty.com* ☾ *Closed Mon. No lunch* ✛ *2:C2.*

NORTHEAST

$$ × **Aviary.** Eschewing many culinary conventions, this visionary Alberta
ASIAN FUSION   Street eatery serves up innovative dishes that sometimes push boundar-
ies but consistently succeed in flavor and execution. The simple menu of small plates (order two to three per person) is influenced by Asian flavors and uses European cooking techniques, combining unusual ingredients that offer pleasing contrasts in flavor and texture. **Known for:** vegetarian tasting menu option; knowledgeable, helpful service; artfully presented food. $ *Average main: $20* ✉ *1733 N.E. Alberta St., Alberta District* ☎ *503/287–2400* ⊕ *www.aviarypdx.com* ☾ *Closed Sun. No lunch* ✛ *2:E1.*

$$$$ × **Beast.** This meat-centric exemplar of Portland's cutting-edge culinary
PACIFIC   scene occupies a nondescript red building with subtle signage. Chef-
NORTHWEST   owner Naomi Pomeroy, who also operates the trendy Expatriate bar
across the street, has appeared on TV's *Top Chef Masters* and garnered countless accolades. **Known for:** communal seating overlooking open kitchen; some of the most creative meat-centric food in the city; sub-lime Sunday brunch. $ *Average main: $102* ✉ *5425 N.E. 30th Ave., Northeast* ☎ *503/841–6968* ⊕ *www.beastpdx.com* ☾ *Closed Mon. and Tues.* ✛ *2:E1.*

$$ × **BTU Brasserie.** This microbrewery in Northeast Portland's Hollywood
CHINESE   district offers a food menu that varies from the usual brewpub format.
Here you'll find Chinese food, with an emphasis on Szechuan fare, and it's some of the best in the city, including *dan dan* noodles with spicy pork and pickled mustard greens, roast-duck noodle soup, and pork-belly *bao* with scallions and hoisin sauce. **Known for:** first-rate house-brewed craft beers; dan dan noodles with spicy pork; very friendly service. $ *Average main: $17* ✉ *5846 Sandy Blvd., Hollywood, Northeast* ☎ *971/407–3429* ⊕ *www.btupdx.com* ☾ *Closed Mon.* ✛ *2:H3.*

$ × **Hat Yai.** A new establishment from the acclaimed chef behind Lang-
THAI   baan and PaaDee, this cozy and casual counter-service eatery takes its
name from a small Thai city near the Malaysian border and its concept

from that region's spicy and delicious fried chicken with sticky rice and rich Malayu-style curries with panfried roti bread. Other treats here uncommon to Thai restaurant culture in the States include fiery turmeric curry with mussels and heady lemongrass oxtail soup. **Known for:** the roti dessert with condensed milk; perfectly crunchy free-range fried chicken; good selection of Asian beers. $ *Average main: $12* ✉ *1605 N.E. Killingsworth St., Northeast* ☎ *503/764–9701* ⊕ *www.hatyaipdx. com* ◷ *Closed Mon.* ✛ *2:D1.*

$$$
PACIFIC
NORTHWEST
Fodor's Choice
★

✕ **Ned Ludd.** Named for the founder of the Luddites, the group that resisted the technological advances of the Industrial Revolution, this Northwest-inspired kitchen prepares its food the most low-tech way possible: in a wood-burning brick oven, over an open flame. Sourcing most of its ingredients locally (or carefully, if they come from afar), Ned Ludd's menu varies completely depending on the season and weather. **Known for:** whole roasted trout with charred leeks; nice selection of craft ciders; earthy and rustic Northwest-inspired interior. $ *Average main: $26* ✉ *3925 N.E. Martin Luther King Blvd., Northeast* ⊕ *www. nedluddpdx.com* ◷ *Closed Mon. and Tues. No lunch* ✛ *2:D2.*

$$$$
ARGENTINE
Fodor's Choice
★

✕ **Ox Restaurant.** Specializing in "Argentine-inspired Portland food," Ox is all about prime cuts of meat prepared well. In a dimly lit dining room with hardwood floors, exposed brick walls, and a bar against the front window, the flannel-shirt-and-white-apron clad waitstaff serves beef, lamb, pork, and fish dishes cooked over flames in a large, hand-cranked grill. **Known for:** the asado Argentino platter (lots of amazing meaty grills); creative side dishes, a few of which could make a full meal; vanilla tres leches cake dessert. $ *Average main: $36* ✉ *2225 N.E. Martin Luther King Blvd., Northeast* ☎ *503/284–3366* ⊕ *www. oxpdx.com* ◷ *No lunch* ✛ *2:D3.*

$
SOUTHERN

✕ **Pine State Biscuits.** Loosen your belt a notch or two before venturing inside this down-home Southern restaurant that's especially beloved for its over-the-top breakfast biscuit fare. Pat yourself on the back, or belly, if you can polish off the Reggie Deluxe (a fluffy house-baked biscuit topped with fried chicken, bacon, cheese, an egg, and sage gravy), a masterful mélange of calorie-laden ingredients. **Known for:** shrimp and grits; arguably the best food stall at the Portland Farmers Market; the massive Reggie Deluxe sandwich. $ *Average main: $7* ✉ *2204 N.E. Alberta St., Alberta District* ☎ *503/477–6605* ⊕ *www.pinestatebiscuits. com* ◷ *No dinner Mon.–Wed.* ✛ *2:E1.*

$
PIZZA

✕ **Pizza Jerk.** The red-checked tablecloths, Tiffany-style lamps, and simple decor of this pizza joint might not inspire high expectations, but just wait until you taste the blistered-crust East Coast–style pies and slices. You can build your own pizza selecting from a long list of ingredients, or choose one of the signature favorites, like the white pie with ricotta and garlic, or the dan dan with sweet pork, chili paste, and mustard greens. **Known for:** thin-crust and cast-iron deep-crust pizzas; interesting side dishes. $ *Average main: $15* ✉ *5028 N.E. 42nd Ave., Northeast* ☎ *503/284–9333* ⊕ *www.pizzajerkpdx.com* ✛ *2:G1.*

$$
BARBECUE

✕ **Podnah's Pit BBQ.** Firing up the smoker at 5 every morning, the pit crew at Podnah's spends the day slow cooking some of the best Texas- and Carolina-style barbecue in the Northwest. Melt-in-your-mouth, oak-smoked brisket, ribs, pulled pork, chicken, and lamb are all served up in a sassy vinegar-based sauce. **Known for:** green-chili mac-and-cheese (when available); daily specials (fried catfish on Friday, smoked lamb on Thursday); casual and lively vibe. [$] *Average main: $16* ✉ *1625 N.E. Killingsworth St., Northeast* ☎ *503/281–3700* 🌐 *www.podnahspit.com* ✥ *2:E1.*

$$ SOUTHERN Fodor's Choice ★ 🍴 **Screen Door.** The line that forms outside this Southern cooking restaurant during weekend brunch and dinner is as epic as the food itself, but you can more easily score a table if you come for weekday breakfast or lunch. A large, packed dining room with canned pickles and peppers along the walls, this Portland hot spot does justice to authentic Southern cooking. **Known for:** fried chicken plate; rotating menu of seasonal side dishes; breakfast or brunch served daily. [$] *Average main: $16* ✉ *2337 E. Burnside St., Northeast* ☎ *503/542–0880* 🌐 *www.screendoorrestaurant.com* ✥ *2:E5.*

$ MEXICAN Fodor's Choice ★ 🍴 **Tamale Boy.** Chef Abel Hernandez hails from Veracruz by way of Mexico City, and while he's adept at preparing tamales—both the Oaxacan style wrapped in banana leaves and the more conventional style wrapped in corn husks (try the version filled with roasted pasilla peppers, onions, corn kernels, and queso fresco), he also turns out fabulous ceviche and *alambre de camarones* (adobe shrimp with bacon and Oaxacan cheese over flat corn tortillas). Be sure to start with an order of table-side guacamole, and the El Diablo margarita with roasted-habanero-infused tequila and mango puree. **Known for:** the El Diablo margarita with roasted-habanero-infused tequila and mango puree; table-side gaucamole; authentic hearty and filling tamales. [$] *Average main: $7* ✉ *1764 N.E. Dekum St., Northeast* ☎ *503/206–8022* 🌐 *www.tamaleboy.com* 🕒 *Closed Mon.* ✥ *2:C3.*

$ CAFÉ FAMILY 🍴 **Tin Shed Garden Cafe.** Sided in metal, this busy restaurant on Alberta Street is known for its hearty breakfasts—namely, its biscuits and gravy, shredded-potato cakes, egg and tofu scrambles, and breakfast burritos; in fact, it's so well known that there can be a long wait for a table for breakfast on weekends. The lunch and dinner menus have creative choices as well, like a creamy artichoke sandwich and a mac and cheese of the day. **Known for:** dog-friendly patio (and special menu); cozy ambience with stone fireplace; picturesque and cheerful outdoor seating. [$] *Average main: $12* ✉ *1438 N.E. Alberta St., Alberta District* ☎ *503/288–6966* 🌐 *www.tinshedgardencafe.com* ✥ *2:D1.*

$$ TAPAS Fodor's Choice ★ 🍴 **Toro Bravo.** The success of this wildly popular and impressively authentic Spanish tapas bar has spawned a popular cookbook and helped spur chef-owner John Gorham to create a restaurant empire in Portland: he operates several other superb eateries around town. This bustling spot with closely spaced tables and a lively vibe caters heavily to groups, as the small-plates format is perfect for sharing. **Known for:** "chef's choice for the table" menu; molten chocolate cake and other rich desserts; extensive sherry list. [$] *Average main: $20* ✉ *120 N.E. Russell St., Northeast* ☎ *503/281–4464* 🌐 *www.torobravopdx.com* 🕒 *No lunch* ✥ *2:C3.*

SOUTHEAST

$$ **Afuri Ramen.** When the acclaimed Japanese ramen chain Afuri decided
RAMEN to open an outpost in the United States in 2016, it chose food-obsessed
Fodor'sChoice Portland—specifically, a modern, high-ceilinged dining room on the
★ trendy Central East Side. They chose Portland, in part because the
exacting culinary team appreciated the city's pristine, glacially fed water
supply, which plays a significant part in the steaming, savory bowls of
yuzu shio (with chicken broth, yuzu citrus, shimeji mushrooms, sea-
soned egg, chashu, endive, and nori), one of a half dozen deeply satis-
fying ramen bowls. **Known for:** relentlessly authentic Japanese ramen;
meat and veggie skewers; flights of premium sake. $ *Average main:*
$18 ✉ *923 S.E. 7th Ave., Southeast* ☎ *503/468–5001* ⊕ *www.afuri.us*
✆ *Closed Mon. No lunch* ✥ *1:H6.*

$ **Apizza Scholls.** The pies at Apizza Scholls, lauded by Anthony Bour-
PIZZA dain, Rachael Ray, and most any pizza lover who visits, deserve the
Fodor'sChoice first-class reputation they enjoy. The greatness of the pies rests not
★ in innovation or complexity, but in the simple quality of the ingredi-
ents. **Known for:** exquisitely crisp handmade crusts; the bacon bianca
pizza (white, with no sauce); interesting beer list. $ *Average main: $14*
✉ *4741 S.E. Hawthorne Blvd., Hawthorne District* ☎ *503/233–1286*
⊕ *www.apizzascholls.com* ✆ *No lunch weekdays* ✥ *2:G5.*

$$$ **Ava Gene's.** Chef Joshua McFadden's fantastic Roman-inspired Italian
ITALIAN eatery ranks among the top tables in town both in popularity and qual-
Fodor'sChoice ity. Capsule-shape lamps dangle from the vaulted ceiling of this buzzy
★ dining room with two long rows of banquette seating and several more
closely spaced tables. **Known for:** pane flatbreads with creative topping;
daily specials, such as rabbit on Thursday and braciole on Saturday;
$70 per person family-style option. $ *Average main: $25* ✉ *3377 S.E.*
Division St., Southeast ☎ *971/229–0571* ⊕ *www.avagenes.com* ✆ *No*
lunch ✥ *2:F6.*

$$ **Bamboo Sushi.** The best sushi spot in Portland is also the most envi-
SUSHI ronmentally sustainable, sourcing its fish conscientiously from fishing
operations that follow eco-friendly guidelines. Try the black cod with
smoked soy and roasted garlic glaze or the house-smoked wild ivory
salmon nigiri. **Known for:** sustainable seafood; stylish decor. $ *Average*
main: $18 ✉ *310 S.E. 28th Ave., Southeast* ☎ *503/232–5255* ⊕ *www.*
bamboosushi.com ✆ *No lunch* ✥ *2:E5.*

$ **Bollywood Theater.** Set beneath a soaring beamed ceiling, and with a
INDIAN welcoming mix of worn wooden seating, kitschy decor, bright fabrics,
and intoxicating smells, this lively restaurant along Division Street's
hoppin' restaurant row specializes in Indian street food and reflects
chef-owner Troy MacLarty's colorful, delicious, authentic vision of
India as experienced on several trips. Order at the counter, and your
food will be brought to you—there's a mix of two-tops and communal
tables, with additional seating on a spacious patio. **Known for:** Goan-
style shrimp; small Indian gourmet market with spices and curries; lively
and fun atmosphere. $ *Average main: $13* ✉ *3010 S.E. Division St.,*
Division ☎ *503/477–6699* ⊕ *www.bollywoodtheaterpdx.com* ✥ *2:F6.*

$ RUSSIAN Fodor's Choice ★ **Broder.** This delightful neighborhood café—one of the most outstanding brunch spots in town—serves fresh and delicious Scandinavian food with fun-to-pronounce names like *friterade applen* (apple fritter) and *aebleskivers* (Danish pancakes). All of the food—the hashes, the baked egg scrambles, the Swedish breakfast boards—is delicious. **Known for:** aebleskivers (Danish pancakes); Swedish-style hash with smoked trout. *Average main: $11 ✉ 2508 S.E. Clinton St., Southeast ☎ 503/736–3333 🌐 www.broderpdx.com ⏲ No dinner ⊕ 2:E6.*

$$$$ PACIFIC NORTHWEST Fodor's Choice ★ **Castagna Restaurant.** Enjoy artful Pacific Northwest cuisine—like grilled halibut, kohlrabi, and mussels, or summer beans, chanterelles, wilted sorrel, and roasted-duck jus—at this tranquil Hawthorne restaurant. Dinner options from chef Justin Woodward's monthly changing menu include either a classic 3-course prix fixe for $98 or a lavish 10-course tasting menu that runs $165; opt for the superb wine pairings for an additional $55 or $75 (with the tasting menu). **Known for:** artfully prepared modern fare; outstanding wine pairings with each prix-fixe menu; tasty and less pricey fare at the café next door. *Average main: $98 ✉ 1752 S.E. Hawthorne Blvd., Hawthorne District ☎ 503/231–7373 🌐 www.castagnarestaurant.com ⏲ Restaurant: Closed Sun.–Tues. No lunch. Café: No lunch ⊕ 2:E6.*

$$$ PACIFIC NORTHWEST **Clarklewis.** In a former warehouse between the Willamette River and the train tracks in the industrial Central East Side, this upscale restaurant serves up inventive, farm-fresh, modern-American cuisine and has an excellent happy hour. The daily changing menu features entrées like fire-grilled lamb with harissa, ratatouille, raisin-and-pine-nut gremolata, and a balsamic glaze, and agnolotti pasta with shishito peppers, Dungeness crab, and mascarpone. **Known for:** family-style $55 prix-fixe menu option; great happy-hour specials on food and drink; light and airy space in great old building in Central East Side. *Average main: $28 ✉ 1001 S.E. Water Ave., Southeast ☎ 503/235–2294 🌐 www.clarklewispdx.com ⏲ Closed Sun. No lunch Sat. ⊕ 1:F6.*

$$$ FRENCH Fodor's Choice ★ **Coquine.** A sunny neighborhood café serving breakfast and lunch daily, Coquine blossoms into a romantic, sophisticated French–Pacific Northwest bistro in the evening. The unfussy storefront space is just steps from Mt. Tabor Park, making it a lovely spot for a meal before or after a leafy stroll. **Known for:** pan-roasted bone-in rib eye steak for two–three; butterscotch pudding with miso-pumpkin butter and chocolate candied pistachios; cheerful setting near Mt. Tabor. *Average main: $27 ✉ 6839 S.E. Belmont St., Southeast ☎ 503/384–2483 🌐 www.coquinepdx.com ⏲ No dinner Mon. and Tues. ⊕ 2:H5.*

$$ SOUTHERN Fodor's Choice ★ **Country Cat.** Pork lovers rejoice: you've found hog heaven. House-cured, slow-cooked country ham and bacon and samplers of pork shoulders, head, and belly await you at this neighborhood craft eatery run by James Beard–nominated chef and in-house butcher Adam Sappington. **Known for:** fantastic (and decadent) brunch served every day; lively bar that serves great Bloody Marys; the fish fry made with beer-battered rockfish. *Average main: $19 ✉ 7937 S.E. Stark St., Southeast ☎ 503/408–1414 🌐 www.thecountrycat.net ⊕ 2:H5.*

$ VIETNAMESE **Ha & VL.** This humble, no-frills banh mi shop amid the many cheap and authentic Asian restaurants on S.E. 82nd stands out not just for its filling sandwiches (these crispy-bread creations come with fillings like spicy Chinese sausage, pork meat loaf, or sardines) but also for the daily featured soup, such as peppery pork-ball noodle soup on Wednesday and Vietnamese turmeric soup, with shrimp cake and sliced pork, on Sunday. There's also a diverse selection of thick milk shakes—top flavors include avocado, mango, and durian. **Known for:** milk shakes in unusual flavors; pork-ball noodle soup (on Wednesday only). [$] *Average main: $6* ✉ *2738 S.E. 82nd Ave., No. 102, Southeast* ☎ *503/772–0103* ⏲ *Closed Tues. No dinner* ✥ *2:H6.*

$$ RUSSIAN Fodor's Choice ★ 🍴 **Kachka.** In a city with a sizable population of Russian immigrants, the success of this Central East Side establishment decorated to resemble a *dasha* is hardly surprising, although it's really the devotion of the city's foodies that resulted in Kachka's white-hot popularity. If you are expecting heavy cuisine, you'll be surprised by the wonderfully creative and often quite light fare, including plenty of shareable small plates, like crispy beef tongue with sweet onion sauce, orange, and pomegranate; panfried sour-cherry *vareniki* (Ukranian dumplings), and—of course—caviar with blini and all the usual accompaniments. **Known for:** extensive craft vodka list; classic chicken Kiev; cherry vareniki (Ukranian dumplings). [$] *Average main: $20* ✉ *720 S.E. Grand Ave., Southeast* ✥ *(moving to 960 S.E. 11th Ave. in 2017)* ☎ *503/235–0059* 🌐 *www.kachkapdx.com* ⏲ *No lunch* ✥ *1:H5.*

$ PIZZA 🍴 **Ken's Artisan Pizza.** Doug-fir beams, old wine barrels, and hungry crowds surround the glowing, beehive-shaped wood oven in the open-kitchen of this thin-crust pizza joint. Ken Forkish, also of Ken's Artisan Bakery and Trifecta Tavern, uses fresh, organic ingredients for the dough, sauces, and toppings of his pies. **Known for:** terrific salads and vegetable sides; the classic margherita pizza with arugula is one of the best in town; solid wine list. [$] *Average main: $15* ✉ *304 S.E. 28th Ave., Southeast* ☎ *503/517–9951* 🌐 *www.kensartisan.com* ⏲ *No lunch* ✥ *2:E5.*

$$$$ THAI Fodor's Choice ★ 🍴 **Langbaan.** Guests reach this tiny, wood-paneled, 24-seat gem with an open kitchen by walking through the adjoining PaaDee restaurant and pushing open a faux bookshelf that's actually a door. Of course, you won't even get this far unless you've called ahead to reserve a table: this very special prix-fixe restaurant, serving the most interesting and consistently delicious Asian food in Portland, is only open Thursday–Sunday, with two seatings per evening. **Known for:** some of the most inventive Thai food in the country; the $30 wine-pairing option is a great value; wonderfully creative and flavorful desserts. [$] *Average main: $75* ✉ *6 S.E. 28th Ave., Southeast* ☎ *971/344–2564* 🌐 *www.langbaanpdx.com* ⏲ *Closed Mon.–Wed. No lunch* ✥ *2:E5.*

$ AMERICAN Fodor's Choice ★ 🍴 **Lardo.** One of several spots around Portland that has become known for advancing the art of sandwich making, Lardo offers a steady roster of about a dozen wonderfully inventive variations, plus one or two weekly specials, along with no-less-impressive sides like maple carrots and escarole Caesar salads. Sandwiches of particular note include the tender Korean-style braised pork shoulder with kimchi, chili mayo, cilantro, and lime, and grilled mortadella with provolone, marinated peppers, and mustard aioli. **Known for:** inviting covered outdoor seating area at Hawthorne; excellent craft-beer and cocktail selection; "dirty fries" topped with pork scraps, marinated peppers, and Parmesan. [$] *Average main: $10* ✉ *1212 S.E. Hawthorne Blvd., Southeast* ☎ *503/234–7786* 🌐 *www.lardosandwiches.com* ✣ *2:D6.*

$$$ STEAKHOUSE Fodor's Choice ★ 🍴 **Laurelhurst Market.** With an artisanal butcher shop anchoring the right side of the building, Laurelhurst Market offers some of the best meaty fare in Portland. Case in point: the Wagyu brisket smoked for 12 hours and served with Thai hazelnut butter, and the beef short ribs braised with red wine and prunes. **Known for:** delicious sandwiches; exhibition kitchen that's fun to watch while dining; surprising amount of meat-free side dishes and salads. [$] *Average main: $27* ✉ *3155 E. Burnside St., Southeast* ☎ *503/206–3097* 🌐 *www.laurelhurstmarket.com* ✣ *2:F4.*

$ CAFÉ Fodor's Choice ★ 🍴 **Lauretta Jean's.** Kate McMillen and Noah Cable's pie-focused operation began as a stall at Portland's Saturday farmers' market at PSU and now comprises a couple of charming, homey, brick-and-mortar cafés, one Downtown, but the most atmospheric along Division Street in Southeast. While it's the delicious pies—with feathery-light crusts and delicious fillings like tart cherry, salted pecan, and chocolate-banana cream—that have made Lauretta Jean's a foodie icon in Portland, these cheerful eateries also serve exceptional brunch fare, including the LJ Classic, a fluffy biscuit topped with an over-easy egg, Jack cheese, bacon, and strawberry jam. **Known for:** salted-caramel apple pie; short but well-curated cocktail list; breakfast sandwich that features the bakery's fluffy biscuits. [$] *Average main: $6* ✉ *3402 S.E. Division St., Division* ☎ *503/235–3119* 🌐 *www.laurettajean.com* 🕒 *No dinner* ✣ *2:F6.*

$$$$ FRENCH Fodor's Choice ★ 🍴 **Le Pigeon.** Specializing in adventurous Northwest-influenced French dishes of extraordinary quality, this cozy and unassuming restaurant consistently ranks among the city's most acclaimed dining venues. The menu changes regularly but often features items like beef-cheek bourguignon, chicken and oxtail with semolina gnocchi, and seared foie gras with chestnut, raisins, bacon, and cinnamon toast (especially exceptional). **Known for:** open kitchen in which diners at the counter can interact with chefs; one of the best burgers in town; grilled dry-aged pigeon with a seasonally changing preparation. [$] *Average main: $33* ✉ *738 E. Burnside St., Southeast* ☎ *503/546–8796* 🌐 *www.lepigeon.com* 🕒 *No lunch* ✣ *1:H3.*

$ CAFÉ 🍴 **Maurice.** Described by baker-owner Kristen Murray as a "modern pastry luncheonette," this dainty West End café with just a handful of wooden booth and counter seats and a minimalist-inspired white-on-white aesthetic serves exquisite French–Scandinavian pastries, cakes, and sandwiches, as well as a full gamut of drinks, including wine, beer, cocktails, teas, and coffee. There's always an interesting *lefse* (Norwegian flatbread) of the day, along with a delicious polenta clafouti with confit of chicken heart. **Known for:** black-pepper cheesecake; varied cocktail list. [$] *Average main: $11* ✉ *921 S.W. Oak St., West End* ☎ *503/224–9921* 🌐 *www.mauricepdx.com* 🕒 *Closed Sun. and Mon.* ✣ *1:C3.*

$$ MODERN ITALIAN 🍴 **Nostrana.** This smart but informal restaurant delivers delicious, thin-crust pizzas and wood-grilled meats and seafood from the large brick oven. Pies carry an assortment of high-quality toppings; the Funghi

Verde pizza—topped with shiitake and maitake mushrooms with house mozzarella and garlic—is one of Nostrana's most popular pies. **Known for:** terrific happy hour deals; smoked rotisserie chicken. [$] *Average main: $22* ✉ *1401 S.E. Morrison St., Southeast* ☎ *503/234–2427* 🌐 *www.nostrana.com* ⏲ *No lunch weekends* ✣ *2:D5.*

$$ MODERN AMERICAN Fodor's Choice ★ 🍴 **Olympia Provisions.** Salumist Elias Cairo made a name for himself throughout the country with his artisanal charcuterie, such as smoked chorizo, pepper-coated capicola, and pork-pistachio pâté, which is sold in fine grocery stores nationally as well as at numerous Portland farmers' markets and gourmet shops. Now Cairo, alongside chef Alex Yoder, have become known for a pair of stellar, meat-centric restaurants—Olympia Provisions Northwest and Olympia Provisions Southeast—in which you can order platters of charcuterie and cheeses along with more eclectic seasonal American fare. **Known for:** lively happy hours; deeply flavorful charcuterie; interesting cocktail selection. [$] *Average main: $22* ✉ *107 S.E. Washington St., Southeast* ☎ *503/954–3663* 🌐 *www.olympiaprovisions.com* ✣ *1:G5.*

$ THAI Fodor's Choice ★ 🍴 **PaaDee.** Adjoining the more celebrated, reservations-only sister restaurant Langbaan, PaaDee serves some of the freshest, most flavorful Thai food in town, and at remarkably fair prices given the complexity of the cooking, the warmth of the staff, and the attractiveness of the dining room, which is on the ground floor of a contemporary condo building at the restaurant-blessed intersection of 28th and Burnside. The kitchen here specializes in traditional Thai comfort fare: grilled squid skewers with chili-lime sauce; wild-caught prawns with lemongrass, scallions, ground rice, and a spicy lime dressing; and sautéed pork belly with basil, chili, green beans, and a fried egg rank among the most popular dishes. **Known for:** fair prices for upscale Thai fare; daily-changing fish entrée, always with a creative preparation. [$] *Average main: $14* ✉ *6 S.E. 28th Ave., Southeast* ☎ *503/360–1453* 🌐 *www.paadeepdx.com* ✣ *2:E5.*

$$ ASIAN Fodor's Choice ★ 🍴 **Pok Pok.** Andy Ricker, the owner of one of Portland's most talked-about restaurants, regularly travels to Southeast Asia to research street food and home-style recipes to include on the menu of this always-hopping spot. Ike's Vietnamese chicken wings, deep-fried in caramelized fish sauce and garlic, are legendary. **Known for:** Ike's Vietnamese chicken wings; charcoal-roasted game hen and other meaty fare; fiery-hot food (although there are plenty of milder dishes—you just have to ask). [$] *Average main: $16* ✉ *3226 S.E. Division St., Division* ☎ *503/232–1387* 🌐 *www.pokpokpdx.com* ✣ *2:F6.*

$$ KOREAN FUSION Fodor's Choice ★ 🍴 **Revelry.** Portland has long trailed its northerly neighbor Seattle when it comes to Korean cuisine. Happily, in 2016, Seattle's renowned Relay Korean restaurant group opened a stylish, industrial-chic restaurant in Portland's white-hot Central East Side. **Known for:** mochi doughnuts with caramel popcorn for dessert; soju cocktails; dinner till midnight most nights (2 am on weekends). [$] *Average main: $16* ✉ *210 S.E. Martin Luther King Blvd., Southeast* ☎ *971/339–3693* 🌐 *www.relayrestaurantgroup.com* ⏲ *No lunch* ✣ *1:G4.*

$ ✗ **Smokehouse Tavern.** *Top Chef* season 14 contestant B.J. Smith oper-
BARBECUE   ates this rather stylish take on a down-home barbecue joint. **Known**
Fodor's Choice   **for:** fall-off-the-bone barbecue brisket; generous sides. $ *Average main:*
★   *$14* ✉ *1401 S.E. Morrison St., Southeast* ☎ *971/279–4850* ⊕ *www.*
smokehousetavernpdx.com ✛ *2:D5.*

$$ ✗ **Taylor Railworks.** The owners of this low-keyed yet sophisticated res-
MODERN   taurant on the ground floor of a handsomely concerted Central East
AMERICAN   Side warehouse describe their food as "borderless American cuisine,"
and although they do source locally and seasonally, it's true that the
contemporary fare—served in small plates portions—draws on differ-
ent parts of the world. Modern takes on old-school classics are part
of the fun here: consider the pig in a blanket of Chinese sausage in a
house-made bao, or pasta noodles à la Johnny with spicy crab, prawns,
and tomatoes. **Known for:** the market fish with daily changing prepa-
ration; terrific raw-bar appetizers; memorable cocktails, many with
Asian influences. $ *Average main: $18* ✉ *117 S.E. Taylor St., Southeast*
☎ *503/208-2573* ⊕ *www.trwpdx.com* ☺ *No lunch Sat.–Mon.* ✛ *1:G6.*

$$ ✗ **Trifecta Tavern.** Baker extraordinaire Ken Forkish (of Ken's Artisan
MODERN   Bakery and Artisan Pizza fame) operates this dapper tavern inside a con-
AMERICAN   verted garage in the industrial Central East Side. The menu reflects the
Fodor's Choice   owner's devotion to wood-fired ovens—there's even a Negroni cocktail
★   infused with charred maple wood on the menu—but you'll also discover
an exhaustive selection of snacks and larger plates that have never met
with an open flame, such as the compressed-watermelon salad with
sheep's milk vinaigrette and spiced almonds. **Known for:** house-baked
breads; impressive selection of shareable small plates; the 18-ounce
"Big-Ass Steak" with wood-fired marrow bones. $ *Average main: $20*
✉ *726 S.E. 6th Ave., Southeast* ☎ *503/841–6675* ⊕ *www.trifectapdx.*
com ☺ *No lunch* ✛ *1:H5.*

$$$ ✗ **Tusk.** With its clean lines and whitewashed walls, Tusk provides a
MIDDLE EASTERN   setting for its colorful, beautifully presented modern Middle Eastern
fare to shine brightly. Think flatbread with salmon roe, squash, mus-
tard oil, and yogurt, and grilled sweet potato with hazelnut tahini and
dukka among the smaller starter plates. **Known for:** extensive selection
of vegetarian small plates; fun vibe for late-night drinks and snacking;
perfectly grilled flatbreads with house-made toppings. $ *Average main:*
$27 ✉ *2448 E. Burnside St., Southeast* ☎ *503/894–8082* ⊕ *www.tusk-*
pdx.com ☺ *No lunch weekdays* ✛ *2:E5.*

WHERE TO STAY

Portland has an unusually rich variety of distinctive, design-driven bou-
tique hotels, historic properties, and charming B&Bs, and while you'll
find the usual mix of budget-oriented, mid-range, and upscale chains
here, if you'd rather avoid cookie-cutter brand-name properties, you're
in the right city.

Although you won't find ultraluxury brands like Four Seasons or W
Hotels, the vast majority of Downtown properties are high-end, with
the rates to prove it, especially during the week when conventions are
in town, and during the summer high season, when many properties

command at least double what they can during the slower, wetter winter months. After a decade of steadily climbing demand but very little new hotel construction, Portland is suddenly booming again—by 2018, some 3,300 new hotel rooms are planned. Upcoming properties—all Downtown unless noted—generating plenty of buzz include the Hi-Lo Hotel (part of Marriott's Autograph Collection), a stylish new AC by Marriott hotel, the Porter Hotel (part of Hilton's new luxe boutique brand, Curio), the Canopy Portland (another new Hilton product, going up in the Pearl District), a Hampton Inn in the Pearl District, the Woodlark Cornelius Hotel (from Portland's own upscale-boutique Provenance Hotels), the historic Grove Hotel in Old Town, the budget-oriented Harlow Hotel in Old Town, the ultrafuturistic Radisson RED Broadway Tower, and what will become the city's largest hotel, a 600-room Hyatt Regency that will adjoin the Oregon Convention Center in the Lloyd District.

A B&B might make a better option than a larger hotel if you're looking for a more personal and authentic Portland experience. Most of Portland's smaller accommodations are in lively neighborhoods abundant with distinctive shopping and dining, and most often, an inn will offer unique guest rooms, deluxe home-cooked breakfasts, and friendly and knowledgeable innkeepers. Airbnb also has a huge inventory in Portland, with many properties in intriguing Eastside neighborhoods.

HOTEL PRICES

Although rates have risen considerably in Portland in recent years as the city's popularity has soared, rates even at upscale Downtown hotels are usually a notch or two lower than what you'd pay in other West Coast cities, such as Seattle and San Francisco. In summer, when the city is abuzz with festivals and festival goers, it can be difficult to find a room in Downtown for under $300 nightly. Most of the time, however, even the more luxurious hotels cost under $250 per night, and there are a lot of options around $175 or less. Outside Downtown, but still within city limits, it is much easier to find rooms in mid-range chains and B&Bs for a little over $100 nightly, and at a handful of reliable budget properties around town *(we've included several in this chapter)*, for under $100 nightly.

If you don't mind a dull but pleasant suburban location, the surrounding towns of Beaverton, Lake Oswego, Gresham, and Vancouver, Washington, abound with chain hotels with rates typically 25% to 50% lower than what you'd pay in Portland, and nearly always with free parking. *Hotel reviews have been shortened. For full information, visit Fodors.com.*

WHAT IT COSTS IN U.S. DOLLARS				
	$	**$$**	**$$$**	**$$$$**
Hotels	under $150	$150–$225	$226–$300	over $300

Hotel prices are the lowest cost of a standard double room in high season.

Use the coordinate (✢ B2) at the end of each listing to locate a site on the corresponding map.

DOWNTOWN

$$ HOTEL
🏨 **Ace Hotel.** The quintessential Portland hipster hotel, the Ace contains a Stumptown Coffee café and Clyde Common restaurant, is a block from Powell's Books and the Pearl District, and is right in the heart of Downtown's ever-trendy West End neighborhood. **Pros:** prime Downtown location; unique design and artwork in each room; free city bicycles available for guests. **Cons:** offbeat decor and hipster vibe isn't for everybody; rooms with private baths push the Ace into the expensive category; some rooms receive street noise. [$] *Rooms from: $190* ✉ *1022 S.W. Stark St., Downtown* ☎ *503/228–2277* 🌐 *www.acehotel.com* 🛏 *78 rooms* 🍴 *No meals* ✥ *1:C4.*

$$$ HOTEL
🏨 **Benson Hotel.** Portland's venerable grande dame may now be overshadowed by several other upscale properties in town in terms of luxury, especially given the steep rates, but the Benson has hosted most every president since it opened in 1913. **Pros:** historic building; beautiful lobby; excellent location. **Cons:** rooms and hallways are a bit dark; many bathrooms are quite small. [$] *Rooms from: $269* ✉ *309 S.W. Broadway, Downtown* ☎ *503/228–2000, 800/716–6199* 🌐 *www.bensonhotel.com* 🛏 *230 rooms, 57 suites* 🍴 *No meals* ✥ *1:C4.*

$$$ HOTEL
🏨 **Courtyard by Marriott–Portland City Center.** More boutique feeling than typical Courtyards, this LEED-certified hotel has individual check-in kiosks in its lobby rather than one big reception desk, and the spacious, tasteful rooms showcase local art and photography. **Pros:** eco-friendly; in the heart of Downtown; good on-site restaurant. **Cons:** only some rooms have tubs; rates are not much lower than some significantly fancier competitors. [$] *Rooms from: $229* ✉ *550 S.W. Oak St., Downtown* ☎ *503/505–5000* 🌐 *www.marriott.com* 🛏 *253 rooms, 3 suites* 🍴 *No meals* ✥ *1:D4.*

$$$ HOTEL FAMILY
🏨 **Embassy Suites Portland–Downtown.** The grand lobby of the former Multnomah Hotel, built in 1912, offers an extravagant welcome to this all-suites hotel located close to both the riverfront and Old Town. **Pros:** central location; atmospheric old building; breakfast and evening drinks and snacks included. **Cons:** surrounding blocks can feel a bit seedy (though still quite safe) at night; no in-and-out privileges in $32 self-park garage across the street. [$] *Rooms from: $279* ✉ *319 S.W. Pine St., Downtown* ☎ *503/279–9000, 800/643–7892* 🌐 *www.embassyportland.com* 🛏 *276 suites* 🍴 *Breakfast* ✥ *1:D4.*

$$$ HOTEL Fodor's Choice ★
🏨 **Heathman Hotel.** From the teak-paneled lobby to the marble fireplaces to the rosewood elevators with Warhol prints at each landing, this wonderfully atmospheric, art-filled 1927 hotel exudes refinement. **Pros:** superior service; central location adjoining Portland Center for the Performing Arts, and a block from Portland Art Museum; outstanding art collection; stellar restaurant. **Cons:** some rooms are small; expensive parking. [$] *Rooms from: $269* ✉ *1001 S.W. Broadway, Downtown* ☎ *503/241–4100, 800/551–0011* 🌐 *portland.heathmanhotel.com* 🛏 *110 rooms, 40 suites* 🍴 *No meals* ✥ *1:C5.*

$$$ HOTEL Fodor's Choice ★
🏨 **Hotel deLuxe.** This retro-glam 1912 boutique hotel with its original chandeliers, gilded ceilings, black-and-white photography (arranged by movie themes), heavy drapes, and hip cocktail lounge evokes Hollywood's Golden Era, but with welcome modern touches like flat-screen

TVs, free Wi-Fi, and iPod docks. **Pros:** fun and artistic vibe; friendly and helpful staff; nice touches like pillow menu, preprogrammed iPods, spiritual book library, and classic movies. **Cons:** standard rooms are a bit compact; location is less central than other Downtown properties. [$] *Rooms from: $229 ✉ 729 S.W. 15th Ave., Downtown ☎ 503/219–2094, 866/986–8085 🌐 www.hoteldeluxeportland.com 🛏 97 rooms, 33 suites 🍴 No meals ⊕ 1:A4.*

$$$ HOTEL 🏨 **Hotel Lucia.** Black-and-white celebrity photos from Pulitzer Prize–winner and native Oregonian David Hume Kennerly, comfy leather chairs, and stylish low-slung furniture adorn the rooms of this nine-story, 1909 European-style boutique hotel in the heart of Downtown. **Pros:** prime location; luxurious amenities; two outstanding restaurants. **Cons:** limited shelf and storage space in the small bathrooms; steep rates during busy times. [$] *Rooms from: $259 ✉ 400 S.W. Broadway, Downtown ☎ 503/225–1717, 866/986–8086 🌐 www.hotellucia.com 🛏 127 rooms, 33 suites 🍴 No meals ⊕ 1:C4.*

$$$ HOTEL 🏨 **Hotel Modera.** Decorated with local artwork, sleek, contemporary furnishings, and wood-and-marble accents, this boutique property is both upscale and accessible, and offers a location convenient to the Southwest Park Blocks and Portland State University. **Pros:** friendly staff; nice courtyard; great bar-restaurant; individually bagged ice in hand-carved chests in every hall. **Cons:** rooms on the small side; no on-site gym (but free passes to nearby 24-hour gym); a 10- to 15-minute walk from West End and Pearl District dining and nightlife. [$] *Rooms from: $234 ✉ 515 S.W. Clay St., Downtown ☎ 503/484–1084, 877/484–1084 🌐 www.hotelmodera.com 🛏 167 rooms, 7 suites 🍴 No meals ⊕ 1:C6.*

$$$$ HOTEL Fodor's Choice ★ 🏨 **Hotel Monaco.** This artsy Downtown Portland outpost of the Kimpton-operated Monaco boutique-hotel brand offers eclectic textiles and patterns, bright spaces and bold colors, quirky amenities like complimentary companion goldfish for your room, and the overall sense that staying here is a lot of fun. **Pros:** sumptuous interior; interesting decor; impeccable service; well-equipped fitness center. **Cons:** design style may not suit all; pricey. [$] *Rooms from: $349 ✉ 506 S.W. Washington St., Downtown ☎ 503/222–0001, 888/207–2201 🌐 www.portland-monaco.com 🛏 86 rooms, 135 suites 🍴 No meals ⊕ 1:D4.*

$$ HOTEL 🏨 **Hotel Rose.** This dapper but reasonably priced boutique property overlooking the Willamette River affords stellar views of the water, easy access to the waterfront park and the events that take place there (Rose Festival, Blues Festival, Gay Pride, and so on), and—as part of the Pineapple Hospitality chain—complimentary pineapple cupcakes during the daily afternoon reception. **Pros:** central location on the riverfront; typically lower rates than many comparable Downtown hotels; lots of perks for the price; easy access to the MAX. **Cons:** rooms not facing the river have dull views. [$] *Rooms from: $179 ✉ 50 S.W. Morrison St., Downtown ☎ 503/221–0711, 877/237–6775 🌐 www.hotelroseportland.com 🛏 140 rooms, 2 suites 🍴 No meals ⊕ 1:D5.*

$$$$ HOTEL Fodor's Choice ★ 🏨 **Hotel Vintage.** This historic landmark takes its theme from Oregon vineyards, with rooms named after local wineries, complimentary wine served every evening, and an extensive collection of Oregon vintages displayed in the tasting room. **Pros:** terrific on-site Italian restaurant

and wine bar; exceptionally helpful and friendly staff; stunning room decor; several over-the-top spectacular suites. **Cons:** pricey parking; some street noise on the lower levels on the Washington Street side. [$] *Rooms from: $325* ✉ *422 S.W. Broadway, Downtown* ☎ *503/228–1212, 800/263–2305* 🌐 *www.vintageplaza.com* 🛏 *96 rooms, 21 suites* 🍴 *No meals* ⊕ *1:C4.*

$$$ HOTEL 🏨 **Mark Spencer Hotel.** This family-owned hotel, with a prime location in the hip West End near Powell's Books and the Pearl District, is one of the better values in town, with most of its warmly decorated and spacious rooms containing well-equipped kitchenettes. **Pros:** commitment to the arts; afternoon tea and cookies and evening local wine tasting; most rooms have kitchenettes. **Cons:** some rooms are a bit dark; street noise can be a problem. [$] *Rooms from: $249* ✉ *409 S.W. 11th Ave., Downtown* ☎ *503/224–3293, 800/548–3934* 🌐 *www.markspencer.com* 🛏 *36 rooms, 66 suites* 🍴 *Breakfast* ⊕ *1:B4.*

$ HOTEL 🏨 **McMenamins Crystal Hotel.** Travelers who appreciate good music and good beer—especially together—love this West End branch of the McMenamin brothers' unorthodox empire, which is home to three bars and a restaurant and is affiliated with the Crystal Ballroom concert venue a block away. **Pros:** historic building with eccentric, rock-star vibe and decor; lots of bars and dining both on-site and on surrounding blocks; shared-bath rooms are rock-bottom affordable. **Cons:** quirky vibe isn't for everyone; shared bath down the hall in most rooms; no TVs. [$] *Rooms from: $110* ✉ *303 S.W. 12th Ave., Downtown* ☎ *503/972–2670, 855/205–3930* 🌐 *www.mcmenamins.com/crystal-hotel* 🛏 *51 rooms, 9 with bath* 🍴 *No meals* ⊕ *1:B3.*

$$$$ HOTEL Fodor's Choice ★ 🏨 **The Nines.** On the top nine floors of a former landmark department store, this swanky hotel, part of the Starwood Luxury Collection, has the city's poshest accommodations, with luxe decor, great views, and two see-and-be-seen restaurants. **Pros:** stunning views; swanky vibe and cool design; two sceney restaurants. **Cons:** rooms facing the atrium and overlooking the bar and restaurant can be noisy; expensive valet-only parking. [$] *Rooms from: $339* ✉ *525 S.W. Morrison St., Downtown* ☎ *503/222–9996, 866/716–8136* 🌐 *www.thenines.com* 🛏 *318 rooms, 13 suites* 🍴 *No meals* ⊕ *1:C5.*

$$$ HOTEL 🏨 **The Paramount Hotel.** This pale-stone, 15-story hotel overlooking Director Park is a few blocks from Pioneer Square, the Arlene Schnitzer Concert Hall, the Portland Art Museum, the MAX, and the streetcar. **Pros:** central location; beautiful granite bathrooms; excellent bar and restaurant off lobby. **Cons:** small fitness facility; parking is expensive. [$] *Rooms from: $249* ✉ *808 S.W. Taylor St., Downtown* ☎ *503/223–9900, 855/215–0160* 🌐 *www.portlandparamount.com* 🛏 *152 rooms, 2 suites* 🍴 *No meals* ⊕ *1:B5.*

$$$$ HOTEL 🏨 **RiverPlace Hotel.** With textured wall coverings, pillows made of Pendleton wool, and a color palette of slate blue, mustard yellow, and a variety of browns, this Kimpton-operated boutique hotel on the banks of the Willamette River captures the look and feel of the Pacific Northwest. **Pros:** stellar views and park-side riverfront location; rooms are spacious and airy; some suites have wood-burning fireplaces. **Cons:** not many restaurants or shops within easy walking distance. [$] *Rooms from: $339*

✉ *1510 S.W. Harbor Way, Downtown* ☎ *503/228–3233, 888/869–3108* 🌐 *www.riverplacehotel.com* 🛏 *39 rooms, 45 suites* 🍴 *No meals* ✣ *1:D6.*

$$$ HOTEL Fodor's Choice ★ 🏨 **Sentinel Hotel.** Formerly known as the Governor Hotel, the grand Sentinel Hotel underwent a $6 million renovation and rebranding in 2014 to take it from historic to hip-historic; all guest rooms and public spaces in the landmark, early-20th-century buildings were brought up-to-date, and the hotel now reflects a very Portland vibe, with locally sourced textiles, furnishings, and goods. **Pros:** indie style meets luxury; central location; spacious, well-designed rooms; well-equipped gym. **Cons:** pricey valet parking. [$] *Rooms from: $259* ✉ *614 S.W. 10th Ave., Downtown* ☎ *503/224–3400, 888/246–5631* 🌐 *www.sentinelhotel.com* 🛏 *76 rooms, 24 suites* 🍴 *No meals* ✣ *1:B4.*

$$$ HOTEL 🏨 **The Westin Portland.** This pale-stone, upscale hotel combines luxury with convenience, with Pioneer Square and the MAX just two blocks away, and West End and Pearl District dining within a 10-minute walk. **Pros:** prime Downtown location (a stone's throw from one of the city's largest, most established food-cart pods); handsome rooms; plush bedding. **Cons:** pricey overnight parking; attractive but not especially distinctive rooms. [$] *Rooms from: $289* ✉ *750 S.W. Alder St., Downtown* ☎ *503/294–9000, 888/625–5144* 🌐 *www.westinportland.com* 🛏 *189 rooms, 16 suites* 🍴 *No meals* ✣ *1:C4.*

OLD TOWN

$ HOTEL Fodor's Choice ★ 🏨 **Society Hotel.** This intimate new boutique hotel with simple, stylish, and affordable rooms just steps from Old Town nightlife and Lan Su Chinese Garden occupies an 1880s former boardinghouse for sailors and retains a quirky and colorful atmosphere. **Pros:** bargain rates; gorgeous rooftop deck; fun and youthful vibe; close to plenty of gay and mainstream bars. **Cons:** rooms are quite basic; neighborhood can get very noisy on weekend evenings. [$] *Rooms from: $109* ✉ *203 N.W. 3rd Ave., Old Town* ☎ *503/445–0444* 🌐 *www.thesocietyhotel.com* 🛏 *39 rooms* 🍴 *No meals* 💳 *No credit cards* ✣ *1:D3.*

PEARL DISTRICT

$$$ HOTEL Fodor's Choice ★ 🏨 **Residence Inn–Pearl District.** This sleek, six-floor, all-suites hotel is the trendy Pearl District's first hotel. **Pros:** clean, modern design both inside and out; best location for proximity to Pearl District businesses; in-room kitchens; many rooms can sleep four to six guests. **Cons:** a little far from Downtown attractions; pricey overnight parking. [$] *Rooms from: $289* ✉ *1150 N.W. 9th Ave., Pearl District* ☎ *503/220–1339, 888/236–2427* 🌐 *www.marriott.com* 🛏 *224 suites* 🍴 *Breakfast* ✣ *1:C1.*

NOB HILL

$$ HOTEL FAMILY Fodor's Choice ★ 🏨 **Inn @ Northrup Station.** Bright colors, bold patterns, and retro designs characterize this Nob Hill hotel containing luxurious suites with full kitchens or kitchenettes. **Pros:** roomy suites have kitchens and feel like home; steps from Nob Hill shopping, dining, and the streetcar; free parking. **Cons:** the bold color scheme isn't for everyone; a 15-minute

walk, or slightly shorter streetcar ride, from Downtown core; in demand so it can be hard to get a reservation. $ *Rooms from: $219* ✉ *2025 N.W. Northrup St., Nob Hill* ☎ *503/224–0543, 800/224–1180* ⊕ *www. northrupstation.com* ⇨ *70 suites* ⦿| *Breakfast* ✛ *2:A4.*

$$
HOTEL
Silver Cloud Inn–Portland. The sole Portland branch of a small, Seattle-area, mid-price hotel chain is just a block from the lively upper end of N.W. 23rd Avenue and a great alternative to the bustle Downtown. **Pros:** free parking; close to Nob Hill boutiques and dining as well as Forest Park hiking trails; easy access to bus and streetcar. **Cons:** gym but no pool; not especially close to Downtown; front rooms face a busy street. $ *Rooms from: $189* ✉ *2426 N.W. Vaughn St., Nob Hill* ☎ *503/242–2400, 800/205–6939* ⊕ *www.silvercloud.com* ⇨ *75 rooms, 6 suites* ⦿| *Breakfast* ✛ *2:A3.*

SOUTHWEST

$$
HOTEL
River's Edge Hotel & Spa. On the edge of Portland's recently developed South Waterfront District and just a 10- to 15-minute drive or bus ride from Downtown, this tranquil boutique property is nestled among trees along the meandering Willamette River. **Pros:** expansive river views; most rooms have balconies; trails nearby for walking and jogging; full-service spa on-site. **Cons:** few restaurants or businesses within walking distance; need a car or bus to get Downtown; only valet ($25) parking is available. $ *Rooms from: $195* ✉ *0455 S.W. Hamilton Ct., Southwest* ☎ *503/802–5800, 888/556–4402* ⊕ *www.riversedgehotel.com* ⇨ *81 rooms, 18 suites* ⦿| *Breakfast* ✛ *2:C6.*

NORTH

$$
B&B/INN
Caravan–The Tiny House Hotel. In keeping with the artsy, idiosyncratic vibe of the surrounding Alberta Arts District, this cluster of itty-bitty custom-built houses-on-wheels offers visitors the chance to experience Portland's unabashed quirky side. **Pros:** a quirky, only-in-Portland experience; in the heart of Alberta's hip retail-dining district; all units have kitchenettes. **Cons:** these houses really are tiny; 15-minute drive or 35-minute bus ride from Downtown; often books up weeks in advance (especially weekends). $ *Rooms from: $155* ✉ *5009 N.E. 11th Ave., Alberta District* ☎ *503/288–5225* ⊕ *www.tinyhousehotel.com* ⇨ *6 cottages* ⦿| *No meals* ✛ *2:D1.*

$
HOTEL
Viking Motel. When this clean, family-run, mid-century motel opened in the late 1970s, it served the nearby shipyard; today, this eco-friendly property is arguably Portland's best bargain lodging, catering to savvy visitors who take the nearby MAX to Downtown Portland. **Pros:** rock-bottom rates (and free parking and Wi-Fi); friendly owners who take great pride in the property's upkeep; just off Interstate 5 and a block from MAX light-rail station. **Cons:** North Portland neighborhood is 15-minute drive north of Downtown; few frills. $ *Rooms from: $79* ✉ *6701 N. Interstate Ave., North* ☎ *503/285–4896, 800/308–5097* ⊕ *www.vikingmotelportland.com* ⇨ *26 rooms* ⦿| *No meals* ✛ *2:B1.*

2

NORTHEAST

$$ HOTEL
DoubleTree by Hilton–Portlandon. This bustling, business hotel maintains a steady customer base in meetings and special events, so you will find all the usual business-friendly perks and luxuries, and—as a leisure traveler—the best rates on weekends. **Pros:** convenient location for light rail, conventions, and concerts and Trail Blazers basketball games; nice views from upper floors. **Cons:** pool is outdoors (and seasonal); hotel can be crowded with conventioneers; surrounding Lloyd District has chains shops and movie theaters but lacks charm. [$] *Rooms from: $158* ✉ *1000 N.E. Multnomah St., Lloyd District/Convention Center* ☎ *503/281–6111, 800/222–8733* 🌐 *www.doubletreeportland.com* 🛏 *458 rooms, 18 suites* 🍴 *No meals* ✢ *2:D4.*

$$$ HOTEL Fodor's Choice ★
Hotel Eastlund. A drab mid-20th-century chain property in Convention Center/Lloyd District morphed into a stylish and slick boutique hotel in 2015. **Pros:** handy location near Moda Center, convention center, and light rail; fashionable rooms with plenty of high-tech perks; see-and-be-seen restaurants with dazzling skyline views. **Cons:** surrounding neighborhood lacks charm and interesting dining options; a bit pricey for this part of town. [$] *Rooms from: $269* ✉ *1021 N.E. Grand Ave., Lloyd District/Convention Center* ☎ *503/235–2100* 🌐 *www.hoteleastlund.com* 🛏 *168 rooms* 🍴 *No meals* ✢ *1:G1.*

$$ B&B/INN Fodor's Choice ★
Lion and the Rose Victorian B&B. Oak and mahogany floors, original light fixtures, and a coffered dining-room ceiling set a tone of formal elegance in this 1906 mansion, while the wonderfully friendly, accommodating, and knowledgeable innkeepers—Dusty and Steve—make sure that you feel perfectly at home. **Pros:** gorgeous house; top-notch service; home-cooked meals. **Cons:** young children not allowed in main house; nearest commercial neighborhood, the Lloyd District, is pretty bland. [$] *Rooms from: $170* ✉ *1810 N.E. 15th Ave., Northeast* ☎ *503/287–9245, 800/955–1647* 🌐 *www.lionrose.com* 🛏 *7 rooms, 1 apartment* 🍴 *Breakfast* ✢ *2:D3.*

$$ HOTEL FAMILY Fodor's Choice ★
McMenamins Kennedy School. In a renovated elementary school on the edge of a trendy Northeast Portland neighborhood, Oregon's famously creative McMenamin brothers hoteliers have created a quirky and fantastical multiuse facility with rooms that feature original schoolhouse touches like chalkboards and cloakrooms and literature-inspired themes, a movie theater, a restaurant, a warm outdoor soaking pool, a brewery, and several small bars. **Pros:** funky and authentic Portland experience; room rates include movies and use of year-round soaking pool; free parking; close to trendy Alberta Arts District. **Cons:** rooms have showers but no tubs; no TVs in rooms; 20-minute drive or 40-minute bus ride from Downtown. [$] *Rooms from: $155* ✉ *5736 N.E. 33rd Ave., Northeast* ☎ *503/249–3983* 🌐 *www.kennedyschool.com* 🛏 *57 rooms* 🍴 *No meals* ✢ *2:F1.*

$$ B&B/INN
Portland's White House Bed and Breakfast. Hardwood floors with Oriental rugs, chandeliers, antiques, and fountains create a warm and romantic mood at this lavish 1910 Greek Revival mansion in the historic Irvington District. **Pros:** over-the-top romantic; excellent service; a short drive or bus ride to several hip East Side restaurant and retail districts. **Cons:** in residential neighborhood a few miles from Downtown;

nearest commercial neighborhood is the rather bland Lloyd District. $ *Rooms from: $165* ⊠ *1914 N.E. 22nd Ave., Northeast* ☎ *503/287–7131, 800/272–7131* ⊕ *www.portlandswhitehouse.com* ⤵ *8 suites* ⍥ *Breakfast* ✛ *2:E3.*

AIRPORT

The airport is about a 20- to 25-minute drive away from Downtown Portland, and as expected you can find a number of chain properties here, all offering much lower rates than comparable Downtown hotels.

$$ **Aloft Portland Airport at Cascade Station.** High-end vibrant design,
HOTEL   sophisticated amenities, and close proximity to the Cascade Station MAX station make the first Aloft in Oregon a standout amid the generally mediocre hotels near the airport. **Pros:** lots of high-tech amenities; welcoming social areas; stylish, spacious rooms. **Cons:** airport location; no sit-down restaurant; no complimentary breakfast. $ *Rooms from: $168* ⊠ *9920 N.E. Cascades Pkwy., Airport* ☎ *503/200–5678, 866/716–8143* ⊕ *www.aloftportlandairport.com* ⤵ *136 rooms* ⍥ *No meals* ✛ *2:H2.*

$$ **Embassy Suites Portland Airport.** Suites in this eight-story atrium hotel,
HOTEL   within view of the airport, come with separate bedrooms, living areas with sleeper sofas, and flat-screen TVs. **Pros:** spacious suites; full breakfast and happy-hour cocktails included; walking distance from Cascade Station chain shops and restaurants. **Cons:** airport location; parking is $10. $ *Rooms from: $157* ⊠ *7900 N.E. 82nd Ave., Airport* ☎ *503/460–3000* ⊕ *www.portlandairport.embassysuites.com* ⤵ *251 suites* ⍥ *Breakfast* ✛ *2:H2.*

SOUTHEAST

$ **Evermore Guesthouse.** Just a block from the trendy dining along South-
B&B/INN   east Portland's hip Division Street, this beautifully restored, 1909 Arts
Fodor's Choice   and Crafts–style mansion contains spacious, light-filled rooms, some
★   with private balconies, claw-foot soaking tubs, and good-size sitting areas; one detached suite has a full kitchen, and a cozy and romantic third-floor room has skylights and pitched ceilings. **Pros:** located in hip, charming neighborhood with many bars and restaurants; reasonably priced with free off-street parking; free laundry and breakfast; distinctive, charming decor. **Cons:** some rooms face busy Cesar Chavez Boulevard; a 15-minute drive or 30-minute bus ride from Downtown. $ *Rooms from: $135* ⊠ *3860 S.E. Clinton St., Richmond* ☎ *503/206–6509, 877/600–6509* ⊕ *www.evermoreguesthouse.com* ⤵ *3 rooms, 3 suites* ⍥ *Breakfast* ✛ *2:F6.*

$ **Jupiter Hotel.** The hip, creative, and adventurous flock to this con-
HOTEL   temporary boutique hotel, formerly a motor inn, adjacent to the Doug Fir Lounge, a bar and restaurant that's also one of the city's most popular concert venues. **Pros:** funky decor and vibe; trendy bar and music club attached; easy access to Downtown. **Cons:** youthful, hipster personality isn't to everyone's taste; request a room on the "chill side" if you want distance from the noisy patio/bar scene; thin walls between rooms. $ *Rooms from: $139* ⊠ *800 E. Burnside St.,*

Southeast ☎ *503/230–9200, 877/800–0004* 🌐 *www.jupiterhotel.com* 🛏 *80 rooms, 1 suite* 🍴 *No meals* ✥ *1:H3.*

$$ B&B/INN 🏨 **Portland Mayor's Mansion.** More than a century ago, Portland Mayor H. Russell Albee resided in this stately redbrick Colonial Revival mansion on the edge of gracious Laurelhurst Park. **Pros:** beautiful rooms with rich period details; views of and easy access to Laurelhurst Park. **Cons:** two rooms share a bath. [$] *Rooms from: $175* ✉ *3360 S.E. Ankeny St., Laurelhurst* ☎ *503/232–3588* 🌐 *www.pdxmayorsmansion.com* 🛏 *4 rooms* 🍴 *Breakfast* ✥ *2:F5.*

NIGHTLIFE AND PERFORMING ARTS

Portland is quite the creative town. Every night top-ranked dance, theater, and musical performers take the stage somewhere in the city. Expect to find never-ending choices for things to do, from taking in true independent films, performance art, and plays, to checking out some of the Northwest's (and the country's) hottest bands at one of the city's many nightclubs or concert venues.

Given the city's unabashed passion for craft cocktails and beer, local wines, and artisanal coffee, it makes sense that Portland abounds with cool lounges, coffeehouses, and bars. Hard-core clubbing and dancing has a bit less of a following here than more casual barhopping, and Portlanders do like to combine noshing and sipping—you'll find an abundance of nightspots serving exceptional food (and often offering great happy-hour deals on victuals and drinks), and quite a few full-service restaurants with popular side bars and lounges. Nightlife and dining really overlap in the Rose City.

EVENT LISTINGS

"A&E, The Arts and Entertainment Guide," published each Friday in the *Oregonian* (🌐 *www.oregonlive.com*), contains listings of performers, productions, events, and club entertainment. *Willamette Week* (🌐 *wweek.com*), published free each Wednesday and widely available throughout the metropolitan area, contains similar, but hipper, listings. The *Portland Mercury* (🌐 *www.portlandmercury.com*), also free, is an even edgier entertainment publication distributed each Wednesday. The glossy newsstand magazine *Portland Monthly* (🌐 *www.pdxmonthly.com*) covers Portland culture and lifestyle and provides great nightlife, entertainment, and dining coverage for the city. The free monthly publication *Portland Family Magazine* (🌐 *www.portlandfamily.com*) has an excellent calendar of events for recreational and educational opportunities for families. *PQ Monthly* (🌐 *www.pqmonthly.com*) is the city's gay publication.

NIGHTLIFE

Portland has become something of a base for up-and-coming alternative-rock bands, which perform in clubs scattered throughout the city. Good jazz groups perform nightly in a handful of bars as well.

Portland's most diverting neighborhoods for barhopping are, not surprisingly, its favored dining districts, too—the West End, Pearl District, and Nob Hill on the west side of the Willamette River, within walking distance (or a streetcar ride) of Downtown hotels; Alberta Street, North Mississippi Avenue, and East Burnside Street in the 20s; the Central East Side, Belmont Street, Hawthorne Boulevard, and Division Street on the East Side. Note that many of the restaurants also double as highly popular nightspots; especially notable for sipping and socializing are Bluehour, BTU Brasserie, Clyde Common, Departure, Interurban, Irving Street Kitchen, Kachka, Revelry, Tusk,and Veritable Quandary.

DOWNTOWN

BARS AND LOUNGES

Fodor's Choice ★ **Driftwood Room.** Once your eyes adjust to the romantically dim lighting, you'll find a curved bar, leather banquette seating, and polished-wood ceilings and walls in this retro-chic bar in the Old Hollywood–themed Hotel deLuxe. The trendy cocktails are garnished with herbs culled from the hotel's garden. ■ TIP→ The happy-hour food menu is one of the best in the city. ⊠ *Hotel deLuxe, 729 S.W. 15th Ave., Downtown* ☎ *503/820–2076* ⊕ *www.hoteldeluxeportland.com.*

Fodor's Choice ★ **Headwaters & Sea Bar at the Heathman.** At the elegant Heathman Hotel, you can sip tea in the eucalyptus-paneled Tea Court or beer, wine, and cocktails in the marble Headwaters restaurant and Sea Bar lounge, a venerable Old World space that received a revamp in 2016 when local celeb chef Vitaly Paley took over. This is one of the city's most popular see-and-be-seen venues, especially before or after shows at nearby theaters and concert halls. ⊠ *Heathman Hotel, 1001 S.W. Broadway, Downtown* ☎ *503/790–7752* ⊕ *www.headwaterspdx.com.*

Huber's Cafe. The city's oldest restaurant (est. 1879) is notable for its old-fashioned feel and iconic Spanish coffee cocktail, which is set aflame at your table. The old bar in the back has great character. Huber's is on the ground floor of the historic Oregon Pioneer Building, which became the snazzy Hi-Lo Hotel in fall 2016. ⊠ *Hi-Lo Hotel, 411 S.W. 3rd Ave., Downtown* ☎ *503/228–5686* ⊕ *www.hubers.com.*

Luc Lac Vietnamese Kitchen. With a reputation as an after-work eating and drinking hangout among local Portland chefs and restaurant workers, this always-hopping Vietnamese joint offers well-executed cocktails crafted with classic liquors and surprising Vietnamese flavors, such as the Single Knight: Four Roses Single Barrel bourbon, pho syrup, Angostura orange bitters, and Lapsang souchong tea ice cube. The kitchen turns out delicious eats until midnight on weekdays and 4 am on weekends. ⊠ *835 S.W. 2nd Ave., Downtown* ☎ *503/222–0047* ⊕ *www.luclackitchen.com.*

Fodor's Choice ★ **Multnomah Whiskey Library.** Smartly dressed mixologists roll drink carts around the seductively clubby room—with beam ceilings, wood panelling, leather club chairs, a wood-burning fireplace, and crystal chandeliers—pouring cocktails table-side. The emphasis, of course, is whiskey and bourbon—Multnomah has such an extensive collection in its "library" that bartenders need rolling ladders to access the bottles perched on the tall shelves lining the exposed-brick walls—but don't overlook the impressive food menu. ⊠ *1124 S.W. Alder St., Downtown* ☎ *503/954–1381* ⊕ *www.multnomahwhiskeylibrary.com.*

Raven & Rose. Popular with the after-work set as well as guests of Downtown hotels, this ornate Victorian two-level carriage house amid Downtown's office towers serves English-style pub fare and a worldly list of beers, wines, and cocktails in the Rookery Bar upstairs. Downstairs, you'll find a main dining room and a small lounge area. There's live music some evenings. ✉ *1331 S.W. Broadway, Downtown* ☏ *503/222–7673* ⊕ *www.ravenandrosepdx.com.*

Saucebox. A sophisticated, often mixed gay/straight crowd flocks here to enjoy colorful cocktails and trendy DJ music, mostly on Friday and Saturday nights. The kitchen turns out consistently good pan-Asian fare. ✉ *214 S.W. Broadway, Downtown* ☏ *503/241–3393* ⊕ *www.saucebox.com.*

COFFEEHOUSES

Case Study Coffee. A first-rate indie alternative to the scads of chain coffeehouses Downtown, Case Study serves exceptional, house-roasted coffee in a variety of formats, from Chemex to Aeropress; they also make their own syrups and serve delicious drinking chocolates. Nibble delectable sweets from local bakeries Nuvrei and Petunia's (the latter is gluten-free). There are two additional locations, one in Hollywood at 5347 N.E. Sandy Boulevard and another in Alberta at 1422 N.E. Alberta Street. ✉ *802 S.W. 10th Ave., Downtown* ☏ *503/477–8221* ⊕ *www.casestudycoffee.com.*

Fodor'sChoice
★
Heart Coffee. Inside this sleek East Burnside coffeehouse, patrons sip coffees from Central America, South America, and Africa, and feast on affogato (homemade coconut ice cream topped with a shot of espresso) while admiring the rather elegant roasting equipment, which looks like a large-scale art installation. Finnish owner Wille Yli-Luoma brings a modern, minimalist aesthetic to this fiercely popular café. There's another location Downtown at 537 S.W. 12th Avenue. ✉ *2211 E. Burnside St., Downtown* ☏ *503/206–6602* ⊕ *www.heartroasters.com.*

GAY AND LESBIAN

Scandals. This low-key bar is the lone remaining LGBT hangout in the West End, which used to be the city's gay nightlife district (it's still a diverse, progressive neighborhood with plenty of mixed hangouts, but the city's gay bars are now spread around the city, although mostly in Old Town). There's a pool table, and light food service noon to closing. The plate-glass windows offer a view of Stark Street, and there's also popular sidewalk seating. ✉ *1125 S.W. Stark St., Downtown* ☏ *503/227–5887* ⊕ *www.scandalspdx.com.*

LIVE MUSIC

McMenamins Crystal Ballroom. With a 7,500-square-foot springy dance floor built on ball bearings to ramp up the energy, this historic former dance hall draws local, regional, and national acts every night but Monday. Past performers include Billy Idol, Jefferson Airplane, Emmylou Harris, Death Cab for Cutie, and the Shins. ✉ *1332 W. Burnside St., Downtown* ☏ *503/225–0047* ⊕ *www.mcmenamins.com.*

PEARL DISTRICT

BARS AND LOUNGES

Hamlet. This tribute to the finest charcuterie and pork products of Europe, including 48-month-aged melt-in-your-mouth Iberico ham, also serves an impressive roster of craft cocktails, some featuring sherries from this classy, intimate bar's extensive list of fortified wines. ⊠ *232 N.W. 12th Ave., Pearl District* ☎ *503/241–4009* ⊕ *www.hamletpdx. com.*

Fodor's Choice ★ **Teardrop Cocktail Lounge.** A swanky, see-and-be-seen bar in the heart of the trendy Pearl District, Teardrop has earned a loyal following for its creative cocktail menu. ⊠ *1015 N.W. Everett St., Pearl District* ☎ *503/445–8109* ⊕ *www.teardroplounge.com.*

Thelonious Wines. This bi-level bottle shop and wine bar differs from others of its kind in that it focuses exclusively on unusual, hard-to-find wines, from small productions of Pinot Noir from outstanding but lesser-known Oregon vineyards to interesting wines from unexpected places (bubbly from Tasmania, dry whites from Slovenia). Several single pours and flights are available, and you can pair your tasting with wine and charcuterie in the cozy upstairs loft with tables fashioned out of wine crates. ⊠ *516 N.W. 9th Ave., Pearl District* ☎ *503/444–7447* ⊕ *www.theloniouswines.com.*

BREWPUBS AND MICROBREWERIES

Fodor's Choice ★ **BridgePort BrewPub.** Sample consistently good craft beers at the oldest microbrewery in Portland, a beautiful brick-and-ivy building that's long been a cornerstone of the Pearl District. Free brewery tours are given on Saturday; call for hours. ⊠ *1313 N.W. Marshall St., Pearl District* ☎ *503/241–3612* ⊕ *www.bridgeportbrew.com.*

Deschutes Brewery & Public House. The Portland branch of the Bend-based Deschutes Brewery typically has more than 25 beers on tap, including nationally acclaimed mainstays Mirror Pond Pale Ale, Inversion IPA, and Black Butte Porter, plus seasonal and experimental brews. There's an extensive menu of well-prepared pub fare, too. ⊠ *210 N.W. 11th Ave., Pearl District* ☎ *503/296–4906* ⊕ *www.deschutesbrewery.com.*

OLD TOWN

GAY AND LESBIAN

Fodor's Choice ★ **C.C. Slaughters Nightclub & Lounge.** The most popular gay and lesbian dance club in the city, "C.C.'s" also has a quieter cocktail bar in front called the Rainbow Room. ⊠ *219 N.W. Davis St., Old Town* ☎ *503/248–9135* ⊕ *www.ccslaughterspdx.com.*

Fodor's Choice ★ **Stag.** Drawing a diverse crowd of hipsters, tourists, and old-school clubbers, this Old Town hot spot cheekily bills itself a "gay gentlemen's lounge." Mounted antlers, leather chairs, and exposed-brick walls lend a rustic air, and male strippers dance on a small stage toward the back of the main room; a side bar contains a pool table. ⊠ *317 N.W. Broadway, Old Town* ☎ *971/407–3132* ⊕ *www.stagpdx.com.*

LIVE MUSIC

Roseland Theater. This spacious theater holds 1,400 people (standing-room only except for the 21+ balcony seating area), primarily stages rock, alternative, and blues shows, plus occasional comedians. Past performers have included Miles Davis, Pearl Jam, the Police, Bonnie Raitt, and Prince. ⊠ *10 N.W. 6th Ave., Old Town* ☎ *855/227–8499* ⊕ *www.roselandpdx.com.*

NOB HILL
BARS AND LOUNGES

Fodor's Choice ★ **The Fireside.** Warmed by an open fire pit and a roaring fireplace, and decorated with lots of wood and leather, this cozy campfire-chic spot on Nob Hill's retail strip offers one of the best happy hours in Northwest, wallet-friendly appetizers made from locally sourced ingredients, and well-crafted cocktails. Try the Dillicious, made with rye whiskey, semidry vermouth, dill tincture, Kümmel liqueur, and lemon zest. ⊠ *801 N.W. 23rd Ave., Nob Hill* ☎ *503/477–9505* ⊕ *www.pdxfireside.com.*

Solo Club. The proprietors of this high-ceilinged haunt in a contemporary apartment building in the up-and-coming Slab Town district like to say that "if you are awake, chances are we're open." Indeed, you can slip in here as early as 6 am for coffee, and then wrap up your evening around 1 am most evenings with a nightcap—the bar is know for its "coolers," mix-and-match concoctions, such as the radler: your choice of draft lager with grapefruit, orange, or lemon soda. There's an extensive menu of nibbles served day and night as well. ⊠ *2110 N.W. Raleigh St., Nob Hill* ☎ *971/254-9806* ⊕ *www.thesoloclub.com.*

NORTH
BREWPUBS AND MICROBREWERIES

Ecliptic Brewing. Fans of boldly flavored brews flock to this spacious, airy brewery and pub at the south end of the Mississippi strip, which also has a spacious patio that's abuzz with revelers on summer afternoons. Founder John Harris is as obsessed with astronomy as he is with beer, hence the cosmic names of beers, which include Quasar Pale Ale and Phobos Single Hop Red Ale. ⊠ *825 N. Cook St., North* ☎ *503/265– 8002* ⊕ *www.eclipticbrewing.com.*

Prost! At the northern end of the hip North Mississippi retail and restaurant strip, Prost! is an airy, amber-lit, contemporary bar specializing in old-school German beers like Spaten Lager, Franziskaner Weissbier, and Erdinger Dunkel Weisse. Nosh on Bavarian pretzels and other Euro snacks or venture next door to one of the East Side's best food-cart pods, Mississippi Marketplace. ⊠ *4237 N. Mississippi Ave., North* ☎ *503/954–2674* ⊕ *www.prostportland.com.*

LIVE MUSIC

Fodor's Choice ★ **Mississippi Studios.** An intimate neighborhood music venue, with a seated balcony and old Oriental rugs covering the standing-room-only floor, Mississippi Studios offers high-quality live music performances every night of the week in a wide range of genres. Between sets, you can jump back and forth from the adjacent BarBar, a hip, comfortable bar with a delicious hamburger and a covered back patio. ⊠ *3939 N. Mississippi, North* ☎ *503/288–3895* ⊕ *www.mississippistudios.com.*

NORTHEAST

BARS AND LOUNGES

Fodor's Choice
★

The Bye and Bye. An Alberta go-to specializing in creative drinks (sample the house favorite, the Bye and Bye, a refreshing concoction of peach vodka, peach bourbon, lemon, cranberry juice, and soda served in a Mason jar) and vegan fare, Bye and Bye has a big covered patio and a festive dining room. The owners also operate several other similarly trendy bars around town, including Century Bar and Sweet Hereafter in Southeast, Victoria Bar in North Portland, and Jackknife at Downtown's Sentinel Hotel. ⊠ *1011 N.E. Alberta St., Northeast* ☎ *503/281–0537* ⊕ *www.thebyeandbye.com.*

Hale Pele. The riotously colorful lighting and kitschy retro-Polynesian decor of this island-inspired tiki bar creates the ideal ambience for sipping tropical cocktails like the fruity Lava Flow (a Hawaiian take on a piña colada) or the potent Cobra's Fang (a mix of grenadine, falernum, dark rum, and mint). The kimchi dog is a highlight among the small plates. ⊠ *2733 N.W. Broadway, Irvington* ☎ *503/662–8454* ⊕ *www.halepele.com.*

Fodor's Choice
★

Expatriate. Operated by Kyle Webster and his wife, celeb-chef partner Naomi Pomeroy of Beast (across the street), this intimate, candlelit spot has a devoted following for its balanced, boozy cocktails and addictively delicious Asian bar snacks, like curried-potato-and-English-pea samosas. Each of the eight nightly cocktails are meticulously crafted, but the Foreign National—a mix of Grey Goose Vodka, Midori Melon Liqueur, Cocchi Americano, fresh lime, ginger syrup, and Pimm's No. 1—is a house favorite. ⊠ *5424 N.E. 30th Ave., Northeast* ☎ *503/805–3750* ⊕ *www.expatriatepdx.com.*

Swift Lounge. The bird-themed Swift Lounge, an endearingly dive-y hipster hangout, offers a menu of Mason-jar cocktails including the Guilty Sparrow (citrus vodka, lemongrass, and house limoncello), the Stoned Finch (cucumber-infused vodka and house elderflower syrup), and the Topless Robin (ginger-lemongrass-infused vodka and apricot brandy). You can order the drinks in two sizes—the 32-ounce "Fatty" or the 16-ounce "Sissy." The weekend "hangover brunch" is quite the scene. ⊠ *1932 N.E. Broadway, Northeast* ☎ *503/288–3333* ⊕ *www.swiftloungepdx.com.*

COFFEEHOUSES

Barista. If you're looking to test-drive a few of Portland's best beans, this dapper café with other locations Downtown, in the Pearl, and on N.E. Alberta is a great option. You'll find Stumptown, Coava, and other fine coffees, as well as a few craft beers and a small selection of high-quality chocolates and desserts. The high-ceilinged Alberta location is the most inviting, with plenty of indoor and outdoor seating. Other locations include 529 S.W. 3rd Avenue (Downtown), 539 N.W. 13th Avenue (Pearl District), and 823 N.W. 23rd Avenue (Nob Hill). ⊠ *1725 N.E. Alberta St., Alberta District* ☎ *503/274–1211* ⊕ *www.baristapdx.com.*

Coffee culture is strong in Portland

SOUTHEAST

BARS AND LOUNGES

Bar Avignon. Drop by this neighborhood wine bar on S.E. Division for one of the neighborhood's best happy hours, and to check out the impressive European-heavy wine selection; there are plenty of interesting bottles as well as about 15 pours by the glass. The staff is friendly and knowledgeable, and the Northwest-French food menu consistently delivers. ✉ *2138 S.E. Division St., Southeast* ☎ *503/517–0808* ⊕ *www. baravignon.com.*

FodorśChoice ★ **Coopers Hall.** Part of the Central East Side's burgeoning wine scene, this urban winery and taproom is set inside a dramatic and spacious Quonset-hut structure, which was once home to an auto-repair shop. Order any of the outstanding wines produced on-site, or delve into the happily esoteric menu of unusual wines from all over the West Coast, with a few French varieties in the mix. The kitchen turns out seriously good food, too. ✉ *404 S.E. 6th St., Southeast* ☎ *503/719–7000* ⊕ *www. coopershall.com.*

Double Dragon. Drop by this festive, low-lit bar for its sassy cocktails, such as the Burnt Reynolds (bourbon, Lapsang souchong honey, lemon, and orange bitters), scene-y crowd, and Saturday-night Baby Ketten Karaoke parties. Stay for the delish Asian bar food, including the eight-hour-braised pork-belly banh mi sandwiches and curried-coconut ramen with chicken and pork. ✉ *1235 S.E. Division St., Southeast* ☎ *503/230–8340* ⊕ *www.doubledragonpdx.com.*

Holocene. Hosting DJ dance nights that range from '90s dance parties to rap/twerk to poetry slams, the 5,000-square-foot former auto-parts warehouse pulls in diverse crowds. It's sometimes closed early in the week; check the online calendar before you visit. ⊠ *1001 S.E. Morrison St., Southeast* ☎ *503/239–7639* ⊕ *www.holocene.org.*

Fodor's Choice **Horse Brass Pub.** A laid-back beer-drinking crowd fills the venerable, ★ dark-wood Horse Brass Pub, as good an English-style pub as you will find in Portland, with 59 beers on tap (including some cask-conditioned varieties). ■ TIP➔ **Try the fish-and-chips.** ⊠ *4534 S.E. Belmont St., Southeast* ☎ *503/232–2202* ⊕ *www.horsebrass.com.*

Loyal Legion. A handsome spot with leather booths and a long central wooden bar, this Central East Side pub carries an eye-opening 99 ales on draft, from local standards to seasonally changing oddballs that delight beer geeks (Ecliptic Orange Giant barley wine, a Yachats Brewing–Loyal Legion collaboration plum-lavender saison). Hefty burgers, Austrian-style wood-smoked pork sausages, and chili-cheddar-smothered fries are among the delicious pub-food accompaniments. ⊠ *710 S.E. 6th Ave., Southeast* ☎ *503/235–8272* ⊕ *loyallegionpdx.com.*

Sapphire Hotel. In the lobby of a former brothel in lively Hawthorne, the deep-red, candlelit Sapphire Hotel serves cocktails, beer, and wine with an intimate, sultry atmosphere. There's a terrific food menu, too, served late and at bargain prices during happy hour. ⊠ *5008 S.E. Hawthorne Blvd., Southeast* ☎ *503/232–6333* ⊕ *www.thesapphirehotel.com.*

Fodor's Choice **Southeast Wine Collective.** This hive of boutique wine-making has an ★ inviting tasting room–cum–wine bar in which you can sample the vinos of several up-and-coming producers. It's open until 10 most evenings, and the energy shifts from low-key tasting space to scene-y wine bar after about 5 pm. You could carve out a full meal from the extensive menu's tapas, salads, baguette sandwiches, and cheese and meats plates. ⊠ *2425 S.E. 35th Pl., Southeast* ☎ *503/208–2061* ⊕ *www.sewinecollective.com.*

Fodor's Choice **Victory Bar.** As beloved for its hefty venison burgers, chorizo spaetzle, ★ and other stick-to-your-ribs bar victuals as for its impressive drinks selection, this dark corner bar with a pressed-tin ceiling is the definitive East Side hipster hangout, retaining a happily unfussy—almost divey—ambience in the face of Division Street's rapid transformation into a busy row of contemporary condos and A-list restaurants. ⊠ *3652 S.E. Division St., Southeast* ☎ *503/236–8755* ⊕ *www.thevictorybar.com.*

BREWPUBS AND MICROBREWERIES

Cascade Brewing. This laid-back brewpub and pioneer of the Northwest sour-beer movement is a good place for friends and sour-beer lovers to share tart flights of several varieties, including Blackcap Raspberry, Kriek, and potent (9.9% ABV) Sang Noir. You'll find 24 rotating taps, small plates and sandwiches to complement the sour beers, and ample outdoor seating. ⊠ *939 S.E. Belmont St., Southeast* ☎ *503/265–8603* ⊕ *www.cascadebrewingbarrelhouse.com.*

Fodor's Choice **Commons Brewery.** This small, artisanal brewery, born in brewer Mike ★ Wright's garage, maintained its small-batch, hands-on approach as it rapidly outgrew its first and second homes and even more rapidly earned a big reputation for exceptionally flavorful farmhouse-style ales. Wright's brews—inspired by European brewing traditions and crafted with local ingredients—have garnered many accolades; the fruit-forward Flemish Kiss and potent Bourbon Little Brother (aged in Heaven Hill bourbon barrels) are especially popular. A nice selection of cheeses and charcuterie are available in the spacious taproom. ✉ *630 S.E. Belmont St., Southeast* ☎ *503/343–5501* ⊕ *www.commonsbrewery.com.*

Hopworks Urban Brewery. A bicycle-themed microbrewery with deftly crafted beer, sandwiches, and pizzas, Hopworks Urban Brewery (HUB for short) occupies an industrial lodge-inspired building that's 100% renewably powered and water neutral. Hopworks BikeBar, located on the bike highway of North Williams, offers similar fare with the same bikey, eco-friendly vibe. ✉ *2944 S.E. Powell Blvd., Southeast* ☎ *503/232–4677* ⊕ *www.hopworksbeer.com.*

COFFEEHOUSES

Fodor'sChoice
★
Coava Coffee Roasters. Located next door to the roastery, the light and open, bamboo wood–filled Coava Coffee Roasters offers some of the highest-quality single-origin, pour-over coffees in the city. There's a second branch in the Hawthorne District. ✉ *1300 S.E. Grand Ave., Southeast* ☎ *503/894–8134* ⊕ *www.coavacoffee.com.*

Stumptown Coffee Roasters. Stumptown Coffee Roasters, which now has locations in several other cities, has three cafés on the east side. At the original site (S.E. Division), organic beans are still roasted on a regular basis. At the Tasting Bar (S.E. Salmon)—adjacent to Stumptown headquarters—patrons can participate in "cuppings," or tastings, at 3 pm each day. Stumptown has other locations around town, including a popular branch inside Downtown's Ace Hotel. ✉ *4525 S.E. Division St., Southeast* ☎ *503/230–7702* ⊕ *www.stumptowncoffee.com.*

Tao of Tea. With soft music and the sound of running water in the background, the Tao of Tea serves more than 80 loose-leaf teas as well as vegetarian snacks and sweets. The company also operates the tearoom inside Old Town's Lan Su Chinese Garden. ✉ *3430 S.E. Belmont St., Southeast* ☎ *503/736–0119* ⊕ *www.taooftea.com.*

Fodor'sChoice
★
Water Avenue Coffee. Java aficionados serious about single-origin coffee favor this Central East Side roastery, which sources its beans from top growers in Colombia, Ethiopia, and Indonesia, roasts on custom-built machines, and provides its house-roasted coffees to many restaurants and cafés around town. There's also a Downtown location. ✉ *1028 S.E. Water Ave., Southeast* ☎ *503/808–7084* ⊕ *www.wateravenuecoffee.com.*

GAY AND LESBIAN

Fodor'sChoice
★
Crush. A favorite gay and lesbian hangout in Southeast, Crush serves up tasty food, strong cocktails, and DJ-fueled dance parties. The front section is mellow and good for conversation, while the back area contains a small but lively dance floor. ✉ *1400 S.E. Morrison St., Southeast* ☎ *503/235–8150* ⊕ *www.crushbar.com.*

LIVE MUSIC

Fodor'sChoice
★
Doug Fir Lounge. Part retro diner and part log cabin, the Doug Fir serves food and booze and hosts DJs and live rock shows from both up-and-coming and established bands most nights of the week. It adjoins the

trendy Hotel Jupiter. ☒ *830 E. Burnside St., Southeast* ☎ *503/231–9663* ⊕ *www.dougfirlounge.com.*

Revolution Hall. Southeast Portland's stately early 1900s former Washington High School building was converted into a state-of-the-art concert hall in 2015, featuring noted pop and world-beat music acts and comedians, from Henry Rollins to Tig Notaro, plus film festivals and other intriguing events. There are two bars on-site, including a roof deck with great views of the Downtown skyline. ☒ *1300 S.E. Stark St., Southeast* ☎ *971/808–5094* ⊕ *www.revolutionhall.com.*

PERFORMING ARTS

For a city of this size, there is truly an impressive—and accessible—scope of talent from visual artists, performance artists, and musicians. The arts are alive, with outdoor sculptural works strewn around the city, ongoing festivals, and premieres of traveling Broadway shows. Top-named international acts, such as David Byrne, Arcade Fire, Joan Baez, and Mumford and Sons regularly include Portland in their worldwide stops.

PERFORMANCE VENUES

Fodor's Choice
★

Arlene Schnitzer Concert Hall. The 2,776-seat Arlene Schnitzer Concert Hall, built in 1928 in an Italian rococo revival style, hosts rock concerts, choral groups, lectures, and concerts by the Oregon Symphony and others. ☒ *Portland Center for the Performing Arts, 1037 S.W. Broadway, Downtown* ☎ *503/248-4335* ⊕ *www.portland5.com.*

Keller Auditorium. With 3,000 seats and outstanding acoustics, Keller Auditorium hosts performances by the Portland Opera and Oregon Ballet Theater, as well as country and rock concerts and touring Broadway shows. ☒ *222 S.W. Clay St., Downtown* ☎ *503/248–4335* ⊕ *www.portland5.com.*

Portland'5 Centers for the Arts. The city's top performing arts complex hosts opera, ballet, rock shows, symphony performances, lectures, and Broadway musicals in its five venues. ☒ *1111 S.W. Broadway, Downtown* ☎ *503/248–4335* ⊕ *www.portland5.com.*

Moda Center. This 21,000-seat facility, formerly known as the Rose Garden, is home to the Portland Trail Blazers basketball team and the site of other sporting events and rock concerts. It's right on the MAX light-rail line, just across from Downtown. ☒ *Rose Quarter, 1 Center Ct., Lloyd District, Northeast* ☎ *503/745–3000* ⊕ *www.rosequarter.com.*

CLASSICAL MUSIC

The Oregon Symphony, established in 1896, is Portland's largest classical group—and one of the largest orchestras in the country.

CHAMBER MUSIC

Chamber Music Northwest. Some of the most sought-after soloists, chamber musicians, and recording artists from the Portland area and abroad perform here during the five-week summer concert series; performances take place at a few different venues, primarily Reed College's Kaul Auditorium and the Lincoln Performance Hall at Portland State University. ☎ *503/294–6400* ⊕ *www.cmnw.org.*

OPERA

Portland Opera. This well-respected opera company performs five productions a year at Keller Auditorium. ⊠ *Keller Auditorium, 222 S.W. Clay St., Downtown* ☎ *503/241–1802, 866/739–6737* ⊕ *www.portlandopera.org.*

ORCHESTRAS

FAMILY

Fodor'sChoice

★

Oregon Symphony. Established in 1896, the symphony is Portland's largest classical group—and one of the largest orchestras in the country. Its season officially starts in September and ends in May, with concerts held at Arlene Schnitzer Concert Hall, but throughout the summer the orchestra and its smaller ensembles can be seen at Waterfront Park and Washington Park for special outdoor summer performances. It also presents about 40 classical, pop, children's, and family concerts each year. ☎ *503/228–1353, 800/228–7343* ⊕ *www.orsymphony.org.*

DANCE

Portland has a wonderful variety of both progressive and traditional dance companies. As part of their productions, many of these companies bring in international talent for choreography and guest performances.

BodyVox. Led by Emmy Award–winning choreographers, BodyVox performs energetic contemporary dance–theater works at its state-of-the-art space in the Pearl District. ⊠ *1201 N.W. 17th Ave., Pearl District* ☎ *503/229–0627* ⊕ *www.bodyvox.com.*

Fodor'sChoice

★

Northwest Dance Project. Founded in 2004, this first-rate contemporary-dance company performs several shows—typically including a world premier or two—each season at different venues around town, including the Newmark Theatre and PSU's Lincoln Performance Hall. ☎ *503/828–8285* ⊕ *www.nwdanceproject.org.*

Oregon Ballet Theatre. This respected company produces several classical and contemporary works a year, including a much-loved holiday *Nutcracker.* Most performances are at Keller Auditorium and the Portland Center for the Arts' Newmark Theatre. ☎ *503/222–5538, 888/922–5538* ⊕ *www.obt.org.*

FILM

The McMenimans "brew theaters" are a great place to catch a flick while chowing down and sipping on local beer. They are not-to-be-missed Portland landmarks when it comes to movie viewing in uniquely renovated buildings that avoid any hint of corporate streamlining.

If you're a film buff, be sure to check out the Northwest Film Center's calendar of events for special screenings and film festivals, with genres that include international, LGBT, and animation.

Fodor'sChoice

★

Bagdad Theater. Built in 1927, the stunningly restored, eminently quirky Bagdad Theater shows first-run Hollywood films on a huge screen and serves pizza, burgers, sandwiches, and McMenamins ales. The Bagdad is a local favorite. ⊠ *3702 S.E. Hawthorne Blvd., Hawthorne District, Southeast* ☎ *503/249–7474* ⊕ *www.mcmenamins.com.*

Hollywood Theatre. A landmark movie theater that showed silent films when it opened in 1926, the not-for-profit Hollywood Theatre screens everything from obscure foreign art films to old American classics and second-run Hollywood hits, and hosts an annual Academy Awards viewing party. ☒ *4122 N.E. Sandy Blvd., Northeast* ☎ *503/281–4215* ⊕ *www.hollywoodtheatre.org.*

Fodor's Choice **Kennedy School Theater.** Furnished with couches and end tables, the Ken-
★ nedy School theater, which is located in a renovated elementary school that also contains a hotel, a restaurant, several bars, and a soaking pool, screens second-run and occasional indie movies. ☒ *5736 N.E. 33rd Ave., Concordia, Northeast* ☎ *503/249–3983* ⊕ *www.mcme-namins.com.*

Laurelhurst Theater. With a classic neon sign out front, the historic Laurelhurst Theater serves beer and pizza and shows excellent second-run features and cult classics for only $4. ☒ *2735 E. Burnside St., Kerns, Laurelhurst* ☎ *503/232–5511* ⊕ *www.laurelhursttheater.com.*

Living Room Theater. The sleek, upscale cinema, which has a lobby restaurant with a full bar, shows 3-D blockbuster, foreign, and independent films in cozy theaters furnished with spacious seats and movable couches and tables. You can dine and drink from your seat. ☒ *341 S.W. 10th Ave., West End* ⊕ *pdx.livingroomtheaters.com.*

Fodor's Choice **Northwest Film Center.** Located adjacent to and operated by the Portland
★ Art Museum, the Northwest Film Center screens art films, documentaries, and independent features, and presents the three-week Portland International Film Festival every February. Films are shown at the Whitsell Auditorium, next to the museum. ☒ *1219 S.W. Park Ave., Downtown* ☎ *503/221–1156* ⊕ *www.nwfilm.org.*

THEATER

From the largest of productions to the smallest of venues, theater comes to life in Portland year-round.

Artists Repertory Theatre. The theater company performs seven to nine productions a year including regional premieres, occasional commissioned works, and classics. ☒ *1515 S.W. Morrison St., Downtown* ☎ *503/241–1278* ⊕ *www.artistsrep.org.*

Imago Theatre. One of Portland's most outstanding innovative theater companies, the Imago specializes in movement-based work for both young and old. ☒ *17 S.E. 8th Ave., Southeast* ☎ *503/231–9581* ⊕ *www.imagotheatre.com.*

FAMILY **Northwest Children's Theater.** This long-running company presents four
Fodor's Choice shows during its fall–spring season, geared to both the toddler and teen
★ set. Performances are staged in the handsome Northwest Neighborhood Cultural Center in Nob Hill. ☒ *1819 N.W. Everett St., Nob Hill* ☎ *503/222–4480* ⊕ *www.nwcts.org.*

FAMILY **Oregon Children's Theatre.** This kid-centric company puts on four to five shows a year for school groups and families at Downtown's Newmark and Winningstad theaters. ☒ *1111 S.W. Broadway, Downtown* ☎ *503/228–9571* ⊕ *www.octc.org.*

Fodor's Choice **Portland Center Stage.** Housed in a handsomely restored 1891 armory,
★ Portland Center Stage puts on contemporary and classical works in the LEED-certified green building between September and June. ☒ *Gerding Theater at the Armory, 128 N.W. 11th Ave., Pearl District* ☎ *503/445–3700* ⊕ *www.pcs.org.*

SPORTS AND THE OUTDOORS

Portlanders avidly gravitate to the outdoors and they're well acclimated to the elements year-round—including winter's wind, rain, and cold. Once the sun starts to shine in spring and into summer, the city fills with hikers, joggers, and mountain bikers, who flock to Portland's hundreds of miles of parks, paths, and trails. The Willamette and Columbia rivers are popular for boating and water sports. Locals also have access to a playground for fishing, camping, skiing, and snowboarding all the way through June, thanks to the proximity of Mt. Hood.

As for competitive sports, Portland is home to the Timbers, a major league soccer team with a devout local fan base, and NBA basketball's beloved Trail Blazers, who play at the Moda Center (aka Rose Quarter) arena, just across the Willamette River from Downtown.

BASKETBALL

Portland Trail Blazers. The NBA's Portland Trail Blazers play their 82-game season in the Moda Center, which can hold up to 20,000 spectators. The MAX train pulls up just a couple blocks from the arena's front door. ⊠ *Moda Center, 1 N. Center Ct., Rose Quarter, North* ☎ *503/797–9600* ⊕ *www.nba.com/blazers.*

BIKING

Biking is a cultural phenomenon in Portland—likely the most beloved mode of transportation in the city. Besides the sheer numbers of cyclists you see on roads and pathways, you'll find well-marked bike lanes and signs reminding motorists to yield to cyclists.

There are more than 340 miles of bicycle boulevards, lanes, and off-street paths in Portland, and the city ushered in the long-anticipated BIKETOWN Portland bike-share program in 2016. Accessible maps, specialized tours, parking capacity (including lockers and sheltered racks Downtown), and bicycle-only traffic signals at confusing intersections make biking in most neighborhoods easy. Cyclists can find the best routes by following green direction-and-distance signs that point the way around town, and the corresponding white dots on the street surface.

Cycling in Portland has evolved into a medium for progressive politics and public service. Several bike co-ops in the city are devoted to providing used bikes at decent prices, as well as to teaching bike maintenance and the economic and environmental benefits of becoming a two-wheel commuter. Check out the helpful Bike Portland (⊕ *www.bikeportland. org*) website for information on regularly scheduled bike events, cycling-related local news and advice, and referrals to reliable bike rental, sales, and repair shops.

BIKE RENTALS

BIKETOWN Portland. Portland's bike-share program, in partnership with Nike and begun in 2016, is affordable and easy to use. There are more than 100 stations throughout the city, and some 1,000 bikes, each with a small basket (helmets are not provided, however, so considering bringing your own). Just choose a plan (single rides start at $2.50 for 30 minutes, and day passes are $12), sign up, and you'll receive an account and PIN number that allows you to take out a bike. ⊠ *Portland* ☎ *866/512–2453* ⊕ *www.biketownpdx.com.*

Fat Tire Farm. For treks in Forest Park, rent mountain bikes at Fat Tire Farm, which is close to the park's Leif Erikson trailhead. The staff here really knows their stuff, from repair and maintenance help to advice on the best trails and routes. ⊠ *2714 N.W. Thurman St., Nob Hill* ☎ *503/222–3276* ⊕ *www.fattirefarm.com.*

Waterfront Bicycle Rentals. For jaunts along the Willamette River, Waterfront Bicycles has everything a visiting bicyclist needs. There is a variety of styles and sizes of bikes to outfit the entire family, including balance bikes for the little rider. To reserve online, book at least 48 hours ahead. Guided bike tours are available as well. ⊠ *10 S.W. Ash St., Suite 100, Downtown* ☎ *503/227–1719* ⊕ *www.waterfrontbikes.com.*

BIKE ROUTES

If you're a social rider, group rides set out from several local shops. Check the events pages of **Bike Gallery** (⊕ *www.bikegallery.com*), **River City Bicycles** (⊕ *www.rivercitybicycles.com*), and **Bike Portland** (⊕ *www.bikeportland.org*).

Bike paths line both sides of the **Willamette River** through Downtown, so you can easily make a mild, several-mile loop through Waterfront Park via the Steel, Hawthorne, Tilikum Crossing, or Sellwood bridges.

Though much of **Forest Park's** 80-plus miles of trails are reserved for hiking and nonbiking activities, there are more than 30 miles of single-track mountain-biking trails and fire lanes open to biking, including Leif Erikson Drive, an 11-mile ride whose dense canopy occasionally gives way to river views. Along the park's trails you may come across old-growth forest as well as some of the park's more than 175 species of animals and birds. To reach the Leif Erikson trailhead, bike up steep Thurman Street or shuttle there via TriMet Bus 15. Maps and information on the trails can be found at ⊕ *www.forestparkconservancy.org.*

Department of Transportation. For information on bike routes and resources in and around Portland, visit the Department of Transportation website (look for the Active Transportation tab). You can download and view maps and learn about upcoming bike-related events and group rides. ⊠ *Portland* ☎ *503/823–5490* ⊕ *www.portlandoregon.gov/transportation.*

PARKS

The variety of Portland's parks ensures that there's something for just about everyone, from the world's smallest park (Mill Ends) to one of the largest urban natural areas in the country (Forest Park). ⇨ *See Exploring for details about other favorite Portland green spaces, including Laurelhurst, Mt. Tabor, and Washington parks.*

2

Fodor's Choice
★

Cathedral Park. Whether it's the view of the imposing and stunning Gothic St. John's Bridge, which rises some 400 feet above the Willamette River, or the historic significance of Lewis and Clark having camped here in 1806, this 23-acre park is divine. Though there's no church, the park gets its name from the picturesque arches supporting the bridge. It's rumored that the ghost of a young girl haunts the bridge, and that may be true, but if you're told that it was designed by the same man who envisioned the Golden Gate Bridge, that's just a popular misconception. Dog lovers, or those who aren't, should take note of the off-leash area. ⊠ *N. Edison St. and Pittsburg Ave., North* ⊕ *www.portlandoregon.gov/parks.*

Fodor's Choice
★

Council Crest Park. The highest point in Portland, at 1,073 feet, this 43-acre bluff-top patch of greenery is a superb spot to take in sunsets and sunrises. Along with nearly 180-degree views of the Portland metro area, a clear day also affords views of the surrounding peaks—Mt. Hood, Mt. St. Helens, Mt. Adams, Mt. Jefferson, and Mt. Rainier. A bronze fountain depicting a mother and child has been erected in the park twice; first in the 1950s and the second in the 1990s. The peaceful piece was stolen in the 1980s, uncovered in a narcotics bust 10 years later, and then returned to the park. Trails connect Council Crest with Marquam Nature Park and Washington Park. ■ TIP➔ **It's quite busy on weekends so visit on a weekday, if possible.** ⊠ *3400 Council Crest Dr., West Hills* ⊕ *www.portlandoregon.gov/parks.*

FAMILY

Peninsula Park & Rose Garden. The "City of Roses" moniker started here, at this park that harks back to another time. The city's oldest (1912) public rose garden (and the only sunken one) houses about 5,000 plantings of roses. The daunting task of deadheading all these flowers is covered in classes taught to volunteers twice a season. The bandstand is a historic landmark, and the last of its kind in the city. This 16-acre North Portland park also contains a 100-year-old fountain, Italian villa–inspired community center, playground, wading pool, tennis and volleyball courts, and picnic tables. ⊠ *700 N. Rosa Parks Way, Piedmont, North* ⊕ *www.portlandoregon.gov/parks.*

FAMILY
Fodor's Choice
★

Sauvie Island. If it's a day to take advantage of gorgeous weather then drive about a half hour northwest of Downtown to Sauvie Island. The island has a wildlife refuge, three beaches (including Collins Beach, which is clothing-optional), superb biking and hiking trails, and several farms offering "u-pick" bounty. To get to the beaches, take U.S. 30 north to Sauvie Island bridge, and turn right; follow N.W. Sauvie Island Road to Reeder Road and follow signs. There's plenty of parking at the beaches, but a permit is required ($10 for a one-day permit, available at the general store at the base of the bridge). ⊠ *N.W. Sauvie Island Rd., Sauvie Island* ⊕ *www.sauvieisland.org.*

FAMILY

Tryon Creek State Natural Area. Portland is chock-full of parks, but this is the only state park within city limits. And at 658 acres, there's plenty of room for all its admirers. The area was logged starting in the 1880s, and the natural regrowth has produced red alder, Douglas fir, big-leaf maple, and western red cedar, giving home to more than 50 bird species. The eastern edge has a paved trail, in addition to 15 miles of trails for bikes, hikers, and horses. Before heading to the trails, stop by the nature center to check out the exhibits and topographical relief map. ✉ *11321 S.W. Terwilliger Blvd., Southwest* ☎ *503/636–4398* ⊕ *www. tryonfriends.org.*

SOCCER

Portland Timbers. Portland's major-league soccer team plays their 34-game season at the Downtown Jeld-Wen Field from March through October. The city has many ardent soccer fans known as the Timbers Army. Sitting near this group means a raucous time with drumming, chanting, and cheers. The MAX stops right by the stadium. ✉ *Jeld-Wen Field, 1844 S.W. Morrison St., Downtown* ☎ *503/553–5555* ⊕ *www. portlandtimbers.com.*

SHOPPING

The shopping landscape in Portland has changed significantly in recent years, perhaps not quite as dramatically as the much-buzzed-about culinary scene, but in similar (pardon the pun) fashion. Specifically, those same hip and indie-spirited neighborhoods around the city that have become hot spots for food and drink—areas like the Pearl District, Downtown West End, Alberta, North Mississippi, North Williams, and Central East Side—are also enjoying a steady influx of distinctive, well-curated boutiques specializing in edgy fashion and jewelry, handcrafted home accessories and household goods, and artisanal foods.

The city's long-standing shopping hubs, including the Downtown core, Nob Hill, and the Hawthorne District continue to support a number of both established and up-and-coming retailers, too. Generally speaking, you'll find more of Portland's nationally known chain stores in these traditional commercial districts, especially around Downtown's Pioneer Courthouse Square, the Pearl District (particularly the lower half of the neighborhood, nearest Burnside Street), and along the lower blocks of Nob Hill's N.W. 23rd Avenue. Additionally, on the East Side, the prosaic but convenient Lloyd Center Mall and surrounding neighborhood has plenty of chain stores.

DOWNTOWN

CLOTHING

Fodor's Choice
★

Frances May. Located in the hip West End section of Downtown, this grandmother-and-granddaughter-owned clothing store is a favorite of stylish local men and women who come for that cool, understated, high-quality look (casual to dressy) that Portlanders are known for. You'll find made-in-America labels like Steven Alan and Rachel Comey as well as European faves like Acne and APC. The Alex Mill cashmere beanies and Carven women's pullovers and sweaters are especially popular during Portland's cool winters. ✉ *1003 S.W. Washington St., Downtown* ☎ *503/227–3402* ⊕ *www.francesmay.com.*

Mario's. Portland's best store for fine men's and women's clothing, Mario's carries designer lines by Prada, Dolce & Gabbana, Etro, and Loro Piana—among others. The store's buyers make regular trips to Italy in search of the latest fashions and trends. There's a *huge* shoe department, too. ⊠ *833 S.W. Broadway, Downtown* ☎ *844/855–4847* ⊕ *marios.mitchellstores.com.*

Nike Portland. It's safe to assume that Nike's flagship retail store, just a short drive from the company's mammoth HQ campus in Beaverton, has the latest and greatest in swoosh-adorned products. The high-tech setting has athlete profiles, photos, and interactive displays. ⊠ *638 S.W. 5th Ave., Downtown* ☎ *503/221–6453* ⊕ *www.nike.com.*

FOOD

Cacao. Chocolate fiends and sweet-tooths get their fix at this inviting storefront shop and café in the West End, which also has a branch inside Downtown's natty Heathman Hotel. Browse the huge selection of ultrafine, single-origin, artisanal chocolates from around the world, or order a cup of luscious and satisfying house-made drinking chocolate. ⊠ *414 S.W. 13th Ave., West End* ☎ *503/241–0656* ⊕ *www.cacaodrink-chocolate.com.*

Moonstruck Chocolate Cafe. Even without getting a nod from Oprah in her magazine, Moonstruck would still be known as a chocolatier extraordinaire. There are three cafés in the Portland metro area, including another Downtown location at Pioneer Place Mall. All offer made-to-order hot chocolate, cocoa, shakes, and mochas, as well as truffles, chocolate bars, and dynamic holiday treats. ⊠ *608 S.W. Alder St., Downtown* ☎ *503/241–0955* ⊕ *www.moonstruckchocolate.com.*

FAMILY
Fodor's Choice
★

Portland Farmers' Market. Running on Saturday mornings and early afternoons year-round, this astoundingly large and diverse farmers' market carries not only Oregon's bounty of flowers and produce (look especially for berries in summer and stone fruits in fall) but also hazelnuts, cheese, delectable baked goods, wines and ciders, and other goodies. It's great for people-watching and souvenir shopping, and several stalls sell great food to eat on-site—be sure to come hungry. If you can't make the Saturday market, check the website for locations of smaller but still very popular versions of the market, held most days during the warmer months at various locations around town. ⊠ *South Park Blocks at S.W. Park Ave. and Montgomery St., Downtown* ☎ *503/241–0032* ⊕ *www. portlandfarmersmarket.org.*

GIFTS

Made in Oregon. This eclectic retail tribute to the Beaver State sells books, smoked salmon, artisan chocolates, local wines, Pendleton woolen goods, carvings made of myrtle wood, and other products made in the state. There are numerous branches around the area, including Portland International Airport and all of the larger shopping malls. ⊠ *Pioneer Place Mall, 340 S.W. Morrison St., Downtown* ☎ *503/241–3630, 866/257–0938* ⊕ *www.madeinoregon.com.*

One-of-a-kind items at Portland Saturday Market

HOUSEHOLD GOODS AND FURNITURE

Boys Fort. If the name of this colorful Downtown emporium brings back memories of hanging out with friends in a rad basement rec room, you'll likely love this offbeat store curated by designers R. Rolfe and Jake France. They've stocked this high-ceilinged shop with a mix of artful items for the hip dude's urban nest, including earthy-hued terra-cotta planters, model sailboats, and mounted wooden faux deer heads, plus old posters and games. ⊠ *902 S.W. Morrison St., Downtown* ☎ *503/567–1015* ⊕ *www.boysfort.com.*

Fodor's Choice
★

Canoe. Form meets function at this stylish, contemporary boutique with a carefully curated selection of clean-lined, modern goods and gifts for every room in the home. You'll find curvy thick-glass bowls, modern lamps with sheer paper shades, polished-stone trays, Bigelow natural-bristle toothbrushes, and Chemex coffee kettles, with some goods produced locally and exclusively for Canoe, and others imported from Asia and northern Europe. ⊠ *1233 S.W. 10th Ave., Downtown* ☎ *503/889–8545* ⊕ *www.canoeonline.net.*

JEWELRY

The Real Mother Goose. Selling mostly handcrafted, unique artistic pieces, current collections can include woodworking, furniture, blown glass, and jewelry. Dangling earrings that incorporate copper wire wrapped around brilliant, colored glass are a customer favorite. The clothing store next door, Changes/Designs to Wear, is part of The Real Mother Goose as well. ⊠ *901 S.W. Yamhill St., Downtown* ☎ *503/223–9510* ⊕ *www.therealmothergoose.com.*

MALLS AND DEPARTMENT STORES

Fodor'sChoice **Union Way.** A modern take on an old-fashioned European shopping
★ arcade, this indoor alley spans one block from Stark to Burnside streets
(right across the street from Powell's Books) and contains about a
dozen diverting boutiques, plus a branch of Little T Bakery and the
trendy Asian restaurant Boxer Ramen. Most of these shops specialize
in apparel and accessories, including Will Leather Goods, Steven Alan
eyewear, and Danner sports and outerwear, but you'll also find Quin
Candy shop and Spruce Apothecary. ⊠ *1022 W. Burnside St., Downtown* ☎ *503/922–0056* ⊕ *www.facebook.com/UnionWayPDX.*

TOYS

Finnegan's Toys and Gifts. Downtown Portland's largest toy store,
Finnegan's stocks artistic, creative, educational, and other types of
toys. ⊠ *820 S.W. Washington St., Downtown* ☎ *503/221–0306* ⊕ *www.
finneganstoys.com.*

OLD TOWN/CHINATOWN

GIFTS

Hand-Eye Supply. One of a handful of intriguing shops that have opened
in Old Town in recent years, Hand-Eye specializes in work wear, studio supplies, tools, and books. But before you write this place off as a
purely utilitarian resource, you should know that the buyers here have
a keen eye for beautifully designed goods. This is first and foremost
an emporium of cool lifestyle goods, including natty gray linen-cotton
work aprons, wood-handled Midori Hamono paring knives, bright-red
Feuerhand camp lanterns, and other stylish curiosities. ⊠ *427 N.W.
Broadway, Old Town* ☎ *503/575–9769* ⊕ *www.handeyesupply.com.*

MARKETS

Fodor'sChoice **Portland Saturday Market.** The open-air Portland Saturday Market, which
★ has been going strong since 1976 and runs from March to December
on weekends (including Sunday, despite the name), is a favorite place
to find one-of-a-kind, handcrafted home, garden, and clothing items—
everything from T-shirts and souvenirs to high-quality sculptures and
housewares. An impressive new pavilion, part of it covered, houses the
more than 300 artisans. ■**TIP→ Don't confuse this crafts-oriented market with the equally popular Portland Farmers' Market.** ⊠ *Tom McCall
Waterfront Park, 2 S.W. Naito Pkwy., adjacent to Burnside Bridge, Old
Town* ☎ *503/222–6072* ⊕ *www.portlandsaturdaymarket.com.*

PEARL DISTRICT

BOOKS

Fodor'sChoice **Oblation Papers.** Employing antique presses and Old World processes,
★ this dapper shop in the Pearl District houses a paper mill, letterpress
shop, and retail store where you can find one-of-a-kind cards, statio-
nery, albums, and journals. The quality, handcrafted cards featuring vintage posters or images of local wildlife make wonderful keepsakes and
gifts. ⊠ *516 N.W. 12th Ave., Pearl District* ☎ *503/223–1093* ⊕ *www.
oblationpapers.com.*

Fodor's Choice
★

Powell's City of Books. The largest retail store of used and new books in the world (with more than 1.5 million volumes), covers an entire city block and rises three stories on the edge of the Pearl District. A local legend, and rightfully so, Powell's also carries rare and collectible books and contains a popular coffeehouse, World Cup. There are also branches in Portland International Airport as well as a large outpost in the heart of the Hawthorne District, with its own coffeehouse, Fresh Pot. ⊠ *1005 W. Burnside St., Pearl District* ☎ *503/228–4651* ⊕ *www. powells.com.*

CLOTHING

Lizard Lounge. Shop until your caffeine levels drop at this expansive men's and women's fashion source in the Pearl, where staff will pour you a complimentary cup of Stumptown coffee as you browse that particularly Portland mix of hip and hipster chic. Lizard Lounge carries everything from major mid-range brands like Levi's and Timberland to higher-end clubbing labels, like G-Star, Nudie Jeans, and Fetch Eyewear. There's also a good selection of gifts and household items, like Field Notes journals and Portland-based Maak Soap Lab bath products. ⊠ *1323 N.W. Irving St., Pearl District* ☎ *503/416–7476* ⊕ *www. lizardloungepdx.com.*

Nau. Specializing in men's and women's sustainable clothing, from rugged hoodies and urbane down jackets to dressier threads made with cotton, Tencel, and other breathable fabrics, Portland-based Nau ships all over the world, but you can try on products and ask questions at this sleek flagship retail store in the Pearl District. ⊠ *304 N.W. 11th Ave., Pearl District* ☎ *503/224–9697* ⊕ *www.nau.com.*

FOOD

Fodor's Choice
★

Smith Teamaker. Tea drinkers rejoice: you don't have to resort to coffee just because you're in Portland. The late founder and legendary tea guru Steve Smith launched two renowned companies, Stash Tea and Tazo, before opening his own company inside a former blacksmith shop on the northwestern edge of the Pearl District. At this handsome tea shop, you can see how the tea is made and packaged, shop teas and accessories, and then sample different varieties at a small tasting bar. Select a tea flight from a menu, try a tea latte, or work your work through an oxidation spectrum—from white to black. The sturdy, pastel-hued boxes in which Smith packages his exquisite, carefully sourced teas make great gifts. ⊠ *1626 N.W. Thurman St., Pearl District* ☎ *503/719–8752* ⊕ *www.smithtea.com.*

GALLERIES

Fodor's Choice
★

First Thursday. This gallery walk the first Thursday of every month gives art appreciators a chance to check out new exhibits while enjoying music and wine. Typically, the galleries, which are largely located in the Pearl District, are open in the evening from 6 to 9, but hours vary. Be prepared for a lively scene including throngs of people, street musicians, and local art vendors, with much of the action along N.W. 13th Avenue between Hoyt and Kearney streets, which is pedestrian only during this event. ⊠ *Pearl District* ☎ *503/227–8519* ⊕ *www.explorethepearl.com.*

J. Pepin Art Gallery. This highly respected contemporary gallery in the Pearl stands out for its unusual mission: the space represents renowned painters, photographers, and others creative spirits who use their experiences coping with mental illness to inspire their work and raise awareness. ✉ *319 N.W. 9th Ave., Pearl District* ☎ *503/274–9614* ⊕ *www. jpepinartgallery.com.*

NOB HILL

CLOTHING

Sloan Boutique. Set among the several fine clothiers on the 700 and 800 blocks of N.W. 23rd Avenue, Sloan Boutique carries a good mix of affordable women's casual and fashion brands, including Kensie, Free People, Kut, and Franco Sarto. The boutique's adjoining space—PlaTform—carries a good selection of trendy shoes and accessories. Sloan has a second branch across the river in Hawthorne. ✉ *738 N.W. 23rd Ave., Nob Hill* ☎ *503/222–6666* ⊕ *www.sloanpdx.com.*

GALLERIES

Laura Russo Gallery. A longtime staple of the Portland arts scene, the Laura Russo Gallery displays contemporary Northwest work of all styles, including landscapes and abstract expressionism. ✉ *805 N.W. 21st Ave., Nob Hill* ☎ *503/226–2754* ⊕ *www.laurarusso.com.*

Twist. This huge space in Nob Hill is well stocked with contemporary American ceramics, glass, furniture, sculpture, and handcrafted jewelry often with a whimsical touch. ✉ *30 N.W. 23rd Pl., Nob Hill* ☎ *503/224–0334* ⊕ *www.twistonline.com.*

JEWELRY

Gem Set Love. Portland's premier estate and vintage jewelry destination, known formerly as Gilt, occupies a dapper Craftsman bungalow along a fashionable stretch of Nob Hill's N.W. 23rd. Inside you'll find an ever-changing inventory of radiant gold and silver rings, bracelets, earrings, and necklaces, many inlaid with dazzling gems. The antique wedding and engagement rings are especially popular. ✉ *720 N.W. 23rd Ave., Nob Hill* ☎ *503/226–0629* ⊕ *www.gem-set-love.com.*

WEST END

MUSIC

Tender Loving Empire. The retail shop of the eponymous Portland indie record label founded by Jared and Brianne Mees carries not only music but also cool hand-printed cards, posters, and T-shirts, along with a hipster-favored selection of lifestyle goods, from coffee-infused soaps and beard oils to do-it-yourself goat-cheese-making kits and screen-printed tote bags. You'll find additional locations on Hawthorne and in Nob Hill. ✉ *412 S.W. 10th Ave., West End* ☎ *503/243–5859* ⊕ *www. tenderlovingempire.com.*

NORTH

FOOD

Fodor'sChoice **The Meadow.** Food writer Mark Bitterman knows a thing or two about
★   salt—he's written two popular books on the subject, and he's the owner
of this tiny purveyor of gourmet finishing salts, some of them smoked or
infused with unusual flavors, like cherry and plums, or saffron. At this
flagship location (there's a second Meadow in Nob Hill, and a third in
Manhattan's West Village) you can also purchase the additional magical
touches you might need to create the perfect dinner party, from Oregon
and European wines and vermouths, to fresh-cut flowers, aromatic
cocktail bitters, and high-quality, single-origin chocolates. ⊠ *3731 N.
Mississippi Ave., North* ☎ *503/974–8349* ⊕ *www.atthemeadow.com.*

HOUSEHOLD GOODS AND FURNITURE

Fodor'sChoice **Beam & Anchor.** Set on a busy street corner several blocks from the North
★   Side's trendy North Mississippi strip, this once-dilapidated warehouse
houses an upstairs workshop for makers of artisanal goods and an
inspiring downstairs retail space where proprietors Robert and Jocelyn
Rahm sell a carefully curated selection of lifestyle goods for every room
in the home, many of them produced locally—some as local as upstairs.
Among the hipster treasures, look for warm and soft camp blankets and
Navajo rugs with vibrant prints, women's jewelry in a variety of simple-
but-beautiful styles, Portland Apothecary bath salts and soaps, and
quite a few larger pieces of distinctive furniture. ⊠ *2710 N. Interstate
Ave., North* ☎ *503/367–3230* ⊕ *www.beamandanchor.com.*

TOYS

Fodor'sChoice **Paxton Gate.** Here, science and biology mix with whimsy and imagina-
★   tion. You'll find everything from taxidermied scorpions and baby goats
to ostrich eggs and ceramic chimes. It's a fascinating and strangely
beguiling mix of goods, and not for the faint of heart. ⊠ *4204 N. Mississippi Ave., North* ☎ *503/719–4508* ⊕ *www.paxtongate.com.*

NORTHEAST

FOOD

FAMILY **Creo Chocolate.** Drop by one of Portland's newest and most acclaimed
artisan bean-to-bar chocolate shops for a tour, or just a taste. Free—and
fascinating—factory tours are given at 11 am Thursday–Saturday, and a
small café doles out chocolates as well as brownies, hot chocolate, and
even chocolate soda. ⊠ *122 N.E. Broadway, Lloyd District/Convention
Center* ☎⊕ *www.creochocolate.com* ⊙ *Closed Sun. and Mon.*

Providore Fine Foods. This sleek gourmet market features the artisan
and local fare of several notable Portland purveyors, including Little T
Baker, Rubinette Produce, Flying Fish Company, Arrosto (which turns
out delicious Mediterranean-style rotisserie chicken), and Pastaworks.
It's a terrific source for picnic supplies, and there's table seating. The
owners also operate Pastaworks at City Market in Nob Hill. ⊠ *2340
N.E. Sandy Blvd., Northeast* ☎ *503/232–1010* ⊕ *www.providorefine-
foods.com.*

2

GALLERIES

Ampersand Gallery & Fine Books. Part art gallery, part media store, this minimalist white-wall space on Alberta Street has monthly shows featuring edgy, contemporary art, and stocks a fascinating trove of photography and art books, vintage travel brochures, curious photography, pulp-fiction novels, and other printed materials of the sort you might find in a chest in a mysterious neighbor's attic. The owners also operate the cute Cord boutique next door, which stocks artfully designed household goods, from handcrafted soaps to aerodynamic coffeepots. ✉ *2916 N.E. Alberta St., Alberta District* ☎ *503/805–5458* ⊕ *www. ampersandgallerypdx.com.*

FAMILY **Last Thursday Arts Walk.** The Alberta Arts District hosts an arts walk
Fodor'sChoice on the last Thursday of each month. This quirky procession along 15
★ blocks of one of the city's favorite thoroughfares for browsing art galleries, distinctive boutiques, and hipster bars and restaurants features street performers and buskers, crafts makers, and food vendors. The street is closed to traffic from 6 to 9:30 pm. ✉ *N.E. Alberta St., Alberta District* ⊕ *www.lastthursdayonalberta.com.*

MUSIC

Fodor'sChoice **Music Millennium.** The oldest record store in the Pacific Northwest, Music
★ Millennium Northwest stocks a huge selection of new and used music in every possible category, including local punk groups. The store also hosts a number of in-store performances, often by top-name artists like Lucinda Williams, Richard Thompson, Sheryl Crow, and Randy Newman. ✉ *3158 E. Burnside St., Laurelhurst* ☎ *503/231–8926* ⊕ *www. musicmillennium.com.*

SOUTHEAST

CLOTHING

Fodor'sChoice **Altar.** A tiny but impressively stocked boutique in a charming, old,
★ Craftsman-style house that also houses the excellent Hazel Room café, Altar is devoted to decorative items, fashion, jewelry, and crafts made by Portlanders. The selection is eclectic and fun—everything from handcrafted soaps made with local beer to geometric-shape brass necklaces. Clothing at Altar is geared mostly to women. ✉ *3279 S.E. Hawthorne Blvd., Hawthorne District* ☎ *503/236–6120* ⊕ *www.altarpdx.com.*

Herbivore Clothing. An animal-rights-minded shop in the Central East Side, Herbivore is a terrific resource if you're seeking clothing and accessories—from cotton-rayon tees and sweaters to braided canvas belts and wallets fashioned out of reclaimed bike and truck tubes—that have been created without the harm or use of animals. There's also a great selection of books on veganism, plus food, health-care products, and gifts. ✉ *1211 S.E. Stark St., Southeast* ☎ *503/281–8638* ⊕ *www. herbivoreclothing.com.*

Fodor'sChoice **Machus.** This small, somewhat under-the-radar, upscale, men's cloth-
★ ier carries arguably the best selection of fashion-forward, emerging labels in the city. In addition to Machus's own private-label dress shirts and tees, check out the form-fitting, refreshingly unadorned Naked

and Famous skinny jeans, stylish sportswear by Knomadik, and edgy, urbane bomber jackets and hoodies from ADYN. You won't find many—or any—pastels or bright prints in here; expect clean classics, with lots of blacks, grays, and whites. ☒ *542 E. Burnside St., Southeast* ☎ *503/206–8626* ⊕ *www.machusonline.com.*

Union Rose. For distinctive women's fashion and accessories designed and made in Portland, check out this boutique in up-and-coming Montavilla. Though there are scores of dresses for any season, including a very good selection of dresses and skirts in plus sizes, there's also plenty of everyday wear, like hoodies and hats. ☒ *7909 S.E. Stark St., Southeast* ☎ *503/287–4242* ⊕ *www.unionrosepdx.com.*

Fodor's Choice
★

Wildfang. This edgy fashion label and shop run by self-proclaimed "tomboys" and "modern-day female Robin Hoods" has earned an international reputation for its gender-bending styles, from brocade lapel blazers and matching trousers to slouchy-fit hoodies. You'll also find beanies, briefs, ties, and trademark "Wild Feminist" snapback caps that make a statement on the street or in the club. ☒ *1230 S.E. Grand Ave., Portland* ☎ *503/208–3631* ⊕ *www.wildfang.com.*

HOUSEHOLD GIFTS AND FURNITURE

House of Vintage. This mammoth 13,000-square-foot shop, just down the street from one of the better Goodwill shops in the city, is de rigueur among vintage aficionados. Inside, you can rifle through the wares of some 60 dealers; bell-bottom jeans and plaid blazers are a big draw, but this time capsule also brims with kitschy ceramic ashtrays, Naugahyde couches, '50s magazines, old-school lunchboxes, and pretty much anything else you might recall from your childhood. ☒ *3315 S.E. Hawthorne Blvd., Hawthorne District* ☎ *503/236–1991* ⊕ *www.houseofvintagenw.com.*

Tilde. With wares that could work just as well in an urban loft as in a cozy country cottage, this compact storefront space is filled with a mix of eye-catching lifestyle goods and functional artwork, including Matt & Nat wallets and bags, lacy steel-and-silver earrings, ceramic bowls and vases, and stylish Nixon watches in bright colors. ☒ *7919 S.E. 13th Ave., Sellwood* ☎ *503/234–9600* ⊕ *www.tildeshop.com.*

OUTDOOR SUPPLIES

Next Adventure Sports. It all about the gear here. Next Adventure Sports carries new and used sporting goods, including camping gear, snowboards, kayaks, and mountaineering supplies. Kayak classes and Outdoor School provide plenty of opportunities to get out and enjoy Oregon like a local. They also operate The Paddle Sports Center, just a few blocks southeast at 624 S.E. 7th Avenue. ☒ *426 S.E. Grand Ave., Southeast* ☎ *503/233–0706* ⊕ *www.nextadventure.net.*

TOYS

FAMILY
Fodor's Choice
★

Cloud Cap Games. There's more than just run-of-the-mill board games at Cloud Cap. For children and grown-ups alike, the games here challenge the mind and provide hours of entertainment. There's a room with tables to play or try out a game. The knowledgeable owners and staff may sit down and join in the fun and are always happy to answer questions and offer suggestions. ☒ *1226 S.E. Lexington St., Sellwood* ☎ *503/505–9344* ⊕ *www.cloudcapgames.com.*

THE OREGON COAST

WELCOME TO THE OREGON COAST

TOP REASONS TO GO

★ **The beaches:** The Oregon Coast has breathtaking beaches, from romantic stretches to creature-teeming tide pools and stunning cliffs that flank many of the beaches.

★ **Shop for blown glass:** Artisanal glass shops dot the coastline—at some, you can even craft your own colorful creations.

★ **Oregon Dunes National Recreation Area:** Whether you're screaming in a dune buggy or scrambling over them on foot, southern Oregon's mountainous sand dunes bring out the kid in anyone who traverses them.

★ **Small-town charms:** You'll find some of the state's most quirky and charming communities along the coast, from hipster-approved Astoria to arty and secluded Port Orford to rustic yet sophisticated Yachats.

★ **Wine and dine:** You don't have to spend a lot to enjoy creatively prepared seafood, artisanal microbrews, and local wines.

1 North Coast. As the primary gateway for both Portlanders and those visiting from neighboring Washington, the north coast is the busiest stretch of Oregon coastline, although it's still rife with secluded coves and funky seaside hamlets. Its lighthouse-dotted shoreline stretches from the mouth of the Columbia River south to Pacific City. The 90-mile region includes the historic working-class fishing town of Astoria and its recent influx of hip cafés, indie boutiques, and restored hotels; family-friendly Seaside with its touristy but bustling boardwalk; art-fueled and refined Cannon Beach; laid-back and stunningly situated Manzanita Beach; and tiny Pacific City, where a colorful fleet of dories dots the wide, deep beach.

2 Central Coast. The 75-mile stretch from Lincoln City to Florence offers whale-watching, incomparable seafood, shell-covered beaches, candy confections, and close-up views of undersea life. At the north end, in Lincoln City visitors can indulge in gaming, shopping, golfing, and beachcombing. The harbor town of Depoe Bay is a center for whale-watching, and nearby Newport offers a stellar aquarium and science center. It's also home to one of Oregon's largest fishing fleets. The less-developed town of Yachats is a true seaside gem with astounding coastal views, where the only demands are to relax and enjoy an increasingly noteworthy restaurant scene. The cute town of Florence and its bustling downtown hugs the Siuslaw River—it's also the northern access point for the Oregon dunes.

3 South Coast. From the heart of Oregon dunes country in Reedsport to the southernmost Oregon town of Brookings, the 134-mile stretch of U.S. 101 is less touristy than points north, but still has mesmerizing beaches, headlands, and coastal rain forests in abundance. Coos Bay and adjacent North Bend make up the region's largest population center. The beach town of Bandon is a world-class golfing destination that's also popular for beachcombing and lighthouse gazing. Ruggedly situated and low-key Port Orford has gorgeous beach landscapes and a growing arts scene, while Gold Beach and Brookings, farther south, are bathed in sunshine.

GETTING ORIENTED

3

Oregon's coastline begins in the north in the town of Astoria, which lies at the mouth of the Columbia River on the Washington state line. It's a slow-going but spectacular 363-mile drive south along U.S. Highway 101 to the small town of Brookings at Oregon's southwestern corner, several miles from the California border. The rugged Coast Range flanks the entire coast to the east, providing a picturesque barrier between the ocean and the lush Willamette, Umpqua, and Rogue valleys, where you'll find Oregon's larger communities, including Portland and Eugene.

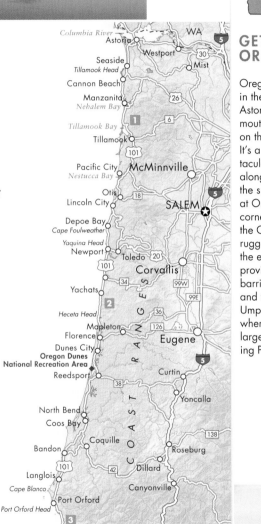

EXPLORING OREGON'S BEST BEACHES

Oregon's 300 miles of public coastline is the backdrop for thrills, serenity, rejuvenation, and romance. From yawning expanses of sand dotted with beach chairs to tiny patches bounded by surf-shaped cliffs, the state's shoreline often draws comparisons to New Zealand.

(above) Surfing the Oregon Coast; (opposite page, top) Oregon Dunes National Recreation Area; (opposite page, bottom) Cannon Beach Sandcastle Contest

Most awe inspiring are the massive rock formations just offshore in the northern and southern sections of the coast, breaking up the Pacific horizon. Beaches along the north coast, from Astoria to Pacific City, are perfect for romantic strolls on the sands. The central-coast beaches, from Lincoln City to Florence, are long and wide, providing perfect conditions for sunbathers, children, clam diggers, horseback riders, and surfers. The southern-coast beaches from Reedsport to Brookings are less populated, ideal for getting away from it all.

In late July and August the climate is kind to sun worshipers. During the shoulder months, keep layers of clothing handy for the unpredictable temperature swings. Winter can be downright blustery, a time that many seaside inns optimistically call "storm-watching season."

GLASS FLOATS: FINDERS KEEPERS

Since 1997, between mid-October and Memorial Day, more than 2,000 handcrafted glass floats made by local artists have been hidden along Lincoln City's 7½-mile public beach. If you happen to come upon one, call the local tourism office (800/452–2151) to register it, and find out which artist made it. While antique glass floats are extremely rare, these new versions make great souvenirs.

THE OREGON COAST'S BEST BEACHES

Cannon Beach. In the shadow of glorious **Haystack Rock,** this beach is wide, flat, and perfect for bird-watching, exploring tide pools, building sand castles, and romantic walks in the sea mist. Each June the city holds a **sand-castle contest,** drawing artists and thousands of visitors. The rest of the year the beach is far less populated. The dapper beachfront town has several of the region's swankiest hotels and finest restaurants, as well as spots for surfing, hiking, and beachcombing.

Pacific City. This beach is postcard perfect, with its colorful fleet of dories sitting on the sand and massive Cape Kiwanda dune flanking the shore to the north. Like Cannon Beach, this town also has a huge (less famous) Haystack Rock that provides the perfect scenic backdrop for horseback riders, beach strollers, and people with shovels chasing sand-covered clams. With safe beach breaks that are ideal for beginners and larger peaks a bit to the south, this is also a great spot for surfers. Winterstorm-watchers love Pacific City, where winds exceeding 75 mph twist Sitka spruce, and tides deposit driftwood and logs on the beach.

Winchester Bay. One reason the Pacific Northwest isn't known for its amusement parks is because nature hurls more thrills than any rattling contraption could ever provide. This certainly is true

at **Oregon Dunes National Recreation Area.** Here riders of all-terrain vehicles (ATVs) will encounter some of the most radical slips, dips, hills, and chills in the nation. It is the largest expanse of coastal sand dunes in North America, extending for 40 miles, from Florence to Coos Bay. More than 1.5 million people visit the dunes each year. For those who just want to swim, relax, hike, and marvel at the amazing expanse of dunes against the ocean, there are spaces off-limits to motorized vehicles. Overlooking the beach is the gorgeous **Umpqua River Lighthouse.**

Samuel H. Boardman State Scenic Corridor. It doesn't get any wilder than this—or more spectacular. The 12-mile strip of forested, rugged coastline between Gold Beach and Brookings is dotted with smaller sand beaches, some more accessible than others. Here visitors will find the amazing **Arch Rock** and **Natural Bridges** and can hike 27 miles of the **Oregon Coast Trail.** Beach highlights include **Whaleshead Beach, Secret Beach,** and **Thunder Rock Cove,** where you might spot migrating gray whales. From the 345-foot-high **Thomas Creek Bridge** you can take a moderately difficult hike down to admire the gorgeous, jagged rocks off **China Beach.**

Updated
by Andrew
Collins

If you aren't from the Pacific Northwest, Oregon's spectacular coastline might still be a secret: it's less visited and talked about than California's coast, but certainly no less beautiful. But in recent decades, the state's reputation for scenic drives and splendid hikes, reasonably priced oceanfront hotels and vacation rentals, low-key towns with friendly, creative vibes, and consistently fresh and well-prepared seafood has garnered increased attention. The true draw here is the beaches, where nature lovers delight at their first sight of a migrating whale or a baby harbor seal sitting on a rock.

Oregon's coastline is open to all; not a grain of its more than 300 miles of white-sand beaches is privately owned. The coast's midsize towns and small villages (you won't find any large cities) are linked by U.S. 101, which runs the length of the state. It winds past sea-tortured rocks, brooding headlands, hidden beaches, historic lighthouses, and tiny ports. This is one of the most picturesque driving routes in the country, and it should not be missed. Embracing it is the vast, indigo-blue Pacific Ocean, which presents a range of moods with the seasons. On summer evenings it might be glassy, and reflect a romantic sunset. In winter the ocean might throw a thrilling tantrum for storm watchers sitting snug and safe in a beachfront cabin.

Active visitors indulge in thrills from racing up a sand dune in a buggy to making par at Bandon Dunes, one of the nation's finest links-style golf courses. Bicyclists pedal along misty coastline vistas, cruising past historic lighthouses. Hikers enjoy breezy, open trails along the sea as well as lush, evergreen-studded treks into the adjoining Coast Range. Boaters explore southern-coast rivers on jet boats while the more adventuresome among them shoot rapids on guided raft trips. If the weather turns, don't overlook indoor venues like the Oregon Coast Aquarium and Columbia River Maritime Museum.

Shoppers appreciate the several art galleries in Newport and Cannon Beach; for more family-oriented shopping fun, giggle in the souvenir shops of Lincoln City and Seaside while eating fistfuls of caramel corn or chewing saltwater taffy.

THE OREGON COAST PLANNER

WHEN TO GO

November through May are generally rainy months (albeit with sporadic stretches of dry and sometimes even sunny days), but once the fair weather comes, coastal Oregon is one of the most gorgeous places on earth. July through September offer wonderful, dry days for beachgoers. Autumn is also a great time to visit, as the warm-enough weather is perfect for crisp beachcombing walks followed by hearty harvest meals paired with ales from the growing crop of craft breweries up and down the coast.

Even with the rain, coastal winter and spring do have quite a following. Many hotels are perfectly situated for storm watching, and provide a romantic experience. Think of a toasty fire, a smooth Oregon Pinot, and your loved one, settled in to watch the waves dance upon a jagged rocky stage.

FESTIVALS

Cannon Beach Sandcastle Contest. It can be tough to find a room—or parking spot—during this single-day mid-June festival that's been going strong for more than 50 years and showcases the amazingly detailed sand constructions of both professional and amateur teams. ⊕ *www.cannonbeach.org.*

Astoria Music Festival. Fans of opera and classical works flock to this increasingly popular festival, which mounts more than 20 performances, over 16 days in late June and early July. ⊕ *www.astoriamusicfestival.org.*

Newport Seafood and Wine Festival. This renowned foodie gathering takes place the last full weekend in February and bills itself the premier seafood and wine event of the Oregon Coast. Dozens of wineries are represented at this expansive celebration, which also features myriad crafts and eateries. ⊕ *www.seafoodandwine.com.*

Cranberry Festival. In Bandon each September this festival in celebration of the town's most famous product (well, after seafood) comprises a fair and parade. ⊕ *www.bandon.com/cranberry-festival.*

GETTING HERE AND AROUND

By far the most practical way to reach and to explore the coast is by car. There's only one small regional airport with limited commercial service, the regional bus lines provide fairly slow and infrequent service from other parts of the state, and there's zero train service. Several two-lane state highways connect the central and northern sections of the coast with the state's two largest cities, Portland and Eugene; the southern portion of the coast is more remote and requires a longer drive.

AIR TRAVEL

From Portland, which has Oregon's largest airport, the drive is about 2 hours to Astoria and Cannon Beach, and 2½ hours to Lincoln City and Newport. If you're headed farther south, you have a few other options, including flying into the regional airport in Eugene, which is served by most major airlines and is a 90-minute drive from Florence; flying into the tiny Southwest Oregon Regional Airport in the coast town of North Bend, which is an hour south of Florence and 2½ hours north of Brookings; flying into Rogue Valley International Airport in Medford, which is a 2½-hour drive from Brookings and a 3-hour drive from Bandon; and flying into Del Norte County Airport in Crescent City, California, which is just a 30-minute drive south of Brookings.

Southwest Oregon Regional Airport has flights to Portland on PenAir (a partner with Alaska Airlines) and to San Francisco and Denver on United Express. The airport has Hertz and Enterprise car-rental agencies as well as cab companies serving the area, including Coos Bay and Bandon.

There are a few shuttle services connecting the airports in Portland and Eugene to the coast, but these tend to be far less economical than renting a car. Caravan Airport Transportation runs a daily shuttle service from Portland International Airport to Lincoln City and on down to Yachats. OmniShuttle provides door-to-door van service from the Eugene airport to the central coast, from Florence down to around Bandon.

Contacts Caravan Airport Transportation. ☎ 503/288–5102 ⊕ www.caravanairporttransportation.com. **OmniShuttle.** ☎ 541/461–7959, 800/741–5097 ⊕ www.omnishuttle.com. **PenAir.** ☎ 800/448–4226 ⊕ www.penair.com. **Southwest Oregon Regional Airport.** ✉ 1100 Airport La., North Bend ☎ 541/756–8531 ⊕ www.cooscountyairportdistrict.com.

BUS TRAVEL

There is bus travel to the coast from Portland and Eugene, but this is a fairly slow and cumbersome way to explore the area. North by Northwest Connector is a nonprofit organization that coordinates travel among five rural transit services in the northwestern corner of the state. From its website, you can plan and book trips from Portland to Astoria, with connecting service between the two along the coast, stopping in Seaside, Cannon Beach, Manzanita, and other communities. Additionally, Northwest Point, operated by MTR Western bus line, has twice-daily bus service from Portland to Cannon Beach, and then up the coast to Astoria; Greyhound handles the company's reservations and ticketing. Pacific Crest Bus Lines connects Florence, Coos Bay, and Reedsport with Eugene every day except Saturday.

Contacts North by Northwest Connector. ⊕ www.nworegontransit.org. **Northwest Point.** ☎ 800/231–2222 ticketing through Greyhound, 541/484–4100 information ⊕ www.oregon-point.com. **Pacific Crest Bus Lines.** ☎ 541/344–6265 ⊕ www.pacificcrestbuslines.com.

CAR TRAVEL

Beautiful U.S. 101 hugs the entire Oregon coastline from Brookings near the California border in the south to Astoria on the Columbia River in the north. The road can be slow in places, especially where it passes through towns and curves over headlands and around coves. In theory, you could drive the entire 345-mile Oregon stretch of U.S 101 in a little under eight hours, but that's without stopping—and, of course, the whole point of driving the coast is stopping regularly to enjoy it. If you want to do a full road trip of the Oregon Coast, give yourself at least three days and two nights; that's enough time to see a few key attractions along the way, enjoy the many scenic viewpoints, and stop to eat and overnight in some small towns along the route.

Several two-lane roads connect key towns on the coast (Astoria, Cannon Beach, Tillamook, Lincoln City, Newport, Waldport, Florence, Reedsport, and Bandon) with the major towns in the Willamette and Rogue valleys (Portland, Eugene, Roseburg). All these roads climb over the Coast Range, meaning the drives tend to be winding and hilly but quite picturesque. Keep in mind that winter storms in the mountains occasionally create slick conditions and even road closures. Always use numbered, paved state roads when crossing the mountains from the valley to the coast, especially in winter; what might appear to be a scenic alternative or shortcut on a map or GPS device is likely an unmaintained logging or forest road that leads through a secluded part of the mountains, without cell service.

RESTAURANTS

Deciding which restaurant has the best clam chowder is just one of the culinary fact-finding expeditions you can embark upon along the Oregon Coast. Chefs here take full advantage of the wealth of sturgeon, chinook, steelhead, and trout that abound in coastal rivers as well as the fresh rockfish, halibut, albacore, and lingcod caught in the Pacific. Fresh mussels, bay shrimp, and oysters are also standard fare in many establishments. Newport's bounty is its Dungeness crab. Razor clams also appear as a succulent addition to many restaurant menus along the coast. You'll find relatively few upscale dining options here, with most of these being in resorts, but quite a few mid-priced urbane bistros emphasizing local seafood and seasonal produce have opened in recent years. They still tend to be casual, but with fine service, art-filled dining rooms, and prices more similar to what you'll find in Portland or Eugene. Most other restaurants tend to be low-key and affordable, many of them catering to both kids and adults. There are plenty of cozy brewpubs and clam shacks, and tasty fish-and-chips are easy to come by. In addition, many Oregon Coast restaurants focus heavily on locally produced wines, beers, and even spirits. *Restaurant reviews have been shortened. For full information visit Fodors.com.*

HOTELS

Compared with other coastal destinations in the United States, the Oregon Coast offers a pretty good value, although during high season in July and August, rates can get fairly steep at some higher-end inns and resorts, especially along the northern stretch of the coastline. Still, you can typically find clean but basic motels and rustic inns, often with beachfront locations, that have nightly rates well below $150, even in high season. Spring and fall rates often drop by 20% to 30%, and in winter—especially on weekdays—a hotel room that costs $250 in July might go for as little as $99. There are plenty of budget- and mid-priced chains in larger towns, but for the most part, the lodging landscape is dominated by family-owned or independent motels and hotels, vacation rentals, and a smattering of distinctive B&Bs.

Properties in much of the north and central coast fill up fast in the summer, so book in advance. Many lodgings require a minimum two-night stay on a summer weekend. *Hotel reviews have been shortened. For full information, visit Fodors.com.*

WHAT IT COSTS IN U.S. DOLLARS			
$	$$	$$$	$$$$
Restaurants	under $16	$16–$22	$23–$30	over $30
Hotels	under $150	$150–$200	$201–$250	over $250

Restaurant prices are the average cost of a main course at dinner, or if dinner is not served, at lunch. Hotel prices are the lowest cost of a standard double room in high season.

VISITOR INFORMATION

Central Oregon Coast Association. ☎ *541/265–2064, 800/767–2064* ⊕ *www.coastvisitor.com.*

Eugene, Cascades & Coast Visitor Center. ✉ *3312 Gateway St., Springfield* ☎ *541/484–5307, 800/547–5445* ⊕ *www.eugenecascadescoast.org.*

Oregon Coast Visitors Association. ☎ *541/574–2679, 888/628–2101* ⊕ *www.visittheoregoncoast.com.*

NORTH COAST

This is the primary beach playground for residents of Portland, and in recent years, increasing numbers of sophisticated cafés, craft breweries and wine bars, colorful art galleries and indie retailers, and smartly restored boutique hotels have opened along this stretch of the Oregon Coast. What distinguishes the region historically from other areas of the coast are its forts, its graveyard of shipwrecks, historic sites related to Lewis and Clark's early visit, and a town—Astoria—that is closer in look and misty temperament to Monterey, California, than any other city in the West. Just south, Cannon Beach and its several high-end hotels feels a bit swankier than any other town in the area.

Every winter Astoria celebrates fisherman poets: hardworking men and women who bare their souls as to what makes their relationship to Oregon's north-coast waters so magical. It's easy to understand their inspiration, whether in the incredibly tempestuous ocean or the romantic beaches.

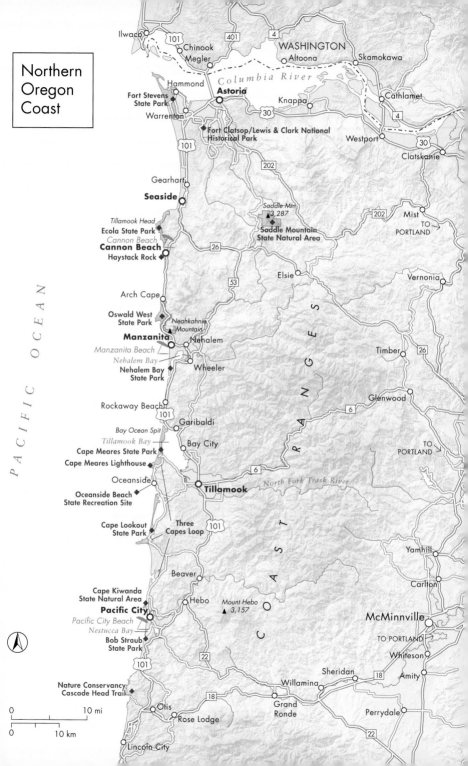

Northern Oregon Coast

Ilwaco
Chinook
101
401
Megler
4
WASHINGTON
Altoona
Skamokawa
Columbia River
Hammond
Astoria
Knappa
Cathlamet
Fort Stevens State Park
Warrenton
30
Westport
4
101
Fort Clatsop/Lewis & Clark National Historical Park
30
Clatskanie
202
Gearhart
Seaside
Saddle Mtn 3,287
Mist
TO PORTLAND
202
Tillamook Head
Ecola State Park
Cannon Beach
Cannon Beach
Haystack Rock
Saddle Mountain State Natural Area
26
Elsie
Vernonia
53
Arch Cape
Oswald West State Park
Neahkahnie Mountain
Manzanita
Nehalem
Timber
26
Manzanita Beach
Nehalem Bay
Wheeler
Nehalem Bay State Park
Glenwood
Rockaway Beach
101
Garibaldi
6
Bay Ocean Spit
Tillamook Bay
Bay City
TO PORTLAND
Cape Meares State Park
Cape Meares Lighthouse
6
Oceanside
Tillamook
North Fork Trask River
Oceanside Beach State Recreation Site
Cape Lookout State Park
Three Capes Loop
101
Yamhill
Beaver
Carlton
Cape Kiwanda State Natural Area
Hebo
Mount Hebo 3,157
McMinnville
Pacific City
Pacific City Beach
Nestucca Bay
Bob Straub State Park
TO PORTLAND
Whiteson
101
22
Sheridan
Amity
Nature Conservancy Cascade Head Trail
18
Willamina
Grand Ronde
Perrydale
Otis
Rose Lodge
18
22
Lincoln City

PACIFIC OCEAN

COAST RANGES

0   10 mi
0   10 km

ASTORIA

96 miles northwest of Portland.

The mighty Columbia River meets the Pacific at Astoria, the oldest city west of the Rockies and a bustling riverfront getaway with a creative spirit and urbane vibe. In recent years the city has reinvented itself, with a greater variety of trendy dining and lodging options, as well as a superb museum dedicated to the Columbia River. Astoria also now cultivates a bit of Portland's hipster vibe, especially when it comes to shopping and nightlife.

It is named for John Jacob Astor, owner of the Pacific Fur Company, whose members arrived in 1811 and established Fort Astoria. In its early days, Astoria was a placid amalgamation of small town and hard-working port city. With rivers rich with salmon, the city relied on its fishing and canning industries. Settlers built sprawling Victorian houses on the flanks of Coxcomb Hill; many of the homes have since been restored and used as backdrops in movies or been converted into bed-and-breakfast inns. Astoria still retains the soul of a fisherman's town, celebrated each February during its FisherPoets Gathering. The town of about 9,500 also has wonderful views from most areas and a richly forested backdrop to the east, yet it remains a working waterfront. There is little public beach access in the town proper; to reach the Pacific, you have to drive a few miles west to Fort Stevens in Warrenton.

GETTING HERE AND AROUND

The northernmost town on the Oregon Coast, Astoria is just across the Columbia River from southwestern Washington via U.S. 101 (over the stunning Astoria-Megler Bridge) and a two-hour drive from Portland on U.S. 30. It only takes about 20 extra minutes to get here from Portland via the more scenic route of U.S. 101 south and U.S. 26 east.

ESSENTIALS

Visitor Information Astoria-Warrenton Area Chamber of Commerce. ⊠ *111 W. Marine Dr.* ☎ *503/325–6311, 800/875–6807* ⊕ *www.oldoregon.com.*

EXPLORING

TOP ATTRACTIONS

Fodor's Choice ★ **Astoria Column.** For the best view of the city, the Coast Range, volcanic Mt. Helens, and the Pacific Ocean, scamper up the 164 spiral stairs to the top of the Astoria Column. When you get to the top, you can throw a small wooden plane and watch it glide to earth; each year some 35,000 gliders are tossed. The 125-foot-high structure sits atop Coxcomb Hill, and was patterned after Trajan's Column in Rome. There are little platforms to rest on if you get winded, or, if you don't want to climb, the column's 500 feet of artwork, depicting important Pacific Northwest historical milestones, are well worth a study. ⊠ *16th St. S* ☎ *503/325–2963* ⊕ *www.astoriacolumn.org* 🅿 *$5 parking (good for an entire year).*

FAMILY
Fodor's Choice ★ **Columbia River Maritime Museum.** One of Oregon's best coastal attractions illuminates the maritime history of the Pacific Northwest and provides visitors with a sense of the perils of guiding ships into the mouth of the Columbia River. Vivid exhibits recount what it was like to pilot a

tugboat and participate in a Coast Guard rescue on the Columbia River Bar. You can tour the actual bridge of a World War II–era U.S. Navy destroyer and the U.S. Coast Guard lightship *Columbia*. Also on display is a 44-foot Coast Guard motor lifeboat, artifacts from the region's illustrious riverboat heyday, and details about Astoria's seafood-canning history. One especially captivating exhibit displays the personal belongings of some of the ill-fated passengers of the 2,000 ships that have foundered here since the early 19th century. In addition, the theater shows an excellent documentary about the river's heritage as well as rotating 3-D films about sea life. At the east end of the property, the city's former railroad depot now houses the museum's Barbey Maritime Center, which offers classes and workshops on maritime culture and wooden boatbuilding. ✉ *1792 Marine Dr.* ☎ *503/325–2323* ⊕ *www.crmm.org* ⬚ *$14.*

Flavel House. The Queen Anne–style mansion helps visitors imagine what life was like for the wealthy in late-19th-century Astoria. It rests on parklike grounds covering an entire city block and has been gorgeously restored, with its three-story octagon tower visible from throughout town. It was built for George Flavel, an influential Columbia River bar pilot and businessman who was one of the area's first millionaires. Visits start in the Carriage House interpretive center. ✉ *441 8th St.* ☎ *503/325–2203* ⊕ *www.cumtux.org* ⬚ *$6.*

FAMILY
Fodor'sChoice
★
Fort Clatsop at Lewis and Clark National Historical Park. See where the 30-member Lewis and Clark Expedition endured a rain-soaked winter in 1805–06, hunting, gathering food, making salt, and trading with the local Clatsops, Chinooks, and Tillamooks. This memorial is part of the 3,200-acre Lewis and Clark National Historical Park and is a faithful replica of the log fort depicted in Clark's journal. The fort lies within a forested wonderland, with an exhibit hall, gift shop, film, and trails. Park rangers dress in period garb during the summer and perform such early-19th-century tasks as making fire with flint and steel. Hikers enjoy the easy 1½-mile Netul Landing trail and the more rigorous but still fairly flat 6½-mile Fort to Sea trail. ✉ *92343 Fort Clatsop Rd.* ☎ *503/861–2471* ⊕ *www.nps.gov/lewi* ⬚ *$5.*

WORTH NOTING

FAMILY
Astoria Riverfront Trolley. Also known as "Old 300," this is a beautifully restored 1913 streetcar that travels for 4 miles along Astoria's historic riverfront, stopping at several points between the Astoria River Inn and the foot of 39th Street (although you can easily flag it down at any point along the route by offering a friendly wave). The hour-long ride gives you a close-up look at the waterfront from the Port of Astoria to the East Morring Basin; the Columbia River; and points of interest in between. ☎ *503/325–6311, 800/875–6807* ⊕ *www.old300.org* ⬚ *$1 per boarding, $2 all-day pass.*

Hanthorn Cannery Museum. Drive or walk over the rickety-seeming (but actually completely sturdy) bridge onto historic Pier 39, which juts out into the Columbia River on the east side of downtown, to visit this small but interesting museum that occupies the oldest extant cannery building in Astoria. It was once operated by Bumble Bee Seafood, and some 30,000 cans of salmon were processed here annually during the plant's late-19th-century heyday. Exhibits and artifacts, including three vintage gill-net boats, some wonderful old photos, and equipment and cans tell the story of the town's—and facility's—canning history. Also on the pier is Coffee Girl café and Rogue Ales Public House. ⊠ *100 39th St.* ☎ *503/325–2502* ⊕ *www.canneryworker.org* ▭ *Free.*

NEED A BREAK

✕ **Coffee Girl. This cozy café inside a 19th-century cannery building on historic Pier 39 has big windows overlooking the river—you can always take your well-crafted espresso or latte with you for a stroll around the pier. Open until late afternoon each day, Coffee Girl also serves tasty quiches, pastries, soups, and grilled panini sandwiches.** ⊠ **100 39th St.** ☎ **503/325–6900** ⊕ **www.thecoffeegirl.com.**

FAMILY **Fort Stevens State Park.** This earthen fort at Oregon's northwestern tip was built during the Civil War to guard the Columbia River against attack. None came until World War II, when a Japanese submarine fired upon it. The fort still has cannons and an underground gun battery, of which tours are available in summer (call for details). The park has year-round camping, with full hookup sites, 11 cabins, and 15 yurts. There are also bike paths, boating, swimming, hiking trails, and a short walk to a gorgeous, wide beach where the corroded skeleton—or the tiny bit that remains of it—of the *Peter Iredale* pokes up through the sand. This century-old English four-master shipwreck is a reminder of the nearly 2,000 vessels claimed by these treacherous waters. ⊠ *100 Peter Iredale Rd., Hammond* ☎ *503/861–3170, 800/551–6949* ⊕ *www. oregonstateparks.org* ▭ *Day use $5 per vehicle.*

FAMILY **Oregon Film Museum.** Housed in the old Clatsop County Jail, this small but engaging museum celebrates Oregon's long history of filmmaking and contains artifacts from and displays about prior productions. The location is apt because it was featured prominently in the famous cult film *The Goonies.* The state's film productions date back to 1908 for *The Fisherman's Bride.* Since then, Oregon has helped give birth to such classics as *The General*, *The Great Race*, *One Flew Over the Cuckoo's Nest*, *Paint Your Wagon*, *Animal House*, and *Twilight*, leading some to call the state Hollywood North. *Kindergarten Cop*, *The Ring II*, *Free Willy I* and *II*, and *Short Circuit* are among those filmed in Astoria. You can download an audio tour of filmed sites (or buy a tour CD for $2) from the Astoria-Warrenton Chamber of Commerce—it's a fun way to see the city's oft-unsung landmarks, especially during the annual Goonies festival, held in June. ⊠ *732 Duane St.* ☎ *503/325–2203* ⊕ *www.oregonfilmmuseum.org* ▭ *$6.*

WHERE TO EAT

$$ ✕ **Astoria Coffeehouse & Bistro.** A source of fine coffee drinks and baked

ECLECTIC goods, this cheerful storefront café has both sidewalk seating and a living-

Fodor's Choice room-like interior decorated with old photos. The always-bustling restau-

★ rant serves consistently well-prepared food, a mix of American classics and international treats. **Known for:** local-rockfish tacos; superb drinks, from coffees to cocktails; Monte Cristo sandwiches. $ *Average main: $19* ⊠ *243 11th St.* ☎ *503/325–1787* ⊕ *www.astoriacoffeehouse.com.*

$ ✕**Blue Scorcher Bakery Café.** "Joyful work, delicious food, and strong
CAFÉ   community" is this family-friendly café's rallying cry. It serves every-
FAMILY   thing from *huevos scorcheros* (poached eggs with rice, beans, cheese,
and salsa) and organic, handcrafted breads to a variety of foods using
local, fair trade, and organic ingredients. **Known for:** vegan and gluten-
free options; children's play area. $ *Average main: $8* ✉ *1493 Duane
St.* ☎ *503/338–7473* ⊕ *www.bluescorcher.com* ☻ *No dinner.*

$$ ✕**Bridgewater Bistro.** In the same complex as the Cannery Pier Hotel,
PACIFIC   this stylish restaurant has great views of the river and bridge to Wash-
NORTHWEST   ington. Inside, high ceilings are supported by ancient fir timbers, and an
extensive menu is strong on creative seafood and meat grills, including
roasted spice-encrusted duck breast with orange marmalade glaze, and
seared wild local salmon with an arugula-strawberry salad and a star
anise–balsamic vinaigrette. **Known for:** Sunday brunch; Columbia River
views. $ *Average main: $22* ✉ *20 Basin St., Suite A* ☎ *503/325–6777*
⊕ *www.bridgewaterbistro.com.*

$ ✕**Buoy Beer Co.** One of the most acclaimed craft brewers on the coast,
AMERICAN   Buoy Beer also serves exceptionally tasty contemporary pub fare in its
warm and inviting taproom, set in a converted 1920s grain warehouse
on the Astoria's riverfront walk—huge windows afford dramatic views
of the Columbia. Seafood figures prominently in many dishes here,
including rockfish-and-chips and bacon-clam chowder, but you'll also
find delicious burgers and meat and cheese boards. **Known for:** hoppy
handcrafted IPAs and strong German-style beers; river views. $ *Average
main: $15* ✉ *1 8th St.* ☎ *503/325–4540* ⊕ *www.buoybeer.com.*

$ ✕**Columbian Cafe & Voodoo Room.** Locals love this funky diner-and-
ECLECTIC   nightclub complex that defies categorization by offering inventive, fresh
seafood, spicy vegetarian dishes, and meats cured and smoked on the
premises. Located next to the historic Columbian Theater, the café
serves simple food, such as crepes with broccoli, cheese, and home-
made salsa for lunch. **Known for:** cocktails and very good pizza in
the Voodoo Room bar; good people-watching. $ *Average main: $12*
✉ *1114 Marine Dr.* ☎ *503/325–2233* ⊕ *www.columbianvoodoo.com/
cafe* ▭ *No credit cards.*

WHERE TO STAY

$$$$ ⊡ **Cannery Pier Hotel.** From every room in this captivating property
HOTEL   there's a gorgeous view of the mighty Columbia River flowing toward
Fodor'sChoice   the Pacific Ocean, and it's almost hypnotic to watch the tugboats shep-
★   herding barges to and fro. **Pros:** amazing river views; great in-room
amenities; hotel hot tub and day spa. **Cons:** pricey; a bit of a walk from
downtown. $ *Rooms from: $309* ✉ *10 Basin St.* ☎ *503/325–4996,
888/325–4996* ⊕ *www.cannerypierhotel.com* ⊸ *46 rooms, 8 suites*
❙◯❙ *Breakfast.*

$ ⊡ **Clementine's B&B.** This painstakingly restored 1888 Italianate Vic-
B&B/INN   torian home is just a couple of blocks up the hill from Flavel House
Museum and a short walk from several fine restaurants and shops.
Pros: superb, multicourse breakfast included; handy downtown loca-
tion. **Cons:** the traditional lacy room decor isn't for everyone. $ *Rooms
from: $122* ✉ *847 Exchange St.* ☎ *503/325–2005* ⊕ *www.clementines-
bb.com* ⊸ *4 rooms, 1 suite* ❙◯❙ *Breakfast.*

$ HOTEL Fodor's Choice ★ 🏨 **Commodore Hotel.** An economical but stylish downtown boutique hotel, the Commodore has become a favorite with young and artsy souls from Portland and Seattle thanks to its vintage-chic aesthetic, large wall murals and photos, and hip Street 14 Cafe off the lobby. **Pros:** hip ambience; wallet-friendly rates; excellent Street 14 Cafe on-site. **Cons:** least expensive rooms share a bath; simple decor. [$] *Rooms from: $89* ✉ *258 14th St.* ☎ *503/325–4747* 🌐 *www.commodoreastoria.com* 🛏 *18 rooms, 10 with shared bath* 🍴 *No meals.*

$$ HOTEL 🏨 **Hotel Elliott.** This atmospheric, five-story hotel stands in the heart of Astoria's historic district and retains the elegance of yesteryear, updated with modern comforts like cozy underfloor heating in the bathrooms. **Pros:** captures the city's historic ambience beautifully; every effort made to infuse the rooms with upscale amenities; popular wine bar. **Cons:** no on-site dining. [$] *Rooms from: $179* ✉ *357 12th St.* ☎ *503/325–2222* 🌐 *www.hotelelliott.com* 🛏 *21 rooms, 11 suites* 🍴 *Breakfast.*

$ HOTEL 🏨 **Norblad Hotel & Hostel.** Formerly a boardinghouse until its recent renovation, the offbeat Norblad occupies a stately two-story 1920s building a few steps from Fort George Brewery. **Pros:** distinctive and quirky vibe; short walk from downtown shopping and dining; bargain-priced rooms. **Cons:** very basic; front desk isn't staffed overnight; most rooms share a bath. [$] *Rooms from: $69* ✉ *443 14th St.* ☎ *503/325–6989* 🌐 *www.norbladhotel.com* 🛏 *12 rooms with shared bath, 1 suite, 2 hostel rooms* 🍴 *No meals.*

NIGHTLIFE

Fodor's Choice ★ **Fort George Brewery.** The spacious taproom and brewery set in a former 1920s auto showroom has plenty of indoor and outdoor seating where you can sample some of the best craft beers on the coast, including the Belgian-style Quick Wit or the oatmeal-infused Sunrise OPA, a light American pale ale. Plenty of seasonal brews appear on the menu as well, along with tasty pub fare. ✉ *1483 Duane St.* ☎ *503/325–7468* 🌐 *www.fortgeorgebrewery.com.*

Inferno Lounge. Just about every seat in this hip bar situated on a pier that juts into the Columbia River offers stupendous water views. Catch the sunset with a well-crafted cocktail and perhaps a few nibbles—Thai shrimp tacos, pork potstickers—from the tapas menu. This place known for house-infused spirits buzzes until midnight or later. ✉ *77 11th St.* ☎ *503/741–3401.*

SHOPPING

Doe & Arrow. This beautifully curated purveyor of urbane women's and men's fashion as well as arty jewelry, hip home accessories, and eco-friendly grooming products occupies a large corner space in downtown's Historic Astor Hotel building. ✉ *380 14th St.* ☎ *503/741–3132* 🌐 *www.doeandarrow.com.*

Josephson's. One of the Oregon Coast's oldest commercial smokehouses, Josephson's uses alder for all processing and specializes in Pacific Northwest chinook and coho salmon. The mouthwatering fish that's smoked on the premises includes hot smoked pepper or wine-maple salmon, as well as smoked halibut, sturgeon, tuna, oysters, mussels, scallops, and prawns by the pound or in sealed gift packs. ✉ *106 Marine Dr.* ☎ *503/325–2190* 🌐 *www.josephsons.com.*

SEASIDE

12 miles south of Astoria on U.S. 101.

As a resort town, Seaside has somewhat spruced up its kitschy, arcade-filled reputation and now supports a bustling tourist trade, with hotels, condominiums, and restaurants lining a traditional promenade. It still has fun games, candy shops, and plenty of carny noise to appeal to young people, but it has added more in the way of shopping and dining that appeals to adults, and it's home to some of the most affordable lodging options on this stretch of the coast. Only 90 miles from Portland, Seaside is often crowded, so it's not the place to come if you crave solitude. Peak times include mid- to late March, when hordes of teenagers descend on the town during spring break; and late June, when the annual Miss Oregon Pageant is in full swing. Just south of town, waves draw surfers to the Cove, a spot jealously guarded by locals, and the dramatic hike along the Oregon Coast Trail to Tillamook Head connects with Cannon Beach's famous Ecola State Park.

3

GETTING HERE AND AROUND

Seaside is about a 90-minute drive from Portland via U.S 26 and a 20-minute drive south of Astoria on coastal U.S. 101.

VISITOR INFORMATION

Seaside Visitors Bureau. ✉ *7 N. Roosevelt Ave.* ☎ *503/738–3097, 888/306–2326* 🌐 *www.seasideor.com.*

EXPLORING

FAMILY **Seaside Aquarium.** The first thing you hear at this relatively small but fun 1930s-era aquarium is the clapping and barking of the harbor seals just inside the door. Located on the 1½-mile beachfront Promenade, the aquarium has jellyfish, giant king crab, octopus, moray eels, wolf eels, and other sea life swimming in more than 30 tanks. The discovery center draws curious kids and grown-ups alike for its hands-on touch tanks of starfish, anemones, and urchins, as well as for a close-up exploration of the most miniature marine life. No restrooms on-site. ✉ *200 N. Promenade* ☎ *503/738–6211* 🌐 *www.seasideaquarium.com* 🎟 *$8.*

WHERE TO EAT

$ DINER 🍴 **Firehouse Grill.** This bustling diner-style café in a former firehouse in downtown Seaside hits the mark with its hearty breakfast fare, including fluffy biscuits with gravy, cinnamon French toast, meat-loaf scrambles, and a couple of lighter options, such as house-made granola with fresh fruit. The excellent Sleepy Monk coffee from Cannon Beach is served, too, as are eye-opening Bloody Marys. **Known for:** hearty breakfasts; halibut tacos at lunch. [$] *Average main: $10* ✉ *841 Broadway* ☎ *503/717–5502* ⏲ *Closed Tues. and Wed. No dinner.*

$$ HAWAIIAN 🍴 **Lilikoi Grill.** You'll find bamboo mats, tropical plants, and knickknacks at this festive Hawaiian-themed restaurant set amid downtown Seaside's souvenir stores and candy shops. The menu mixes island-inspired recipes with both local and Hawaii ingredients. **Known for:**

Kona coffee–braised short ribs; tropical cocktails. [$] *Average main: $19* ✉ *714 Broadway St.* ☎ *503/738–5232* 🌐 *www.lilikoigrill.com* 🕓 *Closed Tues. and Wed. No lunch.*

SPORTS AND THE OUTDOORS

HIKING

Fodor's Choice ★ **Saddle Mountain State Natural Area.** One of the most accessible mountain peaks in the Coast Range, 3,283-foot Saddle Mountain is reached via a challenging but beautiful 2½-mile climb, with a 1,603-foot elevation gain—the reward, on clear days, is a view of the ocean to the west and the Cascade peaks—including Mt. Hood—far to the east. Wear sturdy shoes, and be prepared for sections with steep upgrades. There's a zippy change in the altitude as you climb higher, but the wildflowers make it all worthwhile. The trailhead is well signed off of U.S. 26, the main highway from Portland to Cannon Beach and Seaside. ✉ *Saddle Mountain Rd., off U.S. 26, 20 miles east of Seaside and 70 miles west of Portland* ☎ *800/551–6949, 503/368–5943* 🌐 *www.oregonstateparks.org.*

Tillamook Head. A moderately challenging 7½-mile loop from U.S. 101, south of Seaside, brings you through lushly forested Elmer Feldenheimer Forest Reserve and into the northern end of Cannon Beach's Ecola State Park to a 900-foot-high viewing point, a great place to see the **Tillamook Rock Light Station,** which stands a mile or so off the coast. The lonely beacon, built in 1881 on a straight-sided rock, towers 41 feet above the ocean and was abandoned in 1957. You can also reach this viewing area by hiking north from Indian Beach in Ecola State Park. ✉ *End of Sunset Blvd.* 🌐 *www.oregonstateparks.org.*

CANNON BEACH

25 miles south of Astoria.

Cannon Beach is a mellow but relatively affluent town where locals and part-time residents—many of the latter reside in Portland—come to enjoy shopping, gallery-touring, and dining, the sea air, and the chance to explore the spectacular state parks at either end of the area: Ecola to the north and Oswald West to the south. Shops and galleries selling surfing gear, upscale clothing, local art, wine, coffee, and candies line Hemlock Street, Cannon Beach's main thoroughfare. In late June the town hosts the Cannon Beach Sandcastle Contest, for which thousands throng the beach to view imaginative and often startling works in this most transient of art forms. On the downside, this so-called Carmel of the Oregon Coast is more expensive and often more crowded than other towns along U.S. 101.

GETTING HERE AND AROUND

It's a 90-minute drive east from Portland on U.S. 26 to reach Cannon Beach, which is a 10-minute drive south of Seaside. To make a scenic loop, consider returning to Portland by way of Astoria and U.S. 30 (about 2¼ hours) or Tillamook and Highway 6 (about 2½ hours).

ESSENTIALS

Visitor Information Cannon Beach Chamber of Commerce. ✉ *207 N. Spruce St.* ☎ *503/436–2623* 🌐 *www.cannonbeach.org.*

EXPLORING

EVOO: Cannon Beach Cooking School. School never tasted this good. EVOO Cooking School performs advanced feats of culinary education for large and small groups, set around seasonal or specific food themes. EVOO holds cooking demonstrations, or you can sign up for hands-on courses—both always based on what's local, in season, and tantalizing. They call them dinner shows for a reason: whether or not you remember how to duplicate these recipes at home, you'll have a great time sampling them here. Classes start at $79 per person and include a full meal, with wine pairings for the dinner classes. ⊠ *188 S. Hemlock St.* ☎ *503/436–8555, 877/436–3866* ⊕ *www.evoo.biz.*

Fodor's Choice
★
Haystack Rock. Towering over the broad, sandy beach is a gorgeous, 235-foot-high dome that is one of the most photographed natural wonders on the Oregon Coast. For safety and to protect birding habitats, people are not allowed to climb on the rock, but you can walk right up to its base at low tide. ⊠ *Access beach from end of Gower St.*

WHERE TO EAT

$$
IRISH
Fodor's Choice
★
✕ **Irish Table.** Adjacent to the Sleepy Monk café, this cozy restaurant with a timber-beam ceiling and warm lighting serves seasonal food with an Irish twist, such as potato-kale soup and its heralded Irish lamb stew. Other offerings include a perfect steak and delicate fresh halibut. **Known for:** Irish whiskey selection; friendly service; addictive hot soda bread. $ *Average main: $19* ⊠ *1235 S. Hemlock St.* ☎ *503/436–0708* ⊙ *Closed Wed. and Jan. No lunch.*

$
CAFÉ
✕ **Sleepy Monk.** In a region renowned for artisan coffee, this small roaster brews some of the best espresso and coffee drinks in the state. Sleepy Monk attracts java aficionados on caffeine pilgrimages from near and far eager to sample its certified-organic, fair-trade beans. **Known for:** outstanding coffee. $ *Average main: $5* ⊠ *1235 S. Hemlock St.* ☎ *503/436–2796* ⊕ *www.sleepymonkcoffee.com* ⊙ *Closed Wed. No dinner.*

$$$$
PACIFIC
NORTHWEST
Fodor's Choice
★
✕ **Stephanie Inn Dining Room.** As diners enjoy a romantic view of Haystack Rock, this luxe hotel's sophisticated, supremely romantic dining room prepares a new menu nightly, crafting exquisite dinners using fresh, local ingredients. Diners can expect dishes such as cedar plank–roasted salmon, rack of lamb with chanterelle risotto, and a lemon-curd tart with wild berry sauce. **Known for:** one of the best wine lists on the coast; deft and attentive service; spectacular four-course prix-fixe menu option. $ *Average main: $46* ⊠ *2740 S. Pacific St.* ☎ *503/436–2221, 800/633–3466* ⊕ *www.stephanie-inn.com* ⊙ *No lunch.*

$$$
AMERICAN
✕ **Wayfarer Restaurant.** The dazzling beach and ocean views, especially at sunset, are just part of the story at this casually elegant restaurant at the Surfsand Resort; it's also the top destination in town for a leisurely meal of American food, including plenty of local seafood options, such as sesame-breaded Pacific razor clams with jalapeño-lime jelly, and Oregon-hazelnut-seared sole with a berry beurre blanc. If fish isn't your game, consider the prodigious 22-ounce "tomahawk" rib-eye steak with a Cabernet butter. **Known for:** juicy steaks; razor clams; delicious crab cakes. $ *Average main: $29* ⊠ *1190 Pacific Dr.* ☎ *503/436–1108* ⊕ *www.wayfarer-restaurant.com.*

WHERE TO STAY

$ **Ecola Creek Lodge.** With a quiet, shady courtyard just off the main
HOTEL   road leading into the north side of town, this small, reasonably priced
1940s hotel offers 22 suites and rooms with a mix of configurations,
from two-bedroom units with kitchens to cozy standard rooms. **Pros:**
quiet setting; rooms come in wide range of layouts; good value. **Cons:**
not on the beach; slight walk from downtown shopping. $ *Rooms
from: $136* ⊠ *208 5th St.* ☎ *503/436–2776, 800/873–2749* ⊕ *www.
ecolacreeklodge.com* ↘ *9 rooms, 13 suites* ❘○❘ *No meals.*

$$$$ **Ocean Lodge.** Designed to capture the feel of a 1940s beach resort, this
RESORT   rustic but upscale lodge is perfect for special occasions and romantic getaways. **Pros:** beachfront location; spacious rooms; warm cookies delivered to rooms. **Cons:** expensive; balconies are shared with neighboring
rooms. $ *Rooms from: $289* ⊠ *2864 S. Pacific St.* ☎ *503/436–2241,
888/777–4047* ⊕ *www.theoceanlodge.com* ↘ *45 rooms* ❘○❘ *Breakfast.*

$$$$ **Stephanie Inn.** One of the coastline's most beautiful views is paired
RESORT   with one of its most splendid hotels, where the focus is firmly on
Fodor's Choice   romance, superior service, and luxurious rooms. **Pros:** incredibly plush
★   accommodations; lots of little extras included; top-notch service. **Cons:**
among the highest rates of any hotel in the state; not for families with
younger children; some minimum-night stay requirements. $ *Rooms
from: $479* ⊠ *2740 S. Pacific St.* ☎ *503/436–2221, 800/633–3466*
⊕ *www.stephanie-inn.com* ↘ *27 rooms, 14 suites* ❘○❘ *Breakfast.*

$ **Tolovana Inn.** Set on the beach at the quieter southern end of town,
HOTEL   the large, rambling Tolovana Inn is one of the better-priced options in
FAMILY   this tony seaside community, especially considering that most rooms
enjoy partial or full views of the Pacific. **Pros:** panoramic beach views;
good mix of layouts and room sizes; some units have kitchens. **Cons:**
a 10-minute drive from downtown shops; some rooms are relatively
small; economy rooms have no water view. $ *Rooms from: $134*
⊠ *3400 S. Hemlock St.* ☎ *503/436–2211, 800/333–8890* ⊕ *www.
tolovanainn.com* ↘ *74 rooms, 103 suites* ❘○❘ *No meals.*

SHOPPING

Cannon Beach Art Galleries. The numerous art galleries that line Cannon Beach's Hemlock Street are an essential part of the town's spirit
and beauty. A group of about a dozen galleries featuring beautifully
innovative works in ceramic, bronze, photography, painting, and other
mediums have collaborated to form the Cannon Beach Gallery Group.
You'll find information about exhibits and special events on the website.
⊠ *Hemlock St.* ⊕ *cbgallerygroup.com.*

SPORTS AND THE OUTDOORS
BEACHES

FAMILY   **Cannon Beach and Ecola State Park.** Beachcombers love Cannon Beach for
Fodor's Choice   its often low foamy waves and the wide stretch of sand that wraps the
★   quaint community, making it ideal for fair-weather play or for hunting down a cup of coffee and strolling in winter. This stretch can get
feisty in storms, however, which also makes Cannon Beach a good
place to curl up indoors and watch the show. Haystack Rock rises
235 feet over the beach on the south side of downtown, one of 1,853
protected rocks that's part of the Oregon Ocean Island Wildlife Refuge,

providing a nesting habitat for birds. Continue south past Tolovana Park—a playground located in the flood plain—to find the quiet side of Cannon Beach with a bevy of tide pools and few other souls. To the north of town, the beach gives way to Ecola State Park, a breathtakingly beautiful series of coves and rocky headlands where William Clark spotted a beached whale in 1806 and visitors still come to view them offshore during the twice-yearly migrations. From here, Sitka spruce and barbecues feature along the sands. There are a few excellent trails that hug the sometimes steep cliffs that rise above sand, including a 6½-mile trail first traced by Lewis and Clark, which runs from this spot past the Tillamook Head lookout and all the way to Seaside. **Amenities:** parking; toilets. **Best for:** partiers; sunset; walking. ⊠ *Ocean Ave.* ☎ *503/436–2844, 800/551–6949* ⊕ *oregonstateparks.org* 🖾 *Ecola State Park day use $5 per vehicle.*

MANZANITA

15 miles south of Cannon Beach.

Manzanita is a secluded and gorgeously situated seaside community with only a few more than 500 full-time residents—but a growing following among weekenders from the Willamette Valley means there's one of the highest number of vacation rentals along the northern Oregon Coast here. The village is on a sandy peninsula, peppered with tufts of grass, on the northwestern side of Nehalem Bay, a noted windsurfing destination. It's a fairly laid-back town, but its growing crop of notable restaurants and boutiques has made it increasingly popular with visitors, as does its proximity to beautiful Oswald West State Park.

GETTING HERE AND AROUND

Tiny Manzanita is an easy and picturesque 20-minute drive south of Cannon Beach on coastal U.S. 101; from Portland, it takes just less than two hours to get here.

WHERE TO EAT AND STAY

$$$
MODERN
AMERICAN
Fodor's Choice
★

✕ **Blackbird.** Laid-back and decidedly casual downtown Manzanita received a significant culinary boost with the opening of this sophisticated, locavore-driven bistro. The menu changes often but might feature fried cauliflower with lemon and harissa aioli; ricotta gnocchi with lamb bacon, shaved fennel, basil, and tarragon pesto; or steamed clams with prawns, smoked cippolini onions, and white wine cream—the fresh, uncomplicated food is attractively presented and sings with flavor. **Known for:** dark-chocolate pot de crème; intimate and romantic setting. $ *Average main: $27* ⊠ *503 Laneda Ave.* ☎ *503/368–7708* ⊕ *www. blackbirdmanzanita.com* ⊘ *Closed Sun. No lunch.*

$$
AMERICAN

✕ **Bread and Ocean Bakery.** This small bakery with a simple, cheerful dining room and several more tables on the sunny patio is hugely popular for breakfast and lunch with the many folks who rent cottages in the friendly beach town. Start the morning with slice of quiche or breakfast frittata; tuck into a hefty deli sandwich at lunch. **Known for:** to-go picnic lunches that are great for the beach; craft beers and local wines; decadent cinnamon rolls. $ *Average main: $16* ⊠ *154*

Laneda Ave. ☎ *503/368–5823* 🌐 *www.breadandocean.com* ⏲ *No dinner Sun.–Thurs.*

$ AMERICAN 🍴 **San Dune Pub.** Once a neighborhood dive bar, this 1930s pub has upped its game and become a local magnet for delicious seafood, burgers, sweet-potato fries, grilled-cod tacos, oyster po'boys, and, on Tuesday, baby back ribs. Desserts are worth saving room for here—a few different fresh-fruit and cream pies are always featured. **Known for:** pet-friendly patio; extensive beer selection; live music some evenings. [$] *Average main: $14* ✉ *127 Laneda Ave.* ☎ *503/368–5080* 🌐 *www.sandunepub.com.*

$$ B&B/INN FAMILY 🏨 **Inn at Manzanita.** Shore pines around this 1987 Scandinavian structure give upper-floor patios a tree-house feel, and it's just half a block from the beach. **Pros:** tranquil ambience with a Japanese garden atmosphere; very light and clean; several rooms good for families. **Cons:** two-night minimum stay on weekends; can book up fast in summer. [$] *Rooms from: $179* ✉ *67 Laneda Ave.* ☎ *503/368–6754* 🌐 *www.innatmanzanita.com* 🛏 *13 rooms, 1 suite* 🍽 *No meals.*

SPORTS AND THE OUTDOORS

BEACHES

FAMILY **Manzanita Beach and Nehalem Bay State Park.** The long stretch of white sand that separates the Pacific Ocean from the town of Manzanita is as loved a stretch of coastline as the next, its north side reaching into the shadows of Neahkanie Mountain, right where the mountain puts its foot in the ocean (the mountain itself, which makes for a great hike, lies within Oswald West State Park). The beach is frequented by vacationers, day-trippers, kite flyers, and dogs on its north end, but it extends a breezy 7 miles to the tip of Nehalem Bay State Park, which is accessible on foot over sand or by car along the road. At the south end of the park's parking lot, a dirt horse trail leads all the way to a peninsula's tip, a flat walk behind grassy dunes—you can book horseback rides from **Oregon Beach Rides** (☎ *971/237–6653 www.oregonbeachrides.com*), which has a stable inside the park. Cross to the right for a secluded patch of windy sand on the ocean, or to the left for a quiet, sunny place in the sun on Nehalem Bay, out of the wind. **Amenities:** toilets. **Best for:** sunset; walking. ✉ *Foot of Laneda Ave.* ☎ *503/368–5154, 800/551–6949* 🌐 *www.oregonstateparks.org* 🎟 *Nehalem Bay State Park day use $5 per vehicle.*

RECREATIONAL AREAS

Fodor's Choice ★ **Oswald West State Park.** Adventurous travelers will enjoy a sojourn at one of the best-kept secrets on the Pacific coast, at the base of Neahkahnie Mountain. Park in one of the two free lots on U.S. 101 and hike a half-mile trail to dramatic Short Sand Beach, aka "Shortys," one of the top spots along the Oregon Coast for surfing. It's a spectacular beach with caves and tidal pools. There are several trails from the beach, all offering dazzling scenery; the relatively easy 2½-mile trail to Cape Falcon overlook joins with the Oregon Coast Trail and offers impressive views back toward Shortys Beach. The arduous 5½-mile trail to the 1,680-foot summit of Neahkahnie Mountain (access the trailhead about 2 miles south of the parking lots marked only by a "hikers" sign, or get there via Short Sand Beach) provides dazzling views south for many miles toward the surf, sand, and mountains fringing Manzanita and, in the distance, Tillamook. Come in December or March and you might spot pods of gray whales. ⊠ *U.S. 101, 5 miles north of downtown Manzanita, Arch Cape* ☎ *800/551–6949, 503/368–3575* ⊕ *www.oregonstateparks.org* 🎫 *Free.*

HORSEBACK RIDING

FAMILY **Oregon Beach Rides.** Saddle up for horseback rides at Nehalem Bay State Park, available Memorial Day through Labor Day weekends. Guides take you on a journey along the beach in Manzanita, and reserved rides can last from one to several hours. There's even a romantic sunset trot. It's appropriate for ages six and up. ⊠ *Nehalem Bay State Park, 9500 Sandpiper La., Nehalem* ☎ *971/237–6653* ⊕ *www.oregonbeachrides.com* 🔑 *Reservations essential.*

TILLAMOOK

27 miles south of Manzanita.

More than 100 inches of annual rainfall and the confluence of three rivers contribute to the lush green pastures around Tillamook, probably best known for its thriving dairy industry and cheese factory. The Tillamook County Cheese Factory ships about 50 million pounds of cheese around the world every year. The town itself lies several miles inland from the ocean and doesn't offer much in the way of beachy diversions, but it is the best jumping-off point for driving the dramatic Three Capes Loop, which passes over Cape Meares, Cape Lookout, and Cape Kiwanda and offers spectacular views of the ocean and coastline. The small village of Oceanside, just north of Cape Lookout, has several cute restaurants and shops.

GETTING HERE AND AROUND

Tillamook is a 90-minute drive from Portland on U.S. 26 to Highway 6. It's a winding, pretty, 45-minute drive south of Cannon Beach on U.S. 101, and a one-hour drive north of Lincoln City along the same coastal highway.

VISITOR INFORMATION

Visitor Information Tillamook Coast Tourism. ⊠ *4301 3rd St.* ☎ *503/842–2672, 844/330–6962* ⊕ *www.tillamookcoast.com.*

EXPLORING

FAMILY **Tillamook Cheese Factory.** In high season, hundreds of visitors stop by the largest cheese-making plant on the West Coast to watch the cheese-making process, enjoy free samples, and order delicious ice cream (try the marionberry) from the on-site parlor. Here the rich milk from the area's thousands of Holstein and brown Swiss cows becomes ice cream, butter, and cheddar and Monterey Jack cheeses. The self-guided cheese-making tours don't allow much interaction—you view the operations from a glassed-in mezzanine—but they're free. The store carries a variety of other specialty-food products, including smoked meats, chocolates, jams, and honeys. ⊠ *4175 U.S. 101 N* ☎ *503/815–1300, 800/542–7290* ⊕ *www.tillamookcheese.com.*

Tillamook Naval Air Station Museum. In the world's largest wooden structure, a former blimp hangar south of town displays a fine collection of vintage aircraft from World War II, including a vast trove of artifacts and memorabilia, including war uniforms, photos, and remains from the Hindenburg. The 20-story-high building is big enough to hold half a dozen football fields. ⊠ *6030 Hangar Rd.* ☎ *503/842–1130* ⊕ *www. tillamookair.com* ✉ *$9.50.*

WHERE TO EAT

$$ × **Roseanna's Cafe.** In a rustic 1915 building on the beach, this café is
SEAFOOD right opposite Three Arch Rock, a favorite resting spot for sea lions and puffins. The calm of the beach is complemented in the evening by candlelight and fresh flowers. **Known for:** marionberry cobbler; baked Washington oysters; lovely water views. $ *Average main: $21* ⊠ *1490 Pacific Ave., Oceanside* ☎ *503/842–7351* ⊕ *www.roseannascafe.com.*

SPORTS AND THE OUTDOORS

The **Three Capes Loop**, an enchanting 35-mile byway off U.S. 101, winds along the coast between Tillamook and Pacific City, passing three distinctive headlands—Cape Meares, Cape Lookout, and Cape Kiwanda. Bayocean Road heading west from Tillamook passes what was the thriving resort town of Bayocean, which washed into the sea more than 50 years ago. A road still crosses the levee to Bayocean, and along the beach on the other side you can find the remnants of an old hotel to the north. The panoramic views from the north end of the peninsula are worth the walk. A warm and windless road returns hikers on the bay side.

BEACHES

Oceanside Beach State Recreation Site. This relatively small, sandy cove is a great stop at the midpoint of the cape's loop. It's especially popular with beachcombers in summer for both its shallow, gentle surf and the low-tide bowls and tide pools that make it a great play beach for youngsters. When the water recedes, it also uncovers a tunnel through the north rock face ensconcing the beach, allowing passage to a second, rocky cove. Oceanside's few eateries cater to the crowds: ice cream and quick bites are easily found. Parking in summer, however, is tough. The small lot fills quickly, and a walk through the hilly side streets is sometimes required. **Amenities:** none. **Best for:** walking; partiers. ⊠ *Pacific Ave. at Rosenberg Loop, off Hwy. 131, 3 miles south of Cape Meares, Oceanside* ☎ *800/551–6949, 503/842–3182* ⊕ *www.oregonstateparks.org.*

RECREATIONAL AREAS

Cape Kiwanda State Natural Area. Huge waves pound the jagged sandstone cliffs and caves here, and the much-photographed, 327-foot-high **Haystack Rock** (not to be confused with the 235-foot-tall rock of the same name up in Cannon Beach) juts out of the Pacific Ocean to the south. Surfers ride some of the longest waves on the coast, hang gliders soar above the shore, and beachcombers explore tidal pools and massive sand dunes, and take in unparalleled ocean views. ⊠ *Cape Kiwanda Dr., 1 mile north of Pacific City, Pacific City* ☎ *503/842–3182, 800/551–6949* ⊕ *www.oregonstateparks.org.*

Fodor's Choice **Cape Lookout State Park.** Located about 8 miles south of the beach town
★ Netarts, this park includes a moderately easy (though often muddy)
2-mile trail—marked on the highway as "wildlife viewing area"—that
leads through giant spruces, western red cedars, and hemlocks, and
ends with views of Cascade Head to the south and Cape Meares to
the north. Wildflowers, more than 150 species of birds, and occasional
whales throughout the summer months make this trail a favorite with
nature lovers. The section of the park just north of the trail comprises a
long, curving stretch of beach with picnic areas and campsites. ⊠ *Cape
Lookout Rd. at Netarts Bay Rd.* ☎ *503/842–4981* ⊕ *www.oregonstate-
parks.org* ⊠ *Day use $5.*

Cape Meares State Park. On the northern tip of the Three Capes Loop is
Cape Meares State Park. The restored **Cape Meares Lighthouse,** built
in 1890 and open to the public April through October, provides a
sweeping view over the cliff to the caves and sea lion rookery on the
rocks below. A many-trunked Sitka spruce known as the Octopus Tree
grows near the lighthouse parking lot. ⊠ *3500 Cape Meares Loop, 10
miles west of Tillamook, Oceanside* ☎ *503/842–3182* ⊕ *www.oregon-
stateparks.org* ⊠ *Free.*

PACIFIC CITY

24 miles south of Tillamook.

There's a lot to like about Pacific City, not the least of which is that it's
3 miles off Oregon's busy coastal highway, U.S. 101. That means there's
no backup at the town's only traffic light—a blinking-red, four-way stop
in the center of town. There's just the quiet, happy ambience of a town
whose 1,000-or-so residents live the good life in the midst of extraordinary beauty. There are a few notable dining and hotel options here,
along with some wonderful opportunities for recreation. The beach at
Pacific City is one of the few places in the state where fishing dories
(flat-bottom boats with high, flaring sides) are launched directly into
the surf instead of from harbors or docks. Pacific City's windy climes
tend to keep even the summer months quieter than most.

GETTING HERE AND AROUND
Between Tillamook and Lincoln City, the unincorporated village of
Pacific City is just off U.S. 101 on the south end of the beautiful Three
Capes Loop. It is a two-hour drive from Portland on U.S. 26 to High-
way 6, or a 75-minute drive from Salem via Highway 22.

ESSENTIALS
Visitor Information Pacific City-Nestucca Valley Chamber of Commerce.
☎ *503/392–4340* ⊕ *www.pcnvchamber.org.*

WHERE TO EAT AND STAY
$$ ✕ **Grateful Bread Bakery & Restaurant.** This airy and bright café uses
AMERICAN the cod caught by the local dories for its fish-and-chips. Everything it
FAMILY makes is fresh and from scratch, including delicious breads, pastries,
breakfasts, and pizzas. **Known for:** made-from-scratch pastries; filling
breakfasts of smoked-salmon scrambles and gingerbread pancakes.

[$] *Average main: $16 ⊠ 34805 Brooten Rd. ☎ 503/965–7337 ⊕ www. gratefulbreadbakery.com ⊗ Closed Tues. and Wed. No dinner Mon.*

$ ✕ **Pelican Pub & Brewery.** This beer-lover's favorite stands on the ocean-

AMERICAN   front by Haystack Rock. The microbrewery has garnered consider-

FAMILY   able kudos for its beers, including the Kiwanda Cream Ale and deep, rich Tsunami Stout, while the pub excels with creative comfort fare. **Known for:** occasional brewers dinner with international food and house beer pairings; good children's menu; root beer floats. [$] *Average main: $15 ⊠ 33180 Cape Kiwanda Dr. ☎ 503/965–7007 ⊕ www. pelicanbrewing.com.*

$$$ 🏨 **Inn at Cape Kiwanda.** You won't find a weather-beaten beach cottage

RESORT   here—each of the 35 deluxe, fireplace-warmed rooms has a gorgeous view of Haystack Rock. **Pros:** great views; light and contemporary rooms; terrific restaurants nearby. **Cons:** some rooms have only par-tial water views. [$] *Rooms from: $219 ⊠ 33105 Cape Kiwanda Dr. ☎ 888/965–7001, 503/965–7001 ⊕ www.yourlittlebeachtown.com/inn ↪ 33 rooms, 2 suites ⊙ No meals.*

SPORTS AND THE OUTDOORS

BEACHES

Fodor's Choice   **Pacific City beach.** The town's public beach sits between Cape Kiwanda

★   State Natural Area and Bob Straub State Park. Adjacent to Cape Kiwan-da's massive 240-foot-tall dune, it's a favorite for kids who often climb its bulk just for the thrill of sliding back down again. Hikers also get a thrill from the top, where the view opens on a tiny cove and tide pools below, and the walk down is infinitely easier than the climb. The beach is also popular with tailgaters—it's one of the few places on the Oregon Coast where it's legal to park your vehicle on the sand. Other parking is available off Cape Kiwanda Drive, near the Pelican Pub. For quieter outings, try the Bob Straub. **Amenities:** none. **Best for:** partiers; walking. ⊠ *Cape Kiwanda Dr. ⊕ www.pcnvchamber.org.*

RECREATIONAL AREAS

Fodor's Choice   **Bob Straub State Park.** An often sand-blasting walk along the flat white-

★   sand beach leads down to the mouth of the Nestucca River, considered by many to be the best fishing river on the north coast. The beach along the Pacific is frequently windy, but it's separated from the stiller, warmer side of the peninsula by high dunes. Multiple trails cross the dunes into a forest that leads to small beaches on the Nestucca. Relax here with a book, and easily find stillness and sunshine. It's possible to skip the Pacific stroll all together, and find trails to the Nestucca straight from the parking lot, but it's hard to resist the views from the top of the dunes at the Bob Straub. If you choose the ocean side, pitch your beach-camp in the dunes, not the flat sand, and you'll find respite from the some-times unrelenting wind. ⊠ *Sunset Dr., just south of where Pacific Ave. crosses river ☎ 503/842–3182 ⊕ www.oregonstateparks.org.*

CENTRAL COAST

This is Oregon's coastal playland, drawing families, shoppers, kite flyers, deep-sea fishing enthusiasts, surfers, and dune-shredding daredevils. Although it's a bit touristy and bisected by a rather tatty commercial stretch of U.S. 101, Lincoln City offers a wealth of shops devoted to souvenirs and knickknacks, and visitors can even blow their own glass float at a few local studios. Depoe Bay is popular for whale-watching excursions, and Newport is designated the Dungeness crab capital of the world. As you venture farther south, you'll roll through gorgeous and less developed Yachats and charming Florence to reach the iconic mountains of sand that fall within Oregon Dunes National Recreation Area. Even if you're not intent on making tracks in the sand, the dunes provide vast, unforgettable scenery.

LINCOLN CITY

16 miles south of Pacific City; 90 miles southwest of Portland.

Lincoln City is a captivating destination for families and couples who want to share some time laughing on the beach, poking their fingers in tide pools, and trying to harness wind-bucking kites. Once a series of small villages, Lincoln City is a sprawling town without a center. But the endless tourist amenities make up for a lack of a small-coastal-town ambience. Clustered like barnacles on the offshore reefs are fast-food restaurants, gift shops, supermarkets, candy stores, antiques markets, dozens of motels and hotels, a factory-outlet mall, and a busy casino. Lincoln City is the most popular destination city on the Oregon Coast, but its only real geographic claim to fame is the 445-foot-long D River, stretching from its source in Devil's Lake to the Pacific; *Guinness World Records* lists the D as the world's shortest river.

GETTING HERE AND AROUND

Lincoln City is a 2-hour drive from Portland on Highway 99W and Highway 18, and a 2½-hour drive south of Astoria along coastal U.S. 101.

ESSENTIALS

Visitor Information Lincoln City Visitors & Convention Bureau. ✉ *801 S.W. U.S. 101, Suite 401* ☎ *541/996–1274, 800/452–2151* 🌐 *www.oregoncoast.org.*

WHERE TO EAT

$$$$ PACIFIC NORTHWEST

🍴 **Bay House.** Inside a charming bungalow, this restaurant serves meals to linger over while you enjoy views across sunset-gilded Siletz Bay. The seasonal Pacific Northwest cuisine includes Dungeness crab cakes with roasted-chili chutney, fresh halibut Parmesan, and roast duckling with cranberry compote. **Known for:** extensive wine list; impeccable service. [$] *Average main: $35* ✉ *5911 S.W. U.S. 101* ☎ *541/996–3222* 🌐 *www.thebayhouse.org* 🕒 *Closed Mon. and Tues. No lunch.*

$$ SEAFOOD Fodor's Choice ★

🍴 **Blackfish Café.** Owner and chef Rob Pounding serves simple-but-succulent dishes that blend fresh ingredients from local fishermen and gardeners. His skillet-roasted, "ocean trolled" chinook salmon, basted with fennel lime butter, and Oregon blue-cheese potatoes are flavorful

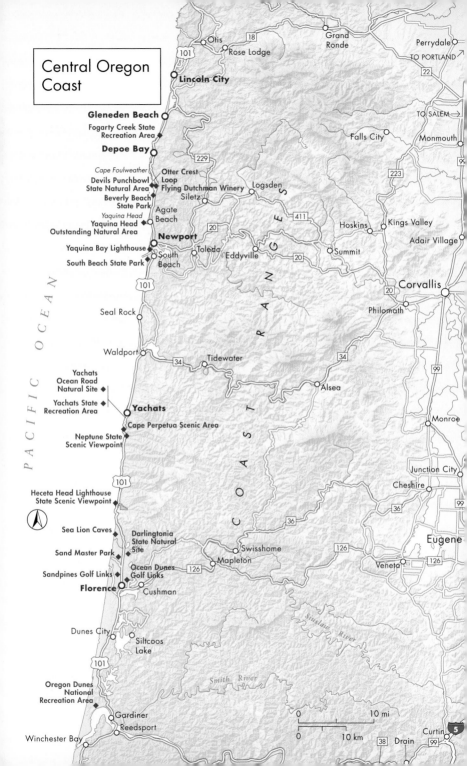

Central Oregon Coast

18
101 Otis
Rose Lodge
Grand Ronde
Perrydale
TO PORTLAND
22
Lincoln City

TO SALEM →

Gleneden Beach
Fogarty Creek State
Recreation Area
Falls City
Monmouth

Depoe Bay
229
223

Cape Foulweather
Otter Crest
Loop
Logsden
411

Devils Punchbowl
State Natural Area
Flying Dutchman Winery
Hoskins
Kings Valley

Beverly Beach
State Park
Siletz
Adair Village

Yaquina Head
Agate
Beach
20

Yaquina Head
Outstanding Natural Area
Summit

Newport
20

Yaquina Bay Lighthouse
Toledo
Eddyville
20
Corvallis

South Beach State Park
South
Beach
20

101
Philomath

Seal Rock

Waldport
Tidewater
34
99

Yachats
Ocean Road
Natural Site
34
Alsea

Yachats State
Recreation Area
Yachats

Cape Perpetua Scenic Area
Monroe

Neptune State
Scenic Viewpoint

101
Junction City

Heceta Head Lighthouse
State Scenic Viewpoint
Cheshire
99

36
36

Sea Lion Caves
Swisshome
126
Eugene

Darlingtonia
State Natural
Site
Mapleton
Veneta
126

Sand Master Park
126

Sandpines Golf Links
Ocean Dunes
Golf Links

Florence
Cushman

Dunes City
Siltcoos
Lake
Siuslaw River

101
Smith River

Oregon Dunes
National
Recreation Area
0   10 mi

Gardiner
0   10 km

Reedsport
38
Drain
99

Winchester Bay
Curtin

5

C O A S T   R A N G E S

P A C I F I C   O C E A N

and perfect. **Known for:** chinook salmon; Ding Dong dessert. $ *Average main: $22* ✉ *2733 N.W. U.S. 101* ☎ *541/996–1007* ⊕ *www.blackfish-cafe.com* ⊙ *Closed Tues.*

$ ✕ **Hearth & Table Kitchen.** The fragrant dishes at this artisan bakery and
AMERICAN   pizzeria look as delicious as they taste—bountiful salads and hefty sand-wiches packed with seasonal ingredients; crispy-crust pizzas crowned with roasted tomatoes, dry-cured salami, pickled jalapenos, and other gourmet ingredients; and fluffy cakes and cupcakes piled high with rich icing. It's a simple, cheerful space: you order at the counter and take a seat at one of the plain wooden tables. **Known for:** creatively topped pizzas; decadent desserts; good beer and wine selection. $ *Average main: $15* ✉ *660 S.E. U.S. 101* ☎ *541/614–0966* ⊕ *www.hearthand-tablekitchen.com* ⊙ *Closed Sun. and Mon.*

$ ✕ **Puerto Vallarta.** Decorated with colorful tapestries and hand-painted
MEXICAN   booths depicting whimsical scenes of Mexico, this festive restaurant consistently prepares some of the best Mexican fare on the coast. Dishes ranges from fairly authentic (tongue tacos, carne asada) to those geared toward American tastes (fajitas, burgers). **Known for:** tortas and tacos; fresh-fruit margaritas. $ *Average main: $12* ✉ *3001 U.S. 101* ☎ *541/994–0300.*

WHERE TO STAY

$ ⌂ **Coho Oceanfront Lodge.** Set on a romantic cliff, the renovated Coho is
HOTEL   a perfect hybrid of family-friendly lodging and a quiet, intimate hide-
FAMILY   away for couples. **Pros:** great value; family-friendly; lots of nice in-room
Fodor'sChoice   amenities. **Cons:** no restaurant. $ *Rooms from: $145* ✉ *1635 N.W.*
★   *Harbor Ave.* ☎ *541/994–3684, 800/848–7006* ⊕ *www.thecoholodge. com* ⇆ *33 studios, 32 suites* ⦿ *Breakfast.*

$ ⌂ **Historic Anchor Inn.** This quirky bungalow might not be for everyone,
B&B/INN   but for those who appreciate a warm, spirited inn with a decidedly inventive and whimsical touch, this is a remarkable find. **Pros:** a memo-rable, truly unique property; everything you need to explore Lincoln City. **Cons:** not on the beach; very quirky and rustic. $ *Rooms from: $99* ✉ *4417 S.W. U.S. 101* ☎ *541/996–3810* ⊕ *www.historicanchorinn. com* ⇆ *19 rooms* ⦿ *Breakfast.*

$$$ ⌂ **Inn at Spanish Head.** Driving up to this upscale resort hotel, you'd
RESORT   think it might be a fairly intimate place, but on further investigation you'll see that the property takes up the entire side of a bluff like a huge staircase. **Pros:** sweeping views of the ocean through floor-to-ceiling windows; good restaurant; easy beach access via elevator; great place to watch winter storms. **Cons:** pricey; isolated setting not within walking distance of many restaurants or shops. $ *Rooms from: $209* ✉ *4009 S.E. U.S. 101* ☎ *541/996–2161, 800/452–8127* ⊕ *www.spanishhead. com* ⇆ *68 rooms, 52 suites* ⦿ *Some meals.*

$$ ⌂ **Surftides.** Built in the 1940s and given a retro-cool makeover in recent
HOTEL   years, this angular five-story hotel enjoys direct access to a wide expanse of beach and is within walking distance of several restaurants along U.S. 101. **Pros:** ocean views; distinctive whimsical decor; good on-site restau-rant. **Cons:** not everybody will appreciate the quirky decor. $ *Rooms from: $179* ✉ *2945 N.W. Jetty Ave.* ☎ *541/994–2191, 800/452–2159* ⊕ *www.surftideslincolncity.com* ⇆ *153 rooms* ⦿ *No meals.*

NIGHTLIFE

Chinook Winds Casino Resort. Oregon's only beachfront casino has a great variety of slot machines, blackjack, poker, keno, and off-track betting. The Rogue River Steakhouse serves a great fillet and terrific appetizers. There's also the Siletz Bay Buffet, the Chinook Seafood Grill, a snack bar, and a lounge. An arcade keeps the kids busy while you are on the gambling floor. Big-name entertainers perform in the showroom. Players can take a break from the tables and enjoy a round of golf at the Chinook Winds Golf Resort next door. ⊠ *1777 N.W. 44th St.* ☎ *541/996–5825, 888/244–6665* ⊕ *www.chinookwindscasino.com.*

SHOPPING

Fodor's Choice
★

Alderhouse Glassblowing. The imaginative crafts folk at this studio turn molten glass into vases and bowls, which are available for sale. It is the oldest glass-blowing studio in the state. ⊠ *611 Immonen Rd.* ☎ *541/996–2483* ⊕ *www.alderhouse.com.*

Culinary Center. Whether she's conducting a small, hands-on class or orchestrating a full-blown cooking demonstration for dozens, executive chef Sharon Wiest loves sharing her passion for Pacific Northwest ingredients. The classes, some of which are led by other noted chefs in the area, offer all sorts of culinary adventures, from baking pizza to making sushi. ⊠ *801 S.W. U.S. 101, Suite 401* ☎ *541/557–1125* ⊕ *www.oregoncoast.org/culinary.*

Jennifer L. Sears Glass Art Studio. Blow a glass float or make a glorious glass starfish, heart, or fluted bowl of your own design (prices start at $65 for a glass float). The studio's expert artisans will guide you every step of the way. It's a fun, memorable keepsake of the coast. ⊠ *4821 S.W. U.S. 101* ☎ *541/996–2569* ⊕ *www.jennifersearsglassart.com.*

Lincoln City Surf Shop. Darn right they surf on the Oregon Coast. Maybe the surfers are dressed from head to toe in wet suits, but they're riding some tasty waves just the same. At Lincoln City's oldest surf shop there's equipment and apparel for purchase or rent. Lessons provide a great family activity, and rates include board, wet suits, hood, and booties. The shop also has a collection of kiteboards, skimboards, and skateboards. ⊠ *4792 S.E. U.S. 101* ☎ *541/996–7433* ⊕ *www.lcsurf-shop.com.*

SPORTS AND THE OUTDOORS

BOATING

Devil's Lake State Recreation Area. Canoeing and kayaking are popular on this small lake just inland from the coast, also loved by coots, loons, ducks, cormorants, bald eagles, and grebes. Visitors can sign up in advance for popular kayaking tours in the summer, for which bird guides are provided. A campground has tent and RV sites as well as yurts. ⊠ *N.E. 6th St., just east of U.S. 101* ☎ *541/994–2002, 800/551–6949* ⊕ *www.oregonstateparks.org.*

OFF THE
BEATEN
PATH

Nature Conservancy Cascade Head Preserve and trail. This dense, green trail winds through a rain forest where 100-inch annual rainfalls nourish 250-year-old Sitka spruces, mosses, and ferns. Emerging from the forest, hikers come upon grassy and treeless Cascade Head, an undulating maritime prairie. There are magnificent views down to the Salmon

River and east to the Coast Range. Continuing along the headland, black-tailed deer often graze and turkey vultures soar in the strong winds. You need to be in fairly good shape for the first and steepest part of the hike, which can be done in about an hour (it's a little over 4 miles round-trip). The 270-acre area has been named a United Nations Biosphere Reserve. ⊠ *Savage Rd. at Headland Circle, 9 miles north of Lincoln City via U.S. 101, Otis* ⊕ *www.nature.org* ✉ *Free* ☉ *Upper trail closed Jan.–mid-July.*

GLENEDEN BEACH

7 miles south of Lincoln City.

Gleneden Beach is a small vacation town known primarily for the famed Salishan Resort, which is perched high above placid Siletz Bay. This expensive collection of guest rooms, vacation homes, condominiums, restaurants, golf fairways, tennis courts, and covered walkways blends into a forest preserve; if not for the signs, you'd scarcely be able to find it.

GETTING HERE AND AROUND

Little Gleneden Beach is a 10-minute drive south of Lincoln City via U.S. 101.

WHERE TO EAT AND STAY

$$$
PACIFIC
NORTHWEST
✕ **Side Door Café.** This dining room, set in an old brick and tile factory with a high ceiling, exposed beams, a fireplace, and many windows, shares its space with Eden Hall performance venue. The menu changes often—fresh preparations have included fire-roasted rack of lamb with vegetable risotto and Northwest bouillabaisse with a lemongrass-saffron-tomato broth. **Known for:** funky and historic industrial setting; creatively prepared seasonal cuisine. $ *Average main: $28* ⊠ *6675 Gleneden Beach Loop Rd.* ☎ *541/764–3825* ⊕ *www.sidedoorcafe.com* ☉ *Closed Mon. and Tues.*

$$
RENTAL
FAMILY
🏠 **Beachcombers Haven vacation rentals.** This cluster of properties is right off the beach, and features spacious one-, two-, or three-bedroom accommodations, some with a hot tub or in-room Jacuzzi. **Pros:** very friendly; well-equipped units with full kitchens; near the beach. **Cons:** some decor is a bit dated; two-night minimum. $ *Rooms from: $189* ⊠ *7045 NW Glen* ☎ *541/764–2252, 800/428–5533* ⊕ *www.beachcombershaven.com* ⇴ *14 units* ❏ *No meals.*

$$$
RESORT
🏠 **Salishan Lodge and Golf Resort.** Secluded and refined, this upscale resort in a hillside forest preserve has long been revered as a luxury weekend getaway as well as a destination for tony corporate retreats, with plenty of reasons to stay on the property. **Pros:** very elegant; secluded resort with a terrific golf course; plenty of activities on the property. **Cons:** ocean views are few; service a bit hit-or-miss considering the steep prices. $ *Rooms from: $229* ⊠ *7760 N. U.S. 101* ☎ *541/764–3600, 800/452–2300* ⊕ *www.salishan.com* ⇴ *205 rooms* ❏ *No meals.*

SPORTS AND THE OUTDOORS

GOLF

Salishan Golf Resort. With a layout designed by Peter Jacobsen, this par-71 course is a year-round treat for hackers and aficionados alike. The front nine holes are surrounded by a forest of old-growth timber, while the back nine holes provide old-school, links-style play. There's an expansive pro shop and a great bar and grill for relaxing after a "rough" day out on the links. High-season greens fees are $99–$119. ✉ 7760 N. U.S. 101 ☎ 541/764–3600, 800/452–2300 ⊕ www.salishan.com.

DEPOE BAY

5 miles south of Gleneden Beach.

Depoe Bay calls itself the whale-watching capital of the world. The small town was founded in the 1920s and named in honor of Charles DePoe of the Siletz tribe, who was named for his employment at a U.S. Army depot in the late 1800s. With a narrow channel and deep water, its tiny harbor is also one of the most protected on the coast. It supports a thriving fleet of commercial and charter fishing boats. The Spouting Horn, a natural cleft in the basalt cliffs on the waterfront, blasts seawater skyward during heavy weather.

GETTING HERE AND AROUND

Depoe Bay lies right between Newport and Lincoln City along U.S. 101—it's a 20-minute drive to either town.

ESSENTIALS

Visitor Information **Depoe Bay Chamber of Commerce.** ✉ 223 S.W. U.S. 101, Suite B ☎ 541/765–2889, 877/485–8348 ⊕ www.depoebaychamber.org.

EN ROUTE Five miles south of Depoe Bay off U.S. 101 (watch for signs), the **Otter Crest Loop,** another scenic byway, winds along the cliff tops. Only parts of the loop are open to motor vehicles, but you can drive to points midway from either end and turn around. The full loop is open to bikes and hiking. British explorer Captain James Cook named the 500-foot-high **Cape Foulweather,** at the south end of the loop, on a blustery March day in 1778—a small visitor center and gift shop at this site affords mesmerizing views, and opportunities to spot whales and other marine life. Backward-leaning shore pines lend mute witness to the 100-mph winds that still strafe this exposed spot. At the viewing point at the **Devil's Punchbowl,** 1 mile south of Cape Foulweather, you can peer down into a collapsed sandstone sea cave carved out by the powerful waters of the Pacific. About 100 feet to the north in the rocky tidal pools of the beach known as **Marine Gardens,** purple sea urchins and orange starfish can be seen at low tide. The Otter Crest Loop rejoins U.S. 101 about 4 miles south of Cape Foulweather near **Yaquina Head,** which has been designated an Outstanding Natural Area. Harbor seals, sea lions, cormorants, murres, puffins, and guillemots frolic in the water and on the rocks below the gleaming, white tower of the **Yaquina Bay Lighthouse.**

Salishan Golf Resort, Gleneden Beach

WHERE TO EAT AND STAY

$$$
PACIFIC
NORTHWEST
Fodor's Choice
★

✕ **Restaurant Beck.** Immensely talented chef-owner Justin Wills presents a short but memorable menu of creatively prepared, modern, Pacific Northwest cuisine each night in this romantic, contemporary dining room at the Whale Cove Inn. The menu changes regularly, with chef Wills sourcing largely from local farms, ranches, and fisheries. **Known for:** panoramic views of Whale Cove; exceptional desserts. $ *Average main: $29* ✉ *Whale Cove Inn, 2345 U.S. 101* ☎ *541/765–3220* ⊕ *www. restaurantbeck.com* ☾ *No lunch.*

$$
SEAFOOD

✕ **Tidal Raves Seafood Grill.** An outstanding purveyor of modern seafood fare, Tidal Raves uses local and sustainable fish and shellfish in preparations inspired by places far and near. A few steaks and vegetarian dishes round out the lengthy menu, which also includes such local classics as Dungeness crab cakes, panko-crusted razor clams, and grilled wild salmon. **Known for:** local Dungeness crab cakes; ocean views. $ *Average main: $22* ✉ *279 U.S. 101* ☎ *541/765–2995* ⊕ *www.tidalraves. com.*

$
HOTEL

🏨 **Clarion Surfrider Resort.** The economical Clarion Surfrider Resort comprises a few two-story clapboard buildings perched on a bluff overlooking the ocean and Fogarty Creek State Park. **Pros:** impressive ocean views; reasonable rates; decent seafood restaurant and bar on-site. **Cons:** rooms have pleasant but perfunctory furniture; not within walking distance of town. $ *Rooms from: $142* ✉ *3115 N.W. U.S. 101* ☎ *541/764–2311* ⊕ *www.choicehotels.com* ↘ *55 rooms* ❍❜ *Breakfast.*

$
B&B/INN

🏨 **Depoe Bay Inn.** This pet-friendly bed-and-breakfast overlooking tiny Depoe Bay Harbor provides a dreamy setting for watching boats and relaxing in a quaint atmosphere. **Pros:** intimate and quite; great breakfasts; peaceful and scenic location. **Cons:** on the bay but no beach. [$] *Rooms from: $129* ✉ *235 S.E. Bay View Ave.* ☎ *541/765–2322, 800/228–0448* 🌐 *www.depoebayinn.com* 🛏 *13 rooms* 🍴 *Breakfast.*

$$$$ B&B/INN Fodor's Choice ★ **Whale Cove Inn.** This small and exquisitely decorated high-end inn overlooks the picturesque cove for which it's named and contains just eight spacious suites, each with a dazzling view of the water. **Pros:** astoundingly good restaurant; stunning building with cushy and spacious suites; terrific ocean views. **Cons:** not a good fit for kids (only those 16 and over are permitted); pricey; not within walking distance of town. [$] *Rooms from: $455* ✉ *2345 U.S. 101* ☎ *541/765–4300, 800/628–3409* 🌐 *www.whalecoveinn.com* 🛏 *8 suites* 🍴 *Breakfast.*

SPORTS AND THE OUTDOORS

RECREATIONAL AREAS

Fogarty Creek State Recreation Area. Bird-watching and viewing the tidal pools are the key draws here, but hiking and picnicking are also popular at this park found along U.S. 101. Wooden footbridges wind through the dense forest and tall cliffs rise above the beach. ✉ *U.S. 101, 3 miles north of Depoe Bay* ☎ *800/551–6949, 541/265–4560* 🌐 *www.oregonstateparks.org* 🎟 *Free.*

NEWPORT

12 miles south of Depoe Bay.

Known as the Dungeness crab capital of the world, Newport offers accessible beaches, a popular aquarium, the coast's premier performing-arts center, and a significant supply of both elegant and affordable accommodations and restaurants. Newport exists on two levels: the highway above, threading its way through the community's main business district, and the old Bayfront along Yaquina Bay below (watch for signs on U.S. 101). With its high-masted fishing fleet, well-worn buildings, seafood markets, art galleries, and touristy shops, Newport's Bayfront is an ideal place for an afternoon stroll. So many male sea lions in Yaquina Bay loiter near crab pots and bark from the waterfront piers that locals call the area the Bachelor Club. Visit the docks to buy fresh seafood or rent a kayak to explore the bay. In 2010 Newport was designated the National Oceanic and Atmospheric Administration's (NOAA) Pacific Marine Operations Center and a $38 million, 5-acre facility (and a port for four ships) opened a year later.

GETTING HERE AND AROUND

Newport is a 2½-hour drive from Portland by way of Interstate 5 south to Albany and U.S. 20 west; the town is a 40-minute drive south along U.S. 101 from Lincoln City, and a 75-minute drive north of Florence.

ESSENTIALS

Visitor Information **Destination Newport.** ✉ *555 S.W. Coast Hwy.* ☎ *503/262–8801, 800/262–7844* 🌐 *www.discovernewport.com.*

TOURS

Marine Discovery Tours. Sea-life cruises, priced from $40 and departing throughout the day, are conducted on a 65-foot excursion boat *Discovery*, with inside seating for 49 people and two viewing levels. The cruise season is March through October. ⊠ *345 S.W. Bay Blvd.* ☎ *800/903–2628, 541/265–6200* ⊕ *www.marinediscovery.com* ✉ *From $36.*

EXPLORING

The Flying Dutchman Winery. Occupying a bluff by the sea, this small, family-owned winery on the Otter Crest Loop enjoys one of the most spectacular locations on the Oregon Coast. Owner Danielle Cutler buys grapes from five Oregon vineyards, and brings them over the Coast Range to its salt-air environment for fermenting. Guests can enjoy its eclectic vintages in the cozy tasting room, or take a quick tour of the oak barrels next door. ⊠ *915 1st St., Otter Rock* ☎ *541/765–2553* ⊕ *www.dutchmanwinery.com.*

FAMILY **Hatfield Marine Science Center.** Interactive and interpretive exhibits at Oregon State University appeal to the kid in everyone. More than just showcasing sea life, the center contains exhibits and holds classes that teach the importance of scientific research in managing and sustaining coastal and marine resources. The staff regularly leads guided tours of the adjoining estuary. ⊠ *2030 S. Marine Science Dr.* ☎ *541/867–0100* ⊕ *www.hmsc.oregonstate.edu* ✉ *$5 suggested donation.*

FAMILY **Oregon Coast Aquarium.** This 4½-acre complex brings visitors face to face with the creatures living in offshore and near-shore Pacific marine habitats: frolicking sea otters, colorful puffins, pulsating jellyfish, and even a 60-pound octopus. There's a hands-on interactive area for children, including tide pools perfect for "petting" sea anemones and urchins. The aquarium houses one of North America's largest seabird aviaries, including glowering turkey vultures. Permanent exhibits include Passages of the Deep, where visitors walk through a 200-foot underwater tunnel with 360-degree views of sharks, wolf eels, halibut, and a truly captivating array of sea life. Large coho salmon and sturgeon can be viewed in a naturalistic setting through a window wall 9 feet high and 20 feet wide. The sherbet-colored nettles are hypnotizing. ⊠ *2820 S.E. Ferry Slip Rd.* ☎ *541/867–3474* ⊕ *www.aquarium.org* ✉ *$22.95.*

FAMILY **Yaquina Bay Lighthouse.** The state's oldest wooden lighthouse was only in commission for three years (1871–74), because it was determined that it was built in the wrong location. Today the well-restored lighthouse with a candy-apple top shines a steady white light from dusk to dawn. Open to the public, it is thought to be the oldest structure in Newport, and the only Oregon lighthouse with living quarters attached. ⊠ *S.W. Government St. at S.W. Martin St.* ☎ *541/265–5679* ⊕ *www.yaquina-lights.org* ✉ *Free, donations suggested.*

FAMILY **Yaquina Head Lighthouse.** The tallest lighthouse on the Oregon Coast Fodor's Choice has been blinking its beacon since its head keeper first walked up its ★ 114 steps to light the wicks on the evening of August 20, 1873. Next to the 93-foot tower is an interpretive center. Bring your camera and call ahead to confirm tour times. ⊠ *N.W. Lighthouse Dr., off U.S. 101, 4 miles north of Newport* ☎ *541/574–3100* ⊕ *www.yaquinalights.org* ✉ *Free. Donations suggested.*

Oregon Coast Aquarium, Newport

WHERE TO EAT

$$ SEAFOOD FAMILY Fodor's Choice ★ 🍴 **Georgie's Beachside Grill.** This stand-alone restaurant for the Hallmark Inns and Resorts serves up some wonderfully innovative dishes. From the sea scallops blackened in house-mixed herbs to flame-broiled halibut with pineapple salsa, the food here lives up to the ocean view. **Known for:** ocean views; excellent breakfasts. [$] *Average main: $20* ✉ *744 S.W. Elizabeth St.* ☎ *503/265–9800* 🌐 *www.georgiesbeachsidegrill.com.*

$$ SEAFOOD FAMILY Fodor's Choice ★ 🍴 **Local Ocean Seafoods.** At this fish market and sleek grill on picturesque Yaquina Bay, the operators purchase fish directly from more than 60 boats in the fishing fleet right outside and take the mission of locally sourced, sustainable seafood seriously. This is also one of few restaurants on the Oregon Coast that doesn't own a deep fryer—even the fish-and-chips are panfried. **Known for:** market with fresh-caught seafood to go; outdoor seating overlooking the bay; flavorful and fragrant Fishwives Stew. [$] *Average main: $21* ✉ *213 S.E. Bay Blvd.* ☎ *514/574–7959* 🌐 *www.localocean.net.*

$ CAFÉ 🍴 **Panini Bakery.** The owner, who operates this local favorite bakery and espresso bar, prides himself on hearty and home-roasted meats, hand-cut breads, sourdough pizza, and friendly service. The coffee's organic, the eggs free range, the orange juice fresh-squeezed, and just about everything is made from scratch. **Known for:** made-from-scratch breakfast fare; outdoor seating. [$] *Average main: $8* ✉ *232 N.W. Coast Hwy.* ☎ *541/265–5033* 💳 *No credit cards.*

$$ PACIFIC NORTHWEST 🍴 **Tables of Content.** The well-plotted prix-fixe menu at the restaurant of the outstanding Sylvia Beach Hotel changes nightly. Chances are that the main dish will be fresh local seafood, perhaps a moist grilled salmon fillet in a Dijonnaise sauce, served with sautéed vegetables, fresh-baked breads,

and rice pilaf; a decadent dessert is also included. **Known for:** convivial family-style dining; rich desserts. $\boxed{\$}$ *Average main: $18* ⊠ *267 N.W. Cliff St.* ☎ *541/265–5428, 888/795–8422* ⊕ *www.sylviabeachhotel.com.*

WHERE TO STAY

$$$
HOTEL
Fodor's Choice
★

🏠 **Inn at Nye Beach.** With a prime beachfront location in the historic Nye Beach section of Newport, this chic, eco-friendly, boutique hotel contains 22 rooms and suites. **Pros:** direct beach access and great views; smartly furnished; contemporary rooms. **Cons:** the complimentary breakfast is very limited (a full one costs extra); views not great from some rooms. $\boxed{\$}$ *Rooms from: $216* ⊠ *729 N.W. Coast St.* ☎ *541/265–2477, 800/480–2477* ⊕ *www.innatnyebeach.com* ⤵ *6 rooms, 16 suites* ⦿| *Breakfast.*

$$
B&B/INN

🏠 **Newport Belle B&B.** This fully operational stern-wheeler is permanently moored at the Newport Marina, where guests have front-row seats to all the boating activity around Yaquina Bay. Rooms are cozy and decorated with nautical memorabilia and Victorian-style furnishings. **Pros:** one-of-a-kind lodging experience; great harbor views. **Cons:** not suitable for kids; need a car to get into town. $\boxed{\$}$ *Rooms from: $160* ⊠ *Dock H, 2126 S.E. Marine Science Dr.* ☎ *541/867–6290* ⊕ *www. newportbelle.com* ☾ *Closed Nov.–early Feb.* ⤵ *5 rooms* ⦿| *Breakfast.*

$
HOTEL

🏠 **Sylvia Beach Hotel.** At this offbeat 1913-vintage beachfront hotel, reading, writing, and conversation eclipse technological hotel-room isolation. **Pros:** distinctive decor; great place to disconnect. **Cons:** no TV, telephone, or Internet access; sharing tables with other guests at mealtimes doesn't suit everyone; least expensive rooms don't have ocean views. $\boxed{\$}$ *Rooms from: $130* ⊠ *267 N.W. Cliff St.* ☎ *541/265–5428, 888/795–8422* ⊕ *www.sylviabeachhotel.com* ⤵ *20 rooms* ⦿| *Breakfast.*

NIGHTLIFE AND PERFORMING ARTS

Fodor's Choice
★

Newport Symphony Orchestra. The only year-round, professional symphony orchestra on the Oregon Coast plays at the 400-seat Newport Performing Arts Center, just a few steps away from the seashore in Nye Beach. Adam Flatt is the music director and conductor, and actor and narrator David Ogden Stiers serves as associate conductor. The orchestra performs a popular series of concerts in the Newport Performing Arts Center September through May, and special events in the summer, including its popular free community concert every July 4. ⊠ *777 W. Olive St.* ☎ *541/574–0614* ⊕ *www.newportsymphony.org.*

SPORTS AND THE OUTDOORS

RECREATIONAL AREAS

Beverly Beach State Park. Seven miles north of Newport, this beachfront park extends from Yaquina Head, where you can see the lighthouse, to the headlands of Otter Rock. It's a great place to fly a kite, surf the waves, or hunt for fossils. The campground is well equipped, with a wind-protected picnic area and a yurt meeting hall. ⊠ *N.E. Beverly Dr., off U.S. 101, 6 miles north of Newport* ☎ *541/265–9278, 800/551–6949* ⊕ *www.oregonstateparks.org* ⊞ *Free.*

Devil's Punchbowl State Natural Area. A rocky shoreline separates the day-use area from the surf. It's a popular whale-watching site and has excellent tidal pools. ⊠ *1st St., off U.S. 101, 8 miles north of Newport, Otter Rock* ☎ *541/265–4560, 800/551–6949* ⊕ *www.oregonstateparks.org* ⊞ *Free.*

South Beach State Park. Fishing, crabbing, boating, windsurfing, hiking, and beachcombing are popular activities at this park that begins just across the Yaquina Bay Bridge from Newport and contains a lovely stretch of beach. Kayaking tours are available for a fee. There's a popular campground, too. ⊠ *U.S. 101 S, 3 miles south of Newport* ☎ *541/867–4715, 800/452–5687* ⊕ *www.oregonstateparks.org.*

Yaquina Head Outstanding Natural Area. Thousands of birds—cormorants, gulls, common murres, pigeon guillemots—make their home just beyond shore on Pinnacle and Colony rocks, and nature trails wind through fields of sea grass and wildflowers, leading to spectacular views. There is also an interpretive center and the historic Yaquina Head Lighthouse. ⊠ *750 N.W. Lighthouse Dr.* ☎ *541/574–3100* ⊕ *www.yaquinalights.org* 🎫 *Free; donations suggested.*

YACHATS

24 miles south of Newport.

The small town of Yachats (pronounced "yah-*hots*") is at the mouth of the Yachats River, and from its rocky shoreline, which includes the highest point on the Oregon Coast, trails lead to beaches and dozens of tidal pools. A relaxed alternative to the more touristy communities to the north, Yachats has all the coastal pleasures without the traffic: B&Bs and oceanfront hotels, some terrific restaurants, deserted beaches, tidal pools, surf-pounded crags, fishing, and crabbing.

GETTING HERE AND AROUND
Yachats lies between Newport and Florence on coastal U.S. 101—it's a 40-minute drive from either town, and a three-hour drive via Interstate 5 and Highway 34 from Portland.

ESSENTIALS
Visitor Information Yachats Visitors Center. ⊠ *241 U.S. 101* ☎ *800/929–0477* ⊕ *www.yachats.org.*

WHERE TO EAT

$

BAKERY

✕ **Bread and Roses Baking.** Artisan breads are handmade in small batches here, along with pastries, muffins, scones, cookies, cinnamon rolls, and desserts. In the bright, yellow-cottage bakery you can also try the daily soup and sandwiches at lunchtime, or just while away the morning with pastries and good coffee. **Known for:** proximity to Yachats State Recreation Area; delicious pastries and baked goods. $ *Average main: $9* ⊠ *238 4th St.* ☎ *541/547–4454* ⊘ *No dinner.*

$

SEAFOOD

FAMILY

✕ **Luna Sea Fish House.** The freshest Dungeness crab around is one of the seasonal attractions in this small weathered restaurant, coming straight from owner Robert Anthony's boat—he catches much of the fish served here using sustainable hook-and-line methods for salmon, cod, and albacore tuna. And in season, he pots the crab seen bubbling in outdoor kettles. **Known for:** on-site market with fresh fish; slumgullion (a rich clam-and-shrimp chowder baked with cheese). $ *Average main: $14* ⊠ *153 N.W. U.S. 101* ☎ *541/547–4794, 888/547–4794* ⊕ *www. lunaseafishhouse.com.*

$$ ✕**ONA Restaurant.** Relatively snazzy for such a laid-back town, this
MODERN popular downtown bistro overlooking the confluence of the Yachats
AMERICAN River and the Pacific is nonetheless unpretentious and relaxed. The spe-
cialty is locally and seasonally sourced Oregon seafood (try the sole over
Dungeness crab and bay shrimp with a rosé cream reduction). **Known
for:** sticky toffee pudding; rockfish-and-chips; great regional wine.
$ *Average main: $22* ✉ *131 U.S. 101 N* ☎ *541/547–6627* ⊕ *www.
onarestaurant.com* ◷ *Closed Wed.–Thurs. in winter.*

$ ✕**Yachats Brewing and Farmstore.** Inside this lively establishment with
ECLECTIC pitched timber ceilings, skylights, and a solarium-style beer garden,
Fodor'sChoice you'll find one of the state's most impressive young craft breweries
★ as well as a taproom specializing in house-fermented ingredients—
everything from kimchi to saurkraut. It may sound like a slightly odd
concept, but it works. **Known for:** unusual craft beers and probiotic
drinks; house-fermented foods. $ *Average main: $14* ✉ *348 U.S. 101
N* ☎ *541/547–3884* ⊕ *www.yachatsbrewing.com.*

WHERE TO STAY

$ 🛏 **Deane's Oceanfront Lodge.** This simple single-story, family-run motel
HOTEL is set on a sweeping stretch of beachfront midway between downtown
Yachats and Waldport. **Pros:** charming rooms; motel has direct ocean
views and beach access; reasonable rates. **Cons:** small rooms; not within
walking distance of dining and shopping. $ *Rooms from: $75* ✉ *7365
U.S. 101 N* ☎ *541/547–3321* ⊕ *www.deaneslodge.com* ⤳ *18 rooms.*

$$$ 🛏 **Overleaf Lodge.** On a rocky shoreline at the north end of Yachats,
HOTEL this rambling romantic three-story hotel enjoys spectacular sunsets and
Fodor'sChoice contains splendidly comfortable accommodations. **Pros:** best hotel in
★ one of the coast's best communities; one of the best full-service spas on
the coast. **Cons:** no restaurant; a bit of a walk from the action. $ *Rooms
from: $225* ✉ *280 Overleaf Lodge La.* ☎ *541/547–4885, 800/338–
0507* ⊕ *www.overleaflodge.com* ⤳ *54 rooms, 4 suites* ⫯⊘⫯ *Breakfast.*

$$ 🛏 **SeaQuest Inn.** Friendly and knowledgeable innkeeper Sherwood
B&B/INN Heineman prepares lavish two-course breakfasts as well as an eve-
ning wine-and-cheese hour at this beautifully designed contemporary
B&B situated along a quiet stretch of U.S. 101 with mesmerizing views
of the sea. **Pros:** tranquil setting; smartly furnished rooms; delicious
breakfast included; all rooms have full or partial ocean views. **Cons:**
a 10- to 15-minute drive from the village of Yachats. $ *Rooms from:
$180* ✉ *95354 U.S. 101 S* ☎ *541/547–3782, 800/341–4878* ⊕ *www.
seaquestinn.com* ⤳ *5 rooms, 1 suite* ⫯⊘⫯ *Breakfast.*

SPORTS AND THE OUTDOORS

RECREATIONAL AREAS

Fodor'sChoice **Cape Perpetua Scenic Area.** The highest vehicle-accessible lookout on
★ the Oregon Coast, Cape Perpetua towers 800 feet above the rocky
shoreline. Named by Captain Cook on St. Perpetua's Day in 1778,
the cape is part of a 2,700-acre scenic area popular with hikers, camp-
ers, beachcombers, and naturalists. General information, educational
movies and exhibits, and trail maps are available at the **Cape Perpetua
Visitors Center,** on the east side of the highway, ½ mile south of Devil's
Churn. The easy 1-mile **Giant Spruce Trail** passes through a fern-filled

rain forest to an enormous 600-year-old Sitka spruce. Easier still is the marked Auto Tour; it begins just north of the visitor center and winds through Siuslaw National Forest to the ¼-mile **Whispering Spruce Trail.** Views from the rustic rock shelter here extend 50 miles north to south, and some 40 miles out to sea. For a more rigorous trek, hike the **St. Perpetua Trail** to the shelter. Other trails lead from the visitor center down along the shore, including a scenic pathway to **Devil's Churn,** next to which a small snack bar sells sandwiches, sweets, and coffee. ✉ *2400 U.S. 101, 3 miles south of Yachats* ☎ *541/547–3289* ⊕ *www. fs.usda.gov/siuslaw* 🚗 *Parking fee $5.*

Neptune State Scenic Viewpoint. Visitors have fun searching for animals, watching the surf, or hunting for agates. The benches set above the beach on the cliff provide a great view of Cumming Creek. It's also a terrific spot for whale-watching. At low tide, beachcombers have access to a natural cave and tidal pools. ✉ *U.S. 101, 4 miles south of Yachats* ☎ *800/551–6949, 541/547–3416* ⊕ *www.oregonstateparks.org* 🚗 *Free.*

Yachats Ocean Road State Natural Site. Drive this 1-mile loop just across the Yachats River from downtown Yachats, and discover one of the most scenic viewpoints on the Oregon Coast. Park along Yachats Ocean Road and scamper out along the broad swath of sand where the Yachats River meets the Pacific Ocean. There's fun to be had playing on the beach, poking around tide pools, and watching blowholes, summer sunsets, and whales spouting. ✉ *Yachats Ocean Rd., just south of U.S. 101 bridge over Yachats River* ☎ *800/551–6949, 541/867–7451* ⊕ *www.oregonstateparks.org.*

Yachats State Recreation Area. The public beach in downtown Yachats is more like the surface of the moon than most other places, and certainly most beaches. A wooden platform overlooks the coastline, where the waves roll in sideways and splash over the rocks at high tide. As is the case throughout most of the town, the beach itself is paralleled by an upland walking trail and dotted with picnic tables, benches, and interpretive signs. Visit to spot the sea lions that frequent this stretch of coast. Or join the intrepid beachcombers who climb the rocks for a closer look at tide pools populated by sea urchins, hermit crabs, barnacles, snails, and sea stars. **Amenities:** parking; toilets. **Best for:** walking; sunset. ✉ *Ocean View Dr., off 2nd St. and U.S. 101* ☎ *800/551–6949, 541/867–7451* ⊕ *www.oregonstateparks.org.*

FLORENCE

25 miles south of Yachats; 64 miles west of Eugene.

The closest beach town to Oregon's second-largest city, Eugene, charming and low-keyed Florence delights visitors with its restored riverfront Old Town and proximity to one of the most remarkable stretches of Oregon coastline. Some 75 creeks and rivers empty into the Pacific Ocean in and around town, and the Siuslaw River flows right through the historic village center. When the numerous nearby lakes are added to the mix, it makes for one of the richest fishing areas in Oregon. Salmon, rainbow trout, bass, perch, crabs, and clams are among the water's treasures. Fishing boats and pleasure crafts moor in Florence's harbor,

3

forming a pleasant backdrop for the town's restored buildings. Old Town has notable restaurants, antiques stores, fish markets, and other diversions. South of town, miles of white sand dunes lend themselves to everything from solitary hikes to rides aboard all-terrain vehicles.

GETTING HERE AND AROUND

It's a 75-minute drive west to Florence on Highway 126 from Eugene and a stunningly scenic 40-minute drive south on U.S. 101 from Yachats. It takes about an hour to drive U.S. 101 south to Coos Bay, a stretch that takes in all of Oregon Dunes National Recreation Area.

ESSENTIALS

Visitor Information **Florence Area Chamber of Commerce.** ⊠ *290 U.S. 101* ☎ *541/997–3128* ⊕ *www.florencechamber.com.*

EXPLORING

Darlingtonia State Natural Site. Six miles south of Sea Lion Caves, on the east side of U.S. 101, is an example of the rich plant life found in the marshy terrain near the coast. It's also a surefire child pleaser. A short paved nature trail leads through clumps of insect-catching cobra lilies, so named because they look like spotted cobras ready to strike. This area is most interesting in May, when the lilies are in bloom. ⊠ *U.S. 101, at Mercer Lake Rd.* ☎ *541/997–3851* ⊕ *www.oregonstateparks.org.*

FAMILY **Sea Lion Caves.** In 1880 a sea captain named Cox rowed a small skiff into a fissure in a 300-foot-high sea cliff. Inside, he was startled to discover a vaulted chamber in the rock, 125 feet high and 2 acres in size. Hundreds of massive sea lions—the largest bulls weighing 2,000 pounds or more—covered every available surface. Cox's discovery would become one of the Oregon Coast's premier attractions, if something of a tourist trap. An elevator near the cliff-top ticket office and kitschy gift shop descends to the floor of the cavern, near sea level, where vast numbers of Steller's and California sea lions relax on rocks and swim about (their cute, fuzzy pups can be viewed from behind a wire fence). This is the only known hauling-out area and rookery for wild sea lions on the mainland in the Lower 48, and it's an awesome sight and sound when they're in the cave, typically only in fall and winter (in spring and summer the mammals usually stay on the rocky ledges outside the cave). You'll also see several species of seabirds here, including migratory pigeon guillemots, cormorants, and three varieties of gulls. Gray whales are sometimes visible during their October–December and March–May migrations. ⊠ *91560 U.S. 101* ✛ *10 miles north of Florence* ☎ *541/547–3111* ⊕ *www.sealioncaves.com* ☜ *$14.*

NEED A
BREAK

✕ **Siuslaw River Coffee Roasters.** This small, homey business serves cups of drip-on-demand coffee—you select the roast and they grind and brew it on the spot. Beans are roasted on-site, muffins and breads are freshly baked, and a view of the namesake river can be savored from the deck out back. ⊠ *1240 Bay St.* ☎ *541/997–3443* ⊕ *www.coffeeoregon.com.*

WHERE TO EAT AND STAY

$$ SEAFOOD

🍴 **Bridgewater Fishhouse.** Freshly caught seafood—20 to 25 choices nightly—is the mainstay of this creaky-floored, Victorian-era restaurant in Florence's Old Town. Whether you opt for patio dining during summer or lounge seating in winter, the eclectic fare of pastas, burgers, salads, and seafood-packed stews is consistently well prepared. **Known for:** live music; happy hour deals; lighter fare in Zebra Lounge. [$] *Average main: $19* ✉ *1297 Bay St.* ☎ *541/997–1133* 🌐 *www.bridgewaterfishhouse.com* 🕑 *Closed Tues.*

$ MODERN AMERICAN

🍴 **Homegrown Public House.** This bustling, intimate gastropub in Old Town Florence—a couple of blocks north of the riverfront—specializes in locally sourced, creatively prepared American fare and offers a well-chosen list of Oregon beers on tap, plus local spirits, iced teas, and kombucha. Stop by for lunch to enjoy the lightly battered albacore fish and hand-cut fries with tartar sauce, or a cheeseburger topped with Rogue blue and served with marinated vegetables and local greens. **Known for:** Sunday brunch; daily market fish special. [$] *Average main: $15* ✉ *294 Laurel St.* ☎ *541/997–4886* 🌐 *www.homegrownpub.com* 🕑 *Closed Mon.*

$$ SEAFOOD Fodor's Choice ★

🍴 **Waterfront Depot Restaurant and Bar.** The detailed chalkboard menu says it all: from the fresh, crab-encrusted halibut to classic duck-and-lamb cassoulet to Bill's Flaming Spanish Coffee, this is a place serious about fresh food and fine flavors. Originally located in the old Mapleton train station, moved in pieces and reassembled in Old Town Florence, the atmospheric tavern has a great view of the Siuslaw River and the Siuslaw River Bridge. **Known for:** patio seating on the river; creative daily specials. [$] *Average main: $20* ✉ *1252 Bay St.* ☎ *541/902–9100* 🌐 *www.thewaterfrontdepot.com* 🕑 *No lunch.*

$$$ B&B/INN Fodor's Choice ★

🏨 **Heceta Head Lighthouse B&B.** On a windswept promontory, this unusual late-Victorian property is one of Oregon's most remarkable bed-and-breakfasts; it is located at Heceta Head Lighthouse State Scenic Viewpoint and owned by a certified executive chef. **Pros:** unique property with a magical setting; exceptionally good food. **Cons:** remote location; expensive, especially considering some rooms share a bath; tends to book up well in advance. [$] *Rooms from: $215* ✉ *92072 U.S. 101, 12 miles north of Florence* ☎ *541/547–3696, 866/547–3696* 🌐 *www.hecetalighthouse.com* 🛏 *6 rooms, 4 with bath* 🍽 *Breakfast.*

$ B&B/INN

🏨 **River House Inn.** On the beautiful Siuslaw River, this property has terrific accommodations and is near quaint shops and restaurants in Florence's Old Town. **Pros:** spacious rooms; great views from most rooms; close proximity to dining and shopping. **Cons:** not on the beach. [$] *Rooms from: $119* ✉ *1202 Bay St.* ☎ *541/997–3933, 888/824–2454* 🌐 *www.riverhouseflorence.com* 🛏 *40 rooms* 🍽 *Breakfast.*

SPORTS AND THE OUTDOORS

RECREATIONAL AREAS

Fodor's Choice ★

Heceta Head Lighthouse State Scenic Viewpoint. A ½-mile trail from the beachside parking lot leads to the oft-photographed Heceta Head Lighthouse built in 1894, whose beacon, visible for more than 21 miles, is the most powerful on the Oregon Coast. More than 7 miles of trails traverse the rocky landscape north and south of the lighthouse, which rises some 200 feet above the ocean. For a mesmerizing view of the

Umpqua Sand Dunes in Oregon Dunes National Recreation Area

lighthouse and Heceta Head, pull over at the scenic viewpoint just north of Sea Lion Caves. ⊠ *U.S. 101, 11 miles north of Florence, Yachats* ☎ *541/547–3416, 800/551–6949* ⊕ *www.oregonstateparks.org* ✉ *Day use $5, lighthouse tours free.*

FAMILY
Fodor'sChoice
★

Oregon Dunes National Recreation Area. The Oregon Dunes National Recreation Area is the largest expanse of coastal sand dunes in North America, extending for 40 miles, from Florence to Coos Bay. The area contains some of the best ATV riding in the United States and encompasses some 31,500 acres. More than 1.5 million people visit the dunes each year, and about 350,000 are ATV users. **Honeyman Memorial State Park,** 515 acres within the recreation area, is a base camp for dune-buggy enthusiasts, mountain bikers, hikers, boaters, horseback riders, and dogsledders (the sandy hills are an excellent training ground). There's a campground, too. The dunes are a vast playground for children, particularly the slopes surrounding cool **Cleawox Lake.** If you have time for just a quick scamper in the sand, stop by the Oregon Dunes Overlook off U.S. 101, 11 miles south of Florence and 11 miles north of Reedsport—it's on the west side of the road, just north of Perkins Lake. ⊠ *Office, 855 U.S. 101, Reedsport* ☎ *541/271–6000* ⊕ *www. fs.usda.gov/siuslaw* ✉ *Day use $5.*

FAMILY
Fodor'sChoice
★

Sandland Adventures. This outfitter provides everything you need to get the whole family together for the ride of their lives. Start off with a heart-racing dune-buggy ride with a professional that will take you careening up, over, down, and around some of the steepest sand in the Oregon Dunes National Recreation Area. After you're done screaming and smiling, Sandland's park has bumper boats, a go-kart track, a miniature golf course, and a small railroad. ✉ *85366 U.S. 101* ☎ *541/997-8087* ⊕ *www.sandland.com.*

GOLF

Ocean Dunes Golf Links. A favorite of locals year-round, this course operated by Three Rivers Casino & Hotel is a straightforward 18 holes that reward great shots and penalize the poor ones. You won't find many sand bunkers, because the narrow course is surrounded by sand dunes. Instead, you'll encounter fairways winding about dunes lined with ball-swallowing gorse, heather, shore pines, and native sea grasses. Pot bunkers guard small greens, and play can get pretty frisky if the frequent wind picks up. However, the course is well drained and playable—even under the wettest conditions. ✉ *3345 Munsel Lake Rd.* ☎ *541/997-3232, 877/374-8377* ⊕ *www.threeriverscasino.com/golf* ⌨ *$99* ⚐ *18 holes, 6055 yards, par 71.*

Sandpines Golf Links. This Scottish Links–style course is playable year-round. Designed by Rees Jones, the outward nine is cut out of pine forest and near blue lakes; and the inward nine provides some undulating fun, with the rolling dunes at the forefront from tee to green. While challenging, the course is generous enough to provide a great day on the links for beginners and more polished players. Sandpines has a fully equipped practice area with a driving range, bunkers, and putting greens. ✉ *1201 35th St.* ☎ *800/917-4653, 541/997-1940* ⊕ *www. sandpines.com* ⌨ *$79* ⚐ *18 holes, 7190 yards, par 72.*

HORSEBACK RIDING

FAMILY **C & M Stables.** Ride year-round along the Oregon Dunes National Recreation Area. The area is rich with marine life, including sea lions, whales, and coastal birds. Sharp-eyed riders also might spot bald eagles, red-tailed fox, and deer. Rides range from hour-long trots to half-day adventures. Children must be at least eight years old for the beach ride or six years old for the dune trail rides. ✉ *90241 U.S. 101 N* ☎ *541/997-7540* ⊕ *www.oregonhorsebackriding.com* ⌨ *From $60.*

SANDBOARDING

FAMILY **Sand Master Park.** Everything you need to sandboard the park's private dunes is right here: board rental, wax, eyewear, clothing, and instruction. The staff is exceptionally helpful, and will get beginners off on their sandboarding adventure with enthusiasm. However, what must be surfed must first be hiked up, and so on. ✉ *5351 U.S. 101* ☎ *541/997-6006* ⊕ *www.sandmasterpark.com.*

SOUTHERN COAST

Outdoors enthusiasts find a natural amusement park along this gorgeous stretch of coast from Reedsport to Brookings. The northern portion has a continuation of the Oregon Dunes National Recreation Area, and is the location of its visitor center. The Umpqua Discovery Center is a perfect trip with (or without) the kids, to learn about the region's history and animals. In Bandon golfers flock to one of the most celebrated clusters of courses in the nation at Bandon Dunes. Lovers of lighthouses, sailing, fishing, crabbing, elk viewing, camping, and water sports may wonder why they didn't venture south sooner.

BAY AREA: COOS BAY AND NORTH BEND

27 miles south of Reedsport on U.S. 101.

The Coos Bay–Charleston–North Bend metropolitan area, collectively known as the Bay Area (population 27,000), is the gateway to rewarding recreational experiences. The town of Coos Bay lies next to the largest natural harbor between San Francisco Bay and Seattle's Puget Sound. A century ago, vast quantities of lumber cut from the Coast Range were milled in Coos Bay and shipped around the world. Coos Bay still has a reputation as a rough-and-ready port city, but with mill closures and dwindling lumber reserves it now looks to tourism and other industries for economic growth. The waterfront is now dominated by an attractive boardwalk with interpretive displays, a casino, and the new home of the Coos History Museum, which opened in 2015.

To see the most picturesque part of the Bay Area, head west from Coos Bay on Newmark Avenue for about 7 miles to **Charleston.** Though it's a Bay Area community, this quiet fishing village at the mouth of Coos Bay is a world unto itself. As it loops into town, the road becomes the Cape Arago Highway and leads to several stunning oceanfront parks.

GETTING HERE AND AROUND

The area lies along a slightly inland stretch of U.S. 101 that's a 40-minute drive south of Reedsport and a 30-minute drive north of Bandon; from the Umpqua Valley and Interstate 5 corridor, Coos Bay is just under two hours' drive west from Roseburg on Highway 42.

Southwest Oregon Regional Airport in North Bend has commercial flights from Portland, Denver, and San Francisco.

ESSENTIALS

Visitor Information Coos Bay—North Bend Visitors & Convention Bureau. ⊠ *50 Central Ave., Coos Bay* ☎ *541/269–0215, 800/824–8486* ⊕ *www.oregonsadventurecoast.com.*

EXPLORING

FAMILY **Cape Arago Lighthouse.** On a rock island just offshore from Charleston near Sunset Bay State Park, this lighthouse has had several iterations; the first lighthouse was built here in 1866, but it was destroyed by storms and erosion. A second, built in 1908, suffered the same fate. The current white tower, built in 1934, is 44 feet tall and towers 100 feet above the ocean. If you're here on a foggy day, listen for its unique foghorn. The lighthouse is connected to the mainland by a bridge. Neither is open to the public, but there's an excellent spot to view this lonely guardian and much of the coastline. From U.S. 101, take Cape Arago Highway to Gregory Point, where it ends at a turnaround, and follow the short trail. ⊠ *Cape Arago Hwy., just north of Sunset Bay State Park, Charleston* ⊕ *www.oregonstateparks.org.*

Charleston Marina Complex. At this bustling marina 8 miles west of Coos Bay, there's a launch ramp, a store with tackle and marine supplies, an RV park, a motel, restaurants, and gift shops. Fishing charters also set out from here. ⊠ *63534 Kingfisher Dr., Charleston* ☎ *541/888–2548* ⊕ *www.charlestonmarina.com.*

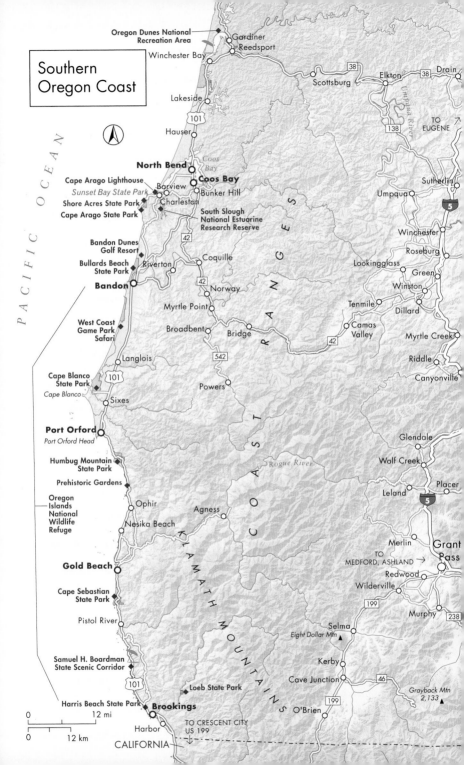

Southern Oregon Coast

PACIFIC OCEAN

Oregon Dunes National Recreation Area
Gardiner
Reedsport
Winchester Bay
Scottsburg
Elkton
Drain
38
38
Lakeside
TO EUGENE
138
101
Hauser
Sutherlin
Coos Bay
North Bend
Cape Arago Lighthouse
Umpqua
Sunset Bay State Park
Barview
Coos Bay
Shore Acres State Park
Charleston
Bunker Hill
5
Cape Arago State Park
South Slough National Estuarine Research Reserve
Winchester
Roseburg
Bandon Dunes Golf Resort
42
Coquille
Lookingglass
Green
Bullards Beach State Park
Riverton
Winston
Bandon
42
Norway
Tenmile
Dillard
Myrtle Point
Camas Valley
Myrtle Creek
West Coast Game Park Safari
Broadbent
Bridge
42
Riddle
Langlois
542
Canyonville
Cape Blanco State Park
101
Powers
Cape Blanco
Sixes
Port Orford
Glendale
Port Orford Head
Wolf Creek
Humbug Mountain State Park
Rogue River
Placer
Prehistoric Gardens
Leland
5
Oregon Islands National Wildlife Refuge
Ophir
Agness
Nesika Beach
Merlin
Grant Pass
TO MEDFORD, ASHLAND →
Gold Beach
Redwood
Wilderville
Cape Sebastian State Park
199
Murphy
238
Pistol River
Selma
Eight Dollar Mtn
Samuel H. Boardman State Scenic Corridor
Kerby
101
Cave Junction
46
Loeb State Park
Grayback Mtn 2,133
Harris Beach State Park
Brookings
199
Harbor
TO CRESCENT CITY US 199
O'Brien
CALIFORNIA

COAST RANGES

KLAMATH MOUNTAINS

0   12 mi
0   12 km

FAMILY **Coos History Museum & Maritime Collection.** This modern 11,000-square-foot museum with expansive views of the Coos Bay waterfront contains an exhaustive collection of memorabilia related to the region's history, from early photos to vintage boats, all displayed in an airy, open exhibit hall with extensive interpretive signage. You'll also find exhibits on Native American history, agriculture, and industry such as logging, shipping, natural history, and mining. ✉ *1210 N. Front St., Coos Bay* ☎ *541/756–6320* 🌐 *www.cooshistory.org* 🎟 *$7.*

FAMILY **South Slough National Estuarine Research Reserve.** The 5,000-acre reserve's fragile ecosystem supports everything from algae to bald eagles and black bears. More than 300 species of birds have been sighted at the reserve, which has an interpretive center with interesting nature exhibits, guided walks (summer only), and nature trails that give you a chance to see things up close. ✉ *61907 Seven Devils Rd., 4 miles south of Charleston, Coos Bay* ☎ *541/888–5558* 🌐 *www.oregon.gov/dsl/ssnerr* 🎟 *Free.*

WHERE TO EAT AND STAY

$$ GERMAN 🍴 **Blue Heron Bistro.** The specialty at this bustling downtown bistro is hearty German fare, but you'll also find a number of local seafood items, as well as sandwiches and lighter dishes, from panfried oysters to meatball sandwiches. The skylit, tile-floor dining room seats about 70 amid natural wood and blue linen. **Known for:** great beer selection; outdoor seating. [$] *Average main: $18* ✉ *100 W. Commercial St., Coos Bay* ☎ *541/267–3933* 🌐 *www.blueheronbistro.net.*

$ SEAFOOD 🍴 **Miller's at the Cove.** Often packed with local fishing and dock workers as well as tourists en route to and from Sunset Bay and nearby state parks, this lively and fun—if at times raucous—sports bar and tavern makes a great dinner or lunch stop for fresh seafood, and watching a game on TV. Favorites here include the fish-and-chips (available with local snapper or cod), oyster burgers, Dungeness crab melts, meatball subs, clam chowder, and Baja-style fish or crab tacos. **Known for:** laid-back ambience; tasty fish tacos; craft beer by the pitcher. [$] *Average main: $11* ✉ *63346 Boat Basin Rd., Charleston* ☎ *541/808–2404* 🌐 *www.millersatthecove.rocks.*

$ B&B/INN FAMILY 🏨 **Coos Bay Manor.** Built in 1912 on a quiet residential street, this 15-room Colonial Revival manor contains original hardwood floors, detailed woodwork, high ceilings, and antiques and period reproductions. **Pros:** very nicely kept and decorated; family-friendly. **Cons:** in busy downtown Coos Bay; a 15-minute drive from the ocean. [$] *Rooms from: $145* ✉ *955 S. 5th St., Coos Bay* ☎ *541/269–1224, 800/269–1224* 🌐 *www.coosbaymanor.com* 🛏 *5 rooms, 1 suite* 🍽 *Breakfast.*

$ RESORT 🏨 **Mill Casino Hotel.** Even if you're not a big fan of gambling, this attractive hotel near the waterfront in North Bend (a short distance north of downtown Coos Bay) makes a handy and fairly economical base for exploring this stretch of the coast. **Pros:** attractive, contemporary rooms; location close to downtown dining and shopping; nice views from rooms in tower. **Cons:** casino can be noisy and smoky. [$] *Rooms from: $114* ✉ *3201 Tremont Ave., North Bend* ☎ *541/756–8800, 800/953–4800* 🌐 *www.themillcasino.com* 🛏 *207 rooms, 10 suites* 🍽 *No meals.*

SPORTS AND THE OUTDOORS

RECREATIONAL AREAS

Cape Arago State Park. The distant barking of sea lions echoes in the air at a trio of coves connected by short but steep trails. The park overlooks the **Oregon Islands National Wildlife Refuge,** where offshore rocks, beaches, islands, and reefs provide breeding grounds for seabirds and marine mammals, including seal pups (the trail is closed in spring to protect them). ✉ *End of Cape Arago Hwy., 1 mile south of Shore Acres State Park, Coos Bay* ☎ *800/551–6949, 541/888–3778* ⊕ *www. oregonstateparks.org* ✑ *Free.*

Fodor'sChoice ★ **Shore Acres State Park.** An observation building on a grassy bluff overlooking the Pacific marks the site that held the mansion of lumber baron Louis J. Simpson. The view over the rugged wave-smashed cliffs is splendid, but the real glory of Shore Acres lies a few hundred yards to the south, where an entrance gate leads into what was Simpson's private garden. Beautifully landscaped and meticulously maintained, the gardens incorporate formal English and Japanese designs. From March to mid-October the grounds are ablaze with blossoming daffodils, rhododendrons, azaleas, roses, and dahlias. In December the garden is decked out with a dazzling display of holiday lights. ✉ *89526 Cape Arago Hwy., 1 mile south of Sunset Bay State Park, Coos Bay* ☎ *800/551–6949, 541/888–2472 info center, 541/888–3732* ⊕ *www. oregonstateparks.org* ✑ *$5 per vehicle day-use fee.*

BANDON

25 miles south of Coos Bay.

Referred to by some who cherish its romantic lure as Bandon-by-the-Sea, Bandon is both a harbor town and a popular vacation spot, famous for its cranberry products and its artists' colony, complete with galleries and shops. Two national wildlife refuges, Oregon Islands and Bandon Marsh, are within the town limits, and a drive along Beach Loop Road, just southwest of downtown, affords mesmerizing views of awesome coastal rock formations, especially around Coquille Point and Face Rock State Scenic Viewpoint. The Bandon Dunes links-style golf courses are a worldwide attraction, often ranked among the top courses in the nation.

Tiny Bandon bills itself as Oregon's cranberry capital—10 miles north of town you'll find acres of bogs and irrigated fields where tons of the tart berries are harvested every year. Each September there's the Cranberry Festival, featuring a parade and a fair.

GETTING HERE AND AROUND

Bandon, on U.S. 101, is a half-hour drive south of Coos Bay and North Bend, and a 2-hour drive north up the coast from the California border; allow 4½ hours to get here from Portland.

ESSENTIALS

Visitor Information Bandon Chamber of Commerce. ✉ *300 2nd St.* ☎ *541/347–9616* ⊕ *www.bandon.com.*

EXPLORING

Bandon Historical Society Museum. In the old city hall building, this museum depicts the area's early history, including Native American artifacts, logging, fishing, cranberry farming, and the disastrous 1936 fire that destroyed the city. The well-stocked gift shop has books, knick-knacks, jewelry, myrtlewood, and other little treasures. ✉ *270 Fillmore St.* ☎ *541/347–2164* 🌐 *www.bandonhistoricalmuseum.org* 🎟 *$3.*

FAMILY Fodor's Choice ★ **Oregon Islands National Wildlife Refuge.** Each of the colossal rocks jutting from the ocean between Bandon and Brookings is protected as part of this 19-acre refuge, in total comprising a string of 1,853 rocks, reefs, islands, and two headland areas spanning 320 miles. Thirteen species of seabirds, totalling 1.2 million birds, nest here, and harbor seals, California sea lions, Steller sea lions, and Northern elephant seals also breed within the refuge. Coquille Point, a mainland unit of Oregon Islands Refuge, is one of many places to observe seabirds and harbor seals. The point overlooks a series of offshore rocks, and a paved trail that winds over the headland ends in stairways to the beach on both sides, allowing for a loop across the sand when tides permit. Visitors are encouraged to steer clear of harbor seals and avoid touching seal pups. A complete list of viewpoints and trails is available online. ✉ *11th St. W and Portland Ave. SW, drive west to road's end for Coquille Point and parking* ☎ *541/347–1470* 🌐 *www.fws.gov/oregoncoast/oregonislands.*

FAMILY **West Coast Game Park Safari.** The "walk-through safari" on 21 acres has free-roaming wildlife (it's the visitors who are behind fences); more than 450 animals and about 75 species, including lions, tigers, snow leopards, lemurs, bears, chimps, cougars, and camels, make it one of the largest wild-animal petting parks in the United States. The big attractions here are the young animals: bear cubs, tiger cubs, whatever is suitable for actual handling. ✉ *46914 U.S. 101, 8 miles south of Bandon on U.S. 101* ☎ *541/347–3106* 🌐 *www.westcoastgameparksafari.com* 🎟 *$17.50.*

WHERE TO EAT

$$ SEAFOOD 🍴 **Edgewaters Restaurant.** This second-story bar above Edgewaters Restaurant has some of the best west-facing views of the ocean from Bandon, and is among few properties in Old Town that don't face north toward the Coquille River. You can sometimes see whales from this spot during whale-watching season. **Known for:** sushi; impressive river and sunset views. [$] *Average main: $18* ✉ *480 1st St.* ☎ *541/347–8500* 🌐 *www.edgewaters.net* 🕒 *Closed Mon. in winter. No lunch Tues.–Thurs.*

$$$ PACIFIC NORTHWEST Fodor's Choice ★ 🍴 **The Loft Restaurant & Bar.** This hip eatery in Bandon's Old Town is notable for chef-owner Kali Fieger's innovative, modern spin on French basics. On the second floor of an old Port of Bandon property, The Loft's vaulted, wood-trimmed ceilings, three-sided view of the Coquille River, and classic wooden tables are all ingredients for an enjoyable meal. **Known for:** gourmet deli and market for to-go goods; artfully presented food. [$] *Average main: $25* ✉ *315 1st St.* ☎ *541/329–0535* 🌐 *www.theloftofbandon.com* 🕒 *Closed Sun. and Mon. No lunch.*

$$$ AMERICAN Fodor's Choice ★ 🍴 **Lord Bennett's.** His lordship has a lot going for him: a cliff-top setting, a comfortable and spacious dining area in a dramatic contemporary building, sunsets visible through picture windows overlooking Face Rock Beach, and occasional live music on weekends. The modern

American menu features plenty of local seafood; try the nut-crusted halibut, blackened red snapper with potato-horseradish crust, or wild prawns with garlic butter and sherry. **Known for:** weekend brunch; some of the best steaks in the area. $ *Average main: $27* ⊠ *1695 Beach Loop Rd.* ☎ *541/347–3663* ⊕ *www.lordbennetts.com* ☾ *No lunch Mon.–Sat.*

$$ × **Tony's Crab Shack & Seafood Grill.** Started in 1989 as a bait and tackle
SEAFOOD shop, Tony's Crab Shack has since become a staple of the Bandon boardwalk, popular with locals and visitors for its crab cakes, fish tacos, crab and bay shrimp sandwich, and smoked Alaskan sockeye. Open only until 6 pm, it's a reliable bet for lunch or perhaps very early dinner. **Known for:** handy boardwalk location; to-go lunch fare that's perfect for a picnic at the beach. $ *Average main: $16* ⊠ *155 1st St.* ☎ *541/347–2875* ⊕ *www.tonyscrabshack.com.*

WHERE TO STAY

$ 🏨 **Bandon Beach Motel.** As its owners like to proclaim, it's all about the
HOTEL view at this low-frills, exceptionally well-kept seaside motel set high
Fodor's Choice on a bluff on Coquille Point and overlooking the smooth beach and
★ rugged offshore rock formations below. **Pros:** terrific value; gorgeous beach views; run by a friendly and helpful family. **Cons:** basic rooms with few bells and whistles; 20-minute walk to downtown; often books up weeks in advance in summer. $ *Rooms from: $130* ⊠ *1090 Portland Ave. SW* ☎ *541/347–9451, 866/945–0133* ⊕ *www.bandonbeachmotel. com* ⤳ *20 rooms* ⦿ *No meals.*

$$$ 🏨 **Bandon Dunes Golf Resort.** This golfing lodge provides a comfortable
RESORT place to relax after a day on the links, with accommodations ranging
Fodor's Choice from single rooms to four-bedroom condos, many with beautiful views of
★ the famous golf course. **Pros:** if you're a golfer, this adds to an incredible overall experience; if not, you'll have a wonderful stay anyway. **Cons:** the weather can be wet and wild in the shoulder-season months. $ *Rooms from: $230* ⊠ *57744 Round Lake Dr.* ☎ *541/347–4380, 888/345–6008* ⊕ *www.bandondunesgolf.com* ⤳ *186 rooms* ⦿ *Some meals.*

SPORTS AND THE OUTDOORS

RECREATIONAL AREA

Bullards Beach State Park. At this rugged park along the north bank of the Coquille River (just across from downtown Bandon but reached via a 3½-mile drive up U.S. 101), you can tour the signal room inside the octagonal **Coquille Lighthouse,** built in 1896 and no longer in use; due to safety concerns, visitors can no longer tour the tower. From turnoff from U.S. 101, the meandering 2-mile drive to reach it passes through the Bandon Marsh, a prime bird-watching and picnicking area. The 4½-mile stretch of beach beside the lighthouse is a good place to search for jasper, agate, and driftwood—the firm sand is also popular for mountain biking. There's a campground with a wide variety of tent and RV sites as well as pet-friendly yurts. ⊠ *52470 U.S. 101, 2 miles north of Bandon* ☎ *800/452–5687, 541/347–2209* ⊕ *www.oregonstateparks.org* ⤳ *Free.*

GOLF

Fodor's Choice ★ **Bandon Dunes Golf Resort.** This windswept, links-style playland for the nation's golfing elite is no stranger to well-heeled athletes flying in to North Bend on private jets to play on the resort's four distinct courses, including the beloved Pacific Dunes layout, many of whose rolling, bunker-laced fairways meander atop high bluffs with breathtaking ocean views. The steep greens fees vary a good bit according to season; they drop sharply during the November–April off season. The expectations at Bandon Dunes are that you walk the course with a caddy—adding a refined, traditional touch. Caddy fees are determined by the player, but it's recommended that you pay $100 per bag, per round. ✉ *57744 Round Lake Dr.* ☎ *541/347–4380, 888/345–6008* 🌐 *www.bandondunesgolf.com* 🎟 *$240–$325* ⛳ *Bandon Dunes Course: 18 holes, 5716 yards, par 72; Bandon Trails Course: 18 holes, 5751 yards, par 71; Old Macdonald Course: 18 holes, 5658 yards, par 71; Pacifc Dunes Course: 18 holes, 5775 yards, par 71.*

3

PORT ORFORD

30 miles south of Bandon.

The westernmost incorporated community in the contiguous United States, Port Orford is surrounded by forests, rivers, lakes, and beaches. The jetty at Port Orford offers little protection from storms, so every night the fishing boats are lifted out and stored on the docks. Commercial fishing boats search for crab, tuna, snapper, and salmon in the waters out of Port Orford, and diving boats gather sea urchins for Japanese markets. Visitors can fish off the Port Orford dock or the jetty for smelt, sardine, herring, lingcod, and halibut. Dock Beach provides beach fishing. The area is a favorite spot for sport divers because of the near-shore, protected reef, and for whale-watchers in fall and early spring.

GETTING HERE AND AROUND

Port Orford is a 30-minute drive south of Bandon and a one-hour drive north of Brookings along U.S. 101.

ESSENTIALS

Visitor Information **Port Orford Visitors Center.** ✉ *520 Jefferson St.* ☎ *541/332–4106* 🌐 *www.enjoyportorford.com.*

EXPLORING

OFF THE BEATEN PATH

Prehistoric Gardens. As you round a bend between Port Orford and Gold Beach, you'll see one of those sights that make grown-ups groan and kids squeal with delight: a huge, open-jawed tyrannosaurus rex, with a green brontosaurus peering out from the forest beside it. You can view 23 other life-size dinosaur replicas on the trail that runs through the property. ✉ *36848 U.S. 101* ☎ *541/332–4463* 🌐 *www.prehistoric-gardens.com* 🎟 *$12.*

WHERE TO EAT AND STAY

$ SEAFOOD FAMILY

🍴 **Crazy Norwegians Fish and Chips.** This quirky and casual hole-in-the-wall in Port Orford excels at what they do: good old-fashioned fish-and-chips. With everything from shrimp to cod to halibut paired with fries, the Crazy Norwegians serve it up with a side of pasta salad or coleslaw. **Known for:** to-go meals to take to the beach or park. [$] *Average main: $11* ✉ *259 6th St.* ☎ *541/332–8601* 🕒 *Closed Mon.*

$$$
MODERN
AMERICAN
Fodor'sChoice
★

✕**Redfish.** Two walls of windows allow diners at the stylish Redfish in downtown Port Orford spectacular ocean vistas, but the views inside are pretty inviting, too, from the modern artwork provided by sister establishment Hawthorne Gallery to the artfully presented and globally influenced food. Start with the Manila clams in lemongrass-coconut red-curry broth or the daily ceviche, before graduating to cedar-plank chinook salmon with mushroom risotto, or organic chicken with truffle grits, garlic-tomato marmalade, and broccoli rabe. **Known for:** crab cakes Benedict at weekend brunch. $ *Average main: $25* ✉ *517 Jefferson St.* ☎ *541/366–2200* ⊕ *www.redfishportorford.com.*

> ### THE FAB 50
>
> U.S. 101 between Port Orford and Brookings, often referred to as the "fabulous 50 miles," soars up green headlands, some of them hundreds of feet high, and past a seascape of cliffs and sea stacks. The ocean is bluer and clearer—though not appreciably warmer—than it is farther north, and the coastal countryside is dotted with farms, grazing cattle, and small rural communities.

$
HOTEL
FAMILY

⌃ **Castaway by the Sea.** This old-school motel operated by friendly proprietor Rockne Berge offers fantastic views from nearly every room, most of which have enclosed sun porches—the simplest and least expensive rooms open to an enclosed breezeway that takes in these same views. **Pros:** within walking distance of local restaurants; panoramic ocean views; reasonable rates. **Cons:** decor is a bit dated; not actually on the beach. $ *Rooms from: $95* ✉ *545 5th St.* ☎ *541/332–4502* ⊕ *www. castawaybythesea.com* ⬎ *9 rooms, 4 suites* ❢❍*No meals.*

$$$$
B&B/INN
Fodor'sChoice
★

⌃ **WildSpring Guest Habitat.** This rustic outpost in the woods above Port Orford blends all the comforts and privacy of a vacation rental with the services of a resort. **Pros:** relaxing, secluded, and private; gorgeous rooms; eco-conscious management. **Cons:** need to drive to the beach and stores. $ *Rooms from: $298* ✉ *92978 Cemetery Loop Rd.* ☎ *541/332–0977, 866/333–9453* ⊕ *www.wildspring.com* ⬎ *5 cabins* ❢❍*Breakfast.*

SPORTS AND THE OUTDOORS
RECREATIONAL AREAS

FAMILY
Battle Rock Park and Port Orford Heads State Park. Stroll the mocha-color sand and admire pristine Battle Rock right in the heart of downtown Port Orford. Named for a battle between white settlers and the Dene Tsut Dah that took place here in 1850, this spot sits just below Port Orford Heads State Park. Atop the bluff that is Port Orford Heads, a trail loops the rocky outcropping between the Pacific and the Port Orford Lifeboat Station, taking in the hillside below, from which crews once mounted daring rescues on the fierce sea. The lifeboat station and adjoining museum is open for tours Wednesday–Monday, 10–3:30. Their motto? "You have to go out... you don't have to come back." ✉ *Port Orford Hwy., Follow signs from U.S. 101* ☎ *800/551-6949, 541/332–6774* ⊕ *www.oregonstateparks.org* ▱ *Free.*

FAMILY
Cape Blanco State Park. Said to be the westernmost point in Oregon and perhaps the windiest—gusts clocked at speeds as high as 184 mph have twisted and battered the Sitka spruces along the 6-mile road from U.S. 101 to the **Cape Blanco Lighthouse.** The lighthouse, atop a 245-foot

headland, has been in continuous use since 1870, longer than any other in Oregon. **Huges House** is all that remains of the Irish settler Patrick Hughes's dairy farm complex built in 1860. No one knows why the Spaniards sailing past these reddish bluffs in 1603 called them *blanco* (white). One theory is that the name refers to the fossilized shells that glint in the cliff face. Campsites at the 1,880-acre park are available on a first-come, first-served basis. Four cabins are available for reservation. ✉ *91814 Cape Blanco Rd., Off U.S. 101, 6 miles north of Port Orford, Sixes* ☎ *541/332–2973, 800/551–6949* ⊕ *www.oregonstateparks.org* 🏷 *Day use and Hughes House tour free; Lighthouse tour $2.*

Humbug Mountain State Park. This secluded, 1,850-acre park, especially popular with campers, usually has warm weather, thanks to the nearby mountains that shelter it from ocean breezes. A 6-mile loop leads to the top of 1,756-foot Humbug Mountain, one of the highest points along the state's coastline. It's a pretty, moderately challenging hike, but the summit is fairly overgrown and doesn't provide especially panoramic views. The campground has tent and RV sites. ✉ *U.S. 101, 6 miles south of Port Orford* ☎ *541/332–6774, 800/551–6949* ⊕ *www.oregonstateparks.org.*

GOLD BEACH

28 miles south of Port Orford.

The fabled Rogue River is one of about 150 U.S. rivers to merit Wild and Scenic status from the federal government. From spring to late fall an estimated 50,000 visitors descend on the town to take one of the daily jet-boat excursions that roar upstream from Wedderburn, Gold Beach's sister city across the bay, into the Rogue River Wilderness Area. Black bears, otters, beavers, ospreys, egrets, and bald eagles are seen regularly on these trips.

Gold Beach is very much a seasonal town, thriving in summer and rather quiet the rest of the year because of its remote location. It marks the entrance to Oregon's banana belt, where mild, California-like temperatures take the sting out of winter and encourage a blossoming trade in lilies and daffodils.

GETTING HERE AND AROUND
It's a 90-minute drive south along U.S. 101 from Coos Bay and North Bend to reach Gold Beach, which is a one-hour drive north of the California border.

ESSENTIALS
Visitor Information Gold Beach Visitors Center. ✉ *94080 Shirley La.* ☎ *541/247–7526, 800/525–2334* ⊕ *www.visitgoldbeach.com.*

WHERE TO EAT

$$$

MODERN
AMERICAN

Fodor's Choice

★

✕ **Anna's by the Sea.** Dining at Anna's by the Sea is like stepping into one man's artisan universe: bowed and wood-trimmed ceilings, handmade cheeses, and blackberry honey lemonade, even a hydroponic herb garden, crafted by owner/head cook Peter Dower. Diners get a dash of personality with their meal service, which offers such choices as rack of lamb with ginger and mint and seared albacore and chicken thighs in chanterelle gravy. **Known for:** outstanding selection of Oregon wines and craft spirits; live music; intimate setting. $ *Average main: $26* ⊠ *29672 Stewart St.* ☎ *514/247–2100* ⊕ *www.annasbythesea.com* ⊘ *Closed Sun.–Tues. No lunch.*

$

AMERICAN

× **Barnacle Bistro.** At this quirky tavern on the main road in downtown Gold Beach, try the fish-and-chips with Asian-style coleslaw and sweet-potato fries, the Dungeness crab–and–bay-shrimp cakes with lemon-dill aioli, the shellfish tacos with a Brazilian coconut-peanut sauce, or any of the enormous burgers. It's reliably good pub fare using produce, meat, and seafood sourced locally, and serving beer from nearby Arch Rock Brewery. **Known for:** beer from nearby Arch Rock Brewery; very reasonable prices. $ *Average main: $14* ⊠ *29805 Ellensburg Ave.* ☎ *541/247–7799* ⊕ *www.barnaclebistro.com* ⊘ *Closed Sun. and Mon.*

$

AMERICAN
FAMILY

× **The Port Hole Café.** A local staple in the old cannery building at the Port of Gold Beach since 1995, this family business has been passed down a generation, and many of the employees are friends and relations who have been tied to it for years. The café overlooks the mouth of the Rogue River, an area with great views but too blustery for outdoor dining. **Known for:** local people-watching; first-rate blueberry pie; fish-and-chips. $ *Average main: $15* ⊠ *29975 Harbor Way* ☎ *541/247–7411* ⊕ *www.portholecafe.com.*

WHERE TO STAY

$

HOTEL
FAMILY

🖼 **Pacific Reef and Resort.** This resort offers a little something for everyone: from comfy, clean, economical rooms in the original renovated 1950s hotel to modern two-story condos with expansive ocean views, king-size beds, full kitchens, and outdoor patios. **Pros:** luxurious condos; full kitchens; glorious water views from the best units. **Cons:** rocky beach; on a busy road. $ *Rooms from: $89* ⊠ *29362 Ellensburg Hwy.* ☎ *541/247–6658* ⊕ *www.pacificreefhotel.com* ⌁ *39 units* ⍾ *Breakfast.*

$$$$

RESORT

Fodor'sChoice

★

🖼 **Tu Tu' Tun Lodge.** Pronounced "too- *too*-tin," this renowned and rather lavish resort is a slice of heaven on the Rogue River, and owner Kyle Ringer is intent on providing his guests with a singular Northwest experience. **Pros:** luxurious, beautifully outfitted rooms; exceptional dining; peaceful location overlooking river. **Cons:** no TV; not well suited for young kids; 15-minute drive from downtown and the ocean. $ *Rooms from: $255* ⊠ *96550 N. Bank Rogue River Rd., 7 miles east of Gold Beach* ☎ *541/247–6664, 800/864–6357* ⊕ *www.tututun.com* ⌁ *16 rooms, 2 suites, 2 cottages* ⍾ *Breakfast.*

SPORTS AND THE OUTDOORS

BOATING

FAMILY

Fodor'sChoice

★

Jerry's Rogue Jets. These jet boats operate from May through September in the most rugged section of the Wild and Scenic Rogue River, offering 64-, 80-, and 104-mile tours, starting at $50 per person. Whether visitors choose a shorter, six-hour lower Rogue scenic trip or an eight-hour white-water trip, folks have a rollicking good time. Its largest vessels are 40 feet long and can hold 75 passengers. The smaller, white-water boats are 32 feet long and can hold 42 passengers. ⊠ *29985 Harbor Way* ☎ *541/247–4571, 800/451–3645* ⊕ *www.roguejets.com.*

FISHING

Five Star Charters. Fishing charter trips range from a five-hour bottom-fish outing to a full-day salmon, steelhead, or halibut charter. They offer all the tackle needed, and customers don't even need experience—they'll take beginners and experts. The outfit has four riverboats, including two drift boats and two powerboats, as well as two ocean boats. They operate year-round. ⊠ *29957 Harbor Way* ☎ *541/247–0217, 888/301–6480* ⊕ *www.goldbeachadventures.com.*

RECREATIONAL AREAS

Cape Sebastian State Scenic Corridor. The parking lots at this scenic area are more than 200 feet above sea level. At the south parking vista you can see up to 43 miles north to Humbug Mountain. Looking south, you can see nearly 50 miles toward Crescent City, California, and the Point Saint George Lighthouse. A deep forest of Sitka spruce covers most of the park. There's a 1½-mile walking trail. ⊠ *U.S. 101, 6 miles south of Gold Beach* ☎ *541/469–2021, 800/551–6949* ⊕ *www.oregonstateparks.org.*

EN ROUTE

Samuel H. Boardman State Scenic Corridor. This 12-mile corridor through beach forests and alongside rocky promontories and windswept beaches contains some of Oregon's most spectacular stretches of coastline, though seeing some of them up close sometimes requires a little effort. About 27 miles of the Oregon Coast Trail weaves its way through this area, a reach dominated by Sitka spruce trees that stretch up to 300 feet and by rocky coast interspersed with sandy beaches. Starting from the north, walk a short path from the highway turnoff to view Arch Rock. The path travels a meadow that blooms in spring time. Down the road, find **Secret Beach**—hardly a secret—where trails run from two parking lots into three separate beaches below. Visit at low tide to make your way through all three, including through a cave that connects to the third beach close to Thunder Rock. At **Thunder Rock**, just north of milepost 345 on U.S. 101, walk west for a 1-mile loop that traces inlets and headlands, edging right up to steep drops. Find the highest bridge in Oregon just south—the **Thomas Creek Bridge**—from which a moderately difficult trail extends to wide, sandy **China Beach**. Find some sun on China Beach, or continue south to walk the unusual sculpted sandstone at **Indian Sands**. Easy beach access is at Whaleshead Beach, where shaded picnic tables shelter the view. From farther south at **Lone Ranch**, climb the grassy hillside to the top of **Cape Ferrelo** for a sweeping view of the rugged coastline, also a great spot for whale-watching in fall and summer. ⊠ *U.S. 101 between Gold Beach and Brookings* ☎ *800/551–6949, 541/469–2021* ⊕ *www.oregonstateparks.org* 🎫 *Free.*

BROOKINGS

27 miles south of Gold Beach on U.S. 101.

The coastal gateway to Oregon if you're approaching from California, Brookings is home to a pair of sterling state parks, one overlooking the ocean and another nestled amid the redwoods a bit inland. It's also a handy base, with some reasonably priced hotels and restaurants—your only overnight option along the 55-mile stretch between Gold Beach and Crescent City. A startling 90% of the pot lilies grown in the United States come from a 500-acre area inland from Brookings. Mild temperatures along this coastal plain provide ideal conditions for flowering plants of all kinds—even a few palm trees, a rare sight in Oregon.

The town is equally famous as a commercial and sportfishing port at the mouth of the turquoise-blue Chetco River. Salmon and steelhead weighing 20 pounds or more swim here.

GETTING HERE AND AROUND

Brookings is the southernmost town on Oregon's coastal 101, just 10 miles north of the California border and a half-hour drive from Crescent City; it's a 2½-hour drive south on U.S. 101 from the Coos Bay and North Bend area. Allow about six hours to get here from Portland via Interstate 5 to Grants Pass and U.S. 199 to Crescent City.

VISITOR INFORMATION

Brookings Harbor Chamber of Commerce. ✉ 97900 *Shopping Center Ave., Suite 14* ☎ *541/469–3181, 800/535–9469* ⊕ *www.brookingsharbor-chamber.com.*

WHERE TO EAT AND STAY

$
AMERICAN
✕ **Superfly Martini Bar & Grill.** The unusual name of this stylish little bar and grill has nothing to do with the Curtis Mayfield '70s funk anthem—rather, owner Ryan Webster named this establishment, which is also an artisanal-vodka distillery, after a fishing fly. Appropriately, the bar serves first-rate cocktails, including a refreshing lemon-basil martini. **Known for:** first-rate cocktails; high-quality pub fare. $ *Average main: $11* ✉ *623 Memory La.* ☎ *530/520–8005* ⊕ *www.superflybooze.com.*

$
AMERICAN
✕ **Vista Pub.** An affordable, friendly, and attractive family-run tavern in downtown Brookings, Vista Pub is known both for its extensive selection of rotating craft beers and tasty but simple comfort food. Try the hefty bacon-cheddar burgers, beer-cheese soup in a bread bowl, thick-cut fries sprinkled with sea salt, fried locally grown zucchini, and smoked-salmon chowder with bacon. **Known for:** tasty pub fare. $ *Average main: $11* ✉ *1009 Chetco Ave.* ☎ *541/813–1638* ⊙ *Closed Mon. and Tues.*

$$
HOTEL
🏨 **Best Western Plus Beachfront Inn.** This spotlessly clean three-story Best Western across the street from the Brookings boat basin has direct beach access and ocean views, making it one of the best-maintained and most appealingly located lodging options along the southern coast. **Pros:** fantastic ocean views; quiet location away from busy U.S. 101; very well kept. **Cons:** rooms don't have much personality; not many restaurants within walking distance. $ *Rooms from: $169* ✉ *16008 Boat Basin Rd.* ☎ *541/469–7779* ⊕ *www.bestwesternoregon.com* ⬎ *102 rooms* ⦿| *Breakfast.*

SPORTS AND THE OUTDOORS

RECREATIONAL AREAS

Fodor'sChoice
★
Harris Beach State Park. The views from the parking areas, oceanfront trails, and beaches at this popular tract of craggy rock formations and evergreen forest are some of the prettiest along the southern Oregon Coast. The proximity to downtown Brookings makes this an easy place to head for morning beachcombing or a sunset stroll. You might see gray whales migrate in spring and winter. Just offshore, Bird Island, also called Goat Island, is a National Wildlife Sanctuary and a breeding site for rare birds. The campground here, with tent and RV sites, is very popular. ✉ *1655 Old U.S. 101* ☎ *541/469–2021, 800/551–6949* ⊕ *www.oregonstateparks.org* ⬏ *Free.*

THE WILLAMETTE
VALLEY AND
WINE COUNTRY

WELCOME TO THE WILLAMETTE VALLEY AND WINE COUNTRY

TOP REASONS TO GO

★ **Swirl and sip:** Each region in the Willamette Valley offers some of the finest vintages and dining experiences found anywhere.

★ **Soar through the air:** Newberg's hot-air balloons will give you a bird's-eye view of Yamhill County's wine country.

★ **Run rapids:** Feel the bouncing exhilaration and the cold spray of white-water rafting on the wild, winding McKenzie River outside Eugene.

★ **Walk on the wild side:** Hillsboro's Jackson Bottom Nature Preserve gives walkers a chance to view otters, beavers, herons, and eagles.

★ **Back the Beavers or Ducks:** Nothing gets the blood pumping like an Oregon State Beaver or University of Oregon Ducks football game.

1 North Willamette Valley. Most visitors begin their journey into wine country here, an area rich with upscale dining, shopping, the arts, and wineries. Close to Portland, North Willamette's communities provide all the amenities of urban life with a whole lot less concrete. Wine enthusiasts will relish the excellent vineyards in Hillsboro and Forest Grove.

2 Yamhill County. This part of the state has undergone a renaissance in the past 20 years, as the world has beaten a path to its door, seeking the perfect Pinot. Many of the Willamette's highest-rated wineries are here. There are gorgeous inns, wine bars, and unforgettable restaurants providing a complete vacation experience.

3 Mid-Willamette Valley. Agriculture is the mainstay of this region; roadsides are dotted with fruit and veggie stands, and towns boast farmers' markets. The flat terrain is ideal for bicycle trips and hikes. The state capitol is Salem, and Oregon State University is in Corvallis.

4 South Willamette Valley. Here visitors soak in natural hot springs, hike in dense forest, run the rapids. Eugene, home to the University of Oregon, has a friendly, youthful vibe, which is enhanced by the natural splendor of the region.

GETTING ORIENTED

The Willamette Valley is a fertile mix of urban, rural, and wild stretching from Portland at the north to Cottage Grove at the south. It is bordered by the Cascade Range to the east and the Coast Range to the west. The Calapooya Mountains border it to the south and the mighty Columbia River runs along the north. Running north and south, Interstate 5 connects communities throughout the valley. In the mid-1800s the Willamette Valley was the destination of emigrants on the Oregon Trail, and today is home to about two-thirds of the state's population. The Willamette Valley is 150 miles long and up to 60 miles wide, which makes it Oregon's largest wine-growing region.

4

Updated by
Margot Bigg

The Willamette (pronounced "wil- *lam*-it") Valley has become a wine lover's Shangri-La, particularly in the northern Yamhill and Washington counties between Interstate 5 and the Oregon Coast, a region that is not only carpeted with vineyards but encompasses small hotels and inns, cozy restaurants, and casual wine bars.

The valley divides two mountain ranges (the Cascade and Coast), and contains more than 500 wineries. The huge wine region is made up of six subappellations: Chehalem Mountains, Ribbon Ridge, Dundee Hills, Yamhill-Carlton, Eola-Amity Hills, and McMinnville. With its incredibly rich soil perfect for growing Pinot Noir, Pinot Gris, Chardonnay, and Riesling, the valley has received worldwide acclaim for its vintages. The region's farms are famous for producing quality fruits, vegetables, and cheeses that are savored in area restaurants. During spring and summer there are many roadside stands dotting the country lanes, and farmers' markets appear in most of the valley's towns. Also delicious are the locally raised lamb, pork, chicken, and beef. The valley also is a huge exporter of plants and flowers for nurseries, with a large number of farms growing ornamental trees, bulbs, and plants.

The valley definitely has an artsy, expressive, and fun side, with its wine and beer festivals, theater, music, crafts, and culinary events. Many residents and visitors are serious runners and bicyclists, particularly in Eugene, so pay close attention while driving.

There's a longstanding collegiate football rivalry between the Oregon State Beavers in Corvallis and University of Oregon Ducks in Eugene; getting a ticket to the annual "Civil War" game between the two teams is a feat in itself. Across the state, but particularly in the Willamette Valley, Oregonians are passionate fans of one team or the other. If you happen to be visiting the area during the event (usually held in October or November), be prepared for some serious traffic and some closed businesses.

THE WILLAMETTE VALLEY AND WINE COUNTRY PLANNER

WHEN TO GO

July to October are the best times to wander the country roads in the Willamette Valley, exploring the grounds of its many wineries. Fall is spectacular, with leaves at their colorful peak in late October. Winters are usually mild, but they can be relentlessly overcast and downright rainy. Visitors not disturbed by dampness or chill will find excellent deals on lodging. In the spring rains continue, but the wildflowers begin to bloom, which pays off at the many gardens and nature parks throughout the valley.

FESTIVALS

International Pinot Noir Celebration. During the International Pinot Noir Celebration in late July and early August, wine lovers flock to McMinnville to sample fine regional vintages along with Pinot Noir from around the world. ⊠ *Box 1310800, McMinnville* ☎ *800/775–4762* ⊕ *www.ipnc.org.*

Oregon Bach Festival. Eugene hosts the world-class Oregon Bach Festival, with 18 summer days of classical music performances. ⊠ *1257 University of Oregon, Eugene* ☎ *541/346–5666, 800/457–1486* ⊕ *oregonbachfestival.com.*

Oregon Country Fair. Every July, the weekend after Independence Day, a small patch of fields and forest right outside of Eugene transforms into an enchanting community celebration known as the Oregon Country Fair. This annual event has been going on since the 1960s and maintains much of its flower-child vibe, with all sorts of parades, live music, puppet shows, face painting, and excellent craft shopping. ⊠ *24207 Oregon 126, Veneta* ☎ *541/343–4298* ⊕ *www.oregoncountryfair.org.*

Wooden Shoe Tulip Fest. Every spring from the end of March through April, visitors to Woodburn's Wooden Shoe Tulip Farm can tiptoe (or walk, or take a hayride) through spectacular fields of brightly hued tulips. Other festival features include wine-tastings, cut-out boards for photos, food booths, and a play area for kids. ⊠ *33814 S. Meridian Rd., Woodburn* ☎ *503/634–2243* ⊕ *www.woodenshoe.com/events/tulip-fest/.*

GETTING HERE AND AROUND

AIR TRAVEL

Portland's airport is an hour's drive east of the northern Willamette Valley. The **Aloha Express Airport Shuttle** and the **Beaverton Airporter** provide shuttle service. **Eugene Airport** is more convenient if you're exploring the region's southern end. It's served by Delta, Alaska/Horizon, American, and United/United Express. The flight from Portland to Eugene is 40 minutes. Smaller airports for private aircraft are scattered throughout the valley.

Rental cars are available at the Eugene airport from Budget, Enterprise, and Hertz. Taxis and airport shuttles will transport you to downtown

Eugene for about $22. **Omni Shuttle** will provide shuttle service to and from the Eugene airport from anywhere in Oregon.

Air Contacts Aloha Express Airport Shuttle. ☎ *503/356–8848* ⊕ *www.aloha-expressshuttle.com.* **Beaverton Airporter.** ☎ *503/760-6565, 866/665-6965* ⊕ *www.beavertonairporter.com.* **Omni Shuttle.** ☎ *541/461–7959, 800/741–5097* ⊕ *www.omnishuttle.com.*

BUS TRAVEL

Buses operated by Portland's **TriMet** network connect Forest Grove, Hillsboro, Beaverton, Tigard, Lake Oswego, and Oregon City with Portland and each other; light-rail trains operated by MAX run between Portland and Hillsboro. Many of the **Lane Transit District** buses will make a few stops to the outskirts of Lane County, such as McKenzie Bridge. All buses have bike racks. **Yamhill County Transit Area** provides bus service for Yamhill County, with links to Hillsboro/MAX, Sherwood/TriMet, and Salem/SAMT.

Bus Contacts Lane Transit District (*LTD*). ☎ *541/682–6100* ⊕ *www.ltd.org.* **Yamhill County Transit Area** (*YCTA*). ☎ *503/472–0457* ⊕ *www.yctransitarea.org.*

CAR TRAVEL

Interstate 5 runs north–south the length of the Willamette Valley. Many Willamette Valley attractions lie not too far east or west of Interstate 5. Highway 22 travels west from the Willamette National Forest through Salem to the coast. Highway 99 travels parallel to Interstate 5 through much of the Willamette Valley. Highway 34 leaves Interstate 5 just south of Albany and heads west, past Corvallis and into the Coast Range, where it follows the Alsea River. Highway 126 heads east from Eugene toward the Willamette National Forest; it travels west from town to the coast. U.S. 20 travels west from Corvallis. Rental cars are available from Budget (Beaverton), Enterprise, and Hertz (both Beaverton, Salem).

RESTAURANTS

The buzzwords associated with fine dining in this region are "sustainable," "farm-to-table," and "local." Fresh salmon, Dungeness crab, mussels, shrimp, and oysters are harvested just a couple of hours away on the Oregon Coast. Lamb, pork, and beef are local and plentiful, and seasonal game appears on many menus. Desserts made with local blueberries, huckleberries, raspberries, and marionberries should not be missed. But what really sets the offerings apart are the splendid local wines that receive worldwide acclaim.

Restaurants in the Willamette Valley are low-key and unpretentious. Expensive doesn't necessarily mean better, and locals have a pretty good nose for good value. Reasonably priced Mexican, Indian, Japanese, and Italian do very well. Food carts in the cities are a growing phenomenon. But there's still nothing like a great, sit-down meal at a cozy bistro for some fresh fish or lamb, washed down with a stellar Pinot Noir. *Restaurant reviews have been shortened. For full information visit Fodors.com.*

HOTELS

One of the great pleasures of touring the Willamette Valley is the incredible selection of small, ornate bed-and-breakfast hotels sprinkled throughout Oregon's wine country. In the summer and fall they can fill up quickly, as visitors come from around the world to enjoy wine tastings at the hundreds of large and small wineries. Many of these have exquisite restaurants right on the premises, with home-baked goods available day and night. There are plenty of larger properties located closer to urban areas and shopping centers, including upscale resorts with expansive spas, as well as national chains that are perfect for travelers who just need a place to lay their heads. *Hotel reviews have been shortened. For full information, visit Fodors.com.*

WHAT IT COSTS IN U.S. DOLLARS			
	$	$$	$$$	$$$$
Restaurants	under $16	$17–$22	$23–$30	over $30
Hotels	under $150	$150–$200	$201–$250	over $250

Restaurant prices are the average cost of a main course at dinner or, if dinner is not served, at lunch. Hotel prices are the lowest cost of a standard double room in high season.

TOURS

Oregon Wine Tours and **EcoTours of Oregon** provide informative guided outings across the Willamette Valley wine country.

Contacts EcoTours of Oregon. ☎ *503/245–1428* ⊕ *www.ecotours-of-oregon. com.* **Oregon Wine Tours.** ☎ *503/681–9463* ⊕ *www.orwinetours.com.*

VISITOR INFORMATION

Contacts Chehalem Valley Chamber of Commerce. ✉ *115 N. College St., Newberg* ☎ *503/538–2014* ⊕ *www.chehalemvalley.org.* **Oregon Wine Country/ Willamette Valley Visitors Association.** ☎ *866/548–5018* ⊕ *www.oregon-winecountry.org.* **Travel Lane County.** ✉ *754 Olive St., Eugene* ☎ *541/484–5307, 800/547–5445* ⊕ *www.eugenecascadescoast.org.* **Travel Yamhill Valley.** ⊕ *www.travelyamhill.com.* **Washington County Visitors Association.** ✉ *12725 S.W. Millikan Way, Suite 210, Beaverton* ☎ *503/644–5555, 800/537–3149* ⊕ *www.oregonswashingtoncounty.com.*

NORTH WILLAMETTE VALLEY

Just outside Portland the suburban areas of Tigard, Hillsboro, and Forest Grove have gorgeous wineries, wetlands, rivers, and nature preserves. The area has a wealth of golfing, biking, and trails for running and hiking, and, appropriately, is home to the headquarters of Nike. From wetlands to residential neighborhoods, it's not unusual to spot red-tail hawks, beavers, and ducks on your route. Shopping, fine dining, and proximity to Portland make this a great area in which to begin your exploration of the Willamette Valley and the wine country.

Vineyard and Valley Scenic Tour. A 60-mile driving route through the lush Tualatin Valley runs between the city of Sherwood in the southern part of the valley and Helvetia at the northern end. The rural drive showcases much of Washington County's agricultural bounty, including many of the county's wineries and farms (some with stands offering seasonal fresh produce and/or U-pick), along with pioneer and historic sites, wildlife refuges, and scenic viewpoints of the Cascade Mountains. For more information, visit the Washington County Visitors Association's tourist center. ⊠ *Washington County Visitors Association, 12725 S.W. Millikan Way, , Suite 210, Beaverton* ☎ *503/644–5555* ⊕ *tualatinvalley.org* ⊗ *Closed weekends.*

HILLSBORO

20 miles southwest of Portland.

Hillsboro offers a wealth of eclectic shops, preserves, restaurants, and proximity to the valley's fine wineries. In the past 20 years Hillsboro has experienced rapid growth associated with the Silicon Forest, where high-tech business found ample sprawling room. Several of Intel's industrial campuses are in Hillsboro, as are the facilities of other leading electronics manufacturers. Businesses related to the town's original agricultural roots remain a significant part of Hillsboro's culture and economy. Alpaca ranches, nurseries, berry farms, nut and fruit orchards, and numerous wineries are among the area's most active agricultural businesses.

GETTING HERE AND AROUND
Hillsboro is about a 45-minute drive west from Portland International Airport. The **Aloha Express Airport Shuttle** and the **Beaverton Airporter** provide shuttle service.

From Downtown Portland it's a short 20-minute car ride, or visitors can ride the MAX light rail. The TriMet Bus Service connects to the MAX light rail in Hillsboro, with connections to Beaverton, Aloha, and other commercial areas.

EXPLORING
Hillsboro Saturday Market. Fresh local produce—some from booths, some from the backs of trucks—as well as local arts and crafts are on sale Saturdays from May through October. Live music is played throughout the day. The market is just a block from the light-rail line. ⊠ *Main St. between 1st and 3rd Aves.* ☎ *503/844–6685* ⊕ *www.hillsboromarkets. org.*

Fodor's Choice   **Ponzi Vineyards.** One of the founding families of Willamette Valley wine,
★   Dick and Nancy Ponzi planted their original estate vineyard in 1970. While you can still visit the historic estate that looks out over these old vines, your best bet is to drop in at their new visitors facility at the winery just 12 miles south of Hillsboro. Here you'll find red and white flights of the current releases, as well as the occasional older vintage from the library. Enjoy table-side wine service indoors around the fireplace, or out on the covered terrace. Antipasti plates are a nice accompaniment to the wine. Pictures on the walls and displays provide

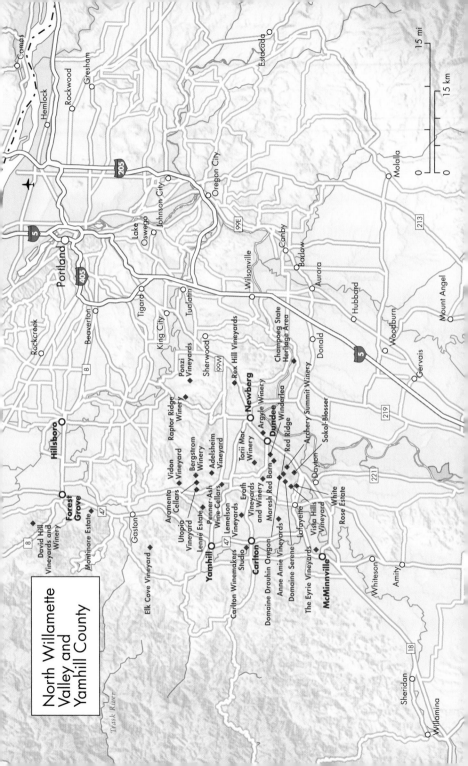

North Willamette Valley and Yamhill County

15 mi

15 km

Trask River

Canada$

Hemlock
Rockwood
Gresham

205

Rockwood

Johnson City

Oregon City

99E

213

Portland

405

Lake
Oswego

Tigard

Wilsonville

Canby

Barlow

Aurora

Hubbard

Mount Angel

5

Woodburn

Gervais

219

Molalla

Rockcreek

Beaverton

King City

Tualatin

99W

Sherwood

Champoeg State
Heritage Area

Donald

8

Ponzi
Vineyards

Rex Hill Vineyards

Newberg

Argyle Winery

Winderlea

Archery Summit Winery

Sokol-Blosser

Hillsboro

Raptor Ridge
Winery

Vidon
Vineyard

Bergstrom
Winery

Adelsheim
Vineyard

Torii Mor
Winery

Dundee

Red Ridge

Dayton

Forest
Grove

David Hill
Vineyards and
Winery

Montinore Estate

47

Aramenta
Cellars

Utopia
Vineyard

Penner-Ash
Wine Cellars

Eroth
Vineyards
and Winery

Maresh Red Barn

221

Gaston

8

Lennè Estate

Lemelson
Vineyards

47

Yamhill

Carlton Winemakers
Studio

Carlton

Domaine Drouhin Oregon

Anne Amie Vineyards

Domaine Serene

Lafayette

Vista Hills
Vineyard

White
Rose Estate

Elk Cove Vineyard

The Eyrie Vineyards

McMinnville

Whiteson

Amity

18

Sheridan

Willamina

a wonderful visual history of this winery that is still family owned and operated. The Ponzi family also launched the BridgePort Brewing Company in 1984, and runs a wine bar and restaurant in Dundee. ✉ *19500 S.W. Mountain Home Rd., Sherwood* ✥ *12 miles south of Hillsboro* ☎ *503/628–1227* 🌐 *www.ponziwines.com* 🎟 *Tastings $20.*

FAMILY **Rice Northwest Museum of Rocks and Minerals.** Richard and Helen Rice began collecting beach agates in 1938, and over the years they developed one of the largest private mineral collections in the United States. The most popular item here is the Alma Rose rhodochrosite, a 4-inch red crystal. The museum (in a ranch-style home) also displays petrified wood from all over the world and a gallery of Northwest minerals—including specimens of rare crystallized gold. Tours are offered Saturday at 2 pm. ✉ *26385 N.W. Groveland Dr.* ☎ *503/647–2418* 🌐 *www.ricenorthwestmuseum.org* 🎟 *$10* ⏲ *Closed Mon. and Tues.*

Washington County Museum and Historical Society. This impressive space on the second floor of the Hillsboro Civic Center houses a range of exhibits focusing on the history and culture of the area. Most of the exhibits include activities for children. ✉ *120 E. Main St.* ☎ *503/645–5353* 🌐 *www.washingtoncountymuseum.org* 🎟 *$6.*

WHERE TO EAT

$ MEXICAN FAMILY 🍴 **Mazatlan Mexican Restaurant.** Although this popular spot is hidden away in a small shopping mall, once you're inside and surrounded by stunning murals and ceramics you'll feel like you're in a charming village. Try the Mazatlan Dinner, a house specialty with sirloin, a chili relleno, and an enchilada, or *arroz con camarones,* prawns sautéed with vegetables. **Known for:** the Mazatlan Dinner; hidden gem in a shopping mall. [$] *Average main: $13* ✉ *20413 S.W. TV Hwy., Aloha* ☎ *503/591–9536* 🌐 *www.mazatlanmexicanrestaurant.com.*

$ JAPANESE 🍴 **Syun Izakaya.** A large assortment of sushi and sashimi, soups, and salads are served in quiet surroundings in the basement of the old Hillsboro Library. Wonderful grilled and fried meats and vegetables are also available, accompanied by a vast sake selection. **Known for:** unique daily specials; a delicious variety of sushi and sashimi. [$] *Average main: $11* ✉ *209 N.E. Lincoln St.* ☎ *503/640–3131* 🌐 *www.syun-izakaya.com* ⏲ *No lunch Sun.*

SPORTS AND THE OUTDOORS

The Tualatin, a slow, meandering river, flows into Hillsboro and along its length offers fantastic opportunities for paddlers who are new to the sport, as well those who are experienced.

RECREATIONAL AREAS

Cook Park. On the banks of the Tualatin River in Tiagrd, east of Hillsboro, this 79-acre park is where local suburbanites gather to enjoy a variety of outdoor activities, and plays host to the annual Festival of Balloons in June. The park has horseshoe pits, a fishing dock, a small boat ramp, picnic shelters, and several walking trails and bike paths. Wildlife includes great blue herons and river otters. ✉ *17005 S.W. 92nd Ave., Tigard* ☎ *503/718–2641* 🌐 *www.tigard-or.gov.*

Jackson Bottom Wetlands Preserve. Several miles of trails in this 710-acre floodplain and woods are home to thousands of ducks and geese, deer, otters, beavers, herons, and eagles. Walking trails allow birders and other animal watchers to explore the wetlands for a chance to catch a glimpse of indigenous and migrating creatures in their own habitats. The **Education Center** has several hands-on exhibits, as well as a real bald eagle's nest that has been completely preserved (and sanitized) for public display. No dogs or bicycles are allowed. ☒ *2600 S.W. Hillsboro Hwy.* ☏ *503/681–6206* ⊕ *www.jacksonbottom.org* 🖅 *$2 suggested donation.*

FAMILY **L.L. "Stub" Stewart State Park.** This 1,654-acre, full-service park has hiking, biking, and horseback riding trails for day use or overnight camping. There are full hookup sites, tent sites, small cabins, and even a horse camp. Lush rolling hills, forests, and deep canyons are terrific for bird-watching, wildflower walks, and other relaxing pursuits. An 18-hole disc golf course winds its way through a dense forest. In case you don't know, in disc golf players throw a disc at a target and attempt to complete the course with the fewest throws. ☒ *30380 N.W. Hwy. 47, Buxton* ☏ *503/324–0606* ⊕ *www.oregonstateparks.org* 🖅 *$5 for day use permit.*

Tualatin River Wildlife Refuge. This sanctuary for indigenous and migrating birds, waterfowl, and mammals is in Sherwood (about 18 miles south of Hillsboro). It is one of only a handful of national urban refuges in the United States and has restored much of the natural landscape common to western Oregon prior to human settlement. The refuge is home to nearly 200 species of birds, 50 species of mammals, 25 species of reptiles and amphibians, and a variety of insects, fish, and plants. It features an interpretive center, a gift shop, photography blinds, and restrooms. This restoration has attracted animals back to the area in great numbers, and with a keen eye, birders and animal watchers can catch a glimpse of these creatures year-round. In May the refuge hosts its Migratory Songbird Festival. ☒ *19255 S.W. Pacific Hwy., Tigard* ☏ *503/625–5944* ⊕ *www.fws.gov/tualatinriver.*

FOREST GROVE

24 miles west of Portland on Hwy. 8.

This small town is surrounded by stands of Douglas firs and giant sequoia, including the largest giant sequoia in the state. There are nearby wetlands, birding, the Hagg Lake Recreation Area, a new outdoor adventure park, and numerous wineries and tasting rooms. To get to many of the wineries, head south from Forest Grove on Highway 47 and watch for the blue road signs between Forest Grove, Gaston, and Yamhill. To the west of town, you'll find some of the oldest Pinot Noir vines in the valley at David Hill Winery.

GETTING HERE AND AROUND

Forest Grove is about an hour's drive west from Portland International Airport. The **Aloha Express Airport Shuttle** and the **Beaverton Airporter** provide shuttle service.

From Downtown Portland it's a short 35-minute car ride with only a few traffic lights during the entire trip. TriMet Bus Service provides bus

David Hill Vineyards and Winery, Forest Grove

service to and from Forest Grove every 15 minutes, connecting to the MAX light rail 6 miles east in Hillsboro, which continues into Portland. Buses travel to Cornelius, Hillsboro, Aloha, and Beaverton.

ESSENTIALS

Forest Grove Chamber of Commerce. ⊠ *2417 Pacific Ave.* ☎ *503/357–3006* ⊕ *www.visitforestgrove.com.*

EXPLORING

David Hill Vineyards and Winery. In 1965 Charles Coury came to Oregon from California and planted some of the Willamette Valley's first Pinot Noir vines on the site of what is now the David Hill Winery. The original farmhouse serves as the tasting room and offers splendid views of the Tualatin Valley. They produce Pinot Noir, some of which comes from the original vines planted by Coury, along with Chardonnay, Gewürztraminer, Merlot, Tempranillo, Pinot Gris, and Riesling. The wines are well made and pleasant, especially the eclectic blend called Farmhouse Red and the estate Riesling. ⊠ *46350 N.W. David Hill Rd.* ☎ *503/992–8545* ⊕ *www.davidhillwinery.com* 🍷 *Tastings from $10.*

Elk Cove Vineyard. Founded in 1974 by Pat and Joe Campbell, this well-established winery covers 600 acres on four separate vineyard sites. The tasting room is set in the beautiful rolling hills at the foot of the coast range overlooking the vines. The focus is on Willamette Valley Pinot Noir, Pinot Gris, and Pinot Blanc. Be sure to also try the limited bottling of their Pinot Noir Rosé if they're pouring it. ⊠ *27751 N.W. Olson Rd., Gaston* ☎ *503/985–7760, 877/355–2683* ⊕ *www.elkcove.com* 🍷 *Tastings from $10.*

Montinore Estate. Locals chuckle at visitors who try to show off their French savvy when they pronounce it "Mont-in-or-ay." The estate, originally a ranch, was established by a tycoon who'd made his money in the Montana mines before he retired to Oregon; he decided to call his estate "Montana in Oregon." Montinore (no "ay" at the end) has 232 acres of vineyards, and its wines reflect the high-quality soil and fruit. Highlights include a crisp Gewürztraminer, a light Müller-Thurgau, an off-dry Riesling, several lush Pinot Noirs, and a delightful white blend called Borealis that's a perfect partner for Northwest seafood. The tasting-room staff is among the friendliest and most knowledgeable in Oregon wine country. ✉ *3663 S.W. Dilley Rd.* ☎ *503/359–5012* ⊕ *www.montinore.com* 🍷 *Tastings $10.*

Pacific University. Founded in 1849, this is one of the oldest educational institutions in the western United States. Concerts and special events are held on the shady campus in the Taylor-Meade Performing Arts Center. ✉ *2043 College Way* ☎ *503/352–6151, 877/722–8648* ⊕ *www. pacificu.edu.*

SakéOne. After the founders realized that the country's best water supply for sake was in the Pacific Northwest, they built their brewery in Forest Grove in 1997. It's one of only six sake brewing facilities in America and produces award-winning sake under three labels, in addition to importing from partners in Japan. The tasting room offers three different flights, including one with a food pairing. Be sure to catch one of the tours, offered daily, where your guide will walk you through every phase of the sake-making process, from milling the rice to final filtration and bottling. ✉ *820 Elm St.* ☎ *503/357–7056, 800/550–7253* ⊕ *www. sakeone.com* 🍷 *Tastings $5.*

WHERE TO STAY

$ | **McMenamins Grand Lodge.** On 13 acres of pastoral countryside, this
HOTEL | converted Masonic rest home has accommodations that run from bunk-bed rooms to a three-room fireplace suite, with some nice period antiques in all. **Pros:** relaxed, friendly brewpub atmosphere. **Cons:** most rooms have shared bathrooms. ⓢ *Rooms from: $50* ✉ *3505 Pacific Ave.* ☎ *503/992–9533, 877/992–9533* ⊕ *www.mcmenamins.com/ grandlodge* ↳ *77 rooms* 🍴 *No meals.*

SPORTS AND THE OUTDOORS

RECREATIONAL AREAS

FAMILY | **Scoggin Valley Park and Henry Hagg Lake.** This beautiful area in the Coast
Fodor'sChoice | Range foothills has a 15-mile-long hiking trail that surrounds the lake.
★ | Bird-watching is best in spring. Recreational activities include fishing, boating, waterskiing, picnicking, and hiking, and a 10½-mile, well-marked bicycle lane parallels the park's perimeter road. ✉ *50250 S.W. Scoggins Valley Rd., Gaston* ☎ *503/846–8715* ⊕ *www.co.washington. or.us/hagglake* 🎟 *$6.*

FAMILY | **Tree to Tree Adventure Park.** At the first public aerial adventure park in the Pacific Northwest—and only the second of its kind in the United States—the aerial adventure course features 19 zip lines and more than 60 treetop elements and obstacles. You can experience the thrills of moving from platform to platform (tree to tree) via wobbly bridges, tight ropes, Tarzan swings, and more. The courses range from beginner to extreme, with certified and trained instructors providing guidance to adventurers. "Woody's Ziptastic Voyage" zip-line tour features six extreme zip lines (including one that is 1,280 feet long), a bridge, and a 40-foot rappel. Harnesses and helmets are provided, and no open-toed shoes are allowed. Reservations are required. ⊠ *2975 S.W. Nelson Rd., Gaston* ☏ *503/357–0109* ⊕ *tree2treeadventurepark.com* ⊠ *Aerial park $49, zip tour $75* ⚲ *Closed mid-Nov.–Feb.*

YAMHILL COUNTY

Yamhill County, at the northern end of the Willamette Valley, has a fortunate confluence of perfect soils, a benign climate, and talented winemakers who craft world-class vintages. In recent years several new wineries have been built in Yamhill County's hills, as well as on its flatlands. While vineyards flourished in the northern Willamette Valley in the 19th century, viticulture didn't arrive in Yamhill County until the 1960s and 1970s, with such pioneers as Dick Erath (Erath Vineyards Winery), David and Ginny Adelsheim (Adelsheim Vineyard), and David and Diana Lett (The Eyrie Vineyards). The focus of much of the county's enthusiasm lies in the Red Hills of Dundee, where the farming towns of Newberg, Dundee, Yamhill, and Carlton have made room for upscale bed-and-breakfasts, spas, wine bars, and tourists seeking that perfect swirl and sip.

The Yamhill County wineries are only a short drive from Portland, and the roads, especially Route 99W and Route 18, can be crowded on weekends—that's because these roads link suburban Portland communities to the popular Oregon Coast.

NEWBERG

24 miles south of Portland on Hwy. 99W.

Newberg sits in the Chehalem Valley, known as one of Oregon's most fertile wine-growing locations, and is called the Gateway to Oregon Wine Country. Many of Newberg's early settlers were Quakers from the Midwest, who founded the school that has become George Fox University. Newberg's most famous resident, likewise a Quaker, was Herbert Hoover, the 31st president of the United States. For about five years during his adolescence, he lived with an aunt and uncle at the Hoover-Minthorn House, now a museum listed on the National Register of Historic Places. Now the town is on the map for the nearby wineries, fine-dining establishments, and a spacious, spectacular resort, the Allison. St. Paul, a historic town with a population of about 325, is about 8 miles south of Newberg, and every July holds a professional rodeo.

GETTING HERE AND AROUND

Newberg is just under an hour's drive from Portland International Airport; **Caravan Airport Transportation** (⊕ *541/994–9645* ⊕ *www.caravanairporttransportation.com*) provides shuttle service. The best way to visit Newberg and the Yamhill County vineyards is by car. Situated on Highway 99W, Newberg is 90 minutes from Lincoln City, on the Oregon Coast. Greyhound provides bus service to McMinnville.

EXPLORING

TOP ATTRACTIONS

Fodor's Choice ★ **Adelsheim Vineyard.** David Adelsheim is the knight in shining armor of the Oregon wine industry—tirelessly promoting Oregon wines abroad, and always willing to share the knowledge he has gained from his long viticultural experience. He and Ginny Adelsheim founded their pioneer winery in 1971. They make their wines from grapes picked on their 230 acres of estate vineyards, as well as from grapes they've purchased. Their Pinot Noir, Pinot Gris, Pinot Blanc, and Chardonnay all conform to the Adelsheim house style of rich, balanced fruit and long, clean finishes. They also make a spicy cool-climate Syrah from grapes grown just outside the beautiful tasting room. Tours are available by appointment. ⊠ *16800 N.E. Calkins La.* ☏ *503/538–3652* ⊕ *www.adelsheim. com* ⊠ *Tastings from $15.*

Bergstrom Winery. Focusing on classic Oregon Pinot Noir and Chardonnay, this family-owned winery produces elegant and refined wines that represent some of the best the Willamette Valley has to offer. The tasting room is surrounded by the Silice Vineyard, and offers beautiful views of several neighboring vineyards as well. French-trained winemaker Josh Bergstrom sources fruit from his estate vineyards and from several other local sites to produce a wide range of single-vineyard Pinots. Enjoy your tasting on the deck on a warm summer day. ⊠ *18215 N.E. Calkins La.* ☏ *503/554–0468* ⊕ *www.bergstromwines.com* ⊠ *Tastings $20.*

Penner-Ash Wine Cellars. Lynn Penner-Ash brings years of experience working in Napa and as Rex Hill's winemaker to the winery that she and her husband Ron started in 1998. Although focused primarily on silky Pinot Noir, Penner-Ash also produces very good Syrah, Viognier, and Riesling. From its hilltop perch in the middle of the Dussin vineyard, this state-of-the-art gravity-flow winery and tasting room offers commanding views of the valley below. ⊠ *15771 N.E. Ribbon Ridge Rd.* ☏ *503/554–5545* ⊕ *www.pennerash.com* ⊠ *Tastings $15.*

Rex Hill Vineyards. A few hundred feet off the busy highway, surrounded by conifers and overlooked by vineyards, Rex Hill seems to exist in a world of its own. The winery opened in 1982, after owners Paul Hart and Jan Jacobsen converted a former nut-drying facility. It produces first-class Pinot Noir, Pinot Gris, Chardonnay, Sauvignon Blanc, and Riesling from both estate-grown and purchased grapes. The tasting room has a massive fireplace, elegant antiques, and an absorbing collection of modern art. Another highlight is the beautifully landscaped garden, perfect for picnicking. ⊠ *30835 N. Hwy. 99W* ☏ *503/538–0666, 800/739–4455* ⊕ *www.rexhill.com* ⊠ *Tastings $15.*

WORTH NOTING

Aramenta Cellars. Owners Ed and Darlene Looney have been farming this land for more than 40 years. In 2000, they planted grape vines after keeping cattle on the property. The winery and tasting room are built on the foundation of the old barn, and Ed makes the wine while Darlene runs the tasting room. Of the 27 acres planted in vines, 20 acres are leased to Archrey Summit for their Looney Vineyard Pinot Noir, and the Looneys farm 7 acres for their own wines which have very limited distribution. If you're looking for a break from all the Pinot Noir, try the Tillie Claret—a smooth Bordeaux blend made with grapes from eastern Washington and southern Oregon. Aramenta offers a great opportunity to interact with farmers who have worked the land for several generations and to taste some great small-production wine. ✉ *17979 N.E. Lewis Rogers La.* ☎ *503/538–7230* ⊕ *www.aramentacellars.com* ✉ *Tastings $10.*

Bravura Cellars. One of the newest additions to the Newberg tasting-room scene, this boutique winery eschews the Pinot Noir prevalent throughout the region in favor of hot-climate varietals—including Zin-fandel, Cab, and even a Ruby Port—all produced in small batches of around 40 to 60 cases. Bravura's wines are only available at the tasting room or online, and every bottle is individually numbered. ✉ *108. S. College St.* ☎ *503/822–5116* ⊕ *www.bravuracellars.com.*

Champoeg State Heritage Area. Pronounced "sham- *poo-ee,*" this 615-acre state park on the south bank of the Willamette River is on the site of a Hudson's Bay Company trading post, granary, and warehouse that was built in 1813. This was the seat of the first provisional government in the Northwest. The settlement was abandoned after a catastrophic flood in 1861, then rebuilt and abandoned again after the flood of 1890. The park's wide-open spaces, groves of oak and fir, modern visitor center, museum, and historic buildings provide vivid insight into pioneer life. Tepees and wagons are displayed here, and there are 10 miles of hiking and cycle trails. ✉ *8239 Champoeg Rd. NE, St. Paul* ☎ *503/678–1251* ⊕ *www.oregonstateparks.org* ✉ *$5 per vehicle.*

Hoover-Minthorn House Museum. In 1885 Dr. Henry Minthorn invited his orphan nephew Herbert "Bertie" Hoover to come west and join the Minthorn family in Newberg. Built in 1881, the restored frame house, the oldest and most significant of Newberg's original structures, still has many of its original furnishings, including the president's boyhood bed and dresser. Hoover maintained his connection to Newberg, and visited several times after his presidency. ✉ *115 S. River St.* ☎ *503/538–6629* ⊕ *hooverminthorn.org* ✉ *$5* ☉ *Closed Jan.; Mar.–Nov., Mon. and Tues.; Dec. and Feb., weekdays.*

Raptor Ridge Winery. The huge windows in the new tasting room look out over the vines of their estate vineyard on the northeast slope of the Chehalem Mountains. If you keep a sharp eye, you may even catch a glimpse of the many raptors (red-tail hawks, sharp-shinned hawks, and kestrels) that give this small winery its name. Raptor Ridge specializes in single-vineyard Pinot Noirs that capture the sense of place of their estate vineyard as well as several other vineyards throughout the Wil-lamette Valley. They also produce Chardonnay, Pinot Gris, and a very nice Tempranillo. During the summer, enjoy your tasting at a table on the outside deck that overlooks the vineyards. Tours of the wine-making facility are available by appointment. ✉ *18700 S.W. Hillsboro Hwy.* ☎ *503/628–8463* ⊕ *www.raptoridge.com* ✉ *Tours with tastings $25* ☉ *Closed mid-Jan.–mid May and mid-Oct.–mid-Dec., Tues. and Wed.*

Utopia Vineyard. Take a trip back in time to when the Oregon wine industry was much smaller and more intimate. Utopia owner and winemaker Daniel Warnhius moved north from California looking for a vineyard site that would produce world-class Pinot Noir, and he found this location with the right combination of location, climate, and soil structure. In the tasting room, you're likely to be served by Daniel himself. In addition to several great Pinot Noirs, they also produce a bright, crisp Chardonnay, and a Pinot Noir Rosé. ✉ *17445 N.E. Ribbon Ridge Rd.* ☎ *503/687–1671* 🌐 *utopiawine.com* 🎟 *Tastings $15* 🕓 *Closed weekdays Dec.–Apr.*

Vidon Vineyard. This small Newberg-area winery produces seven varieties of Pinot Noir along with small batches of Chardonnay, Pinot Gris, Viognier, Tempranillo, and Syrah. While the wines are enough to merit a visit to Vidon's hilltop tasting room, those with an interest in the science of wine-making will likely get a kick out of chatting with physicist-turned-winemaker Donald Hagge, who has applied his background to come up with some innovative ways to make and store wine. ✉ *17425 N.E. Hillside Dr.* ☎ *503/538–4092* 🌐 *www.vidonvineyard.com* 🎟 *Tastings $20.*

4

WHERE TO EAT AND STAY

$$$$ MODERN AMERICAN 🍴 **Jory.** This exquisite hotel dining room is named after one of the soils in the Oregon wine country. Chef Sunny Jin sources the majority of his ingredients locally, many from the on-site garden. **Known for:** Oregon-centric wine list; locally sourced ingredients. [$] *Average main: $35* ✉ *The Allison Inn, 2525 Allison La.* ☎ *503/554–2525, 877/294–2525* 🌐 *www.theallison.com.*

$$$$ RESORT 🏨 **The Allison Inn & Spa.** At this luxurious, relaxing base for exploring the region's 200 wineries, each bright, comfortable room includes a gas fireplace, original works of art, a soaking tub, impressive furnishings, bay-window seats, and views of the vineyards from the terrace or balcony. **Pros:** outstanding on-site restaurant; excellent gym and spa facilities; located in the middle of wine country. **Cons:** not many nearby off-property activities other than wine tasting. [$] *Rooms from: $405* ✉ *2525 Allison La.* ☎ *503/554–2525, 877/294–2525* 🌐 *www.theallison.com* 🛏 *85 rooms.*

$$$ B&B/INN 🏨 **Le Puy A Wine Valley Inn.** This beautiful wine country retreat caters to wine enthusiasts with amenities that include wine bars in each individually decorated room, along with hot tubs and gas fireplaces in some. **Pros:** beautiful surroundings; lots of nice architectural and decorative touches. **Cons:** a distance from sights other than wineries. [$] *Rooms from: $235* ✉ *20300 N.E. Hwy. 240* ☎ *503/554–9528* 🌐 *lepuy-inn.com* 🛏 *8 rooms* 🍽 *Breakfast.*

NIGHTLIFE AND PERFORMING ARTS

FAMILY **99W Drive-in.** Ted Francis built this drive-in in 1953, and operated it until his death at 98; the business is now run by his grandson. The first film begins at dusk. ✉ *3110 Portland Rd. (Hwy. 99W)* ☎ *503/538–2738* 🌐 *www.99w.com* 🎟 *$8; vehicles with single occupant $12* 🕓 *Closed Mon.–Thurs.*

SPORTS AND THE OUTDOORS

BALLOONING

Hot-air balloon rides are nothing less than a spectacular, breathtaking thrill—particularly over Oregon's beautiful Yamhill County.

Fodor's Choice ★ **Vista Balloon Adventures.** Enjoy floating gently above beautiful Oregon wine country as the sun rises behind the vines. Your FAA-licensed pilot will take the balloon up about 1,500 feet and can often steer the craft down to skim the water, then up to view hawks' nests. A brunch is served upon returning to the ground. ⊠ *1050 Commerce Pkwy.* ☎ *503/625–7385, 800/622–2309* ⊕ *www.vistaballoon.com* 🖃 *$220 per person.*

DUNDEE

3 miles southwest of Newberg on Hwy. 99W.

Dundee used to be known for growing the lion's share (more than 90%) of the U.S. hazelnut crop. Today, some of Oregon's top-rated wineries are just outside Dundee, and the area is now best known for wine tourism and wine bars, bed-and-breakfast inns, and restaurants.

GETTING HERE AND AROUND

Dundee is just under an hour's drive from Portland International Airport; **Caravan Airport Transportation** provides shuttle service.

What used to be a pleasant drive through quaint Dundee on Highway 99W now can be a traffic hassle, as it serves as the main artery from Lincoln City on the Oregon Coast to suburban Portland. Others will enjoy wandering along the 25 miles of Highway 18 between Dundee and Grande Ronde, in the Coast Range, which goes through the heart of the Yamhill Valley wine country.

Contacts Caravan Airport Transportation. ☎ *541/994–9645* ⊕ *www.caravanairporttransportation.com.*

EXPLORING

TOP ATTRACTIONS

Fodor's Choice ★ **Archery Summit Winery.** The winery that Gary and Nancy Andrus, owners of Pine Ridge winery in Napa Valley, founded in the 1990s has become synonymous with premium Oregon Pinot Noir. Because they believed that great wines are made in the vineyard, they adopted such innovative techniques as narrow spacing and vertical trellis systems, which give the fruit a great concentration of flavors. In addition to the standard flight of Pinot Noirs in the tasting room, you can call ahead and reserve a private seated tasting or a tasting paired with small bites or a tour of the winery and, weather permitting, a walk out to the vineyard. You're welcome to bring a picnic, and as at many Oregon wineries, you can bring your dog, too. ⊠ *18599 N.E. Archery Summit Rd., Dayton* ☎ *503/864–4300* ⊕ *www.archerysummit.com* 🖃 *Tastings $20.*

Argyle Winery. A beautiful establishment, Argyle has its tasting room in a Victorian farmhouse set amid gorgeous gardens. The winery is tucked into a former hazelnut processing plant—which explains the Nuthouse label on its reserve wines. Since Argyle opened in 1987, it has consistently produced sparkling wines that are crisp on the palate, with an aromatic, lingering finish and bubbles that seem to last forever. And these sparklers cost about a third of their counterparts from California. The winery also produces Chardonnay, dry Riesling, Pinot Gris, and Pinot Noir. ⊠ *691 Hwy. 99W* ☎ *503/538–8520, 888/427–4953* ⊕ *www.argylewinery.com* ✉ *Tastings $15.*

Fodor's Choice **Domaine Drouhin Oregon.** When the French winery magnate Robert
★ Drouhin ("the Sebastiani of France") planted a vineyard and built a winery in the Red Hills of Dundee back in 1987, he set local oenophiles abuzz. His daughter Veronique is now the winemaker and produces silky and elegant Pinot Noir and Chardonnay. Ninety acres of the 225-acre estate has been planted on a hillside to take advantage of the natural coolness of the earth and to establish a gravity-flow winery. No appointment is needed to taste the Oregon wines, but if you can plan ahead for the tour (reservations required), you can taste Oregon and Burgundy side-by-side. ⊠ *6750 N.E. Breyman Orchards Rd., Dayton* ☎ *503/864–2700* ⊕ *www.domainedrouhin.com* ✉ *Tastings $15* ⊗ *Closed mid-Oct.–May, Mon. and Tues.*

Winderlea. The tasting room looks over the acclaimed former Goldschmidt vineyard, first planted in 1974, and the view can be enjoyed on the outside deck on a warm summer day. Winemaker Robert Brittan crafts lush Pinot Noir and Chardonnay from several nearby vineyards in both single-vineyard offerings and blends from multiple vineyards. Proceeds from the tasting fee are donated to Salud, a partnership between Oregon winemakers and local medical professionals to provide healthcare services for Oregon's seasonal vineyard workers and their families. ⊠ *8905 N.E. Worden Hill Rd* ☎ *503/554–5900* ⊕ *www.winderlea.com* ✉ *Tastings $20.*

WORTH NOTING

Dobbes Family Estate. Joe Dobbes makes a lot of wine, but he's definitely not a bulk winemaker. He provides custom wine-making services to many Oregon wineries that are too small to have their own winery or winemaker. But he also makes several lines of his own wine, ranging from his everyday "Wine By Joe" label to the premium Dobbes Family Estate label featuring great Pinot Noir, Syrah, Sauvignon Blanc, Viognier, and Grenache Blanc. In addition to a few single vineyard Pinot Noir bottlings, Dobbes focuses on blends from multiple vineyards to provide consistent, balanced, and interesting wines. Two different tasting flights are available in the tasting room, and seated tastings and tours can be arranged by appointment. ⊠ *240 S.E. 5th St.* ☎ *503/538–1141* ⊕ *www.joedobbeswines.com* ✉ *Tastings $15.*

Domaine Serene. This world-class winery in Dundee's Red Hills is a well-regarded producer of Oregon Pinot Noir and Chardonnay. Bring a picnic and enjoy the beautiful grounds of the estate. As an alternative to the standard drop-in tasting in the high-ceiling tasting room, call ahead to reserve a tour or private seated tasting, which includes an extended flight of rare wines. ⊠ *6555 N.E. Hilltop La., Dayton* ☎ *503/864–4600, 866/864–6555* ⊕ *www.domaineserene.com* ✉ *Tastings $20.*

The Dundee Bistro's Wine and Bubble Bar. Located right on the main highway between Portland and wine country, The Dundee Bistro's Wine

Continued on page 196

The Willamette Valley is Oregon's premier wine region. With a milder climate than any growing area in California, cool-climate grapes like Pinot Noir and Pinot Gris thrive here, and are being transformed into world-class wines.

There may be fewer and smaller wineries than in Napa, but the experience is often more intimate. The winemaker himself may even pour you wine.

Touring is easy, as most wineries are well marked, and have tasting rooms with regular hours. Whether you're taking a day trip from Portland, or staying for a couple of days, here's how to get the most out of your sipping experience.

By Dave Sandage and John Doerper

Above and right, Willamette Valley

Wine Tasting
in the
Willamette
Valley

OREGON'S WINES: THEN AND NOW

Rex Hill Vineyards

THE EARLY YEARS

The French made wine first—French Canadians, that is. In the 1830s, retired fur trappers from the Hudson's Bay Company started to colonize the Willamette Valley and planted grapes on the south-facing buttes. They were followed by American settlers who made wine.

Although wine-making in the region languished after these early efforts, it never quite vanished. A few wineries hung on, producing wines mainly for Oregonians of European descent.

It wasn't until the 1970s that the state's wine industry finally took off. Only after a group of young California winemakers started making vinifera wines in the Umpqua and Willamette Valleys and gained international acclaim for them, did Oregon's wines really take hold.

WINEMAKING TODAY

Today, Oregon's wine industry is racing ahead. Here the most prolific white and red grapes are Pinot Gris and Pinot Noir, respectively. Other prominent varietals include Riesling, Gewürztraminer, Viognier, Chardonnay, Carbernet Franc, and Syrah.

The wine industry in Oregon is still largely dominated by family and boutique wineries that pay close attention to quality and are often keen to experiment. That makes traveling and tasting at the source an always-interesting experience.

OREGON CERTIFIED SUSTAINABLE WINE

The latest trend in Oregon winemaking is a dedication to responsible grape growing and winemaking. When you see the Oregon Certified Sustainable Wine (OCSW) logo on the back of a wine bottle, it means the winery ensures accountable agricultural and winemaking practices (in conjunction with agencies such as USDA Organic, Demeter Biodynamic, the Food Alliance, Salmon-Safe, and Low Input Viticulture and Enology) through independent third-party certification. For more information on Oregon Certified Sustainable wines and participating wineries, check ⊕ www.ocsw.org.

WINE TASTING PRIMER

Ordering and tasting wine—whether at a winery, bar, or restaurant—is easy once you master a few simple steps.

LOOK AND NOTE

Hold your glass by the stem and look at the wine in the glass. Note its color, depth, and clarity.

For whites, is it greenish, yellow, or gold? For reds, is it purplish, ruby, or garnet? Is the wine's color pale or deep? Is the liquid clear or cloudy?

SWIRL AND SNIFF

Swirl the wine gently in the glass to intensify the scents, then sniff over the rim of the glass. What do you smell? Try to identify aromas like:

- **Fruits**—citrus, peaches, berries, figs, melon

- **Flowers**—orange blossoms, honey, perfume

- **Spices**—baking spices, pungent, herbal notes

- **Vegetables**—fresh or cooked, herbal notes

- **Minerals**—earth, steely notes, wet stones

- **Dairy**—butter, cream, cheese, yogurt

- **Oak**—toast, vanilla, coconut, tobacco

- **Animal**—leathery, meaty notes

Are there any unpleasant notes, like mildew or wet dog, that might indicate that the wine is "off?"

SIP AND SAVOR

Prime your palate with a sip, swishing the wine in your mouth. Then spit in a bucket or swallow.

Take another sip and think about the wine's attributes. Sweetness is detected on the tip of the tongue, acidity on the sides of the tongue, and tannins (a mouth-drying sensation) on the gums. Consider the body—does the wine feel light in the mouth, or is there a rich sensation? Are the flavors consistent with the aromas? If you like the wine, try to pinpoint what you like about it, and vice versa if you don't like it.

Take time to savor the wine as you're sipping it—the tasting experience may seem a bit scientific, but the end goal is your enjoyment.

WINE TOURING AND TASTING

Wine tasting at Argyle and Rex Hill

WHEN TO GO

In high season (June through October) and on weekends and holidays during much of the year, wine-country roads can be busy and tasting rooms are often crowded. If you prefer a more intimate tasting experience, plan your visit for a weekday.

To avoid the frustration of a fruitless drive, confirm in advance that wineries of interest will be open when you plan to visit.

Choose a designated driver for the day: Willamette wine-country roads are often narrow and curvy, and you may be sharing the road with bicyclists and wildlife as well as other wine tourists.

IN THE TASTING ROOM

Tasting rooms are designed to introduce newcomers to the pleasures of wine and to the wines made at the winery. At popular wineries you'll sometimes have to pay for your tasting, anything from a nominal $2 fee to $30 and up for a tasting that might include a glass you can take home. This fee is often deducted if you buy wine before leaving.

WHAT'S AN AVA?

AVAs (American Viticultural Areas) are geographic winegrowing regions that vaguely reflect the French concept of terroir, or "sense of place." The vineyards within a given AVA have similar characteristics such as climate, soil types, and/or elevation, which impart shared characteristics to the wines made from grapes grown in that area. AVAs are strictly geographic boundaries distinct from city or county designations. AVAs can also be subdivided into sub-AVAs; each of the AVAs mentioned here is actually part of the larger Willamette Valley AVA.

Each taste consists of an ounce or two. Feel free to pour whatever you don't finish into one of the dump buckets on the bar. If you like, rinse your glass between pours with a little water. Remember, those sips add up, so pace yourself. If you plan to visit several wineries, try just a few wines at each so you won't suffer from palate fatigue, when your mouth can no longer distinguish subtleties. It's also a good idea to bring a picnic lunch, which you can enjoy on the deck of a winery, taking in the surrounding wine country vistas.

FALL FOLIAGE

In autumn, Willamette Valley vineyards are particularly stunning as the leaves change color.

DAY TRIP FROM PORTLAND

With nearly 150 vineyards, the Chehalem Mountain and Ribbon Ridge AVAs offer widely varied soil types and diverse Pinot Noirs. The region is less than an hour away from Portland.

Ponzi Vineyards

CHEHALEM MOUNTAIN AND RIBBON RIDGE AVAS

❶ PONZI VINEYARDS
First planted in 1970, Ponzi has some of Oregon's oldest Pinot Noir vines. In addition to current releases, the tasting room sometimes offers older library wines. **Try:** *Arneis, a crisp Italian white varietal.*
✉ 19500 SW Mountain Home Rd., Sherwood
☎ 503/628-1227
🌐 www.ponziwines.com

❷ REX HILL VINEYARDS
Before grapevines, the Willamette Valley was widely planted with fruits and nuts. Enjoy classic Oregon Pinot Noir in this tasting room built around an old fruit and nut drying facility. **Try:** *dark and spicy Dundee Hills Pinot Noir.*
✉ 30835 N. Hwy. 99W, Newberg
☎ 800/739-4455
🌐 www.rexhill.com

❸ VERCINGETORIX (VX) VINEYARD
This 10-acre vineyard sits in the middle of a 210-acre farm near the Willamette River. The tasting room is in one of the barns; a relaxed, friendly atmosphere for sampling. **Try:** *crisp and refreshing Pinot Blanc.*
✉ 8000 N.E. Parrish Rd., Newberg
☎ 503/538-9895
🌐 www.vxvineyard.com

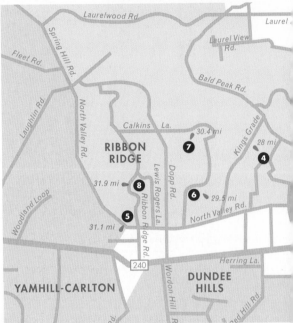

❹ FOX FARM VINEYARDS TASTING ROOM
In addition to offering their own wines, this multi-winery tasting room in downtown Newberg features samples from several small local producers. The menu changes periodically.
✉ 606 E. First St., Newberg
☎ 503/538-8466
🌐 www.foxfarmvineyards.com

❺ UTOPIA VINEYARD
The tasting room at this small Oregon winery is quite intimate—you'll likely be served by the winemaker himself. **Try:** *light and slightly sweet Rosé.*
✉ 17445 N.E. Ribbon Ridge Rd., Newberg
☎ 503/298-7841
🌐 www.utopiawine.com

Vercingetorix (VX) Vineyard

Adelsheim Vineyard

Rex Hill

Pinot Gris grapes

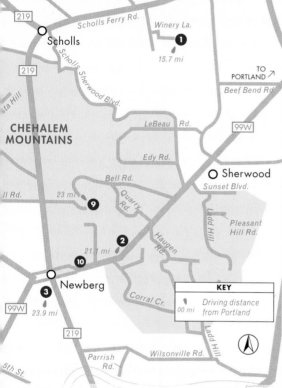

❽ ARAMENTA CELLARS

A small, family-run operation that offers tastings in its winery, built on the foundation of an old barn. The on-site vineyard grows primarily Pinot Noir and Chardonnay. **Try:** *smooth and structured Tillie Claret.*

✉ 17979 N.E. Lewis Rogers La., Newberg
☏ 503/538-7230
🌐 www.aramentacellars.com

STOP FOR A BITE

❾ JORY RESTAURANT

Located within the luxurious Allison Inn and Spa, Jory serves creative dishes that highlight the bounty of the Willamette Valley.

✉ 2525 Allison La., Newberg
☏ 503/554-2526
🌐 www.theallison.com

❿ SUBTERRA

Casual fine dining in a wine cellar atmosphere underneath the Dark Horse wine bar. The menu features global cuisine and a good selection of local wines.

✉ 1505 Portland Rd., Newberg
☏ 503/538-6060
🌐 www.subterrarestaurant.com

KEY

	Driving distance
00 mi	from Portland

❻ ADELSHEIM VINEYARD

One of Oregon's older Pinot Noir producers, Adelsheim has just opened a new tasting room inside its modern winery, with friendly, knowledgeable employees. **Try:** *dark and smoky Elizabeth's Reserve Pinot Noir.*

✉ 16800 N.E. Calkins La., Newberg
☏ 503/538-3652
🌐 www.adelsheim.com

❼ BERGSTROM WINERY

A beautiful tasting room, but the real high point here is the classic Oregon Pinot Noir sourced from several of its estate vineyards as well as other local sites. **Try:** *earthy Bergstrom Pinot Noir.*

✉ 18215 N.E. Calkins La., Newberg
☏ 503/554-0468
🌐 www.bergstromwines.com

TWO DAYS IN WINE COUNTRY

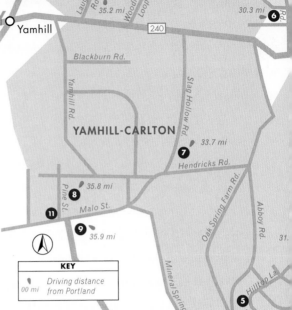

DAY 1

DUNDEE HILLS AVA

The Dundee Hills AVA is home to some of Oregon's best known Pinot Noir producers. Start your tour in the town of Dundee, about 30 miles southwest of Portland, then drive up into the red hills and enjoy the valley views from many wineries.

❶ ARGYLE WINERY

If you don't want to drive off the beaten path, this winery is right on Highway 99W in Dundee. They specialize in sparkling wines, but also make very nice still wines. **Try:** *crisp Brut Rosé.*

✉ 691 Hwy. 99 W, Dundee
☎ 503/538-8520
🌐 www.argylewinery.com

❷ PONZI WINE BAR

This tasting room close to Argyle has a nice selection of local wines. It's a good choice for those who want to sample a large selection side-by-side. **Try:** *bright and fruity Ponzi Pinot Gris.*

✉ 100 S.W. 7th St., Dundee
☎ 503/554-1500
🌐 www.ponziwines.com

❸ ARCHERY SUMMIT

An Oregon Pinot Noir pioneer, Archery Summit features memorable wines and equally pleasing views. Call in advance to schedule a tour of the winery and aging caves. **Try:** *dark and rich Premier Cuvée Pinot Noir.*

✉ 18599 NE Archery Summit Rd., Dayton
☎ 503/864-4300
🌐 www.archerysummit.com

❹ DOMAINE DROUHIN OREGON

Started in the late 1980s by the Drouhin family of Burgundy fame, this winery makes notable Oregon Pinot Noir, as well as Chardonnay. **Try:** *smooth and earthy Willamette Valley Pinot Noir.*

✉ 6750 Breyman Orchards Rd., Dayton
☎ 503/864-2700
🌐 www.domainedrouhin.com

❺ VISTA HILLS VINEYARD

The so-called Treehouse is arguably the most stunning tasting room in Oregon. Sample wine made from estate fruit on a deck that overlooks the vineyards of the Dundee Hills. **Try:** *fruity Treehouse Pinot Noir.*

✉ 6475 N.E. Hilltop La., Dayton
☎ 503/864-3200
🌐 www.vistahillsvineyard.com

DAY 2

YAMHILL-CARLTON AVA

To the west of the Dundee Hills AVA is the horseshoe-shaped Yamhill-Carlton AVA. Vineyards here are found on the slopes that surround the towns of Yamhill and Carlton. Carlton has become a center of wine tourism, and you could easily spend a day visiting tasting rooms in town.

❻ PENNER-ASH WINE CELLARS

This state-of-the-art winery and tasting room is atop a hill with an excellent view of the valley below. **Try:** *smooth and dark Shea Vineyard Pinot Noir.*

✉ 15771 N.E. Ribbon Ridge Rd., Newberg
☎ 503/554-5545
🌐 www.pennerash.com

Penner-Ash Wine Cellars

Ponzi Wine Bar

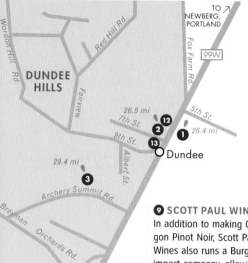

STOP FOR A BITE

⑪ THE HORSERADISH WINE AND CHEESE BAR
Located in downtown Carlton, The Horseradish offers a wide selection of local wines as well as cheese from around the world. The sandwiches and small plates make for a great quick lunch.
✉ 211 W. Main St., Carlton
☎ 503/852-6656
🌐 www.thehorseradish.com

⑫ DUNDEE BISTRO
A favorite of winemakers, Dundee Bistro serves seasonal local ingredients paired with Willamette Valley wines. Enjoy outdoor seating, or watch chefs work in the open kitchen inside.
✉ 100-A S.W. 7th St., Dundee
☎ 503/554-1650
🌐 www.dundeebistro.com

⑬ TINA'S
The warm and intimate Tina's features dishes made with seasonal ingredients, organic vegetables, and free-range meats. Stop by for lunch Tuesday–Friday, or nightly dinner.
✉ 760 Hwy. 99 W, Dundee
☎ 503/538-8880
🌐 www.tinasdundee.com

⑦ LEMELSON VINEYARDS
Although it specializes in single-vineyard Pinot Noir, Lemelson also makes several crisp white wines. The deck overlooking the vineyards is perfect for picnics. Try: *crisp and fruity Riesling.*
✉ 12020 N.E. Stag Hollow Rd., Carlton
☎ 503/852-6619
🌐 www.lemelsonvineyards.com

⑧ TYRUS EVAN WINE
Well-known winemaker Ken Wright's second label features big reds. The tasting room is in the historic Carlton train station. Try: *bold and spicy Del Rio Claret.*
✉ 120 N. Pine St., Carlton
☎ 503/852-7070
🌐 www.tyrusevanwine.com

⑨ SCOTT PAUL WINES
In addition to making Oregon Pinot Noir, Scott Paul Wines also runs a Burgundy import company, allowing you to taste locally grown Pinot Noir alongside some of the best Burgundies. Try: *structured and elegant La Paulée Pinot Noir.*
✉ 128 S. Pine St., Carlton
☎ 503/852-7300
🌐 www.scottpaul.com

⑩ LENNÉ ESTATE
Lenné specializes in highly regarded Pinot Noir, although it's often pouring a couple of non-Pinot wines from other wineries as well. The tasting room in a small stone building overlooks the vineyards. Try: *complex and earthy Estate Pinot Noir.*
✉ 18760 Laughlin Rd., Yamhill
☎ 503/956-2256
🌐 www.lenneestate.com

and Bubble Bar offers the opportunity to sample wines from both the Ponzi Winery and small local producers without straying far from the beaten path. The tasting menu features current releases of Ponzi wines, as well as a rotating selection of other local wines. If you've had enough wine for a while, you can also get snacks, Italian coffee, or a craft beer to enjoy in the comfortable tasting room. ✉ *100 S.W. 7th St.* ☎ *503/554–1500* ⊕ *www.dundeebistro.com.*

Erath Vineyards Winery. When Dick Erath opened one of Oregon's pioneer wineries more than a quarter century ago, he focused on producing distinctive Pinot Noir from grapes he'd been growing in the Red Hills since 1972—as well as full-flavored Pinot Gris, Pinot Blanc, Chardonnay, Riesling, and late-harvest Gewürztraminer. The wines are excellent and reasonably priced. In 2006 the winery was sold to Washington State's giant conglomerate Ste. Michelle Wine Estate. The tasting room is in the middle of the vineyards, high in the hills, with views in nearly every direction; the hazelnut trees that covered the slopes not so long ago have been replaced with vines. The tasting-room terrace, which overlooks the winery and the hills, is a choice spot for picnicking. Crabtree Park, next to the winery, is a good place to stretch your legs after a tasting. ✉ *9409 N.E. Worden Hill Rd.* ☎ *503/538–3318, 800/539–9463* ⊕ *www.erath.com* 🍷 *Tastings $15.*

Maresh Red Barn. When Jim and Loie Maresh planted 2 acres of vines in 1970, theirs became the fifth vineyard in Oregon and the first on Worden Hill Road. The quality of their grapes was so high that some of the Dundee Hills' best and most famous wineries soon sought them out. When the wine industry boomed in the 1980s, the Mareshes decided they might as well enjoy some wine from their renowned grapes, now planted on 45 acres of their land. They transformed their old barn into a tasting room, where you can taste and purchase exceptional Chardonnay, Pinot Noir, Pinot Gris, Riesling, and Sauvignon Blanc made by several acclaimed local winemakers from Maresh family grapes. ✉ *9325 N.W. Worden Hill Rd.* ☎ *503/537–1098* ⊕ *www.vineyardretreat.com* ☉ *Closed Dec.–Feb. and Mar.–Thanksgiving, Mon.–Thurs.*

Red Ridge. A good place to clean your palette after all that wine tasting is Red Ridge, home to the first commercial olive mill in the Pacific Northwest. Stop by the gift shop to taste some of the farm's signature oils or head out back to see an old-fashioned (and not-in-use) olive press imported from Spain. Free tours are available June through September, daily at 11; if you're in town in November, don't miss the annual Olio Nuovo Festival, where you can taste extra virgin oil in its freshly milled and unfiltered state. ✉ *5510 N.E. Breyman Orchards Rd., Dayton* ☎ *503/864–8502* ⊕ *redridgefarms.com.*

Fodor's Choice
★

Sokol Blosser. One of Yamhill County's oldest wineries (it was established in 1971) makes consistently excellent wines and sells them at reasonable prices. Set on a gently sloping south-facing hillside and surrounded by vineyards, lush lawns, and shade trees, it's a splendid place to learn about wine. A demonstration vineyard with several rows of vines contains the main grape varieties and shows what happens to them as the seasons unfold. Winery tours are available daily at 11. ✉ *5000 Sokol*

Blosser La. ✥ *3 miles west of Dundee off Hwy. 99W* ☎ *503/864–2282, 800/582–6668* 🌐 *www.sokolblosser.com* 🎫 *Tastings $15, tours $40.*

Torii Mor Winery. One of Yamhill County's oldest vineyards, established in 1993, makes small quantities of handcrafted Pinot Noir, Pinot Gris, and Chardonnay and is set amid Japanese gardens with breathtaking views of the Willamette Valley. The gardens were designed by Takuma Tono, the same architect who designed the renowned Portland Japanese Garden. The owners, who love all things Japanese, named their winery after the distinctive Japanese gate of Shinto religious significance; they added a Scandinavian mor, signifying "earth," to create an east-west combo: "earth gate." Jacques Tardy, a native of Nuits Saint Georges, in Burgundy, France, is the current winemaker. Under his guidance Torii Mor wines have become more Burgundian in style. ✉ *18323 N.E. Fairview Dr.* ☎ *503/538–2279* 🌐 *www.toriimorwinery.com* 🎫 *Tastings $15.*

4

Vista Hills Vineyard. The Treehouse tasting room here is arguably the most beautiful in Oregon. Step out onto the deck and enjoy the view from underneath the towering trees. Vista Hills is a bit different from its neighbors in that there is no winery but several well-known local winemakers create wine from the vineyard grapes to sell under the Vista Hills label. The result is a range of distinctive wine styles, all made from the same vineyard. Also available are Hawaiian chocolate and coffee from their sister farm in Kona. ✉ *6475 Hilltop La., Dayton* ☎ *503/864–3200* 🌐 *www.vistahillsvineyard.com* 🎫 *Tastings $15.*

White Rose Estate. Like many of its better-known neighbors in the Dundee Hills, White Rose Estate produces elegant Pinot Noir that reflects the land where it is grown. In addition to their own estate vineyard, they purchase grapes from several highly regarded vineyards around the Willamette Valley. They describe their wines as "neoclassical," using traditional techniques in the vineyard, and state-of-the-art equipment and handling in the winery. Somewhat unusual for Oregon, most of the wines have a fairly high percentage of whole clusters included during fermentation, giving the wines more complexity and a bit of spice. ✉ *6250 N.E. Hilltop La., Dayton* ☎ *503/864–2328* 🌐 *www.whiteroseestate.com* 🎫 *Tastings $15.*

WHERE TO EAT

$$$ CONTEMPORARY

🍴 **Dundee Bistro.** The Ponzi wine family are capable restaurateurs as well and use Northwest organic foods such as Draper Valley chicken, Carlton Farms pork, and locally produced wines, fruits, vegetables, nuts, mushrooms, fish, and meats. Vaulted ceilings provide an open feeling inside, warmed by abundant fresh flowers and the works of local Oregon artists. **Known for:** part of the Ponzi wine family. [$] *Average main: $25* ✉ *100-A S.W. 7th St.* ☎ *503/554–1650* 🌐 *www.dundeebistro.com.*

$ PACIFIC NORTHWEST FAMILY

🍴 **Red Hills Market.** Serving great sandwiches, salads, and pizza, this is the perfect stop for a quick lunch in the middle of a day of wine tasting, or a casual no-frills dinner at the end of the day. Many of the sandwiches feature locally made charcuterie and cheeses, and the pizzas range from traditional Margarita to a spicy chorizo, blue cheese, and arugula. **Known for:** great stop during wine tasting; takeout options.

$ *Average main: $12* ✉ *155 S.W. 7th St.* ☎ *971/832–8414* 🌐 *www.redhillsmarket.com.*

$$$$ FRENCH Fodor's Choice ★ 🍴 **Tina's.** Chef–proprietors Tina and David Bergen bring a powerful one-two punch to this Dundee favorite that often lures Portlanders away from their own restaurant scene. The couple shares cooking duties—Tina does the baking and is often on hand to greet you, and David brings his experience as a former caterer and employee of nearby Sokol Blosser Winery to the table, ensuring that you have the right glass of wine to match your course. **Known for:** attracting Portland foodies; delicious homemade soups. $ *Average main: $35* ✉ *760 Hwy. 99W* ☎ *503/538–8880* 🌐 *www.tinasdundee.com* 🕒 *No lunch Sun. and Mon.*

WHERE TO STAY

$$$ B&B/INN Fodor's Choice ★ 🏨 **Dundee Manor Bed and Breakfast.** This 1908-built traditional home on expansive grounds is filled with treasures and collectibles that add intrigue to each themed room: African, Asian, European, and North American. **Pros:** terrific amenities; lots of activities; attentive staff. **Cons:** few rooms; closed January and February. $ *Rooms from: $225* ✉ *8380 N.E. Worden Hill Rd.* ☎ *503/554–1945, 888/262–1133* 🌐 *www.dundeemanor.com* 🕒 *Closed Jan. and Feb.* 🛏 *4 rooms* 🍽 *Breakfast.*

$$ HOTEL 🏨 **The Inn at Red Hills.** These spacious and extremely comfortable rooms, each with its own layout, offer plenty of local flavor, from the materials in the building, to the wines served and the ingredients used in the kitchen. **Pros:** contemporary, stylish surroundings; close to many wineries. **Cons:** located on the main highway through town rather than the country. $ *Rooms from: $179* ✉ *1410 N. Hwy. 99W* ☎ *503/538–7666* 🌐 *www.innatredhills.com* 🛏 *20 rooms* 🍽 *No meals.*

YAMHILL-CARLTON

14 miles west of Dundee.

Just outside the small towns of Carlton and Yamhill are neatly combed benchlands and hillsides, an American Viticultural Area (AVA) established in 2004, and home to some of the finest Pinot Noir vineyards in the world. Carlton has exploded with many small tasting rooms in the past few years, and you could easily spend an entire day tasting wine within three or four blocks. The area is a gorgeous quilt of nurseries, grain fields, and orchards. Come here for the wine tasting, but don't expect to find too much else to do.

GETTING HERE AND AROUND

Having your own car is the best way to explore this rural region of Yamhill County, located a little more than an hour's drive from Portland International Airport. The towns of Yamhill and Carlton are about an hour's drive from Downtown Portland, traveling through Tigard, to Newberg and west on Highway 240.

EXPLORING

TOP ATTRACTIONS

Lemelson Vineyards. This winery was designed from the ground up to be a no-compromises Pinor Noir production facility with an eye to Willamette Valley aesthetics, and the highlight is a diverse range of single-vineyard Pinot Noirs. But don't neglect the bright Pinot Gris and Riesling, perfect with seafood or spicy fare. The spacious high-ceiling tasting room is a great place to relax and take in the view through the floor-to-ceiling windows, or bring a picnic and enjoy the deck on a warm summer day. ✉ *12020 N.E. Stag Hollow Rd., Carlton* ☎ *503/852–6619* ⊕ *www.lemelsonvineyards.com.*

Lenné Estate. The small stone building that houses the tasting room is surrounded by the estate vineyard and looks like something right out of Burgundy. Steve Lutz was looking for the perfect site to grow Pinot Noir and bought the property in 2000. In addition to offering his own rich and elegant estate Pinot Noirs for tasting, he often pours other varietals from other wineries. ✉ *18760 N.E. Laughlin Rd., Yamhill* ☎ *503/956–2256* ⊕ *www.lenneestate.com* ▭ *$10* ⊙ *Closed Mon.–Wed.*

WORTH NOTING

Anne Amie Vineyards. Early wine country adopters Fred and Mary Benoit established this hilltop winery as Chateau Benoit in 1979. When the winery changed hands in 1999, it was renamed Anne Amie and has been concentrating on Pinot Blanc, Pinot Gris, and Pinot Noir, but still makes a dry Riesling. In addition, they also make Syrah and a Bordeaux blend from eastern Washington grapes. Both the tasting room and the picnic area have spectacular views across the hills and valleys of Yamhill County. ✉ *6580 N.E. Mineral Springs Rd., Carlton* ☎ *503/864–2991* ⊕ *www.anneamie.com* ▭ *Tastings $15.*

Carlton Winemakers Studio. Oregon's first cooperative winery was specifically designed to house multiple small premium wine producers. This gravity-flow winery has up-to-date wine-making equipment as well as multiple cellars for storing the different makers' wines. You can taste and purchase bottles from the different member wineries: Andrew Rich, Asilda, Bachelder, Dukes Family Vineyard, Hamacher Wines, Lazy River Vineyard, Merriman Wines, Mad Violets, Omero, Retour Wine Co., Trout Lily Ranch, Utopia Vineyard, and Wahle Vineyards and Cellars. The emphasis is on Pinot Noir, but more than a dozen other types of wines are poured, from Cabernet Franc to Gewürztraminer to Mourvèdre on a rotating basis. The selection of wines available to taste changes every few days. ✉ *801 N. Scott St., Carlton* ☎ *503/852–6100* ⊕ *www.winemakersstudio.com* ▭ *Tastings from $22.*

Ken Wright Cellars Tasting Room. Carlton's former train depot is now the tasting room for Ken Wright Cellars and his warm-climate label, Tyrus Evan. The winery specializes in single-vineyard Pinot Noirs, each subtly different from the next depending on the soil types and grape clones. The wines are poured side by side, giving you an opportunity to go back and forth to compare them. The Tyrus Evan wines are quite different from the Ken Wright Pinots: they are warm-climate varieties like Cabernet Franc, Malbec, Syrah, and red Bordeaux blends, from grapes Wright buys from vineyards in eastern Washington and southern Oregon. You can also pick up cheeses and other picnic supplies, as well as wine country gifts and souvenirs. ✉ *120 N. Pine St., Carlton* ☎ *503/852–7010* ⊕ *www.kenwrightcellars.com* ▭ *Tastings from $20.*

Scott Paul Tasting Room and Winery. Pinot Noir fans, listen up: this small spot in the center of Carlton not only makes Pinot Noir from Oregon grapes, but it also imports and sells Pinot Noirs from Burgundy (as well as grower Champagne). The mainstay Pinot Noirs made from local grapes are Audrey, the finest wine of the vintage, and La Paulée, a selection of the best lots of each vintage. In addition, they'll make several other Pinots customized to the widely variable growing conditions each year in Oregon. All are splendid examples of the wines that can be made from this great, challenging grape. The tasting room, a quaint redbrick building, is across the street from the winery. Tours are by appointment only. Wine seminars are offered periodically, and private guided tastings are available by appointment. ✉ *128 S. Pine St., Carlton* ☎ *503/852–7300* ⊕ *www.scottpaul.com* 🍷 *Tastings $10* ⊘ *Closed Mon. and Tues.*

WHERE TO EAT

$ ✕ **The Horse Radish.** The perfect stop in the middle of a day of wine tasting offers a wide selection of artisan cheese and meats, as well as a great lunch menu. Pick up some sandwiches and a soup or salad to go, and you're all set for a picnic at your favorite winery. **Known for:** live music on Friday and Saturday nights; tasting room featuring Marshall Davis wines. $ *Average main: $8* ✉ *211 W. Main St., Carlton* ☎ *503/852–6656* ⊕ *www.thehorseradish.com* ⊟ *No credit cards.*

PACIFIC
NORTHWEST

MCMINNVILLE

11 miles south of Yamhill on Hwy. 99 W.

The Yamhill County seat, McMinnville lies in the center of Oregon's thriving wine industry. There is a larger concentration of wineries in Yamhill County than in any other area of the state. Among the varieties are Chardonnay, Pinot Noir, and Pinot Gris. Most of the wineries in the area offer tours and tastings. McMinnville's downtown area has a few shops worth a look; many of the historic district buildings, erected 1890–1915, are still standing, and are remarkably well maintained.

GETTING HERE AND AROUND

McMinnville is a little more than an hour's drive from Downtown Portland; **Caravan Airport Transportation** provides shuttle service to Portland International Airport. McMinnville is just 70 minutes from Lincoln City on the Oregon Coast, and 27 miles west of Salem.

ESSENTIALS

Visitor Information Visit McMinnville. ✉ *328 N.E. Davis St., Suite 1* ☎ *503/857–0182* ⊕ *visitmcminnville.com.*

EXPLORING

FAMILY
Fodor's Choice
★

Evergreen Aviation and Space Museum and Wings and Waves Waterpark. Howard Hughes' *Spruce Goose,* the largest plane ever built and constructed entirely of wood, is on permanent display, but if you can take your eyes off the giant you will also see more than 45 historic planes and replicas from the early years of flight and World War II, as well as the postwar and modern eras. Across the parking lot from the aviation museum is the space museum with artifacts that include a German V-2 rocket and a Titan missile, complete with silo and launch control room. The adjacent Wings and Waves Waterpark (separate admission) has 10 waterslides, including one that starts at a Boeing 747-100 that sits on *top* of the building. The IMAX theater is open daily and features several different films each day. There's a museum store and two cafés, as well as ongoing educational programs and special events. ⊠ *500 N.E. Michael King Smith Way* ☎ *503/434–4185* ⊕ *www.evergreenmuseum. org* ⤳ *$27, includes IMAX movie; $33 waterpark.*

The Eyrie Vineyards. When David Lett planted the first Pinot Noir vines in the Willamette Valley in 1965, he was setting in motion a series of events that has caused Willamette Valley Pinot Noir to be recognized as among the best in the world. Affectionately known as Papa Pinot, Lett, along with several other pioneering winemakers nurtured the Oregon wine industry to what it is today. Today David's son Jason Lett is now the winemaker and vineyard manager, and continues to make Pinot Noir, Pinot Gris, and Chardonnay that reflect the gentle touch that has always characterized Eyrie wines. In recent years, many small wineries have sprung up in the neighborhood around this historic winery. ⊠ *935 N.E. 10th Ave.* ☎ *503/472–6315, 888/440–4970* ⊕ *www.eyrievineyards.com* ⤳ *Tastings $10.*

4

NEED A BREAK

✕ **Serendipity Ice Cream.** Historic Cook's Hotel, built in 1886, is the setting for a true, old-fashioned ice-cream-parlor experience. Try a sundae, and take home cookies made from scratch. Known for: locally made ice cream (dairy- and sugar-free varieties). ⊠ *502 N.E. 3rd St.* ☎ *503/474–9189* ⊕ *serendipityicecream.com.*

WHERE TO EAT AND STAY

$$$$
CONTEMPORARY

✕ **Joel Palmer House.** Wild mushrooms and truffles are the stars at this 1857 home, named after an Oregon pioneer, that is now on the National Register of Historic Places. There are three small dining rooms, each seating about 15 people. **Known for:** mushrooms, mushrooms, mushrooms; three-course prix-fixe menu; Chef Christopher's Mushroom Madness Menu. Ⓢ *Average main: $50* ⊠ *600 Ferry St., Dayton* ☎ *503/864–2995* ⊕ *www.joelpalmerhouse.com* ☾ *Closed Sun. and Mon. No lunch.*

$$$
ITALIAN
Fodor's Choice
★

✕ **Nick's Italian Cafe.** Famed for serving Oregon's wine country enthusiasts, this fine-dining venue is a destination for a special evening or lunch. Modestly furnished but with a voluminous wine cellar, Nick's serves spirited and simple food, reflecting the owner's northern Italian heritage. **Known for:** five-course prix-fixe with wine pairings; expansive wine cellar. Ⓢ *Average main: $26* ⊠ *521 N.E. 3rd St.* ☎ *503/434–4471* ⊕ *nicksitaliancafe.com.*

$
HOTEL

⊓ **Hotel Oregon.** Rooms in the former Elberton Hotel, built in 1905, have tall ceilings and high windows, are outfitted in late-Victorian furnishings, and filled with whimsical art—sometimes serene, often bizarre—as well as photos and sayings scribbled on the walls. **Pros:** inexpensive; casual and lively; plenty of food and drink on the premises. **Cons:** shared baths for most rooms; those seeking upscale ambience should look elsewhere. Ⓢ *Rooms from: $60* ⊠ *310 N.E. Evans*

St. ☎ *503/472–8427, 888/472–8427* 🌐 *www.mcmenamins.com* 🛏 *42 rooms* 🍴 *No meals.*

$$ B&B/INN Fodor's Choice ★ 🏨 **Joseph Mattey House Bed & Breakfast.** The four upstairs rooms in this Queen Anne Victorian mansion are whimsically named after locally grown grape varieties and are decorated in keeping with the character of those wines: crisp white furnishings in the Chardonnay Room, dark-wood pieces and reddish wine accents in the Pinot Noir room. **Pros:** refined bed-and-breakfast atmosphere. **Cons:** not many modern amenities in the rooms. [$] *Rooms from: $175* ✉ *10221 N.E. Mattey La.* ✣ *Off Hwy. 99 W, ¼ mile south of Lafayette* ☎ *503/434–5058* 🌐 *www.matteyhouse.com* 🛏 *4 rooms* 🍴 *Breakfast.*

NIGHTLIFE AND PERFORMING ARTS

Spirit Mountain Casino and Lodge. Located 24 miles southwest of McMinnville on Highway 18, this popular gambling getaway is owned and operated by the Confederated Tribes of the Grande Ronde Community of Oregon. The 90,000-square-foot casino has more than a thousand slots, as well as poker and blackjack tables, roulette, craps, Pai Gow poker, keno, bingo, and off-track betting. Big-name comedians and rock and country musicians perform in the 1,700-seat concert hall, and there's an arcade for the kids. Complimentary shuttle service from Portland and Salem is available. Dining options include an all-you-can-eat buffet, a deli, and a café. ✉ *27100 S.W. Salmon River Hwy., Grand Ronde* ☎ *503/879–2350, 800/760–7977* 🌐 *spiritmountain.com.*

MID-WILLAMETTE VALLEY

While most of the wineries are concentrated in Washington and Yamhill counties, there are several finds in the mid–Willamette Valley that warrant extending a wine enthusiast's journey. There are also flower, hops, berries, and seed gardens scattered throughout Salem, Albany, and Corvallis. The huge number of company stores concentrated on Interstate 5 will have you thinking about some new Nikes, and Oregon State University will have you wearing orange and black long after Halloween is over. Be aware that many communities in this region are little more than wide spots in the road. In these tiny towns you might find only a gas station, a grocery store, a church or two, and a school. Watch out for any "School Crossing" signs: Oregon strictly enforces its speed-limit laws.

SALEM

24 miles from McMinnville, south on Hwy. 99W and east on Hwy. 22, 45 miles south of Portland on I–5.

The state capital has a rich pioneer history, but before that it was the home of the Calapooia Indians, who called it Chemeketa, which means "place of rest." Salem is said to have been renamed by missionaries. Although trappers and farmers preceded them in the Willamette Valley, the Methodist missionaries had come in 1834 to minister to Native Americans, and they are credited with the founding of Salem. In 1842 they established the first academic institution west of the Rockies, which is now known as Willamette University. Salem became the capital when Oregon achieved statehood in 1859 (Oregon City was the capital of the Oregon Territory). Salem serves as the seat to Marion County as well as the home of the state fairgrounds. Government ranks as a major industry here, while the city's setting in the heart of the fertile Willamette Valley stimulates rich agricultural and food-processing industries. More than a dozen wineries are in or near Salem. The main attractions in Salem are west of Interstate 5 in and around the Capitol Mall.

GETTING HERE AND AROUND

Salem is located on Interstate 5 with easy access to Portland, Albany, and Eugene. **Hut Portland Airport Shuttle** provides transportation to Portland International Airport, which is one hour and 15 minutes away. Salem's McNary Field no longer has commercial airline service, but serves general aviation aircraft.

Bus transportation throughout Salem is provided by **Cherriots**. Amtrak operates regularly, and its train station is located at 500 13th Street SE.

ESSENTIALS

Contacts Cherriots. ⊕ *www.cherriots.org.* **Hut Portland Airport Shuttle.** ☎ *503/364–4444* ⊕ *www.portlandairportshuttle.com.*

Visitor Information Salem Convention & Visitors Center. ✉ *181 High St. NE* ☎ *503/581–4325, 800/874–7012* ⊕ *www.travelsalem.com.*

EXPLORING

TOP ATTRACTIONS

Oregon Garden. Just outside the town of Silverton, a 25-minute drive from Salem, the Oregon Garden showcases the botanical diversity of the Willamette Valley and Pacific Northwest. Open 365 days a year, the 80-acre garden features themed plots ranging from a conifer forest to medicinal plants. There also a whimsical children's garden complete with a model train, and another garden featuring the agricultural bounty of the area. A free narrated tram tour operates from April to October allowing visitors an overview of the garden before exploring on their own. ✉ *879 W. Main St., Silverton* ☎ *503/874–8100, 877/674–2733* ⊕ *www.oregongarden.org* ✉ *$12* ⊗ *Closed Jan.–Mar., Mon.–Thurs. and Nov.–Dec., Mon.–Wed.*

FAMILY **Willamette Heritage Center at The Mill.** Take a trip back in time to experience the story of Oregon's early pioneers and the industrial revolution. The **Thomas Kay Woolen Mill Museum** complex (circa 1889), complete with working waterwheels and millstream, looks as if the workers have just stepped away for a lunch break. Teasel gigging, napper flock bins, and the patented Furber double-acting napper are but a few of the machines and processes on display. The **Jason Lee House,** the **John D. Boon Home,** and the **Methodist Parsonage** are also part of the village. There is nothing grandiose about these early pioneer homes, the oldest frame structures in the Northwest, but they reveal a great deal about domestic life in the wilds of Oregon in the 1840s. ✉ *1313 Mill St. SE* ☎ *503/585–7012* ⊕ *www.willametteheritage.org* ✉ *$7* ⊗ *Closed Sun.*

Witness Tree Vineyard. Named for the ancient oak that towers over the vineyard (it was used as a surveyor's landmark in the 1850s), this winery

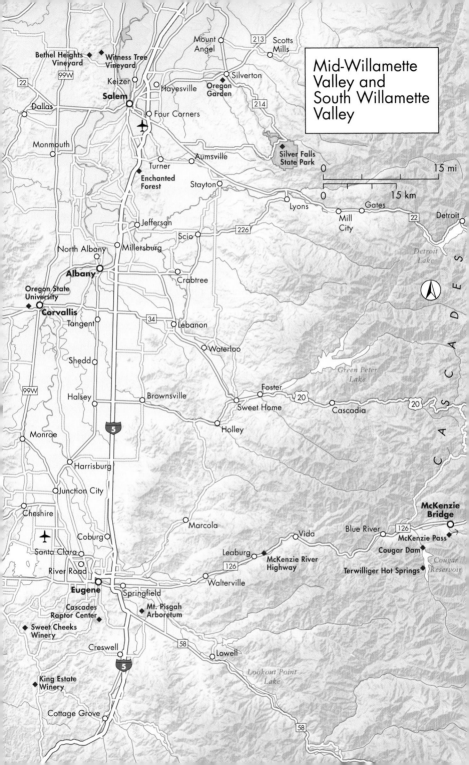

Mount
Angel
Scotts
Mills
213
Bethel Heights
Vineyard
Witness Tree
Vineyard
Keizer
Silverton
22
99W
Hayesville
Oregon
Garden
Salem
Dallas
214
Four Corners
Monmouth
Aumsville
Silver Falls
State Park
0   15 mi
Turner
Enchanted
Forest
Stayton
0   15 km
Jefferson
Lyons
Gates
Detroit
Scio
226
Mill
City
22
North Albany
Millersburg
Detroit
Lake
Albany
Crabtree
CASCADES
Oregon State
University
Corvallis
Tangent
34
Lebanon
Shedd
Waterloo
Green Peter
Lake
99W
Halsey
Brownsville
Foster
Sweet Home
20
Cascadia
20
Monroe
Holley
Harrisburg
Junction City
McKenzie
Bridge
Cheshire
Marcola
Vida
Blue River
126
McKenzie Pass
Coburg
Leaburg
McKenzie River
Highway
Cougar Dam
Santa Clara
126
Terwilliger Hot Springs
Cougar
Reservoir
River Road
Walterville
Eugene
Springfield
Cascades
Raptor Center
Mt. Pisgah
Arboretum
Sweet Cheeks
Winery
Creswell
58
Lowell
5
Lookout Point
Lake
King Estate
Winery
Cottage Grove
58

Mid-Willamette
Valley and
South Willamette
Valley

produces premium Pinot Noir made entirely from grapes grown on its 100-acre estate nestled in the Eola Hills northwest of Salem. The vineyard also produces limited quantities of estate Chardonnay, Viognier, Pinot Blanc, Dolcetto, and a sweet dessert wine called Sweet Signé. Tours are available by appointment. ⊠ *7111 Spring Valley Rd. NW* ☎ *503/585–7874* ⊕ *www.witnesstreevineyard.com* ⬚ *Tastings from $5* ⊙ *Closed May–Oct., Mon. and Mar. and Apr., Nov.–mid-Dec., Mon.–Wed.*

WORTH NOTING

Bethel Heights Vineyard. Founded in 1977, Bethel Heights was one of the first vineyards planted in the Eola Hills region of the Willamette Valley. It produces Pinot Noir, Chardonnay, Pinot Blanc, and Pinot Gris. The tasting room has one of the most glorious panoramic views of any winery in the state; its terrace and picnic area overlook the surrounding vineyards, the valley below, and Mt. Jefferson in the distance. ⊠ *6060 Bethel Heights Rd. NW* ☎ *503/581–2262* ⊕ *www.bethelheights.com* ⬚ *Tastings $10* ⊙ *Closed Mon.*

Bush's Pasture Park. These 105 acres of rolling lawn and formal English gardens include the remarkably well-preserved Bush House, an 1878 Italianate mansion at the park's far-western boundary. It has 10 marble fireplaces and virtually all of its original furnishings, and can be visited only on informative tours. Bush Barn Art Center, behind the house, exhibits the work of Northwest artists and has a sales gallery. ⊠ *600 Mission St. SE* ☎ *503/363–4714* ⊕ *www.salemart.org* ⬚ *House $6.*

Elsinore Theatre. This flamboyant Tudor Gothic vaudeville house opened on May 28, 1926, with Edgar Bergen in attendance. Clark Gable (who lived in nearby Silverton) and Gregory Peck performed on stage. The theater was designed to look like a castle, with a false-stone front, chandeliers, ironwork, and stained-glass windows. It's now a lively performing arts center with a busy schedule of bookings, and there are concerts on its Wurlitzer pipe organ. ⊠ *170 High St. SE* ☎ *503/375–3574* ⊕ *www.elsinoretheatre.com.*

FAMILY **Gilbert House Children's Museum.** This is a different kind of kids' museum; an amazing place to let the imagination run wild. Celebrating the life and the inventions of A.C. Gilbert, a Salem native who became a toy manufacturer and inventor, the historic houses included many themed interactive rooms along with a huge outdoor play structure. In addition to the children's activities, many beloved toys created by A.C. Gilbert are on display, including Erector sets and American Flyer trains. The wide range of indoor and outdoor interactive exhibits will appeal to children (and adults) of all ages. ⊠ *116 Marion St. NE* ☎ *503/371–3631* ⊕ *www.acgilbert.org* ⬚ *$8* ⊙ *Closed Mon. in fall and winter.*

Mount Angel Abbey. This Benedictine monastery on a 300-foot-high butte was founded in 1882 and is the site of one of two Modernist buildings in the United States designed by Finnish architect Alvar Aalto. A masterpiece of serene and thoughtful design, Aalto's library opened its doors in 1970, and has become a place of pilgrimage for students and aficionados of modern architecture. ⊠ *1 Abbey Dr., St. Benedict*

Oregon Capitol building in Salem

⊕ *18 miles from Salem; east on Hwy. 213 and north on Hwy. 214*
☎ *503/845–3030* ⊕ *www.mountangelabbey.org* ✉ *Free* ⊙ *Closed Sun.*

Oregon Capitol. A brightly gilded bronze statue of the *Oregon Pioneer* stands atop the 140-foot-high Capitol dome, looking north across the Capitol Mall. Built in 1939 with blocks of gray Vermont marble, Oregon's Capitol has an elegant yet austere neoclassical feel. East and west wings were added in 1978. Relief sculptures and deft historical murals soften the interior. Tours of the rotunda, the House and Senate chambers, and the governor's office leave from the information center under the dome. ✉ *900 Court St. NE* ☎ *503/986–1388* ⊕ *www.oregon-legislature.gov* ✉ *Free* ⊙ *Closed weekends.*

Willamette University. Behind the Capitol, across State Street but half a world away, are the brick buildings and grounds of Willamette University, the oldest college in the West. Founded in 1842, Willamette has long been a breeding ground for aspiring politicians. **Hatfield Library,** built in 1986 on the banks of Mill Stream, is a handsome brick-and-glass building with a striking campanile; tall, prim **Waller Hall,** built in 1867, is one of the oldest buildings in the Pacific Northwest. ✉ *900 State St.* ☎ *503/370–6300* ⊕ *www.willamette.edu* ⊙ *Closed weekends.*

EN
ROUTE **Enchanted Forest.** South of Salem, the Enchanted Forest is the closest thing Oregon has to a major theme park. The park has several attractions in forestlike surroundings, including a Big Timber Log Ride. On it, you ride logs through flumes that pass through a lumber mill and the woods. The ride—the biggest log ride in the Northwest—has a 25-foot roller-coaster dip and a 40-foot drop at the end. Other attractions include the Ice Mountain Bobsled roller coaster, the Haunted

House, English Village, Storybook Lane, the Fantasy Fountains Water Light Show, Fort Fearless, and the Western town of Tofteville. ✉ *8462 Enchanted Way SE, Turner* ✣ *7 miles south of Salem at Exit 248 off I–5* ☎ *503/363–3060, 503/371–4242* 🌐 *www.enchantedforest.com* 🎟 *$11.75, rides cost extra* ⏲ *Closed Apr. and Labor Day–end of Sept., weekdays, and Nov.–Mar.*

WHERE TO EAT AND STAY

$$ ITALIAN Fodor's Choice ★ 🍴 **DaVinci.** Salem politicos flock to this two-story downtown gathering spot for Italian-inspired dishes cooked in a wood-burning oven. No shortcuts are taken in the preparation, so don't come if you're in a rush. **Known for:** pasta made in-house; good wines by the glass; live music. [$] *Average main: $24* ✉ *180 High St. SE* ☎ *503/399–1413* 🌐 *www.davincisofsalem.com* ⏲ *No lunch.*

$$ HOTEL 🏨 **Grand Hotel in Salem.** Large rooms, with comfortable and luxurious furnishings, are the best in town, a good base for guests attending shows and meetings at Salem Conference Center or touring the region. **Pros:** spacious rooms; centrally located. **Cons:** some street noise; lacks character. [$] *Rooms from: $169* ✉ *201 Liberty St. SE* ☎ *503/540–7800, 877/540–7800* 🌐 *www.grandhotelsalem.com* 🛏 *193 rooms* 🍽 *Breakfast.*

$ RESORT 🏨 **Oregon Garden Resort.** Bright, spacious, and tastefully decorated rooms, each with a fireplace and a private landscaped patio or balcony, neighbor the Oregon Garden (admission is included in the rates). **Pros:** gorgeous grounds; luxurious rooms; pool and plenty of other amenities. **Cons:** a distance from other activities. [$] *Rooms from: $115* ✉ *895 W. Main St., Silverton* ☎ *503/874–2500* 🌐 *www.oregongardenresort.com* 🛏 *103 rooms* 🍽 *Breakfast.*

SHOPPING

Reed Opera House. These days the 1869 opera house in downtown Salem contains an eclectic collection of locally owned stores, shops, restaurants, bars, and bakeries, everything from art galleries to tattoo parlors. Its Trinity Ballroom hosts special events and celebrations. ✉ *189 Liberty St. NE* ☎ *503/391–4481* 🌐 *www.reedoperahouse.com.*

Woodburn Company Stores. Located 18 miles north of Salem just off Interstate 5 are more than 100 brand-name outlet stores, including Nike, Calvin Klein, Bose, Gymboree, OshKosh B'Gosh, Ann Taylor, Levi's, Chico's, Fossil,The North Face, and Columbia Sportswear. There's also a small playground and a couple of places to eat. ✉ *1001 Arney Rd., Woodburn* ☎ *503/981–1900, 888/664–7467* 🌐 *www.woodburncompanystores.com.*

SPORTS AND THE OUTDOORS

RECREATIONAL AREAS

Silver Falls State Park. Hidden amid old-growth Douglas firs in the foothills of the Cascades, this is the largest state park in Oregon (8,700 acres). South Falls, roaring over the lip of a mossy basalt bowl into a deep pool 177 feet below, is the main attraction here, but 13 other waterfalls—half of them more than 100 feet high—are accessible to hikers. The best time to visit is in the fall, when vine maples blaze with brilliant color, or early spring, when the forest floor is carpeted with trilliums and yellow violets. There are picnic facilities and a day lodge; in winter you can cross-country ski. Camping facilities include tent and trailer sites, cabins, and a horse camp. ⊠ *20024 Silver Falls Hwy. SE, Sublimity* ☎ *503/873–8681, 800/551–6649* ⊕ *www.oregonstateparks. org* ⌕ *$5 per vehicle.*

Willamette Mission State Park. Along pastoral lowlands by the Willamette River, this serene park holds the largest black cottonwood tree in the United States. A thick-barked behemoth by a small pond, the 275-year-old tree has upraised arms that bring to mind J.R.R. Tolkien's fictional Ents. Site of Reverend Jason Lee's 1834 pioneer mission, the park also offers quiet strolling and picnicking in an old orchard and along the river. The Wheatland Ferry, at the north end of the park, began carrying covered wagons across the Willamette in 1844 and is still in operation today. ⊠ *Wheatland Rd.* ✛ *8 miles north of Salem, I–5 Exit 263* ☎ *503/393–1172, 800/551–6649* ⊕ *www.oregonstateparks.org* ⌕ *$5 per vehicle.*

ALBANY

20 miles from Salem, south on I–5 and west on U.S. 20.

Known as the grass-seed capital of the world, Albany has some of the most historic buildings in Oregon. Some 700 buildings, scattered over a 100-block area in three districts, include every major architectural style developed in the United States since 1850. The area is listed on the National Register of Historic Places. Eight covered bridges can also be seen on a half-hour drive from Albany. Oregon has the largest collection of covered bridges in the western United States, and the Willamette Valley has more than 34 of the wooden structures.

GETTING HERE AND AROUND
Albany is located on Interstate 5 with easy access to Portland, Salem, and Eugene. Portland International Airport is one hour, 40 minutes away, and the Eugene airport is one hour away to the south. Several shuttle services are available from both airports.

Albany Transit System provides two routes for intercity travel. The Linn-Benton loop system provides for transportation between Albany and Corvallis. Albany is served by Amtrak.

ESSENTIALS
Visitor Information Albany Visitors Association. ⊠ *110 3rd Ave. SE* ☎ *541/928–0911, 800/526–2256* ⊕ *www.albanyvisitors.com.*

EXPLORING
Albany Historic Carousel and Museum. It's not often that you get to watch a carousel being built, but that's exactly what's happening here. Craftsmen and volunteers from the Albany area have come together to contribute thousands of hours to carving and painting a huge array of whimsical carousel creatures ranging from traditional horses to giant frogs and dragons. They hope to have the carousel in operation in 2017, but there have been plenty of delays in the project so it's best to call ahead. In the meantime you can enjoy watching the creations come together, as well

as viewing many historical carousel artifacts in the museum. ✉ *250 S.W. Broadalbin St.* ☎ *541/791–3340* 🌐 *albanycarousel.com.*

WHERE TO EAT

$ HUNGARIAN 🍴 **Novak's Hungarian.** Since 1984, the Novak family has been a delightful fixture in Albany's dining scene. Whether you're ordering Hungarian hash and eggs in the morning or chicken paprika served over homemade Hungarian pearl noodles for dinner, you can't go wrong in this establishment. **Known for:** good, hearty Hungarian fare; locally sourced ingredients; familial atmosphere. [$] *Average main: $14* ✉ *208 2nd St. SW* ☎ *541/967–9488* 🌐 *www.novakshungarian.com.*

$$ ECLECTIC Fodor's Choice ★ 🍴 **Sybaris.** A rotating menu at this fine bistro in Albany's historic downtown changes monthly and features flavorful cuisine at reasonable prices. The restaurant strives to ensure that most of the ingredients, including the lamb, eggs, and vegetables, are raised within 10 miles. **Known for:** reasonable prices; menu changes monthly; locally sourced products. [$] *Average main: $20* ✉ *442 1st Ave. W* ☎ *541/928–8157* 🌐 *www.sybarisbistro.com* ⏲ *Closed Sun. and Mon. No lunch.*

CORVALLIS

10 miles southwest of Albany on U.S. 20.

Corvallis is a small city that's best known as the home of Oregon State University and its Beavers athletic teams. Driving the area's economy are a growing engineering and high-tech industry, a burgeoning wine industry, and more traditional local agricultural crops, such as grass and legume seeds. The town and its environs offer plenty of outdoor activities as well as scenic attractions, from covered bridges to wineries and gardens.

GETTING HERE AND AROUND

Corvallis Transit System (CTS) operates eight bus routes throughout the city. **Hut Shuttle** provides transportation between Corvallis and the Portland airport, located one hour, 53 minutes away. **OmniShuttle** provides transportation between Corvallis and the Eugene airport, 50 minutes away. Corvallis Municipal Airport is a public airport 4 miles south of the city.

ESSENTIALS

Visitor Information **Corvallis Tourism.** ✉ *420 N.W. 2nd St.* ☎ *541/757–1544, 800/334–8118* 🌐 *www.visitcorvallis.com.*

EXPLORING

Oregon State University. It's a thrill to be on campus on game day, when students are a sea of orange and black cheering on their beloved Beavers. This 400-acre campus, west of the city center, was established as a land-grant institution in 1868. OSU has more than 26,000 students, many of them studying the university's nationally recognized programs in conservation biology, agricultural sciences, nuclear engineering, forestry, fisheries and wildlife management, community health, pharmacy, and zoology. ✉ *15th and Jefferson Sts.* ☎ *541/737–1000* 🌐 *oregonstate.edu.*

WHERE TO EAT AND STAY

$$$ LATIN AMERICAN

🍴 **Del Alma.** This multilevel waterfront eatery gives every table a nice view of the river and puts a modern spin on tapas, bringing unexpected flavors and textures to classic Latin food. The menu features both tapas and larger dishes, with a strong emphasis on seafood and beef. **Known for:** tapas; Latin-inspired cocktails; great river views. [$] *Average main: $28* ✉ *136 S.W. Washington Ave.* ☎ *541/753–2222* 🌐 *delalmarestaurant.com* 🕑 *Closed Sun. No lunch.*

$$$ MODERN AMERICAN Fodor's Choice ★

🍴 **Gathering Together Farm.** When spring arrives, it means that the organic farmers outside of Philomath are serving their bounty. Fresh vegetables, pizzas, local lamb, pork, and halibut are frequent highlights on a menu that features simple fresh ingredients impeccably prepared. **Known for:** coppa; organic produce from collective of local farms. [$] *Average main: $25* ✉ *25159 Grange Hall Rd., Philomath* ☎ *541/929–4270* 🌐 *www.gatheringtogetherfarm.com* 🕑 *No dinner Tues. or Wed.*

$ HOTEL Fodor's Choice ★

🏨 **Boulder Falls Inn.** One of the chicest places to stay in the area, this business-boutique hotel features sleek rooms and suites filled with locally produced furniture, many of which look out on a huge koi pond surrounded by an authentic Japanese garden. **Pros:** sleek rooms; excellent dining; on-site Japanese garden. **Cons:** location somewhat removed from area attractions. [$] *Rooms from: $120* ✉ *505 Mullins Dr., Lebanon* ☎ *541/405–7025* 🌐 *boulderfallsinn.com* 🛏 *84 rooms* 🍽 *Breakfast.*

SPORTS AND THE OUTDOORS

RECREATIONAL AREAS

Fodor's Choice ★

Siuslaw National Forest. The forest, starting just 2 miles from Corvallis and extending to the coast, includes the Oregon Dunes National Recreation Area and the Cape Perpetua Interpretive Center. Within the park is the highest point in the Coast Range, Mary's Peak (4,097 feet), offering panoramic views of the Cascades, the Willamette Valley, and the rest of the Coast Range. On a clear day you can see as far as the Pacific Ocean. There are several picnicking areas, more than 10 miles of hiking trails, and a small campground, as well as stands of noble fir and alpine meadows. You can access Mary's Peak from Highway 34 between Corvallis and Newport and the central coast. Several other major highways (Highways 26, 6, 18, 26, and 126) also run through the forest between the Willamette Valley and the coast, providing access to recreation areas. ✉ *Forest office, 3200 S.W. Jefferson Way* ☎ *541/750–7000* 🌐 *www.fs.fed.us/r6/siuslaw* 🎟 *$5 per vehicle at some recreation sites.*

SWIMMING

FAMILY

Osborn Aquatic Center. This is not your ordinary lap pool. There are waterslides, a water channel, water cannons, and floor geysers. The indoor pools are open all year. ✉ *1940 N.W. Highland Dr.* ☎ *541/766–7946* 🌐 *www.corvallisoregon.gov/index.aspx?page=57* 🎟 *$6.*

SOUTH WILLAMETTE VALLEY

Lane County rests at the southern end of the Willamette Valley, encompassing Eugene, Springfield, Drain, McKenzie Bridge, and Cottage Grove. Visitors can enjoy a wide range of outdoor activities such as running, fishing, swimming, white-water rafting, and deep-woods hiking along the McKenzie River, while Eugene offers great food, shopping, and the arts. There are plenty of wineries to enjoy, too, as well as cheering on the Oregon Ducks. To the west lies the Oregon Dunes Recreation Area, and to the east are the beautiful central Oregon communities of Sisters, Bend, and Redmond.

4

EUGENE

63 miles south of Corvallis on I–5.

Eugene was founded in 1846, when Eugene Skinner staked the first federal land-grant claim for pioneers. Eugene is consistently given high marks for its "livability." As the home of the University of Oregon, a large student and former-student population lends Eugene a youthful vitality and countercultural edge. Full of parks and oriented to the outdoors, Eugene is a place where bike paths are used, pedestrians *always* have the right-of-way, and joggers are so plentiful that the city is known as the Running Capital of the World. Shopping and commercial streets surround the Eugene Hilton and the Hult Center for the Performing Arts, the two most prominent downtown buildings. During football season you can count on the U of O Ducks being the primary topic of most conversations.

GETTING HERE AND AROUND

Eugene's airport has rental cars, cabs, and shuttles that make the 15-minute trip to Eugene's city center. By train, Amtrak stops in the heart of downtown. Getting around Lane County's communities is easy with **Lane Transit District** public transportation. Eugene is very bicycle-friendly.

ESSENTIALS

Visitor Information Travel Lane County. ⊠ *754 Olive St.* ☎ *541/484–5307, 800/547–5445* ⊕ *www.eugenecascadescoast.org.*

EXPLORING

TOP ATTRACTIONS

FAMILY **Cascades Raptor Center.** This birds-of-prey nature center and hospital hosts more than 30 species of birds. A visit is a great outing for kids, who can learn what owls eat, why and where birds migrate, and all sorts of other raptor facts. Some of the full-time residents include turkey vultures, bald eagles, owls, hawks, falcons, and kites. ⊠ *32275 Fox Hollow Rd.* ☎ *541/485–1320* ⊕ *www.eraptors.org* 🏷 *$8* ⊘ *Closed Mon.*

Eugene Saturday Market. Held every Saturday from April through the middle of November, the Saturday Market is a great place to browse for handicrafts, try out local food carts, or simply kick back and people-watch while listening to live music at the Market Stage. ⊠ *126 E. 8th Ave.* ☎ *541/686–8885* ⊕ *www.eugenesaturdaymarket.org.*

Fresh produce at a farmers' market in Eugene

King Estate Winery. One of Oregon's largest producers is known for their crisp Pinot Gris and silky Pinot Noir and boasts the world's largest organic vineyard. The visitors center offers wine tasting and production tours, and the restaurant highlights local meats and organic produce grown in the estate gardens. ✉ *80854 Territorial Rd.* ☎ *541/942–9874* ⊕ *www.kingestate.com* 🍷 *Tastings $10* ☒ *Closed Mon. and Tues. in winter.*

Lane County Farmers' Market. Across the street from the Eugue Saturday Market, the Lane County market offers produce grown or made in Oregon. Hours and days vary throughout the year. ✉ *Corner of 8th Ave. and Oak St.* ☎ *541/431–4923* ⊕ *www.lanecountyfarmersmarket. org/markets* ☒ *Closed Jan.*

Ninkasi Brewing Company. Named after the Sumerian goddess of fermentation, Ninkasi has grown from a little start-up in 2006 to a major supplier of craft beer. Its flagship beer, Total Domination IPA, is signature Northwest, with bold flavor and lots of hops. Visit the tasting room and enjoy a tasting flight or a pint, either indoors or on the patio. The beer menu changes often and includes a few hard-to-find limited-production beers. If you'd like a little food to go with your beer, you'll usually find one of Eugene's many food carts right there on the patio. Free brewery tours are offered daily. ✉ *272 Van Buren St.* ☎ *541/344–2739* ⊕ *www. ninkasibrewing.com.*

WORTH NOTING

Alton Baker Park. This parcel of open land on the banks of the Willamette River is named after the late publisher of Eugene's newspaper, the *Register-Guard,* and is the site of many community events. Live music is performed in summer at the Cuthbert Amphitheater. There's fine hiking and biking on a footpath that runs along the river for the length of the park, and an 18-hole disc golf course. Also worth seeing is the Whilamut Natural Area, an open space with 13 "talking stones," each with an inscription. ✉ *200 Day Island Rd.* ☎ *541/682–4906* ⊕ *www. altonbakerpark.com/.*

Jordan Schnitzer Museum of Art. Works from the 20th and 21st centuries are a specialty in these handsome galleries on the University of Oregon campus. They feature works by many leading Pacific Northwest artists, and European, Korean, Chinese, and Japanese works are also on view, as are 300 works commissioned by the Works Progress Administration in the 1930s and '40s. You can also view an ever-changing collection of important works from private collections by internationally recognized artists through the museum's Masterworks On Loan program. ✉ *1430 Johnson La.* ☎ *541/346–3027* ⊕ *jsma.uoregon.edu* 🎟 *$5* ⊗ *Closed Mon. and Tues.*

FAMILY **Mount Pisgah Arboretum.** This beautiful nature preserve near southeast Eugene includes extensive all-weather trails, educational programs for all ages, and facilities for special events. Its visitor center holds workshops and features native amphibian and reptile terraria; microscopes for exploring tiny seeds, bugs, feathers, and snakeskins; "touch me" exhibits; reference books; and a working viewable beehive. ✉ *34901 Frank Parrish Rd.* ☎ *541/747–3817* ⊕ *www.mountpisgaharboretum. org* 🎟 *Parking $4.*

FAMILY **Science Factory.** Formerly the Willamette Science and Technology Center (WISTEC), and still known to locals by its former name, Eugene's imaginative, hands-on museum assembles rotating exhibits designed for curious young minds. The adjacent **planetarium,** one of the largest in the Pacific Northwest, presents star shows and entertainment events. ✉ *2300 Leo Harris Pkwy.* ☎ *541/682–7888* ⊕ *www.sciencefactory.org* 🎟 *$4 for exhibit hall or planetarium, $7 for both* ⊗ *Closed Oregon Ducks home football games; exhibit hall Mon. and Tues.; planetarium weekdays.*

Sweet Cheeks Winery. This estate vineyard lies on a prime sloping hillside in the heart of the Willamette Valley appellation. It also supplies grapes to several award-winning wineries. Bring a picnic and enjoy the amazing view from the lawn outside the tasting room, or take advantage of the food available for purchase. Friday-night tastings are embellished with cheese pairings and live music. ✉ *27007 Briggs Hill Rd.* ☎ *541/349–9463, 877/309–9463* ⊕ *www.sweetcheekswinery.com* ⊗ *Closed Sun. and Mon.*

University of Oregon. The true heart of Eugene lies southeast of the city center at its university. Several fine old buildings can be seen on the 250-acre campus; **Deady Hall,** built in 1876, is the oldest. More than 400 varieties of trees grace the bucolic grounds, along with outdoor sculptures that include *The Pioneer* and *The Pioneer Mother.* The two bronze figures by Alexander Phimster Proctor were dedicated to the men and women who settled the Oregon Territory and less than a generation later founded the university. ✉ *1585 E. 13th Ave.* ☎ *541/346–1000* 🌐 *www.uoregon.edu.*

University of Oregon Museum of Natural and Cultural History. Relics on display are devoted to Pacific Northwest anthropology and the natural sciences. Highlights include the fossil collection of Thomas Condon, Oregon's first geologist, and a pair of 9,000-year-old sandals made of sagebrush. ✉ *1680 E. 15th Ave.* ☎ *541/346–3024* 🌐 *natural-history.uoregon.edu* 🎫 *$5* 🕒 *Closed Mon.*

WHERE TO EAT

$ PACIFIC NORTHWEST Fodor's Choice ★

🍴 **The CiderHouse at WildCraft Cider Works.** With the laid-back atmosphere of a brewpub and a long list of house-crafted ciders, this casual spot is a great place to try out WildCraft's locally celebrated dry ciders. The menu is equally impressive with Oregon-style comfort food ranging from mac and cheese with truffle oil to sesame tofu brochettes. **Known for:** house-crafted ciders; Oregon-style comfort food. [$] *Average main: $14* ✉ *390 Lincoln St.* ☎ *541/735–3506* 🌐 *wildcraftciderworks.com* 🕒 *Closed Sun. and Mon.*

$$ PACIFIC NORTHWEST

🍴 **Grit Kitchen and Wine.** You know you're in for local, seasonal ingredients when the chalkboard in this intimate place right across the street from the Ninkasi Brewery in Eugene's eccentric Whiteaker neighborhood lists nearly 20 local farmers and purveyors who are suppliers. The menu changes often, depending on what's in season. **Known for:** the weekly changing four-course feast; Northwest cuisine; products and ingredients come from 20 local farmers and purveyors. [$] *Average main: $21* ✉ *1080 W. 3rd St.* ☎ *541/343–0501* 🌐 *gritkitchen.com* 🕒 *No lunch.*

$$$ FRENCH

🍴 **Marché.** Located in the bustling Fifth Street Market, this renowned Eugene restaurant works with more than a dozen local farmers to bring fresh, local organic food to the table. Specialties include salmon, halibut, sturgeon, and beef tenderloin, braised pork shoulders, and outstanding local oysters paired with an extensive wine list featuring lots of Oregon wines. **Known for:** fresh Sunday beignets; sourced from a dozen local farmers; located in Fifth Street Market. [$] *Average main: $30* ✉ *296 E. 5th Ave.* ☎ *541/342–3612* 🌐 *www.marcherestaurant.com.*

$$$ ITALIAN

🍴 **Ristorante Italiano.** The chef uses fresh local produce from the restaurant's own farm, but this bistro-style café across from the University of Oregon is best known for its authentic Italian cuisine, with a heavy emphasis on fresh local seafood. The menu changes according to the season, but staples include delicious salads and soups, ravioli, grilled chicken, pizza, and sandwiches. **Known for:** seasonal menus; outdoor seating. [$] *Average main: $26* ✉ *Excelsior Inn, 754 E. 13th Ave.* ☎ *541/342–6963, 800/321–6963* 🕒 *No lunch Sat.*

WHERE TO STAY

$ B&B/INN

🏨 **Campbell House.** One of the oldest structures in Eugene, built in 1892, combines architectural details and a mixture of century-old antiques and reproductions to lend each of the rooms a distinctive personality. **Pros:** classic architecture; comfortable rooms; well-kept grounds. **Cons:** rooms lack some of the amenities of nearby hotels. [$] *Rooms* *from: $129* ✉ *252 Pearl St.* ☎ *541/343–1119, 800/264–2519* 🌐 *www.campbellhouse.com* 🛏 *18 rooms* 🍴 *Breakfast.*

$$ B&B/INN Fodor's Choice ★ 🏨 **C'est la Vie Inn.** Listed on the National Register of Historic Places, this 1891 Queen Anne Victorian bed-and-breakfast provides Old World comfort and modern-day amenities in its luxurious and romantic guest rooms. **Pros:** outstanding service and value. **Cons:** few rooms. [$] *Rooms from: $160* ✉ *1006 Taylor St.* 🌐 *cestlavieinn.com* 🛏 *4 rooms* 🍴 *Breakfast.*

$ B&B/INN Fodor's Choice ★ 🏨 **Excelsior Inn.** Quiet sophistication, attention to architectural detail, and rooms furnished in a refreshingly understated manner, each with a marble-and-tile bath and some with fireplaces, suggest a European inn. **Pros:** romantic accommodations; excellent service and restaurant. **Cons:** formal in a casual town. [$] *Rooms from: $135* ✉ *754 E. 13th Ave.* ☎ *541/342–6963, 800/321–6963* 🌐 *www.excelsiorinn.com* 🛏 *14 rooms* 🍴 *Breakfast.*

$$$$ HOTEL 🏨 **Inn at the 5th.** This upscale boutique hotel, set among the shops and restaurants of the trendy Fifth Street Public Market, features subtly elegant rooms and suites. **Pros:** most rooms have fireplaces; great location surrounded by boutiques and restaurants. **Cons:** no self-parking. [$] *Rooms from: $259* ✉ *205 E. 6th Ave.* ☎ *541/743–4099* 🌐 *www.innat5th.com* 🛏 *69 rooms* 🍴 *No meals.*

NIGHTLIFE AND PERFORMING ARTS

Hult Center for the Performing Arts. This is the locus of Eugene's cultural life. Renowned for the quality of its acoustics, the center has two theaters that are home to Eugene's symphony and opera. ✉ *1 Eugene Center* ☎ *541/682–5087 administration, 541/682–5000 tickets* 🌐 *www.hultcenter.org.*

Fodor's Choice ★ **Oregon Bach Festival.** Conductor Helmuth Rilling leads the internationally known Oregon Bach Festival every summer. Concerts, chamber music, and social events—held mainly in Eugene at the Hult Center and the University of Oregon School of Music but also in Corvallis and Florence—are part of this three-week event. ✉ *1 Eugene Center* ☎ *541/682–5000 for tickets, 800/457–1486 for information* 🌐 *oregonbachfestival.com.*

SPORTS AND THE OUTDOORS

BIKING AND JOGGING

The **River Bank Bike Path,** originating in Alton Baker Park on the Willamette's north bank, is a level and leisurely introduction to Eugene's topography. It's one of 120 miles of trails in the area. **Prefontaine Trail,** used by area runners, travels through level fields and forests for 1½ miles.

RECREATIONAL AREAS

FAMILY **Dexter State Recreation Site.** A 20-minute drive southeast of Eugene on the western shores of Dexter Reservoir, this recreation site offers disc golf, picnic areas, boat launches, and plenty of hiking. ✣ *Hwy. 58, between mileposts 11 and 12.*

FAMILY **Skinner Butte Park.** Rising from the south bank of the Willamette River, this forested enclave provides the best views of any of the city's parks; it also has the greatest historic cachet, since it was here that Eugene

Skinner staked the claim that put Eugene on the map. Children can scale a replica of Skinner Butte, uncover fossils, and cool off under a rain circle. Skinner Butte Loop leads to the top of Skinner Butte, traversing sometimes difficult terrain through a mixed-conifer forest. ⊠ *248 Cheshire Ave.* ☎ *541/682–4800* ⌨ *Free.*

SHOPPING

Fifth Street Public Market. Tourists coming to the Willamette Valley, especially to Eugene, can't escape without experiencing the Fifth Street Public Market in downtown Eugene. There are plenty of boutiques and crafts shops, a large gourmet food hall with a bakery, and restaurants serving sushi, pizza, and seafood. ⊠ *296 E. 5th Ave.* ☎ *541/484–0383* ⊕ *www.5stmarket.com.*

Valley River Center. The largest shopping center between Portland and San Francisco has five department stores, including Macy's and JCPenney, plus 130 specialty shops and a food court. ⊠ *293 Valley River Center* ☎ *541/683–5513* ⊕ *www.valleyrivercenter.com.*

MCKENZIE BRIDGE

58 miles east of Eugene on Hwy. 126.

On the beautiful McKenzie River, lakes, waterfalls, and covered bridges surround the town of McKenzie Bridge and wilderness trails in the Cascades. Fishing, skiing, backpacking, and rafting are among the most popular activities in the area.

GETTING HERE AND AROUND

McKenzie Bridge is about an hour from Eugene, on Highway 126. It is just 38 miles from Hoodoo Ski Area, but its proximity can be deceiving if the snow is heavy. Bend also is close at 64 miles to the east.

EXPLORING

McKenzie River Highway. Highway 126, as it heads east from Eugene, is known as the McKenzie River Highway. Following the curves of the river, it passes grazing lands, fruit and nut orchards, and the small riverside hamlets of the McKenzie Valley. From the highway you can glimpse the bouncing, bubbling, blue-green McKenzie River, one of Oregon's top fishing, boating, and white-water rafting spots, against a backdrop of densely forested mountains, splashing waterfalls, and jet-black lava beds. The small town of McKenzie Bridge marks the end of the McKenzie River Highway and the beginning of the 26-mile McKenzie River National Recreation Trail, which heads north through the Willamette National Forest along portions of the Old Santiam Wagon Road. ⊠ *McKenzie Bridge.*

OFF THE
BEATEN
PATH

McKenzie Pass. Just beyond McKenzie Bridge, Highway 242 begins a steep, 22-mile eastward climb to McKenzie Pass in the Cascade Range. The scenic highway, which passes through the Mt. Washington Wilderness Area and continues to the town of Sisters, is generally closed November through June because of heavy snow. Novice motorists take note, this is not a drive for the timid: it's a challenging exercise in negotiating tight curves at quickly fluctuating, often slow speeds—the skid marks on virtually every turn attest to hasty braking—so take it slow, and don't be intimidated by cars on your tail itching to take the turns more quickly. The route is closed to trucks and large trailers and motor homes. ✉ *McKenzie Bridge.*

WHERE TO EAT AND STAY

$ AMERICAN FAMILY 🍴 **Takoda's Restaurant.** A popular roadside café serves burgers, sandwiches, great soups, salads, pizza, and daily specials. The burger selection includes not only beef, but seafood, chicken, turkey, and veggie options. **Known for:** great burger options; video game room for kids. [$] *Average main: $11* ✉ *91806 Mill Creek Rd., Milepost 47.5 McKenzie Hwy., Blue River* ☎ *541/822–1153* 🌐 *www.takodasrainbow.com.*

$ RESORT FAMILY 🏨 **Belknap Hot Springs Resort.** A pleasant lodge, with comfortable though not luxurious rooms, and a campground with both tent trailer sites, are nestled onto the banks of the beautiful McKenzie River. **Pros:** hot springs; wooded location. **Cons:** 14-day cancellation policy; two-night minimum on weekends; trailers and motor homes detract from the rustic atmosphere. [$] *Rooms from: $120* ✉ *59296 Belknap Springs Rd.* ☎ *541/822–3512* 🌐 *www.belknaphotsprings.com* 🛏 *19 rooms, 7 cabins* 🍽 *Breakfast.*

$ B&B/INN Fodor's Choice ★ 🏨 **Eagle Rock Lodge.** These wood-paneled rooms filled with quilts and gorgeous custom furniture are surprisingly luxurious and provide a romantic, relaxing riverside retreat in the woods. **Pros:** great location on the McKenzie River; comfortable atmosphere. **Cons:** a distance from nonoutdoor activities. [$] *Rooms from: $130* ✉ *49198 McKenzie Hwy., Vida* ☎ *541/822–3630, 888/773–4333* 🌐 *www.eaglerocklodge.com* 🛏 *8 rooms* 🍽 *Breakfast.*

SHOPPING

Organic Redneck. On the way to McKenzie Bridge from Eugene, this farm stand offers seasonal, certified organic produce grown right on the family's farm. Blueberries are the specialty here, and they've got dried versions available for those who visit out of season. ✉ *44382 Mckenzie Hwy., Leaburg* ☎ *541/896–3928* 🌐 *www.ogredneck.com.*

SPORTS AND THE OUTDOORS

GOLF

Tokatee Golf Club. Ranked one of the best golf courses in Oregon by *Golf Digest*, this 18-hole beauty is tucked away near the McKenzie River with views of the Three Sisters Mountains, native ponds, and streams. *Tokatee* is a Chinook word meaning "a place of restful beauty." The course offers a practice range, carts, lessons, rentals, a coffee shop and snack bar, and Wi-Fi. ✉ *54947 McKenzie Hwy.* ☎ *541/822–3220, 800/452–6376* 🌐 *www.tokatee.com* 🎫 *18 holes $49; 9 holes $29* 🏌 *9 or 18 holes, 6806 yards, par 72.*

RECREATIONAL AREAS

Cougar Dam and Reservoir. Four miles outside of McKenzie Bridge is the highest embankment dam ever built by the Army Corps of Engineers—452 feet above the streambed. The resulting reservoir, on the South Fork McKenzie River, covers 1,280 acres. The dam generates 25 megawatts of power, and includes a fish collection and sorting facility, and a temperature control tower to keep the downstream water at a suitable temperature for spawning. The public recreation areas are in

4

the Willamette National Forest. You can visit the dam year-round, but some campgrounds are open only from April to September. ⊠ *Willamette National Forest, Forest Rd. 19* ☎ *541/822–3381* 💲 *Free.*

Terwilliger Hot Springs (Cougar Hot Springs). Bring a towel and enjoy the soaking pools in this natural hot-springs area. Located an hour east of Eugene off of Highway 126, the pools are a short hike from the parking area, and include a changing area. Soaking aficionados will find Terwilliger to be rustic, which many regard as an advantage, though the popularity of this beautiful spot can be a drawback. The pools are in a forest of old-growth firs and cedars, and just downstream is a beautiful lagoon complete with waterfall that is also suitable for swimming. Clothing is optional. ⊠ *Off Forest Rd. 19, Blue River* ☎ *541/822–3381* 💲 *$6.*

FodorsChoice
★
Willamette National Forest. Stretching 110 miles along the western slopes of the Cascade Range, this forest boasts boundless recreation opportunities, including waterfall exploration, camping, hiking, boating, ATV riding, and winter sports. It extends from the Mt. Jefferson area east of Salem to the Calapooya Mountains northeast of Roseburg, encompassing 1,675,407 acres. ⊠ *3106 Pierce Pkwy., Suite D, Springfield* ☎ *541/225–6300* ⊕ *www.fs.usda.gov/willamette.*

WHITE-WATER RAFTING

FAMILY **High Country Expeditions.** Raft the white waters of the McKenzie River on a guided full- or half-day tour. You'll bounce through rapids, admire old-growth forest, and watch osprey and blue herons fishing. The outfit provides life jackets, splash gear, wet suits, booties (if requested), boating equipment, paddling instructions, river safety talk, a three-course riverside meal, and shuttle service back to your vehicle. Full-day trips are $90, half-day trips $60. ⊠ *Belknap Hot Springs Resort, 59296 N. Belknap Springs Rd.* ☎ *541/822–8288, 888/461–7238* ⊕ *www.highcountryexpeditions.com.*

5

THE COLUMBIA RIVER GORGE AND MT. HOOD

WELCOME TO THE COLUMBIA RIVER GORGE AND MT. HOOD

TOP REASONS TO GO

★ **Orchards and vineyards:** Dozens of farm stands selling apples, pears, peaches, cherries, and berries, and wine-tasting rooms are open to visitors around Hood River.

★ **Outdoor rec mecca:** From kiteboarding in the Columbia River to mountain biking the slopes of Mt. Hood to hiking among the roaring waterfalls of the Gorge, this is a region tailor-made for adventure junkies.

★ **Historico-luxe:** Grand dames like Timberline Lodge and the Columbia Gorge Hotel exude history and architectural distinction.

★ **Road-tripping:** From Portland, you can make a full 250-mile loop through the Gorge out to Goldendale, Washington, returning to Hood River and then circling Mt. Hood to the south.

★ **Hop havens:** The Gorge/ Hood area has a fast-growing proliferation of taprooms, from Stevenson's tiny Walking Man Brewing to Pfriem, in Hood River.

1 **Columbia River Gorge.** The dams of the early 20th century transformed the Columbia River from the raging torrent that vexed Lewis and Clark in 1805 to the breathtaking but comparatively docile waterway that hosts kiteboarders and windsurfers today. Auto visitors have been scoping out the Gorge's picturesque bluffs and waterfalls for quite a while now—the road between Troutdale and The Dalles, on which construction began in 1913, was the country's first planned scenic highway.

2 **Mt. Hood.** Visible from 100 miles away, Mt. Hood (or simply "the Mountain," as some Portlanders call it) is the kind of rock that commands respect. It's holy ground for mountaineers, more than 10,000 of whom make a summit bid each year. Sightseers are often shocked by the summer snows, but skiers rejoice, keeping the mountain's resorts busy year-round. Mingle with laid-back powderhounds and other outdoorsy types in the hospitality villas of Welches and Government Camp.

GETTING ORIENTED

The mighty Columbia River flows west through the Cascade Range, past the Mt. Hood Wilderness Area, to Astoria. It's a natural border between Oregon and Washington to the north, and bridges link roads on both sides of the Gorge at Biggs Junction, The Dalles, Hood River, and Cascade Locks. The Gorge's watery recreation corridor stretches from Portland's easternmost suburbs past Hood River and The Dalles out to Maryhill and Goldendale, Washington. For portions of that drive, Mt. Hood looms to the southwest. While the massive peak feels remote, the snowcapped heights are just 60 miles east of Portland. Hood River drains the mountain's north side, emptying into the Columbia at its namesake town. Follow the river upstream and you'll trade the warm, low-elevation climes of the Gorge for the high country's tall pines and late-season snows.

Updated
by Andrew
Collins

Volcanoes, lava flows, Ice Age floodwaters, and glaciers were nature's tools of choice when carving a breathtaking, nearly 100-mile landscape now called the Columbia River Gorge. Proof of human civilization here reaches back 31,000 years, and excavations near The Dalles have uncovered evidence that salmon fishing is a 10,000-year-old tradition in these parts. In 1805 Lewis and Clark discovered the Columbia River, the only major waterway that leads to the Pacific. Their first expedition was a treacherous route through wild, plunging rapids, but their successful navigation set a new exodus in motion.

Today the river has been tamed by a comprehensive system of hydroelectric dams and locks, and the towns in these parts are laid-back recreation hamlets whose residents harbor a fierce pride in their shared natural resources. Sightseers, hikers, and skiers have long found contentment in this robust region, officially labeled a National Scenic Area in 1986. They're joined these days by epicures scouring the Columbia's banks in search of farm-to-table cuisine, artisanal hop houses, and top-shelf vino. Highlights of the Columbia River Gorge include Multnomah Falls, Bonneville Dam, the rich orchard and vineyard land of Hood River, and Maryhill Museum of Art. Sailboaters, windsurfers, and kiteboarders take advantage of the blustery Gorge winds in the summer, their colorful sails decorating the waterway like windswept confetti.

To the south of Hood River are all the alpine attractions of the 11,250-foot-high Mt. Hood. With more than 2.2 million people living just up the road in greater Portland, you'd think this mountain playground would be overrun, but it's still easy to find solitude in the 300,000-acre wilderness surrounding the peak. Some of the world's best skiers take advantage of the powder on Hood, and they stick around in summertime for the longest ski season in North America at Palmer Snowfield, above Timberline Lodge.

THE COLUMBIA RIVER GORGE AND MT. HOOD PLANNER

WHEN TO GO

Winter weather in the Mt. Hood area is much more severe than in Portland and the Willamette Valley, and occasionally rough conditions permeate the Gorge, too. Rarely, Interstate 84 closes because of snow and ice. If you're planning a winter visit, be sure to carry plenty of warm clothes. High winds and single-digit temps are par for the course around 6,000 feet—the elevation of Timberline Lodge on Mt. Hood—in January. Note that chains are sometimes required for traveling over mountain passes.

Temperatures in the Gorge are mild year-round, rarely dipping below 30°F in winter and hovering in the high 70s in midsummer. As throughout Oregon, however, elevation is often a more significant factor than season, and an hour-long drive to Mt. Hood's Timberline Lodge can reduce those midsummer temps by 20–30 degrees. Don't forget that the higher reaches of Mt. Hood retain snow year-round.

In early fall, look for maple, tamarack, and aspen trees around the Gorge, bursting with brilliant red and gold color. No matter the season, the basalt cliffs, the acres of lush forest, and that glorious expanse of water make the Gorge one of the West's great scenic wonders.

GETTING HERE AND AROUND

The Columbia Gorge, which is easily accessed from Portland, is best explored by car. The same is generally true for the Mt. Hood area, but in season, the area ski resorts do have shuttle services from Portland and the airport. Even light exploring of the region, however, requires an automobile—take heart that the driving in these parts is scenic and relatively free of traffic. Just keep in mind that winter storms can result in road closures around Mt. Hood and, occasionally, even in the Gorge. It's just a 20-minute drive east of Portland to reach the beginning of the Columbia Gorge, in Troutdale. From Portland it's a one-hour drive to Hood River, a 90-minute drive to Mt. Hood, and a two-hour drive to Goldendale, Washington *(the farthest-away point covered in this chapter)*.

CAR TRAVEL

Interstate 84 is the main east–west route into the Columbia River Gorge, although you can also reach the area on the Washington side via slower but quite scenic Highway 14, which skirts the north side of the river. U.S. 26, which leads east from Portland, is the main route into the Mt. Hood area.

The scenic Historic Columbia River Highway (U.S. 30) from Troutdale to just east of Oneonta Gorge passes Crown Point State Park and Multnomah Falls. Interstate 84/U.S. 30 continues on to The Dalles. Highway 35 heads south from Hood River to the Mt. Hood area, intersecting with U.S. 26 near Government Camp. From Portland, the Columbia Gorge–Mt. Hood Scenic Loop is the easiest way to fully explore the Gorge and the mountain. Take Interstate 84 east to Troutdale and then follow U.S. 26 east to Mt. Hood, then take Highway 35 north to Hood River and Interstate 84 back to Portland. Or make the loop in reverse.

RESTAURANTS

A prominent locavore mentality pervades western Oregon generally, and low elevations around the Gorge mean long growing seasons for dozens of local producers. Fresh foods grown, caught, and harvested in the Northwest dominate menus in the increasingly sophisticated restaurants in the Gorge, especially in the charming town of Hood River, and up around Mt. Hood. Columbia River salmon is big, fruit orchards proliferate around Hood River, delicious huckleberries flourish in Mount Hood National Forest, and the Gorge nurtures a glut of excellent vineyards. Additionally, even the smallest towns around the region have their own lively brewpubs with consistently tasty pub fare and tap after tap of craft ales. In keeping with the region's green and laid-back vibe, outdoor dining is highly popular. *Restaurant reviews have been shortened. For full information visit Fodors.com.*

HOTELS

The region is close enough that you could spend a day or two exploring the Gorge and Mt. Hood, using Portland hotels as your base. The best way to fully appreciate the Gorge, however, is to spend a night or two—look to Hood River and The Dalles for the largest selections of lodging options, although you'll also find some noteworthy resorts, motels, and B&Bs in some of the towns between Portland and Hood River, on both sides of the river. There are a couple of run-of-the-mill motels in Goldendale, but otherwise, you won't find any accommodations in the region east of The Dalles. The slopes of Mt. Hood are dotted with smart ski resorts, and towns like Government Camp and Welches have a mix of rustic and contemporary vacation rentals. The closer you are to Mt. Hood in any season, the earlier you'll want to reserve. With ski country working ever harder to attract summer patrons, Mt. Hood resorts like Timberline Lodge and Mt. Hood Skibowl offer some worthwhile seasonal specials. *Hotel reviews have been shortened. For full information, visit Fodors.com.*

WHAT IT COSTS IN U.S. DOLLARS			
	$	$$	$$$	$$$$
Restaurants	under $16	$17–$22	$23–$30	over $30
Hotels	under $151	$151–$200	$201–$250	over $250

Restaurant prices are the average cost of a main course at dinner or, if dinner is not served, at lunch. Hotel prices are the lowest cost of a standard double room in high season.

TOURS

EverGreen Escapes. The energetic crew at this highly respected tour operator provides both regularly scheduled and customizable tours of the Gorge (with themes that range from wine to hiking) and Mt. Hood, where options include hiking and snowshoeing. ☎ *503/252–1931, 866/203–7603* ⊕ *www.evergreenescapes.com* ✉ *From $135.*

Explore the Gorge. Customizable tours of the Gorge, Mt. Hood, and the Hood River Valley explore everything from the Lewis and Clark Trail to the region's microbreweries. ☎ *800/899–5676* ⊕ *www.explorethegorge. com* ✉ *From $180.*

Martin's Gorge Tours. Wine tours, waterfall hikes, and spring wildflower tours are among the popular trips offered by this Portland-based guide. ☎ *503/349–1323* ⊕ *www.martinsgorgetours.com* ✉ *From $49.*

Mt. Hood Adventure. The only outfitter on Mt. Hood that rents snowmobiles and offers snowmobile tours is also a well-respected tour company for snowshoe tours and sleigh rides in winter, and mountain hikes, biking trips, and boat excursions on area rivers—the shop is also a good place to buy gear and ask for advice on outdoorsy activities in the area. ✉ *88335 Government Camp Loop Rd., Government Camp* ☎ *503/715–2175* ⊕ *www.mthoodadventure.com* ✉ *From $111; snowmobile tours from $189.*

VISITOR INFORMATION

Columbia River Gorge Visitors Association. ☎ *509/427–8911* ⊕ *www.crgva. org.*

Mt. Hood Territory. ☎ *800/424–3002, 503/655–8490* ⊕ *www.mthoodterritory.com.*

COLUMBIA RIVER GORGE

When glacial floods carved out most of the Columbia River Gorge at the end of the last Ice Age, they left behind massive, looming cliffs where the river bisects the Cascade mountain range. The size of the canyon and the wildly varying elevations make this small stretch of Oregon as ecologically diverse as anyplace in the state. In a few days along the Gorge you can mountain bike through dry canyons near The Dalles, hike through temperate rain forest in Oneonta Gorge, and take a woodland wildflower stroll just outside Hood River. At night you'll be rewarded with historic lodging and good food in one of a half dozen mellow river towns and one very bustling one, Hood River. The country's second federally designated National Scenic Area remains exceptionally inviting.

HISTORIC COLUMBIA RIVER HIGHWAY

U.S. 30, paralleling I–84 for 22 miles between Troutdale and Interstate Exit 35.

The oldest scenic highway in the United States is a construction marvel that integrates asphalt path with cliff, river, and forest landscapes. Paralleling the interstate, U.S. 30 climbs to forested riverside bluffs, passes

Columbia River Gorge

WASHINGTON

Yacolt

Goldendale Observatory State Park
Goldendale

Blockhouse
Brockhouse
Centerville

Klickitat

Husum
141

Carson
14

TO FALL CREEK FALLS

Camas
Washougal

Rooster Rock State Park

TO PENDLETON

Cliffs
Rufus
Maryhill
Wishram
Biggs

Maryhill Museum of Art

84

Columbia Gorge Discovery Center/ Wasco County Historical Museum

The Dalles Lock and Dam
Dallesport
The Dalles

Celilo Park

142
Lyle Mayer State Park

Syncline Winery
Bingen
Mosier

White Salmon

84

Aniche Cellars
Hood

Hood River
Marchesi Vineyards

Gorge White House
Glassometry Studio
Hood River Lavender Farm

Fort Dalles Museum
Chenoweth

197

Moro
Grass Valley

Maupin
197

Dufur

197

Columbia Gorge-Mt. Hood Scenic Highway

216
Tygh Valley
Wamic

216
Wapinitia

Columbia River

Odell
35

Dee
281

Mt. Hood Railroad
Parkdale

35

Mt. Hood
▲

Mt. Hood
see detail map

26

TO BEND

Warm Springs Indian Res.

Columbia River Gorge National Scenic Area

Columbia Gorge Interpretive Center Museum
Bridge of the Gods
Cascade Locks
Stevenson
14
Bonneville Dam and Fish Hatchery
North Bonneville

Beacon Rock State Park
Ainsworth State Park
Oneonta Gorge
Multnomah Falls

Historic Columbia River Hwy.

Wahtum Lake
Lost Lake
Lost Lake Resort

Pacific Coast Trail

Mt. Hood National Forest

Mount Hood Village
Brightwood
Rhododendron
Government Camp

Salmon River
Pacific Coast Trail

Timothy Lake

30

Vista House at Crown Point
Historic Columbia River Hwy.

84
Troutdale

GREATER PORTLAND

Boring
Sandy
26
224

Estacada

224

10 mi
10 km

half a dozen waterfalls, and provides access to hiking trails leading to still more falls and scenic overlooks. Completed in 1922, the serpentine highway was the first paved road in the Gorge built expressly for automotive sightseers. Technically, the Historic Columbia River Highway extends some 74 miles to The Dalles, but much of that is along modern Interstate 84—the 22-mile western segment is the real draw.

GETTING HERE AND AROUND

U.S. 30 heads east out of downtown Troutdale, but you can also access the route from Interstate 84 along the way, via Exit 22 near Corbett, Exit 28 near Bridal Veil Falls, Exit 31 at Multnomah Falls, and Exit 35, where it rejoins the interstate.

ESSENTIALS

Visitor Information Multnomah Falls Visitor Center. ⊠ *53000 E. Historic Columbia River Hwy., Exit 31 off I-84, 15 miles east of Troutdale, Bridal Veil* ☎ *503/695-2372* ⊕ *www.multnomahfallslodge.com.*

EXPLORING

FAMILY
Fodor'sChoice
★

Multnomah Falls. A 620-foot-high double-decker torrent, the second-highest year-round waterfall in the nation, Multnomah is by far the most spectacular of the Gorge cataracts east of Troutdale. You can access the falls and Multnomah Lodge via a parking lot at Exit 31 off Interstate 84, or via the Historic Columbia River Highway; from the parking area, a paved path winds to a bridge over the lower falls. A much steeper, though paved, 1.1-mile trail climbs to a viewing point overlooking the upper falls, and from here, unpaved but well-groomed trails join with others, allowing for as much as a full day of hiking in the mountains above the Gorge, if you're up for some serious but scenic trekking. Even the paved ramble to the top will get your blood pumping, but worth it to avoid the crowds that swarm the lower falls area in every season. ⊠ *53000 E. Historic Columbia River Hwy., 15 miles east of Troutdale, Bridal Veil* ☎ *503/695-2376* ⊕ *www.multnomah-fallslodge.com.*

Oneonta Gorge. Following the old highway east from Multnomah Falls, you come to a narrow, mossy cleft with walls hundreds of feet high. Oneonta Gorge is most enjoyable in summer, when you can walk up the streambed through the cool green canyon, where hundreds of plant species—some found nowhere else—flourish under the perennially moist conditions. At other times of the year, take the trail along the west side of the canyon. The clearly marked trailhead is 100 yards west of the gorge, on the south side of the road. The trail takes you to Oneonta Falls, about ½ mile up the stream, where it links with an extensive regional trail system exploring the region's bluffs and waterfalls. Bring boots or submersible sneakers—plus a strong pair of ankles—because the rocks are slippery. On hot days, many hikers wade or swim in the creek at the base of the falls. ⊠ *E. Historic Columbia River Hwy., Cascade Locks* ✛ *2 miles east of Exit 31 off I-84 and Multnomah Falls* ☎ *541/308-1700* ⊕ *www.fs.usda.gov/crgnsa.*

Fodor'sChoice
★

Vista House at Crown Point. A two-tier octagonal structure perched on the edge of this 730-foot-high cliff offers unparalleled 30-mile views up and down the Columbia River Gorge. The building dates to 1917,

its rotunda and lower level filled with displays about the Gorge and the highway. Vista House's architect Edgar Lazarus was the brother of Emma Lazarus, author of the poem displayed at the base of the Statue of Liberty. The property is part of the Crown Point State Scenic Corridor, which is administered by the Oregon State Parks office. ✉ *40700 E. Historic Columbia River Hwy., Corbett* ✥ *10 miles east of Troutdale* ☎ *503/344–1368* 🌐 *www.vistahouse.com* 🎫 *Free.*

WHERE TO EAT AND STAY

$$ AMERICAN 🍴 **Multnomah Falls Lodge.** Vaulted ceilings, stone fireplaces, and exquisite views of Multnomah Falls are complemented by friendly service and reliably good American fare at this landmark restaurant, which is listed on the National Register of Historic Places. Consider the smoked salmon starter with apple-huckleberry compote, cod fish-and-chips, or the elk burger with aged Tillamook cheddar and garlic-sesame mayo. **Known for:** amazing waterfall views; champagne Sunday brunch. [$] *Average main: $21* ✉ *53000 Historic Columbia River Hwy., Bridal Veil* ✥ *Exit 31 off I–84, 15 miles east of Troutdale* ☎ *503/695–2376* 🌐 *www.multnomahfallslodge.com.*

$ RESORT Fodor's Choice ★ 🏨 **McMenamins Edgefield.** Set in 74 acres of gardens, murals, orchards, and vineyards, this Georgian Revival manor that once housed the county poor farm is now operated by Northwest brewers and hospitality innovators par excellence Mike and Brian McMenamin. **Pros:** plenty of eating and drinking choices; large variety of rooms and prices; great spa; on-site movie theater; live music events. **Cons:** this busy place can get pretty crowded; no TVs, phones, or air-conditioning in the rooms; most rooms share baths. [$] *Rooms from: $110* ✉ *2126 S.W. Halsey St., Troutdale* ☎ *503/669–8610, 800/669–8610* 🌐 *www.mcmenamins.com* 🛏 *114 rooms* 🍽 *No meals.*

SPORTS AND THE OUTDOORS

RECREATIONAL AREAS

Rooster Rock State Park. The most famous beach lining the Columbia River is right below Crown Point. Three miles of sandy beaches, panoramic cascades, and a large swimming area makes this a popular spot. True naturists appreciate that one of Oregon's two designated nude beaches is at the east end of Rooster Rock, and that it's not visible to conventional sunbathers—the area is especially popular with Portland's LGBT community. Rooster Rock is 9 miles east of Troutdale, and it's accessible only via the interstate. ✉ *I–84, Exit 25, 9 miles east of Troutdale, Corbett* ☎ *503/695–2261* 🌐 *www.oregonstateparks.org* 🎫 *Day use $5 per vehicle.*

CASCADE LOCKS

7 miles east of Oneonta Gorge on Historic Columbia River Hwy. and I–84; 30 miles east of Troutdale on I–84.

In pioneer days, boats needing to pass the bedeviling rapids near the town of Whiskey Flats had to portage around them. The locks that gave the town its new name were completed in 1896, allowing waterborne passage for the first time. In 1938 they were submerged beneath the new Lake Bonneville when the Bonneville Lock and Dam became one

Dog Mountain Trail, Columbia River Gorge National Scenic Area

of the most massive Corps of Engineers projects to come out of the New Deal. The town of Cascade Locks hung on to its name, though. A historic stern-wheeler still leads excursions from the town's port district, and the region's Native American tribes still practice traditional dip-net fishing near the current locks.

GETTING HERE AND AROUND

Cascade Locks is 45 miles east of Portland and 20 miles west of Hood River on Interstate 84. The town is also home to Bridge of the Gods ($2 toll), which featured prominently in the 2014 movie *Wild* and is the only auto bridge crossing the Columbia River (it connects with Stevenson, Washington) between Portland and Hood River.

EXPLORING

FAMILY **Bonneville Dam.** President Franklin D. Roosevelt dedicated the first federal dam to span the Columbia in 1937. Its generators (visible from a balcony on a self-guided tour or up close during free guided tours offered daily in summer and on weekends the rest of the year) have a capacity of more than a million kilowatts, enough to supply power to more than 200,000 single-family homes. There's an extensive visitor center on Bradford Island, complete with underwater windows where gaggles of kids watch migrating salmon and steelhead as they struggle up fish ladders. The best viewing times are between April and October. In recent years the dwindling runs of wild Columbia salmon have made the dam a subject of much environmental controversy. ⊠ *I–84, Exit 40 , follow signs 1 mile to visitor center* ☎ *541/374–8820* ⊕ *www.nwp. usace.army.mil.*

FAMILY **Bonneville Fish Hatchery.** Built in 1909 and operated by the Oregon Fish & Wildlife Department, the largest state-operated fish hatchery is next door to Bonneville Dam. Visitors can view the fishponds in which chinook, coho, and steelhead spawn—October and November are the most prolific times. Other ponds hold rainbow trout (which visitors can feed) and mammoth Columbia River sturgeon, some exceeding 10 feet in length. ✉ *70543 N.E. Herman Loop, off exit 40 of I–84* ☎ *541/374–8393* 🌐 *www.dfw.state.or.us.*

Cascade Locks Marine Park. This riverfront park is the home port of the 500-passenger stern-wheeler *Columbia Gorge*, which churns upriver, then back again, on one- and two-hour excursions through some of the Columbia River Gorge's most impressive scenery, mid-May to early October; brunch and dinner cruises are also available. The ship's captain discusses the Gorge's fascinating 40-million-year geology and pioneering spirits and legends, such as Lewis and Clark, who once triumphed over this very same river. The park itself, which includes a pedestrian bridge to leafy and tranquil Thunder Island, is a lovely spot for picnicking, and Thunder Island Brewing—at the west end of the park—serves first-rate craft beers. ✉ *Marine Park, S.W. Portage Rd.* ☎ *541/224–3900, 800/224–3901* 🌐 *www.portlandspirit.com* *Cruises from $28* *Reservations essential.*

WHERE TO EAT AND STAY

$ AMERICAN **Thunder Island Brewing.** Hikers, boaters, and others exploring the Gorge gather at this laid-back, funky brewpub with several tables inside, as well as a large patio with picnic tables overlooking the Columbia River, Marine Park, and the little island for which the brewery is named. Order a glass of hoppy Pacific Crest Trail Pale Ale or malty Scotch Porter, and enjoy it with one of the light dishes from the short menu. **Known for:** great beer from on-site brewery; smoked-fish and charcuterie platters; stellar river views from outdoor dining area. *Average main: $8* ✉ *515 S.W. Portage Rd.* ☎ *971/231–4599* 🌐 *www.thunderislandbrewing.com.*

$$ HOTEL **Best Western Plus Columbia River Inn.** The draw here is an enviable setting with great views of the Columbia River and Bridge of the Gods—many rooms, which are done in soft tans and grays and hung with framed black-and-white photos of the Gorge, overlook the river, as does a deck in back and the breakfast room. **Pros:** excellent river views; handy location midway between Portland and Hood River; spotless, modern rooms. **Cons:** cookie-cutter furnishings; some rooms face away from the river. *Rooms from: $159* ✉ *735 Wa Na Pa St.* ☎ *541/374–8777, 800/780–7234* 🌐 *www.bwcolumbiariverinn.com* *62 rooms* *Breakfast.*

SPORTS AND THE OUTDOORS

HIKING

Pacific Crest Trail. Cascade Locks bustles with grubby thru-hikers refueling along the 2,650-mile Canada-to-Mexico Pacific Crest Trail, which was immortalized in the 2014 movie, *Wild* starring Reese Witherspoon. Check out a scenic and strenuous portion of it, heading south from the trailhead at Herman Creek Horse Camp, just east of town. The route heads up into the Cascades, showing off monster views of the Gorge.

Backpackers out for a longer trek will find idyllic campsites at Wahtum Lake, 14 miles south. You can also access the trail from the free parking area at Toll House Park, by the Bridge of the Gods. ⊠ *Off N. W. Forest La., 1 mile east of downtown* ☎ *541/308–1700* ⊕ *www.pcta.org.*

STEVENSON, WASHINGTON

Across the river from Cascade Locks via the Bridge of the Gods and 1 mile east on Hwy. 14.

With the Bridge of the Gods toll bridge spanning the Columbia River above the Bonneville Dam, Stevenson acts as a sort of "twin city" to Cascade Locks on the Oregon side. Tribal legends and the geologic record tell of the original Bridge of the Gods, a substantial landslide that occurred here sometime between AD 1000 and 1760, briefly linking the two sides of the Gorge before the river swept away the debris. The landslide's steel namesake now leads to tiny Stevenson, where vacationers traverse quiet Main Street, which has a few casual eateries and shops. Washington's Highway 14 runs through the middle of town, and since the cliffs on the Oregon side are more dramatic, driving this two-lane highway actually offers better views.

GETTING HERE AND AROUND

From the Oregon side of the Gorge, cross the Columbia River at the Bridge of the Gods ($2 toll).

ESSENTIALS

Visitor Information Skamania County Chamber of Commerce. ⊠ *167 N.W. 2nd St., Stevenson* ☎ *509/427–8911, 800/989–9178* ⊕ *www.skamania.org.*

EXPLORING

Bridge of the Gods. For a magnificent vista 135 feet above the Columbia, as well as a short and quick (despite its 15 mph speed limit) route between Oregon and Washington, $2 will pay your way over the grandly named bridge that Reese Witherspoon memorably strolled across in the 2014 movie, *Wild.* Hikers cross the bridge from Oregon to reach the Washington segment of the **Pacific Crest Trail**, which picks up just west of the bridge. ⊠ *Off Hwy. 14, Stevenson* ⊕ *portofcascadelocks. org/bridge-of-the-gods/.*

FAMILY **Columbia Gorge Interpretive Center Museum.** A petroglyph whose eyes seem to look straight at you, "She Who Watches" or "Tsagaglalal" is the logo for this museum. Sitting among the dramatic basaltic cliffs on the north bank of the Columbia River Gorge, the museum explores the life of the Gorge: its history, culture, architecture, legends, and much more. Younger guests enjoy the reenactment of the Gorge's formation in the Creation Theatre, and the 37-foot-high fish wheel, a device like a mill wheel equipped with baskets for catching fish, from the 19th century. Historians appreciate studying the water route of the Lewis and Clark Expedition. There's also an eye-opening exhibit that examines current environmental impacts on the area. ⊠ *990 S.W. Rock Creek Dr., Stevenson* ☎ *509/427–8211, 800/991–2338* ⊕ *www.columbiagorge.org* 🎫 *$10.*

WHERE TO EAT AND STAY

$ AMERICAN 🍴 **Big River Grill.** A tradition with hikers, bikers, fishermen, and scenic drivers out exploring the Gorge, especially for weekend breakfast but also at lunch and dinnertime, this colorful roadhouse in the center of town is festooned with license plates, vintage signs, and kitschy artwork. Grab a seat at the counter or in one of the high-back wooden booths, and tuck into grilled wild salmon sandwich, chicken-fried chicken with eggs, home-style meat loaf with buttermilk-garlic mashed potatoes, and other hearty, reasonably priced fare. **Known for:** grilled wild salmon sandwiches; weekend breakfast; hiker and biker crowd. [$] *Average main: $16* ✉ *192 S.W. 2nd St., Stevenson* ☎ *509/427–4888* 🌐 *www.thebigrivergrill.com.*

$$$ PACIFIC NORTHWEST Fodor's Choice ★ 🍴 **Cascade Room at Skamania Lodge.** At Skamania Lodge's signature restaurant, with its stunning views of sky, river, and cliff scapes, the chef draws on local seafood and regionally sourced meats. Try dishes like a Dungeness crab tower with avocado, beet coulis, and basil oil; and bacon-cured Carlton Farms pork chops. **Known for:** stunning Gorge views; lavish Sunday brunch. [$] *Average main: $26* ✉ *Skamania Lodge, 1131 S.W. Skamania Lodge Way, Stevenson* ☎ *509/427–7700* 🌐 *www.skamania.com.*

$ AMERICAN 🍴 **Red Bluff Tap House.** With exposed-brick walls, varnished wood tables, and a sleek long bar, this downtown gastropub excels both with its extensive craft-beer and drinks selection and its modern take on comfort food. Snack on shareable starters like deep-fried brussels sprouts with pork belly and apple-cider reduction and smoked salmon flatbread. **Known for:** ample selection of craft beers and Columbia Gorge wines; fish-and-chips. [$] *Average main: $13* ✉ *256 2nd St., Stevenson* ☎ *509/427–4979* 🌐 *www.redblufftaphouse.com.*

$$$ RESORT FAMILY Fodor's Choice ★ 🏨 **Skamania Lodge.** This warm, woodsy lodge on an expansive, verdant swath of forest and meadows impresses with a multitude of windows overlooking in the surrounding mountains and Gorge, an outstanding array of recreational facilities, and handsome, Pacific Northwest–chic accommodations, many with fireplaces and all with views. **Pros:** just a 45-minute drive from Portland but feels secluded and totally relaxing; plenty of fun outdoorsy activities; first-rate spa and dining facilities. **Cons:** expensive for a large family; can get crowded—sometimes there's a wait for a table in the dining room. [$] *Rooms from: $229* ✉ *1131 S.W. Skamania Lodge Way, Stevenson* ☎ *509/427–7700, 800/221–7117* 🌐 *www.skamania.com* 🛏 *254 rooms* 🍽 *No meals.*

NIGHTLIFE AND PERFORMING ARTS

Walking Man Brewing. This sunshiny patio and cozy interior are great spots for creative pizzas and a sampling the dozen-or-so craft ales. After a couple of pints of the strong Homo Erectus IPA and Knuckle Dragger Pale Ale, you may go a little ape. Live music on summer weekends skews twangy and upbeat. ✉ *240 S.W. 1st St., Stevenson* ☎ *509/427–5520* 🌐 *www.walkingmanbeer.com.*

SPORTS AND THE OUTDOORS
RECREATIONAL AREA

Fodor's Choice ★ **Beacon Rock State Park.** For several hundred years this 848-foot rock was a landmark for river travelers, including Native Americans, who recognized this point as the last rapids of the Columbia River. Lewis and Clark are thought to have been the first white men to see the volcanic remnant. Even most casual hikers can make the steep but safe trek up to the top of the rock—allow about 45–60 minutes round-trip. More serious hikers should head to the trailhead for Hamilton Mountain, which is reached via a beautiful, though arduous, 8-mile ramble over a roaring waterfall, through dense temperate rain forest, and finally up to 2,400-foot summit with breathtaking views up and down the Gorge. ⊠ *34841 Hwy. 14, Skamania* ✛ *7 miles west of Bridge of the Gods* ☎ *509/427–8265* ⊕ *www.parks.wa.gov* 🎫 *$10.*

Falls Creek Falls. You'll find one of the most spectacular waterfalls hikes in the Northwest in the Wind River section of 1½-million-acre Gifford Pinchot National Forest. The large, free parking area (with restrooms) is at the end of graded, unpaved forest road off paved Wind River Road, about 20 miles north of Stevenson. The trail meanders through dense forest and crosses a couple of sturdy suspension bridges en route to the more spectacular Lower Falls (a relatively easy 3½-mile round-trip). If you're up for more of an adventure, continue to the Upper Falls overlook, which adds about 3 more miles and makes it a loop hike—parts of this section are quite steep. ⊠ *End of NF 057, Carson* ✛ *16 miles north of Carson via Wind River Rd. and NF 3062* ☎ *509/395–3400* ⊕ *www.fs.usda.gov/main/giffordpinchot.*

HOOD RIVER

20 miles east of Cascade Locks and 60 miles east of Portland on I–84.

This picturesque riverside community of about 7,200 residents affords visitors spectacular views both of the Columbia River and snowcapped Mt. Hood. More than 40 civic and commercial buildings date from 1893 to the 1930s, some of which are listed in the National Register of Historic Places.

Hood River is the dining and lodging hub of the Gorge, with an increasingly respected bounty of urbane farm-to-table restaurants, up-and-coming craft breweries and wine-tasting rooms, and nicely curated shops and art galleries. Little wonder this is one of the most popular weekend getaways among Portlanders, all the more so since the surrounding countryside abounds with orchards and vineyards, making it a favorite destination for fans of U-pick farmsteads and tasting rooms. Hood River wineries grow a broader range of grapes than Oregon's more famous Willamette Valley, and wine touring has become a favorite activity in the area.

GETTING HERE AND AROUND
Reach Hood River from Portland by driving 60 miles east on Interstate 84, or from Mt. Hood by heading 40 miles north on Highway 35.

ESSENTIALS

Visitor Information Hood River County Chamber of Commerce. ✉ *720 E. Port Marina Dr.* ☎ *541/386–2000, 800/366–3530* ⊕ *www.hoodriver.org.*

EXPLORING

Cathedral Ridge Winery. Run by fourth-generation winemaker Michael Sebastiani, this vineyard has racked up countless ribbons and awards from wine festivals and publications, and *Wine Press Northwest* called it one of the region's best wine-country picnic spots. Popular varietals include Riesling, Pinot Gris, and Syrah. ✉ *4200 Post Canyon Dr.* ☎ *800/516–8710* ⊕ *www.cathedralridgewinery.com.*

Fruit Loop. Either by car or bicycle, tour the quiet country highways of Hood River Valley, which abounds with more than 25 fruit stands, a handful of U-pick berry farms, and about 10 wineries. You'll see apples, pears, cherries, and peaches fertilized by volcanic soil, pure glacier water, and a conducive harvesting climate. Along the 35 miles of farms are a host of outlets for delicious baked goods, wines, flowers, and nuts. While on the loop, consider stopping in the small town of **Parkdale** to lunch, taste beer at Solera Brewery, and snap a photo of Mt. Hood's north face. ✉ *Hood River* ✛ *Begins just east of downtown at State St. and Hwy. 35* ⊕ *www.hoodriverfruitloop.com.*

Glassometry Studios. Artist and teacher Laurel Marie Hagner operates this colorful gallery and sculpture garden just off the Hood River Fruit Loop, near the village of Odell. You can admire the larger-than-life, riotously vibrant glass sculptures with a walk through the garden, watch live glass-blowing demonstrations (and take classes) in the studio, and browse the fanciful yet absolutely functional vases, bowls, drinking glasses, decanters, and decorative glass art in the studio. ✉ *3015 Lower Mill Dr.* ☎ *541/354–3015* ⊕ *www.glassometry.com* ☉ *Closed Mon.–Wed.*

Fodor's Choice
★

Gorge White House. You'll find pretty much everything the Hood River Valley is famous for growing and being produced at this picturesque, century-old farm anchored by a Dutch Colonial farmhouse and surrounded by acres of U-pick flowers, apple and peach trees, and blackberry and blueberry bushes. After strolling through the farm fields, stop inside the main house to sample wines—the tasting room carries one of the largest selections of Columbia River wines in the region. Out back, there's a farm store, another tasting room serving local craft beer and cider, and a garden patio with seating and a food-truck-style café serving delicious strawberry salads, pulled-pork sandwiches, pear pizzas, and other light fare. ✉ *2265 Hwy. 35* ☎ *541/386–2828* ⊕ *www.thegorgewhitehouse.com.*

Hood River Lavender Farm. Part of the joy of visiting this organic U-pick lavender farm that harvests some 75 varieties of the plant is the beautiful drive up the hill from Odell's orchards and vineyards. Stroll through the fields of lavender, relax in a chair taking in mesmerizing views of Mt. Hood and Mt. Adams, or peruse the huge selection of lavender products in the gift shop—everything from lip balms and shampoo to infused teas and dried lavender bouquets. ✉ *3801 Straight Hill Rd.* ☎ *541/354–9917* ⊕ *www.hoodriverlavender.com.*

OFF THE
BEATEN
PATH

Lost Lake Resort. One of the most-photographed sights in the Pacific Northwest, this lake's waters reflect towering Mt. Hood and the thick forests that line its shore. Cabins and campsites are available for overnight stays, and because no motorboats are allowed on Lost Lake, the area is blissfully quiet. ✉ *9000 Lost Lake Rd., Dee ✢ 25 miles southwest of Hood River via Hwy. 35 and Hwy. 281* ☎ *541/386–6366* ⬚ *Day use $8.*

Fodor's Choice
★

Marchesi Vineyards. Somewhat unusual for the Pacific Northwest, this boutique winery with a small, airy tasting room and a verdant garden patio specializes in Italian varietals—Moscato, Primitivo, Dolcetto, Sangiovese, Barbera, Nebbiolo, and a few others. Owner Franco Marchesi hails from Italy's Piemonte region, and he's earned serious kudos for his finesse as a winemaker. ✉ *3955 Belmont Dr.* ☎ *541/386–1800* ⊕ *www.marchesivineyards.com.*

FAMILY

Mt. Hood Railroad. Scenic passenger excursions along a small rail line established in 1906 offer a picturesque and relaxing way to survey Mt. Hood and the Hood River Valley. Chug alongside the Hood River through vast fruit orchards before climbing up steep forested canyons, glimpsing Mt. Hood along the way. There are several trip options, from $30: a four-hour excursion (serves light concessions), dinner, brunch, and several themed trips, like murder-mysteries and Old West robberies, and a family-popular holiday-inspired Polar Express train runs throughout much of November and December. Exceptional service is as impressive as the scenery. ✉ *110 Railroad Ave.* ☎ *541/386–3556, 800/872–4661* ⊕ *www.mthoodrr.com* ◷ *Closed Jan.–Apr.*

Mt. Hood Winery. In addition to producing increasingly acclaimed wine—with particularly impressive Pinot Gris, dry Rosé, Zinfandel (which is seldom bottled in these parts), Pinot Noir, Barbera, and Syrah—this winery adjacent to the long-running Fruit Company (fruit and gift baskets) has a beautiful, contemporary tasting room with gorgeous Mt. Hood views from inside and the expansive patio. ✉ *2882 Van Horn Dr.* ☎ *541/386–8333* ⊕ *www.mthoodwinery.com* ◷ *Closed Dec.–Feb.*

Viento Wines. Focused more on whites than most of the winemakers in the Gorge region, Viento has a stunning tasting room with vaulted ceilings, soaring windows, and a large patio overlooking the on-site vineyard of Riesling grapes. This is a lovely space for tasting and chatting with fellow oenophiles. Notable wines here include a crisp Grüner Veltliner, a food-friendly Brut Rosé, and one of the better Oregon Pinot Noirs you'll find in the Hood River region. ✉ *301 Country Club Rd.* ☎ *541/386–3026* ⊕ *www.vientowines.com.*

NEED A
BREAK

✗ **Doppio Coffee + Lounge.** Sunshine fills the small dining room and outdoor seating area of this high-ceilinged, contemporary downtown coffee bar that serves fine espresso drinks as well as local wines and craft beers. It's great for light snacking—there's a nice selection of baked goods and fine chocolates—but there are also substantial grilled panini sandwiches, salads, and soups. **Known for:** rich Ghiradelli hot chocolate; great selection of Columbia Gorge wines by the glass. ✉ *310 Oak St.* ☎ *541/386–3000* ⊕ *www.doppiohoodriver.com* ◷ *No dinner.*

Vineyards in the Hood River Valley

FAMILY **Western Antique Aeroplane and Automobile Museum.** Housed at Hood River's tiny airport (general aviation only), the museum's impressive, meticulously restored, propeller-driven planes are all still in flying condition. The antique steam cars, Model Ts, and sleek Depression-era sedans are road-worthy, too. Periodic car shows and an annual fly-in draw thousands of history buffs and spectators. ⊠ *1600 Air Museum Rd., off Hwy. 281* ☎ *541/308–1600* ⊕ *www.waaamuseum.org* ✈ *$14.*

WHERE TO EAT

$ ✕ **Broder Øst.** Portland's wildly popular modern Scandinavian restaurant
SCANDINAVIAN Broder has opened a branch just off the lobby of downtown's historic Hood River Hotel. Breakfast and lunch are the main event, although dinner is served during the busy summer months. **Known for:** Danish favorites like pancakes with lingonberry sauce; covered sidewalk tables overlooking bustling Oak Street. $ *Average main: $11* ⊠ *Hood River Hotel, 102 Oak St.* ☎ *541/436–3444* ⊕ *www.brodereast.com* ⊗ *No dinner Mon. and Tues. or Sept.–May.*

$$$ ✕ **Celilo Restaurant.** Refined and relaxing, this high-ceilinged restaurant
PACIFIC in a contemporary downtown building is popular both for dinner and
NORTHWEST enjoying a glass of local wine in the bar. Deftly crafted Pacific Northwest fare—order the cast-iron-skillet seafood-and-chorizo roast or duck-leg confit if it's on the menu. **Known for:** one of the best local wine lists in the Gorge; attractive sidewalk seating. $ *Average main: $25* ⊠ *16 Oak St.* ☎ *541/386–5710* ⊕ *www.celilorestaurant.com* ⊗ *No lunch Mon.–Thurs.*

$$ ✕ **Kin.** Several Czech dishes have been added to the otherwise farm-to-
ECLECTIC table Northwest menu that includes orecchiette pasta with merguez

sausage, mint, and fava beans, and hearty goulash with potato gnocchi. Kin doesn't serve lunch, but is justly popular for Sunday brunch. **Known for:** Sunday brunch; impressive Eurocentric wine list. $ *Average main:* $19 ⌧ 110 5th St. ☎ 541/387–0111 ⊕ www.kineatery.com ⊘ Closed Mon. and Tues. No lunch.

$$

PIZZA

Fodor's Choice

★

× **Solstice Wood Fire Cafe.** It can be hard to score a table on weekends in this snazzy space along the Hood River waterfront. Wood-fire-grilled pizzas with unusual toppings—such as the Cherry Girl, layered with local cherries, spicy chorizo, goat cheese, mozzarella, and marinara sauce—bring the crowds. **Known for:** creative pizzas; wood-fired mac-n-cheese; s'mores. $ *Average main: $17* ⌧ 501 Portway Ave. ☎ 541/436–0800 ⊕ www.solsticewoodfirecafe.com.

$$

AMERICAN

× **Stonehedge Gardens.** Each of the four dining rooms in the restored 1898 home has a distinct personality, from cozy to verdant to elegant, but the tiered patio is where summer diners gather. The kitchen tends toward the traditional side, specializing in classics like steak Diane and filet mignon. Just when you think your meal is complete, along comes the Flaming Bread Pudding. **Known for:** gorgeous outdoor seating amid lovely gardens; flaming bread pudding. $ *Average main: $23* ⌧ 3405 Wine Country Ave. ☎ 541/386–3940 ⊕ www.stonehedgeweddings.com ⊘ Closed Mon. No lunch.

WHERE TO STAY

$$

HOTEL

▦ **Best Western Plus Hood River Inn.** This low-slung, rambling hotel beside the Hood River Bridge offers some of the best river views of any hotel in the Gorge, and many units have private balconies or patios on the water; the deluxe accommodations have full kitchens, fireplaces, and Jacuzzi tubs. **Pros:** riverfront location with great views; good restaurant and lounge. **Cons:** a little pricey in summer; downtown shopping and dining not within walking distance. $ *Rooms from: $179* ⌧ 1108 E. Marina Way ☎ 541/386–2200, 800/828–7873 ⊕ www.hoodriverinn. com ⇱ 194 rooms ⦿ Breakfast.

$$

HOTEL

FAMILY

Fodor's Choice

★

▦ **Columbia Cliff Villas Hotel.** This elegant condo-style compound on a sheer cliff overlooking the Columbia River contains some of the plushest accommodations in the region—units have one to three bedrooms, fireplaces, terraces or patios, stone-and-tile bathrooms, and fine linens. **Pros:** private apartment-style accommodations; great river views; sophisticated decor and top-flight amenities. **Cons:** no restaurant or fitness center on-site. $ *Rooms from: $189* ⌧ 3880 Westcliff Dr. ☎ 541/490–8081, 866/912–8366 ⊕ www.columbiacliffvillas.com ⇱ 37 suites ⦿ No meals.

$$$$

HOTEL

▦ **Columbia Gorge Hotel.** Charming though somewhat dated-looking period-style rooms at this grande dame of Gorge hotels are fitted out with plenty of wood, brass, and antiques and overlook the Gorge, impeccably landscaped formal gardens, or a 208-foot-high waterfall. **Pros:** historic structure built by Columbia Gorge Highway visionary Simon Benson; unbeatable Gorge views; full-service spa. **Cons:** smallish rooms with rather dated decor; rooms facing away from river pick up noise from nearby Interstate 84; often books up with weddings on summer and fall weekends. $ *Rooms from: $255* ⌧ 4000 Westcliff

Dr. ☎ *541/386–5566, 800/345–1921* 🌐 *www.columbiagorgehotel.com* 🛏 *40 rooms* 🍴 *No meals.*

$ HOTEL

🏨 **Hood River Hotel.** In the heart of the lively and hip business district, steps from great restaurants and shops, this handsomely restored building has a grand, Old West facade, behind which are simple rooms with tasteful period-style antiques and a few larger suites that have kitchenettes and large sitting rooms. **Pros:** excellent downtown location; good-value rafting and ski packages; antiques-heavy interiors have feel of a European inn. **Cons:** smallish rooms; no king-size beds; rooms in back have great river views but tend to receive some freeway noise. [$] *Rooms from: $129* ✉ *102 Oak St.* ☎ *541/386–1900, 800/386–1859* 🌐 *www.hoodriverhotel.com* 🛏 *41 rooms* 🍴 *Breakfast.*

$$$ B&B/INN Fodor's Choice ★

🏨 **Sakura Ridge.** The five warm but sleekly furnished rooms of this contemporary lodge-style B&B on a 72-acre farm on the south side of town offer magical panoramas of Mt. Hood amid a welcome absence of clutter. **Pros:** spectacular mountain views; rustic yet urbane decor; lush gardens and orchards on the grounds. **Cons:** secluded location is a 15-minute drive from downtown; closed in winter. [$] *Rooms from: $205* ✉ *5601 York Hill Rd.* ☎ *541/386–2636, 877/472–5872* 🌐 *www.sakuraridge.com* ⏲ *Closed Nov.–Mar.* 🛏 *5 rooms* 🍴 *Breakfast.*

$$ B&B/INN

🏨 **Villa Columbia B&B.** The five guest rooms in this handsomely maintained 1911 Craftsman-style bed-and-breakfast are a tasteful but eclectic mix of older and newer pieces; all are named for famous Oregon rivers, and from the Columbia River room you're actually treated to a fine view of the Gorge. **Pros:** helpful, knowledgeable innkeepers; proximity to downtown galleries, restaurants, and brewpubs; decor is upscale but unfussy. **Cons:** river views are somewhat obstructed by trees and other houses; on a busy street. [$] *Rooms from: $189* ✉ *902 Oak St.* ☎ *541/386–6670* 🌐 *www.villacolumbia.com* 🛏 *5 rooms* 🍴 *Breakfast.*

NIGHTLIFE AND PERFORMING ARTS

Brian's Pourhouse. A cute downtown cottage with a spacious deck serves excellent, eclectic food, but is even better known as a later-in-the-evening spot. It's the favored place in town to enjoy a cocktail or glass of wine and perhaps a sweet nosh—the Dutch apple pie with caramel sauce, whipped cream, and ice cream is memorable. ✉ *606 Oak St.* ☎ *541/387–4344* 🌐 *www.brianspourhouse.com.*

Double Mountain Brewery & Taproom. Notable for its European-style beers, including the rich Black Irish Stout and the refreshing Kölsch, Double Mountain also produces seasonal cherry-infused Kriek ales and a hoppy India Red Ale. The bustling, homey downtown taproom is also a great source for pizzas, salads, and sandwiches. ✉ *8 4th St.* ☎ *541/387–0042* 🌐 *www.doublemountainbrewery.com.*

Full Sail Tasting Room and Pub. A glass-walled microbrewery with a windswept deck overlooking the Columbia, Full Sail was a pioneer brewpub in Oregon, helping to put Hood River on the map as a major beer hub. Free, on-site brewery tours are given daily at 1, 2, 3, and 4 pm. ✉ *506 Columbia St.* ☎ *541/386–2247* 🌐 *www.fullsailbrewing.com.*

Fodor's Choice ★

Pfriem Family Brewers. Inside a striking new building on the Columbia River, Pfriem (pronounced "freem") is all about the marriage of

Belgium's brewing traditions and Oregon's decidedly hoppy style. The brewery has quickly vaulted to the top echelon of Northwest craft beer makers, earning accolades for its heady Belgian Strong Blonde and one of the best IPAs in the state. The on-site restaurant serves stellar pub fare, too, including mussels and fries, vegan Moroccan stew, and house-made bratwurst. ✉ *707 Portway Ave.* ☎ *541/321–0490* ⊕ *www. pfriembeer.com.*

SPORTS AND THE OUTDOORS

KAYAKING

Gorge Paddling Center. Whether you want to practice your Eskimo roll in the safety of a pool, run the Klickitat River in an inflatable kayak, or try out a stand-up paddleboard on the Columbia, the Gorge's premier kayak guides can arrange the trip. Book online, by phone, or at the Kayak Shed downtown. ✉ *101 N. 1st St.* ☎ *541/806–4190* ⊕ *www. gorgekayaker.com.*

WINDSURFING

Big Winds. The retail hub for Hood River's windsurfing and kiteboarding culture also rents gear and provides windsurfing lessons for beginners. Lessons and clinics begin at $79. ✉ *207 Front St.* ☎ *541/386–6086, 888/509–4210* ⊕ *www.bigwinds.com.*

WHITE SALMON, WASHINGTON

5 miles north of Hood River on Hwy. 14.

Tiny White Salmon, which sits on a bluff with commanding views of the Columbia River as well as the town of Hood River, is a good base for exploring the Washington side of the eastern end of the Gorge. A few noteworthy restaurants and shops in the village center cater to hikers, kayakers, and wine- and beer-tasting aficionados checking out this quieter but similar scenic counterpart to Hood River. Several first-rate wineries have opened in the rural communities just west and east of White Salmon along Highway 14.

The Coyote Wall trail, accessed about 5 miles east of town off Highway 14 at Courtney Road, affords hikers unobstructed views of the Columbia River and the surrounding mountains, including Mt. Hood. The trail leads from a disused section of roadway up a gradual slope, through tall grass and wildflower meadows, from sea level to an elevation of 1,900 feet. You can descend the way you came up or by looping back down through an intriguing valley of basalt rock formations—the full round-trip is about 8 miles, but you could hike part of the way up the trail and back, taking in the impressive vistas, in less than an hour. Drive north of town about 20 miles on Highway 141 to reach secluded Trout Lake, the access point for hiking and recreation in and around 12,281-foot Mt. Adams, which is visible from many points in the Gorge.

GETTING HERE AND AROUND

You reach White Salmon by driving across the Hood River Bridge (toll $1), turning east onto Highway 14, and then north in the small village of Bingen onto Highway 141—it's a 10-minute drive from Hood River.

ESSENTIALS

Mt. Adams Chamber of Commerce. ✉ *1 Heritage Plaza, off Hwy. 14, just west of Hood River Bridge, White Salmon* ☎ *509/493–3630* 🌐 *www.mtadamschamber.com.*

EXPLORING

Aniche Cellars. Just a short drive west of White Salmon, this friendly boutique winery has one of the prettiest tasting-room settings in the area—it's high on Underwood Mountain, with outdoor seating that affords spectacular views looking east toward Hood River and deep into the Gorge. The cleverly named wines here—Puck, an Albarino–Pinot Gris blend; Three Witches, a Rhône-style blend of Cinsault, Carignan, and Counoise—are paired with little amuse-bouche-style nibbles, typically chocolate, prosciutto, or fruit. The winery also has a tasting room in downtown Hood River. ✉ *71 Little Buck Creek Rd., Underwood* ☎ *360/624–6531* 🌐 *www.anichecellars.com.*

Fodor's Choice ★ **Syncline Wines.** The focus at this intimate winery is predominantly on elegant, full-bodied Rhône-style wines. The friendly, knowledgeable tasting-room has garnered plenty of awards for its aromatic Cuvée Elena Grenache-Syrah-Mourvedre blend, as well as a first-rate standalone Syrah, and several racy, dry whites—Picpoul, Grenache Blanc, Gruner Veltliner—that seem tailor-made for the Gorge's warm summer nights. Note that several other outstanding small wineries—Domaine Pouillon, Memaloose, and COR Cellars among them—are in the same rural town, 10 miles east of White Salmon. ✉ *111 Balch Rd., Lyle* ☎ *509/365–4361* 🌐 *www.synclinewine.com* 🕒 *Closed Mon.–Wed.*

WHERE TO EAT

$$ PACIFIC NORTHWEST Fodor's Choice ★ 🍴 **Henni's Kitchen & Bar.** It's well worth venturing across the Columbia from Hood River to this jewel of a neighborhood tavern, which serves well-priced, creatively prepared international fare with a decided Northwest focus—think kale fritters with romesco sauce, Thai red curry with local flat-iron steak, and classic fish-and-chips. This is hearty comfort food, but with healthy and fresh ingredients. **Known for:** good cocktails; eclectic menu. [$] *Average main: $18* ✉ *120 E. Jewett Blvd., White Salmon* ☎ *509/493–1555* 🌐 *www.henniskitchenandbar.com* 🕒 *No lunch.*

NIGHTLIFE

Everybody's Brewing. Head to this festive downtown brewpub for seriously impressive beers, with the potent Big Brother Imperial IPA (7.7% ABV) and orange-peel-enhanced Daily Bread Common Ale leading the way. There's live music many evenings, and tasty pub fare, too. ✉ *151 E. Jewett Blvd., White Salmon* ☎ *509/637–2774* 🌐 *www.everybodysbrewing.com.*

SPORTS AND THE OUTDOORS

Wet Planet Whitewater. This outfitter just outside White Salmon offers half- and full-day white-water rafting trips on the White Salmon, Wind, Klickitat, Hood, and Tieton rivers, which rank among some of the top waterways for this activity in the region. The Wind and Hood rivers contain stretches of hairy Class IV–Class V rapids (previous experience is required), but the other trips are suitable for beginners. The company also offers kayaking instruction and trips. ⊠ *860 Hwy. 141, Husum* ☎ *509/493–8989, 877/390–9445* ⊕ *www.wetplanetwhitewater.com.*

THE DALLES

20 miles east of Hood River on I–84.

The Dalles lies on a crescent bend of the Columbia River where it narrows and once spilled over a series of rapids, creating a flagstone effect. French voyagers christened it *dalle,* or "flagstone." The Dalles is the seat of Wasco County and the trading hub of north-central Oregon. It gained fame early in the region's history as the town where the Oregon Trail branched, with some pioneers departing to travel over Mt. Hood on Barlow Road and the others continuing down the Columbia River. This may account for the small-town, Old West feeling that still permeates the area. Several historic Oregon moments as they relate to The Dalles' past are magnificently illustrated on eight murals painted by renowned Northwest artists, located downtown within short walking distance of one another.

GETTING HERE AND AROUND

From Hood River, it's a 22-mile drive east on Interstate 84 to reach The Dalles. Alternatively, you can take the slightly slower and more scenic Highway 14, on the Washington side of the Columbia, from White Salmon to U.S. 197, which leads you into town via The Dalles Bridge.

ESSENTIALS

Visitor Information The Dalles Area Chamber of Commerce. ⊠ *404 W. 2nd St.* ☎ *541/296–2231, 800/255–3385* ⊕ *www.thedalleschamber.com.*

EXPLORING

FAMILY **Columbia Gorge Discovery Center–Wasco County Historical Museum.** Exhibits and artwork at this expansive, contemporary museum just off Interstate 84 as you approach The Dalles from the west highlight the geological history of the Columbia Gorge, back 40 million years when volcanoes, landslides, and floods carved out the area. History exhibits focus on 10,000 years of Native American life and exploration of the region by white settlers, from Lewis and Clark to the early-20th-century engineers who developed the Historic Columbia River Highway. ⊠ *5000 Discovery Dr.* ☎ *541/296–8600* ⊕ *www.gorgediscovery.org* ⊠ *$9.*

The Dalles Lock and Dam. At this hydroelectric dam 50 miles east of the Bonneville Dam, you can tour a visitor center, which is located on the Oregon side of the river at Seufert Park, with surprisingly even-handed exhibits presenting differing perspectives on the Columbia River dams, with input from farmers, utility companies, environmentalists, and indigenous tribes. There's also a surreal live feed of salmon and sturgeon scaling the fish ladder. Call ahead for the guided tours, which include the powerhouse and fish ladder, offered most weekends. Photo ID required. ⊠ *3545 Bret Clodfelter Way* ✛ *2 miles east of The Dalles, off I-84, Exit 87 or Exit 88* ☎ *541/296–9778* ⊕ *www.nwp.usace.army. mil* ⊠ *Free.*

Fort Dalles Museum. The 1856-vintage Fort Dalles Surgeon's Quarters ranks among the state's oldest history museums. The first visitors came through the doors in 1905. On display in authentic hand-hewn log buildings, originally part of a military base, are the personal effects of some of the region's settlers and a collection of early automobiles. The entrance fee gains you admission to the Swedish log-style **Anderson Homestead** museum across the street, which also displays pioneer artifacts. ✉ *500 W. 15th St.* ☎ *541/296–4547* 🌐 *www.fortdallesmuseum.org* 🎟 *$5.*

Sunshine Mill Winery. You won't find many wineries situated in more unusual buildings than Quenett, which operates out of a early 1900s flour mill with huge grain elevators that soar over the southern end of The Dalles's downtown. Inside this dramatic old structure that nearly fell to the wrecking ball before winemakers James and Molli Martin bought it, you'll find the tasting room for Quenett, which produces first-rate Grenache, Viognier, Barbera, and a Chardonnay–Viognier–Sauvignon- Blanc–Semillon blend. You can also order cheese boards and other snacks, and sample wines from the company's other line, Copa Di Vino, an inexpensive brand of single-serving table wines sold throughout the country. ✉ *901 E. 2nd St.* ☎ *541/298–8900* 🌐 *www.sunshinemill.com.*

5

WHERE TO EAT AND STAY

$ AMERICAN 🍴 **Baldwin Saloon.** The walls of this historic downtown watering hole and restaurant are an engagingly authentic mix of landscape art and early American oil-painting erotica. The immense, traditional menu runs the gamut from pastas to fish-and-chips to burgers—portions are substantial. **Known for:** conversation-starting art; dinner accompanied by the saloon's 1894 piano; delicious bouillabaisse. [$] *Average main: $13* ✉ *205 Court St.* ☎ *541/296–5666* 🕒 *Closed Sun.*

$ CAFÉ 🍴 **Petite Provence.** This popular downtown bistro-bakery-dessertery, which also has branches in Portland, serves delicious eggs, crepes, and croissants for breakfast; hot and cold sandwiches and salads for lunch, and fresh-baked pastries and breads (you can take a loaf home). For lunch, consider the Columbia River steelhead fillet with hazelnut crust, served over sautéed leeks and roasted artichokes. **Known for:** delicious French pastries; nice selection of wines. [$] *Average main: $11* ✉ *408 E. 2nd St.* ☎ *541/506–0037* 🌐 *www.provencepdx.com* 🕒 *No dinner.*

$ HOTEL Fodor's Choice ★ 🏨 **Celilo Inn.** A prototypical retro motor lodge gone high-design, with exterior-entry rooms and a '50s light-up motel sign that disguise a slick, boutique feel, commands a hilltop overlooking the Columbia River and Dalles Dam. Flat-screen TVs, pillow-top mattresses, and smart decorating come standard, and the outdoor pool and patio are mighty inviting during The Dalles' dry summers. **Pros:** sexy design; terrific wine-touring packages; most rooms have great views. **Cons:** not all rooms have views; those on the far end feel very away from the front desk. [$] *Rooms from: $119* ✉ *3550 E. 2nd St.* ☎ *541/769–0001* 🌐 *www.celiloinn.com* 🛏 *46 rooms* 🍽 *No meals.*

$ HOTEL 🏨 **Fairfield Inn & Suites.** Although it's part of Marriott's mid-range brand, this four-story hotel a couple of blocks from Interstate 84 does have the brightest and most up-to-date rooms in the eastern end of the Gorge, with spacious work areas, comfy bedding, mini-refrigerators, microwaves, and marble-accent bathrooms. **Pros:** upscale rooms at reasonable prices; nice indoor pool and fitness center. **Cons:** bland location on the west side of town that's a bit of a long walk from downtown. [$] *Rooms from: $139* ✉ *2014 W. 7th St.* ☎ *541/769–0753, 800/306–1665* 🌐 *www.marriott.com* 🛏 *80 rooms* 🍴 *Breakfast.*

SPORTS AND THE OUTDOORS

RECREATIONAL AREAS

Celilo Park. Named for the falls that challenged spawning salmon here in the pre-dam days, this favorite spot for windsurfers also has swimming, sailboarding, fishing, and both tent and RV camping. ✉ *The Dalles* ✥ *13 miles east of The Dalles, off I–84 Exit 97* ☎ *541/296–1181* 🎫 *Free.*

Fodor's Choice ★ **Mayer State Park.** Views from atop the park's Rowena Crest bluff are knockout, especially during the March and April wildflower season, and there are a couple of fairly short and scenic hikes that lead from the bluff parking lot (off U.S. 30, 13 miles west of The Dalles, and 6 miles east of Mosier). The 3½.-mile (round-trip) trek up to McCall Point is especially scenic—it affords great views of Mt. Hood. The lower part of the park hugs the Columbia River and is accessed from I–84; here the activities include swimming, boating, fishing, and picnicking. ✉ *Exit 76 off Interstate 84 , Lower Mayer State Park access* ☎ *800/551–6949* 🌐 *www.oregonstateparks.org* 🎫 *Day use $5 per vehicle.*

GOLDENDALE, WASHINGTON

34 miles northeast of The Dalles via Hwy. 14 and U.S. 97.

Although the actual town of Goldendale lies about 12 miles north of the Columbia River, this easygoing community is a good base for exploring the eastern end of the Gorge. It's home to one of the few notable restaurants in this vast but sparsely populated section of the Columbia River Valley, and it also has a couple of basic motels, a small downtown with a few funky cafés and shops, and the small but excellent Goldendale Observatory State Park. Views on the drive to Goldendale and in town itself are some of the most dramatic in the drier, eastern reaches of the Gorge—you'll see soaring white wind turbines lining the grassy bluffs and cliffs on both sides of the river, and along U.S. 97 as it leads into Goldendale, you can see the snowcapped summit of Washington's 12,281-foot Mt. Adams, which receives a little less attention than its southerly twin, Mt. Hood, but is actually taller and every bit as dramatic.

GETTING HERE AND AROUND

Although it's quickest to drive east along Interstate 84 and then north on U.S. 97 to reach Goldendale (a total of 34 miles) and the attractions around Maryhill, it takes only a few extra minutes and is far more scenic to cross the Columbia via The Dalles Bridge into Washington and drive east on Highway 14 to U.S. 97.

ESSENTIALS

Greater Goldendale Chamber of Commerce. ✉ *903 E. Broadway St., Goldendale* ☎ *509/773–3400* 🌐 *www.goldendalechamber.org.*

EXPLORING

FAMILY **Goldendale Observatory State Park.** This 5-acre park on a 2,100-foot-elevation bluff just north of Goldendale's compact downtown contains one of the nation's largest public telescopes, and the town's remote location, far from the lights of any cities, is ideal. Fascinating astronomy programs and sky-watching events are held during the day and evening, year-round. ✉ *1602 Observatory Dr., Goldendale* ☎ *509/773–3141* ⊕ *www.goldendaleobservatory.com* ✉ *$10 day pass* ☾ *Closed Apr.–Sept., Mon. and Tues.; Oct.–Mar., Mon.–Thurs.*

Fodor's Choice **Maryhill Museum of Art.** A wonderfully eclectic mix of artworks, including
★ the largest assemblage of Rodin works outside France; posters, glasswork, and ephemera related to the modern-dance pioneer Loïe Fuller; an impressive cache of Native American artifacts; furniture and art that belonged to another Hill companion, Queen Marie of Romania; an art nouveau glass collection; and a large collection of mostly Victorian-era European and American landscape paintings: they're all housed within the walls of a grandiose mansion built rather improbably in the middle of nowhere by Sam Hill, the man who spearheaded the development of a scenic highway through the Columbia Gorge. The main Beaux-Arts building dates to 1914, and a daring, beautifully executed, LEED-certified modern wing, extends from the back, with a terraced slope overlooking the Columbia River—it contains the museum café, a lovely spot for lunch. The extensive, harmoniously landscaped grounds include a sculpture garden and pathways along the Gorge rim. ✉ *35 Maryhill Museum of Art Dr., Goldendale* ✛ *Off Hwy. 14, 3 miles west of junction with U.S. 97* ☎ *509/773–3733* ⊕ *www.maryhillmuseum. org* ✉ *$9* ☾ *Closed mid-Nov.–mid-Mar.*

Fodor's Choice **Maryhill Winery.** Just down the road from Maryhill Museum, this large
★ winery enjoys the same phenomenal views up and down the Gorge. The largest tasting room in the Gorge has a good-size gift shop as well as a market selling cheese, charcuterie, and other gourmet goodies. Maryhill produces dozens of wines at a variety of prices—the reserves, including stellar Cabernet Franc, Cabernet Sauvignon, Malbec, and Chardonnay, tend to earn most acclaim. In summer, the outdoor amphitheater on the grounds hosts a series of pop concerts. ✉ *9774 Hwy. 14, Goldendale* ☎ *509/773–1976, 877/627–9445* ⊕ *www.maryhillwinery.com.*

Stonehenge Memorial. Built by Maryhill Museum founder Sam Hill, this full-scale replica of England's legendary Neolithic stone creation was constructed in 1918 as the nation's first memorial to servicemen who perished in World War I. The memorial is a five-minute drive east of the museum, on a promontory overlooking the Columbia River. ✉ *Stonehenge Dr., Goldendale* ✛ *Off Hwy. 14, just east of U.S. 97* ☎ *509/773–3733* ⊕ *www.maryhillmuseum.org* ✉ *Free.*

WHERE TO EAT

$ ✕ **Glass Onion.** Visitors to small, unpretentious Goldendale will be sur-
MODERN prised to find one of the culinary gems of the Columbia Gorge in the
AMERICAN center of town, set within a cozy, beautifully restored house hung with
Fodor's Choice local artwork. Chef Matt McGowan sources seasonal ingredients from
★ local farms and purveyors, serves a great selection of local beers and

wines, and keeps the price of everything on his menu at least $10 below what you'd pay in Hood River or Portland. **Known for:** homemade desserts; reasonable prices; nice selection of Gorge wines and beers. [$] *Average main: $13* ✉ *604 S. Columbus Ave., Goldendale* ☎ *509/773–4928* 🌐 *www.theglassonionrestaurant.com* 🕒 *Closed Sun.–Tues.*

MT. HOOD

The Multnomah tribe call Mt. Hood "Wy'East," named, according to popular legend, for a jealous lover who once sparred over a woman with his rival, Klickitat. When their fighting caught the Great Spirit's attention, Wy'East and Klickitat were transformed into two angry, smoke-bellowing mountains—one became Washington's Mt. Adams, the other became Mt. Hood. Wy'East has mellowed out a bit since then, but the mountain is still technically an active volcano, and it's had very minor, lava-free eruptive events as recently as the mid-1800s.

Today Mt. Hood is better known for the challenge it poses to climbers, its deep winter snows, and a dozen glaciers and snowfields that make skiing possible nearly year-round. Resort towns and colorful hospitality villages are arranged in a semicircle around the mountain, full of ski bars and rental cabins that host hordes of fun-loving Portlanders each weekend. In every direction from the postcard-perfect peak, the million-acre Mount Hood National Forest spreads out like a big green blanket, and more than 300,000 acres of that are designated wilderness. Mule deer, black bears, elk, and the occasional cougar share the space with humans who come to hike, camp, and fish in the Pacific Northwest's quintessential wild ecosystem.

AROUND THE MOUNTAIN

About 60 miles east of Portland on I–84 and U.S. 26, and 42 miles south of Hood River via Hwy. 35 and U.S. 26.

Majestically towering 11,245 feet above sea level, Mt. Hood is what remains of the original north wall and rim of a volatile crater. Although the peak no longer spews ash or fire, active vents regularly release steam high on the mountain. The mountain took its modern moniker in 1792, when a crew of the British Royal Navy, the first recorded Caucasians sailing up the Columbia River, spotted it and named it after a famed British naval officer by the name of—you guessed it—Hood.

Mt. Hood offers the longest ski season in North America, with three major ski areas and some 30 lifts, as well as extensive areas for cross-country skiing and snowboarding. Many of the ski runs turn into mountain-bike trails in summer. The mountain is also popular with climbers and hikers. In fact, some hikes follow parts of the Oregon Trail, and signs of the pioneers' passing are still evident.

GETTING HERE AND AROUND

From Portland, U.S. 26 heads east into the heart of Mount Hood National Forest, while Highway 35 runs south from Hood River along the mountain's east face. The roads meet 60 miles east of Portland, near Government Camp, forming an oblong loop with Interstate 84 and the

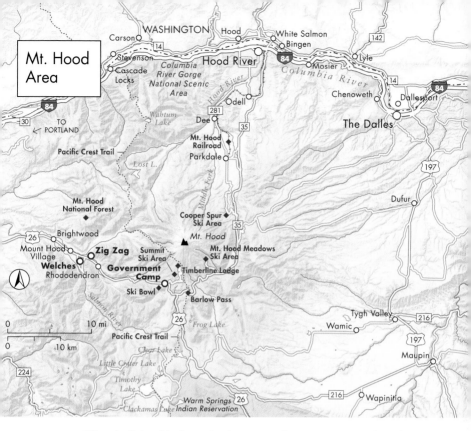

Historic Columbia Gorge Highway. It's about a 75-minute drive from Downtown Portland to Government Camp via U.S. 26. **Sea to Summit**—call for timetables and pickup and drop-off sites—offers shuttle service from Portland International Airport and Downtown Portland hotels to all of the Mt. Hood resorts; the fare is $50 each way, with discounted lift-ticket and ski-rental packages available. Additionally, the **Mt. Hood Express** bus line operates daily and links the villages along the corridor—including Welches, Government Camp, and Timberline Lodge—to the Portland suburb of Sandy, which you can get to via TriMet commuter bus. This option is slower (it takes 2½ to 3 hours each way from the airport or Downtown to Timberline Lodge, for example) than a direct shuttle but costs just $2, plus $2.50 for TriMet bus fare to Sandy.

Contacts Mt. Hood Express. ☎ *503/668–3466* ⊕ *www.mthoodexpress.com.* **Sea to Summit.** ☎ *503/286–9333* ⊕ *www.seatosummit.net.*

ESSENTIALS

Visitor Information Mt. Hood Area Chamber of Commerce. ☎ *503/622–3017* ⊕ *www.mthoodchamber.com.* **Mount Hood National Forest Headquarters.** ✉ *16400 Champion Way, Sandy* ☎ *503/668–1700* ⊕ *www.fs.usda.gov/mthood.*

EXPLORING

Fodor's Choice ★ **Mount Hood National Forest.** The highest spot in Oregon and the fourth-highest peak in the Cascades, "the Mountain" is a focal point of the 1.1-million-acre forest, an all-season playground attracting around 3 million visitors annually. Beginning 20 miles southeast of Portland, it extends south from the Columbia River Gorge for more than 60 miles and includes more than 311,400 acres of designated wilderness. These woods are perfect for hikers, horseback riders, mountain climbers, and cyclists. Within the forest are more than 80 campgrounds and 50 lakes stocked with brown, rainbow, cutthroat, brook, and steelhead trout. The Sandy, Salmon, Clackamas, and other rivers are known for their fishing, rafting, canoeing, and swimming. Both forest and mountain are crossed by an extensive trail system for hikers, cyclists, and horseback riders. The **Pacific Crest Trail,** which begins in British Columbia and ends in Mexico, crosses at the 4,157-foot-high Barlow Pass. As with most other mountain destinations within Oregon, weather can be temperamental, and snow and ice may affect driving conditions as early as October and as late as June. Bring tire chains and warm clothes as a precaution.

Since this forest is close to the Portland metro area, campgrounds and trails are potentially crowded over the summer months, especially on weekends. If you're planning to camp, get info and permits from the Mount Hood National Forest Headquarters. Campgrounds are managed by the U.S. Forest Service and a few private concessionaires, and standouts include a string of neighboring campgrounds on the south side of Mt. Hood: Trillium Lake, Still Creek, Timothy Lake, Little Crater Lake, Clackamas Lake, Summit Lake, Clear Lake, and Frog Lake. Each varies in what it offers and in price. The mountain overflows with day-use areas. From mid-November through April, all designated Winter Recreation Areas require a Sno-Park permit, available from the U.S. Forest Service and many local resorts and sporting goods stores. ✉ *Headquarters, 16400 Champion Way, Sandy* ☎ *503/668–1700* 🌐 *www.fs.usda.gov/mthood* 🎟 *Day pass $5.*

WHERE TO EAT AND STAY

$$$$ PACIFIC NORTHWEST 🍴 **Cascade Dining Room.** Vaulted wooden beams and a wood-plank floor, handcrafted furniture, handwoven drapes, and a lion-size stone fireplace set the scene in Timberline Lodge's esteemed restaurant, from which views of neighboring mountains are enjoyed, except when snow drifts cover the windows. The atmosphere is traditional and historic, but chef Jason Stoller Smith is a former wine-country *wunderkind* whose resume includes orchestrating a salmon bake at the White House. **Known for:** taste of Oregon lunch buffet; chef demonstrations; historic setting. [$] *Average main: $38* ✉ *27500 E. Timberline Rd., Timberline Lodge* ☎ *503/272–3104* 🌐 *www.timberlinelodge.com.*

$$ RESORT FAMILY Fodor's Choice ★ 🏨 **Timberline Lodge.** Guest rooms are simple, rustic, and charming (a handful of them lack private baths), but don't expect a cushy experience—the reason for staying here is the location and setting. **Pros:** a thrill to stay on the mountain itself; great proximity to all snow activity; amazing architecture. **Cons:** rooms are small and the least expensive ones have shared bathrooms; views from rooms are often completely

A snowboarder catches some air on Mt. Hood.

blocked by snow in winter; carloads of tourists. ⓢ *Rooms from: $160*
⊠ *27500 E. Timberline Rd., Timberline Lodge* ☎ *503/272–3311,
800/547–1406* ⊕ *www.timberlinelodge.com* ↝ *70 rooms* ⥾ *Some
meals.*

SPORTS AND THE OUTDOORS
DOWNHILL SKIING

FAMILY   **Cooper Spur Mountain Resort.** On the northern slope of Mt. Hood, Cooper
Spur caters to families and has one double chair and a tow rope. The
longest run is 2/3 mile, with a 350-foot vertical drop. Facilities and
services include rentals, instruction, repairs, and a ski shop, day lodge,
snack bar, and restaurant. Call for hours. ⊠ *10755 Cooper Spur Rd.,
Mount Hood* ⚓ *Follow signs from Hwy. 35 for 2½ miles to ski area*
☎ *541/352–6692* ⊕ *www.cooperspur.com.*

Timberline Lodge & Ski Area. The longest ski season in North America
unfolds at this full-service ski area, where the U.S. ski team conducts
summer training. Thanks to the omnipresent Palmer Snowfield, it's
the closest thing to a year-round ski area in the Lower 48 (it's typically closed for just a few weeks in September). Timberline is famous
for its Palmer chairlift, which takes skiers and snowboarders to the
high glacier for summer skiing. There are five high-speed quad chairs,
one triple chair, and one double. The top elevation is 8,500 feet, with
a 3,700-foot vertical drop, and the longest run is 3 miles. Facilities
include a day lodge with fast food and a ski shop; lessons and equipment rental and repair are available. Parking requires a Sno-Park permit. The Palmer and Magic Mile lifts are popular with both skiers and

sightseers. ✉ *27500 E. Timberline Rd., Timberline Lodge* ☎ *503/272–3311* 🌐 *www.timberlinelodge.com.*

GOVERNMENT CAMP

54 miles east of Portland on I–84 and U.S. 26, and 42 miles south of Hood River via Hwy. 35 and U.S. 26.

This alpine resort village with a bohemian vibe has several hotels and restaurants popular with visitors exploring Mt. Hood's ski areas and mountain-biking and hiking trails. "Govy" is also just a 12-mile drive up the hill from Welches, which also has restaurants and lodging.

GETTING HERE AND AROUND

Government Camp is on U.S. 26, which is often called the Mt. Hood Corridor. It's about 55 miles east of Portland and just down the hill from Timberline Lodge.

WHERE TO EAT AND STAY

$ AMERICAN 🍴 **Charlie's Mountain View.** Old and new ski swag plasters the walls, lift chairs function as furniture, and photos of famous (and locally famous) skiers and other memorabilia are as abundant as the menu selections. Open-flame-grilled steaks and hamburgers are worthy here, and the happy hour crowd shares plates piled high with waffle fries. **Known for:** live music on weekends; apple dumplings (in season); rowdy and fun vibe. [$] *Average main: $9* ✉ *88462 E. Government Camp Loop* ☎ *503/272–3333* 🌐 *www.charliesmountainview.com/eats.*

$$ EASTERN EUROPEAN 🍴 **Glacier Haus Bistro.** This lively, family-operated spot in the center of Government Camp is a good bet for a simple snack and espresso drink or a full meal. Pizzas and sandwiches are an option, but locals especially love the Eastern European standards, such as Hungarian beef goulash, Wiener schnitzel, and Bavarian sausages with sauerkraut and garlic-mashed potatoes. **Known for:** hearty Eastern European fare; family-friendly ambience. [$] *Average main: $17* ✉ *88817 E. Government Camp Loop Rd.* ☎ *503/272–3471* 🌐 *www.glacierhaus.com* 🕒 *Closed Mon. and Oct.*

$ AMERICAN 🍴 **Mt. Hood Brewing.** Producing finely crafted beers—Multorporter Smoked Porter, Ice Axe IPA, Highland Meadow Blond Ale, and others—since the early '90s, this casual brewpub with stone walls, a fireplace, and both booth and table seating buzzes in the early evening for après-ski dining and drinking. It's popular for its creative comfort food, including poutine with fontina cheese and peppercorn demi-glace, cast-iron-skillet-baked fondue, Alsatian pizza topped with smoked ham and crème fraîche, barbecue pulled-pork-and-porter sandwiches. **Known for:** root-beer—and beer—ice cream floats; cast-iron fondue. [$] *Average main: $13* ✉ *87304 E. Government Camp Loop* ☎ *503/272–3172* 🌐 *www.mthoodbrewing.com.*

$ HOTEL 🏨 **Best Western Mt. Hood Inn.** Clean, well maintained, and inexpensive, all rooms have microwaves and refrigerators, and some have kitchenettes and whirlpool tubs. **Pros:** central location; clean and modern rooms; great value. **Cons:** cookie-cutter decor and design. [$] *Rooms from: $136* ✉ *87450 E. Government Camp Loop* ☎ *503/272–3205, 800/780–7234* 🌐 *www.bestwesternoregon.com* 🛏 *57 rooms* 🍽 *Breakfast.*

$$ RESORT FAMILY Fodor's Choice ★ **Collins Lake Resort.** Comprising 66 poshly furnished chalets with fireplaces and dozens of other amenities, scattered around an alpine lake, this contemporary, 28-acre compound is the cushiest accommodations option in the Mt. Hood area. **Pros:** within walking distance of Government Camp restaurants and bars; spacious layouts are ideal for groups and families. **Cons:** steepest rates in town. [$] *Rooms from: $190* ✉ *88149 E. Creek Ridge Rd.* ☎ *503/928–3498, 800/234–6288* 🌐 *www.collinslakeresort.com* 🛏 *66 condos* 🍴 *No meals.*

SPORTS AND THE OUTDOORS

DOWNHILL SKIING

Fodor's Choice ★ **Mt. Hood Meadows Ski Resort.** The mountain's largest resort has more than 2,150 skiable acres, 85 runs, five double chairs, six high-speed quads, a top elevation of 9,000 feet, a vertical drop of 2,777 feet, and a longest run of 3 miles. If you're seeking varied, scenic terrain with plenty of trails for all skiing abilities, this is your best choice among the region's ski areas. Facilities include a day lodge, nine restaurants, two lounges, a ski-and-snowboard school, a children's learning center with daycare, and two ski shops with equipment rentals. ✉ *Hwy. 35* ✣ *10 miles east of Government Camp* ☎ *503/337–2222* 🌐 *www.skihood.com.*

FAMILY **Mt. Hood Skibowl.** The ski area closest to Portland is also known as "America's largest night ski area," with 34 runs lighted each evening. It has 960 skiable acres serviced by four double chairs and five surface tows, a top elevation of 5,100 feet, a vertical drop of 1,500 feet, and a longest run of 3 miles. You can take advantage of two day lodges, a mid-mountain warming hut, four restaurants, and two lounges. Sleigh rides are conducted, weather permitting, and a hugely popular tubing and adventure park has several tubing hills, plus music, LED lights, and a laser show. In summer the resort morphs into the Adventure Park at Skibowl, with mountain biking, zip lines, bungee jumping, a five-story free-fall Tarzan Swing, disc golf, and kid-friendly tubing and alpine slides. ✉ *87000 E. U.S. 26* ☎ *503/272–3206* 🌐 *www.skibowl.com.*

SHOPPING

Govy General Store. Good thing this is a really nice grocery store, because it's the only one for miles around. Govy General stocks all the staples, plus a nice selection of gourmet treats like cheeses and chocolates. It's also a full-service liquor store and your one-stop shop for Mt. Hood sweatshirts, postcards, and other keepsake tchotchkes. **TIP→** Grab your Sno-Park permit here in winter. ✉ *30521 E. Meldrum St.* ☎ *541/272–3107* 🌐 *www.govygeneralstore.com.*

WELCHES AND ZIGZAG

12 miles west of Government Camp and 40 miles east of Portland.

One of a string of small communities known as the Villages at Mt. Hood, Welches's claim to fame is that it was the site of Oregon's first golf course, built at the base of Mt. Hood in 1928. Another golf course is still going strong today, and summer vacationers hover around both towns for access to basic services like gas, groceries, and dining. Others come to pull a few trout out of the scenic Zigzag River or to access trails and streams in the adjacent Salmon–Huckleberry Wilderness.

GETTING HERE AND AROUND

Most of Welches is found just off U.S. 26, often called the Mt. Hood Corridor here, about 45 miles east of Portland.

WHERE TO EAT AND STAY

$$$ MODERN AMERICAN

🍴 **Altitude.** The flagship restaurant at the Resort at The Mountain aims for a sleek, modernist look in its glitzy—for the rustic Mt. Hood region at least—dining room with recessed lighting and contemporary art. The kitchen ably handles standards like bacon-wrapped beef tenderloin with huckleberry sauce and hazelnut-crusted baked halibut, along with a few adventurous dishes like braised pork cheek with pickled shallots and pan-seared polenta. **Known for:** popular lounge with lighter menu; nice views of resort's greenery. [$] *Average main: $26* ✉ *Resort at The Mountain, 68010 E. Fairway Ave., Welches* ☎ *503/622–2214* 🌐 *www.mthood-resort.com* 🕘 *No lunch.*

$$ AMERICAN Fodor's Choice ★

🍴 **The Rendezvous Grill & Tap Room.** "Serious food in a not-so-serious place" is the slogan of this casual roadhouse with surprisingly sophisticated food—it's been a locals' favorite since it opened back in mid-'90s. For a joint many miles from the coast, the 'Vous sure does a nice job with seafood, turning out appetizing plates of sautéed shrimp, Willapa Bay oysters, Dungeness crab, and char-grilled wild salmon. **Known for:** surprisingly sophisticated menu; house-infused vodkas; great outdoor seating. [$] *Average main: $21* ✉ *67149 E. U.S. 26, Welches* ☎ *503/622–6837* 🌐 *www.thevousgrill.com* 🕘 *Closed Mon.*

$ RENTAL

🏨 **The Cabins Creekside at Welches.** Affordability, accessibility to recreational activities, and wonderful hosts make these cabins with knotty-pine vaulted ceilings, log furnishings, and full-size kitchens a great lodging choice in the Mt. Hood area. **Pros:** family-run; quiet, off-highway location; anglers will benefit from the Thurmans' fly-fishing savvy. **Cons:** no dining within walking distance; no cabin-side parking; simple but clean, functional furnishings. [$] *Rooms from: $109* ✉ *25086 E. Welches Rd., Welches* ☎ *503/622–4275* 🌐 *www.mthoodcabins.com* 🛏 *10 cabins* 🍽 *No meals.*

$$ RENTAL

🏨 **Mt. Hood Vacation Rentals.** Doggedly determined to ensure a great time for the two- and four-pawed vacationer alike, this company welcomes the family pet into the majority of its homes/cabins/condos, yet the properties are still on the upscale side: you'll find fireplaces/wood-burning stoves, hot tubs, river views, and full kitchens. **Pros:** knowledgeable, hospitable staff; gorgeous homes nestled throughout the Mt. Hood area; many secluded sites; family- and pet-friendly. **Cons:** bring your own shampoo; two- to five-night minimum. [$] *Rooms from: $175* ✉ *67898 E. Hwy. 26, Welches* ☎ *866/921–1757* 🌐 *www.mthoodrentals.com* 🛏 *32 units* 🍽 *No meals.*

$$ RESORT

🏨 **Resort at The Mountain.** In the evergreen-forest foothills of Mt. Hood, this expansive resort is popular year-round both with outdoorsy sorts and couples seeking romantic hideaways. **Pros:** every sport available; plenty of choices in room size. **Cons:** there will be crowds; may not appeal to those who are not fans of golf. [$] *Rooms from: $188* ✉ *68010*

E. Fairway Ave., Welches ☎ 503/622–3101, 877/439–6774 ⊕ www.
theresort.com ⊋ 157 rooms ⟟⟠ No meals.

SPORTS AND THE OUTDOORS

FISHING

The Fly Fishing Shop. This heritage shop full of self-proclaimed "fish-aholics" has been peddling flies and guiding trips for three decades. Drop in to ask about the huge variety of customizable float trips (from $500), clinics, and by-the-hour walking trips for seasonal steelhead and salmon ($50 an hour). Great nearby rivers include the glacial-fed Sandy and its tributary the Zigzag, which hides some native cuthroat. ✉ 67296 E. U.S. 26, Welches ☎ 503/622–4607, 800/266–3971 ⊕ www.
flyfishusa.com.

Ron Lauzon's Fly Fishing School. Knowledgeable and highly respected fishing expert Ron Lauzon offers private and group lessons and instruction, and also leads guided float and wading trips. He knows the top trout- and steelhead-fishing sites in the region like no other. ✉ Sandy ☎ 503/622–3634 ⊕ www.theflyfishinginstructor.com.

GOLF

The Courses. The three 9-hole tracks at the Resort at the Mountain include the Pine Cone Nine, Oregon's oldest golf course, built on a rented hayfield in 1928—you can mix any combination of the three courses to complete a full 18-hole round. There's also a lighted 18-hole putting course that's popular with families and adults working on their short game. ✉ 68010 E. Fairway Ave., Welches ☎ 503/622–3151, 800/669–4653 ⊕ mthood-resort.com ⌷ $50–$70 for 18 holes ⚐. Pine Cone: 9 holes, 3299 yards, par 36. Foxglove: 9 holes, 3106 yards, par 36. Thistle: 9 holes, 2956 yards, par 34.

CENTRAL OREGON

WELCOME TO CENTRAL OREGON

TOP REASONS TO GO

★ **Become one with nature:** Central Oregonians live on the flanks of the Cascade Range and are bracketed by rock formations, rivers, lakes, forests, ancient lava flows, and desert badlands. Bring your golf clubs, carabiners, snowboard, or camera, and explore deeper.

★ **Visit Bend:** Downtown Bend is lively and walkable, with a variety of appealing restaurants, galleries, and stores.

★ **Kick back at Sunriver:** This family-oriented resort has bike paths, river trails, horse stables, tennis courts, a golf course, and several restaurants.

★ **Check out the craftbrewing scene:** With nearly three dozen breweries—and more on the horizon—you can discover nearly any type of beer that fits your tastes.

★ **Discover the Old West:** Cowboy towns, such as Sisters and Prineville, offer a glimpse into what life was like when the West was wild.

1 West Central Oregon. The western portion of central Oregon ranges from lush and green in the Cascades to dry and full of conifers down to the Deschutes River. It's the side with the ski areas, the high mountain lakes, most of the resorts, and the rushing waters. The region's largest town is Bend, and it straddles the forested west and the harshly beautiful east.

2 East Central Oregon. East of the Deschutes River this land is marked by rugged buttes, tough junipers, and bristly sagebrush. It's a place that still hugs the edge of the wilderness, with weathered barns, painted desert hills, a caldera holding two popular lakes, and some world-class rock climbing.

GETTING ORIENTED

Central Oregon provides a natural meeting place between the urban west side and the rural east side. It nestles neatly below the Columbia River basin and is drained by the Deschutes River, which flows from south to north. Skiers and snowboarders flock to winter sports areas on the western edge, anglers head to the Deschutes, the Metolius, and the Cascade Lakes, and climbers, campers, rockhounds, and wanderers explore the arid landscapes on the east side. Bend, the largest town for more than 120 miles in any direction, sits roughly in the center of this region.

6

Updated by
Jon Shadel

After a day on the Sunriver bike paths, a first-time visitor from Europe shook her head. "This place is paradise," she declared. It's easy to see why she thought so. Central Oregon has snowfields so white they sharpen the edges of the mountains; canyons so deep and sudden as to induce vertigo; air so crisp that it fills the senses; water that ripples in mountain lakes so clear that boaters can see to the bottom, or rushes through turbulent rapids favored by rafters.

A region born of volcanic tumult is now a powerful lure for the adventurous, the beauty-seeking, and even the urbane—Bend has grown into a sophisticated city of 87,000-plus, a magnet for people retreating from larger, noisier city centers. For most visitors Bend is the sunny face of central Oregon, a haven for hikers, athletes, and aesthetes, but with the charm and elegance of much larger cities.

From Bend it's easy to launch to the attractions that surround it. To the northwest, Camp Sherman is a stunning place to fish for rainbow trout or kokanee. The Smith Rocks formation to the north draws climbers and boulderers, and, to the south, Lava Lands and the Lava River Caves fascinate visitors more than 6,000 years after they were chiseled out of the earth. The Oregon Badlands Wilderness to the east draws hikers and horseback riders wanting to connect with the untamed landscape. Lake Billy Chinook to the north is a startling oasis, where summer visitors drift in houseboats beneath the high walls of the Deschutes River canyon. The Deschutes River itself carries rafters of all descriptions, from young families to solo adventurers.

The area's natural beauty has brought it a diverse cluster of resorts, whether situated on the shores of high mountain lakes or cradling golf courses of startling green. They dot the landscape from the dry terrain around Warm Springs to the high road to Mt. Bachelor.

CENTRAL OREGON PLANNER

WHEN TO GO

Central Oregon is a popular destination year-round. Skiers and snowboarders come from mid-December through March, when the powder is deepest and driest. During this time, guests flock to the hotels and resorts along Century Drive, which leads from Bend to Mt. Bachelor. In summer, when temperatures reach the upper 80s, travelers are more likely to spread throughout the region. But temperatures fall as the elevation rises, so take a jacket if you're heading out for an evening at the high lakes or Newberry Crater.

You'll pay a premium at the mountain resorts during ski season, and Sunriver and other family and golf resorts are busiest in summer. It's best to make reservations as far in advance as possible; six months in advance is not too early.

GETTING HERE AND AROUND

AIR TRAVEL

Visitors fly into **Redmond Municipal Airport–Roberts Field** (RDM), about 17 miles north of downtown Bend. Rental cars are available for pickup at the airport from several national agencies. The **Redmond Airport Shuttle** provides transportation throughout the region (reservations requested); a ride from the airport to addresses within Bend costs about $40. Taxis are available at curbside, or can be summoned from the call board inside the airport. Portland's airport is 160 miles northwest of Bend, and daily flights connect the two cities.

Air Contacts Redmond Airport Shuttle. ☎ *541/382–1687, 888/664–8449* ⊕ *www.redmondairportshuttle.net.* **Redmond Municipal Airport–Roberts Field** (RDM). ✉ *2522 S.E. Jesse Butler Circle, Redmond* ☎ *541/548–0646* ⊕ *www. flyrdm.com.*

BUS TRAVEL

The **Central Oregon Breeze,** a regional carrier, runs one bus a day each way between Portland and Bend, with stops in Redmond and Madras. **Cascades East Transit** is Bend's intercity bus service, and connects Redmond, La Pine, Madras, Prineville, Bend, and Sisters. Trips from the airport require reservations. **Greyhound** also serves the area with direct routes from Bend to Eugene and Salem, with connections onward to Portland.

Bus Contacts Cascades East Transit. ✉ *334 Hawthorn Ave., Bend* ☎ *541/385–8680, 866/385–8680* ⊕ *www.cascadeseasttransit.com.* **Central Oregon Breeze.** ✉ *2045 N.E. Hwy. 20, Bend* ☎ *541/389–7469, 800/847–0157* ⊕ *www.cobreeze.com.* **Greyhound Bend.** ✉ *334 N.E. Hawthorne Ave., Bend* ☎ *541/923–1732* ⊕ *www.greyhound.com.*

CAR TRAVEL

U.S. 20 heads west from Idaho and east from the coastal town of Newport into central Oregon. U.S. 26 goes southeast from Portland to Prineville, where it heads northeast into the Ochoco National Forest. U.S. 97 heads north from California and south from Washington to Bend. Highway 126 travels east from Eugene to Prineville; it connects with

U.S. 20 heading south (to Bend) at Sisters. Major roads throughout central Oregon are well maintained and open throughout the winter season, although it's always advisable to have tire chains in the car. Some roads are closed by snow during winter, including Oregon 242. Check the **Oregon Department of Transportation's TripCheck** (⊕ *www.trip-check.com*) or call **ODOT** (☎ *800/977–6368*).

FESTIVALS

Bend Film Festival. This popular local film festival takes place in October. ✉ *1000 N.W. Wall St., Suite 260, Bend* ☎ *541/388–3378* ⊕ *www.bendfilm.org*.

Bend Summer and Fall Festival. Downtown Bend is blocked off with food, crafts, art booths, and music in July and September. ✉ *Box 1424, Bend* ☎ *541/508–4280* ⊕ *www.bendfestivals.com*.

Oregon Winterfest. February brings music, food, brews, wine, ice carving, and other winter sports to Bend's Old Mill District. ✉ *Bend* ⊕ *www.oregonwinterfest.com*.

Pole, Pedal, Paddle. Bend's popular ski, bike, run, and kayak or canoe race is held in May. ✉ *Bend* ☎ *541/388–0002* ⊕ *www.pppbend.com*.

Sisters Folk Festival. A celebration of American music is held in September. ✉ *Sisters* ☎ *541/549–4979* ⊕ *www.sistersfolkfestival.org*.

Sisters Outdoor Quilt Show. The second Saturday in July, Sisters transforms into a Western town covered with colorful quilts hanging from building exteriors. ✉ *Sisters* ☎ *541/549–0989* ⊕ *www.sistersoutdoorquiltshow.org*.

Sisters Rodeo. Multiple rodeo and community events, held annually for more than 70 years, take place over a weekend in June. ✉ *67637 U.S. 20, south of Sisters, Sisters* ☎ *541/549–0121, 800/827–7522* ⊕ *www.sistersrodeo.com*.

RESTAURANTS

The center of culinary ambition is in downtown Bend, but good restaurants also serve diners in Sisters, Redmond, Prineville, and the major resorts. Styles vary, but many hew to the Northwest preference for fresh foods grown, caught, and harvested in the region.

Central Oregon also has many down-home places and family-friendly brewpubs, and authentic Mexican restaurants have emerged to win faithful followings in Prineville, Redmond, Madras, and Bend. *Restaurant reviews have been shortened. For full information visit Fodors.com.*

HOTELS

Central Oregon has lodging for every taste, from upscale resort lodges to an in-town brewpub village, eclectic bed-and-breakfasts, rustic Western inns, and a range of independent and chain hotels and motels. If you're drawn to the rivers, stay in a pastoral fishing cabin along the Metolius near Camp Sherman. If you came for the powder, you'll want a ski-snowboard condo closer to the mountain. For soaking up the atmosphere, you might favor one of downtown Bend's luxurious hotels, or Old St. Francis, the Catholic school–turned-brewpub village. *Hotel reviews have been shortened. For full information, visit Fodors.com.*

WHAT IT COSTS IN U.S. DOLLARS				
	$	**$$**	**$$$**	**$$$$**
Restaurants	under $17	$17–$24	$25–$30	over $30
Hotels	under $150	$150–$200	$201–$250	over $250

Restaurant prices are the average cost of a main course at dinner, or if dinner is not served, at lunch. Hotel prices are the lowest cost of a standard double room in high season.

TOURS

Cog Wild Bicycle Tours. One- and multiday mountain bike tours are offered for people of all skill levels and interests. ✉ *255 S.W. Century Dr., Suite 201, Bend* ☎ *541/385–7002* ⊕ *www.cogwild.com* 🖃 *From $170.*

Sun Country Tours. A longtime provider of raft and tube trips on central Oregon rivers offers rafting excursions that range from two hours to full days May through September. ✉ *531 S.W. 13th St., Bend* ☎ *541/382–6277* ⊕ *www.suncountrytours.com* 🖃 *From $59.*

Fodor'sChoice ★ **Wanderlust Tours.** Popular and family-friendly half-day or evening excursions are offered around Bend, Sisters, and Sunriver. Options include kayaking, canoeing, snowshoeing, and caving. ✉ *61535 S. Hwy. 97, Suite 13, Bend* ☎ *541/389–8359* ⊕ *www.wanderlusttours.com* 🖃 *From $75.*

VISITOR INFORMATION

Central Oregon Visitors Association. ✉ *57100 Beaver Dr., Bldg. 6, Suite 130, Sunriver* ☎ *541/389–8799, 800/800–8334* ⊕ *www.visitcentral-oregon.com.*

6

WEST CENTRAL OREGON

Sunshine, crisp pines, pure air, rushing waters, world-class skiing and snowboarding at Mt. Bachelor, destination golf resorts, a touch of the frontier West at Sisters, an air of sophistication in Bend—the forested side of central Oregon serves up many recreational flavors. The area draws young couples, seniors, families, athletes, and adventurers, all of whom arrive with a certain sense of purpose, but also with an appreciation for the natural world. Travelers will have no problem filling a week in central Oregon's western half with memorable activities, from rafting to enjoying some sensational meals.

BEND

160 miles southeast of Portland.

Bend, Oregon's largest city east of the Cascades, is once more one of the fastest-growing cities in the state, recovering abundantly from the hard-hitting recession. Construction is booming and new businesses seem to open every day. The people of Bend continue to enjoy an enviable climate, proximity to skiing, dynamic lifestyle, and a reputation as

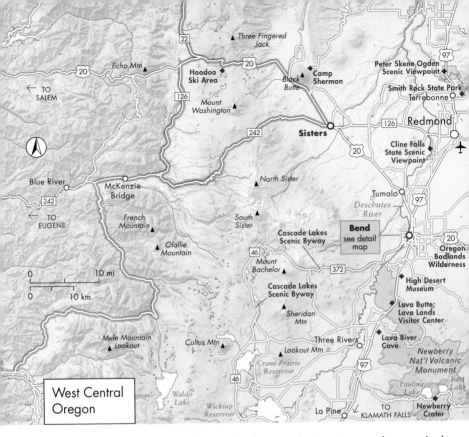

West Central Oregon

a playground and recreational escape. At times it seems that everybody in Bend is an athlete or a brewer, but it remains a tolerant, welcoming town, conscious of making a good first impression. Bend's heart is an area of about four square blocks, centered on Wall and Bond streets. Here you'll find boutique stores, galleries, independent coffee shops, brewpubs, fine restaurants, lively nightlife establishments, and historic landmarks such as the Tower Theatre, built in 1940. A few traditional barbershops and taverns are also spread around, keeping it real.

Neighboring Mt. Bachelor, though hardly a giant among the Cascades at 9,065 feet, is blessed by an advantage over its taller siblings—by virtue of its location, it's the first to get snowfall, and the last to see it go. Inland air collides with the Pacific's damp influence, creating skiing conditions immortalized in songs by local rock bands and raves from the ski press.

GETTING HERE AND AROUND
Portlanders arrive via car on U.S. 20 or U.S. 26, and folks from the mid–Willamette Valley cross the mountains on Oregon 126. Redmond Municipal Airport, 17 miles to the north, is an efficient hub for air travelers, who can rent a car or take a shuttle or cab into town. **Greyhound** also serves the area with direct routes to Eugene and Salem. The **Central Oregon Breeze,** a privately operated regional carrier, runs daily

between Portland and Bend, with stops in Redmond and Madras. Bend is served by a citywide bus system called **Cascades East Transit,** which also connects to Redmond, La Pine, Sisters, Prineville, and Madras. To take a Cascades East bus between cities in central Oregon, reservations are not required but recommended. *For more on bus travel to and from Bend, see Getting Here and Around in the Central Oregon Planner.*

If you're trying to head out of or into Bend on a major highway during the morning or 5 pm rush, especially on U.S. 97, you may hit congestion. Parking in downtown Bend is free for the first two hours (three hours at the centrally located parking garage), or park for free in the residential neighborhoods just west of downtown. In addition to the car-rental counters at the airport, Avis, Budget, Enterprise, and Hertz also have rental locations in Bend.

ESSENTIALS

Visitor Information Bend Chamber of Commerce. ⊠ *777 N.W. Wall St., Suite 200* ☎ *541/382–3221* ⊕ *www.bendchamber.org.* **Visit Bend/Bend Visitor Center.** ⊠ *750 N.W. Lava Rd., Suite 160* ☎ *541/382–8048, 877/245–8484* ⊕ *www.visitbend.com.*

EXPLORING

FAMILY **Des Chutes Historical Museum.** The Deschutes County Historical Society operates this museum, which was originally built as a schoolhouse in 1914. Exhibits depict historical life in the area, including a pioneer schoolroom, Native American artifacts, and relics from the logging, ranching, homesteading, and railroading eras. ⊠ *129 N.W. Idaho Ave.* ☎ *541/389–1813* ⊕ *www.deschuteshistory.org* 🔳 *$5.*

Deschutes Brewery. Central Oregon's first and most famous brewery produces and bottles its beer in this facility separate from the popular brewpub. Take a free tour at 1 pm every day and learn from the beer-obsessed staff; be sure to make reservations online or by phone since groups fill quickly. The tour ends in the tasting room and gift shop, where participants get to try samples of the fresh beer. ⊠ *901 S.W. Simpson Ave.* ☎ *541/385–8606* ⊕ *www.deschutesbrewery.com.*

Drake Park and Mirror Pond. At its western edge, downtown Bend slopes down to these 13 acres of manicured greensward and trees lining the edge of the Deschutes, attracting flocks of Canada geese as well as strollers from downtown. Various events, such as music festivals, occur in the park during the summer months. Note the 11-foot-high wheel log skidder, harkening back to Bend's logging industry in the early 20th century, when four draft horses pulled the wheel to move heavy logs. ⊠ *Bounded on the west by N.W. Brooks St. and Drake Park; N.W. Lava Rd. on the east; N.W. Franklin Ave. to the south; and N.W. Greenwood Ave. to the north* ⊕ *www.downtownbend.org.*

FAMILY Fodor's Choice ★ **High Desert Museum.** The West was actually wild, and this combo museum/zoo proves it. Kids will love the up-close-and-personal encounters with Gila monsters, snakes, porcupines, birds of prey, Vivi the bobcat, and Snowshoe the lynx. Characters in costume take part in the Living History series, where you can chat with stagecoach drivers, boomtown widows, pioneers, homesteaders, and sawmill operators. Peruse the 110,000-square-feet of indoor and outdoor exhibits, such

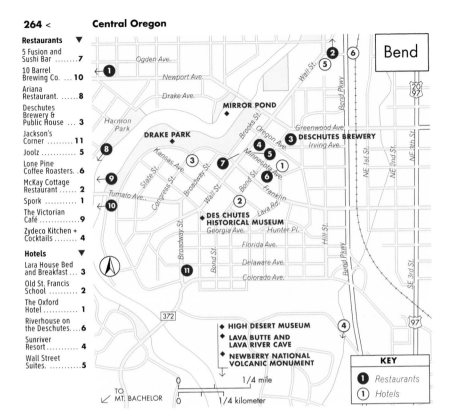

as Spirit of the West and a historic family ranch, to experience how the past can truly come alive. ⊠ *59800 S. Hwy. 97, 7 miles south of downtown Bend* ☎ *541/382–4754* ⊕ *www.highdesertmuseum.org* ✉ *$15 May–Oct., $12 Nov.–Apr.*

FAMILY   **Newberry National Volcanic Monument and Lava Lands.** The last time hot lava flowed from Newberry Volcano was about 13 centuries ago. The north end of the monument has several large basalt flows, as well as the 500-foot **Lava Butte** cinder cone—a coal-black and scorched-red, symmetrical mound thrust from the depths 7,000 years ago. The cone is now home to the **Lava Lands Visitor Center,** which features interpretive exhibits that explain the volcanic and early human history of the area. **Lava River Cave,** a 1-mile-long lava tube, takes about 90 minutes to explore on your own with a lantern (available for rent, $5). On the south end of the monument, an unpaved road leads to beautiful views from **Paulina Peak.** Along the shores of **Paulina Lake** and **East Lake,** you can hike, fish, camp, or stay at the rustic resorts. You can also hike a trail to **Paulina Falls,** an 80-foot double waterfall. The monument offers 100 miles of summer trails, and may be accessible during winter months, depending on snowmelt, for snowmobiling, snowshoeing, and skiing. ⊠ *58201 S. Hwy. 97* ☎ *541/593–2421* ⊕ *www.fs.usda.gov/*

Paulina Falls in Newberry National Volcanic Monument

centraloregon 🚗 *$5 per vehicle* ⊙ *Lava River Cave closes Oct. 1 to protect bat population.*

EN ROUTE **Cascade Lakes Scenic Byway.** For 66 miles, this nationally designated Scenic Byway meanders past a series of high mountain lakes and is good for fishing, hiking, and camping in the summer months. (Much of the road beyond Mt. Bachelor is closed by snow during the colder months.) To find, take Century Drive/Oregon 372 out of Bend and follow it around Mt. Bachelor. To complete as a loop, take U.S. 97 to return. ✉ *Bend* ⊕ *www.visitbend.com.*

WHERE TO EAT

$$$
AMERICAN
Fodor's Choice
★

✕ **Ariana Restaurant.** Bendites craving a fine-dining experience flock to this upscale New American restaurant, housed in a Craftsman bungalow just west of downtown. Top Northwest ingredients are transformed into French-, Italian-, and Spanish-inspired dishes, which pair perfectly with the extensive wine list. **Known for:** intimate atmosphere; special-occasion meals; decadent desserts. 💲 *Average main: $30* ✉ *1304 N.W. Galveston Ave.* ☎ *541/330–5539* ⊕ *www.arianarestaurantbend.com.*

$
AMERICAN

✕ **Deschutes Brewery & Public House.** Established in 1988, Bend's original brewpub remains a happening spot to get a taste of the city's beer scene. The menu includes a diverse lineup of craft brews, including rotating seasonals, and pub food, such as hearty burgers on house-made brioche rolls. **Known for:** central Oregon–inspired brews; crowded dining room. 💲 *Average main: $15* ✉ *1044 N.W. Bond St.* ☎ *541/382–9242* ⊕ *www. deschutesbrewery.com.*

$$$
ASIAN FUSION

✕ **5 Fusion and Sushi Bar.** Elegant combinations of sushi and other dishes fill the senses with color, texture, and tastes and are presented as pieces

Central Oregon Brewery Boom

With nearly three dozen breweries and counting, central Oregon rivals the Portland metro area for brewpubs per capita, but it only hit the map as a beer travel destination in recent years.

Since the first microbrewery opened its doors in 1988 (Deschutes Brewery in downtown Bend), the industry has continued to grow and expand. Each brewery and brewpub approaches the craft beer experience in an original manner, often supported by locals and a combination of live music, good food, unique marketing, experimental brews, and good ole standbys that keep pint glasses and growlers filled.

Residents may buoy the industry, but breweries in turn support the community. Local artists design labels, many beer proceeds go to neighborhood causes, and brews are continually concocted with local events and culture in mind.

BEND ALE TRAIL

Pick up a Bend Ale Trail brochure, or download the app, to guide you through 15 of Bend's breweries. Stop at each brewery, have a taste or a pint, and receive a stamp in your passport. Once you've visited 10 locations, drop by the Bend Visitor Center to receive the prize: a durable silicone pint glass.

---

of art. Everything about this dining experience is exciting, from the background music to the IPA sushi roll to the horizontal waterfall hanging from the ceiling. **Known for:** inventive sushi; craft cocktails. $ *Average main: $25* ✉ *821 N.W. Wall St.* ☎ *541/323–2328* ⊕ *www.5fusion. com* ⊗ *No lunch.*

$ ✕ **Jackson's Corner.** This family-friendly community restaurant is housed
AMERICAN in an unassuming vintage building tucked into a neighborhood near
FAMILY downtown. The eclectic menu leans heavily on locally grown and organic dishes, such as seasonal market salads, house-made pasta dishes, and brick-oven pizza. **Known for:** pasta made fresh daily; kid-friendly table-side service. $ *Average main: $12* ✉ *845 N.W. Delaware Ave.* ☎ *541/647–2198* ⊕ *www.jacksonscornerbend.com/.*

$$ ✕ **Joolz.** Joolz offers vibrant Middle Eastern food with an Oregon flair;
MIDDLE EASTERN try the small plates like Oregon lamb meatballs and cauliflower with tahini dipping sauce, or mains such as a local free-range longhorn beef burger or Pacific seafood tagine. The chef, raised in Beirut, is the son of a Lebanese father and Oregonian mother (who is rumored to still make the family's melt-in-your-mouth spiced date cake). **Known for:** extensive small plates menu; happy hour cocktail deals (4–9 pm at the bar). $ *Average main: $17* ✉ *916 N.W. Wall St.* ☎ *541/388–5094* ⊕ *www.joolzbend.com* ⊗ *No lunch.*

$ ✕ **Lone Pine Coffee Roasters.** Tucked down Tin Pan Alley, just paces from
CAFÉ The Oxford Hotel, this micro-roaster and café crafts espresso drinks
Fodor's Choice with single-origin coffee and house-made syrups. A hip crowd descends
★ on the shop mid-morning for a light breakfast of pastries delivered daily from Bend's Sparrow Bakery; show up early to snatch a flaky Ocean Roll. **Known for:** skilled baristas; house-roasted coffee; breakfast

sweets. [$] *Average main: $5* ✉ *845 Tin Pan Alley* ☎ *541/306–1010* 🌐 *www.lonepinecoffeeroasters.com* 🕒 *No lunch or dinner.*

$ AMERICAN 🍴 **McKay Cottage Restaurant.** This breakfast and lunch spot is housed in a 1916 pioneer cottage, where locals relax throughout its cozy rooms and spill over onto the porch and patio below. The menu is long on comfort food, including fresh scones and sticky buns, and servers are friendly and attentive. **Known for:** cheesy omelets and scrambles; gluten-free options. [$] *Average main: $12* ✉ *62910 O.B. Riley Rd.* ☎ *541/383–2697* 🌐 *www.themckaycottage.com* 🕒 *No dinner.*

$ INTERNATIONAL 🍴 **Spork.** Bend's favorite food cart–turned–restaurant offers a globally inspired and healthy menu with an intimate and trendy decor. Try Peruvian stir-fry, Thai steak salad, coconut green curry, or organic tofu tacos. **Known for:** eclectic, wide-ranging menu; globally inspired house cocktails; popular for takeout. [$] *Average main: $12* ✉ *937 N.W. Newport Ave.* ☎ *541/390–0946* 🌐 *www.sporkbend.com.*

$ AMERICAN 🍴 **10 Barrel Brewing Co.** This trendy brewpub supplies good beer and compatible food. Pizzas are hand tossed daily, salads are fresh, and sandwiches are varied. **Known for:** innovative brews; comfort pub food; noisy crowds. [$] *Average main: $12* ✉ *1135 N.W. Galveston Ave.* ☎ *541/678–5228* 🌐 *www.10barrel.com.*

6

$ AMERICAN 🍴 **The Victorian Café.** In a renovated house on the west side of Bend, this breakfast and lunch place offers a wide selection of surprising combinations of egg Benedict, such as the Caribbean Benedict with Cuban seasoned ham, mango, and black beans. There's often a long wait on weekends, so order a Bloody Mary or a "Man-mosa" (a mimosa in a pint glass) to enjoy around the outdoor fireplace. **Known for:** extensive menu of conventional brunch fare; big, boozy breakfast cocktails. [$] *Average main: $16* ✉ *1404 N.W. Galveston Ave.* ☎ *541/382–6411* 🌐 *www.victoriancafebend.com* 🕒 *No dinner.*

$$ AMERICAN 🍴 **Zydeco Kitchen & Cocktails.** The blended menu of Northwest specialties and Cajun influences has made this trendy but welcoming restaurant (named after a style of Creole music) a popular lunch and dinner spot. On the menu, fillet medallions, chicken, and pasta sit alongside jambalaya and redfish dishes. **Known for:** gluten-free menu; well-curated wine list; expert bartenders. [$] *Average main: $23* ✉ *919 N.W. Bond St.* ☎ *541/312–2899* 🌐 *www.zydecokitchen.com* 🕒 *No lunch weekends.*

WHERE TO STAY

$$ B&B/INN 🏨 **Lara House Bed and Breakfast.** Located in a manicured residential neighborhood across from Drake Park, guests will feel at home at this historically grand and cherished Bend house. **Pros:** clean lines and an uncluttered feel; downtown is a short walk away; wine hour every evening. **Cons:** no pets or kids; can be crowded during peak travel times; check-in only 4–6 or by prior arrangement. [$] *Rooms from: $200* ✉ *640 N.W. Congress St.* ☎ *541/388–4064, 800/766–4064* 🌐 *www.larahouse.com* 🛏 *6 rooms* 🍽 *Breakfast.*

$$ RESORT 🏨 **Old St. Francis School.** Part of the eclectic McMenamins brand of pubs, movie theaters, and hotels, this charming and fun outpost in a restored 1936 Catholic schoolhouse has classrooms turned into lodging quarters, restaurant and bars, a brewery, a stage, a mosaic-tile soaking pool, and a movie theater with couches and food service. **Pros:** a

self-contained destination village, yet only footsteps from downtown Bend and Drake Park; quirky, unique stay; kids and pets welcome. **Cons:** few modern appliances. $ *Rooms from: $155* ⊠ *700 N.W. Bond St.* ☎ *541/382–5174, 877/661–4228* ⊕ *www.mcmenamins.com* ⇨ *60 rooms* ⎜⊘⎜ *No meals.*

$$$$
HOTEL
Fodor'sChoice
★
⛓ **The Oxford Hotel.** Stepping into the sleek, high-ceilinged lobby tells you you've found a new kind of accommodation in central Oregon, with stylish Northwest interiors and elegantly spacious rooms. **Pros:** generous and environmentally sustainable amenities; luxurious spa and fitness room; loaner bikes in summer months; exceptional service. **Cons:** on the exterior, property appears inconspicuously wedged into a half block on the edge of downtown. $ *Rooms from: $349* ⊠ *10 N.W. Minnesota Ave.* ☎ *877/440–8436* ⊕ *www.oxfordhotelbend.com* ⇨ *59 rooms* ⎜⊘⎜ *No meals.*

$$
HOTEL
FAMILY
⛓ **Riverhouse on the Deschutes.** Freshly renovated, this lodge-inspired hotel and convention center overlooks the Deschutes River and appeals to family travelers with its indoor and outdoor pools, hot tubs, and on-site dining. **Pros:** large, simply decorated standard rooms and suites; convenient facilities for family and business travelers; dining and shopping nearby. **Cons:** rooms lack character; not ideal for those looking to walk downtown. $ *Rooms from: $189* ⊠ *3075 N. Business Hwy. 97* ☎ *541/389–3111* ⇨ *221 rooms* ⎜⊘⎜ *No meals.*

$$$$
RESORT
FAMILY
Fodor'sChoice
★
⛓ **Sunriver Resort.** Central Oregon's premier family playground and luxurious destination resort encapsulates so many things that are distinctive about central Oregon, from the mountain views and winding river, to the biking, rafting, golfing, skiing, and family or romantic getaways. **Pros:** many activities for kids and adults; much pampering in elegant lodge facilities; close to The Village at Sunriver. **Cons:** when visitors throng the shops, restaurants, and bike paths, it can feel as if an entire city has relocated here. $ *Rooms from: $259* ⊠ *17600 Center Dr., 15 miles south of Bend on Hwy. 97, Sunriver* ☎ *800/801–8765* ⊕ *www.sunriver-resort.com* ⇨ *245 rooms, 284 houses* ⎜⊘⎜ *No meals.*

$$$
HOTEL
⛓ **Wall Street Suites.** Built in the 1950s as a motel and renovated with stunning pine, hardwood, tile, and iron a few years ago, these spacious suites and rooms are both stylishly contemporary and cozy. **Pros:** close to downtown; pet-friendly; nice amenities and TVs. **Cons:** next to a busy and complicated intersection. $ *Rooms from: $224* ⊠ *1430 Wall St.* ☎ *541/706–9006* ⊕ *www.wallstreetsuitesbend.com* ⇨ *4 suites, 13 rooms.*

NIGHTLIFE

The Astro Lounge. Bend's take on a space-age cocktail haven comes complete with specialty martinis and cosmic-looking interior. ⊠ *939 N.W. Bond St.* ☎ *541/388–0116* ⊕ *www.astroloungebend.com* ⊘ *Closed Sun.*

Bend Brewing Company. A long-standing brewery, founded in 1995, BBC (as it is affectionately called by locals) offers about 10 different types of beers on tap. It's located on the second floor above the brewpub, where diners and drinkers can look up through windows to the tanks above. Because space is limited for brewing, BBC focuses not on the quantity of beer, but the quality. ⊠ *1019 N.W. Brooks St.* ☎ *541/383–1599* ⊕ *www. bendbrewingco.com.*

Sunriver Resort

Crux Fermentation Project. Housed in a converted auto repair shop, this industrial-chic and experimental brewery has no flagship beer. Instead, the brewmaster, a Deschutes Brewery alum, produces an ever-changing variety of pale ales and other craft brews, all of which are on tap in the lively tasting room. On-site food carts and a sprawling patio make this a popular hangout in summer months. ✉ *50 S.W. Division St.* ☎ *541/385-3333* ⊕ *www.cruxfermentation.com.*

Level 2. After a day of shopping, or before concertgoing at the amphitheater, sip on a perfectly mixed cocktail at this trendy Old Mill District urban-esque lounge. The rich chai martini is a delectable winter treat. ✉ *360 S.W. Powerhouse Dr.* ☎ *541/323–5382.*

900 Wall Restaurant and Bar. In a historic corner brick building on a downtown Bend crossroads, this sophisticated restaurant and bar serves hundreds of bottles and about 50 different wines by the glass, earning it the Wine Spectator Award of Excellence. ✉ *900 N.W. Wall St.* ☎ *541/323–6295* ⊕ *www.900wall.com.*

SPORTS AND THE OUTDOORS

BIKING

U.S. 97 north to the Crooked River Gorge and Smith Rock and the route along the **Cascade Lakes Highway** out of Bend provide bikers with memorable scenery and a good workout. **Sunriver** has more than 30 miles of paved bike paths.

Hutch's Bicycles. Road, mountain, and kids' bikes can be rented at this shop as well as a location at 725 N.W. Columbia Street. ✉ *820 N.E. 3rd St.* ☎ *541/382–6248 3rd St. shop, 541/382–9253 Columbia St. shop* ⊕ *www.hutchsbicycles.com.*

BOATING AND RAFTING

A popular summer activity is floating the Deschutes River at your own pace.

Bend Whitewater Park. The first white-water park in Oregon, at McKay Park in the Old Mill District, is the result of an extensive renovation to a 1915 dam, which previously made this section of the Deschutes River impassable. Three separate channels below the dam cater to rafters, kayakers, tubers, and even surfers. ✉ *166 S.W. Shevlin Hixon Rd.* ☎ *541/389–7275* ⊕ *www.bendparksandrec.org.*

Riverbend Park. In Bend, rent an inner tube at Riverbend Park from a kiosk operated from Memorial Day to Labor Day by **Sun Country Tours** and float an hour and a half downriver to Drake Park, where you can catch a shuttle back for a minimal cash fee. ✉ *799 S.W. Columbia St.* ☎ *541/389–7275* ⊕ *www.bendparksandrec.org.*

Tumalo Creek Kayak & Canoe. Rent a kayak or stand-up paddleboard and enter the river from the store's backyard, but be prepared to paddle upriver before a leisurely float downstream. ✉ *805 S.W. Industrial Way, Suite 6* ☎ *541/317–9407* ⊕ *tumalocreek.com.*

RECREATIONAL AREAS

Deschutes National Forest. This 1½-million-acre forest has 20 peaks higher than 7,000 feet, including three of Oregon's five highest mountains, more than 150 lakes, and 500 miles of streams. If you want to park your car at a trailhead, some of the sites require a Northwest Forest Pass; day-use passes are also needed May through September at many locations for boating and picnicking. Campgrounds are operated by a camp host. ✉ *63095 Deschutes Market Rd.* ☎ *541/383–5300* ⊕ *www. fs.usda.gov/centraloregon* ✉ *Park pass $5.*

SKIING

Many Nordic trails—more than 165 miles of them—wind through the Deschutes National Forest.

FAMILY **Mt. Bachelor.** This is alpine resort area has 60% of downhill runs that are rated advanced or expert, with the rest geared for beginner and intermediate skiers and snowboarders. One of 10 lifts takes skiers all the way to the mountain's 9,065-foot summit. One run has a vertical drop of 3,265 feet for thrill-seekers, and the longest of the 88 runs is 4 miles. Facilities and services include equipment rental and repair, a ski school, retail shop, and day care; you can enjoy seven restaurants, three bars, and six lodges. Other activities include cross-country skiing, a tubing park, sled-dog rides, snowshoeing, and in summer, hiking, biking, disc-golfing and chairlift rides. The 35 miles of trails at the **Mt. Bachelor Nordic Center** are suitable for all abilities.

During the off-season, the lift to the **Pine Marten Lodge** provides sightseeing, stunning views, and fine sunset dining. Visitors can play disc golf on a downhill course that starts near the lodge. At the base of the mountain, take dry-land dogsled rides with four-time Iditarod musher Rachael Scdoris. ✉ *13000 S.W. Century Dr.* ☎ *541/382–7888, 800/829–2442* ⊕ *www.mtbachelor.com* ✉ *Lift tickets $52–$92 per day; kids 5 and under free.*

SHOPPING

In addition to Bend's compact downtown, the Old Mill District draws shoppers from throughout the region. Chain stores and franchise restaurants have filled in along the approaches to town, especially along U.S. 20 and U.S. 97.

Cowgirl Cash. This funky Western outfitter buys and sells vintage boots and Western apparel. You never know exactly what you'll find, but you can expect a fair share of leather, turquoise, silver, and, always, boots. It's a quirky and welcome feature of the downtown scene but closed Thursday–Sunday in the winter. ✉ *924 N.W. Brooks St.* ☎ *541/678–5162* ⊕ *www.cowgirlcashbend.com.*

Dudley's BookShop Cafe. This independent bookseller offers Wi-Fi, a small café, and seating areas that attract interesting people who meet amidst new and used books to participate in all kinds of activities, from tango classes to philosophical debates. ✉ *135 N.W. Minnesota Ave.* ☎ *541/749–2010* ⊕ *www.dudleysbookshopcafe.com.*

Goody's. If the aroma of fresh waffle cones causes a pause on your downtown stroll, you've probably hit one of central Oregon's favorite soda fountain and candy shops. Try the Oreo cookie ice cream, a local favorite, or the homemade chocolate. If you purchase a stuffed toy animal that calls the store home, expect for it to smell sweetly for weeks to come. ✉ *957 N.W. Wall St.* ☎ *541/389–5185* ⊕ *www.goodyschocolates.com.*

Hot Box Betty. This fun, lively shop sells high fashion for women, carrying boutique clothing and designer handbags. ✉ *903 N.W. Wall St.* ☎ *541/383–0050* ⊕ *www.hotboxbetty.com.*

Newport Avenue Market. In business for more than 20 years, this favorite local grocer not only offers a large selection of organic and gourmet foods, but also sells items such as high-end kitchen supplies and humorous gifts. Pick up a pair of squirrel underwear—it's as small as you might expect. ✉ *1121 N.W. Newport Ave.* ☎ *541/382–3940* ⊕ *www.newportavemarket.com.*

Old Mill District. Bend was once the site of one of the world's largest sawmill operations, with a sprawling industrial complex along the banks of the Deschutes. In recent years the abandoned shells of the old factory buildings have been transformed into an attractive shopping center, a project honored with national environmental awards. National chain retailers can be found here, along with restaurants, boutiques, a 16-screen multiplex and IMAX movie theater, and the Les Schwab Amphitheater that attracts nationally renowned artists, local bands, and summer festivals. ✉ *450 S.W. Powerhouse Dr.* ☎ *541/312–0131* ⊕ *www.theoldmill.com.*

Oregon Body & Bath. If adventures in the high desert's arid climate have left your skin feeling dry and dehydrated, head to this body and bath boutique in downtown Bend for locally made soaps, lotions, bath bombs, and body butters. The store also stocks home goods, such as fragrant candles and scents. ✉ *1019 N.W. Wall St.* ☎ *541/383–5890* ⊕ *www.oregonbodyandbath.com.*

Patagonia@Bend. A helpful staff sells stylishly comfortable and environmentally friendly outdoor clothing, equipment, and footwear at a Patagonia concept store that is locally owned. ⊠ *1000 N.W. Wall St., Suite 140* ☎ *541/382–6694* ⊕ *www.patagoniabend.com.*

Pine Mountain Sports. Part of Bend's fleet of outdoors stores, this shop sells high-quality clothing, energy bars, and the locally famous Hydro Flask water bottles. Recreation equipment such as mountain bikes, backcountry skis, and snowshoes are also available for rent or purchase. ⊠ *255 S.W. Century Dr.* ☎ *541/385–8080* ⊕ *www.pinemountainsports.com.*

Silverado Jewelry Gallery. Showcasing dazzling pieces of silver, turquoise, pearls, and everything in between, it will be difficult not to exit the store without being moved by a stunning piece of jewelry that appeals to all tastes. ⊠ *1001 N.W. Wall St., Suite 101* ☎ *541/322–8792* ⊕ *www.silveradogallery.com.*

SISTERS

21 miles northwest of Bend.

If Sisters looks as if you've stumbled into the Old West, that's entirely by design. The town strictly enforces an 1800s-style architecture. Rustic cabins border ranches on the edge of town, and you won't find a stoplight on any street. Western storefronts give way to galleries, the century-old hotel now houses a restaurant and bar, and a bakery occupies the former general store. Although its population is just a little more than 2,000, Sisters increasingly attracts visitors as well as urban runaways who appreciate its tranquillity and charm. If you're driving over from the Willamette Valley, note how the weather seems to change to sunshine when you cross the Cascades at the Santiam Pass and begin descending toward the town.

Black Butte, a perfectly conical cinder cone, rises to the northwest. The Metolius River/Camp Sherman area to the west is a special find for fly-fishermen and abounds with springtime wildflowers.

GETTING HERE AND AROUND

Travelers from Portland and the west come to Sisters over the Santiam Pass on Oregon 126. This is also the route for visitors who fly into Redmond Municipal Airport, rent a car, and drive 20 miles west. Those coming from Bend drive 21 miles northwest on U.S. 20. **Cascades East,** a regional bus carrier, runs routes between Sisters and the Redmond airport by reservation.

ESSENTIALS

Visitor Information Sisters Chamber of Commerce. ⊠ *291 E. Main Ave.* ☎ *541/549–0251* ⊕ *www.sisterscountry.com.*

EXPLORING

Camp Sherman. Surrounded by groves of whispering yellow-bellied ponderosa pines, larch, fir, and cedars and miles of streamside forest trails, this small, peaceful resort community of about 250 full-time residents (plus a few stray cats and dogs) is part of a designated conservation area. The area's beauty and natural resources are the big draw: the spring-fed Metolius River prominently glides through the community. In the early 1900s Sherman County wheat farmers escaped the dry summer heat by migrating here to fish and rest in the cool river environment, making Camp Sherman one of the first destination resorts in central Oregon. As legend has it, to help guide fellow farmers to the spot, devotees nailed a shoebox top with the name "camp sherman" to a tree at a fork in the road. Several original buildings still stand from the early days, including some cabins, a schoolhouse, and a tiny railroad chapel. Find the source of local information at the Camp Sherman Store & Fly Shop, built in 1918, adjacent to the post office. ✉ *25451 S.W. Forest Service Rd. 1419, 10 miles northwest of Sisters on U.S. 20, 5 miles north on Hwy. 14.* ☎ *541/595–6711* 🌐 *www.campshermanstore.com.*

NEED A BREAK

🍴 Sisters Bakery. In a rustic Western-looking former general store built in 1925, Sisters Bakery turns out high-quality pastries, doughnuts, and specialty breads from 5 am to 5 pm. The bakery serves Bend's Strictly Organic coffee, and harkens back to a time when doughnuts were simple and tasty. ✉ ***251 E. Cascade St.*** ☎ ***541/549-0361*** 🌐 ***www.sistersbakery.com.***

6

WHERE TO EAT

$ AMERICAN FAMILY Fodor's Choice ★ 🍴 **The Cottonwood Cafe.** Formerly the much-celebrated Jen's Garden, the owners opened this new breakfast and lunch concept in the same cute cottage in 2015. The new family-oriented menu focuses on comfortable café standbys, such as eggs Benedict and slow-roasted pulled pork sandwiches. **Known for:** festive brunch ambience; pup-friendly patio. [$] *Average main: $12* ✉ *403 E. Hood Ave.* ☎ *541/549–2699* 🌐 *www.intimatecottagecuisine.com* 🕒 *Closed Wed. fall and winter.*

$ AMERICAN 🍴 **The Depot Café.** A railroad theme prevails at this main-street rustic café. A miniature train circles above as the kitchen dishes out sandwiches, salads, and dinner specials. **Known for:** minitrain. [$] *Average main: $12* ✉ *250 W. Cascade St.* ☎ *541/549–2572* 🌐 *www.sistersdepot.com* 🕒 *No breakfast Mon.–Thurs.*

$$$ AMERICAN 🍴 **Kokanee Café.** The remarkable restaurant near the banks of the Metolius River draws diners from across the mountains to sample artful Northwest dishes at this homey hideaway with a paneled dining room and warm-weather porch. Local lamb, fresh fish, and vegetarian options are presented with creative elegance. **Known for:** menu focused on local and sustainably sourced meat; extensive wine list. [$] *Average main: $30* ✉ *25545 S.W. Forest Service Rd. 1419, Camp Sherman* ☎ *541/595–6420* 🌐 *www.kokaneecafe.com* 🕒 *Closed Oct.–Apr. No lunch.*

$ ITALIAN 🍴 **The Open Door.** Serving simple and light Italian fare, such as panini and flatbread pizzas, this quaint and cozy restaurant and wine bar offers a different homemade pasta dish every night for dinner. The interior is an eclectic mix of mismatched tables and chairs, which opens into a gallery displaying Northwest artwork. **Known for:** romantic, artsy ambience; good wine list. [$] *Average main: $16* ✉ *303 W. Hood Ave.* ☎ *541/549–6076* 🌐 *www.theclearwatergallery.com* 🕒 *Closed Sun.*

$ AMERICAN 🍴 **Sno Cap Drive In.** Since 1945, this burger joint has been serving iconic burgers, sandwiches, fries, milk shakes, and ice cream to residents and visitors. Be prepared for long lines out the doors, as travelers driving across the mountain often plan to stop here for lunch. **Known for:** authentic drive-in fare; creamy and thick milk shakes; long lines in summer months. [$] *Average main: $8* ✉ *380 W. Cascade Ave.* ☎ *541/549–6151.*

WHERE TO STAY

$$ RESORT FAMILY Fodor's Choice ★ 🏨 **FivePine Lodge.** At this luxurious Western-style resort resembling a forest lodge, high-end furnishings were built by Amish craftsmen. **Pros:** top-quality amenities, like the Kohler waterfall tubs; peaceful atmosphere, but conveniently located on the fringes of downtown Sister. **Cons:** slightly set back from U.S. 20, where traffic is sometimes heavy; some cabins are close to neighbors. [$] *Rooms from: $189* ✉ *1021 Desperado Trail* ☎ *541/549–5900, 866/974–5900* 🌐 *www.fivepinelodge.com* 🛏 *8 rooms, 24 cabins* 🍴 *Breakfast.*

$$$ RESORT 🏨 **Suttle Lodge.** The hospitality company behind the hip Ace Hotel Portland reopened this lakefront resort in 2016 after an extensive renovation, enhancing the whimsical charm of the grand light-flooded lodge and rustic cabins. **Pros:** hip accommodations in a peaceful setting; on-site restaurant and bar; year-round accessibility to outdoor sports. **Cons:** no air-conditioning; cell reception is spotty. [$] *Rooms from: $248* ✉ *13300 U.S. Hwy. 20, 13 miles northwest of Sisters* ☎ *541/638–7001* 🌐 *www.thesuttlelodge.com* 🛏 *11 rooms, 14 cabins* 🍴 *Breakfast.*

$$$$ RENTAL 🏨 **Metolius River Resort.** Each of the immaculate, individually owned cabins that nestle amid the pines and aspen at this peaceful resort has splendid views of the sparkling Metolius River, decks furnished with Adirondack chairs, a full kitchen, and a fireplace. **Pros:** privacy; cabins feel like home—a very luxurious home; fall asleep and wake up to the sound of the river. **Cons:** no additional people (even visitors) allowed; no cell-phone service; bring supplies on winter weekdays when Camp Sherman closes down. [$] *Rooms from: $265* ✉ *25551 S.W. Forest Service Rd. 1419, Camp Sherman* ✥ *Off U.S. 20, northeast 10 miles from Sisters, turn north on Camp Sherman Rd., stay to left at fork (1419), and then turn right at only stop sign* ☎ *800/818–7688* 🌐 *www.metoliusriverresort.com* 🛏 *11 cabins* 🍴 *No meals.*

NIGHTLIFE

Fodor's Choice ★ **Sisters Saloon & Ranch Grill.** Pass through the swinging saloon doors into this Old West watering hole, originally built more than a century ago as the Hotel Sisters. Head to the bar, which is decorated with a mural of cancan dancers, weathered saddles hanging on the wall, and a mounted stuffed buffalo head. Under new ownership, the menu remains rooted in ranch favorites but gets updated with vegetarian-friendly offerings. ✉ *190 E. Cascade Ave.* ☎ *541/549–7427* 🌐 *www.sisterssaloon.net.*

Three Creeks Brewing Co. Currently Sisters' only brewery, Three Creeks offers a selection of beers at its brewing facility and brewpub that play on Northwest culture and the outdoor lifestyle. The brewery is visible from the brewpub, which serves a wide range of burgers, pizzas, salads, and other bar mainstays. Order a frothing pint of the popular Knotty Blonde, or try one of their seasonal brews. ✉ *721 Desperado Ct.* ☎ *541/549–1963* 🌐 *www.threecreeksbrewing.com.*

SHOPPING

Hop in the Spa. America's first beer spa takes advantage of the medicinal, nonintoxicating, and detoxifying qualities of hops and other beer ingredients. Call ahead to schedule a microbrew soak and massage, or one of the other beer-centric spa packages. ⊠ *371 W. Cascade Ave.* ☎ *844/588–6818* ⊕ *www.hopinthespa.com.*

Paulina Springs Books. Select a book from the discounted staff recommendation table, or from categories such as history, outdoor recreation, field guides, regional, science, and fiction. Sisters' leading independent bookstore also sells toys and games, and has a substantial young readers section. ⊠ *252 W. Hood Ave.* ☎ *541/549–0866* ⊕ *www.paulinasprings. com.*

Stitchin' Post. Owned by a mother-and-daughter team, the famous knitting, sewing, and quilting store opened its doors in 1975. The spacious store not only inspires the senses with colorful fabric, patterns and yarns, but also conducts classes throughout the year. The Sisters Outdoor Quilt Show, annually held the second Saturday of July, is the largest in the world and intertwines its origins with the store's early years. ⊠ *311 W. Cascade St.* ☎ *541/549–6061* ⊕ *www.stitchinpost.com.*

SPORTS AND THE OUTDOORS

FISHING

Fly-fishing the Metolius River attracts anglers who seek a challenge.

Camp Sherman Store & Fly Shop. This local institution, center of life in the tiny riverside community, sells gear and provides information about where and how best to fish. ⊠ *25451 Forest Service Rd. 1419, Camp Sherman* ☎ *541/595–6711* ⊕ *www.campshermanstore.com.*

Fly and Field Outfitters. This large Bend-based supplier of gear also sets anglers up with expert guides. ⊠ *35 S.W. Century Dr., Bend* ☎ *866/800–2812* ⊕ *www.flyandfield.com.*

RECREATIONAL AREAS

Metolius Recreation Area. On the eastern slope of the Cascades and within the 1.6-million-acre Deschutes National Forest, this bounty of recreational wilderness is drier and sunnier than the western side of the mountains, giving way to bountiful natural history, outdoor activities, and wildlife. There are spectacular views of jagged, 10,000-foot snow-capped Cascade peaks, looming high above the basin of an expansive evergreen valley clothed in pine.

Five miles south of **Camp Sherman** (2 miles to head waters), the dark and perfectly shaped cinder cone of **Black Butte** rises 6,400 feet. At its base the **Metolius River** springs forth. Witness the birth of this "instant" river by walking a short paved path embedded in ponderosa forest, eventually reaching a viewpoint with the dramatic snow-covered peak of **Mt. Jefferson** on the horizon. At this point, water gurgles to the ground's surface and pours into a wide trickling creek cascading over moss-covered rocks. Within feet it funnels outward, expanding its northerly flow; becomes a full-size river; and meanders east alongside grassy banks and a dense pine forest to join the Deschutes River downstream. Within the 4,600-acre area of the Metolius and along the river, there are ample resources for camping, hiking, biking, and floating.

Enjoy fly-fishing for rainbow, brown, and bull trout in perhaps the best spot within the Cascades. ✉ *Off Hwy. 20, 9 miles northwest of Sisters, Camp Sherman* ⊕ *www.metoliusriver.com.*

SKIING

Hoodoo Ski Area. On a 5,703-foot summit, this winter sports area has more than 800 acres of skiable terrain. With 32 runs and five lifts, skiers of all levels will find suitable thrills. Upper and lower Nordic trails are surrounded by silence, and an inner tube run and night skiing round out the range of activities. At a 60,000-square-foot lodge at the mountain's base you can take in the view, grab a bite, shop, or rest your weary feet. The ski area has kids' activities and child-care services available. Lift tickets range from $10 to $51, depending on the type and day. ✉ *U.S. 20, 20 miles northwest of Sisters* ☎ *541/822–3799* ⊕ *www.hoodoo.com.*

EAST CENTRAL OREGON

East of the Cascades, central Oregon changes to desert. The land is austere, covered mostly in sage and juniper, with a few hardy rivers and great extrusions of lava, which flowed or was blasted across the prehistoric landscape. In recent years resorts have emerged to draw west-side residents weary of the rain. They come over to bask in the sun and to soak up the feeling of the frontier, reinforced by ranches and resilient towns like Redmond and Prineville. They also come to fish and boat on the man-made lakes near Culver and Prineville.

REDMOND

20 miles east of Sisters; 17 miles northeast of Bend.

Redmond sits at the western end of Oregon's high desert, a handful of miles from the Deschutes River and within minutes of several lakes. It is a place where desert ranches meet runways, as it serves as the regional hub for air travel. It is the town nearest to Eagle Crest Resort and Smith Rock, a magnet for rock climbers. As with Deschutes County, Redmond has experienced rapid growth in the state during the past 10 years, largely owing to a dry and mild climate and year-round downhill and cross-country skiing, fishing, hiking, mountain biking, and rockhounding. Still, this is no gentrified resort town à la Bend, as a stroll through the compact and historic downtown will attest. A few blocks of vintage buildings remain, but north–south traffic hustles through the city core, with most residents in neighborhoods strung out to the west. Centennial Park is a small but attractive open space with fountains and an expansive lawn, aspen trees, flowers, and a kiosk selling drinks and ice cream. The park is a great place for the kids to play in the splash fountain on a hot summer's day. A clock tower contains a time capsule buried in 2010, marking the centennial celebration of Redmond's founding.

GETTING HERE AND AROUND

A couple of highways—U.S. 97 and Oregon 126—cross in Redmond. U.S. 97 carries travelers north and south to Washington and California, and Highway 126 runs between Sisters in the west to Prineville in the

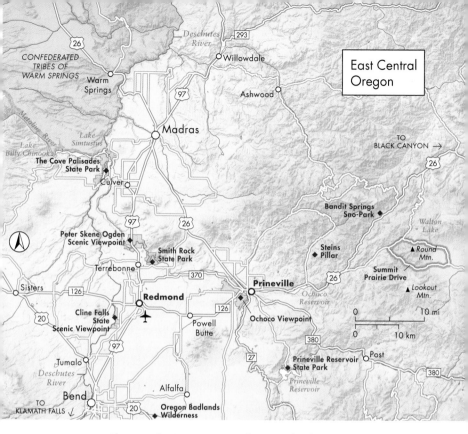

east. If you're driving on U.S. 26 from Portland, stop at **The Museum at Warm Springs** (☎ 541/553–3331 ⊕ *www.museumatwarmsprings.org*) at the Confederated Tribes of Warm Springs Reservation for a look at Native American artifacts, culture and history. Taxis and the **Redmond Airport Shuttle** ferry travelers to the Redmond Municipal Airport. Two bus lines, the **Central Oregon Breeze** and **Cascades East Transit,** serve Redmond. The Central Oregon Breeze links Bend, Redmond, Madras, and Portland, and Cascades East runs buses to and from Redmond and Madras, Prineville, and Bend. Passengers should call to ensure a ride.

ESSENTIALS

Visitor Information Redmond Chamber of Commerce and Convention Visitor's Bureau. ⌂ 446 S.W. 7th St. ☎ 541/923–5191 ⊕ www.visitredmondoregon.com.

EXPLORING

OFF THE BEATEN PATH

The Cove Palisades State Park. Many people who drive through this part of north central Oregon are more intent on their distant destinations than on the arid landscape they're passing through. But venture down the two-lane roads to this mini Grand Canyon of red-rock cliffs and gorges 14 miles west of small-town Madras. On a clear day a column of snow-capped Cascades peaks lines the horizon during the drive from town.

Lake Billy Chinook, a glittering oasis amid the rocks, snakes through the park. It's formed by the Deschutes, Metolius, and Crooked rivers.

The park is accessible year-round, but high season is summertime, when families camp on the lakeshore and houseboats drift unhurriedly from cliff to cleft. The lake is renowned for its wildlife, from the lake's bull trout to turkey vultures that fill the sky with their cries. Nature lovers also flock to the park in February for the annual eagle watch. The Crooked River Day Use Area is the most immediately accessible part of the park, a great place to cast a line into the water, launch a boat, or raid your picnic basket. Nearby is the Cove Palisades Marina, where you can rent fishing and houseboats, clean fish, and buy sandwiches and boat supplies, including kids' water toys.

In addition to 10 miles of hiking trails, The Cove Palisades has a driving loop around its craggy rim. Near the Ship Rock formation, you may see petroglyphs carved into a boulder by indigenous people who moved through the area centuries ago.

Two full-service campgrounds have full hookups, electrical sites with water, and tent sites, boat slips, and cabins. ✉ *7300 Jordan Rd., Off U.S. 97, 27 miles north of Redmond, Culver* ☎ *541/546–3412, 800/551–6949, 800/452–5687* 🌐 *www.oregonstateparks.org* 🎟 *Day use $5 per vehicle.*

Peter Skene Ogden Scenic Viewpoint. Even the most seasoned traveler may develop vertigo peering from the cliff top into a deep river canyon. It is a view that gives insight into why Oregon's high desert looks the way it does, with sheer drops and austere landscapes. You'll want to take pictures, but hang on to your camera. ✉ *U.S. 97 N, 9 miles north of Redmond* ☎ *800/551–6949* 🌐 *www.oregonstateparks.org.*

WHERE TO EAT AND STAY

$$$ STEAKHOUSE 🍴 **Brickhouse.** An elegant dining experience in Redmond can be found at this wood-tables-and-brick-wall restaurant, which specializes in steaks and chops but also offers attractive plates of seafood, especially shellfish. You can get lost in the list of cocktails and wines from Oregon and around the world. **Known for:** USDA Prime–graded steaks; well-stocked bar. [$] *Average main: $30* ✉ *412 S.W. 6th St.* ☎ *541/526–1782* 🌐 *www.brickhousesteakhouse.com* 🕒 *Closed Sun and Mon. No lunch.*

$$ MEXICAN FUSION 🍴 **Diego's Spirited Kitchen.** Near the "Redmond Est. 1910" sign that straddles downtown 6th Street, this fusion restaurant serves both Mexican and classic American dishes. Answer to "senorita" and "senor" as the bartender hand-squeezes limes for fresh margaritas while considering the good 'ole five-way grilled ham and cheese sandwich, or the more adventurous pork carnitas raviolis. **Known for:** generous portions of satisfying, if unremarkable, Tex-Mex fare; classic drinks menu. [$] *Average main: $20* ✉ *447 S.W. 6th St.* ☎ *541/316–2002.*

$$ AMERICAN 🍴 **Terrebonne Depot.** An old train depot is the setting for a meal that can match the stunning views of the Smith Rock cliffs. Offering an array of reasonably priced, tasty dishes, the kitchen plays it straight down the middle with nicely seasoned salmon, chicken, and pasta. **Known for:** a reliable dining option near Smith Rock; standard pub fare, such as nachos and juicy burgers. [$] *Average main: $18* ✉ *400 N.W. Smith*

Rock Way ☎ *541/548–5030* ⏲ *Closed Tues. year-round and Mon. Labor Day–Memorial Day.*

$$ RESORT FAMILY 🏨 **Eagle Crest Resort.** On high-desert grounds covered with juniper and sagebrush, accommodations include vacation rental houses as well as rooms and suites, some with fireplaces, clustered in a single building. **Pros:** a full-service resort with a spa, three 18-hole golf courses, restaurants; great for kids; pet-friendly. **Cons:** there can be crowds, kids, and pets; clean but not luxurious. [$] *Rooms from: $158* ✉ *1522 Cline Falls Hwy., 5 miles west of Redmond* ☎ *541/923–2453, 888/306–9643* 🌐 *www.eagle-crest.com* 🛏 *100 rooms, 70 town houses* 🍴 *No meals.*

NIGHTLIFE

Wild Ride Brew. Occupying a block on the edge of downtown, Wild Ride's tasting room and outdoor patio bustles late into the evening thanks to a quartet of food carts serving meals until the bartenders stop pouring. As its name suggests, the brewery takes a cue from the locals' adventurous lifestyles and names each beer for various "wild rides"—from motorcycles to skiing to rock climbing. Tours of the brewing facilities are available by appointment. ✉ *332 S.W. 5th St.* ☎ *541/516–8544* 🌐 *www.wildridebrew.com.*

6

SPORTS AND THE OUTDOORS

RECREATIONAL AREAS

Cline Falls State Scenic Viewpoint. Picnicking and fishing are popular at this 9-acre rest area commanding scenic views on the Deschutes River. You'll feel free from civilization here. ✉ *Hwy. 126, 4 miles west of Redmond* ☎ *800/551–6949* 🌐 *www.oregonstateparks.org.*

ROCK CLIMBING

Fodor's Choice ★ **Smith Rock State Park.** Eight miles north of Redmond, this park is world famous for rock climbing, with hundreds of routes of all levels of difficulty. A network of trails serves both climbers and families dropping in for the scenery. In addition to the stunning rock formations, the Crooked River, which helped shape these features, loops through the park. You might spot golden eagles, prairie falcons, mule deer, river otters, and beavers. Due to the environmental sensitivity of the region, the animal leash law is strongly enforced. It can get quite hot in midsummer, so most prefer to climb in the spring and fall. The stunning scenery—specifically, a view of the river curving through the high rocks—was adopted by Deschutes Brewery for its Twilight Summer Ale label. ✉ *9241 N.E. Crooked River Dr., Off U.S. 97* ☎ *541/548–7501, 800/551–6949* 🌐 *www.oregonstateparks.org* 🎟 *Day use $5 per vehicle.*

Smith Rock Climbing Guides. Professionals with emergency medical training take visitors to the Smith Rock formation for climbs of all levels of difficulty; they also supply equipment. Guided climbs—you meet at Smith Rock—can run a half day or full day, and are priced according to the number of people. ✉ *Smith Rock State Park, Terrebonne* ☎ *541/788–6225* 🌐 *www.smithrockclimbingguides.com.*

PRINEVILLE

18 miles east of Redmond.

Prineville is the oldest town in central Oregon, and the only incorporated city in Crook County. Tire entrepreneur Les Schwab founded his regional empire here, and it remains a key hub for the company. In more recent years, Facebook and Apple have chosen Prineville as the location for data centers. Surrounded by verdant ranch lands and the purplish hills of the Ochoco National Forest, Prineville will likely interest you chiefly as a jumping-off point for some of the region's more secluded outdoor adventures. The area attracts thousands of anglers, boaters, sightseers, and rockhounds to its nearby streams, reservoirs, and mountains. Rimrocks nearly encircle Prineville, and geology fans dig for free agates, limb casts, jasper, and thunder eggs. Downtown Prineville consists of a handful of small buildings along a quiet strip of Highway 26, dominated by the Crook County Courthouse, built in 1909. Shopping and dining opportunities are mostly on the basic side.

GETTING HERE AND AROUND

Travelers approaching Prineville from the west on Oregon 126 descend like a marble circling a funnel, dropping into a tidy grid of a town from a high desert plain. It's an unfailingly dramatic way to enter the seat of Crook County, dominated by the courthouse on N.E. Third Street, aka Highway 26, the main drag. Prineville is 19 miles east of Redmond Municipal Airport. If you're coming to Prineville from the airport, it's easiest to rent a car and drive. However, two bus lines, **Central Oregon Breeze** and **Cascades East Transit,** run routes.

ESSENTIALS

Visitor Information Ochoco National Forest Office. ✉ *3160 N.E. 3rd St.* ☎ *541/416–6500* ⊕ *www.fs.usda.gov/centraloregon.* **Prineville-Crook County Chamber of Commerce and Visitor Center.** ✉ *185 N.E. 10th St.* ☎ *541/447–6304* ⊕ *www.visitprineville.org.*

EXPLORING

A.R. Bowman Memorial Museum. A tough little stone building (it was once a bank, and banks out here needed to be solid) is the site of the museum of the Crook County Historical Society. The 1910 edifice is on the National Register of Historic Places, with the inside vault and teller cages seemingly untouched. Prominent in the museum are old guns, relics from the lumber mills, and Native American artifacts that define early Prineville. An expansion houses a research library and life-size representations of an Old West street. ✉ *246 N. Main St.* ☎ *541/447–3715* ⊕ *www.bowmanmuseum.org* 🎫 *Free* ⊗ *Closed Jan.*

SCENIC ROUTE

Summit Prairie Drive. The scenic drive winds past Lookout Mountain, Round Mountain, Walton Lake, and Big Summit Prairie. The prairie abounds with trout-filled creeks and has one of the finest stands of ponderosa pines in the state; wild horses, coyote, deer, and sometimes even elk roam the area. The prairie can be glorious between late May and June, when wildflowers with evocative names like mule ears, paintbrush, checkermallow, and Peck's mariposa lily burst into bloom. ✉ *Prineville* ⊹ *From*

Prineville, head 16 miles east on Hwy. 26, go right on County Rd. 123, turn east and travel 8½ miles to Forest Rd. 42, turn southeast and travel 9½ miles to Forest Rd. 4210 ☎ 541/416–6500.

Ochoco Viewpoint. This is a truly fantastic scenic overlook that commands a sweeping view of the city, including the prominent Crook County Courthouse built in 1909, and the hills, ridges, and buttes beyond. ⊠ *U.S. Hwy. 126, ½ mile west of Prineville.*

WHERE TO EAT AND STAY

$$ ✕ **Barney Prine's Steakhouse & Saloon.** Prineville is home to a startlingly
STEAKHOUSE appealing restaurant and saloon named after one of the town's founders. It's a good place to get a filet mignon, pepper steak, slow-smoked prime rib, 1-pound rib-eye steak, or other cuts. **Known for:** Old West ambience; long wait times on weekends. $ *Average main: $20* ⊠ *389 N.W. 4th St.* ☎ *541/447–3333* ⊕ *www.barneyprines.com* ⊗ *No lunch.*

$ ✕ **Tastee Treet.** Open since 1957, this local establishment is renowned for
DINER its traditional burgers, hand-cut french fries, and milk shakes. Saunter
FAMILY up to the horseshoe-shaped counter to sit on swiveling stools and chat with locals, or talk with out-of-towners, some of whom never miss a chance to drop by while passing through. **Known for:** old-school burger joint menu; greasy deep-fried appetizers. $ *Average main: $9* ⊠ *493 N.E. 3rd St.* ☎ *541/447–4165.*

$$$$ ☖ **Brasada Ranch.** Enjoy a luxurious guest-ranch resort with spacious
RESORT suites and cabins with fireplaces and decks, all offering authentic
Fodor'sChoice Western experiences and pristine modern amenities in the midst of
★ exquisite views on 1,800 acres. **Pros:** helpful staff; range of on-site facilities and activities; serene views of mountain horizons. **Cons:** not all units have hot tubs; morning light seeps through wood-slatted shades. $ *Rooms from: $289* ⊠ *16986 S.W. Brasada Ranch Rd., Powell Butte* ☎ *866/373–4882* ⊕ *www.brasada.com* ⟿ *8 suites, 63 cabins* ⚑ *No meals.*

SPORTS AND THE OUTDOORS

FISHING

It's a good idea to check the **Oregon Department of Fish and Wildlife's** (⊕ *ww.dfw.state.or.us*) recreation report before you head out.

Ochoco Reservoir. This lake is annually stocked with fingerling trout, and you might also find a rainbow, bass, or brown bullhead tugging on your line. ⊠ *Hwy. 26, 6 miles east of Prineville* ☎ *541/447–1209* ⊕ *www. ccprd.org* ⛺ *Campsites $16.*

HIKING

Pick up maps at the Ochoco National Forest office for trails through the nearly 5,400-acre **Bridge Creek Wilderness** and the demanding Black Canyon Trail (11½ miles one-way with a hazardous river crossing in spring) in the **Black Canyon Wilderness.** The 1½-mile **Ponderosa Loop Trail** follows an old logging road through ponderosa pines growing on hills. In early summer wildflowers take over the open meadows. The trailhead begins at Bandit Springs Rest Area, 29 miles east of Prineville on U.S. 26. A 2-mile, one-way trail winds through old-growth forest and mountain meadows to **Steins Pillar,** a giant lava column with panoramic views;

6

be prepared for a workout on the trail's poorly maintained second half, and allow at least three hours for the hike. To get to the trailhead, drive east 9 miles from Prineville on U.S. 26, head north (to the left) for 6½ miles on Mill Creek Road (also signed as Forest Service Road 33), and head east (to the right) on Forest Service Road 500.

RECREATIONAL AREAS

Ochoco National Forest. Twenty-five miles east of the flat, juniper-dotted countryside around Prineville, the landscape changes to forested ridges covered with tall ponderosa pines and Douglas firs. Sheltered by the diminutive Ochoco Mountains and with only about a foot of rain each year, the national forest, established in 1906 by President Theodore Roosevelt, manages to lay a blanket of green across the dry, high desert of central Oregon. This arid landscape—marked by deep canyons, towering volcanic plugs, and sharp ridges—goes largely unnoticed except for the annual influx of hunters during the fall. The Ochoco, part of the old Blue Mountain Forest Reserve, is a great place for camping, hiking, biking, and fishing in relative solitude. In its three wilderness areas—Mill Creek, Bridge Creek, and Black Canyon—it's possible to see elk, wild horses, eagles, and even cougars. ⊠ *Office, 3160 N.E. 3rd St. (U.S. 26)* ☎ *541/416–6500* ⊕ *www.fs.usda.gov/recmain/ochoco.*

Oregon Badlands Wilderness. This 29,000-acre swath of Oregon's high desert was designated a national wilderness in 2009, following the longtime advocacy of Oregonians enamored by its harshly beautiful landscape riven by ancient lava flows and home to sage grouse, pronghorn antelope, and elk. Motorized vehicles are prohibited, but visitors can ride horses on designated trails and low-impact hikers are welcome. Bring a camera to capture the jagged rock formations, birds, and wildflowers. ⊠ *BLM Office, 3050 N.E. 3rd St. (U.S. 26)* ☎ *541/416–6700* ⊕ *www.blm.gov/or/wilderness/badlands.*

Prineville Reservoir State Park. Mountain streams flow out of the Ochoco Mountains and join together to create the Crooked River, which is dammed near Prineville. Bowman Dam on the river forms this park, where recreational activities include boating, swimming, fishing, hiking, and camping. Some anglers return here year after year, although temperatures can get uncomfortably hot and water levels relatively low by late summer. The reservoir is known for its bass, trout, and crappie, with fly-fishing available on the Crooked River below Bowman Dam. ⊠ *19020 S.E. Parkland Dr.* ☎ *541/447–4363, 800/452–5687* ⊕ *www. oregonstateparks.org* ⊠ *Campsites $21–$31.*

SKIING

Bandit Springs Sno-Park. A network of cross-country trails starts here at a rest area. Designed for all levels of skiers, the trails traverse areas near the Ochoco Divide and have great views. ⊠ *U.S. 26, 29 miles east of Prineville.*

Oregon Department of Motor Vehicles Prineville. The office can provide the required Sno-Park permits. ⊠ *Ochoco Plaza, 1595 E. 3rd St., Suite A-3* ☎ *541/447–7855* ⊕ *www.oregondmv.com.*

CRATER LAKE
NATIONAL PARK

WELCOME TO CRATER LAKE NATIONAL PARK

TOP REASONS TO GO

★ **The lake:** Cruise inside the caldera basin and gaze into the extraordinary sapphire-blue water of the country's deepest lake, stopping for a ramble around Wizard Island.

★ **Native land:** Enjoy the rare luxury of interacting with totally unspoiled terrain.

★ **The night sky:** Billions of stars glisten in the pitch-black darkness of an unpolluted sky.

★ **Splendid hikes:** Accessible trails spool off the main roads and wind past colorful bursts of wildflowers and cascading waterfalls.

★ **Lake-rim lodging:** Spend the night perched on the lake rim at the rustic yet stately Crater Lake Lodge.

1 Crater Lake. The park's focal point, this nonrecreational, scenic destination is known for its deep blue hue.

2 Wizard Island. Visitors can take boat rides to this protruding landmass rising from the western section of Crater Lake; it's a great place for hiking and picnicking.

3 Mazama Village. About 5 miles south of Rim Drive, the village is your best bet for stocking up on snacks, beverages, and fuel.

4 Cleetwood Cove Trail. The only designated trail to hike down the caldera and reach the lake's edge is on the rim's north side off Rim Drive; all boat tours leave from the dock at trail's end.

GETTING ORIENTED

Crater Lake National Park covers 183,224 acres, and only a relatively small portion of it encompasses the lake for which it's named. In southern Oregon less than 75 miles from the California border, the park is surrounded by several Cascade Range forests, including the Winema and Rogue River national forests. The town of Klamath Falls, 50 miles south of the park, has the most convenient Amtrak stop; Ashland and Medford, to the southwest, are 73 miles and 85 miles, respectively, from the park's southern (Annie Spring) entrance. Roseburg is 85 miles northwest of the park's northern entrance, which is open only seasonally.

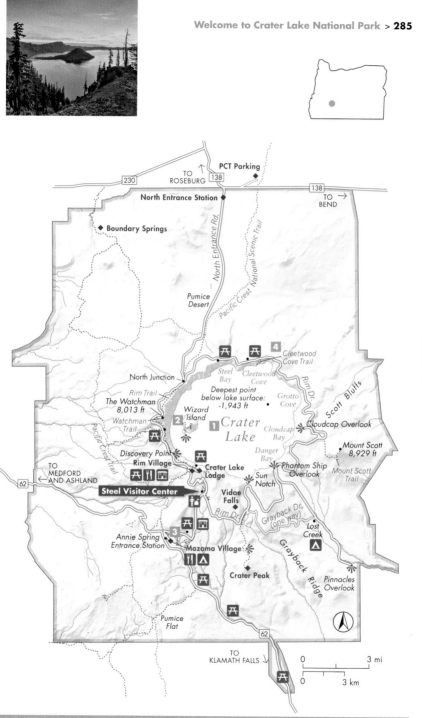

PCT Parking

TO
ROSEBURG 138

230

North Entrance Station

138 TO →
BEND

◆ Boundary Springs

North Entrance Rd.

Pumice
Desert

Pacific Crest National Scenic Trail

4 Cleetwood
Cove Trail

Steel
Bay

Cleetwood
Cove

Rim Dr.

Scott Bluffs

North Junction

Deepest point
below lake surface:
-1,943 ft

Grotto
Cove

Rim Trail
The Watchman
8,013 ft

Wizard
Island

2

1 Crater
Lake

Cloudcap
Bay

Cloudcap Overlook

Watchman
Trail

Mount Scott
8,929 ft

Pacific Crest Trail

Discovery Point
Rim Village

Danger
Bay

Phantom Ship
Overlook

Mount Scott
Trail

TO
MEDFORD
AND ASHLAND

62

Crater Lake
Lodge

Sun
Notch

Steel Visitor Center

Vidae
Falls

Rim Dr.

Grayback Dr.
(one way)

Lost
Creek

3

Annie Spring
Entrance Station

Mazama Village

Grayback Ridge

Pinnacles
Overlook

Crater Peak

Pumice
Flat

62

TO
KLAMATH FALLS ↓

0   3 mi

0   3 km

7

Updated by Andrew Collins

The pure, crystalline blue of Crater Lake astounds visitors at first sight. More than 5 miles wide and ringed by cliffs almost 2,000 feet high, the lake was created approximately 7,700 years ago, following Mt. Mazama's fiery explosion. Days after the eruption, the mountain collapsed on an underground chamber emptied of lava. Rain and snowmelt filled the caldera, creating a sapphire-blue lake so clear that sunlight penetrates to a depth of 400 feet (the lake's depth is 1,943 feet). Crater Lake is both the clearest and deepest lake in the United States—and the ninth deepest in the world.

For most visitors, the star attractions of Crater Lake are the lake itself and the breathtakingly situated Crater Lake Lodge. Although it takes some effort to reach it, Wizard Island is another outstanding draw. Other park highlights include the natural, unspoiled beauty of the forest and the geological marvels you can access along the Rim Drive.

CRATER LAKE PLANNER

WHEN TO GO

The park's high season is July and August. September and early October tend to draw smaller crowds. From October well into June, nearly the entire park closes due to heavy snowfall. The road is kept open just from the South Entrance to the rim in winter, except during severe weather. Early summer snowmelt often creates watery breeding areas for large groups of mosquitoes. Bring lots of insect repellent in June and July, and expect mosquito swarms in the early morning and at sunset. They can also be a problem later in the summer in campgrounds and on the Cleetwood Cove Trail, so pack repellent if you plan on camping or hiking. You might even consider a hat with mosquito netting.

FESTIVALS AND EVENTS

Oregon Shakespeare Festival. More than 400,000 Bard lovers descend on charming downtown Ashland (85 miles from Crater Lake) for this nearly yearlong festival that presents works by Shakespeare and other past and contemporary playwrights. ✉ *Ashland* ☎ *541/482–4331* ⊕ *www.osfashland.org.*

PLANNING YOUR TIME

CRATER LAKE IN ONE DAY

Begin at the **Steel Visitor Center,** a short drive from Annie Spring, the only park entrance open year-round. The center's interpretive displays and a short video describe the forces that created the lake and what makes it unique. From here, begin circling the crater's rim by heading northeast on **Rim Drive,** allowing an hour to stop at overlooks—be sure to check out the Phantom Ship rock formation in the lake—before you reach the trailhead of **Cleetwood Cove Trail,** the only safe and legal way to access the lake. If you're game for a good workout, hike down the trail to reach the dock at trail's end and hop aboard a **tour boat** for a two-hour ranger-guided excursion. If you'd prefer to hike on your own, instead take the late-morning shuttle boat to **Wizard Island** for a picnic lunch and a trek to the island's summit.

Back on Rim Drive, continue around the lake, stopping at the **Watchman Trail** for a short but steep hike to this peak above the rim, which affords a splendid view of the lake and a broad vista of the surrounding southern Cascades. Wind up your visit at **Crater Lake Lodge.** Allow time to wander the lobby of this 1915 structure that perches right on the rim. Dinner at the lodge's restaurant, overlooking the lake, caps the day.

7

GETTING HERE AND AROUND

Rogue Valley International–Medford Airport (MFR) is the nearest commercial airport. About 75 miles southwest of the park, it is served by Alaska, Allegiant, Delta, and United airlines and has rental cars. Amtrak trains stop in downtown Klamath Falls, 50 miles south of the park. Car rentals are available.

Crater Lake National Park's South Entrance, open year-round, is off Highway 62 in southern Oregon. If driving here from California, follow Interstate 5 north to Medford and head east on Highway 62, or take U.S. 97 north past Klamath Falls, exiting northwest on Highway 62. From Portland, Oregon, allow from 5½ to 6 hours to reach the park's South Entrance, via Interstate 5 through the city of Grants Pass. In summer, when the North Entrance is open, the drive from Portland takes just 4½ hours via Interstate 5, Highway 58 (through Oakridge), U.S. 97, and Highway 138. If coming from Portland in summer, staying at an Oakridge or Chemult motel the night before your arrival will have you fairly close to the park the following morning.

Most of the park is accessible only from late June or early July through mid-October. The rest of the year, snow blocks park roadways and entrances except Highway 62 and the access road to Rim Village from Mazama Village. Rim Drive is typically closed because of snow from mid-October to mid-July, and you could encounter icy conditions at any time of year, particularly in the early morning.

PARK ESSENTIALS

PARK FEES AND PERMITS

Admission to the park is $15 per vehicle, good for seven days. For all overnight trips, backcountry campers and hikers must obtain a free wilderness permit at Canfield Ranger Station, which is at the park headquarters adjacent to Steel Visitor Center and open daily 9–5 from mid-April through early November, and 10–4 the rest of the year.

PARK HOURS

Crater Lake National Park is open 24 hours a day year-round; however, snow closes most park roadways from October to June. Lodging and dining facilities usually are open from late May to mid-October. The park is in the Pacific time zone.

CELL-PHONE RECEPTION

Cell-phone reception in the park is unreliable, although generally it works around Crater Lake Lodge and Mazama Village, which also have public phones.

EDUCATIONAL OFFERINGS

RANGER PROGRAMS

FAMILY **Boat Tours.** The most popular way to tour Crater Lake itself is on a two-hour ranger-led excursion aboard a 37-passenger launch. The first narrated tour leaves the dock at 9:30 am; the last departs at 3:45 pm. Four of the 10 daily boats stop at Wizard Island, where you can get off and reboard three or six hours later. Two of these trips act as shuttles, with no ranger narration. They're perfect if you just want to get to Wizard Island to hike. The shuttles leave at 8:30 and 11:30 and return to Cleetwood Cove at 12:45 and 3:35 respectively. To get to the dock you must hike down Cleetwood Cove Trail, a strenuous 1.1-mile walk that descends 700 feet in elevation along the way; only those in excellent physical shape should attempt the hike. Bring adequate water with you. Purchase boat-tour tickets at Crater Lake Lodge, at the top of the trail, or through reservations. Restrooms are available at the top and bottom of the trail. ⊠ *Crater Lake National Park* ✢ *Access Cleetwood Cove Trail off Rim Dr., 11 miles north of Rim Village* ☎ *541/594–2255, 888/774–2728 reservations* ⊕ *www.craterlakelodges.com/activities* ⬛ *$32 shuttle, $40 guided tour, $57 guided tour with island drop-off.*

FAMILY **Junior Ranger Program.** Kids ages 6–12 learn about Crater Lake while earning a Junior Ranger patch in daily sessions during summer months at the Rim Visitor Center, and year-round they can earn a badge by completing the Junior Ranger Activity Booklet, which can be picked up at either visitor center. ☎ *541/594–3100* ⊕ *www.nps.gov/crla/learn/kidsyouth.*

TOURS

Main Street Adventure Tours. This Ashland-based outfitter's guided tours in southern Oregon include seven-hour ones to Crater Lake. During these tours, available year-round, participants are driven around part of the lake and, seasonally, given the chance to take a boat tour. Along the way to the park there are stops at the Cole M. Rivers Fish Hatchery, the Rogue River Gorge, and Lake of the Woods. ⊠ *Ashland* ☎ *541/482–9852* ⊕ *www.ashland-tours.com* ⬛ *From $179.*

RESTAURANTS

There are just a few casual eateries and convenience stores within the park, all near the main (southern) entrance. For fantastic upscale dining on the caldera's rim, head to the Crater Lake Lodge. Outside the park, Klamath Falls has a smattering of good restaurants, and both Medford and Ashland abound with first-rate eateries serving farm-to-table cuisine and local Rogue Valley wines. *Restaurant reviews have been shortened. For full information visit Fodors.com.*

HOTELS

Crater Lake's summer season is relatively brief, and Crater Lake Lodge, the park's main accommodation, is generally booked up a year in advance. If you are unable to get a reservation, check availability as your trip approaches—cancellations do happen on occasion. The other in-park option, the Cabins at Mazama Village, also books up early in summer. Outside the park there are a couple of options in nearby Prospect, and numerous lodgings in Klamath Falls, Medford, Ashland, and Roseburg. Additionally, if visiting the park via the North Entrance in summer, you might consider staying in one of the handful of motels in Oakridge and Chemult. Even Bend is an option, as it's just a two-hour drive from North Entrance, which is only slightly longer than the drive from Ashland to the main entrance. *Hotel reviews have been shortened. For full information, visit Fodors.com.*

WHAT IT COSTS				
	$	$$	$$$	$$$$
Restaurants	under $13	$13–$20	$21–$30	over $30
Hotels	under $100	$100–$150	$151–$200	over $200

Restaurant prices are the average cost of a main course at dinner, or if dinner is not served, at lunch. Hotel prices are the lowest cost of a standard double room in high season.

VISITOR INFORMATION

Park Contact Information Crater Lake National Park. ☎ *541/594–3000* ⊕ *www.nps.gov/crla.*

Park Literature and Information Crater Lake Natural History Association. ☎ *541/594–3111* ⊕ *www.craterlakeoregon.org.*

VISITOR CENTERS

Rim Visitor Center. In summer you can obtain park information at the center, take a ranger-led tour, or stop into the nearby Sinnott Memorial, which has a small museum and a 900-foot view down to the lake's surface. In winter, snowshoe walks are offered on weekends and holidays. A short walk away, the Rim Village Gift Store and cafeteria are the only services open in winter. ⊠ *Rim Dr., 7 miles north of Annie Spring entrance station* ☎ *541/594–3000* ⊕ *www.nps.gov/crla.*

Steel Visitor Center. Open year-round, the center, part of the park's headquarters, has restrooms, a first-aid station, a small post office, and a shop that sells books, maps, and postcards. There are fewer exhibits than at comparable national park visitor centers, but you can view an engaging 22-minute film, *Crater Lake: Into the Deep*, which describes the lake's formation and geology and examines the area's cultural history. ⊠ *Rim Dr., 4 miles north of Annie Spring entrance station* ☎ *541/594–3000* ⊕ *www.nps.gov/crla.*

EXPLORING

SCENIC DRIVES

Fodor's Choice
★
Rim Drive. Take this 33-mile scenic loop for views of the lake and its cliffs from every comparable angle. The drive takes two hours not counting frequent stops at overlooks and short hikes that can easily stretch this to a half day. Rim Drive is typically closed due to heavy snowfall from mid-October to mid-June, and icy conditions can be encountered any month of the year, particularly in early morning. ⊠ *Crater Lake National Park* ✛ *Drive begins at Rim Village, 7 miles from (Annie Spring) South Entrance; from North Entrance, follow North Entrance Rd. south for 10 miles* ⊕ *www.nps.gov/crla.*

HISTORIC SITES

Fodor's Choice
★
Crater Lake Lodge. Built in 1915, this imposing log-and-stone structure was designed in the classic style of Western national park lodges, and the original lodgepole-pine pillars, beams, and stone fireplaces are still intact. The lobby, fondly refer▮▮▮o as the Great Hall, serves as a warm, welcoming gathering place where you can play games, socialize with a cocktail, or gaze out of the many windows to view spectacular sunrises and sunsets by a crackling fire. Exhibits off the lobby contain historic photographs and memorabilia from throughout the park's history. ⊠ *Rim Village, just east of Rim Visitor Center* ⊕ *www.craterlake-lodges.com.*

SCENIC STOPS

Cloudcap Overlook. The highest road-access overlook on the Crater Lake rim, Cloudcap has a westward view across the lake to Wizard Island and an eastward view of Mt. Scott, the volcanic cone that is the park's highest point. ⊠ *Crater Lake National Park* ✛ *2 miles off Rim Dr., 13 miles northeast of Steel Visitor Center* ⊕ *www.nps.gov/crla.*

Discovery Point. This overlook marks the spot at which prospectors first spied the lake in 1853. Wizard Island is just northeast, close to shore. ⊠ *West Rim Dr., 1½ miles north of Rim Village* ⊕ *www.nps.gov/crla.*

Mazama Village. In summer, a campground, cabin-style motel, amphitheater, gas station, and small store are open here. No gasoline is available in the park from mid-October to mid-May. Snowfall determines when the village and its facilities open and close for the season. Hours vary; call ahead. ⊠ *Mazama Village Rd., off Hwy. 62, near Annie Spring entrance station* ☎ *541/594–2255, 888/774–2728* ⊕ *www.craterlake-lodges.com.*

CLOSE UP

Wildlife in Crater Lake

Wildlife in the Crater Lake area flourishes in the water and throughout the surrounding forest.

SALMON AND TROUT

Two primary types of fish swim beneath the surface of Crater Lake: kokanee salmon and rainbow trout. Kokanees average about 8 inches in length, but they can grow to nearly 18 inches. Rainbow trout are larger than the kokanee but are less abundant in Crater Lake. Trout—including bull, Eastern brook, rainbow, and German

brown—swim in the park's many streams and rivers.

ELK, DEER, AND MORE

Remote canyons shelter the park's elk and deer populations, which can sometimes be seen at dusk and dawn feeding at forest's edge. Black bears and pine martens—cousins of the short-tailed weasel—also call Crater Lake home. Birds such as hairy woodpeckers, California gulls, red-tailed hawks, and great horned owls are more commonly seen in summer in forests below the lake.

Phantom Ship Overlook. From this point you can get a close look at Phantom Ship, a rock formation that resembles a schooner with furled masts and looks ghostly in fog. ⊠ *East Rim Dr., 7 miles northeast of Steel Visitor Center* ⊕ *www.nps.gov/crla.*

Pinnacles Overlook. Ascending from the banks of Sand and Wheeler creeks, unearthly spires of eroded ash resemble the peaks of fairy-tale castles. Once upon a time, the road continued east to a former entrance. A path now replaces the old road and follows the rim of Sand Creek (affording more views of pinnacles) to where the entrance arch still stands. ⊠ *Pinnacles Rd., 12 miles east of Steel Visitor Center* ⊕ *www. nps.gov/crla.*

Sun Notch. It's a relatively easy ¼-mile hike through wildflowers and dry meadow to this overlook, which has views of Crater Lake and Phantom Ship. Mind the cliff edges. ⊠ *East Rim Dr., 4.4 miles east of Steel Visitor Center* ⊕ *www.nps.gov/crla.*

Fodor's Choice
★

Wizard Island. The volcanic eruption that led to the creation of Crater Lake resulted in the formation of this magical island a quarter mile off the lake's western shore. The views at its summit—reached on a somewhat strenuous 2-mile hike—are stupendous.

Getting to the island requires a strenuous 1.1-mile hike down (and later back up) the steep Cleetwood Cove Trail to the cove's dock. There, board either the shuttle boat to Wizard Island or a Crater Lake narrated tour boat that includes a stop on the island. If you opt for the latter, you can explore Wizard Island a bit and reboard a later boat to resume the lake tour.

The hike to Wizard Summit, 763 feet above the lake's surface, begins at the island's boat dock and steeply ascends over rock-strewn terrain; a path at the top circles the 90-foot-deep crater's rim. More moderate is the 1.8-mile hike on a rocky trail along the shore of Wizard Island, so called because William Steel, an early Crater Lake booster, thought

7

its shape resembled a wizard's hat. ⊠ *Crater Lake National Park* ⊹ *Access Cleetwood Cove Trail off Rim Dr., 11 miles north of Rim Village* ☎ *541/594–2255, 888/774–2728* ⊕ *www.craterlakelodges.com/activities* ⛴ *Shuttle boat $32, tour boat $57.*

SPORTS AND THE OUTDOORS

FISHING

Fishing is allowed in the lake, but you may find the experience frustrating—in such a massive body of water, the problem is finding the fish. Try your luck near the Cleetwood Cove boat dock, or take poles on the boat tour and fish off Wizard Island. Rainbow trout and kokanee salmon lurk in Crater Lake's aquamarine depths, and some grow to enormous sizes. You don't need a state fishing license, but to protect the lake's pristine waters, the park service prohibits the use of worms, fish eggs, and even some artificial bait (such as powerbait); check with the visitor center for guidance on permissible bait. Private boats are prohibited on the lake.

HIKING

EASY

Castle Crest Wildflower Trail. This short half-mile loop that passes through a spring-fed meadow is one of the park's flatter hikes. Wildflowers burst into full bloom here in July. *Easy.* ⊠ *Crater Lake National Park* ⊹ *Trailhead: East Rim Dr., across street from Steel Visitor Center parking lot.*

Godfrey Glen Trail. This 1.1-mile loop trail is an easy stroll through an old-growth forest with canyon views. Its dirt path is accessible to wheelchairs with assistance. *Easy.* ⊠ *Crater Lake National Park* ⊹ *Trailhead: Mission Valley Rd., 2.4 miles south of Steel Visitor Center.*

MODERATE

Annie Creek Canyon Trail. This somewhat challenging 1.7-mile hike loops through a deep stream-cut canyon, providing views of the narrow cleft scarred by volcanic activity. This is a good area to look for flowers and deer. *Moderate.* ⊠ *Mazama Campground, Mazama Village Rd.* ⊹ *Trailhead: behind amphitheater between D and E campground loops.*

Boundary Springs Trail. If you feel like sleuthing, take this moderate 5-mile round-trip hike to the headwaters of the Rogue River. The trail isn't well marked, so a detailed trail guide is necessary. You'll see streams, forests, and wildflowers along the way before discovering Boundary Springs pouring out of the side of a low ridge. *Moderate.* ⊠ *Crater Lake National Park* ⊹ *Trailhead: pullout on Hwy. 230, near milepost 19, about 5 miles west of Hwy. 138.*

Watchman Peak Trail. This is one of the park's best and most easily accessed hikes. Though it's just 1.6 miles round-trip, the trail climbs more than 400 feet—not counting the steps up to the actual lookout, which has great views of Wizard Island and the lake. *Moderate.*

⊠ *Crater Lake National Park* ✛ *Trailhead: at Watchman Overlook, Rim Dr., 3.8 miles northwest of Rim Village, west side of lake.*

DIFFICULT

Cleetwood Cove Trail. This strenuous 2.2-mile round-trip hike descends 700 feet down nearly vertical cliffs along the lake to the boat dock. Be in very good shape before you tackle this well-maintained trail—it's the hike back up that catches some visitors unprepared. Bring along plenty of water. *Difficult.* ⊠ *Crater Lake National Park* ✛ *Trailhead: on Rim Dr., 11 miles north of Rim Village, north side of lake.*

Fodor's Choice
★

Mt. Scott Trail. This strenuous 4.4-mile round-trip trail takes you to the park's highest point—the top of Mt. Scott, the oldest volcanic cone of Mt. Mazama, at 8,929 feet. The average hiker needs 90 minutes to make the steep uphill trek—and nearly 60 minutes to get down. The trail starts at an elevation of about 7,679 feet, so the climb is not extreme, but the trail is steep in spots. The views of the lake and the broad Klamath Basin are spectacular. *Difficult.* ⊠ *Crater Lake National Park* ✛ *Trailhead: 14 miles east of Steel Visitor Center on Rim Dr., across from road to Cloudcap Overlook.*

Pacific Crest Trail. You can hike a portion of the Pacific Crest Trail, which extends from Mexico to Canada and winds through the park for 33 miles. For this prime backcountry experience, catch the trail off Highway 138 about a mile east of the North Entrance, where it heads south and then toward the west rim of the lake and circles it for about 6 miles, then descends down Dutton Creek to the Mazama Village area. You'll need a detailed map for this hike; check online or with the PCT association (*www.pcta.org*). *Difficult.* ⊠ *Crater Lake National Park* ✛ *Trailhead: at Pacific Crest Trail parking lot, off Hwy. 138, 1 mile east of North Entrance.*

SKIING

There are no maintained ski trails in the park, although some backcountry trails are marked with blue diamonds or snow poles. Most cross-country skiers park at Rim Village and follow a portion of West Rim Drive toward Wizard Island Overlook (4 miles). The road is plowed to Rim Village, but it may be closed temporarily due to severe storms. Snow tires and chains are essential. The park's online brochure (available at ⊕ *www.nps.gov/crla*) lists additional trails and their length and difficulty.

SWIMMING

Swimming is allowed in the lake, but it's generally popular only on hot days and among the hardiest of souls. Made up entirely of snowmelt, Crater Lake is very cold—about 45°F to 56°F in summer. The lagoons on Wizard Island and at Cleetwood Cove are your only real choices—but swimming is only advisable when the air temperature rises above 80°F, relatively rare.

WHERE TO EAT

$$
AMERICAN
FAMILY

✕**Annie Creek Restaurant.** This family-friendly dining spot in Mazama Village serves hearty if unmemorable comfort fare, and service can be hit or miss. Blue cheese–bacon burgers, Cobb salads, sandwiches, pizzas, lasagna, and a tofu stir-fry are all on the menu. **Known for:** large portions. $ *Average main: $13* ✉ *Mazama Village Rd. and Ave. C, near Annie Spring entrance station* ☎ *541/594–2255* ⊕ *www.craterlakelodges.com/dining-shopping* ☾ *Closed late Sept.–early Apr.*

$$$$
PACIFIC
NORTHWEST
Fodor's Choice
★

✕**Dining Room at Crater Lake Lodge.** The only sophisticated dining option inside the park, the dining room is magnificent, with a large stone fireplace and views of Crater Lake's clear-blue waters. Breakfast and lunch are enjoyable here, but the dinner is the main attraction, with tempting dishes such as smoked salmon crostini with roasted beets and goat cheese, elk chops with a huckleberry-walnut glaze, and bison meat loaf with a mushroom-Merlot sauce. **Known for:** well-prepared steak; rustic and historic atmosphere; views of the lake. $ *Average main: $33* ✉ *Crater Lake Lodge, 1 Lodge Loop Rd.* ☎ *541/594–2255* ⊕ *www.craterlakelodges.com* ☾ *Closed mid-Oct.–mid-May.*

PICNIC AREAS

Godfrey Glen Trail. In a small canyon abuzz with songbirds, squirrels, and chipmunks, this picnic area has a south-facing, protected location. The half dozen picnic tables here are in a small meadow; there are also a few fire grills and a pit toilet. ✉ *Crater Lake National Park* ✛ *2.4 miles south of Steel Visitor Center* ⊕ *www.nps.gov/crla.*

Highway 62. Set in the fir, spruce, and pine forests of the Cascades' dry side, the three picnic areas along the southern portion of this route have tables, some fire grills, and pit toilets, but no drinking water. Picnickers who mind traffic noise should head farther into the park. ✉ *Crater Lake National Park* ✛ *2, 4, and 7 miles southeast of Annie Spring entrance station on Hwy. 62* ⊕ *www.nps.gov/crla.*

Rim Drive. About a half dozen picnic-area turnouts encircle the lake; all have good views, but they can get very windy. Most have pit toilets, and a few have fire grills, but none have running water. ✉ *Rim Dr.* ⊕ *www.nps.gov/crla.*

Rim Village. This is the only park picnic area with running water. The tables are set behind the visitor center, and most have a view of the lake below. There are flush toilets inside the visitor center. ✉ *Rim Dr., south side of lake, by Crater Lake Lodge, Rim Village* ⊕ *www.nps.gov/crla.*

Vidae Falls. In the upper reaches of Sun Creek, the picnic tables here enjoy the sound of the small falls across the road. There is a vault toilet, and a couple of fire grills. ✉ *Rim Dr., 3 miles east of Steel Visitor Center, near Crater Peak turnoff* ⊕ *www.nps.gov/crla.*

Fodor's Choice
★

Wizard Island. The park's best picnic venue is on Wizard Island; pack a lunch and book yourself on one of the early-morning boat tour departures, reserving space on an afternoon return. There are no formal picnic areas and just pit toilets, but you'll discover plenty of sunny and shaded spots where you can enjoy a quiet meal and appreciate the astounding scene that surrounds you. The island is accessible by

Best Campgrounds in Crater Lake

Tent campers and RV enthusiasts alike will enjoy the heavily wooded and well-equipped setting of Mazama Campground. Lost Creek Campground is much smaller, with minimal amenities and a more "rustic" Crater Lake experience. Pack bug repellent and patience if camping in the snowmelt season.

Lost Creek Campground. The 16 small, remote tent sites here are usually available on a daily basis; in July and August arrive early to secure a spot. The cost is $10 nightly. ⊠ *3 miles south of Rim Rd. on Pinnacles Spur Rd. at Grayback Dr.* ☏ *541/594–3100.*

Mazama Campground. This campground is set well below the lake caldera in the pine and fir forest of the Cascades not far from the main access road (Highway 62). Drinking water, showers, and laundry facilities help ensure that you don't have to rough it too much. About half the 200 spaces are pull-throughs, some with electricity and a few with hookups. The best tent spots are on some of the outer loops above Annie Creek Canyon. Tent sites cost $22, RV ones $31. ⊠ *Mazama Village, near Annie Spring entrance station* ☏ *541/594–2255, 888/774–2728* ⊕ *www.craterlakelodges.com.*

boat only, and to get to the boat dock you must hike down 1.1 miles. The hike back up is strenuous. ⊠ *Crater Lake ✛ To get to boat dock, access Cleetwood Cove Trail, off Rim Dr., 11 miles north of Rim Village* ⊕ *www.craterlakelodges.com/activities/volcano-boat-cruises.*

7

WHERE TO STAY

$$$
HOTEL

🛏 **The Cabins at Mazama Village.** In a wooded area 7 miles south of the lake, this complex is made up of several A-frame buildings and has modest rooms with two queen beds and a private bath. **Pros:** clean and well-kept facility. **Cons:** lots of traffic into adjacent campground. Ⓢ *Rooms from: $152* ⊠ *Mazama Village, near Annie Spring entrance station* ☏ *541/594–2255, 888/774–2728* ⊕ *www.craterlakelodges.com* 🕙 *Closed mid-Oct.–late May* ⇄ *40 rooms* ❐| *No meals.*

$$$
HOTEL
Fodor's Choice
★

🛏 **Crater Lake Lodge.** The period feel of this 1915 lodge on the caldera's rim is reflected in its lodgepole-pine columns, gleaming wood floors, and stone fireplaces in the common areas. **Pros:** ideal location for watching sunrise and sunset reflected on the lake; exudes rustic charm; excellent restaurant. **Cons:** books up far in advance; some rooms have tubs only, no shower; relatively simple furnishings and basic amenities; small rooms; no air-conditioning. Ⓢ *Rooms from: $180* ⊠ *1 Lodge Loop Rd., Rim Village, east of Rim Visitor Center* ☏ *541/594–2255, 888/774–2728* ⊕ *www.craterlakelodges.com* 🕙 *Closed mid-Oct.–mid-May* ⇄ *71 rooms* ❐| *No meals.*

8

SOUTHERN OREGON

Visit Fodors.com for advice, updates, and bookings

WELCOME TO SOUTHERN OREGON

TOP REASONS TO GO

★ **Discover Oregon's other wine regions:** The under-rated Umpqua and Rogue River wine regions offer pic-turesque pastoral views and numerous tasting rooms.

★ **Go underground:** Explore deep into mysterious under-ground chambers and marble caves at Oregon Caves National Monument.

★ **Shakespeare Festival:** The acclaimed Oregon Shakespeare Festival draws drama lovers to Ashland nine months a year, presenting a wide variety of both classic and contemporary theater.

★ **Enjoy quaint towns:** Southern Oregon's own throwback to the Old West, Jacksonville abounds with well-preserved buildings while Ashland claims one of the prettiest downtowns in the state.

★ **Get wet and wild:** Each fall more than 1 mil-lion waterfowl descend upon Klamath Basin National Wildlife Refuge Complex. The Rogue River is Oregon's white-water-rafting capital, and the entire region is laced with stunning hiking trails.

1 **Umpqua Valley.** Known increasingly for its up-and-coming wineries, including superb Abacela, this valley is home to tiny and historic Oakland, bustling Roseburg and its family-friendly Wildlife Safari park, and the Umpqua River Scenic Byway, a particularly scenic route to the northern (summer only) entrance of Crater Lake.

2 **Rogue Valley.** This fertile, mild-temperature region that extends from Grants Pass southeast through Medford and down to Ashland takes in the most populous communi-ties in the area—it's also the gateway for reach-ing Klamath Falls, to the east, and the remote but fascinating Oregon Caves National Monument to the southwest. The Oregon Shakespeare Festival and an abundance of historic build-ings have turned Ashland into a hub of arts, dining, and fine bed-and-break-fasts. Grants Pass, which also has a lively downtown restaurants and boutiques district, is the launch point for some of the best white-water rafting around, while Medford and historic Jacksonville are surrounded by vineyards and farms that produce some of the state's tastiest local edibles, from pears to Pinot Gris.

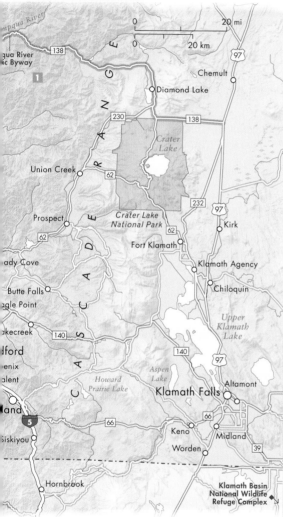

GETTING ORIENTED

To locals, southern Oregon really refers to the southwestern corner of the state, encompassing the Rogue and several other river valleys that lie between the Coast and Cascade mountain ranges, from a little north of Roseburg down to the California border. The area is due south of Eugene and the Willamette Valley, and has a lush, hilly, and fertile terrain that lends itself perfectly to agriculture and wine-making. Towns in the valleys, such as Ashland and Roseburg, have elevations ranging from about 500 to 2,000 feet, while peaks to the east, in the Cascade Range, rise as high as 9,000 feet. This area is also the gateway to Crater Lake National Park—many visitors to that park overnight in Medford or Ashland, which are about 85 miles away.

8

Updated by Andrew Collins

Southern Oregon begins where the verdant lowlands of the Willamette Valley give way to a complex collision of mountains, rivers, and ravines. The intricate geography of the "Land of Umpqua," as the area around Roseburg is somewhat romantically known, signals that this is territory distinct from neighboring regions to the north, east, and west.

Wild rivers—the Rogue and the Umpqua are legendary for fishing and boating—and twisting mountain roads venture through the landscape that saw Oregon's most violent Indian wars and became the territory of a self-reliant breed. "Don't-Tread-on-Me" southern Oregonians see themselves as markedly different from fellow citizens of the Pacific Wonderland. In fact, several early-20th-century attempts to secede from Oregon (in combination with northern California) and proclaim a "state of Jefferson" survive in local folklore and culture. That being said, Ashland and parts of the surrounding area have steadily become more progressive and urbane in recent decades, as wineries, art galleries, and farm-to-table restaurants continue to proliferate. The mix of folks from all different political, social, and stylistic bents is a big part of what makes southern Oregon so interesting—and appealing.

Some locals describe this sun-kissed, sometimes surprisingly hot landscape as Mediterranean; others refer to it as Oregon's banana belt. It's a climate built for slow-paced pursuits and a leisurely outlook on life, not to mention agriculture—the region's orchards, farms, and increasingly acclaimed vineyards have lately helped give southern Oregon cachet among food and wine aficionados. The restaurant scene has grown partly thanks to a pair of big cultural draws, Ashland's Oregon Shakespeare Festival and Jacksonville's open-air, picnic-friendly Britt Festivals concert series.

Roseburg, Medford, and Klamath Falls are also all popular bases for visiting iconic Crater Lake National Park *(see Chapter 7)*, which lies at the region's eastern edge, about two hours away by car. Formed nearly 8,000 years ago by the cataclysmic eruption of Mt. Mazama, this stunningly clear-blue lake is North America's deepest.

SOUTHERN OREGON PLANNER

WHEN TO GO

Southern Oregon's population centers, which all lie chiefly in the valleys, tend to be warmer and quite a bit sunnier than Eugene and Portland to the north, receiving almost no snow in winter and only 2 to 3 inches of rain per month. In summer, temperatures regularly climb into the 90s, but the low humidity makes for a generally comfortable climate. This makes most of the region quite pleasant to visit year-round, with spring and fall generally offering the best balance of sunny and mild weather.

The exceptions, during the colder months, are southern Oregon's mountainous areas to the east and west, which are covered with snow from fall through spring. Some of the roads leading from the Umpqua and Rogue valleys up to Crater Lake are closed because of snow from mid-October through June, making summer the prime time to visit.

FESTIVALS

Britt Festivals. ✉ *Britt Festival Pavilion, 350 1st St., Jacksonville* ☎ *541/773–6077* ⊕ *www.brittfest.org.*

Fodor's Choice ★ **Oregon Shakespeare Festival.** Ashland's biggest attraction is this festival of Shakespeare and other plays, which runs mid-February through early November. Book tickets and lodging well in advance. ✉ *15 S. Pioneer St., Ashland* ☎ *541/482–4331* ⊕ *www.osfashland.org.*

Winter Wings Festival. Each February, nature enthusiasts flock to the Klamath Basin for the Winter Wings Festival, the nation's oldest birding festival. ✉ *Box 354, Klamath Falls* ☎ *877/541–2473* ⊕ *winterwingsfest. org.*

GETTING HERE AND AROUND

AIR TRAVEL

Medford's Rogue Valley International Airport (MFR) is the state's third-largest facility, with direct flights to Denver, Los Angeles, Portland, Salt Lake City, San Francisco, and Seattle, and service by Allegiant, Alaska, Delta, and United. Most national car-rental branches are at the airport. A few taxi and shuttle companies provide transportation from the airport to other towns in the area; these are used mostly by locals, as a car is the only practical way to explore this relatively rural part of Oregon. The one exception is Ashland, where many attractions, restaurants, and accommodations are within walking distance. Cascade Airport Shuttle offers door-to-door service from the airport to Ashland for about $30 to $35. Among taxi companies, Valley Cab serves the Rogue Valley region, with fares costing $2.75 base per trip, plus $2.75 per mile thereafter.

Roseburg is a 75-mile drive from Oregon's second-largest airport, in Eugene (EUG). Ashland is about 300 miles south of the state's largest airport, in Portland, and 350 miles north of San Francisco. Although it's often cheaper to fly into these larger airports than it is to Medford, what you lose in gas costs, time, and inconvenience will likely outweigh any savings.

Contacts Cascade Airport Shuttle. ☎ *541/488–1998, 888/760–7433* ⊕ *www. cascadeshuttle.com.* **Rogue Valley International Airport.** ☎ *541/772–8068*

8

⊕ *www.jacksoncountyor.org/airport.* **Valley Cab.** ☎ *541/772–1818* ⊕ *www. myvalleycab.com.*

CAR TRAVEL

Unquestionably, your best way to explore the region is by car, although most of Ashland's key attractions, hotels, and dining are downtown and within walking distance of one another. Interstate 5 runs north–south the length of the Umpqua and Rogue river valleys, linking Roseburg, Grants Pass, Medford, and Ashland. Many regional attractions lie not too far east or west of Interstate 5. Jacksonville is a short drive due west from Medford. Highway 138 winds scenically along the Umpqua River east of Roseburg to the less-visited northern end of Crater Lake National Park. Highway 140 leads from Medford east to Klamath Falls, which you can reach from Bend via U.S. 97.

RESTAURANTS

Southern Oregon's dining scene varies greatly from region to region, with the more tourism-driven and upscale communities of Ashland, Jacksonville, and Grants Pass leading the way in terms of sophisticated farm-to-table restaurants, hip coffeehouses, and noteworthy bakeries and wine bars. Other larger towns in the valleys, including Roseburg and Medford, have grown in culinary stature and variety of late, while Klamath Falls and Cave Junction have few dining options of note. In the former communities you'll find chefs emphasizing Oregon-produced foods; regional wines, including many from the Rogue and Umqua valleys, also find their way onto many menus. *Restaurant reviews have been shortened. For full information visit Fodors.com.*

HOTELS

Ashland has the region's greatest variety of distinctive lodgings, from the usual low- to mid-priced chain properties to plush B&Bs set in restored Arts and Crafts and Victorian houses. Nearby Jacksonville also has several fine, upscale inns. Beyond that, in nearly every town in southern Oregon you'll find an interesting B&B or small hotel, and in any of the key communities along Interstate 5—including Roseburg, Grants Pass, and Medford—a wide variety of chain motels and hotels. Rooms in this part of the state book up earliest in summer, especially on weekends. If you're coming to Ashland or Jacksonville, try to book at least a week or two ahead. Elsewhere, you can usually find a room in a suitable chain property on less than a day's notice. *Hotel reviews have been shortened. For full information, visit Fodors.com.*

WHAT IT COSTS IN U.S. DOLLARS			
$	$$	$$$	$$$$
Restaurants under $16	$16–$22	$23–$30	over $30
Hotels under $150	$150–$200	$201–$250	over $250

Restaurant prices are the average cost of a main course at dinner or, if dinner is not served, at lunch. Hotel prices are the lowest cost of a standard double room in high season.

TOURS

FAMILY **Hellgate Jetboat Excursions.** You'll see some of Oregon's most magnificent scenery on these excursions, which depart from the Riverside Inn in Grants Pass. The 36-mile round-trip runs through Hellgate Canyon and takes two hours. There is also a five-hour, 75-mile round-trip from Grants Pass to Grave Creek, with a stop for a meal on an open-air deck (cost of meal not included). Trips are available May through September, conditions permitting. ☎ *541/479–7204, 800/648–4874* ⊕ *www. hellgate.com* ✉ *From $31.*

Wine Hopper Tours. Getting to know the region's more than 125 wineries can be a challenge to visitors, especially when you factor in having to drive from tasting room to tasting room. This outfitter with knowledgeable guides leads seven-hour tours leaving daily from Ashland, Medford, and Jacksonville—the day includes a tour of a winery, picnic lunch, and tasting at a few of the area's top producers. ☎ *541/476– 9463, 855/550–9463* ⊕ *www.winehoppertours.com* ✉ *From $89.*

VISITOR INFORMATION

Southern Oregon Visitors Association. ⊕ *www.southernoregon.org.*

UMPQUA VALLEY

The northernmost part of southern Oregon, beginning about 40 miles south of Eugene and the Willamette Valley, the rural and sparsely populated Umpqua Valley is the gateway to this part of the state's sunny and relatively dry climate. As you drive down Interstate 5 you'll descend through twisting valleys and climb up over scenic highlands. In summer you can follow the dramatic Umpqua River Scenic Byway (Highway 138) east over the Cascades to access Crater Lake from the north—it's the prettiest route to the lake. Within the Umpqua Valley, attractions are relatively few, but this area has several excellent wineries, some of the best river fishing in the Northwest, and one of the region's top draws for animal lovers, the Wildlife Safari park.

ROSEBURG

73 miles south of Eugene on Interstate 5.

Fishermen the world over hold the name Roseburg sacred. The timber town on the Umpqua River attracts anglers in search of a dozen popular fish species, including bass, brown and brook trout, and chinook, coho, and sockeye salmon. The native steelhead, which makes its run to the sea in the summer, is king of them all.

The north and south branches of the Umpqua River meet up just north of Roseburg. The roads that run parallel to this river provide spectacular views of the falls, and the North Umpqua route also provides access to trails, hot springs, and the Winchester fish ladder. White-water rafting is also popular here, although not to the degree that it is farther south in the Rogue Valley.

About 80 miles west of the northern gateway to Crater Lake National Park and in the Hundred Valleys of the Umpqua, Roseburg produces innovative, well-regarded wines. Wineries are sprouting up throughout the mild, gorgeous farm country around town, mostly within easy reach of Interstate 5.

GETTING HERE AND AROUND

Roseburg is the first large town you'll reach driving south from Eugene on Interstate 5. It's also a main access point into southern Oregon via Highway 138 if you're approaching from the east, either by way of Crater Lake or U.S. 97, which leads down from Bend. And from the North Bend–Coos Bay region of the Oregon Coast, windy but picturesque Highway 42 leads to just south of Roseburg. It's a 75-mile drive north to Eugene's airport, and a 95-mile drive south to Rogue Valley Airport in Medford.

ESSENTIALS

Visitor Information Roseburg Visitors & Convention Bureau. ⊠ *410 S.E. Spruce St.* ☎ *541/672–9731, 800/440–9584* ⊕ *www.visitroseburg.com.*

EXPLORING

Fodor's Choice
★

Abacela Vineyards and Winery. The name derives from an archaic Spanish word meaning "to plant grapevines," and that's exactly what this winery's husband-wife team did not so very long ago. Abacela released its first wine in 1999 and has steadily established itself as one of the best wineries outside the Willamette Valley. Hot-blooded Spanish Tempranillo is Abacela's pride and joy, though inky Malbec and torrid Sangiovese also highlight a repertoire heavy on Mediterranean varietals, which you can sample in a handsome, eco-friendly tasting room. ⊠ *12500 Lookingglass Rd.* ☎ *541/679–6642* ⊕ *www.abacela.com.*

Douglas County Museum. One of the best county museums in the state surveys 8,000 years of human activity in the region. The fossil collection is worth a stop, as is the state's second-largest photo collection, numbering more than 24,000 images, some dating to the 1840s. ⊠ *123 Museum Dr.* ☎ *541/957–7007* ⊕ *www.umpquavalleymuseums.org* ⊟ *$8.*

FAMILY
Fodor's Choice
★

Wildlife Safari. Come face-to-face with some 500 free-roaming animals at the 600-acre drive-through wildlife park. Inhabitants include alligators, bobcats, cougars, gibbons, lions, giraffes, grizzly bears, Tibetan yaks, cheetahs, Siberian tigers, and more than 100 additional species. There's also a petting zoo, a miniature train, and elephant rides. The admission price includes two same-day drive-throughs. This nonprofit zoological park is a respected research facility with full accreditation from the American Zoo and Aquarium Association, with a mission to conserve and protect endangered species through education and breeding programs. ⊠ *1790 Safari Rd., Winston* ☎ *541/679–6761* ⊕ *www. wildlifesafari.net* ⊟ *$18.*

WHERE TO EAT AND STAY

$$
AMERICAN

✕ **Brix.** This handsome downtown American bistro with exposed-brick walls, curving leather banquettes, and high ceilings serves reasonably priced breakfast and lunch fare daily, and somewhat more upscale dinners. Start the day with blueberry–lemon zest pancakes or eggs Benedict topped with wild salmon. **Known for:** mix of affordable and upscale dishes; impressive wine and cocktail list. [$] *Average main: $19* ✉ *527 S.E. Jackson St.* ☎ *541/440–4901* ☷ *No dinner Sun.*

$$
AMERICAN
FAMILY

✕ **Tolly's.** Most folks head to this sweetly nostalgic restaurant in the center of tiny and historic Oakland—18 miles north of Roseburg—for inexpensive lunch (including exceptionally good burgers) or to enjoy an old-fashioned soda or malt downstairs in the Victorian ice-cream parlor. Most nights, however, you can dine upstairs in the oak- and antiques-filled dining room on deftly prepared creative American cuisine. **Known for:** Sunday brunch; historic vibe. [$] *Average main: $18* ✉ *115 N.E. Locust St., Oakland* ☎ *541/459–3796* ⊕ *www.tollysgrill. com* ☷ *No dinner Mon.–Wed.*

$$$
B&B/INN
Fodor's Choice
★

🛏 **The Steamboat Inn.** The world's top fly-fishermen converge at this secluded forest inn, high in the Cascades above the North Umpqua River; others come simply to relax in the reading nooks or on the decks of the riverside guest cabins nestled below soaring fir trees. **Pros:** good option if en route to Crater Lake; access to some of the best fishing in the West; peaceful escape. **Cons:** far from any towns or cities. [$] *Rooms from: $205* ✉ *42705 N. Umpqua Hwy., 38 miles east of Roseburg on Hwy. 138, near Steamboat Creek, Idleyld Park* ☎ *541/498–2230, 800/840–8825* ⊕ *www.thesteamboatinn.com* ⇄ *8 cabins, 5 cottages, 2 suites, 5 houses* ⌑ *No meals.*

SPORTS AND THE OUTDOORS

FISHING

You'll find some of the best river fishing in Oregon along the Umpqua, with smallmouth bass, shad, steelhead, salmon (coho, chinook, and sockeye), and sturgeon—the biggest reaching 10 feet in length—among the most prized catches. In addition to the Steamboat Inn, several outfitters in the region provide full guide services, which typically include all gear, boats, and expert leaders. There's good fishing in this region year-round, with sturgeon and steelhead at their best during the colder months, chinook and coho salmon thriving in the fall, and most other species prolific in spring and summer.

Big K Guest Ranch. Set along a 10-mile span of the upper Umpqua River near Elkton (about 35 miles north of Roseburg), Big K is a 2,500-acre guest ranch. Accommodations are geared primarily to groups and corporate retreats, but the ranch offers individual eight-hour fishing trips starting at $400 for one or two anglers, and two-day/three-night fishing and lodging packages (meals included) for around $900 per person. Adventures include fly-fishing for smallmouth bass and summer steelhead, as well as spin-casting and drift-boat fishing. ✉ *20029 Hwy. 138 W., Elkton* ☎ *541/584–2295, 800/390–2445* ⊕ *www.big-k.com.*

Oregon Angler. One of the state's most respected and knowledgeable guides, Todd Hannah, specializes in jet-boat and drift-boat fishing excursions along the famed "Umpqua Loop," an 18-mile span of river that's long been lauded for exceptional fishing. Full-day trips start at $200 per person. ✉ *1037 Maupin Rd., Elkton* ☎ *800/428–8585* ⊕ *www.theoregonangler.com.*

8

RAFTING

There's thrilling Class III and higher white-water rafting along the North Umpqua River, with several outfitters providing trips ranging from a few hours to a few days throughout the year.

North Umpqua Outfitters. Since 1987, this trusted provider has offered half-, full-, and two-day rafting and kayaking trips, starting at $105 per person, along the frothy North Umpqua. ⊠ *Box 158, Idleyld Park* ☎ *888/454–9696* ⊕ *www.umpquarivers.com.*

ROGUE VALLEY

Encompassing the broad, curving, southeasterly swath of towns from Grants Pass through Medford down to Ashland, the mild and sun-kissed Rogue Valley is southern Oregon's main population center, and also where you'll find the bulk of the region's lodging, dining, shopping, and recreation.

Interstate 5 cuts through the valley en route to northern California, but venture away from the main thoroughfare to see what makes this part of Oregon so special, including the superb—if underrated—wineries. With warmer temperatures, this area is conducive to many more grape varieties than the Willamette Valley—from reds like Syrah, Tempranillo, and Cabernet Sauvignon to increasingly well-known Old World whites like Viognier and Pinot Gris. Foodies are drawn to the region's abundance of local food producers, from nationally acclaimed cheese makers and chocolatiers to farms growing pears, blackberries, and cherries. Access to excellent food has helped turn the small but artsy city of Ashland into one of Oregon's top restaurant destinations, with nearby communities also growing in culinary cachet. Additionally, the area's reputation for performing arts, which manifests itself in the famed Oregon Shakespeare Festival in Ashland and Britt Music Festival in historic Jacksonville, continues to grow.

Flanked by 1.8-million-acre Rogue–Siskiyou National Forest, which has rangers' offices near Grants Pass and Medford, the Rogue Valley is a hub of outdoor recreation, from fishing and white-water rafting along its clear rivers to mountain biking, hiking, and even skiing in the higher elevations—peaks in the Cascade Range, to the east, rise to nearly 10,000 feet. Klamath Falls lies technically a bit east of the Rogue Valley but shares the region's abundance of unspoiled wilderness and opportunities for getting in touch with nature.

GRANTS PASS

70 miles south of Roseburg on I–5.

"It's the Climate!" So says a confident 1950s vintage neon sign presiding over Josephine County's downtown. Grants Pass bills itself as Oregon's white-water capital: the Rogue River, preserved by Congress in 1968 as a National Wild and Scenic River, runs right through town. Downtown Grants Pass is a National Historic District, a stately little enclave of 19th-century brick storefronts housing a mix of folksy businesses harking back to the 1950s and newer, trendier cafés and boutiques. It's all

Kayaking Rainey Falls on the Rogue River

that white water, however, that compels most visitors—and not a few moviemakers (*The River Wild* and *Rooster Cogburn* were both filmed here). If the river alone doesn't serve up enough natural drama, the sheer rock walls of nearby Hellgate Canyon rise 250 feet.

GETTING HERE AND AROUND

Grants Pass is easily reached via Interstate 5, and it's also where U.S. 199 cuts southwest toward Oregon Caves National Monument and, eventually, the northernmost section of California's coast (and Redwood National Park). Many visitors to the southern Oregon coastline backtrack inland up U.S. 199 to create a scenic loop drive, ultimately intersecting with Interstate 5 at Grants Pass. Medford's airport is a 30-mile drive south.

ESSENTIALS

Visitor Information Grants Pass Tourism. ✉ *198 S.W. 6th St.* ☎ *541/476–7574* ⊕ *travelgrantspass.com.*

EXPLORING

Fodor's Choice ★ **Troon Vineyards.** Few winemakers in southern Oregon have generated more buzz than Troon, whose swank tasting room and winery is patterned after a French country villa. Troon produces relatively small yields of exceptional wines more typical of Sonoma than Oregon (Malbec and Zinfandel are the heavy hitters), but they also plant less typical U.S. varietals, such as Vermentino and Sangiovese. The winery is 14 miles southeast of downtown Grants Pass, in the northern edge of the Applegate Valley; there's a second Troon tasting room in Carlton, in the Willamette Valley. ✉ *1475 Kubli Rd.* ☎ *541/846–9900* ⊕ *www. troonvineyard.com.*

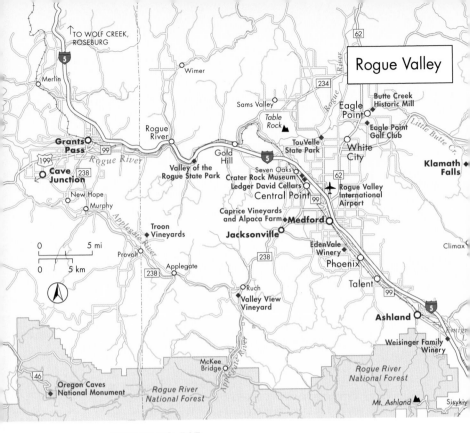

WHERE TO EAT

$$ **✕ Blondie's Bistro.** Sophisticated but affordable Blondie's serves glob-
ECLECTIC ally inspired food and cocktails in a dapper downtown space with
high ceilings and hardwood floors—the lone aesthetic drawback is the
sometimes boisterous acoustics. The kitchen, however, prepares first-
rate food, including an especially good list of starters, from Portuguese-
style steamed clams with herbed sausage to a substantial Mediterranean
antipasto platter. **Known for:** live music some nights; popular happy
hour. $ *Average main: $19* ⊠ 226 S.W. G St. ☎ 541/479–0420 ⊕ *www.
blondiesbistro.com.*

$ **✕ Gtano's.** Set in a nondescript downtown shopping center, this cozy
LATIN AMERICAN and welcoming restaurant is cheerful inside, and the kitchen turns out
superb Nuevo Latino cuisine. Specialties include the starter of Puerto
Rico "nachos," with Jack cheese, black beans, chicken, grilled pine-
apples, and mango salsa; and hearty main dishes, many of them focused
on seafood, such as Colombian-style prawns with butter, garlic, and a
tropical sauce. **Known for:** fresh-fruit margaritas; guacamole prepared
table-side. $ *Average main: $13* ⊠ 218 S.W. G St. ☎ 541/507–1255
⊙ *Closed Sun.*

$ ✕**Ma Mosa's.** Sustainability is the name of the game at this lively café in
AMERICAN downtown Grants Pass, with a cozy dining room of colorfully painted
Fodor's Choice tables and mismatched chairs, and a large adjacent patio with picnic
★ tables and lush landscaping. The kitchen sources from local farms and
purveyors to create beer-battered fried chicken and waffles, kale Caesar
salads, and line-caught-fish tacos with seasonal slaw and house-made
salsa. **Known for:** refreshing mimosa cocktails at brunch; pet-friendly
patio. $ *Average main: $10* ✉ *118 N.W. E St.* ☎ *541/479–0236* ⊕ *www.*
mamosas.com ⊘ *Closed Mon. No dinner.*

$ ✕**Twisted Cork Wine Bar.** With a mission to showcase southern Ore-
WINE BAR gon's fast-growing reputation for acclaimed vino, this dapper, art-
Fodor's Choice filled space lends a bit of urbane sophistication to downtown Grants
★ Pass. In addition to pouring varietals from throughout the Umpqua
and Rogue valleys, Twisted Cork carries wines from more than 115
wineries throughout the Northwest, along with a few from California.
Known for: local ports and dessert wines; shareable platters of cheese
and charcuterie; reasonably priced food. $ *Average main: $15* ✉ *210*
S.W. 6th St. ☎ *541/295–3094* ⊕ *www.thetwistedcorkgrantspass.com*
⊘ *Closed Sun. and Mon.*

WHERE TO STAY

$$ ⌂**Lodge at Riverside.** The pool and many rooms overlook the Rogue
HOTEL River as it passes through downtown, and all but a few rooms, fur-
nished with stylish country house–inspired armoires, plush beds, and
oil paintings, have private balconies or patios; suites have river-rock
fireplaces and Jacuzzi tubs. **Pros:** central location; attractive modern
furnishings; landscaped pool overlooks Rogue River. **Cons:** no restau-
rant on-site. $ *Rooms from: $155* ✉ *955 S.E. 7th St.* ☎ *541/955–0600,*
877/955–0600 ⊕ *www.thelodgeatriverside.com* ⤵ *29 rooms, 4 suites*
⍟ *Breakfast.*

$$$ ⌂**Weasku Inn.** Pacific Northwest–inspired art, handmade furnishings,
B&B/INN and fine fabrics fill a rambling timber-frame home overlooking the
Fodor's Choice Rogue River, 11 handsomely outfitted cabins, and an A-frame bun-
★ galow to comprise the most luxurious accommodations between Ashland and Eugene. **Pros:** set directly on the Rogue River; impeccably
decorated; fireplaces in many rooms. **Cons:** 10-minute drive east of
downtown; among the highest rates in the region. $ *Rooms from: $209*
✉ *5560 Rogue River Hwy.* ☎ *541/471–8000, 800/493–2758* ⊕ *www.*
weaskuinn.com ⤵ *5 rooms, 12 cabins* ⍟ *Breakfast.*

SPORTS AND THE OUTDOORS

RAFTING

More than a dozen outfitters guide white-water rafting trips along the
Rogue River in and around Grants Pass. In fact, this stretch of Class III
rapids ranks among the best in the West. The rafting season lasts from
about July through August and often into September, and the stretch
of river running south from Grants Pass, with some 80 frothy rapids, is
exciting but not treacherous, making it ideal for novices, families, and
others looking simply to give this enthralling activity a try.

Morrisons Rogue Wilderness Adventures. If you're up for an adventure that
combines rafting with overnight accommodations, consider booking

one of these exciting excursions that run along a 34-mile stretch of the Rogue River. They last for four days and three nights, with options for both lodge and camping stays along the way. Half- and full-day trips are also available. ⊠ *8500 Galice Rd., Merlin* ☎ *800/336–1647, 541/476–3825* ⊕ *www.rogueriverraft.com* 🖃 *From $65.*

Orange Torpedo Trips. One of the most reliable operators on the Rogue River offers half-day to several-day trips, as well as relaxed dinner-and-wine float trips along a calmer stretch of river. Klamath and North Umpqua river trips are also available. ⊠ *210 Merlin Rd., Merlin* ☎ *541/479–5061, 800/635–2925* ⊕ *www.orangetorpedo.com* 🖃 *From $49.*

RECREATIONAL AREAS

Rogue River–Siskiyou National Forests, Grants Pass. In the Klamath Mountains and the Coast Range of southwestern Oregon, the 1.8-million-acre forest contains the 35-mile-long Wild and Scenic section of the Rogue River, which races through the Wild Rogue Wilderness Area, and the Illinois and Chetco Wild and Scenic rivers, which run through the 180,000-acre Kalmiopsis Wilderness Area. Activities include whitewater rafting, camping, and hiking, but many hiking areas require trail-park passes. ⊠ *Off U.S. 199* ☎ *541/618–2200* ⊕ *www.fs.usda. gov/rogue-siskiyou.*

Valley of the Rogue State Park. A 1¼-mile hiking trail follows the bank of the Rogue, the river made famous by novelist and fisherman Zane Grey. There's a campground along 3 miles of shoreline with full RV hookups as well as yurts (some of them pet-friendly). There are picnic tables, walking trails, playgrounds, and restrooms. The park is 12 miles east of downtown Grants Pass. ⊠ *3792 N. River Rd., Gold Hill* ☎ *541/582–1118, 800/551–6949* ⊕ *www.oregonstateparks.org.*

MEDFORD

30 miles southeast of Grants Pass on I–5.

Medford is the professional, retail, trade, and service hub for eight counties in southern Oregon and northern California. As such, it offers more professional and cultural venues than might be expected for a city of its size (with a population of about 80,000). The workaday downtown has shown signs of gentrification and rejuvenation in recent years, and in the outskirts you'll find several major shopping centers and the famed fruit and gourmet-food mail-order company Harry & David.

Lodging tends to be cheaper in Medford than in nearby (and easily accessible) Ashland or Jacksonville, although cookie-cutter chain properties dominate the hotel landscape. It's also 71 miles southwest of Crater Lake and 80 miles northeast of the Oregon Caves, making it an affordable and convenient base for visiting either.

GETTING HERE AND AROUND

Medford is in the heart of the Rogue Valley on Interstate 5, and is home to the state's third-largest airport, Rogue Valley International. A car is your best way to get around the city and surrounding area.

ESSENTIALS

Visitor Information **Medford Visitors & Convention Bureau.** ✉ *1314 Center Dr.* ☎ *541/776–4021, 800/469–6307* 🌐 *www.travelmedford.org.*

EXPLORING

Crater Rock Museum. Jackson County's natural history and collections of the Roxy Ann Gem and Mineral Society are on display at this quirky, 12,000-square-foot museum in Central Point (6 miles northwest of Medford). Fossils, petrified wood, fluorescent rocks, and precious minerals from throughout Oregon and elsewhere in the West are included, plus works of glass by renowned artist Dale Chihuly. ✉ *2002 Scenic Ave., Central Point* ☎ *541/664–6081* 🌐 *www.craterrock.com* 🎟 *$7.*

EdenVale Winery. Four miles southwest of downtown Medford amid a bucolic patch of fruit orchards, this winery and tasting room, called the Rogue Valley Wine Center, adjoins a rather grand 19th-century white-clapboard farmhouse surrounded by flower beds and vegetable gardens. Inside the tasting room you can sample and buy not only EdenVale's noted reds and late-harvest whites but also other respected labels from vineyards throughout the region. ✉ *2310 Voorhies Rd.* ☎ *541/512–2955* 🌐 *www.edenvalewines.com.*

Ledger David Cellars. Sandwiched handily between Rogue Creamery and Lillie Belle Chocolates in the small downtown of Central Point, this boutique winery produces an interesting portfolio of wines that have rapidly begun to earn praise at competitions and from critics. Standouts include a bright, balanced Chenin Blanc and a berry-forward, medium-body Sangiovese. Enjoy your tasting on the patio if it's a nice day. ✉ *245 N. Front St., Central Point* ☎ *541/664–2218* 🌐 *www.ledgerdavid.com.*

8

WHERE TO EAT AND STAY

$$ TAPAS 🍴 **Elements Tapas Bar.** A stylish ambience and a taste of impressively authentic Spanish fare—these are the draws of this handsome tapas restaurant in downtown Medford's turn-of-the-20th-century "Goldy" building. Pass around plates of mussels in romesco sauce, apricot-braised-pork empanadas, chorizo-studded Andalucian paella, and lamb-sausage flatbread, while sampling selections from the lengthy beer and cocktail menus. **Known for:** late-night dining; Sunday brunch; extensive beer, wine, and cocktail selection. [$] *Average main: $20* ✉ *101 E. Main St.* ☎ *541/779–0135* 🌐 *www.elementsmedford.com* 🕒 *No lunch.*

$ BURGER 🍴 **Jaspers Cafe.** This cute roadhouse-style building a few miles northwest of downtown Medford has made a name for itself serving obscenely large, decadently topped, and deliciously crafted burgers. Polish off the Jasperado, with chorizo, salsa verde, and a fried egg, and you probably won't be experiencing any hunger pains for the rest of the day. **Known for:** unusual game burgers (such as kangaroo and antelope); tasty sides—sweet potatoes, pork pot stickers. [$] *Average main: $7* ✉ *2739 N. Pacific Hwy.* ☎ *541/776–5307* 🌐 *www.jasperscafe.com.*

$ HOTEL 🏨 **Inn on the Commons.** This recently revamped and rebranded (formerly a Red Lion) mid-price hotel is within walking distance of downtown Medford's restaurants and shops. **Pros:** prettier and more distinctive decor than most of Medford's chain properties; a branch of Ashland's excellent Larks restaurant is on-site; guests receive free passes to health club across the street. **Cons:** some rooms have street and freeway traffic noise. [$] *Rooms from: $99* ✉ *200 N. Riverside Ave.* ☎ *541/779–5811, 866/779–5811* 🌐 *www.innatthecommons.com/* 🛏 *118 rooms* 🍴 *Breakfast.*

$ HOTEL 🏨 **Rodeway Inn–Medford.** If you're on a budget and seeking a simple and immaculately clean base camp, check into this friendly, family-run '50s vintage motor court on the city's south side. **Pros:** vintage charm; convenient to sights in Medford as well Jacksonville and Ashland; super low rates. **Cons:** few amenities and luxuries; rather dated (though that's part of the charm). [$] *Rooms from: $60* ✉ *901 S. Riverside Ave.* ☎ *541/776–9194, 877/424–6423* 🌐 *www.rodewayinnmedford.com* 🛏 *40 rooms* 🍴 *Breakfast.*

NIGHTLIFE AND PERFORMING ARTS

Jefferson Spirits. This hip nightspot has helped to spur downtown Medford's ongoing renaissance by creating a swanky environment for hobnobbing and enjoying creating craft cocktails, like the locally inspired Rogue Pear, with whiskey, pear, and a splash of lemon juice. Barrel-aged cocktails are a specialty, and you'll also find local and international wines and mostly Oregon beers. ✉ *404 E. Main St.* ☎ *541/622–8190* 🌐 *www.jeffersonspirits.com.*

SPORTS AND THE OUTDOORS

FISHING

With close access to some of the best freshwater fishing venues in the Northwest, Medford has several companies that lead tours and provide gear.

Carson's Guide Service. Based 22 miles north of Medford along Highway 62 (toward Crater Lake), Carson's provides expert instruction and knowledge of many of the area's rivers, including the Rogue, Sixes, Umpqua, Coquille, Elk, and Chetco, as well as several lakes. Steelhead, salmon, shad, and smallmouth bass are the most common catches. ✉ *595 Ragsdale Rd., Trail* ☎ *541/261–3279* 🌐 *www.fishwithcarson.com.*

Fishing The Rogue. These experienced outfitter offers half- and full-day guided steelhead and salmon fishing trips in heated boats, with all gear provided, on the Rogue and Umpqua rivers as well as some of the waterways that flow down toward the southern Oregon Coast. These trips are great for all skill and experience levels, even beginners—expert instruction is included. ☎ *541/326–9486* 🌐 *www.fishingtherogue.com.*

HIKING

Fodor's Choice ★ **Table Rock.** One of the best venues for hiking in the Rogue Valley comprises a pair of monolithic rock formations that rise some 700 to 800 feet above the valley floor about 10 miles north of Medford and just a couple of miles north of TouVelle State Park. Operated by a partnership between the Bureau of Land Management and the Nature Conservancy, the Table Rock formations and surrounding 4,864 acres of wilderness afford panoramic valley views from their summits. You reach Lower Table Rock by way of a moderately challenging 5.4-mile round-trip trail, and Upper Table Rock via a shorter (2.8-mile round-trip) and less-steep route. The trailheads to these formations are a couple of miles apart—just follow the road signs from Table Rock Road, north of

TouVelle State Park (reached from Exit 33 of Interstate 5). ⊠ *Off Table Rock Rd., Central Point* ☎ *541/618–2200* ⊕ *www.blm.gov.*

RECREATIONAL AREAS

Rogue River–Siskiyou National Forest, Medford. Covering 2 million acres, this immense tract of wilderness woodland has fishing, swimming, hiking, and skiing. Motorized vehicles and equipment—even bicycles—are prohibited in the 113,000-acre Sky Lakes Wilderness, south of Crater Lake National Park. Its highest point is the 9,495-foot Mt. McLoughlin. Access to most of the forest is free, but there are fees at some trailheads. ⊠ *Forest Office, 3040 Biddle Rd.* ☎ *541/618–2200* ⊕ *www.fs.fed.us/r6/rogue-siskiyou.*

OFF THE
BEATEN
PATH

Rogue River Views. Nature lovers who want to see the Rogue River at its loveliest can take a side trip to the Avenue of the Boulders, Mill Creek Falls, and Barr Creek Falls, off Highway 62, near Prospect, which is about 45 miles northeast of Medford—it's a scenic one-hour drive, and it's on the way to Crater Lake. Here the wild waters of the upper Rogue foam past volcanic boulders and the dense greenery of the Rogue River National Forest. ⊠ *Hwy. 62, Prospect.*

FAMILY

Rogue Valley Family Fun Center. You'll find an impressive array of kids' games and recreation at this complex just off Exit 33 of Interstate 5 (about 5 miles north of Medford). Miniature golf, batting cages, a golf driving range, bumper boats, and go-karts are among the offerings, and there's also a video arcade and game room. ⊠ *1A Peninger Rd., Central Point* ☎ *541/664–4263* ⊕ *www.rvfamilyfuncenter.com.*

SHOPPING

Harry & David. Famous for their holiday gift baskets, Harry & David is based in Medford and offers hour-long tours of its huge facility on weekdays at 9:15, 10:30, 12:30, and 1:45. The tours cost $5 per person, but the fee is refunded if you spend a minimum of $40 in the mammoth Harry & David store, great for snagging picnic supplies to carry with you on any winery tour. Reservations are recommended, as space is limited. ⊠ *1314 Center Dr.* ☎ *541/864–2278, 877/322–8000* ⊕ *www.harryanddavid.com.*

Fodor's Choice
★

Lillie Belle Farms. Next door to Rogue River Creamery, this artisan chocolatier handcrafts outstanding chocolates using local, often organic ingredients. A favorite treat is the Smokey Blue Cheese ganache made with Rogue River blue, but don't overlook the dark-chocolate–marionberry bonbons (made with organic marionberries grown on-site) or the delectable hazelnut chews. Most unusual, however, is the chocolate-covered bacon, coated in chipotle and brown sugar, hand-dipped in chocolate, and sprinkled with sea salt. ⊠ *211 N. Front St., Central Point* ☎ *541/664–2815* ⊕ *www.lilliebellefarms.com.*

Fodor's Choice
★

Rogue Creamery. Just a few miles up the road from Medford in the little town of Central Point, you'll find one of the nation's most respected cheese makers, started in 1935 by Italian immigrants. Current owners Cary Bryant and David Gremmels bought the company in 2002, and promptly won one of the highest honors for cheese making, the London World Cheese Award. You can purchase any of the company's stellar cheeses here, from Smokey Blue to a lavender-infused cheddar, and you can watch the production through a window on most days. Delicious grilled-cheese sandwiches and local wines and beers are also available—enjoy them at one of the sidewalk tables outside. ✉ *311 N. Front St., Central Point* ☎ *541/664–1537, 866/396–4704* ⊕ *www. roguecreamery.com.*

JACKSONVILLE

5 miles west of Medford on Hwy. 238.

This perfectly preserved town founded in the frenzy of the 1851 gold rush has served as the backdrop for several Western flicks. It's easy to see why. Jacksonville is one of only a small number of towns corralled into the National Register of Historic Places lock, stock, and barrel. These days, living-history exhibits offering a glimpse of pioneer life and the world-renowned Britt Festivals of classical, jazz, and pop music are the draw, rather than gold. Trails winding up from the town's center lead to the festival amphitheater, mid-19th-century gardens, exotic madrona groves, and an intriguing pioneer cemetery.

GETTING HERE AND AROUND

Most visitors to Jacksonville come by way of Medford, 5 miles east, on Highway 238—it's a scenic drive over hilly farmland and past vineyards. Alternatively, you can reach the town coming the other way on Highway 238, driving southeast from Grants Pass. This similarly beautiful drive through the Applegate Valley takes about 45 minutes.

ESSENTIALS

Visitor Information Jacksonville Visitor Center. ✉ *185 N. Oregon St.* ☎ *541/899–8118* ⊕ *www.jacksonvilleoregon.org.*

EXPLORING

FAMILY **Caprice Vineyards and Alpaca Farm.** Among the many vineyards throughout the Rogue Valley, Caprice stands out both for producing well-balanced wines (including a quite tasty oak-aged Cabernet Sauvignon) and for having a herd of curious, friendly alpacas, which makes this a fun stop for the entire family. You can admire and even pet the alpacas; shop for sweaters, scarves, and fiber art in the small boutique; and sip wine while snacking on cheese and charcuterie on the tasting room or on the shaded patio. Although technically in the town of Central Point, the vineyard is just over a mile up the road from Jacksonville's historic downtown. ✉ *970 Old Stage Rd., Central Point* ☎ *541/499–0449* ⊕ *www.capricevineyards.com.*

FAMILY **Jacksonville Cemetery.** A trip up the winding road—or, better yet, a hike
Fodor's Choice via the old cart track marked Catholic access—leads to the resting place of
★ the clans (the Britts, the Beekmans, and the Orths) that built Jacksonville. You'll also get a fascinating, if sometimes unattractive, view of the social dynamics of the Old West: older graves (the cemetery is still in use) are strictly segregated, Irish Catholics from Jews from Protestants. A somber granite plinth marks the pauper's field, where those who found themselves on the losing end of gold-rush economics entered eternity anonymously. The cemetery closes at sundown. ✉ *Cemetery Rd. at N. Oregon St., follow signs from downtown* ☎ *541/826–9939* ⊕ *www.friendsjvillecemetery.org.*

Valley View Vineyard. Perched on a bench in the scenic Applegate Valley, you can sample acclaimed Chardonnay, Viognier, Rousanne, Merlot, Tempranillo, Pinot Noir, and Cabernet Franc while soaking up some of the best views in southern Oregon. The valley's especially sunny, warm climate produces highly acclaimed vintages. Founded in the 1850s by pioneer Peter Britt, the vineyard was reestablished in 1972. A restored pole barn houses the winery and tasting room. ✉ *1000 Upper Applegate Rd., 10 miles southwest of downtown* ☎ *541/899–8468, 800/781–9463* 🌐 *www.valleyviewwinery.com.*

WHERE TO EAT AND STAY

$$ BARBECUE 🍴 **Back Porch Bar & Grill.** For an excellent, mid-priced alternative to Jacksonville's more upscale eateries, head to this roadhouse-style clapboard building six blocks northeast of the town's historic main drag. Authentic central Texas–style barbecue is served here: char-grilled red-hot sausage, slow-cooked pork ribs, chicken-fried steak, and ½-pound burgers, plus a few seafood and pasta dishes. **Known for:** tangy slow-cooked barbecue; laid-back atmosphere. [$] *Average main: $18* ✉ *605 N. 5th St.* ☎ *541/899–8821* 🌐 *www.backporchjacksonville.com.*

$$ PACIFIC NORTHWEST 🍴 **Déjà Vu Bistro.** This classy but unpretentious wine bar and bistro resides inside downtown Jacksonville's historic McCully House Inn. Seasonal dishes include a summertime starter of pan-roasted brussels sprouts, heirloom cherry tomatoes, crumbled goat cheese, and balsamic vinegar, and the entrée of coffee-rubbed flat iron steak with local green beans, roasted red potatoes, and stone-ground mustard sauce. **Known for:** predinner wine tasting; delicious house-made gelato for dessert. [$] *Average main: $20* ✉ *McCully House Inn, 240 E. California St.* ☎ *541/899–1942* 🌐 *www.dejavubistrowinebar.com* 🕒 *Closed Mon. and Tues. No lunch.*

$$$ ECLECTIC Fodor's Choice ★ 🍴 **Gogi's.** Visitors sometimes miss this small, low-key restaurant just down the hill from Britt Gardens—it's a favorite of foodies and locals, though, for sophisticated international cuisine. The menu changes regularly, but has featured a tower of roasted beets and chèvre topped with toasted walnuts and a balsamic-truffle reduction, followed by prosciutto-wrapped quail with cauliflower, asparagus, and roasted mushrooms. **Known for:** terrific Sunday brunch; artful and innovative dishes; discerning wine list. [$] *Average main: $26* ✉ *235 W. Main St.* ☎ *541/899–8699* 🌐 *www.gogisrestaurant.com* 🕒 *Closed Mon. and Tues. No lunch Wed.–Sat.*

$$ B&B/INN 🏨 **Jacksonville Inn.** The spotless pioneer period antiques and the wealth of well-chosen amenities (fireplaces, saunas, whirlpool tubs, double steam showers) at this 1861-vintage inn evoke what the Wild West might have been had Martha Stewart been in charge. **Pros:** in heart of downtown historic district; one of the town's most historically significant buildings; very good restaurant on-site. **Cons:** rather old-fashioned decor for some tastes. [$] *Rooms from: $159* ✉ *175 E. California St.* ☎ *541/899–1900, 800/321–9344* 🌐 *www.jacksonvilleinn.com* 🛏 *8 rooms, 4 cottages* 🍽 *Breakfast.*

$$ B&B/INN Fodor's Choice ★ 🏨 **TouVelle House B&B.** This six-bedroom inn set inside a grand 1916 Craftsman-style home a few blocks north of Jacksonville's tiny commercial strip manages that tricky balance between exquisite and comfy. **Pros:** situated on a gentle bluff surrounded by beautiful gardens; downtown dining is a five-minute walk away; knowledgeable and friendly hosts. **Cons:** a couple of rooms require climbing two flights of stairs to third floor. [$] *Rooms from: $159* ✉ *455 N. Oregon St.* ☎ *541/899–8938* 🌐 *www.touvellehouse.com* 🛏 *6 rooms* 🍽 *Breakfast.*

SHOPPING

Jacksonville's historic downtown has several engaging galleries, boutiques, and gift shops. It's best just to stroll along California Street and its cross streets to get a sense of the retail scene.

Jacksonville Company. Drop by to browse the stylish selection of handbags, footwear, and women's apparel. MOTO Jeans, Brighton, Nicole Shoes, Kersh sweaters, and Bernardo Footwear are among the top brands carried here. ⊠ *115 W. California St.* ☎ *541/899–8912.*

Jacksonville Mercantile. The racks of this gourmet-food store abound with sauces, oils, vinegars, jams, and tapenades. Watch for Lillie Belle Farms lavender–sea salt caramels, and the shop's own private-label Merlot-wine jelly. ⊠ *120 E. California St.* ☎ *541/899–1047* ⊕ *www.jacksonvillemercantile.com.*

ASHLAND

20 miles southeast of Jacksonville and 14 miles southeast of Medford on I–5.

As you walk Ashland's hilly streets, it seems like every house is a restored Victorian or Craftsman operating as an upscale B&B, though that's not nearly all there is to this town: the Oregon Shakespeare Festival attracts thousands of theater lovers to the Rogue Valley every year, from late February to early November (though tourists don't start showing up en masse until June). That influx means that Ashland is more geared toward the arts, more eccentric, and more expensive than its size (about 21,000 people) might suggest. The mix of well-heeled theater tourists, bohemian students from Southern Oregon University, and dramatic show folk imbues the town with some one-of-a-kind cultural frissons. The stage isn't the only show in town—skiing at Mt. Ashland and the town's reputation as a secluded getaway and growing culinary destination keep things hopping year-round.

GETTING HERE AND AROUND

Ashland is the first town you'll reach on Interstate 5 if driving north from California, and it's the southernmost community in this region. You can also get here from Klamath Falls by driving west on winding but dramatic Highway 66. Cascade Airport Shuttle offers door-to-door service from the airport to Ashland for about $30 to $35. A car isn't necessary to explore downtown and to get among many of the inns and restaurants, but it is helpful if you're planning to venture farther afield or visit more than one town, which most visitors do.

ESSENTIALS

Visitor Information Ashland Chamber of Commerce and Visitors Information Center. ⊠ *110 E. Main St.* ☎ *541/482–3486* ⊕ *www.ashlandchamber.com.*

EXPLORING

FAMILY
Fodor's Choice
★

Lithia Park. The Allen Elizabethan Theatre overlooks this park, a 93-acre jewel that is Ashland's physical and psychological anchor. The park is named for the town's mineral springs, which supply a water fountain by the band shell as well as a fountain on the town plaza—be warned that the slightly bubbly water has a strong and rather disagreeable taste.

Lithia Park, Ashland

Whether thronged with colorful hippie folk and picnickers on a summer evening or buzzing with joggers and dog walkers in the morning, Lithia is a well-used, well-loved, and well-tended spot. On weekends from March through early November, the park plays host to a lively artisans' market, and free concerts take place Thursday evenings in summer. Each June the Oregon Shakespeare Festival opens its outdoor season by hosting the Feast of Will in the park, with music, dancing, bagpipes, and food. Tickets ($15) are available through the festival box office (☎ 541/482–4331 ⊕ *www.osfashland.org*). ✉ *W. Fork and S. Pioneer Sts.* ⊕ *www.ashland.or.us.*

Schneider Museum of Art. At the edge of the Southern Oregon University campus, this museum includes a light-filled gallery devoted to special exhibits by Oregon, West Coast, and international artists. The permanent collection has grown considerably over the years, and includes pre-Columbian ceramics and works by such notables as Alexander Calder, George Inness, and David Alfaro Siqueiros. Hallways and galleries throughout the rest of the 66,000-square-foot complex display many works by students and faculty. ✉ *1250 Siskiyou Blvd.* ☎ *541/552–6245* ⊕ *www.sou.edu/sma.*

FAMILY **ScienceWorks Hands-On Museum.** Geared toward kids but with some genuinely fascinating interactive exhibits that will please curious adults, too, this 26,000-square-foot science museum is close to Southern Oregon University campus. In the main hall, you can explore touch-friendly exhibits on nanotechnology and sports science, and Discovery Island has curious games and puzzles geared to tots under age five. There's outdoor fun amid the plantings and pathways in the xeriscape Black Bear Garden, as well as a weather station, solar-power nursery, and kid-appropriate climbing wall. ✉ *1500 E. Main St.* ☎ *541/482–6767* ⊕ *www.scienceworksmuseum.org* ⚐ *$10.*

Weisinger Family Winery. Just a short drive from downtown Ashland's wine bars and tasting rooms, Weisinger occupies a leafy hilltop with broad views of the surrounding mountains. Specialties here include a fine Malbec, a well-respected Viognier, and a nicely balanced Tempranillo. ✉ *3150 Siskiyou Blvd.* ☎ *541/488–5989, 800/551–9463* ⊕ *www.weisingers.com.*

WHERE TO EAT

$$$
PACIFIC
NORTHWEST
Fodor'sChoice
★

✕ **Alchemy.** Meticulous attention to detail, with regard both to preparation and presentation, are hallmarks of this refined contemporary Pacific Northwest restaurant inside the plush Winchester Inn, just a few blocks from the Shakespeare Festival theaters. Typically artful creations from the seasonal menu include a starter of goat cheese gnocchi seared in brown butter with chorizo and apricots and a tender 14-day dry-aged Oregon filet mignon cooked *sous vide* with sunchoke puree. **Known for:** lighter and less spendy fare in the bistro; the best filet mignon in town. Ⓢ *Average main: $28* ✉ *Winchester Inn, 35 S. 2nd St.* ☎ *541/488–1115* ⊕ *www.alchemyashland.com* ☾ *No lunch.*

$$$$
ECLECTIC
Fodor'sChoice
★

✕ **Amuse.** Northwest-driven French cuisine here is infused with seasonal, organic meat and produce. You might sample braised cheek and grilled tenderloin of pork with herb spaetzle, Savoy cabbage, and pomegranate molasses, or charcoal-grilled ruby trout with pole beans, heirloom tomatoes, and horseradish. **Known for:** amazing desserts; terrific coffee and pastries at sister establishment, Mix Sweet Shop. Ⓢ *Average main: $31* ✉ *15 N. 1st St.* ☎ *541/488–9000* ⊕ *www.amuserestaurant.com* ☾ *Closed Mon. No lunch.*

$$$
AMERICAN

✕ **Larks.** In a swanky yet soothing dining room off the lobby of the historic Ashland Springs Hotel, Larks pairs the freshest foods from local farms with great wines, artisan chocolate desserts, and drinks. Modern interpretations of comfort food are the order of the day, with servings such as homemade meat loaf with grilled-onion ketchup and smoked Brie–and–cheddar grits; Southern fried chicken with bacon pan gravy; and double-cut pork chops with grilled peach compote. **Known for:** cheesecake with daily-rotating flavor; outstanding Sunday brunch; pretheater dining. Ⓢ *Average main: $25* ✉ *Ashland Springs Hotel, 212 E. Main St.* ☎ *541/488–5558* ⊕ *www.larksrestaurant.com.*

$
AMERICAN
Fodor'sChoice
★

✕ **Morning Glory.** Breakfast reaches new heights in an eclectically furnished, blue Craftsman-style bungalow across the street from Southern Oregon University. The extraordinarily good food emphasizes breakfast fare—omelets filled with crab, artichokes, Parmesan, and smoked-garlic cream; Tandoori tofu scrambles with cherry-cranberry chutney; lemon-poppy waffles with seasonal berries; and cranberry-hazelnut French toast with lemon butter. **Known for:** large portions; long lines; crab omelet and crab melt. Ⓢ *Average main: $12* ✉ *1149 Siskiyou Blvd.* ☎ *541/488–8636.*

$$$
PACIFIC
NORTHWEST
Fodor'sChoice
★

✕ **New Sammy's Cowboy Bistro.** The loyal legion of foodies fond of this cult favorite a few miles northwest of Ashland, in the small town of Talent, have been known to make reservations weeks in advance, especially on weekends. The stucco Southwest-style roadhouse is surrounded by orchards and gardens, whose bounty finds its way into the exquisite—and mostly organic—Northwestern fare. **Known for:** artful desserts; funky yet romantic ambience; farm-to-table ingredients. [$] *Average main: $27* ✉ *2210 S. Pacific Hwy.* ☎ *541/535–2779* 🌐 *www.newsammyscowboybistro.com* 🕒 *Closed Sun.–Tues.*

$$ MODERN AMERICAN 🍴 **Peerless Restaurant & Bar.** This cosmopolitan, neighborhood bistro and wine bar anchors the up-and-coming Railroad District, on the north side of downtown, just a few blocks from Main Street and the Shakespeare theaters. It's adjacent to the Peerless Hotel, a stylish little property with the same creative spirit and hipster vibe of the restaurant. **Known for:** delicious desserts; first-rate cocktails; farm-to-table American fare. [$] *Average main: $19* ✉ *265 4th St.* ☎ *541/488–6067* 🌐 *www.peerlesshotel.com* 🕒 *Closed Sun. and Mon. No lunch.*

WHERE TO STAY

The Oregon Shakespeare Festival has stimulated one of the most extensive networks of B&Bs in the Northwest—more than 30 in all. High season for Ashland-area bed-and-breakfasts is June–October.

Ashland B&B Network. The network provides referrals and has an online booking system for about two dozen of the town's top inns. 🌐 *www.stayashland.com.*

$$$$ B&B/INN 🏨 **Ashland Creek Inn.** Every plush suite in this converted late-19th-century mill has a geographic theme—the Normandy is outfitted with rustic country French prints and furniture, while Moroccan, Danish, and New Mexican motifs are among the designs in other units—and each sitting room–bedroom combo has its own entrance, a full kitchen or kitchenette, and a deck just inches from burbling Ashland Creek. **Pros:** exceptionally good breakfasts; peaceful but central location; enormous suites. **Cons:** expensive for this part of the state; limited common areas. [$] *Rooms from: $295* ✉ *70 Water St.* ☎ *541/482–3315* 🌐 *www.ashlandcreekinn.com* 🛏 *10 suites* 🍽 *Breakfast.*

$ HOTEL Fodor's Choice ★ 🏨 **Ashland Hills Hotel & Suites.** Hoteliers Doug and Becky Neuman (who also run the excellent Ashland Springs Hotel and Lithia Springs Resort) transformed this long-shuttered '70s-era resort into a stylish yet affordable retro-cool compound, retaining the property's fabulous globe lights, soaring lobby windows, and beam ceilings while adding many period-style furnishings. **Pros:** great value; terrific restaurant on-site; attractive grounds, including patio and sundeck. **Cons:** just off the interstate a 10-minute drive from downtown; some rooms face parking lot. [$] *Rooms from: $140* ✉ *2525 Ashland St.* ☎ *541/482–8310, 855/482–8310* 🌐 *www.ashlandhillshotel.com* 🛏 *152 rooms, 70 suites* 🍽 *Breakfast.*

$$ HOTEL 🏨 **Ashland Springs Hotel.** Ashland's stately 1925 landmark hotel towers seven stories over the center of downtown, with 70 rooms done with a preponderance of gentle fall colors and unconventional decor—think French-inspired botanical-print quilts and lampshades with leaf designs. **Pros:** rich with history; upper floors have dazzling mountain views; the excellent Larks restaurant is on-site. **Cons:** central location translates to some street noise and bustle; some rooms are on the small side. [$] *Rooms from: $185* ✉ *212 E. Main St.* ☎ *541/488–1700, 888/795–4545* 🌐 *www.ashlandspringshotel.com* 🛏 *70 rooms* 🍽 *Breakfast.*

$$ B&B/INN Fodor's Choice ★ **Chanticleer Inn.** At this courtly, 1920 Craftsman-style bed-and-breakfast, owner Ellen Campbell has given the rooms a tasteful, contemporary flair with muted, nature-inspired colors and Arts and Crafts furnishings and patterns. **Pros:** rooms all have expansive views of the Cascade Mountains; only eco-friendly products are used; exceptional breakfasts. **Cons:** it's intimate and homey, so fans of larger and more anonymous lodgings may prefer a bigger inn or hotel. [$] *Rooms from: $175* ✉ *120 Gresham St.* ☎ *541/482–1919* 🌐 *www.ashland-bed-breakfast.com* 🛏 *6 rooms* 🍴 *Breakfast.*

$$$ B&B/INN FAMILY **The Winchester Inn.** Rooms and suites in this upscale Victorian have character and restful charm—some have fireplaces, refrigerators, and wet bars, and private exterior entrances, and most are well suited to having one or two children in the room. **Pros:** the adjacent Alchemy wine bar and restaurant serve outstanding international fare; one of the more child-friendly B&Bs in town; surrounded by lush gardens. **Cons:** among the more expensive lodgings in town. [$] *Rooms from: $225* ✉ *35 S. 2nd St.* ☎ *541/488–1113, 800/972–4991* 🌐 *www.winchesterinn.com* 🛏 *11 rooms, 9 suites* 🍴 *Breakfast.*

NIGHTLIFE AND PERFORMING ARTS

With its presence of college students, theater types, and increasing numbers of tourists (many of them fans of local wine), Ashland has developed quite a festive nightlife scene. Much of the activity takes place at bars inside some of downtown's more reputable restaurants in the center of town.

Fodor's Choice ★ **Caldera Tap House.** In addition to operating a full-service restaurant at their brewing facility out at 590 Clover Lane, just off Interstate 5, Exit 14, this highly acclaimed Ashland craft-beer maker with wide distribution throughout the Northwest also has this tap room downtown. Here you can sample the signature Hopportunity Knocks IPA, Old Growth Imperial Stout, and an extensive selection of tasty apps, burgers, and pub fare. ✉ *31 Water St.* ☎ *541/482–7468* 🌐 *www.calderabrewing.com.*

Liquid Assets. Popular early in the evening and late at night with those attending Shakespeare Festival plays up the street, this handsome wine bar and restaurant serves delicious modern-American food, from truffled popcorn and beef tartare to substantial fare. But as the name suggests, the favorite assets here are drinkable, including wines by the glass and a huge selection of bottles priced at retail (there's a modest $5 cork fee). Creative cocktails and local microbrews are also served. ✉ *96 N. Main St.* ☎ *541/482–9463* 🌐 *www.liquidassetswinebar.com.*

Fodor's Choice ★ **Oregon Shakespeare Festival.** From mid-February to early November, more than 100,000 Bard-loving fans descend on Ashland for some of the finest Shakespearean productions you're likely to see outside of London—plus works by both classic (Ibsen, O'Neill) and contemporary playwrights. Eleven plays are staged in repertory in the 1,200-seat Allen Elizabethan Theatre, an atmospheric re-creation of the Fortune Theatre in London; the 600-seat Angus Bowmer Theatre, a state-of-the-art facility typically used for five different productions in a single season; and the 350-seat Thomas Theatre, which often hosts productions of new or experimental work. The festival, which dates to 1935, generally operates close to capacity, so it's important to book ahead. ✉ *15 S. Pioneer St.* ☎ *541/482–4331, 800/219–8161* 🌐 *www.osfashland.org.*

SPORTS AND THE OUTDOORS

MULTISPORT OUTFITTERS

Adventure Center. This respected Ashland company offers "mild to wild" outdoor expeditions, including white-water rafting, fishing, and bike excursions. ✉ *40 N. Main St.* ☎ *541/488–2819, 800/444–2819* ⊕ *www.raftingtours.com.*

RAFTING

Noah's River Adventures. This long-running outfitter provides white-water rafting and wilderness fishing trips throughout the region—the company can lead single- or multiple-day adventures along the mighty Rogue River as well as just across the border, in northern California, on the Salmon and Scott rivers. ✉ *53 N. Main St.* ☎ *541/488–2811* ⊕ *www.noahsrafting.com.*

SKIING

Mt. Ashland Ski Area. This winter-sports playground in the Siskiyou Mountains is halfway between San Francisco and Portland. The ski runs average more than 265 inches of snow each year. There are 23 trails, virtually all of them intermediate and advanced, in addition to chute skiing in a glacial cirque called the bowl. Two triple and two double chairlifts accommodate a vertical drop of 1,150 feet; the longest of the runs is 1 mile. Facilities include rentals, repairs, instruction, a ski shop, a restaurant, and a bar. A couple of days a week, usually Thursday and Friday, there's also lighted twilight skiing until 9 pm. Anytime of year the drive up the twisting road to the ski area is incredibly scenic, affording views of 14,162-foot Mt. Shasta, some 90 miles south in California. ✉ *Mt. Ashland Access Rd., off Exit 6 from I–5, 18 miles south of downtown* ☎ *541/482–2897* ⊕ *www.mtashland.com* ✍ *Lift ticket $48.*

SHOPPING

Dagoba Organic Chocolate. A few miles' drive south of town you'll find the retail outlet of this company that produces those small, handsomely packed, superfine chocolate bars sold in fancy-food shops and groceries throughout the country. Although Hershey Company now owns the company, Dagoba was founded in Ashland, and its operation remains here, where a small retail shop—open weekdays only—sells its goods. ✉ *1105 Benson St.* ☎ *866/608–6944* ⊕ *www.dagobachocolate.com.*

KLAMATH FALLS

65 miles east of Ashland via Hwy. 66; 75 miles east of Medford via Hwy. 140.

The Klamath Basin, with its six national wildlife refuges, hosts the largest wintering concentration of bald eagles in the contiguous United States and the largest concentration of migratory waterfowl on the continent. Each February nature enthusiasts from around the world flock here for the Winter Wings Festival, the nation's oldest birding festival.

The Nature Conservancy has called this largest wetland basin west of the Mississippi the Western Everglades, but humans have significantly damaged the ecosystem through farming and development. More than 25% of vertebrate species in the area are now endangered or threatened.

As recently as the 1980s, about 6 million birds used the area every year; today that number is down to 2 to 3 million. Environmental organizations have succeeded in reversing some of the damage, and today more than 350 birds species visit the refuge.

Apart from being a handy base for visiting the refuges and Crater Lake, the actual town of Klamath Falls is somewhat prosaic and often overlooked by visitors traveling the Interstate 5 corridor, but it does have a nice little museum. With a population of about 21,000 people, the city stands at an elevation of 4,100 feet, on the southern shore of Upper Klamath Lake. The highest elevation in Klamath County is the peak of Mt. Scott, at 8,926 feet. There are more than 82 lakes and streams in Klamath County, including Upper Klamath Lake, which covers 133 square miles.

GETTING HERE AND AROUND

Klamath Falls lies along U.S. 97, one of the Northwest's main north–south routes—it's a prime stop between Bend, 140 miles north, and Weed, California, about 70 miles south. You can also get here from the Rogue Valley, either by way of Highway 66 from Ashland or Highway 140 from Medford, which is home to the nearest airport (about a 90-minute drive).

ESSENTIALS

Visitor Information Meet Me In Klamath. ⊠ *205 Riverside Dr.* ☎ *541/882–1501, 800/445–6728* ⊕ *www.meetmeinklamath.com.*

EXPLORING

Fodor'sChoice
★
Klamath Basin National Wildlife Refuge Complex. As many as 1,000 bald eagles make Klamath Basin their rest stop, amounting to the largest wintering concentration of these birds in the contiguous United States. Located along the Pacific Flyway bird migration route, the nearly 40,000 acres of freshwater wetlands in this complex of six different refuges serve as a stopover for nearly 1 million waterfowl in the fall. Any time of year is bird-watching season; more than 400 species of birds—including about 15 types of raptors—have been spotted in the Klamath Basin. For a leisurely excursion by car, follow the tour routes in the Lower Klamath and Tule Lake refuges—the latter has a superb bookstore and visitor center and is also a short drive from Lava Beds National Monument. ⊠ *Tule Lake Refuge Visitor Center, 4009 Hill Rd., Tulelake* ✛ *27 miles south of Klamath Falls via Hwy. 39* ☎ *530/667–2231* ⊕ *www.fws.gov/refuge/tule_lake* ✉ *Free.*

Klamath County Museum. The anthropology, history, geology, and wildlife of the Klamath Basin are explained at this extensive museum set inside the city's historic armory building, with special attention given to the hardships faced by early white settlers. Also part of the museum's domain are the Baldwin Hotel Museum and Fort Klamath Museum. ⊠ *1451 Main St.* ☎ *541/883–4208* ⊕ *museum.klamathcounty.org* ✉ *$5.*

WHERE TO EAT AND STAY

$$
AMERICAN
✕ **Basin Martini Bar.** Although the name of this elegant storefront spot in the heart of the downtown historic district suggests an option for evening cocktails, the bar is just as well regarded for its reliably tasty dinner fare—New York strip steaks, burgers topped with Crater Lake blue cheese, and bacon-wrapped scallops are among the highlights. There's seating

in a handful of comfy booths or at stools along the modern bar. **Known for:** well-prepared craft cocktails; decadent mac-and-cheese. $ *Average main: $17 ⊠ 632 Main St.* ☏ *541/884–6264* ☉ *Closed Sun. No lunch.*

$ ╳ **Gathering Grounds Cafe.** Although this bustling coffeehouse with comfortable seating and exposed-brick walls is a hot spot for espresso drinks

CAFÉ made from house-roasted coffee beans, it's also a great option for grabbing healthful, flavorful picnic items. Fresh-fruit parfaits and croissant and English muffin sandwiches are popular for breakfast. **Known for:** delicious panini sandwiches at breakfast and lunch; best coffee in town, roasted in-house. $ *Average main: $9 ⊠ 116 S. 11th St.* ☏ *541/887–8403* ⊕ *www.gatheringgroundscafe.com* ☉ *Closed Sun. No dinner.*

$ ⛳ **Running Y Ranch Resort.** Golfers rave about the Arnold Palmer–designed

RESORT course at this 3,600-acre resort in a juniper-and-ponderosa–shaded can-

FAMILY yon overlooking Upper Klamath Lake. **Pros:** kids enjoy indoor pool; walkers and joggers have 8 miles of paved trails. **Cons:** may be too far off the beaten path for some. $ *Rooms from: $149 ⊠ 5500 Running Y Rd., 8 miles north of Klamath Falls* ☏ *541/850–5500* ⊕ *www.runningy. com* ↘ *82 rooms, 43 houses* ⦿ *No meals.*

SPORTS AND THE OUTDOORS

MULTISPORT OUTFITTERS

The Ledge Outdoor Store. For advice, gear, clothing, books, and maps for hiking, birding, mountaineering, canoeing, camping, and fishing throughout the area, visit this extensively stocked shop in downtown Klamath Falls, which carries all kinds of equipment, and also offers guided fly-fishing trips. ⊠ *369 S. 6th St.* ☏ *541/882–5586* ⊕ *www.yetiledge.wordpress.com.*

CAVE JUNCTION

8

30 miles southwest of Grants Pass via U.S. 199; 60 miles west of Jacksonville via Hwy. 238 and U.S. 199.

One of the least populated and most pristine parts of southern Oregon, the town of Cave Junction and the surrounding Illinois Valley attract outdoors enthusiasts of all kinds for hiking, backpacking, camping, fishing, and hunting. Expect rugged terrain and the chance to view some of the tallest Douglas fir trees in the state. Other than those passing through en route from Grants Pass to the northern California coast via U.S. 199, most visitors come here to visit the Oregon Caves National Monument, one of the world's few marble caves (formed by erosion from acidic rainwater). Sleepy Cave Junction makes an engaging little base camp, its main drag lined with a handful of quirky shops, short-order restaurants, and gas stations.

GETTING HERE AND AROUND

Cave Junction lies along U.S. 199, the main road leading from Grants Pass. You can also reach Cave Junction by heading west from Jacksonville on Highway 238 to U.S. 199. From Cave Junction, head east on Highway 46 to reach Oregon Caves National Monument. Cave Junction is about a 75-minute drive southwest of Medford's regional airport. Alternatively, the small airport (served by PenAir, with service from Portland) in Crescent City, California, is the same distance.

ESSENTIALS

Visitor Information Illinois Valley Chamber of Commerce. ✉ *201 Caves Hwy. (Hwy. 46), just off U.S. 199* ☎ *541/592–3326* ⊕ *www.cavejunction.com.*

EXPLORING

Bridgeview Vineyard and Winery. The producers of the well-distributed and reasonably priced Blue Moon wines (known especially for Riesling, Chardonnay, Pinot Gris, and Merlot), as well as more premium vintages such as Black Beauty Syrah and a very nice reserve Pinot Noir, established the winery in 1986, and—despite skepticism from observers—have gone on to tremendous success. There's a second tasting room, open summer only, in the Applegate Valley, near Grants Pass. ✉ *4210 Holland Loop Rd.* ☎ *541/592–4688* ⊕ *www.bridgeviewwine.com.*

Fodor's Choice ★ **Oregon Caves National Monument.** Marble caves, large calcite formations, and huge underground rooms shape this rare adventure in geology. Guided cave tours take place on the hour in late spring and fall, and every half hour in June, July, and August. The 90-minute half-mile tour is moderately strenuous, with low passageways, twisting turns, and more than 500 stairs; children must be at least 42 inches tall to participate. Cave tours aren't given in winter. Above ground, the surrounding valley holds an old-growth forest with some of the state's largest trees. ⚠ **GPS coordinates for the caves often direct drivers onto a mostly unpaved forest service road meant for four-wheel-drive vehicles. Instead, follow well-signed Highway 46 off U.S. 199 at Cave Junction, which is also narrow and twisting in parts; RVs or trailers more than 32 feet long are not advised.** ✉ *19000 Caves Hwy. (Hwy. 46), 20 miles east of U.S. 199, 140 miles southwest of Crater Lake* ☎ *541/592–2100* ⊕ *www.nps.gov/orca* 🎟 *Park free, tours $10.*

WHERE TO STAY

$
HOTEL
FAMILY
⌂ **Oregon Caves Chateau.** This six-story wood-frame lodge, virtually unchanged since it was built in 1934, has a rustic authenticity and steep gabled roofs, while the simple rooms, all with their original furnishings, have canyon or waterfall views. **Pros:** on the grounds of the national monument; historic and funky personality; wonderfully tranquil setting. **Cons:** no-frills rooms; no Internet or phones (and very limited cell reception); location well out of the way if you aren't visiting the caves. 🖫 *Rooms from: $109* ✉ *20000 Caves Hwy.* ☎ *541/592–3400* ⊕ *www.oregoncaveschateau.com* ☾ *Closed early Nov.–early May* ⌐ *23 rooms* ⦚❙ *No meals.*

$
B&B/INN
FAMILY
⌂ **Out 'n' About.** You sleep among the leaves in the tree houses of this extraordinary resort—the highest is 37 feet from the ground, one has an antique claw-foot bath, and another has separate kids' quarters connected to the main room by a swinging bridge. **Pros:** kids love the Swiss Family Robinson atmosphere; it truly feels at one with the surrounding old-growth forest; amazingly quiet and peaceful. **Cons:** accommodations are extremely rustic; some units don't have bathrooms; two-night minimum during week and three-night minimum weekends during spring to fall. 🖫 *Rooms from: $140* ✉ *300 Page Creek Rd.* ☎ *541/592–2208* ⊕ *www.treehouses.com* ⌐ *15 tree houses, 1 cabin* ⦚❙ *Breakfast.*

9

EASTERN
OREGON

WELCOME TO EASTERN OREGON

TOP REASONS TO GO

★ **Wallowa wonder:** The usually snowcapped peaks of the Wallowa Range ornament one of the West's most overlooked alpine playgrounds, with Wallowa Lake resting at its base and Hells Canyon beckoning nearby.

★ **Historic Baker City:** See architecture from Oregon's mining-era heyday in Baker City's authentically restored downtown, where a short walking tour takes you past more than 100 historic buildings, many of which now contain indie boutiques and cafés.

★ **Snow day:** The family-friendly Anthony Lakes Ski Area offers skiing, snowboarding, and miles of Nordic trails.

★ **Rodeo:** Pendleton's famous rodeo attracts 50,000 people every September, but the cowboy mystique sticks around all year.

★ **Otherworldly scenery:** The buff-color, crumpled-looking Painted Hills seem to change hues throughout the day.

1 East Gorge. Near the majestic Colombia River Gorge, the high plains around Umatilla and Pendleton are the heart of Oregon's ranching and agricultural communities. "Let 'er buck!" is the rallying cry at the hugely popular Pendleton Round-Up rodeo, a phrase that sets the tone for the whole region's rootin', tootin' vibe.

2 Northeast Oregon. The superlative Wallowa and Blue Mountains dominate this corner of the state. The peaks that once presented formidable obstacles to Oregon Trail pioneers later lured generations of miners with their mineral bounty. These days, both ranges attract bands of hikers, mountain bikers, and other adventure types. In former frontier towns like Joseph and Baker City, old-school ranchers and cowboys mingle with a swelling population of artisans, foodies, and creative spirits.

GETTING ORIENTED

At its eastern end, Oregon begins in a high, sage-scented desert plateau that covers nearly two-thirds of the state's 96,000 square miles. To the north, the border with Washington follows the Colombia River, then stretches eastward across the Colombia River Plateau to meet the Snake River, itself forming much of the state's eastern border with Idaho. East-central Oregon is carved out by the forks and tributaries of the John Day River, the country's third-largest undammed waterway. Its north–south course to the Columbia marks an invisible line extending southward, separating eastern Oregon from central Oregon's high plateaus and Cascade foothills. To the south, the Nevada border is an invisible line slicing through a high, desolate region sometimes known as the Oregon outback—it's one of the most sparsely settled areas in the lower 48 states.

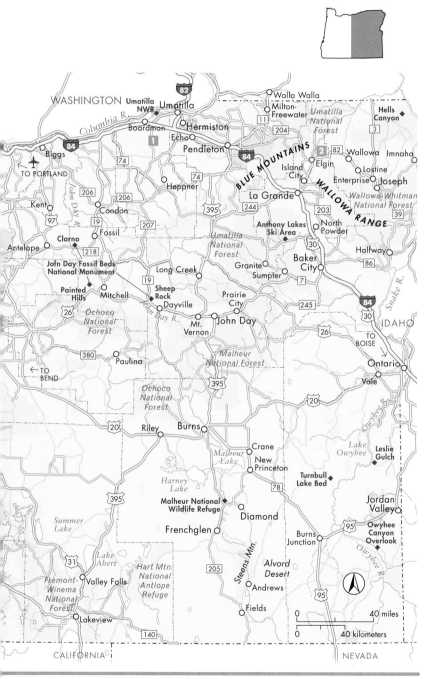

WASHINGTON

Columbia R.

TO PORTLAND

84

Biggs

Kent

97

Antelope

Clarno

John Day Fossil Beds
National Monument

Painted
Hills

Mitchell

26

Ochoco
National
Forest

← TO
BEND

380

Paulina

20

Riley

Summer
Lake

31

Lake
Abert

Fremont-
Winema
National
Forest

Lakeview

140

CALIFORNIA

Umatilla
NWR

Umatilla

Boardman

82

Hermiston

Echo

Pendleton

1

84

206

74

206

74

Heppner

Condon

Fossil

19

207

218

Long Creek

19

Sheep
Rock

Dayville

John Day R.

Mt.
Vernon

John Day

Malheur
National Forest

395

Burns

Malheur
Lake

Crane

New
Princeton

Harney
Lake

78

Malheur National
Wildlife Refuge

Diamond

Frenchglen

395

Hart Mtn.
National
Antelope
Refuge

205

Steens Mtn.

Alvord
Desert

Andrews

Fields

Valley Falls

Walla Walla

Milton-
Freewater

11

204

Umatilla
National
Forest

Hells
Canyon

3

82

Wallowa

Imnaha

Elgin

Island
City

Lostine

Enterprise

Joseph

La Grande

244

BLUE MOUNTAINS

WALLOWA RANGE

Wallowa-Whitman
National Forest

203

North
Powder

39

Anthony Lakes
Ski Area

Granite

Sumpter

Baker
City

7

Halfway

86

30

245

84

30

IDAHO

TO
BOISE

Ontario

Vale

20

Snake R.

Prairie
City

26

Ochoco
National
Forest

9

Lake
Owyhee

Leslie
Gulch

Turnbull
Lake Bed

Jordan
Valley

Burns
Junction

95

Owyhee
Canyon
Overlook

Owyhee R.

95

0   40 miles

0   40 kilometers

NEVADA

Updated by
Jon Shadel

Travel east from The Dalles, Bend, or any of the foothill communities blossoming in the shade of the Cascades, and you'll find a very different side of Oregon. The air is drier, clearer, and often pungent with the smell of juniper. The vast landscape of sharply folded hills, wheat fields, and mountains shimmering in the distance evokes the mythic Old West. There is a lonely grandeur in eastern Oregon, a plainspoken, independent spirit that can startle, surprise, and enthrall.

Much of eastern Oregon consists of national forest and wilderness, and the population runs the gamut from spur-janglin' cowboys to conservationists and urban expats. This is a world of ranches and rodeos, pickup trucks and country-Western music. For the outdoor-adventure crowd, it's one of the West's last comparatively undiscovered playgrounds.

Some of the most important moments in Oregon's history took place in the towns of northeastern Oregon. The Oregon Trail passed through this corner of the state, winding through the Grande Ronde Valley between the Wallowa and Blue mountain ranges. The discovery of gold in the region in the 1860s sparked a second invasion of settlers, eventually leading to the displacement of the Native American Nez Perce and Paiute tribes. Pendleton, La Grande, and Baker City were all beneficiaries of the gold fever that swept through the area. Yet signs of even earlier times have survived, especially visible in the John Day Fossil Beds, with fragments of saber-toothed tigers, giant pigs, and three-toed horses.

Recreation and tourism are gaining a foothold in eastern Oregon today, but the region still sees only a fraction of the visitors that drop in on Mt. Hood or the coast each year. For off-the-beaten-path types, eastern Oregon's mountains and high desert country are as breathtaking as any landscape in the West, and you'd be pretty hard-pressed to get farther from the noise and distractions of city life.

EASTERN OREGON PLANNER

WHEN TO GO

Though skiers and snowboarders appreciate the Blues and the Wallowas in winter, summer is eastern Oregon's primary travel season. It comes late in the state's northeast corner, where snow can remain on the mountains until July, and May flurries aren't uncommon at lower elevations. July and August are the best months for wildflowers in the high northeast, and they're also the only months when many remote-but-scenic Forest Service roads are guaranteed to be open.

Summer temps in northeast Oregon generally level out in the 80s around July and August. In midwinter, 20-degree days are the norm. Bear in mind: elevation varies greatly in eastern Oregon, and this can render seasonal averages pretty meaningless. It's not uncommon to gain or lose several thousand feet during the course of an hour's drive, and for much of the year this can mean the difference between flip-flops and snow boots.

GETTING HERE AND AROUND

AIR TRAVEL

Eastern Oregon Regional Airport at Pendleton is not serviced by any major airline, but San Francisco–based airline, Boutique Air, runs flights between Pendleton and Portland. There's a Hertz car-rental agency on-site. Across the Washington border, Tri-Cities Airport is just 35 miles from Hermiston and 70 miles from Pendleton and has service on Allegiant, Delta, Alaska/Horizon, and United Express from several major cities in the West. If visiting Baker City or other communities in the eastern edge of the region, your best bet is flying into Boise, which is about a two-hour drive from Baker City. To reach the John Day region, it's easiest to fly into Bend, which is 2½ to 3 hours away.

Contacts **Eastern Oregon Regional Airport at Pendleton.** ☎ 541/276–7754 ⊕ www.pendleton.or.us/pendleton-airport. **Tri-Cities Airport.** ☎ 509/547–6352 ⊕ www.flytricities.com.

BUS TRAVEL

The major Greyhound route travels along Interstate 84, passing through Pendleton Baker City, and Ontario, but buses are an extremely impractical way to get around the vast distances of this part of the state.

Contacts **Greyhound.** ☎ 800/231–2222 ⊕ www.greyhound.com.

CAR TRAVEL

Virtually all visitors to eastern Oregon get around by car. Interstate 84 runs east along the Columbia River and dips down to Pendleton, La Grande, Baker City, and Ontario. U.S. 26 heads east from Prineville through the Ochoco National Forest, passing the three units of the John Day Fossil Beds. U.S. 20 travels southeast from Bend in central Oregon to Burns. U.S. 20 and U.S. 26 both head west into Oregon from Idaho.

In all these areas, equip yourself with chains for winter driving, and remember that many roads are closed by snow and can remain inaccessible for months. Check the **Oregon Department of Transportation's TripCheck** (⊕ *www.tripcheck.com*) or call **ODOT** (☎ *800/977–6368*).

Four-wheel drive is beneficial on a lot of eastern Oregon's designated Scenic Byways. Plan ahead for gas, since service stations can be few and far between. They often close early in small towns, and because drivers in Oregon can't legally pump their own gas, you'll be out of luck until morning.

RESTAURANTS

Chef-driven restaurants serving anything beyond traditional pub fare and hearty steaks are rare on the eastern Oregon range, but it's not hard to find a tasty, authentic meal if you know where to look. Restaurants around the Wallowas, in particular, have a burgeoning locavore-organic ethos: locally grown produce abounds, farmers' markets are a big draw, and the rural county even has its own Slow Food chapter. A few noteworthy brewpubs have also cropped up around Pendleton, the Wallowas, and Baker City.

Elsewhere in the high desert, an entrenched ranching culture means big eating: farm-boy breakfasts and steak house after spur-jangling steak house. Generations of *braceros* (Hispanic laborers) have left their mark on the region's culinary scene as well, and excellent taquerias can be found in even the dustiest ranch towns. Pack a lunch if you're touring more remote areas, where traveler services are few and far between. *Restaurant reviews have been shortened. For full information visit Fodors.com.*

HOTELS

Chain hotels are easy to find in the Gorge and in bigger towns like Baker City and Pendleton, but elsewhere, small motels and bed-and-breakfasts are more typical. Properties described as "rustic" or "historic" aren't kidding around—a lot of the region's lodging hasn't seen a major renovation since the Eisenhower administration.

Triple-digit rates are an anomaly in eastern Oregon, and you'd have to work pretty hard to spend more than $150 on a night's lodging. Remember, much of eastern Oregon shuts down in the off-season, so don't count on winter lodging without calling first. *Hotel reviews have been shortened. For full information, visit Fodors.com.*

WHAT IT COSTS IN U.S. DOLLARS				
	$	$$	$$$	$$$$
Restaurants	under $16	$16–$22	$23–$30	over $30
Hotels	under $150	$150–$200	$201–$250	over $250

Restaurant prices are the average cost of a main course at dinner, or if dinner is not served, at lunch. Hotel prices are the lowest cost of a standard double room in high season.

TOURS

Hells Canyon Adventures. From May through October, Hells Canyon Adventures leads full- and half-day jet-boat tours of the country's deepest gorge. ☎ *800/422–358, 541/785–3352* ⊕ *www.hellscanyonadventures.com* ✉ *From $60.*

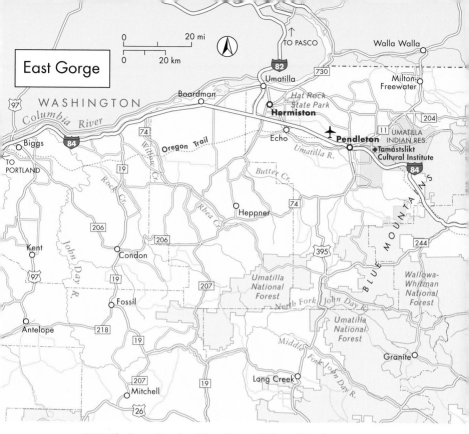

TREO Bike Tours. Local guides offer multiday, all-inclusive tours and customize routes based on the interest of groups. ☎ 541/676–5840 ⊕ *www.treobiketours.com* ☞ *From $450.*

VISITOR INFORMATION

Eastern Oregon Visitors Association. ☎ *800/332–1843* ⊕ *www.visiteasternoregon.com.*

EAST GORGE

Heading east along the interstate through the beige flats and monoculture croplands between Hermiston and Pendleton, you could be forgiven for supposing that the most interesting part of Oregon was behind you. But just off the beaten path in the East Gorge country are seasonal wetlands chock-full of avian wildlife, roadside relics of the Old West, and dusty frontier towns undergoing commercial rebirths. Parks like Hat Rock State Park offer boaters and anglers access to the vast Columbia River Gorge, one of the country's most impressive waterways. A few dozen miles away in Pendleton, one of the world's largest and oldest rodeos anchors a town with an unexpectedly hip dining and shopping scene. Look south and east to where the river plateau gives way to the forested foothills of the Blue Mountains.

HERMISTON

188 miles east of Portland; 30 miles west of Pendleton.

Although its population is just more than 17,000, Hermiston is the urban service center for nearly three times that many people in the expansive and productive agricultural industry that surrounds it. Irrigated farmlands and ranch lands produce livestock and crops, including alfalfa, potatoes, corn, and wheat. But the most popular export is the watermelons: the confluence of sandy loam soil, dry days, and cool nights creates the sugary magic that makes for the Hermiston brand of extraordinarily tasty fruit. Named for Robert Louis Stevenson's unfinished novel, *The Weir of Hermiston,* the city has more than 75 acres of parks, with the Columbia River just 6 miles to the north and the Umatilla River and Blue Mountains nearby.

GETTING HERE

Nearly all visitors arrive by car, but commercial flights do land at the Tri-Cities Airport in Pasco, Washington, 37 miles north. From Portland, it's a three-hour drive on Interstate 84.

VISITOR INFORMATION

Hermiston Chamber of Commerce. ⊠ *415 S. U.S. 395* ☎ *541/567–6151* ⊕ *www.hermistonchamber.com.*

EXPLORING

Echo. Ten miles south of Hermiston, just off Interstate 84, lies a little town at the intersection of the Oregon Trail and the transcontinental railroad. On the short walking tour of downtown, approximately an hour, mounted plaques tell the story of the town's historic buildings, including the Chinese House/ON&R Railroad Museum (now filled with railroad artifacts) and 10 sites on the National Register of Historic Places. Other draws include a fun pub, the Wheat and Barley, and a small winery, Sno Road. ⊠ *Oregon Trail Rd. at N. Thielson St., 1 mile south of I–84 at Exit 188* ☎ *541/376–8411* ⊕ *www.echo-oregon.com.*

WHERE TO EAT AND STAY

$$

PACIFIC
NORTHWEST

Fodor's Choice

★

✕ **Walker's Farm Kitchen.** In this rich agricultural region, it makes sense that downtown Hermiston is home to a restaurant with a strong farm-to-table ethos, along with a great list of regional craft beers and wines. The restaurant occupies a simple gray Craftsman bungalow with a charming dining room that befits the unpretentious cuisine. **Known for:** fresh, locally sourced ingredients; rotating specials menu. Ⓢ *Average main: $21* ⊠ *920 S.E. 4th St.* ☎ *541/289–3333* ⊙ *Closed Sun. and Mon. No dinner Tues. and Wed.*

$

HOTEL

🛏 **Oxford Suites Hermiston.** The region's most attractive and best-maintained hotel, this relatively upscale (for the area) chain property has spacious rooms, all with large sitting areas with work desks and sofas. **Pros:** complimentary breakfast and evening snacks; convenient location. **Cons:** most of the "suites" are really just large rooms with sitting areas; dated, cookie-cutter decor. Ⓢ *Rooms from: $115* ⊠ *1050 N. 1st St.* ☎ *541/564–8000, 888/545–7848* ⊕ *www.oxfordsuiteshermiston. com* 🛏 *114 rooms, 12 suites* ⦿ *Breakfast.*

PENDLETON

200 miles east of Portland; 130 miles east of The Dalles.

At the foot of the Blue Mountains amid waving wheat fields and cattle ranches, Pendleton is a quintessential Western town with a rip-roaring history. It was originally acquired in a swap for a couple of horses, and the town's history of wild behavior was evident from the first city ordinance, which outlawed public drunkenness, fights, and shooting off one's guns within the city limits. But Pendleton is also the land of the Umatilla Tribe—the herds of wild horses that once thundered across this rolling landscape were at the center of the area's early Native American culture (today the tribe operates the Wildhorse Resort & Casino). Later Pendleton became an important pioneer junction and home to a sizable Chinese community. The current cityscape still carries the vestiges of yesteryear, with many of its century-old homes still standing, from simple farmhouses to stately Queen Anne Victorians.

Given its raucous past teeming with cattle rustlers, saloons, and bordellos, the largest city in eastern Oregon (population 17,000) looks unusually sedate. But all that changes in September when the **Pendleton Round-Up** draws thousands.

GETTING HERE

Nearly all visitors arrive by car on Interstate 84. Pendleton does have the region's only airport, the Eastern Oregon Regional Airport, but it is not currently serviced by any major airlines.

VISITOR INFORMATION

Pendleton Chamber of Commerce. ⊠ *501 S. Main St.* ☎ *541/246–7411, 800/547–9811* ⊕ *www.travelpendleton.com.*

EXPLORING

Fodor's Choice ★ **Pendleton Underground Tours.** This 90-minute tour transports you below ground and back through Pendleton's history of gambling, girls, and gold. The Underground Tours depict town life from more than a century ago (when 32 saloons and 18 brothels were operating in full swing) to the 1953 closure of the Cozy Rooms, the best-known bordello in town. The Underground Tour eventually resurfaces, climbing the "31 Steps to Heaven" to those Cozy Rooms where madam Stella Darby reigned. The secret gambling lairs, opium dens, and bathhouses that lie directly below the pavement will give you a whole new perspective of the streets of Pendleton. Reservations are required. ⊠ *31 S.W. Emigrant Ave.* ☎ *541/276–0730* ⊕ *www.pendletonundergroundtours.org* ✉ *$15* ☞ *No children under 6.*

Pendleton Woolen Mills. Pendleton's most significant source of name-recognition in the country comes from this mill, home of the trademark wool plaid shirts and colorful woolen Indian blankets. This location is the company's blanket mill; there's also a weaving mill in the Columbia Gorge town of Washougal, Washington, near Portland and about three hours west of Pendleton. If you want to know more about the production process, the company gives 20-minute tours on weekdays (call for tour times). The mill's retail store stocks blankets and clothing with good bargains on factory seconds. ⊠ *1307 S.E. Court Pl.* ☎ *541/276–6911* ⊕ *www.pendleton-usa.com.*

FAMILY   **Round-Up Hall of Fame Museum.** The museum's collection spans the rodeo's history since 1910, with photographs—including glamorous glossies of prior Rodeo Queens and the Happy Canyon Princesses (all Native American)—as well as saddles, guns, and costumes. A taxidermied championship bronco named War Paint is the museum's cool, if-slightly creepy, prize artifact. ⊠ *1114 S.W. Court Ave., across from Round-Up grounds* ☏ *541/278–0815* ⊕ *www.pendletonhalloffame.com* ▧ *$5.*

FAMILY   **Tamástslikt Cultural Institute.** Located at the Wildhorse Resort and Casino, this impressive 45,000-square-foot interpretive center depicts history from the perspective of the Cayuse, Umatilla, and Walla Walla tribes (*Tamástslikt* means "interpret" in the Walla Walla native language). An art gallery showcases the work of local and regional tribal artists, and on Saturday in summer you can visit the adjacent Living Culture Village, Naami Nishaycht, and watch a variety of talks and demonstrations on everything from tepee-building to traditional community games. There's also a museum gift shop, a theater showing a short film about the tribe's heritage, and a café. ⊠ *47106 Wildhorse Blvd.* ☏ *541/429–7700* ⊕ *www.tamastslikt.org* ▧ *$10.*

WHERE TO EAT

$ ✕ **Great Pacific Wine & Coffee Co.** Set in a stately 1880s former masonic
CAFÉ   lodge in downtown Pendleton, what began as a coffeehouse and wine bar has expanded over the years into a full restaurant serving reasonably priced salads, sandwiches, soups, pizzas, and appetizers. The food tends toward traditional American café fare, with focaccia topped with Kalamata olives and chèvre, smoked-salmon Caesar salads, and barbecue-pork pizzas among the favorites. **Known for:** extensive selection of beer and wine; Naples-style pizza; live music on most weekends. $ *Average main: $9* ⊠ *403 S. Main St.* ☏ *541/276–1350* ⊕ *www.greatpacific.biz* ☾ *Closed Sun.*

$$$ ✕ **Hamley Steakhouse.** A large downtown complex of Western-style brick
STEAKHOUSE   and log cabin buildings holds a steak house, café, and saloon, and captures Pendleton's cowboy heritage with its stunningly ornate interior. The swanky steak house is open for dinner only, the saloon serves a lighter bar menu (and produces its own whiskey), and the café serves breakfast and lunch. **Known for:** meat-heavy menu of steaks and burgers; Old West ambience with 19th century mahogany bar and period memorabilia. $ *Average main: $28* ⊠ *8 S.E. Court St.* ☏ *541/278–1100* ⊕ *www.hamleysteakhouse.com.*

$ ✕ **The Prodigal Son.** A cavernous and historic former car dealership houses
AMERICAN   this hip brewpub, which also has a kitchen serving tasty pub food, such as Tillamook cheeseburgers and beer-battered fish-and-chips. Since it opened in 2010, it's become known for its nicely crafted beers, including the heady Max Power IPA, faintly tart Huckleberry Wheat beer, and robust Bruce/Lee Porter. **Known for:** laid-back, saloon-inspired atmosphere; rotating tap list of seasonal beers. $ *Average main: $12* ⊠ *230 S.E. Court Ave.* ☏ *541/276–6090* ⊕ *www.prodigalsonbrewery.com* ☾ *Closed Mon.*

$ ✕ **Rainbow Cafe.** A downtown institution since 1883, this historic saloon
AMERICAN   hasn't changed much in more than a hundred years. Locals donning cowboy hats and leather boots still belly up to the bar seven days a week for no-frills breakfast, lunch, and dinner. **Known for:** truly authentic Old West ambience; colorful and talkative regulars. $ *Average main:*

$10 ✉ *209 S. Main St.* ☎ *541/276–4120* 🌐 *www.rainbowcafependleton.com* 💳 *No credit cards.*

WHERE TO STAY

$ B&B/INN Fodor's Choice ★ **The Pendleton House Bed & Breakfast.** This gorgeous, 6,000-square-foot pink stucco home in Pendleton's North Hill neighborhood dates to 1917 and abounds with handsome decorative details, including Chinese silk wallpaper and custom woodwork; it's a grand reminder that the Old West had its share of wealth and worldly sophistication. **Pros:** glorious home with lavishly decorated rooms; small pets allowed; quiet location just across the river from downtown. **Cons:** most rooms share a bath. [$] *Rooms from: $135* ✉ *311 N. Main St.* ☎ *541/276–8581* 🌐 *www.pendletonhousebnb.com* 🛏 *5 rooms, 1 with bath* 🍴 *Breakfast.*

$ RESORT **Wildhorse Resort & Casino.** Situated on a sweeping mesa 6 miles southeast of downtown Pendleton, this contemporary hotel at Wildhorse Resort (operated by the Umatilla tribe) offers plenty of perks even if you're not a gamer. **Pros:** great views and stylish decor in tower hotel; lots of amenities and dining options on-site; scenic location outside town. **Cons:** casino can be noisy and reeks of cigarette smoke; a 15-minute drive from downtown restaurants; rooms in courtyard building feel a bit dated, and some still allow smoking. [$] *Rooms from: $95* ✉ *46510 Wildhorse Blvd.* ☎ *800/654–9453* 🌐 *www.wildhorseresort.com* 🛏 *300 rooms* 🍴 *No meals.*

$ B&B/INN **Working Girls Hotel.** From boardinghouse to bordello to affordable and historic inn, this refurbished 1890s edifice owned and operated by Pendleton Underground Tours advertises its "Old West Comfort" with a large vertical sign hanging from the side of the building. **Pros:** centrally located in downtown Pendleton; fun decor; very affordable. **Cons:** bathrooms are down the hall; no children or pets allowed. [$] *Rooms from: $85* ✉ *17 S.W. Emigrant Ave.* ☎ *541/276–0730* 🌐 *www.pendletonundergroundtours.org* 🛏 *4 rooms with 2 shared baths, 1 suite* 🍴 *Breakfast.*

SPORTS AND THE OUTDOORS

FISHING

Blue Mountain Anglers and Fly Shop. Oregon's largest full-service fly shop east of the Cascades also has a fishing school and information about angling in the area; the focus here is on fishing in the Umatilla River for steelhead, trout, and salmon. ✉ *1847 Westgate Pl.* ☎ *541/966–8770* 🌐 *www.bluemountainanglers.com.*

RODEO

FAMILY Fodor's Choice ★ **Pendleton Round-Up.** More than 50,000 people roll into town during the second full week in September for one of the oldest and most prominent rodeos in the United States. With its famous slogan of "Let 'er Buck," the Round-Up features eight days of parades, races, beauty contests, and children's rodeos, culminating in four days of rodeo events. Vendors line the length of Court Avenue and Main Street, selling beadwork and curios, while country bands twang in the background. ✉ *1205 S.W. Court Ave.* ☎ *541/276–2553, 800/457–6336* 🌐 *www.pendletonroundup.com.*

SHOPPING

Hamley & Co. Western Store & Custom Saddlery. On-site craftspeople at this Western superstore fashion hand-tooled saddles considered among the best in the world. You'll also find authentic cowboy/cowgirl gear and quality leather products, plus gifts and art. The store is next to Hamley's massive—and gorgeous—steak house, saloon, and café. ⊠ *30 S.E. Court Ave.* ☎ *541/278–1100* ⊕ *www.hamleyco.com.*

Fodor's Choice ★ **Montana Peaks Hat Co.** If the custom-sized felt hats in this shop and workspace look familiar, it's for good reason—the owners of Montana Peaks have outfitted celebrities and major Hollywood stars. They'll happily size anyone's head for a hat with their rare 19th-century equipment. ⊠ *24 S.W. Court Ave.* ☎ *541/215–1400* ⊕ *www.montanapeaks. net* ☉ *Closed Sun. and Wed.*

NORTHEAST OREGON

No part of eastern Oregon repudiates the region's reputation for flat and barren landscapes quite like its lush and mountainous northeast corner. The Wallowa Mountains are among the most underrated outdoor recreation hot spots in the Rockies, with 565 square miles of backpacker-friendly wilderness, abundant wildlife, and proximity to Hells Canyon, North America's deepest gorge. The nearby Blue Mountains are no slouches either, home to some of the state's best alpine and Nordic skiing. Towns like Baker City, Enterprise, Joseph, and La Grande have transitioned more thoroughly than much of the region from pastoral and extractive economies to hospitality and recreation, making them eastern Oregon's de facto capitals of art, food, and culture. Each city has a vibrant downtown with a growing number of sophisticated galleries and boutiques, and you'll find locals swapping fish stories and trail tales in one of the area's excellent brewpubs. Baker City in particular has maintained its mining-era integrity—the restored Geiser Grand Hotel is a must-visit, especially for history buffs.

LA GRANDE

52 miles southeast of Pendleton.

Home to Eastern Oregon University, a small state college, La Grande is a quiet little city of 13,000, which sits at the center of the Grand Ronde Valley. It's a convenient stop if you're heading to the Wallowa Mountains and La Grande's historic frontier character charms visitors. The city started life in the late 1800s as a farming community. It grew slowly while most towns along the Blue Mountains were booming or busting in the violent throes of gold-fueled stampedes. When the railroad companies were deciding where to lay their tracks through the valley, a clever local farmer donated 150 acres to ensure that the Iron Horse would run through La Grande. With steam power fueling a new boom, the town quickly outgrew its neighbors, took the title of county seat from fading Union City. Today the city is home to a handful of attractions and restaurants, and makes a good base for hiking and other outdoor adventures in the mountains.

GETTING HERE

La Grande sits at the intersection of Interstate 84 and Highway 82, the primary route through the Wallowa Valley to Joseph and Enterprise. It's a 4-hour drive from Portland and 2½ hours from Boise, Idaho.

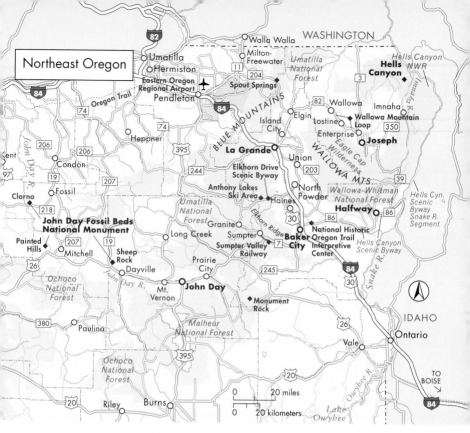

VISITOR INFORMATION

La Grande Visitor Center. ✉ *207 Depot St.* ☎ *541/963–8588, 800/848–9969* ⊕ *www.unioncountychamber.org.*

EXPLORING

Oregon Trail Interpretive Park at Blue Mountain Crossing. Trace the steps of Oregon Trail pioneers at this nature park in the Blue Mountains, where pine trees still bear the scars made by passing covered wagons more than 150 years ago. Signs along the various non-paved hiking trails highlight the history of the journey West. ✉ *La Grande* ☎ *541/523–6391* ⊕ *www.fs.usda.gov/wallowa-whitman* ✉ *$5 per vehicle* ☉ *Closed mid-Sept.–early May.*

WHERE TO EAT AND STAY

$
CAFÉ
✗ **Joe and Sugar's.** If you want to remain an anonymous tourist, don't visit Joe and Sugar's. You can't avoid being chatted up by the funny, friendly, and helpful owner of this sweet-smelling café and coffee shop that's popular for breakfast, lunch, and light snacks. **Known for:** home-style omelets; self-serve coffee bar; chatty locals. $ *Average main: $8* ✉ *1119 Adams Ave.* ☎ *541/975–5282* ▬ *No credit cards.*

$$$
AMERICAN
✗ **Ten Depot Street.** In a stylish historic brick building, Ten Depot Street serves an eclectic menu of classic American favorites, everything from burgers to hearty steak and seafood dishes. Start off your evening with

a drink at the adjoining bar—there's a very nice wine list. **Known for:** upscale, if a bit dated, ambience; live music on Tuesday and Thursday; attentive service. [$] *Average main: $23* ✉ *10 Depot St.* ☎ *541/963–8766* 🌐 *www.tendepotstreet.com* 🕒 *Closed Sun. No lunch.*

$ HOTEL **Historic Union Hotel.** Cast-iron Victorian lampposts frame the entrance to this funky three-story, redbrick hotel about 15 miles south of La Grande. **Pros:** bargain rates; atmospheric old building in a historic town. **Cons:** no TV or phones in rooms; property is a bit dated; front view of a trailer park doesn't impress. [$] *Rooms from: $89* ✉ *326 N. Main St., Union* ☎ *541/562–1200* 🌐 *www.theunionhotel.com* 🛏 *15 rooms* 🍴 *Breakfast.*

JOSEPH

6 miles southeast of Enterprise.

The area around Wallowa Lake was the traditional home of the Nez Perce Indians—the town of Joseph is named for Chief Joseph, their famous leader. The peaks of the Wallowa Mountains, typically snow-covered until July, tower 5,000 feet above the regional tourist hubs of the town. Joseph itself isn't much more than a nice Main Street speckled with shops, galleries, brewpubs, and cafés. Follow Main Street a mile out of town, though, to reach the gorgeous Wallowa Lake, where you'll find a whole separate hospitality village of rental cabins, outfitters, go-karts, and ice-cream stands. The busy area on the south end of the lake is also the site of two of the most popular access points for the mountains, the Wallowa Lake trailhead and the Wallowa Lake Tramway.

GETTING HERE

Highway 82 ends at Joseph, which is reachable primarily by car.

VISITOR INFORMATION

Joseph Chamber of Commerce. ✉ *Kiosk at Main St. and Joseph Ave.* ☎ *541/432–1015* 🌐 *www.josephoregon.com.*

EXPLORING

Valley Bronze of Oregon. This impressive gallery displays sculptures by the many artists who cast their work at the nearby foundry, plus quite a few international pieces. The foundry itself is a half mile away; call ahead for reservations and to confirm hours. Your tour guide will lead you there after the group has gathered at the gallery. ✉ *18 S. Main St.* ☎ *541/432–7445* 🌐 *www.valleybronzegallery.com* 🎟 *Gallery free, tours $15.*

Wallowa County Farmers Market. More than just a cluster of produce tents, Joseph's Saturday markets are the social hub of the community. Grab groceries or treats from rows of veggie vendors, specialty-food producers, and sustainable-cattle ranchers, then hang around for live outdoor music and bronze-sculpture street art. The market is also held in Enterprise on Thursday afternoons (4–7 pm), on the Wallowa County Courthouse lawn. ✉ *Main St. and Joseph Ave.* 🌐 *www.wallowacountyfarmersmarket.com.*

NEED A BREAK

Red Horse Coffee Traders. In this modest yellow clapboard cottage in downtown Joseph, you can sample some of the finest coffee in eastern Oregon. The owners roast carefully sourced, organic, fair-trade beans and

serve a selection of sandwiches, breakfast burritos, and baked goods. Known for: the best cup of coffee for miles; simple breakfast and lunch fare to go. ✉ *306 N. Main St.* ☎ *541/432-3784* 🌐 *www.redhorsecoffeetraders.com.*

Wallowa County Museum. Joseph's history museum has a small but poignant collection of artifacts and photographs chronicling the flight of the Nez Perce, a series of battles against the U.S. Army that took place in the late 1870s. Built as a bank in 1888, the building was robbed in 1896, an event commemorated by a number of the museum's artifacts, including a massive old safe and some yellowing newspaper accounts. ✉ *110 S. Main St.* ☎ *541/432-6095* 🌐 *www.co.wallowa.or.us/community_services/museum* 🎟 *$4.*

Wallowa Lake Tramway. The steepest tram in North America rises 3,700 feet in 15 minutes, rushing you up to the top of 8,150-foot Mt. Howard. Vistas of mountain peaks, forest, and Wallowa Lake far below will dazzle you, both on the way up and at the summit. Early and late in the season, 2½ miles of cross-country skiing trails await at the top, and the interpretive trails are open for hiking during the snowless months of midsummer, as are mountain-bike trails. A casual lunch is available at the Summit Grill and Alpine Patio, but keep in mind that it's more about the view than the sometimes uneven food and service. ✉ *59919 Wallowa Lake Hwy.* ☎ *541/432-5331* 🌐 *www.wallowalaketramway.com* 🎟 *$31.*

EN ROUTE

Wallowa Mountain Loop. This is a relatively easy way to take in the natural splendor of the Eagle Cap Wilderness and reach Baker City without backtracking to La Grande. The three-hour trip from Joseph to Baker City, designated the Hells Canyon Scenic Byway, winds through the national forest and part of Hells Canyon Recreation Area, passing over forested mountains, creeks, and rivers. Before you travel the loop, check with the Forest Service about road conditions; the route can be impassable when snowed over. From Joseph, take Highway 350 east for 8 miles, turn south onto Forest Service Road 39, and continue until it meets Highway 86, which winds past the town of Halfway and then continues to Baker City. ✉ *Begins at Hwy. 82 and Hwy. 350* ☎ *541/426-5546* 🌐 *www.fs.usda.gov/wallowa-whitman.*

9

WHERE TO EAT AND STAY

$ CAFÉ

🍴 **Old Town Cafe.** Both the keen early riser ready for the day's adventure and the groggy late-sleeper up for a lazy afternoon will find bottomless cups of coffee and hearty breakfast standbys at this stalwart café smack in the middle of Joseph's main strip. **Known for:** French toast made with house-baked bread; sunny breakfast classics; breakfast served till close. [$] *Average main: $9* ✉ *8 S. Main St.* ☎ *541/432-9898* 🌐 *www.oldtowncafejoseph.com* 🕒 *No dinner.*

$$ EASTERN EUROPEAN

🍴 **Vali's Alpine Restaurant.** This rustic and inviting Wallowa Lake institution serves a rotating, single-entrée menu of classic Hungarian dishes like cabbage rolls and goulash, with seatings at 5 and 7 pm; call ahead for reservations. The featured dish changes according to the day of the week—recently, schnitzel on Sundays, chicken paprikas on Thursday, and more. **Known for:** a wide-ranging, rotating menu. [$] *Average main: $18* ✉ *59811 Wallowa Lake Hwy.* ☎ *541/432-5691* 🌐 *www.*

Teepees overlooking Joseph Canyon

valisrestaurant.com 🛒 *No credit cards* ⊘ *Closed Mon. and Tues. (also Wed.–Fri. in fall and spring) and Dec.–Mar. No lunch.*

$$ 🛏 **Bronze Antler B&B.** This cozy 1920s Craftsman bungalow on the south
B&B/INN end of downtown Joseph is along Main Street, a short walk from local
Fodor's Choice shops and restaurants; it's surrounded by perennial gardens laced with
★ pathways and containing a bocce court and picnic area. **Pros:** beautiful
grounds with great mountain views; friendly and helpful innkeepers;
smartly furnished rooms. **Cons:** on the slightly busy main road through
town. $ *Rooms from: $150* ✉ *309 S. Main St.* ☎ *541/432–0230*
🌐 *www.bronzeantler.com* ⟿ *3 rooms, 1 suite* ⦿| *Breakfast.*

$ 🛏 **Wallowa Lake Lodge.** At this friendly 1920s lodge, handmade replicas
HOTEL of the structure's original furniture fill a large common area with a
massive fireplace. **Pros:** affordable; a visual and historical treat; staff
goes out of its way to accommodate. **Cons:** no TV, phones, or Internet;
closed in winter; rooms are quite rustic and simple. $ *Rooms from:
$115* ✉ *60060 Wallowa Lake Hwy., Wallowa Lake* ☎ *541/432–9821*
🌐 *www.wallowalakelodge.com* ⟿ *22 rooms, 8 cabins* ⦿| *No meals.*

SHOPPING

Fodor's Choice **Arrowhead Chocolates.** Take a break from browsing at Joseph's several
★ galleries and boutiques to indulge in first-rate caramels and truffles at
this popular downtown shop. You'll also find rich, hot mochas that
blend chocolate with Portland's Stumptown coffee. The sweets come in
novel flavors, including caramels topped with alder-smoked sea salt and
lavender-honey chocolate truffles. ✉ *100 N. Main St.* ☎ *541/432–2871*
🌐 *www.arrowheadchocolates.com.*

ToZion. Check out the well-curated collection of fair-trade clothing, soaps, skin-care products, Buddha statuary, jewelry, pottery, and artwork at this colorful two-story boutique carrying both local and international goods. ⊠ *200 N. Main St.* ☎ *541/432–0745* ⊘ *Closed Mon. and Tues.*

SPORTS AND THE OUTDOORS

HORSEBACK RIDING

Eagle Cap Wilderness Pack Station. Book a short or full-day guided summer pack trip from the south end of Wallowa Lake into the Eagle Cap Wilderness. ⊠ *59761 Wallowa Lake Hwy.* ☎ *541/432–4145, 541/962–5900* ⊕ *www.eaglecapwildernesspackstation.com.*

RAFTING AND BOATING

Wallowa Lake Marina. From May to mid-September, you can rent paddleboats, motorboats, rowboats, and canoes by the hour or by the day. ⊠ *Marina La., south end of Wallowa Lake, off Hwy. 351* ☎ *541/432–9115* ⊕ *www.wallowalakemarina.com.*

Winding Waters River Expeditions. Experienced river guides at this Joseph-based company lead white-water rafting and kayaking trips, as well as fly-fishing outings, on the Snake River and the nearby Grande Ronde and Salmon rivers. ⊠ *Joseph* ☎ *888/906–3816, 541/886–5078* ⊕ *www. windingwatersrafting.com.*

RECREATIONAL AREAS

Eagle Cap Wilderness. At more than 360,000 acres, this is the largest wilderness area in Oregon, encompassing most of the Wallowa range with 535 miles of trails for hard-core backpackers and horseback riders. Most of the popular trailheads are along Eagle Cap's northern edge, accessible from Enterprise or Joseph, but you also can find several trailheads 20 to 30 miles southeast of La Grande along Route 203. Some areas of the wilderness are accessible year-round, while the high-elevation areas are accessible only for a few months in summer. To park at many trailheads you must purchase a Northwest Forest Pass for $5 per day, or $30 per year. To hike into the wilderness, you also need to get a free permit that will alert rangers of your plans. ⊠ *Wallowa Mountains Ranger Office, 201 E. 2nd St.* ☎ *541/426–5546* ⊕ *www. fs.usda.gov/detail/wallowa-whitman.*

Wallowa Lake. A few miles south of Joseph proper on Highway 351 (or the Wallowa Lake Highway), sparkling, blue-green Wallowa Lake is the highest body of water in eastern Oregon (elevation 5,000 feet). Boating and fishing are popular, and the lake supports a whole vacation village on its southern end, complete with cabins, restaurants, and miniature golf. ⊠ *Wallowa Lake Hwy.*

FAMILY
Fodor's Choice
★

Wallowa Lake State Park. On the south shore of beautiful Wallowa Lake, just a 10-minute drive south of downtown Joseph, this alpine park with a highly popular campground is surrounded on three sides by 9,000-foot-tall snowcapped mountains. Popular activities include fishing and powerboating on the lake, plus hiking wilderness trails, horseback riding, and canoeing. Nearby are a marina, bumper boats, miniature golf, and the tramway to the top of Mt. Howard. ⊠ *72214*

9

DID YOU KNOW?

The Eagle Cap Wilderness area is one of Oregon's premier backpacking destinations, with more than 500 miles of trails. It is home to more than 50 alpine lakes, including the highest lake in Oregon, Legore Lake.

Marina La., off Hwy. 351 ☎ *541/432–4185, 800/551–6949* ⊕ *www.*
oregonstateparks.org 🖃 *Day use $5 per vehicle.*

Fodor'sChoice **Wallowa Mountains.** Forming a rugged U-shape fortress between Hells
★ Canyon on the Idaho border and the Blue Mountains, the Wallowas are
sometimes called the American Alps or Little Switzerland. The granite
peaks in this range are between 5,000 and 9,000 feet in height. Dotted
with crystalline alpine lakes and meadows, rushing rivers, and thickly
forested valleys that fall between the mountain ridges, the Wallowas
have a grandeur that can take your breath away. Bighorn sheep, elk,
deer, and mountain goats populate the area. Nearly all the trails in the
Wallowa Mountains are at least partially contained within the Eagle
Cap Wilderness. The offices and visitor center for the mountains are
in Joesph at the Wallowa Mountains ranger office of Wallowa-Whitman National Forest, but you can access different parts of the range
from different towns in the region, including Enterprise, La Grande,
and Baker City. ⊠ *Wallowa Mountains Ranger Office, 201 E. 2nd St.*
☎ *541/426–5546* ⊕ *www.fs.usda.gov/detail/wallowa-whitman.*

Rainbow trout, kokanee, and mackinaw are among the species of fish
in 300-foot-deep, 4-mile-long Wallowa Lake. You can picnic on the
water at several moored docks.

HELLS CANYON

30 miles northeast of Joseph; 80 miles east of Baker City.

This remote place along the Snake River is the deepest river-carved
gorge in North America (7,900 feet), with many rare and endangered
animal species. There are three different routes from which to view
and experience the canyon, though only one is accessible year-round.

GETTING HERE

Many seasonal National Forest Service roads access Hells Canyon from
Imnaha east of Joseph and the Wallowa Mountain Loop. Four-wheel
drive can be necessary on certain roads, but National Forest Road 39
is paved the entire way; check with rangers at the Wallowa Mountains
Ranger Office in Joseph for road conditions and trip-planning advice.
Even in perfect conditions, these forest roads can be slow going; allow
two to three hours, for instance, to drive the 50-mile Wallowa Mountain Loop. Most float trips originate from the Hells Canyon Creek site
below the Hells Canyon Dam.

VISITOR INFORMATION

Hells Canyon Chamber of Commerce. ☎ *541/742–4222* ⊕ *www.hellscan-*
yonchamber.com.

EXPLORING

Hells Canyon. Most travelers take a scenic peek from the overlook on
the 45-mile **Wallowa Mountain Loop**, which follows Route National Forest Road 39 (part of the Hells Canyon National Scenic Byway) from
just east of Halfway on Route Highway 86 to just east of Joseph on
Route Highway 350. At the junction of Route National Forest Road
39 and National Forest Road 3965, take the 6-mile round-trip spur to
the 5,400-foot-high rim at Hells Canyon Overlook. This is the easiest

way to get a glimpse of the canyon, but be aware that National Forest Road Route 39 is open only during summer and early fall. During the late fall, winter, and spring the best way to experience Hells Canyon is to follow a slightly more out-of-the-way route along the **Snake River Segment** of the Wallowa Mountain Loop. Following Snake River Road north from Oxbow, the 60-mile round-trip route winds along the edge of Hells Canyon Reservoir on the Idaho side, crossing the Snake River at Hells Canyon Dam on the Oregon-Idaho border. In some places the canyon is 10 miles wide. There's a visitor center near the dam, and hiking trails continue on into the Hells Canyon Wilderness and National Recreation Area. Be sure you have a full tank before starting out, since there are no gas stations anywhere along the route. If you're starting from Joseph, you also have the option of heading to the **Hat Point Overlook**. From Joseph, take Route Highway 350 northeast to Imnaha, a tiny town along the Imnaha River. From there, National Forest Road 4240 leads southeast to Route Highway 315, which in turn heads northeast up a steep gravel road to the overlook. This route is also open only during the summer. Carry plenty of water. ⊠ *Enterprise.*

SPORTS AND THE OUTDOORS

FISHING AND BOATING

Hells Canyon Adventures. Book a fishing trip or jet-boat excursion on the Snake River through Hells Canyon with this well-respected company that offers half- and full-day trips. ⊠ *Oxbow* ☎ *541/785–3352, 800/422–3568* ⊕ *www.hellscanyonadventures.com* 🖻 *From $85.*

RECREATIONAL AREAS

Hells Canyon National Recreation Area. This is the site of one of the largest elk herds in the United States, plus 422 other species, including bald eagles, bighorn sheep, mule deer, white-tailed deer, black bears, bobcats, cougars, beavers, otters, and rattlesnakes. The peregrine falcon has also been reintroduced here. Part of the area was designated as Hells Canyon Wilderness, in parts of Oregon and Idaho, with the establishment of the Hells Canyon National Recreation Area in 1975. Additional acres were added as part of the Oregon Wilderness Act of 1984, and the recreation area currently extends across more than 652,000 wild and rugged acres. Nine hundred miles of trails wind through the wilderness area, closed to all mechanized travel. If you want to visit the wilderness it must be on foot, mountain bike, or horseback. Three of its rivers (the Snake, Imnaha, and Rapid) have been designated as Wild and Scenic. Environmental groups have proposed the creation of Hells Canyon National Park to better manage the area's critical habitat. You can access the canyon from several points—see the website for an overview map. ⊠ *Wallowa Mountains Office, 201 E. 2nd St., Joseph* ☎ *541/426–5546* ⊕ *www.fs.usda.gov/wallowa-whitman.*

HALFWAY

63 miles southeast of Joseph; 40 miles south of Hells Canyon Dam; 55 miles east of Baker City.

Halfway, the closest town to Hells Canyon, got its name because it was midway between the town of Pine and the gold mines of Cornucopia.

The mines are long gone now, but this small (population just under 300), straightforward town on the southern flanks of the Wallowas has an appealing main street and a quiet rural flavor. Most visitors to Halfway are prepping for Hells Canyon or passing through along the scenic Wallowa Mountain Loop.

GETTING HERE

Halfway is reachable by car on Highway 86, part of the Hells Canyon National Scenic Byway. Interstate 84 at Baker City is 55 miles east. The summer-only Wallowa Mountain Loop road leads to Joseph, a scenic three-hour drive through the mountains.

WHERE TO STAY

$

B&B/INN

Inn at Clear Creek Farm. Amid 170 acres of orchards, ponds, woods, and fields on the southeastern flank of the Wallowa Mountains, this 1912 Craftsman-style farmhouse is a comfortable rural retreat on a working ranch. **Pros:** glorious views; peaceful and secluded; many recreational activities available. **Cons:** not exactly on the beaten path. $ *Rooms from: $100* ⊠ *48212 Clear Creek Rd., off Fish Lake Rd., 3½ miles north of Halfway* ☎ *541/742–2238* ⊕ *www.clearcreekinn. com* ⤳ *5 rooms 1 suite* �‖○‖ *Breakfast; Some meals.*

$

B&B/INN

Pine Valley Lodge. From the outside, this lodge on Main Street is constructed like many others built in eastern Oregon during the timber boom of the late 1920s, using wood from the original mines' construction. **Pros:** nicely updated rooms; recreation options close by. **Cons:** in a tiny remote town with few services and amenities. $ *Rooms from: $110* ⊠ *163 N. Main St.* ☎ *541/742–2027* ⊕ *www.pvlodge.com* ⤳ *8 rooms, 5 suites, 1 cottage* �‖○‖ *Breakfast.*

SHOPPING

Halfway Whimsical. Look past the silly name to find a cool artists' co-op chockablock full of landscape photography, textile art, and handcrafted jewelry. Some of the gallery's more "whimsical" items are clever remixes of household materials—think lamps made of toasters and jewelry made from cutlery. ⊠ *231 Gover La.* ☎ *541/742–6040.*

BAKER CITY

44 miles south of La Grande; 305 miles southeast of Portland; 114 miles south of Joseph.

During the 1860s gold rush, Baker City was the hub of the action. Many smaller towns dried up after the gold rush, but Baker City transformed itself into the seat of the regional logging and ranching industries that are still around today. Remnants of its turn-of-the-20th-century opulence, when it was the largest city between Salt Lake and Portland, are still visible in the many restored Victorian houses and downtown storefronts, many of which now hold distinctive boutiques, design shops, and cafés.

Baker City may not have that much gold left in its surrounding hills—but what hills they are. The Wallowas and Eagle Cap, the Elkhorn Ridge of the Blue Mountains, the Umatilla National Forest, the Wallowa-Whitman, Hells Canyon, Monument Rock—the panorama almost completes a full circle. Outdoor enthusiasts flock here for the climbing, fishing, hunting, waterskiing, canoeing, hiking, cycling, and skiing. It seems Baker City's gold rush has been supplanted by the "green rush."

GETTING HERE

Baker City is easily accessed by Interstate 84, a five-hour drive east of Portland and a two-hour drive west of Boise, Idaho. The city is the hub for several smaller highways as well, including scenic Highway 7 through the Blue Mountains to John Day.

VISITOR INFORMATION

Baker County Chamber of Commerce and Visitors Center. ✉ *490 Campbell St.* ☎ *541/523–5855, 800/523–1235* ⊕ *www.visitbaker.com.*

EXPLORING

Baker Heritage Museum. Located in a stately brick building that once housed the community's swimming pool, Baker's history center has one of the most impressive rock collections in the West. Assembled over a lifetime by a local amateur geologist, the Cavin-Warfel Collection includes thunder eggs, glowing phosphorescent rocks, and a 950-pound hunk of quartz. Other exhibits highlight pioneering, ranching, gold mining, and antique furniture. ✉ *2480 Grove St.* ☎ *541/523–9308* ⊕ *www. bakerheritagemuseum.com.*

Adler House Museum. The museum also operates the nearby Adler House Museum, an 1889 Italianate house that was once home to an eccentric publishing magnate and philanthropist. ✉ *2305 Main St.* ✉ *$6.*

EN
ROUTE

Elkhorn Drive Scenic Byway. This scenic 106-mile loop winds from Baker City through the Elkhorn Range of the Blue Mountains. Only white-bark pine can survive on the range's sharp ridges and peaks, which top 8,000 feet; spruce, larch, Douglas fir, and ponderosa pine thrive on the lower slopes. The route is well marked; start in Baker City on Highway 7, head west to Sumpter, turn onto County Road 24 toward Granite, turn north on Forest Road 73 and take that over Granite Pass and eventually by Anthony Lakes ski area to Haines, and then return to Baker City along U.S. 30. ✉ *Baker City.*

Fodor'sChoice
★

National Historic Oregon Trail Interpretive Center. Head 5 miles east of Baker City to this sprawling facility, containing 12,000 square feet of galleries, for a superb exploration of pioneer life in the mid-1800s. From 1841 to 1861 about 300,000 people made the 2,000-mile journey from western Missouri to the Columbia River and the Oregon Coast, looking for agricultural land in the West. A simulated section of the Oregon Trail will give you a feel for camp life and the settlers' impact on Native Americans; an indoor theater presents movies and plays. A 4-mile round-trip trail winds from the center to the actual ruts left by the wagons. ✉ *22267 Hwy. 86* ☎ *541/523–1843* ⊕ *www.blm.gov/or/ oregontrail* ✉ *$8.*

Sumpter Valley Railway. Though the original track was scrapped in 1947, an all-volunteer workforce has rebuilt more than 7 miles of track on the railroad's original right-of-way. Today the train operates along a 5-mile route in Sumpter. The historic trains leave from the McEwen and Sumpter stations; call ahead for departure information. A few additional fall foliage runs and Christmas trains are offered in October and December respectively. ✉ *211 Austin St., 22 miles west of Bakery City via Hwy. 7, Sumpter* ☎ *541/894–2268, 866/894–2268* 🌐 *www.sumptervalleyrailroad.org* 🎟 *$20.*

WHERE TO EAT AND STAY

$$ AMERICAN Fodor's Choice ★ 🍴 **Barley Brown's Brewpub.** It's the "Cheers" of Baker City—and everyone knows owner Tyler's name. A frequent winner at American beer festivals, Barley Brown's is just as famous in the area for their food, which is prepared with locally sourced ingredients (the hand-cut fries are Baker County potatoes) and hormone-free beef for burgers and other tasty grub. **Known for:** crowds in high-season; award-winning craft beer; locally sourced ingredients. [$] *Average main: $16* ✉ *2190 Main St.* ☎ *541/523–4266* 🌐 *www.barleybrownsbeer.com.*

$ MODERN AMERICAN 🍴 **Earth & Vine Art & Wine Gallery.** A chic little café on the ground-floor corner of one of Baker's numerous historic buildings, Earth & Vine sticks to sandwiches, flatbread pizza, fondue, and other simple treats. Regional varieties occupy much of the short wine list, but owner Mary Ellen Stevenson keeps many more bottles in the cellar than she prints on the menu, so ask for a recommendation. **Known for:** hosting local art and music events; slow but friendly service. [$] *Average main: $14* ✉ *2001 Washington Ave.* ☎ *541/523–1687.*

$ HOTEL 🏨 **Bridge Street Inn.** Right off Main Street, the Bridge Street Inn is one of the least expensive motels in town and with rooms that are clean and reliable, it's an excellent option if you're looking to save money. **Pros:** inexpensive; centrally located. **Cons:** walls can be a little thin; no-frills decor. [$] *Rooms from: $65* ✉ *134 Bridge St.* ☎ *541/523–6571* 🛏 *41 rooms* 🍽 *Breakfast.*

$ HOTEL Fodor's Choice ★ 🏨 **Geiser Grand Hotel.** Built in 1889, the stately Gesier Grand sits like the dowager duchess of Main Street, her cupola clock tower cutting a sharp figure against a wide Baker City sky—the Italianate Renaissance Revival beauty was once known as the finest hotel between Portland and Salt Lake City, and it's still one of the best. **Pros:** great downtown location; fascinating history. **Cons:** rooms, while well appointed, are decidedly old-fashioned and not to everyone's taste. [$] *Rooms from: $109* ✉ *1996 Main St.* ☎ *541/523–1889, 888/434–7374* 🌐 *www.geisergrand.com* 🛏 *30 rooms* 🍽 *No meals.*

SHOPPING

MAD Habit Boutique. Whimsical crafts and decorative goods are sold at this large downtown boutique on historic Main Street, along with jewelry and women's clothing. Be sure to say hello to the friendly shop cats, Earl and Pearl, whose images appear on the shop's own line of greeting cards. ✉ *1798 Main St.* ☎ *541/829–3157* 🕒 *Closed Sun. and Mon.*

No. 1911. This hip but unpretentious lifestyle and home-accessories shop stocks an eclectic assortment of goods, from whimsical Ames Bros. T-shirts to one-of-a-kind antiques. You'll also find soaps, balms, and lotions from U.S. Apothecary, Ranch Organics, and Duke Cannon Supply Co. ✉ *1911 Main St.* ☎ *541/523–4321* 🕒 *Closed Sun. and Mon.*

SPORTS AND THE OUTDOORS

FAMILY **Anthony Lakes Ski Area.** Find some of the state's best powder at this hill in the Wallowa-Whitman National Forest, along with a vertical drop of 900 feet and a top elevation of 8,000 feet. There are 21 trails, one triple

Historic Baker City mural in downtown Baker City

chairlift, and a 30-km cross-country network. Snowboards are permitted. ✉ *47500 Anthony Lake Hwy., 35 miles northwest of Baker City, North Powder* ☎ *541/856–3277* ⊕ *www.anthonylakes.com* 🎫 *Lift tickets $35.*

JOHN DAY

80 miles west of Baker City; 150 miles east of Bend.

More than $26 million in gold was mined in the John Day area. The town was founded shortly after gold was discovered there in 1862. Yet John Day is better known to contemporaries for the plentiful outdoor recreation it offers and for the nearby John Day Fossil Beds. The town is also a central location for trips to the Malheur National Wildlife Refuge and the towns of Burns, Frenchglen, and Diamond to the south.

As you drive west through the dry, shimmering heat of the John Day Valley on U.S. 26, it may be hard to imagine this area as a humid subtropical forest filled with lumbering 50-ton brontosauruses and 50-foot-long crocodiles. But so it was, and the eroded hills and sharp, barren-looking ridges contain the richest concentration of prehistoric plant and animal fossils in the world.

GETTING HERE
The town is a scenic, 90-minute drive from Baker City on Highways 7 and 26. To the west, it's about a three-hour drive to Bend via U.S. 26.

VISITOR INFORMATION
Grant County Chamber of Commerce. ✉ *301 W. Main St.* ☎ *551/575–0547, 800/769–5664* ⊕ *www.gcoregonlive.com.*

EXPLORING

Grant County Historical Museum. Two miles south of John Day, Canyon City is a small town that feels as if it hasn't changed much since the Old West days. Memorabilia from the gold rush is on display at the town's small museum, along with Native American artifacts and antique musical instruments. Drop in at the neighboring pioneer jail, which the locals pilfered years ago from a nearby crumbling ghost town. ✉ *101 S. Canyon City Blvd., Canyon City* ☎ *541/575–0362, 541/575–0509 off-season* 🌐 *www.gchistoricalmuseum.com* 🎟 *$4* 🕒 *Closed Sun.*

Fodor's Choice ★ **Kam Wah Chung State Heritage Site.** This ramshackle building operated by the state park system was a trading post on The Dalles Military Road in 1866 and 1867, then later served as a general store, a Chinese labor exchange for the area's mines, a doctor's shop, and an opium den. Listed on the National Register of Historic Places, the museum is an extraordinary testament to the early Chinese community in Oregon. Tours are on the hour with groups limited to 10 people; if you miss it, you can always catch the 19-minute video lecture given by the curator. ✉ *125 N.W. Canton St.* ☎ *541/575–2800, 800/551–6949* 🌐 *www.oregonstateparks.org* 🎟 *Free.*

WHERE TO EAT AND STAY

$ AMERICAN FAMILY 🍴 **Outpost Pizza, Pub & Grill.** The Outpost occupies one of the sleekest spaces in town: a large building with a log-cabin exterior, a vast entry lobby, and a bright, spacious, high-ceiling dining room. The kitchen serves creative pizzas and has a lengthy menu of standard entrées including burgers, steak, seafood, salads, and quesadillas. **Known for:** typical steak-house menu; large pizzas. [$] *Average main: $11* ✉ *201 W. Main St.* ☎ *541/575–0250* 🌐 *www.outpostpizzapubgrill.com.*

$ AMERICAN 🍴 **Squeeze-In Restaurant & Deck.** This casual downtown eatery serves three meals a day and has a sunny deck overlooking Canyon Creek as well as a bustling, casual dining room. Regulars pile in at breakfast for buttermilk pancakes and biscuits with sausage gravy. **Known for:** all-day breakfast; dog-friendly outdoor deck. [$] *Average main: $13* ✉ *423 W. Main St.* ☎ *541/575–1045* 🌐 *www.squeeze-in.com* 🕒 *No dinner Sun.*

$ HOTEL 🏨 **Dreamers Lodge.** The outside of this hotel is quite dated if a bit fun in a retro sense, but the rooms themselves are a definite step up from the exterior, with comfortable armchairs as well as microwaves, refrigerators, and flat-screen TVs in all the rooms. **Pros:** good value; central location. **Cons:** very basic. [$] *Rooms from: $59* ✉ *144 N. Canyon Blvd.* ☎ *541/575–0526, 800/654–2849* 🌐 *www.dreamerslodge.com* 🛏 *25 rooms* 🍽 *No meals.*

JOHN DAY FOSSIL BEDS NATIONAL MONUMENT

40 miles west of John Day; 150 miles south of Pendleton.

Fodor's Choice ★ The geological formations that compose this peculiar monument cover hundreds of square miles and preserve a diverse record of plant and animal life spanning more than 40 million years of the Age of Mammals. The national monument itself is divided into three units: Sheep Rock, Painted Hills, and Clarno—each of which looks vastly different and tells a different part of the story of Oregon's history. Each unit has

John Day Fossil Beds

picnic areas, restrooms, visitor information, and hiking trails. The main visitor center is in the Sheep Rock Unit, 40 miles northwest of John Day; Painted Hills and Clarno are about 70 and 115 miles northwest of John Day, respectively. If you only have time for one unit of the park, make it Painted Hills, where the namesake psychedelic mounds most vividly expose the region's unique geology.

GETTING HERE

Reach the Sheep Rock Unit of the John Day Fossil Beds Monument driving 38 miles west of John Day on U.S. 26, then 2 miles north on Highway 19. The Painted Hills unit is an additional 35 miles west on U.S. 26. To reach the Clarno unit, follow Highway 19 north from the Sheep Rock Unit, 60 miles northwest to Fossil. From Fossil, drive west on Highway 218 for 20 miles to the entrance. Be prepared to stop for frequent roadside interpretive exhibits between the three units. From other towns in central and eastern Oregon, it's a two-hour drive to the Sheep Rock Unit from The Dalles and Redmond, and a two-hour drive from Bend to the Painted Hills unit.

VISITOR INFORMATION

Thomas Condon Paleontology Center. ⊠ *32651 Hwy. 19, 2 miles north of U.S. 26, Kimberly* ☎ *541/987–2333* ⊕ *www.nps.gov/joda.*

EXPLORING

Clarno. The 48-million-year-old fossil beds in this small section have yielded the oldest remains in the John Day Fossil Beds National Monument. The drive to the beds traverses forests of ponderosa pines and sparsely populated valleys along the John Day River before traveling through a landscape filled with spires and outcroppings that attest to the region's volcanic past. A short trail that runs between the two parking lots contains fossilized evidence of an ancient subtropical forest. Another trail climbs ½ mile from the second parking lot to the base of the Palisades, a series of abrupt, irregular cliffs created by ancient volcanic mud flows. ✉ *Hwy. 218, 18 miles west of Fosseil* ☎ *541/987–2333* 🌐 *www.nps.gov/joda.*

Painted Hills. The fossils at Painted Hills, a unit of the John Day Fossil Beds National Monument, date back about 33 million years, and reveal a climate that has become noticeably drier than that of Sheep Rock's era. The eroded buff-color hills reveal striking red and green striations created by minerals in the clay. Come at dusk or just after it rains, when the colors are most vivid. If traveling in spring, the desert wildflowers are most intense between late April and early May. Take the steep, ¾-mile **Carroll Rim Trail** for a commanding view of the hills or sneak a peek from the parking lot at the trailhead, about 2 miles beyond the picnic area. A few Forest Service roads lead north toward the Spring Basin Wilderness and the town of Antelope, but these can only be managed safely by high-clearance vehicles and when dry. ✉ *37375 Bear Creek Rd., off U.S. 26, 9 miles west of Mitchell, Mitchell* ☎ *541/987–2333* 🌐 *www.nps.gov/joda.*

Sheep Rock. The **Thomas Condon Paleontology Center** at Sheep Rock serves as the area's primary visitor center, with a museum dedicated to the fossil beds, fossils on display, in-depth informational panels, handouts, and an orientation movie. Two miles north of the visitor center on Highway 19 is the impressive **Blue Basin**, a badlands canyon with sinuous blue-green spires. Winding through this basin is the ½-mile **Island in Time Trail**, where trailside exhibits explain the area's 28-million-year-old fossils. The 3-mile Blue Basin Overlook Trail loops around the rim of the canyon, yielding some splendid views. Blue Basin is a hike with a high effort-to-reward ratio, and in summer rangers lead interpretive jaunts Friday to Sunday at 10 am. ✉ *32651 Hwy. 19, Kimberly* ☎ *541/987–2333* 🌐 *www.nps.gov/joda.*

WHERE TO STAY

$ B&B/INN

🏨 **Fish House Inn and RV Park.** One of the few places to stay near the Sheep Rock fossil beds is 9 miles east, in the small town of Dayville, where the piscatory touches at this lovely inn include fishing gear, nets, and framed prints of fish. **Pros:** very low rates; fun atmosphere; ground floor of main house is great for a group traveling together. **Cons:** no food service other than the small mercantile shop. [$] *Rooms from: $55* ✉ *110 Franklin St., Dayville* ☎ *541/987–2124* 🌐 *www.fishhouseinn.com* 🛏 *5 rooms, 3 with bath; 1 suite* 🍴 *No meals.*

$ HOTEL Fodor's Choice ★

🏨 **Hotel Condon.** A popular option for visitors exploring the Clarno (35 miles south) and Painted Hills (60 miles south) sections of John Day Fossil Beds National Monument, this three-story 1920 redbrick hotel anchors the small town of Condon, which is also fairly close to the Columbia Gorge, about 70 miles southeast of The Dalles. **Pros:** grand old small-town hotel; friendly staff; large rooms with comfy furnishings. **Cons:** few dining options in the area; remote location. [$] *Rooms from: $149* ✉ *202 S. Main St., Condon* ☎ *541/384–4624, 800/201–6706* 🌐 *www.hotelcondon.com* 🛏 *12 rooms, 8 suites* 🍴 *Breakfast.*

TRAVEL SMART
OREGON

GETTING HERE AND AROUND

Except for Portland, you'll need a car to enjoy Oregon's cities, towns, coast, mountains, and wine country. Portland has outstanding public transportation options, such as a light rail (that goes to the airport), streetcar, buses, and taxis. This is not the case in most other towns in the state, so even if bus or train service exists between two points, you'll need a car to get around once you reach your destination.

▌ AIR TRAVEL

Flying times to Portland are about 5 hours from New York, 4 hours from Chicago, 2½ from Los Angeles, and 3¼ hours from Dallas.

AIRPORTS
Portland International Airport (PDX) is an efficient and modern airport with service to and from most major national and a growing number of international destinations. It's a relatively uncrowded facility, and both check-in and security lines tend to proceed quickly. It's also easily accessible from Downtown Portland, both by car and public transit. It serves as the primary gateway to the state, with connections to a handful of smaller airports, including Bend, Coos Bay, Eugene, and Medford.

Airport Info Portland International Airport (PDX). ☎ 503/460–4234, 877/739–4636 ⊕ www.flypdx.com.

GROUND TRANSPORTATION
PDX is 30 minutes by car from Downtown Portland, and is served by taxi ($38–$45), Lyft and Uber ride-sharing app service ($20–$28), light rail and bus ($2.50), and airport shuttle service ($14 one-way, $24 round-trip).

Contacts Blue Star Airporter. ☎ 503/249–1837 ⊕ www.bluestarbus.com.

▌ BOAT TRAVEL

CRUISES
From early April through early November, a few cruise lines offer excursions focused specifically on the Pacific Northwest, usually along the Columbia River, leaving from Portland. **Un-Cruise Adventures** (formerly America Safari Cruises) offers seven-day excursions (some of them wine-themed) along the Columbia and Snake rivers, calling at Richland (with access to Walla Walla), Clarkston–Hells Canyon, The Dalles, Hood River, Bonneville Dam, Portland, and Astoria.

American Cruise Lines runs seven-day excursions from February through April along the Columbia and Snake rivers, departing either from Portland or Clarkston (WA), on a Victorian-style stern-wheeler, the *Queen of the West.*

American Cruise Lines. ☎ *800/460–4518* ⊕ *www.americancruiselines.com.*

Un-Cruise Adventures. ☎ *888/862–8881* ⊕ *www.uncruise.com.*

▌ BUS TRAVEL

Greyhound buses travel to and within Oregon, providing frequent service to major cities, such as Portland, Eugene, and Medford. A cheap alternative is BoltBus, which offers inexpensive daily fares between Eugene and Portland, and service farther north up to Seattle, Bellingham, and Vancouver, BC.

Bus Info BoltBus. ☎ 877/265–8287 ⊕ www.boltbus.com. **Greyhound Lines.** ☎ 800/231–2222 ⊕ www.greyhound.com.

In Portland, TriMet operates one of the finest mass transit systems in the country with buses connecting to MAX light rail stations, which provide faster service to the airport and suburban areas. Most buses stop every 15 minutes or so most of the day, every day. Service is less frequent outside rush hour. A single fare is $2.50, a daily pass is $5, a weekly pass is $26, and a monthly, unlimited pass is $100.

TriMet Mass Transit. ☎ *503/238–7433* ⊕ *trimet.org.*

▌ CAR TRAVEL

Interstate 5 is the major north–south conduit for western Oregon (the most populous part of the state) and provides a straight shot at high speeds from California to Washington—provided there aren't traffic snarls due to slick conditions or summer road construction. Most of Oregon's largest cities, such as Portland, Salem, Eugene, Medford, and Ashland, are along Interstate 5. This makes driving between the major hubs the most practical way of exploring the state, as bus and train service is limited, and once outside Portland you'll need a car to get around.

For those who have the time, traveling U.S. 101 is an attraction in itself, as it hugs the Oregon Coast the entire length of the state with its incredibly scenic road. Make sure you want to commit to the coastal drive, which may be slow going in some parts, before getting on U.S. 101, because jumping back and forth to Interstate 5 adds a great deal of time to your trip.

The Cascade Range cuts through the middle of Oregon, which means that east–west journeys often wind through mountain passes, and can be either simply breathtaking (summer) or beautiful, slow, and treacherous (winter).

Interstate 84 is northern Oregon's major east–west artery—it enters the majestic Columbia River Gorge near Portland and continues east to Hood River, The Dalles, Pendleton, LaGrande, and Baker City. U.S. 26 provides access to Mt. Hood from Portland and eventually connects with U.S. 97, leading to Bend.

TRAVEL TIMES FROM PORTLAND BY CAR	
Bend	3½–4 hours
Crater Lake National Park	4½–5 hours
Columbia River Gorge/ Mt. Hood	1½ hours
Willamette Valley	1½–2 hours

CAR RENTALS

Unless you only visit Portland, you will need to rent a car for at least part of your trip.

Rates in Portland begin around $30 a day and $150 a week, not including the 17% tax if you rent at the airport (you can avoid this by renting Downtown or elsewhere in metro Portland, where a number of the major agencies have offices). Note that summer rates can be steep (easily as much as $65 per day or $300 per week for a compact); book as far in advance as possible, and if you find a good deal, grab it. All the major agencies are represented here.

In Oregon, you must be 21 to rent a car. Non-U.S. citizens need a reservation voucher, passport, driver's license, and insurance for each driver.

GASOLINE

The first thing visitors notice in Oregon is that except in some very rural counties or late at night at some self-service pumps, it is illegal for customers to pump their own gas. Gas stations are plentiful in major metropolitan areas and along major highways such as Interstate 5. Major credit and debit cards are accepted, and stations often stay open late, except in rural areas, where you may drive long stretches without a refueling opportunity.

PARKING

Oregon communities offer plenty of on-street parking and pay lots. In certain urban areas, specifically Portland, there are sections of town where street parking is metered and can be hard to find, particularly during festivals and special events. Mass transit in Portland is a plentiful and efficient alternative.

ROAD CONDITIONS

Winter driving can present challenges; in coastal areas the mild, damp climate contributes to frequently wet roadways. Snowfall generally occurs only once or twice a year on the coast and in the valleys, but when snow does fall, traffic grinds to a halt and roadways become treacherous and stay that way until the snow melts.

Tire chains, studs, or snow tires are essential equipment for winter travel in mountain areas, which receive plenty of snow starting as early as October and running well into the middle of spring. If you're planning to drive into high elevations, be sure to check the weather forecast beforehand. Even the main-highway mountain passes can close because of snow conditions. In winter, state and county highway departments operate snow-advisory telephone lines that give pass conditions.

ROADSIDE EMERGENCIES

Emergency Services AAA Oregon.
☎ *800/222-4357* ⊕ *www.oregon.aaa.com.*
Oregon State Police. ☎ *503/378-3720*
⊕ *www.oregon.gov/OSP.*

RULES OF THE ROAD

Oregon drivers tend to be fairly polite and slower going, which can be a bit maddening for those in a hurry. Bicyclists are plentiful in Oregon cities and rural highways; drivers need to be especially alert to avert accidents, including when opening the car door after parking.

Car seats are compulsory for children under four years *and* 40 pounds; older children are required to sit in booster seats until they are eight years old *and* 80 pounds.

Oregon is a hands-free state. It is illegal to talk or text on a cell phone while operating a motor vehicle, and doing so will net you a hefty fine. Use a wireless headset device if you need to stay connected.

▌ TAXI TRAVEL

Portland has several reliable taxi companies and is also well served by ride-share companies, such as Uber and Lyft. It can be expensive to get around town by cab, however, and you need to call for a taxi, as it's very difficult to hail them on the street. In Portland the flag-drop rate is $2.50 and then $2.90 per mile, and Uber and Lyft trips typically cost a fraction of the price. Make sure to ask whether the driver takes credit cards, whether there's a minimum fare, and whether there are charges for extra passengers. Other charges may include waiting times and airport minimums. Other larger communities in the state have at least one or two taxi companies, but you'll generally find that a couple of cab rides per day costs about the same as a daily car-rental rate.

▌ TRAIN TRAVEL

Amtrak has daily service to the Pacific Northwest from the Midwest and California. The Coast Starlight begins in Los Angeles; makes stops throughout California, western Oregon, and Washington; and terminates in Seattle. There are stops in both Portland and Eugene (as well as Salem, Albany, Chemult, and Klamath Falls); the 2½-hour trip between Portland and Eugene costs $21–$50.

Amtrak's Cascades begins in Vancouver, British Columbia; makes stops in Seattle, Tacoma, Portland, and Salem; and terminates in Eugene. The trip from Seattle to Portland takes roughly 3½ hours and costs $26–$63 for a coach seat; this is a pleasant alternative to the rather dull drive along Interstate 5. The Empire Builder begins in Chicago; makes stops in Milwaukee, WI; St. Paul, MN; Spokane, WA; and other cities before arriving in Portland. The journey from Spokane to Portland is 7 hours ($44–$120), with part of the route running through the Columbia River Gorge.

Train Info Amtrak. ☎ *800/872-7245* ⊕ *www. amtrak.com.*

ESSENTIALS

■ ACCOMMODATIONS

The lodgings we list are the cream of the crop in each price category. We always list the facilities that are available, but we don't specify whether they cost extra; when pricing accommodations, always ask what's included and what costs extra. Properties are assigned price categories based on a standard double room in high season (excluding holidays), and excluding tax and service charges. Oregon room taxes range from 6% to 11.5%. *For price categories, see individual chapters.*

APARTMENT AND HOUSE RENTALS

An alternative to staying in a hotel is to spread out a bit and relax in a vacation rental. There are plenty of choices, particularly along the Oregon Coast, near Mt. Hood, and in central Oregon resort areas near Bend. Renting an apartment or a house is an especially attractive idea for long-term visitors or large groups and families.

Contacts ForGetaway. ⊕ *www.forgetaway. com.* **Home Away.** ⊕ *www.homeaway.com.* **Vacasa.** ☎ *503/345–9399* ⊕ *www.vacasa.com.*

BED-AND-BREAKFASTS

Oregon is renowned for its range of bed-and-breakfast options, which are found everywhere from busy urban areas to casual country farms and windswept coastal retreats. Many bed-and-breakfasts in Oregon provide full gourmet breakfasts, and some have kitchens that guests can use. Other popular amenities to ask about are fireplaces, jetted bathtubs, and outdoor hot tubs. The regional bed-and-breakfast organizations listed can provide information on reputable establishments. Another excellent resource is Airbnb, which is well represented throughout the state and is especially helpful if you're looking to stay in Portland's hip East Side, which has few hotels and commercial B&Bs.

Contacts Airbnb. ☎ *855/424–7262* ⊕ *www.airbnb.com.* **Bed & Breakfast.com.** ☎ *512/322–2710* ⊕ *www.bedandbreakfast.com.* **Bed & Breakfast Inns Online.** ☎ *800/215–7365* ⊕ *www.bbonline.com.* **BnB Finder.com.** ☎ *888/469–6663* ⊕ *www. bnbfinder.com.* **Oregon Bed and Breakfast Guild.** ☎ *800/944–6196* ⊕ *www.obbg.org.*

CAMPING

Oregon has excellent state-run campgrounds. Half accept advance camping reservations, and the others are first come, first served. Campgrounds range from primitive tent sites to parks with yurts, cabins, and full hookups. Sites are located in and around Oregon's more spectacular natural sites, be it on the coast, the Cascade Range, or near the wine country. Privately operated campgrounds sometimes have extra amenities such as laundry rooms and swimming pools. For more information, contact the state or regional tourism department.

Campground Reservations Oregon Parks and Recreation Department. ☎ *800/452–5687 reservations* ⊕ *www.oregonstateparks. org.*

■ COMMUNICATIONS

INTERNET

Like the rest of the country, Oregon is well wired and virtually all hotels, most coffeehouses, and many other businesses offer Wi-Fi, which is typically free except at a handful of mostly upscale hotels that cater to business travelers.

■ EATING OUT

Oregon has been a pioneer in the now ubiquitous farm-to-table movement. Pacific Northwest cuisine highlights regional seafood, locally raised meat, and organic produce. Farm stands are plentiful in the rural areas and are definitely worth a stop; almost all cities have at least a weekly farmers' market, and Portland has them daily most of the year.

All of Oregon's cities and prominent towns have some genuinely stellar dining options. Portland has become one of the top foodie destinations in the country, and Bend, Eugene, Ashland, Hood River, the Willamette Valley, and several towns along the coast—most notably Astoria, Cannon Beach, and Newport—have a few superb restaurants specializing in locavore-driven cuisine. Portland has also become quite famous for its wealth of food carts.

Oregon's wines are well regarded throughout the world, particularly those produced in the Willamette Valley and, increasingly, the Rogue Valley in southern Oregon and Columbia Gorge around Hood River. It's also one of the top states in the country for craft breweries, microdistilleries, and artisan coffee roasters. Portland again leads the way when it comes to beer, booze, and beans, but Bend, Hood River, and Astoria also have several nationally acclaimed producers, and you'll find notable brewpubs and coffeehouses throughout the state, even in small towns. The restaurants listed *in the chapters* are among the best in each price category. *For price categories, see individual chapters.*

MEALS AND MEALTIMES
Unless otherwise noted, the restaurants listed *in this guide* are open daily for lunch and dinner. Most people eat dinner between 6 and 9 pm, although in many rural areas—including some coastal towns—some restaurants close by 8 or 8:30, especially on weeknights.

RESERVATIONS AND DRESS
Regardless of the venue, it's a good idea to inquire whether reservations are needed on a weekend evening. We only mention them specifically when reservations are essential (there's no other way you'll ever get a table) or when they are not accepted. For popular restaurants, book as far ahead as you can (often a week is more

than ample), and reconfirm as soon as you arrive. (Large parties should always call ahead to check the reservations policy.) We mention dress only when men are required to wear a jacket or a jacket and tie, although these policies are virtually unheard of in Oregon.

WINE, BEER, AND SPIRITS
Oregon's largest concentration of wineries is in the Willamette Valley between the northern Cascades and the coast, but you'll also find vibrant wine regions in the Rogue Valley and Columbia Gorge. The Oregon Wine Board maintains a helpful website, with facts, history, and information on local wineries—Oregon has more than 700 wine-making operations, most of them open to the public.

Oregon has more than 250 microbreweries, with plenty of festivals and events celebrating its brews. The Oregon Brewers Guild also has links to breweries and information on events.

You must be 21 to buy alcohol in Oregon.

Contacts Oregon Brewers Guild. ⊕ *www. oregonbeer.org.* **Oregon Wine Board.** ⊕ *www. oregonwine.org.*

∎ HOURS OF OPERATION

Oregon store hours are fairly typical compared to the rest of the United States. Major department stores or shops in the downtown areas including Portland generally follow the 10-to-6 rule, but you should always phone ahead if you have your heart set on visiting a smaller shop. Never assume that a store is open on Sunday, even in the major cities; many smaller shops have truncated Saturday hours as well. Thankfully, coffeehouses tend to keep regular and long hours, so you'll have no problem finding one to kill time in if you have to wait for a store to open.

Note that bars in Oregon close at 2 am, with last call coming as early as 1:30.

▍MONEY

Prices are given for adults. Substantially reduced fees are almost always available for children, students, and senior citizens.

In Portland, Downtown parking meters take credit cards.

▍PACKING

It's all about the layers here, as there's no other way to keep up with the weather, which can morph from cold and overcast to warm and sunny and back again in the course of a few hours, especially in spring and early fall. Summer days are warm and more consistent, but evenings can cool off substantially. August and September are the glorious, warm, clear months that remind Oregonians why they live there. Bring an umbrella or raincoat for unpredictable fall and winter weather. Hikers will want to bring rain gear and a hat with them, even if they're visiting in summer; insect repellent is also a good idea if you'll be hiking along mountain trails or beaches.

▍SAFETY

The greatest dangers in the Northwest are becoming lost or suffering an accident in the great outdoors. Don't hike alone, and make sure you bring enough water plus basic first-aid items. If you're not an experienced hiker, stick to tourist-friendly spots such as the well-marked trails in the national parks; if you have to drive 30 miles down a Forest Service road to reach a trail, it's possible you might be the only one hiking on it.

▍TAXES

Oregon has no sales tax, although many cities and counties levy a tax on lodging and services. Room taxes, for example, vary from 6% to 11.5%.

▍TIME

Most of Oregon is in the Pacific time zone, except for Malheur County in eastern Oregon, which is in the mountain time zone.

▍VISITOR INFORMATION

Travel Oregon. ☎ *800/547–7842* ⊕ *www.traveloregon.com.*

Travel Portland. ☎ *503/275–8355, 877/678–5263* ⊕ *www.travelportland.com.*

INDEX